THE PSYCHOLOGICAL ASSESSMENT OF PRESIDENTIAL CANDIDATES

THE
PSYCHOLOGICAL
ASSESSMENT
OF PRESIDENTIAL
CANDIDATES

Stanley A. Renshon

with a foreword by Alexander L. George

Routledge
New York   London

Published in 1998 by
Routledge
29 West 35th Street
New York, NY 10001

Published in Great Britain by
Routledge
11 New Fetter Lane
London EC4P 4EE

Errata
Chap. 12
Page 316, line 28: "martial" should read "marital."
Chap. 13
Page 340, line 10: change "five" to "four."
Page 341, line 2: change "Fourth" to "Third."
Page 341, line 38: change "Fifth" to "Fourth."
Bibliography
Page 487, line 2: "Kelley" should read "Kelly."

Library of Congress Cataloging-in-Publication Data

Renshon, Stanley A.
    The psychological assessment of presidential candidates / by Stanley
A. Renshon : with a foreword by Alexander L. George.
        p.   cm.
    Originally published: New York : New York University Press, c1996.
    ISBN 0-415-92146-5 (pbk.)
    1. Presidential candidates—United States—Psychology.   I. Title.
    [E176. 1.R396   1998]
    320—dc21   98-11839
                                                                  CIP

10 9 8 7 6 5 4 3 2 1

For my wife, Judith:
warm, thoughtful, intelligent, sensitive,
and loving partner through life.

Contents

Foreword
by Alexander L. George

The duties, tasks, and responsibilities we have assigned to the president have grown enormously in magnitude and complexity since the depression of the 1930s. The role of the federal government expanded rapidly, and this trend was accompanied by the belief that we must look to the president as the "engine of progress," the savior of the political system, the fulcrum of the entire governmental system. Given the emergence of this "heroic" conception of the presidency, it naturally followed that the president should be given additional resources and powers needed to perform the critical tasks that only he could be expected to discharge effectively. The White House grew enormously in numbers and activities and, indeed, became a "miniaturization" of the entire executive branch.

No one who favored the enhancement of the role and powers of the presidency anticipated the results of this trend. The president's job has become so complex and so demanding that it virtually defies accurate description in comprehensible terms. Any reasonably successful effort to describe the president's job, such as Thomas Cronin's *The State of the Presidency* (1975), only serves to raise sober questions regarding the ability of any incumbent president to perform the job effectively with any degree of consistency.

Indeed, it has become harder than ever to state confidently what the qualifications are for the job and who can be expected to perform them effectively and acceptably. Some years ago, experts on the presidency, having Harry Truman in mind, could quip (somewhat facetiously but also with a degree of seriousness) that however inadequately prepared or personally unsuited for the presidency a man might appear to be, the presidency would bring out the best in him, and the nation would somehow be adequately served. But this concept of the presidency as a kind of "reform school" fell into disfavor. After Lyndon B. Johnson, Vietnam, Richard M. Nixon, and Watergate, a gloomier view of the presidency took hold which viewed it as a job that seemed to bring out not the best but the worst in each new incumbent. Until Watergate, Americans were more interested in doing what was necessary to strengthen the presidency in order to enhance the *performance* of any incumbent of the White House than they were concerned about his *accountability*.

These two developments—the historical trend towards a much more complex and demanding set of presidential duties and the dismay generated by gross abuse and misuse of presidential power—do much to explain the tendency of the electorate to regard "character" as a major requirement for the office. "Character" became for many of us the answer to the difficult question, "What are the essential qualifications for performing the increasingly complex and difficult responsibilities of the enhanced presidency?" And "character" seemed the best explanation for misuse and abuse of presidential power.

Overlooked was the disconcerting fact that the politician's role in our political system and—the apparent requirements for political advancement and success may activate in some of those who participate in the political game darker sides of personality and may reward unsavory skills and behaviors. As Willard Gaylin (1973) put it, the nature of politics—as of business—may attract sociopathic and paranoid personality types: "The capacity to be ruthless, driving, and immoral, if also combined with intelligence and imagination, can be a winning combination in politics as well as in commerce. . . . Sociopathic and paranoid personality traits that are most dangerous in people of power are precisely those characteristics most suitable for the attainment of power in a competitive culture such as ours." One need not subscribe fully to Gaylin's unsettling observation to recognize that in underlines the importance of the character of candidates for high office.

This book provides an important, much-needed analysis of this central aspect of American political life. The issue of the character and psychological suitability of candidates for the presidency has received increasing attention and emphasis in presidential campaigns in recent decades. Some observers would go so far as to say that character has been *the* dominant issue in the last few elections. And the issue of character will almost certainly be central in 1996 and for decades to come.

The author, Stanley Renshon, is highly qualified for the assignment he undertakes in this book. He traces the historical evolution of the growing preoccupation with the character issue. Efforts to assess the "psychological suitability" of candidates for this high office in the past have had a markedly subjective and political cast. Nowhere was this more flagrantly evident than in the *FACT* magazine survey in 1964 in which over 2,000 psychiatrists were asked to judge whether Barry Goldwater was "psychologically fit" to serve as president, which Renshon discusses in Chapter 5. Comments offered by respondents in the *FACT* survey indicated that there was virtually no agreement about what qualities would make a leader psychologically fit or unfit for the office. Moreover, there was disturbing evidence that quite a few of the evaluations of Goldwater's fitness were influenced by the respondent's own political values and preferences.

Renshon is fully aware that the reasons for subjective and political judgments of the character and psychological suitability of candidates are deep-seated and will persist. Yet, he proposes a framework that should help to discipline and reduce the subjective and political underpinnings of such assessments. This he attempts by developing a theoretical framework for the analysis of character, drawing on the best available discussions of this important component of personality, and linking it with an incisive analysis of the main requirements for effective performance in the presidency. Renshon argues persuasively that three aspects of character—"ambition," "integrity," and "relatedness"—stand out in influencing the caliber of one's performance in the presidency. He addresses three questions: how to define "character," how to identify it in leaders, and how to evaluate its impact. Renshon's discussion of character and personality are psychologically informed without being tied to any particular psychoanalytic school; his theory of character is accessible to the general reader, focusing as it does on observable behavior. Moreover, he recognizes that much more than character affects performance of presidential duties.

Renshon here formulates a theory of presidential performance that focuses on two basic tasks any incumbent of that office will face: leadership and decision making. In his discussion of decision making Renshon quite rightly emphasizes the importance of the quality of judgment exercised by an incumbent as opposed to the nature of the procedures followed and the technical "rationality" of the decisions taken. As for the task of presidential leadership, about which so much has been said, Renshon emphasizes that leadership should manifest itself in performing three tasks: "mobilization," "orchestration," and "consolidation." Linking character and presidential performance, he points out that each of these leadership tasks requires different skills and that each engages the three components of character differently. Finally, Renshon illustrates the importance of the interplay between character and performance in incisive commentaries on several presidents and candidates for the presidency.

More and more newsprint and media attention are directed at presidential candidates and elections with every passing campaign. And yet we continue to muddle forward, fumbling with the issue of character and presidential psychology. With this important book, we no longer need to reinvent the wheel every four years.

 *Acknowledgments*

I have worked on this book over a substantial period of time and, in the process, have benefited from the work and efforts of a number of friends and colleagues. Their help and support have been crucial, and I am happy to have this opportunity to acknowledge them.

It will be clear to any reader of this book that my attempt to develop a framework for the analysis of psychological suitability and presidential performance builds on the work of Harold D. Lasswell, Alexander L. George, Fred I. Greenstein, and James David Barber. My intellectual debt to their work is evident in what follows, and I acknowledge it with appreciation.

A number of my colleagues gave me their valuable time and observations on drafts of this work and have measurably improved whatever merit this book contains. I am very appreciative of Asher Arian, James David Barber, Fred I. Greenstein, and Barbara Kellerman for their time and good advice on various aspects of the manuscript, both substantive and organizational.

Key aspects of the manuscript were clarified in presentations to the International Society of Political Psychology (1991), the American Political Science Association Meetings (1972), the Clinton Presidency Conference held at the City University of New York Graduate Center (1993), the Training and Research Institute for Self Psychology (1994), and the Policy Sciences Symposium at Yale University (1994).

I am very indebted to my colleagues at the Training and Research Institute for Self Psychology (TRISP), where I received my psychoanalytic training and where I am a senior faculty member. My training, supervision, and teaching have helped to clarify a number of important aspects of this work, I am particularly appreciative of the support and helpful theoretical discussions over the years with Harry Paul and Richard Ulman.

A number of scholars helped to clarify my work, and I would like to express my appreciation to Lloyd Etheredge, Ronald Heifetz, Margaret G. Hermann, Edwin P. Hollinder, David Longly, Bruce Mazlish, Michael

Nelson, Jerrold M. Post, William McKinley Runyan, Peter Suedfeld, and Stephen Wayne for doing so.

I would especially like to express my deep appreciation to Alexander L. George for his many pages of incisive and helpful comments and questions. Many pages of correspondence between us have helped clarify my thinking in a number of points. While theoretical differences between us remain, the manuscript and I have benefited enormously from his wise questions and helpful observations.

My graduate assistant, Ann E. Zemaitis, deserves special mention. Her sharp editorial eye and questioning mind were instrumental in clarifying aspects of the manuscript. I am much indebted to her.

This work was supported in part by two grants to the author from the City University of New York Faculty Research Award Program. I appreciate the help from those awards.

A number of people at New York University Press have worked diligently on this book. Despina Papazoglou Gimbel, managing editor at the press, supervised the copyediting and production of the book with attention and care. Joanna L. Mullins did an excellent job of copyediting the manuscript. Finally, I wish to express my sincere appreciation to Niko Pfund, editor in chief at the press, for his support and encouragement of my work. Every author should be so fortunate.

My family, Judith, David, and Jonathan, have been a sustaining source of great pleasure and pride in my life and throughout my writing.

Prologue

We are accustomed to thinking of the use of depth psychology to assess presidential candidates as a recent development in our public life. In fact, the first public application of psychoanalytic theory to the assessment of an American presidential candidate was undertaken in the United States over eighty years ago by Morton Prince, M. D., a follower of Sigmund Freud. In 1912, he wrote an article that appeared in the Sunday magazine section of *The New York Times*, titled "Roosevelt as Analyzed by the New Psychology." The article immediately created a controversy that directly reached Freud in Vienna.

From the standpoint of contemporary concerns with the psychological suitability of presidential candidates, the article was decidedly circumscribed in perspective and concern. The thrust of the article was to analyze former president Theodore Roosevelt's failure to support his party's nominee William Howard Taft in spite of Roosevelt's repeatedly stated intention not to run for a third term as an independent candidate, which he eventually did. Prince wishes to show how the "new psychology" could make sense of apparently contradictory statements and behaviors on Roosevelt's part concerning his intentions.

Prince (1912, 1) begins by stating that "Roosevelt might as well be introduced into a textbook of the new psychology to illustrate its principles." These principles, of course, are the cornerstones of psychoanalytic theory (for example, conflicting wishes, the use of repression, and the role of ambivalence). The thrust of Prince's analysis is that Roosevelt had ambivalent feelings about his renunciation of any intention to run again for the presidency. The wish to become a candidate for a third term was therefore repressed but came into public view in the form of inappropriately strong feelings about relatively minor matters and other verbal and behavioral "slips." For example, a story appeared in the newspapers in early June which reported that Roosevelt would support Taft. Roosevelt heatedly denounced this report as a "deliberate invention," in spite of the fact that he was repeatedly proclaiming his noncandidacy. From this and similar public events, Prince surmises that Roosevelt had a preconscious (not unconscious) wish to be president again, which conflicted with his friendship with Taft (it was Roosevelt, Prince notes, who had helped get Taft the nomination) and the political custom of two-term presidencies.

Prince did not accuse the former president of duplicity. Indeed, in answer to the question of whether Roosevelt deceived the public with his frequent statements of not wishing to be a candidate, Prince noted (1912, 2) that "psychology is more charitable than history and we can, from this point of view, acquit Mr. Roosevelt of intended duplicity at that time." One cannot be responsible for the wish one has no knowledge of, which is an interesting problem for the democratic theory of leadership accountability.

By the standards of contemporary concerns with character, Prince's analysis was quite tame, although it generated strong reactions at the time. Prince merely stated that Roosevelt had conflicting feelings about a political decision, which he could resolve only over time (as evidenced by his at first vague, then active stance toward the nomination). There was no suggestion of abnormality. The thrust of the article is that Roosevelt's behavior illustrated principles of psychological functioning seen universally. Nor was there any suggestion that Roosevelt was unable or unfit to govern because of his unresolved conflicts toward seeking the presidency, which were, after all, resolved by his candidacy.

There was also no indication that (or in what ways) either Roosevelt or the public would have been better served if he were more in touch with his feelings earlier, although such a case could surely have been made. Prince suggests that Roosevelt's support of moves by groups opposed to Taft arose from his own as yet unknown desire also to become a candidate, or in other terms, that "the subconscious wish in its new form was unconsciously determining his thoughts to encourage these policies" (1912, 2). Prince argued only that Roosevelt was not aware of his motives, not that they were pathological or even inappropriate. Indeed, neither word appears in the article.

While psychoanalytic theory was, from the outset, applied outside of psychotherapeutic consultations, and while Freud seemed willing, and, even eager to apply his theory in nontherapeutic settings,[1] he was at first uneasy about applying psychoanalytic theory to the evaluation of political leadership. His response to the first attempt by one of his followers to do so was sharp and critical. His criticisms, however, may have owed as much to the particular circumstances of the fledgling movement at that period as to concerns of ethics and privacy. Moreover, Freud appears to have changed his position later in his career.

On April 21, 1912, Freud wrote Carl Jung a letter (McGuire 1978, 500), enclosing a copy of the Prince article, and noted:

I want to bring up a matter that may warrant your intervention. As you can see from the enclosure, Morton Prince has made use of psi for a personal attack on Roosevelt, which seems to be creating quite a stir over there. In my opinion such a thing is absolutely inadmissible, an infringement on privacy, which to be sure is not greatly respected in America.

Freud invited Jung to comment on this development (presumably reflecting Freud's perspective) during Jung's forthcoming trip to the United States, which the later promised to do (McGuire 1978, 501), calling Prince a "mudslinger." Another member of Freud's inner circle, Ernst Jones, wrote a brief attack on Prince's article which appeared in *Zentralbatt* that same year. After reading a draft of Jones's piece, Freud wrote to Jung (McGuire 1978, 507), "I would like to append the blame that is not expressed by Jones," so the published version of the article contained the following footnote (McGuire 1978, 508 n. 3): "We should like to emphasize that we do not favor the tendency to exploit psychoanalysis for the invasion of privacy—The Editors."

Freud's strong reaction is somewhat puzzling when considered solely on the basis of the article's content. There was, after all, no suggestion of abnormality in Prince's article, no psychoanalytic reconstruction of early history of development, and no real treatment of the "deeper" (and the more controversial) aspects of the unconscious, such as orality, sadism, and the like. All that was suggested by Prince was that Roosevelt had preconscious thoughts of which he was not fully aware, and that the mechanism of repression had been used to a limited degree. Perhaps it was the later, with its early association with "neurosis," that was a source of difficulty. The invasion-of-privacy argument, while certainly a reasonable concern, is hard to justify in these limited circumstances. The criticism is also somewhat odd, given that by 1905, Freud had published his case study of Dora, a young woman who was alive at the time.

Another possible argument is that persons have some inherent right not to have their motives analyzed publicly without their explicit consent. This was not an argument that Freud made. Had he done so, it would have been somewhat paradoxical, since just seven years before he had publicly advocated (1906) that judges undertake systematic familiarization with psychoanalytic theory because it could aid them in distinguishing truth from deception and thus, help them to determine guilt or innocence. Freud's proposal to render public verdicts based on such psychological understanding is hardly consistent with another's right not to be subjected to this analysis.

A more plausible possibility for Freud's response to this analysis is that at this time Freud was very much concerned with professional and public acceptance of his work and did not welcome the unnecessary and adverse publicity that came with novel applications of an as yet controversial theory. Prince (1912, 1) certainly did not help matters by publicly challenging Roosevelt "to submit himself to what is technically called a psychoanalysis" if he denied the truth of Prince's analysis.

Freud appears to have moved closer to accepting the propriety of such analyses later in his career. In his introduction to his controversial study with William Bullitt of Woodrow Wilson, Freud disclaims any intention to do more than provide a psychological analysis of the former president, yet he concludes his introduction by noting, "We cannot however deny that, in this case as in all cases, a more intimate knowledge of the man may lead to a more exact estimate of his achievements" (Freud and Bullitt 1966, xix). If psychoanalysis was not yet to be placed in the service of the contemporary assessment of psychological suitability, it could at least provide perspective.

The questions of whether it is legitimate to undertake this task, whether it is possible to accomplish it, and (if it is) how it might be done are the subjects of this analysis.

Introduction: Does the President's Character Still Matter?

President's Response to Questions of Character:

Question: Following up on Peter's earlier question, to what degree do you think the president, any president, is a role model in his private behavior? And does that not justify questions about private behavior that might otherwise be considered intrusive?

President Clinton: Well, these are questions you need to ask and answer without my involvement for the simple reason that our consensus about that over time has been . . . has changed dramatically.[1]

As Alexander Hamilton hoped,[2] the modern presidency has become an engine of energy and progress. When Franklin D. Roosevelt forged a public-presidential partnership that displaced the congressional-presidential partnership which had preceded it, he made the presidency the center of the American political universe. Thereafter, presidents would be responsible for managing the economy, and soon, under Presidents Truman and Eisenhower, they became responsible for national security as well. After a Senate career building large legislative monuments reflecting his power as the majority leader, President Lyndon Johnson did not think it overreaching to declare the president responsible for solving pressing social problems like poverty and discrimination. And from there, President Clinton found it a natural step to initiate a national discussion on race that would point to a new presidential role, that of managing issues of cultural diversity and conflicts. These escalating expectations resulted in a fundamental realignment of

1

candidate motivation and presidential psychology. Traditionally, presidential candidates were required to reconcile their real capacities, and just as real limitations, with their desire to gain office. Most choose decisively in favor of their ambitions.

Today, however, ambition is not enough. Because the presidency now occupies an important position at the intersection of the public's many hopes and fears, aspiring candidates must also reconcile the mismatch between the public's expectations and their, or any president's, realistic ability to deliver on them. Caught between their ambitions and realism, many candidates have succumbed to the temptation to substitute promises for candor and market-tested phrases for honest public discussion. Once in office, therefore, they must further reconcile their real ability to satisfactorily accomplish public purposes with the expectations they have created.[3]

It was not always like this. In the past, Americans were optimistic about progress, but more realistic and accepting of the hard work, determination, and sacrifice that were necessary to accomplish it. They wanted a president who could and did get things done, but in a way that was consistent with the personal integrity they expected. And, while Americans wanted competence, they also wanted a president who embodied their best ideals, and those of the country—a person of public stature and reputation of whom they could be justifiably proud whether they fully agreed with him or not.

In the two years since this book was first published, that understanding has been called into question by the apparent paradox of a president whose personal ethics and political skills seem inversely related, but whose job ratings have remained high. For example, in an April 1998 *Washington Post* poll, 65% of those asked said they approved of the way President Clinton was handling the presidency. Yet, the same poll found that only 35% thought him honest and trustworthy, and only 29% felt he had high personal moral and ethical standards.[4] The theory of character put forward within these pages does not view character as a president's supreme virtue (or failing) to be judged by public approval ratings, but rather as a set of patterns, rooted in his inner psychology, that he brings to every circumstance. His ambitions, his adherence to ideals and values as well as his relationships with others are central not only to his own psychological functioning, but to the ways he chooses to carry out the responsibilities of his office. However, this book also makes clear that as useful as this theory might be, ultimately it is the public's responsibility to decide.

Do these conflicting poll ratings of President Clinton mean that after two decades of intense public concern with "character issues," these issues no longer matter? Do Americans no longer care what kind of person occupies the office? If that is true, what could possibly account for this dramatic and unexpected change? Has the public grown more sophisticated, more cynical, or simply more realistic? The answers to these questions are at the heart of this book.

Performance=A, Personal Ethics=F: Conflicting Evidence and Explanations of the Public's Response to the Unfolding Clinton Scandals

A number of substantive explanations have been put forward to explain what some suggest is a dramatic shift in the public's stance toward evaluating a president's character and performance. Some are plausible, others are not.[5] Some are consistent with available evidence of the public's views, others are not. Many are certainly inconsistent with each other. Yet, examining the most plausible explanations briefly in turn, allows us to gain a deeper understanding of the triangulation between presidential character and performance on one hand, and public judgments about these matters on the other.

Excess Is Appealing: Most, but not all, explanations of the Clinton paradox (high ratings in job performance coupled with low personal ratings) take for granted that the president's behavior may be understandable, perhaps excusable, but certainly not desirable. However, some argue that it is precisely the president's excesses that make him attractive. Lydia Saad, managing editor of the Gallop polls, argues that "people seem to like a big man with a reputation that is larger than life," and that President Clinton "seems to prosper from something we can't poll for, unspoken affection for leaders who live large—large life, large appetites, large loves."[6]

The problem with this theory is that no data exists to support it. Quite the contrary.[7] In February 1998, Princeton Survey Research Associates found that while 69% approved of the president's policies, only 42% said that they liked him personally. In a December 1997 poll which asked Americans whether they would rather have their child grow up to be like Bill Clinton or Bill Gates, 47% picked the Microsoft CEO and just 24%

preferred the president (another 20% found neither appealing). This is hardly evidence of admiration.

Public Ambivalence: Making judgments about the limits of privacy and the relationship between personal behavior and public responsibilities for a candidate or president is no easy matter, factually or emotionally. That process is riddled with conflict, both self-initiated and encouraged by others. Whether the facts can be established is one issue, what they mean is another, and what one must do given the two, quite another. Facts which lead to unavoidable conclusions impose a burden of guilt on those who clearly see their responsibilities, but can't act.

The Psychological Assessment of Presidential Candidates points out that the conflicts generated by these kinds of character issues first surfaced in 1988 with Gary Hart, a front runner for the Democratic Party's presidential nomination with a reputation for philandering. When he announced his candidacy, his family by his side, he promised a campaign and presidency of the highest moral standards. Asked about the rumors of his infidelity, he denied them, inviting reporters to follow him around. Acting on a tip, they did and watched as he spent the weekend with a woman who wasn't his wife. In spite of attempts to create a narrative that could, if you were so inclined, account for these and other facts that emerged, Hart's presidential bid collapsed. Reacting to these facts, the public was conflicted and angry, at both Hart and the reporters who uncovered the story, as the following interview attests:[8]

Woman: Well, I think his private life is his own business.
Interviewer: It wouldn't affect whether or not you would vote for him?
Woman: Yeah, it makes a big difference to me.
Interviewer: His private life does?
Woman: Yes.
Interviewer: Should the press report on his private life?
Woman: No.
Interviewer: How are you going to know about it?
Woman: I would have felt better if I didn't know about it.
Interviewer: You don't want to know?
Woman: No, I don't.
Interviewer: But it does affect the way you vote, right?
Woman: It certainly does.

Evidence of similar ambivalence is easy to find in the case of President Clinton's behavior and the allegations that surround it. For example,

64% of the public thinks the president's alleged affair with a 21-year old intern is a private matter having to do with his personal life and not having to do with his job as president. The same 64% say that the public doesn't need to know the details of the president's relationship with the intern. However, 61% of the public think it is important to know if the president encouraged her to lie.[9] How it would be possible to find this out without learning more of the details of their relationship is unclear.

These anomalies have led some to argue that the public is confused because it says "it is waiting for proof . . . but . . . already think they know the truth, yet profess not to care about it."[10] The public is not necessarily confused, just severely conflicted.

The Decline of Public Attention: Americans approaching the latest Clinton controversies with the ambivalent wish that they would just vanish[11] have been frustrated and disappointed. Failing that, an alternative is for the public to do what the scandals won't. They can disappear.

In fact, rapt attention to politics has rarely been the defining characteristic of the American public. Robert Samuelson notes that "Most Americans view freedom from politics as part of their well-being." The Englishman James Bryce, who visited this country in 1881 and wrote *The American Commonwealth* noted, "Never once have I heard American politics discussed, except when I or some other European brought the subject on the carpet."[12] In 1997, the Pew Research Center for the People and the Press reported that among its twenty most closely watched stories in 1997 only three were concerned with politics, and none ranked higher than thirteenth. The story which headed the list was Princess Diana's death.

Americans' declining interest in politics can be seen in other numbers as well. In the 1992 presidential election, ordinarily a high point of the public's political interest and participation, only 55.2% of those eligible to vote registered and did so. Four years later, that number had declined to 48.8% in spite of new laws which made registering to vote easier than at any time in this country's history. The reasons for this are themselves complex. They reflect historical preference for limited government which had the effect of reducing the public and enlarging the private spheres in this country. The structure and arrangement of American political institutions also favors incremental pragmatism over massive and potentially divisive change. This tendency is reinforced, and no doubt partially a result of, the public's own political beliefs. Americans overwhelmingly tend to be either moderate or conservative, rather than liberal.[13] While not quite the "end of ideology," which Daniel Bell anticipated in 1960,[14] it is true that, with certain clear exceptions, divisive and mobilizing public issues have been the exception and not the rule historically in the United States. Does this mean that the public believes that the country has no important problems to address? Hardly. In spite of the fact that the economy is doing well, which clearly helps the president, a January 1998 poll found that half of a representative national sample thought that the country was "seriously off on the wrong track."[15] In another survey, many said they were satisfied with the performance of the economy but gravely concerned about other problems, particularly the moral health of the nation and its families, and the issues of crime, moral health, as well as education, race, homelessness, and immigration.[16]

So, why, at a time when the public has substantial concerns about the direction of the country even as the economy is booming, isn't there more concern with the myriad scandals swirling around the Clinton administration? One possible explanation put forward by some is that the public is more "mature" and "sophisticated" about sexual matters.

The Low(er) Moral Expectations Theory: This theory starts out with the view that modern presidents are judged in the context of past presidents' private lives, about which the public has learned after they have been in office. Or, as *New York Times* columnist Anthony Lewis put it, "Greatness in leadership does not depend on sexual purity."[17]

Eighty-five percent of the public agree that "other presidents have had equally bad private lives," (Harris, February 25). Given that some of these presidents are held in public esteem (FDR, JFK), it is not surprising that 84% (CBS/*New York Times*, February 23) think "someone can be a good president even if you disapprove of his personal life." Moreover, this theory, some said, applies with particular force to President Clinton. Democratic pollster Peter Hart argued that discussions about the public's view of presidential morality assumed that "this is a person with high moral standards. In truth, they've never believed that."[18]

The Psychological Assessment of Presidential Candidates points out, however, that not all extramarital relationships are psychologically or politically synonymous. Singular long-term relationships suggest one psychology, serial sometimes multiple relationships another. FDR's relationship with Lucy Mercer was singular, took place fourteen years before he entered the White House and was serious enough to lead him to consider divorce.[19] John F. Kennedy's relationship with Judith Exner, among many others, Gary Hart's multiple relationships, and Bill Clinton's extramarital relationships and episodes (one admitted to by himself, others acknowledged by the women involved) represent a wholly different psychology. While greatness in leadership does not depend on sexual purity, it does depend on trust.

The Rise of Public Mistrust: In 1958, at the end of the Eisenhower administration, almost 75% of the American public thought they could trust the government in Washington to do what is right "just about always," or "most of the time."[20] By 1998 those figures had been exactly reversed with 75% of the public believing you could not trust Washington to do what is right "just about always," or "most of the time." The number of people who thought the government looked out for the interests of the common person rather than themselves took a parallel nosedive from 70% in 1958 to 20% in 1994.

These numbers appear to be independent of the president's job approval ratings or even the health of the economy. The *Washington Post* poll found that 75% of its respondents did not trust the government to do what is right—a view that was shared even by those who had prospered the most during the last four years. A recent Pew Research Center analysis of the causes of the decline of trust in government concluded, "Discontent with political leaders and lack of faith in the political system are principal factors that stand behind public distrust of government. Much of that criticism involves the honesty and ethics of government leaders."[21] In other words, it is the action of leaders themselves, their integrity and morality, which affect the degree of the public's trust. From this perspective, the scandals surrounding the Clinton presidency have the paradoxical effect of insulating him from their consequences.

The increasing public mistrust of politics and major American political institutions helps explain why Americans might turn *away* from politics. However, it doesn't really answer Republican presidential candidate Bob Dole's plaintive question during the last presidential campaign, "Where's the outrage?" One clue is found in the Pew Research Center study ("Deconstructing Distrust") which reported that 56% of the public described themselves as frustrated with the government, while only 12% described themselves as angry. However, this doesn't explain why the public remains more frustrated than angry.

A firmer clue is found in the answers to a question which is ordinarily asked as part of a set of questions on trust in government. This one asks respondents to agree or disagree with the proposition that "public officials care (or don't care) about what people like me think." A September 1956 ANES poll found that 53% of the public thought public officials did care, and only 37% thought they did not. However, by August 1976, a CBS/*New York Times* poll found that only 26% of the public now thought they did, while 71% though they did not. Finally, a March 1994 ABC/*Washington Post* poll found that 32% thought they did, and 67% thought not. In answer to the question, "Where's the outrage?" these data suggest that the public response may well be "why bother?"

Scandal Fatigue: While politics are not central to most Americans' lives, after eight years of successive controversies that began during the Clinton candidacy in 1991, even those that have tried to follow them are likely to be emotionally and intellectually tired.[22] Some controversies have been major (Mr. Clinton's relationship with Gennifer Flowers, "Filegate"[23]), some have been minor (whether he tried marijuana). Most have been complicated.

Whitewater is hard to follow because the actors and actions under investigation have spanned the years from Clinton's days as governor right into his years as president (Vincent Foster, disappearing, then miraculously reappearing records). Others, like the 1996 campaign finance scandals have involved the Democratic National Committee (DNC), the Teamsters' Union, the White House, and some political advocacy groups in a variety of schemes. Some of these are clearly illegal and individuals have been criminally indicted, others are merely ethically questionable (White House coffees for big donors), while still others are legal but distasteful (renting out the Lincoln Bedroom in exchange for campaign contributions).

The sheer number of legitimate ethical questions, actual and potential criminal indictments, and allegations (some serious, some marginal) surrounding the president and his administration have made keeping up with them close to a full-time job. In many of these numerous and complex controversies, the public has also had to sort through which ones are private, personal matters and which ones are not. However, no understanding of the paradox of questionable ethical behavior and high poll ratings can hope to prove adequate without examining the role of the administration's comprehensive, tough, and substantially successful efforts to disparage its critics, discredit its accusers, and provide many, often conflicting explanations of events in an effort to raise doubt, fatigue, and ambivalence.

Just What Are the Facts?: A corollary of the fact that Americans prefer not to pay attention to politics is that while they can be counted on to give their opinions, these opinions are not well informed. Only 24% of the public could name both their U. S. Senators, and 67% could not name their congressional representative.[24] The Pew Research Center reported that only 20% of those under age 30, 23% of those between 30 and 49, and 29% of people over 50 paid close attention to the news.[25] Or, to put it another way, over 70% of every age group didn't do what is minimally necessary to be well informed. The Pew Research Center also reports that as of June 1992, 45% strongly or moderately agreed with the statement that they were generally bored with what went on in Washington. By July of 1994, that figure had risen to 51%.

So, summing up the public's informational stance regarding government, we might say this: They prefer to be free from politics, and have grown increasingly mistrustful of it in good measure because of the questionable ethical conduct of leaders, who, the public feels, don't care much about what people think. Under these circumstances it hardly seems a good use of precious time to be politically attentive, and most are not.

As a result, many, if not most, Americans lack a substantive foundation, aside from any party loyalty, which would allow them to place the numerous facts arising out of the Clinton sandals into a framework of analysis and understanding. However, even if there were fewer facts to understand and judge, and the public were less ambivalent or reticent about doing so, they would still have to contend with the administration's no-holds-barred defense strategy.[26]

This strategy consists of contesting the authenticity of every presented fact by whatever means possible in as strong or outraged a tone as possible. The first line of defense is to deny the facts or, when that proves impossible, to contest their relevance or the meaning attributed to them. If that fails, and even if it doesn't, create new issues wherever possible. And, of course, wherever possible attack the credibility, character, and motivation of anyone who questions your behavior. The point is not so much to introduce exculpatory evidence, or to provide straight forward explanations, but rather to create doubt. So, if you are accused of having an affair with a 21-year-old intern, emphatically deny it, note that there are legitimate questions being raised, and emphasize how hard you are working on getting answers to them. Later you can say that your previous denial represents all that needs to be said in spite of new evidence of at least three dozen unexplained White House visits by that same intern.[27]

Or, demand that your opponent stop leaking confidential court information. If his response is that you are orchestrating the leaks for your own purposes, deny it and file publicly announced court motions to stop the leaks. If you are not vindicated by the court, complain loudly and publicly of a "prosecutorial public relations offensive," giving the impression that the prosecutor's single newly hired spokesman is more partisan or loose with the facts than the large White House staff devoted to the president's defense. Since reporters keep their sources confidential, it will be almost impossible to pinpoint the origins of any leaks, but doing so is hardly the real point. If a prosecutor, or anyone, makes you the issue, make certain they become the issue instead. Raise every question possible, from the serious (Mr. Starr's decision, quickly reversed, to leave his responsibilities to take up a position financed in part by an opponent of the administration) to the superficial, and don't worry if your accusations are religiously insensitive (Mr. Starr is suspect because he sings hymns while jogging). The primary purpose is to discredit the person, and any damaging evidence this person brings to the public's attention about the president.[28]

It would be naive to expect that any president, accused of a wide range of dishonest and illegal behavior, would quietly acquiesce to opponents' views of himself. It is especially unthinkable for a president like Mr. Clinton, who firmly believes the best of himself—that his motives are pure, his behavior understandable and more often beyond reproach, and that his troubles are solely attributable to his enemies.[29]

Given the state of information in the American public, their ambivalence, their reluctance, their alienation from politics, as well as the view that leaders don't care what people think anyway—the administration's strategy seems clear. Create as much conflict as possible thereby feeding public ambivalence, reluctance, and turmoil. Blunt the force of the facts you can't dispute and settle in to a determined stall, wounded but still in office as the last years of your presidency ebb.

The Public–Private Distinction: Privacy is psychologically important for any person, including the president. There are important distinctions to be drawn between the president's private and public lives. This book offers some basis on which to make these distinctions.

And, in fact, this is precisely what the public appears to be doing.[30] An NBC/*Wall Street Journal* poll (5 March, 1998) found that 65% believed that "the public has become more realistic and accepts that political leaders should be judged on job performance, not personal life." In that same poll, 67% felt that the president should be able to withhold "certain private matters." A *New York Times*/CBS poll (23 February, 1998) reported that a majority of 59% found it "understandable [that] he would not tell the truth about his sex life."

Certainly, the *Washington Post*, and other polls, show that the public is able to and does make the distinction between the president's ethical and moral character (rated low) and his abilities as a president (rated high). During the same period that the public saw Mr. Clinton as having low moral standards and being dishonest and untrustworthy, they also saw him as understanding the problems of "people like you" (56%) and being a strong leader (62%). And while only 40% of the public thought he "shared the moral values that most Americans try to live by," the public was willing to give him credit for making progress since 1994 on a range of domestic issues.[31]

The capacity to distinguish is a hallmark of intelligence. Therefore, critics of the substantive quality of American public opinion might well take heart. However, the question here is not only whether Americans can, or should make such distinctions, but also what is the most appropriate way to handle these distinctions, once they are made.

Public Judgement, If at All, at a Snail's Pace: In his recent study of suburban middle class values, Alan Wolfe noted that Americans seem to have added an eleventh commandment to the original ten: "Thou shalt not judge."[32] The "non-judgmentalism of middle class Americans" in matters of religion, family, and other personal values emerges as his book's major finding. He attributes it to an emphasis on pragmatism rather than values in the making of tough personal decisions, a reluctance to second-guess the tough choices of other people, and an ambivalence, or confusion, as the "default" moral position. It is only a short step from this stance to a reluctance in making any adverse judgments about political life as well, and Wolte is not surprised that this has happened. Wolfe notes that this reluctance is found among Democrats and Republicans alike. However, this conflicts with Ladd's data, to be discussed shortly, which reveals partisan differences in making judgments about the president.

Wolfe notes in another context that Washington "is a place where the values of the 1960s and the values of corporate America have come together," both being extremely relativistic and adverse to making judgments.[33] There is an important distinction to be drawn between being slow in making judgments, and being adverse to making them. Why Americans now seem more adverse than slow is a question left unanswered by Wolfe, but is nonetheless critical in understanding the public's response to the unfolding scandals. Some think they have found the answer to this question: self-interest. In particular, they point to a robust economy.

"It's the Economy, Stupid": Low unemployment, low inflation, and a roaring stock market have all combined to lift the president's approval ratings for job performance. A *Washington Post*/ABC news poll concluded that the president "clearly benefits from good economic times."[34] His job approval rating in that poll stood at 68% among those who thought the economy was doing well, and only 24% among those who thought the economy was not doing so well. Among those Americans who said they were personally better off now than they were four years ago, 68% approved of the job Clinton is doing, a view shared by only 42% of those whose finances had suffered.[35]

The answer to the question of why the country's strong economic performance has helped to insulate the president emerges in more in-depth interviews with the public. After conducting a series of interviews in a suburban New Jersey town, reporters found a consensus that the country must move beyond the Lewinsky matter, "mostly out of concern that further investigation could bring about changes in the White House and uncertainty about the future—from the economy to an Al Gore presidency."[36] At base, however, the worry about the undermining of the Clinton Presidency by the news media, the independent counsel, or the president himself, was that it could jeopardize this moment of relative prosperity. Or, in other words, self-interest appears to trump concerns with presidential morality.[37] Somewhat paradoxically, what started out as a puzzle of the president's behavior, led to questions regarding the public's psychology and values.

The President as the Perfect Embodiment of the Age: A critical link exists between the leader and his times. Martin Luther, for example, poised between tradition and Reformation, gave voice not only to his own religious doubts, but to the barely spoken yet pervasive questions of his time. More recently, Winston Churchill was viewed by his countrymen as indispensable to their country's survival during World War II, but not after it ended. Leaders, especially when they are freely chosen as they are in the United States, will partially, if not substantially, reflect the psychology and values of those who select them.

It remains to ask, then: How can Americans be characterized? Some look around and see evidence of the erosion of the values and beliefs that were instrumental in developing this country. They see America fast becoming a country where people want dispensations from inconvenient rules and standards.[38] Can't get into the college of your choice because of low test scores or poor grades? No problem. We'll simply create a new special category for you that exempts you from the standards that others need to surmount. Are you a young woman a point shy of a record, who breaks her foot? No problem. We'll arrange a special uncontested shot for you. You live in a commonwealth that would like to become America's fifty-first state, but your official language is Spanish and you are not anywhere close to meeting the requirements of the other fifty states? No problem. Some in Congress, hoping for political advantage, will create special rules for your admission.

It is not a far stretch from these examples to tolerating a president whose moral fitness standards would not be tolerated in any CEO, professor, military commander, or anyone else in a position of power and responsibility. In a review of a psychologically framed biography of President Clinton and his administration, written shortly before the '96 presidential election, Richard Restak wrote that "social commentators have suggested that Americans have reached a time in our history when we no longer care about the integrity of our leaders . . . when many are infatuated with the superficial charm that masks ruthlessness and ambition, . . . a time when leadership translates into glibness and a facility for mouthing empty expressions of concern. . . . If these commentators are correct . . . Americans need look no further for their ideal leader: They already have their man."[39]

Do the Polls Reflect or Encourage Public Ambivalence?: Almost all the data used to support speculation about the demise of the public's concern with character issues are potentially fatally flawed. The problem is not the wording of questions which can influence public responses, although they can only answer the specific questions put to them. Nor is it the distinction which Americans prefer to make between their own lack of interest in any details about the president's private life, and what they see as other Americans' more direct, prurient interest in these matters.[40] Rather, begin with the public's reluctance to make judgments. Then consider the fact that surveys require people to do exactly that, in front of a stranger, and often over the phone no less.[41] Add to this the most basic finding on the psychology of groups, namely that hearing like-minded people express their views helps lower a person's inhibition in expressing his own."[42] Thus, in a series of focus groups brought together to ascertain the public's view of welfare reform, participants had no difficulty passing judgment and even expressing outrage at those who took advantage of the system.[43]

Focus groups run the risk of having dominant personalities sway the less committed or more compliant ones. However, anonymous telephone surveys run the risk of underestimating people's concern simply because of their reluctance to express it publicly and that to a stranger. Paradoxically, if this is accurate, polls may wind up encouraging the very behavior they report. After all, if a person is reluctant to make judgments publicly, and polls report that reluctance is now the "conventional wisdom," they would seem even less likely to express a contrary view to someone they didn't know and perhaps even to someone they did know.

Partisan Judgments?: Public identification with political parties, which has been declining for years, does play a role in organizing public views of the president's behavior. Ladd found that "Democrats are far more inclined than Republicans to defend the president, criticize his opponents, and oppose the very idea of removing him from office."[44] This was a reversal of Watergate-related partisan evaluations.

The reason for the partisan divide may seem obvious. Democrats defend "their man" and the programs he advocates, while Republicans favor neither. But there may be deeper currents here. Identification with a political party reflects more than agreement with its policies. It also reflects agreement with its premises.

Do you believe that welfare encourages people to become dependent on government and that if government did less, people could and would take more responsibility for themselves? This is a traditional conservative policy view which is consistent with conservative understanding of human psychology. Do you believe that swift, certain, and strong punishment is more likely to have an impact on criminals' thinking than well-meaning, but diffuse efforts to eradicate "root causes"? If so, you probably support a host of traditionally conservative "get tough" criminal policies which are consistent with the understanding of criminal motivation that underlies them.

Americans may be reluctant to pass judgments, but conservatives seem quite able to do so with those who ignore what they consider to be responsible, morally respectable, legitimately expectable behavior. In diverse policy areas—for example, abortion, crime, and welfare where personal psychology is seen to play as much of a role as social circumstances, conservatives are much more likely than liberals to make personal and policy judgments, often adverse, about others.[45]

Now, consider this: In 1994, 73% of Americans who identified themselves as conservative also identified with the Republican Party. Rank and file Republicans, therefore, were much more likely than their liberal Democratic counterparts to make adverse judgments about their fellow citizens, especially when that behavior violated "traditional" standards and values. Perhaps that willingness has now carried over to the president as well. Perhaps the "traditional" expectation that the president should be honest as well as competent is the basis for having adverse views of this president's behavior. In a country that is reluctant to "pass judgment," has the Republican Party become the home of those willing to do so?

Conclusion

Some have argued that the lack of a large groundswell of public outrage and calls for the president's impeachment show that the public no longer cares about character issues. In doing so, they appear to accept the president's dishonest and possibly unlawful behavior as a fact, and argue for our disinterest on the grounds of public indifference. Yet, funeral services for alleged demise of public concern with the president's character and behavior seem premature.

Americans may be slow or reluctant to judge, uninterested or uninformed about politics, put off by what they see to some degree through a partisan lens, frustrated in their search for clarity by the strategic sowing of confusion and controversy, and reluctant to jeopardize economic well-being. Yet, for all that, the public is conflicted and concerned, not disinterested. Their ambivalence does lead to avoidance, but it also reflects a reluctant, unpleasant and, for the president, politically damaging knowledge. Certainly that information is unwanted, but that doesn't necessarily make it unimportant.

The many explanations of how the president can keep his performance high, while his personal ratings are low overlook one important fact. A number of Americans are willing and do make adverse moral judgments about the president. In a March 1998 *Washington Post* poll,

58% of the public thought the president was not honest or trustworthy, 64% though he didn't have high personal and moral standards, 61% thought he had engaged in a pattern of sexual misconduct, and 47% thought that pattern was important and relevant. Fifty percent thought the president had broken the law by lying under oath about sexual misconduct or by encouraging others to lie under oath, and 72% said that whether he did it was an important issue. Assuming that was true, and offered the following choices—he should: resign or be impeached; be formally reprimanded by Congress but stay in office, apologize to the country but no further action is taken; or, no action taken at all—37% favored resignation, 22% a formal reprimand, 21% an apology, and 16% no action.

Finally, it is important to keep in mind that the special prosecutor has yet to make his report. It will, almost certainly, be severely damaging to the president. Whether Mr. Clinton's high job approval ratings will survive intact after the report becomes public and its implications are digested, is extremely doubtful.

Our only other modern experience with such issues has been with Richard Nixon and Watergate. Then, as now, the public was slow to judge, reluctant to reach the conclusions that the unfolding facts clearly pointed toward, and aware of the awesome political implications of so doing. Yet even then, just two weeks before Mr. Nixon was forced to resign, 35% saw him as a man of integrity, a greater proportion than so credit Bill Clinton today.[46]

Moreover, is it clear that the public will be slow to judge should allegations prove accurate that the frenzied search for campaign contributions led the president to overrule his advisors and allow sensitive missile technology to be given to the People's Republic of China. The public may be ambivalent about, or willing to overlook, a president driven by the pursuit of his own personal pleasures. However, it is extremely unlikely that it will be as tolerant of a president driven by the pursuit of his own reelection, especially if in the process it concludes, as Congress has, that he failed to act in "the national interest."[47]

Whether Mr. Clinton remains in office is not the most relevant, or even necessarily the most important indication of whether character is, will be, or should be important in our selection of presidents. The evidence presented herein suggests that it is still important, although, it is still conflicted public territory. Even leaving aside the question of ordinary American ambivalence to looking into private matters, this is hardly surprising.

Americans are reluctant to judge others, even as standards for making any judgments are called into question. Yet, they view with concern the level of violence on the airwaves and in their schools, the decline of merit as a principle for rewarding accomplishment, and the growing acceptability of intrusive, offensive, and legally suspect personal behavior. In this atmosphere, is there any reason to expect that the presidency would be exempt from the larger moral and ethical questions with which this country now struggles? Bill Clinton's presidency may prove more important as a symbolic reflection of this struggle, than its triumphant embodiment.

Moreover, there already is evidence that character *will be* important in coming presidential elections. Democratic Party front runner Al Gore's reputation for probity will doubtlessly be an asset if it can survive his association with the president. On the Republican side as well, Representative John Kasich (R–Ohio) is already making ethics comparisons as basis of his candidacy. Jimmy Carter's emphasis on integrity in the wake of the Nixon resignation helped gain him the White House. Even if "scandal fatigue" helps to save the Clinton presidency, it is unlikely that their "empathic rogue" will be a presidential mantle any future candidate will choose, or successfully be allowed, to wear.

Finally, even if the public remains conflicted and reluctant to make judgments about character of the individuals it places in office, does that require those who professionally understand its importance to become mute? True, the public is the ultimate, but ambivalent judge of these matters. And yes, drawing reasonable lines between public and private is a difficult task.

However, the paradoxical but basic psychological fact remains: Character is indivisible. A president who is dishonest in his public dealings will not be less so in his private ones. And a president who is not to be trusted in his private dealings is not likely to be more trustworthy in his public ones.

The Psychological Assessment of Presidential Candidates argues that a president's psychology and the patterns it gives rise to, *are* central to how he sees and carries out his responsibilities. Before Richard Neustadt's magisterial *Presidential Power*[48] changed the way scholars looked at the presidency, its occupants were seen to wear many hats: commander-in-chief, head of his party, etc. Neustadt's paradigm-shifting insight was that they all sat on the same head. That insight is no less true for a president: character, interior psychology, and choices in carrying out his public responsibilities.

The issue of presidential character and how to assess it has, if anything, become more relevant in light of the political, legal, and ultimately ethical problems of the Clinton administration.

Notes

1. "The President's News Conference (April 30, 1998)," *Weekly Compilation of Presidential Documents*, 4 May, 1998, 34:18, p. 747.
2. Alexander Hamilton, James Madison, and John Jay, *The Federalist Papers, with an introduction by Clinton Rossiter.* (New York: New American Library, 1961) No. 70.
3. See for example the prescient analysis by Daniel Boornstin, *The Image.* (New York: Vintage 1988). For a recent illustration of "pseudo-events" in the arena of presidential leadership see Meg Greenfield, "Leadership by Presentation," *Newsweek*, 9 March 1998, p. 68.
4. *The Washington Post*, 5 April 1998. Unless otherwise cited, all data drawn from the *The Washington Post* polling results on the Clinton scandals can be found at: http://www.washingtonpost.com/wpsrv/politics/polls/vault/stories/data040598.htm.
5. Among the least plausible is one that argued that the public excused the president's behavior because he was "widely viewed . . . as a member of the family." No evidence for this speculation is presented, and none of the many polls that address the public's view of the president give the slightest support for it. See Peter Rubin, "Family Man," *The New Republic*, 27 April 1998, p. 12.
6. Ron Suskind, "What's Sex Got to Do with it? In the World of Politics, Quite a Bit," *The Wall Street Journal*, 24 March 1998, A1. The quotes which follow are drawn from this article.
7. The poll numbers which follow in the paragraph are drawn from Everett Carll Ladd, "Nixon, Clinton, and the Polls," *The Wall Street Journal*, 1 April, 1998, A18.
8. Transcript, *MacNeil/Lehrer NewsHour*, 18 December 1987, p. 8.
9. The preceding figures are drawn from James Bennet and Janet Elder, "Despite Intern, President Stays in Good Graces," *The New York Times*, 24 February 1998, A15.
10. That is, for example, the conclusion of James Q. Wilson. See for example, his "Making Sense of the Polls," *The Wall Street Journal*, 13 February, 1998, A18.
11. Thirty-four percent of the public expressed the wish that Special Prosecutor Ken Starr would wrap up his investigation of the president, and another 35% wanted to impose some time limits on it. Only 27% of the public surveyed were willing to grant as much time as needed to conclude the investigation. See Dan Balz and Claudia Deane,"Poll Finds Impatience With Ongoing Starr Investigation, *The Washington Post*, 5 April, 1998, A1.
12. The two preceding quotes are drawn from Robert J. Samuelson, "Why Clinton Is Surviving," *Newsweek*, 6 April 1998, p. 40.

13. Surveys from the American National Election Studies conducted by the University of Michigan and the National Opinion Research Center at the University of Chicago found that the average percentage of Americans identifying themselves as either "moderate" or "conservative" was 75% for the years 1972–1994. See Stephen J. Wayne et al, *The Politics of American Government, Second Edition* (New York: St. Martin's Press, 1997) p. 216.

14. Daniel Bell, *The End of Ideology* (Glencoe, Ill.: The Free Press, 1960.)

15. See Richard Morin and Claudia Deane, "Poll Shows Americans More Satisfied with U.S.," *The Washington Post*, 21 January 1998, A6.

16. Richard Morin. "Poll Finds Pessimism on U.S. Course," *The Washington Post*, 29 August 1997; A1.

17. Anthony Lewis, "Sex and Leadership," *The New York Times*, 28 February 1998, A19.

18. Kathleen Hall Jamieson, "That Clear Line Between Public and Private Conduct," *The Washington Post National Weekly Edition*, 30 March, 1998, p. 21.

19. Doris Kearns Goodwin, *No Ordinary Time: Franklin and Eleanor Roosevelt: The Homefront in World War II.* (New York: Simon and Schuster, 1994); see also Dorothy Rabinowitz, "TV: The President and the Polls," *The Wall Street Journal*, 2 February 1998, A20.

20. Charles Murray, "Americans Remain Wary of Washington," *The Wall Street Journal*, 23 December 1997, A14; Stephen J. Wayne et al., op. cit., p. 219.

21. Pew Research Center for the People and the Press, "Deconstructing Distrust: How Americans View Government," 10 March 1998; for other views of the cause of the decline of public trust see Joseph S. Nye, Jr. et al. (Eds), *Why People Don't Trust Government* (Cambridge, Ma: Harvard University Press, 1997.)

22. For example, see Jonathan Alter, "Depleting His Account," *Newsweek*, 13 April 1998, p. 34.

23. See editorials, "The FBI Files Flap," and "The FBI Files Flap: Take 2," *The Washington Post National Weekly Edition*, 24–30 June 1996, A24.

24. See Stephen J. Wayne, et al., op. cit., p. 210.

25. Pew Research Center for the People and the Press, "The Times Mirror News Interest Index: 1989–1995," no. 7.

26. Howard Kurtz, *Spin Cycle: Inside the Clinton Propaganda Machine.* (New York: The Free Press, 1998.)

27. James Bennet, "Clinton Emphatically Denies an Affair with Ex-Intern," *The New York Times*, 26 January 1998, A1; "Excerpts from Clinton's News Conference on Investigations and Middle East," *The New York Times*, 1 May 1998, A24–25; Don Van Natta, Jr. and John M. Broder, "Logs at White House Show 3 Dozen Visits by Lewinsky," *The New York Times*, 3 February 1998, A1.

28. To some degree that strategy appears to be working. *Washington Post* polls found that in January 1998, 36% of the public had an unfavorable opinion of Mr. Starr. By March 1998 that figure had risen to 43%. A majority thought that he was less interested in finding out the truth than in hurting the president.

20   *Introduction*

See Dan Balz and Claudia Deane, "Poll Finds Impatience With Ongoing Starr Investigation," *The Washington Post*, April 5, 1998, A01; Howard Kurtz, "Starr Accused of PR Offensive on Leaks," *The Washington Post*, 17 May 1998, A10.

29. "The President's News Conference (April 30, 1998)," *Weekly Compilation of Presidential Documents*, 4 May 1998, 34:18, p. 734.

30. Kathleen Hall Jamieson, "That Clear Line Between Public and Private Conduct," *The Washington Post National Weekly Edition*, 30 March 1998, p. 21.

31. Richard L. Burke, "Clinton Job Rating Remains High Despite Doubts on Moral Values," *The New York Times*, 27 January 1998, A1.

32. The quotes which follow are drawn from Alan Wolfe, *One Nation, After All: What Middle Class Americans Really Think About God, Country, Family, Racism, Welfare, Immigration, Homosexuality, Work, The Right, The Left, and Each Other.* (New York: Viking, 1998) pp. 54, 71, 107, 110.

33. Julia Duin, "America seen as less judgmental, less Christian," *The Washington Times*, 22 March 1998, p. 12. Elsewhere, Professor Wolfe is quoted as saying that, "the unwillingness of Americans to judge each other is one of the great triumphs of the '60s." See G. Pascal Zachary, "Straight-Laced Public Yawns at Scandal," *The Wall Street Journal*, 9 February 1998, B1.

34. Richard Morin and Claudia Deane, "Poll Shows Americans More Satisfied With U.S.," *The Washington Post*, 21 January 1998, A6.

35. Richard Morin. "Poll Finds Pessimism on U.S. Course," *The Washington Post*, 29 August 1997, A1.

36. Dan Barry and Jennifer Preston, "Clinton finds Support in Town's Prosperity," *The New York Times*, 26 February 1998, A1.

37. For example, one political scientists says after reviewing the survey data that, "Public support for Clinton will be more affected by the future performance of the economy than by the clarity of the evidence concerning the charges against him." See John Zaller, "Monica Lewinsky's Contribution to Political Science," *PS: Political Science & Politics*, 31:2, p. 186.

38. For example, see Wesley Pruden, "Pruden on Politics: A Perfect Expression for a Gelded Age," *The Washington Times*, 13 March 1998, p. 22.

39. Richard Restak, M. D., "Psychobiographer Puts Clinton on the Couch—and Finds Nixon," *Insight*, 10 June 1996, p. 32.

40. On this matter, see Richard L. Burke, "Clinton's O.K. in the Polls, Right?" *The New York Times*, 15 March 1998, wk1.

41. The public's increasing unwillingness to respond to survey requests has become a matter of concern to pollsters. Reputable non-partisan surveys must now share the public with advocacy polls. This includes so called "push surveys" used by both political parties, in which a survey is a thinly disguised effort at negative advertising (Do you know that Congressman X favors lowering social security payments to needy elders? How do you feel about that?).

42. See, for example, the early work of A. Paul Hare, Edgar F. Borgatta, and Robert F. Bales, (eds.). *Small Groups: Studies in Social Interaction.* (New York: Knopf, 1967).

43. Steve Farkas and Jean Johnson, "The Values We Live by: What Americans

Want from Welfare Reform," New York: Public Agenda, 1996. See also Herbert Asher, *Polling and the Public: What Every Citizen Should Know. 4th Ed.* (Washington, D.C.: 1998) p. 116.

44. Everett Carll Ladd, "Nixon and Watergate Revisited," *The Public Perspective*, April/May 1998, p. 28.

45. Stanley C. Brubaker, "Can Liberals Punish?" *American Political Science Review*, 1988, 82: pp. 821–36.

46. Ibid., p. 32.

47. John F. Harris and Juliet Eilperin, "House Rebukes Clinton on China Satellite Export," *The Washington Post*, 21 May 1998, A1.

48. Richard A. Neustadt, *Presidential Power* (New York: Wiley, 1960).

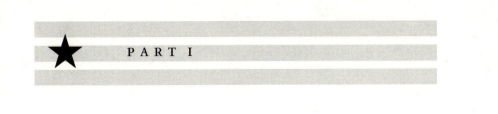

PART I

The Concept of
Psychological Suitability

ONE

The Psychological Suitability of
Presidents in an Era of Doubt

The emergence of psychological suitability as a dimension of leadership evaluation can be seen now at all levels of the political system, but nowhere is it more pronounced than in the assessment of presidential candidates. Questions of character, judgment, temperament, and experience have become a routine part of the presidential campaign process. What was once peripheral is now central.

Looking back on the past quarter century of presidential campaigns, two related but distinctive sets of concerns about the personal and psychological characteristics of presidential candidates are discernible. The first revolves around the emotional well-being and psychological functioning of presidential candidates. The issue of suitability in this instance is raised in terms of the "mental health" of the candidates. It is expressed in such questions as whether the leader is emotionally stable, adequately rational, and appropriate in his assumptions, beliefs, and judgment.

More recently, a second set of concerns has emerged that centers on issues of character and leadership. Questions here focus on a presidential candidate's integrity, judgment, motivations, and ways of dealing with issues of power and its responsibilities. Is the candidate honest? Does he have a clear set of values and ideals? Does he have the capacity to accomplish them?[1] Can he be trusted with political power? Is his judgment or leadership enhanced or endangered by aspects of his personality or character?

The Concept of Psychological Suitability

Concerns with character and presidential leadership are central to exploring the issue of *psychological suitability*. Generally defined, psychological suitability refers to the fit (or lack thereof) between the personal skills and capacities of a candidate and the ability to perform effectively within the confines of what a particular political role of office offers in the way of resources and opportunities.[2]

The concept of psychological suitability is in every sense a term of political psychology theory. It is psychological because the personal abilities and limitations that a candidate brings to the office have an important bearing on his performance as president. They of necessity reflect his character and more general psychological functioning.

The psychological domain of the term has both an intrapsychic and an interpersonal dimension. Generally, the first refers to psychological elements that are primarily "within" the individual, such as motivations, identifications, and assumptions. The term *interpersonal* generally refers to those psychological elements that reflect a person's relationships with others. In reality, there is some overlap between the two domains, for some aspects of character are often expressed in particular kinds of relations with others. Many intrapsychic elements have consequences for the ways in which the president will relate to others.

Ambition, which I argue later is one building block of character and thus clearly an intrapsychic element, also has direct implications for a president's interpersonal relations. A president with strong ambition may try to bend others to his will or find other methods to satisfy his ambition, with consequences for how he treats others.

Good personal and political judgment, too, reflects both intrapsychic and interpersonal elements. The reflective analytic skills that underlie good judgment represent the integration of a number of characterological elements and cognitive processes.[3] Too much ambition, for example, may inhibit the capacity for good judgment in several ways, one of which may be to rely too little on advisers who do not mirror or agree with ambitious aspirations.

Finally, psychological suitability must be examined in the context of particular performance settings. Not every ability or limitation is equally relevant for all political offices. Some character elements and skills matter more for some positions, and some limitations are far more cause for concern. The term also has political referents that must be addressed. The presidency, like any political office in a democracy, exists in institutional, constitutional, and historical contexts. These set the framework within which political power is exercised and evaluated.

The concept of psychological suitability suggests that there is a range of personal skills and limitations that directly fit or fail to fit with the nature of a particular office. That fit shapes how effectively the officeholder exercises political power within the office. The range is not infinitely malleable. The basic character elements we will examine can be linked in a number of ways with a candidate's political and leadership style, but they must be present for the candidate to have a strong chance of effective performance.

The Emergence of Concern with Issues of Psychological Suitability

Concern with the personal characteristics of presidential candidates is not entirely a recent development. Calling into question the personal traits of one's opponent was at one time a robust part of American campaign life. As Wattenberg (1991, 81) notes, "Scurrilous attacks on candidates' personal lives were commonplace in the nineteenth century." An examination of presidential campaigns in the last century and the beginning of this one will bring to light many examples of a candidate's private life and behavior being called into question in an effort to influence the campaign. In 1802, for example, Thomas Jefferson was accused of keeping a slave mistress, and during the 1884 presidential campaign, Grover Cleveland was publicly confronted by his opponents with charges that he had fathered an illegitimate child.

Then, as now, these kinds of public accusations were a form of partisan politics whose function was to discredit an individual's candidacy. However, unlike now, the charges were presented as illustrations of the candidate's moral failure, not of a personality or character deficit. Nor did they reflect any serious consideration of what might be the relationship between these allegations and a person's actual performance in office.

In more recent times also presidential candidates' personal characteristics have played some role in presidential elections. Harry Truman's combativeness and his "give 'em hell" campaign of 1948 and Dwight D. Eisenhower's image as a wise and kindly elder statesman are two among many possible reminders that there has been for some time a certain sensitivity to the importance of personal attributes for presidential leadership. Yet these concerns have become particularly acute in the last three presidential elections, and the question is why. Is concern with presidential character primarily a creation of the media? Is it a passing concern, one that is likely to disappear as a public issue?

I think the answer to both of these questions is no. Concern with the character and psychology of presidential candidates is not an epiphenomenon; nor is it likely to disappear in the immediate future. The reasons I suggest for this lie in the convergence of six interrelated sets of factors, which I examine below.

A first cause grows out of the public's experience over the last quarter century with two aspects of presidential performance. One is the rise of public concern over the nuclear issue. The other is the public's response to several presidencies that were perceived as deeply flawed, even failed. These presidencies were flawed as much by the character of the presidents as by failed policy. These experiences have reinforced the public's sense that the president's psychology is important.

A second, parallel set of factors is related to a decline in the belief in effective policy solutions. The failure to find lasting policy solutions to urgent social problems, regardless of which party is in power, has lead to deepening distrust that any solutions are possible. The decline in public faith in the efficiency of policy has in turn fueled the search for leadership, which it is hoped will prevail where policy has not.

A third factor has been the shift in the relationships among political ideology, policy views, political parties, and presidential contenders. At one time it was possible to predict presidential policy from a candidate's political party or ideology. As this has become more difficult, attention on the candidates themselves has become reinforced.

Fourth, leaders themselves have become more important. They have become the focal point of increasing public expectations and responsibilities. At the same time, the instruments associated with powerful leadership positions have grown. I do not wish to deny here the importance of complex social and economic factors such as global interdependence, only to point out that these elements have contributed to the importance of leaders.

Each of these four elements would seem to play an important role. However, I think two further developments helped to propel these issues to their contemporary importance. One was the emergence of a set of theoretical and conceptual tools with which to frame the problem of psychological suitability. That set of theories is drawn from the study of the psychology of leadership and from political psychology generally. Such theories have become the public vehicle by which candidates are now assessed.

This development must be considered in relation to an additional, very important factor. There now exists a body of persons with extensive public access and power who are ready and increasingly willing to ask questions regarding psychological suitability. They are collectively "the media" but encompass a wide variety of roles, including newspaper reporters, columnists, journalists, television reporters, and commentators. Moreover, not only are these persons willing to ask such questions but they now have a variety of academic and public experts available and willing to try and answer them. The result is that psychological assessments have to a large degree become institutionalized, largely because of the continued activity of these groups.

The Nuclear Weapons and "Mental Health" Issue

The development of concern with the psychological suitability of presidential candidates over the last twenty-five years owes part of its early impetus to fears regarding nuclear weapons. This connection first surfaced in the presidential campaign of 1964, and thereafter it appeared repeatedly.

In 1964, Democratic presidential nominee Lyndon Johnson ran against Senator Barry Goldwater, a conservative Republican. Goldwater was perceived as very hard-line on foreign policy, especially in U.S.–Soviet relations. He was also perceived by a number of people as an ideological extremist who might very well believe that it was better to be dead than red.

That campaign marked the first time that psychological suitability, framed in terms of mental health and emotional stability, was a manifest issue in a presidential election. In the election Lyndon Johnson explicitly characterized his opponent as emotionally unsuited to have his finger on the nuclear button. During the campaign, the Democratic Party aired an extremely controversial commercial that explicitly linked the Republican candidate with the possibility of nuclear war.

The 1964 presidential campaign also marked the first and only time that a sample of psychiatrists, members of the American Psychiatric Association, was polled on the psychological suitability of a political candidate. During the campaign, a now-defunct magazine called *FACT* sent out a survey to all the members of the American Psychiatric Association, asking them to assess the mental health of Senator Goldwater and his psychological suitability for the presidency. (That survey and its implications will be examined in chapter 5.)

In May 1970, concerns about President Nixon's psychological well-being were raised when, after a decision to bomb Cambodia resulted in violent, nationwide protests, Nixon decided to take a late-night, 4:30 a.m. tour of the Lincoln Memorial. Safire's (1975, 201–12) detailed description of that evening makes clear that White House aides were very concerned about Nixon's mental state. Nixon's personal physician, Walter Tkach, is noted as being present at the memorial (Safire 1975, 208), although he is not mentioned as being in the original party that left the White House.

In 1972 the issue of psychological suitability framed in terms of mental health and emotional stability surfaced when it was revealed that the Democratic nominee for vice president, Senator Thomas Eagleton, had been hospitalized three times for depression and had received shock treatments on two of those occasions. Eagleton at first refused to resign from the ticket but eventually did so under enormous pressure. His resignation marks the first time in modern history that a nominee for the second highest office in our system was forced to resign because of questions raised about his mental health. (The diagnostic and political controversy surrounding Eagleton's revelations about his treatment for depression will be examined in chapter 6.)

In July 1979, President Carter left Washington for his Camp David retreat. Once there, he suddenly and unexpectedly canceled what had been billed as a major policy address to the nation. Thereafter, in quick succession, numerous advisers, academic theorists, labor leaders, and others were seen shuttling in and out of the camp, all under the watchful eyes of the press. Jimmy Carter was reconsidering his presidency.

After many days of private consideration amid mounting public speculation, Carter moved quickly and dramatically. Three members of his cabinet were fired, and several others offered their resignations and had them accepted. Carter further ordered that hundreds of top-level staff members be reevaluated as part of his attempt to chart a new direction for his administration.

Public and political reaction was both dramatic and strong. Presidents in the past had replaced cabinet members, even more than one, but these replacements had usually been more widely spaced and had occurred after reelection, when some change is expected. In this case President Carter replaced an unexpectedly large number quickly and after a mysterious, in some ways unprecedented, retreat during the normally uneventful summer season.

The reaction of the public and especially of members of the House and

Senate was dramatic. Senator Ted Stevens of Alaska wondered aloud in a public interview whether President Carter "might not be having some sort of mental problem" (Smith 1979). After he repeated this statement on the Senate floor, the majority leader, Robert C. Byrd, characterized his comments as "caustic and out of order" and Stevens retreated, but just a little. "I don't think anyone's saying he's crazy," Stevens explained, "but the pressures on him are just so great, we are wondering if he is having some sort of breakdown" (Smith 1979). Then Senator Lowell Weicker of Connecticut, in discussing President Carter's response to his political problems, was moved to point out, "We have no way of removing a president who lacks capacity for the job, unless he's at the point where he has to be chased down by nets" (*Miami Herald,* 10 August 1979, 1E).

One striking aspect of this incident was the direct public speculation about the state of Carter's mind and the anxiety that his behavior generated. That public anxiety was taken seriously enough to elicit denials from the president's wife and reassuring comments from colleagues and the press. As if to reassure the public, the *New York Times* duly noted that President Carter had addressed an advisory committee of the White House Conference on Families, "speaking quietly, but with fervor" (Smith 1979). At the same time, Governor Hugh Gallen of New Hampshire met with reporters after seeing the president and assured them that he had found the president "cool and in complete control of himself." Even the president's wife, Rosalynn, found it necessary to comment several times the next day, during a cross-country tour, that the president was "happy, healthy [and] confident," at another point repeating, "The president is healthy" and "We're having a wonderful time in the White House" (Seifman 1979).

It seems clear in retrospect that the dramatic nature of Carter's moves startled observers, as did the rapidity with which they were taken. Sudden, dramatic moves by a president with a reputation for deliberateness and dispassionate analysis tended to heighten concern. Carter himself clearly was not sensitive to how these moves might be perceived by the public and that people might not come to the proper conclusion, namely, that the president simply wished to remove himself for a brief period from the daily responsibilities of government to reflect on his administration and make needed corrections.

The question of psychological suitability framed in terms of emotional well-being, especially as it is connected with the president's ultimate authority over the use of nuclear weapons, continues to be raised in presidential elections. In 1984, Democratic candidate Walter Mondale ran against incumbent Ronald Reagan and tried to raise the same sense of uneasiness about Reagan that Lyndon Johnson had done with Barry Goldwater. Once again, as in 1964, the Democrats fielded a political commercial that raised the issue of whose finger citizens would prefer to have on the nuclear trigger, but this time without achieving the desired effect.

In 1988 rumors surfaced that Democratic presidential candidate Michael S. Dukakis had seen a psychiatrist for treatment of depression. The candidate denied the rumors (Toner 1988) but was forced to release a detailed medical history (Rosenthal 1988) in response to President Reagan's remark that he "would not pick on an invalid." Meanwhile, some commentators (Nelson 1988) questioned why it was necessary to persecute candidates for seeking psychiatric help, while others noted that seeking help during a crisis might represent "healthy common sense" (*New York Times,* 5 August 1988, 24).

With the decline of U.S.–Soviet hostility and the lessening of the likelihood of nuclear conflict between the two countries, direct concern with the president's psychological well-being (mental health) during presidential campaigns has appeared to recede. Still, the issue comes up in a somewhat indirect form in discussions of which candidate is better able to deal with crisis; or as George Bush put it during the 1992 campaign, "When that crisis call comes in to the White House in the middle of the night, who would you like to have answer the phone?"

Questions of psychological suitability, defined broadly in terms of judgment and emotional stability, have been present in almost every presidential election since 1964. The issue of the stability of the person whose hand rests on the "nuclear trigger" clearly fueled this concern. However, George Bush's request that Americans carefully consider whom they would prefer to have in office during a crisis suggests that this concern has not fully receded and may take other forms with the end of the cold war.

Character Issues and Flawed Presidencies: Public Distrust

The emergence of the public's concern with character issues cannot be traced to any specific, dramatic issue, as was the case with questions of emotional stability. Rather, it appears to have emerged gradually from a damaging set of historical experiences related to the exercise of political power. Ironically, it was Lyndon Johnson, the first presidential candidate to publicly and directly raise the issue of his opponent's emotional stability and suitability, who by his own behavior in office helped to raise the issue of character.

In 1964, Lyndon Johnson ran against Senator Barry Goldwater, a conservative Republican with a reputation as a very strong advocate of military power. Johnson positioned himself politically in the campaign as the candidate of peace as well as reason. The issue of the use of American military force came up during the campaign in connection with the presence of American advisers in Vietnam. There was concern at the time that the United States was becoming involved, step by step, in a process that would lead to the commitment of U.S. troops in defense of South Vietnam. Johnson told the American public during the campaign that he would never send American boys 8,000 miles away to fight a war that should be fought by Asian boys (Barber 1992a, 26). This was a promise that he reneged on soon after winning the election and entering office.

The history of the Johnson administration's public deception regarding the intentions, rationale, and conduct of American involvement in Vietnam is familiar. Presidents had deceived the public before, but rarely had the costs of a policy decided in secret, and maintained with a minimum of public candor, been so evident or so tragic. One measure of the toll Johnson's policies took on public trust can be seen in the following sets of figures.

When researchers at the University of Michigan's Survey Research Center asked a national sample of Americans in 1958 how much of the time they could trust the federal government to do what is right—just about always, most of the time, or only some of the time—only 22 percent of the public thought they could *not* trust the government all or most of the time (Miller 1974). In 1964, at the start of the Johnson presidency, that number remained at 22 percent. However, two years into the Johnson administration the number had risen to 31 percent, and by 1968, the end of Johnson's presidency, the number had reached 37 percent (Miller 1974, 952, Table 1). While not all of the decline in public trust can be directly attributed to Johnson himself or his Vietnam policy in particular, there is evidence that his behavior in office did play an important role. For example, in 1968, 56 percent of those who rated Johnson's presidential performance as "poor" had low levels of trust in government (Citrin 1974, 977, Table 2).

It seems plausible in retrospect that the public's experience with the Johnson presidency began the process of increasing awareness that character counts. Why did this realization begin to develop? One possible answer lies in the directness and the magnitude of the consequences of Johnson's Vietnam policies. This was not a deception uncovered decades after the fact. Nor was it a single, perhaps understandable deception (like Eisenhower's original denial of the U-2 flight over the Soviet Union) in a generally truthful administration. Rather, it was a series of deceptions carried out before an increasingly skeptical public that led to disastrous, public, and long-term consequences.

Questions about President Johnson's honesty in connection with his Vietnam policies are important. However, they are not the sole reason for the public's increasing concern with character issues. The next step in that process occurred with the 1968 presidential campaign and election. In that campaign, Richard M. Nixon attempted for a second time in his career to gain the presidency.

The campaign began on a characterological note in the form of speculations about the "new Richard Nixon." These were fueled in part by some apparent changes in Nixon's style (he was seen as more mature and less combative than in previous years). Nixon won the presidency and accomplished a number of goals in his domestic and foreign policy agendas. Four years later, he won an overwhelming electoral victory but was forced to resign in the face of impeachment proceedings for abuses of presidential power and obstruction of justice.

Both Johnson and Nixon were, in many areas and respects, enormously skilled presidents. In neither Johnson's nor Nixon's case was policy or political competence the issue. Both of these presidents were able and experienced leaders with substantial records of accomplishment. Politics did not cause (although it may have exacerbated) their problems. Rather, their difficulties can be traced directly to their efforts to manipulate and deceive other administration officials, members of Congress, and the American public, efforts that ultimately proved self-defeating. Their errors in exercising power, while political in consequence, were ultimately psychological and ethical in origin.

The Decline of Faith in Policy Solutions

Many have argued that policy debate has been eclipsed (some would say, replaced) by issues of psychological suitability. The solution proposed by some, therefore, is to dispense with the latter so that campaigns can return to their proper purpose, which is the discussion of policy. This is an appealing but flawed remedy. It is flawed because the decline of policy debate and the rise of character issues are related to each other in complex ways.

The wish to replace discussion of character issues with policy debate neglects the fact that it is the president who is at the center of policy formulation and implementation. The effectiveness of policy is related in part to the policy judgment and political skills of a president. If these skills, which are part of the package of personal characteristics that are addressed by "character issues," are poor, policy formulation and implementation will suffer.

However, there is another aspect to the decline of policy debate that lies somewhat outside the realm of presidential character, that is, the efficacy of policy itself. Americans have traditionally been optimistic about their ability to solve problems and, consequently, great believers in the idea of progress. It seemed only reasonable, therefore, to believe, as was the case in the 1960s, that an emphasis on pragmatic politics coupled with a growing command of developing social technologies would usher in a period of prosperity. This combination would at the same time confront and eradicate major social problems such as poverty and welfare. In the international system, superior military power would assure the triumph of our policies where the virtue of our positions was not otherwise persuasive.

From our present perspective this view seems somewhat naive, but it is worth asking what factors are related to the rise of public skepticism. In the international arena, one plausible answer is that in the period from 1948 to 1988, Americans were forced to face the fact that there were limits to the U.S. ability to accomplish its policy purposes abroad. A partial list of the historical experiences that reinforced the idea of limits might include the fight to stalemate in Korea, the (apparent) rise to scientific and military parity of the Soviet Union, the decline of colonial systems, the failures of U.S. policy in Vietnam, the failure to bring about a comprehensive Middle East settlement, and so on.

Even in the post–cold war period with the demise of the former Soviet Union, American power has come up against limits. American interventions in Somalia, Rwanda, Bosnia, and even Haiti have proved to be difficult policy undertakings. While the existence of the former Soviet Union no doubt played a major role in limiting American power, its demise suggests there was more to these limits than the efforts of one major adversary.

The paradox of enormous formal power coupled with limited ability to effect outcomes also has its counterpart in domestic policy. It was the hope of many that important domestic public issues of the past few decades— poverty, welfare, and the environment, to name just three—would yield to a combination of technical solutions and large-scale government intervention. However, this has not proved to be the case, for a number of complex, interrelated reasons. One is that many social programs begun as presidential initiatives were put into place without adequate evaluation or monitoring. Cronin (1975, 242) notes, in speaking of the large-scale social programs initiated in the 1960s, "Former White House aides now admit that these capabilities were overtaxed and ineffective throughout the nineteen sixties. Alternatives seldom were evaluated carefully, and effectiveness was rarely calculated accurately."

A result was that costs were substantially underestimated and expected and actual results overinflated. A 1980 report by the Advisory Commission on Intergovernmental Relations concluded that "an unmanageable, wasteful and unaccountable system of domestic aid programs" had been partially responsible for the "rising public discontent with government at all levels" (Herbers 1980).

The "war on poverty," to use one example, has not come close, much less succeeded, in eradicating poverty. While some groups have been helped, others have fallen farther behind (Wilson 1987). Adding to policy difficulties is the fact that social forces frequently lead to the development of new forms of the problem, in addition to older ones. For example, recent data indicate that white middle-aged and older women who have been widowed or divorced are experiencing poverty in increasing numbers, joining other, more traditional high-risk groups.

Not only have social problems proved difficult to eradicate but policy solutions have sometimes brought with them their own set of problems.[4] As a result, the efficacy and therefore the public legitimacy of such programs have increasingly become problematic.[5] Additionally, the recognition of social and policy problems took many years and was acknowledged only to a limited degree, and even then with enormous reluctance. Frank public discussion of many issues became (and continues to be) difficult. When Daniel Moynihan (1969) released his report on social and economic strains affecting minority families, he was denounced by many as a racist. So while there was a growing sense among the public that policy solutions were failing to accomplish their purposes, real discussion of the issues as a foundation for introducing meaningful changes was stymied by a lack of candor.[6]

Since 1964, presidents often have attempted to solve public problems and not succeeded. They have not, however, generally taken the lead in encouraging discussion of the problems and the real prospects for success. Presidents have increasingly substituted optimism for candor, and as a result, government and policy itself have become suspect.

One effect has been a dramatic decline in public confidence in the government's ability to solve such problems. When a January 1993 CBS/ *New York Times* poll asked whether "you think that, in general, [government] creates more problems than it solves . . . [or] solves more problems than it creates," 69 percent choose the former and only 22 percent the latter (Ladd 1993, 16). Not surprisingly, in a Voter Research and Surveys (VRS) exit poll, taken on the day of the 1992 election, that asked voters whether they wanted government to provide more services while raising taxes or government that cost less while providing fewer services, 55 percent of the voters opted for less government (Ladd 1993, 16).

In the absence of faith in government's ability to provide policy solutions, the public has turned increasingly toward the search for leadership, which, it is hoped, will prevail where particular programs have not. In place of policies, citizens now seek visions from presidential candidates.

Generally, citizens have been offered little real information during presidential campaigns about how, specifically, the presidential candidates will proceed. One can attribute some of this to a natural reluctance on the part of candidates to engage in frank public discussion of sensitive policy issues, which might prove politically damaging. Presidential election campaigns may be the least likely context in which to have such discussions. They mark the point at which the ambition that led to joining the race in the first place shapes the eventual difficulties of governing and leading once the election has been won.

It is possible to look at this simply as a matter of ambition gone awry. Candidates generally run for the presidency to win the right to govern and lead. They do so because they believe they should occupy the office and will perform more ably than their opponents. It is a small psychological step from this view to the belief that one's presence in the office will be "better" for the country and offer an opportunity then to accomplish the difficult policy tasks of government.

Such a set of beliefs involves some wishful thinking, a reflection of self-deception with public consequences. However, it also reflects two other, accurate appraisals. First, to accomplish political and policy purposes one must be in a position to do so. Second, the capacity to educate the public about policy issues is one part of presidential leadership. It is true that once in office a president can do and say things that were simply not possible as a candidate. The problem, therefore, is not only that candidates have failed to educate the public during election campaigns but that they have failed to do so as presidents.

It is, of course, also possible that presidential candidates are truly per-plexed and find it increasingly difficult to honestly offer viable solutions to complex public problems. Traditional ideologically framed policies do not appear to provide an adequate map to help them. Meanwhile, the public is demanding answers.

Concern with character issues has developed out of disappointed public expectations for performance in two areas, namely, presidential and policy efficacy. In analyzing the decline of policy debate, it is important to distinguish between the decline of the importance of policy and decline in the public's expectation of policy efficacy. It is the latter, not the former, that has been a central factor in the rise of character issues.

Presidential Candidates, Political Parties, and Ideology: From Clarity to Ambiguity

Political parties have traditionally performed evaluating functions for citizens' assessments of presidential candidates. One such function arose from the stamp of legitimacy that a party nomination conferred on the candidate who obtained it. Voters could be assured that such a person had been selected by and had obtained the approval of many party regulars who knew and presumably trusted him to lead and represent them.

However, the rules of the nomination process have dramatically changed. Control has passed for the most part from a cadre of party officials to a series of presidential primaries. Candidates' organization and support have bypassed traditional bases of party support.

This decoupling is related to several factors. There has been a public decline in support for the traditional parties, a decline of party-line voting, and a decline of party identification (Wattenberg 1991, 47–65; see also Wattenberg 1990). These trends have coincided with the rise of candidate-centered politics.

Somewhat less commented upon is the other critical evaluation function of parties, that which arose from their ideologies and platforms. One of the most persistent findings of early voter research was that parties served as a "filter" through which citizens assessed the candidates (Campbell, Gurrin, and Miller 1954; Campbell, Converse, Miller, and Stokes 1960). Knowing that a presidential candidate was running as the standard-bearer for one of the political parties conveyed something concrete about a candidate. It reflected his political identity, suggesting for whom and what he stood.

It also, in broad but nonetheless important ways, keyed the public to a presidential candidate's policy positions. It was not that party positions defined the candidates ideologically and programmatically, although this was true to some degree. Rather, the political identities of the presidential candidates were similar to their party ideologies and the two were thus reinforcing. Making a choice for the Democrat (Lyndon Johnson) or for the Republican (Barry Goldwater) in 1964, or choosing Ronald Reagan (the Republican) or Walter Mondale (the Democrat) as the candidate in 1984, were essentially related choices. Each candidate's political philosophy and persona were reflected in the official and unofficial policy views of his party. The coherence and stability of this link provided the public with a broad but nonetheless accurate indication of how the successful presidential candidate would proceed and where he would lead if elected.

The rise of character issues is in part a reflection of the attenuation of the link between presidential candidates and their political personas on the one hand and party ideology and policy on the other. It is not entirely clear why this has happened. One can argue that a "regression toward the mean" has taken place between the political parties. This view has much to recommend it. Political parties whose platforms and candidates have reflected too narrow an ideological spectrum, as did the Republicans in 1964 and the Democrats in 1984, have suffered electoral losses. This is a powerful political incentive toward moderation.

However, what is true for political parties has also become true of the presidential candidates themselves. There is a powerful political incentive for candidates to blur ideological and policy distinctions. It appears to be a preferred strategy. One result is further to decouple the candidate's political persona and policy ideology from the traditional "filtering" function of political party labels. Voters can no longer rely on party labels to inform them of the policy approaches of a party's candidates. Deprived of this source of information, they must make their own way through the haze of blurred political personas of the candidates. The result is an increasing emphasis on the candidates themselves.

One can trace some of these developments to the presidency of Richard Nixon. Nixon was a Republican, but one who rejected discussions of whether he was "conservative" or "liberal." He saw himself as "pragmatic" rather than ideological, and his policies tended to follow from that. Was Nixon a conservative anticommunist? Yes, for the most part. Was he prepared to engage in strategic negotiations with his adversaries? Yes, when possible. Did Nixon's anticommunist views keep him from forging a new relationship with China? No, they did not.

In domestic policy one can observe the same blending of ideological strands. Nixon was "tough on crime," in both rhetoric and policy. Yet the "conservative" Republican president was not a mortal foe of the liberal welfare programs; indeed, he attempted to reform and improve several of these programs. In answer to the question of whether Nixon was a moderate, liberal, or conservative, one would have to answer, in truth, "It depends on the issue."

One can see similar trends in the Carter candidacies in 1976 and 1980. Carter, a southern Democrat, ran on a personal platform in which supporting a "strong defense" and being "tough on criminals" played prominent roles. Was Carter a traditional Democratic liberal? No, not really. Was he a "conservative"? In some respects, yes, but in others, no. Carter, like Nixon before him, campaigned and governed as a pragmatist, not as an ideologue.

In the presidential election of 1988, the same trends are observable for both major party candidates. George Bush, the Republican candidate, had so blended and moderated his views on many policy issues that numerous analyses were written that asked, "Who is George Bush?" In the area of civil rights, for example, Bush was known to be generally supportive but against the use of quotas and other preferential systems for minorities. His Democratic opponent, Michael Dukakis, completely disavowed any political ideology, liberal or conservative, Democratic or Republican. His campaign slogan that the election was "about competence, not ideology" reflected, in the most pristine form, an attempt by a candidate to bypass ideology and the labeling and filtering function that it served.

One continues to see evidence of the trend in the 1992 presidential campaign. President Clinton's campaign promised a candidate who reflected a "new Democratic party," presumably one that was unlike its predecessor. His policy positions, expressed in general terms, continued the trend of blending positions. Thus candidate Clinton was for "a strong America" but also promised to drastically reduce the military budget. He was a supporter of social welfare programs but promised to "end welfare as we know it" during his presidency. The "New Democrat" was one who blended, if not transcended, liberal and conservative ideologies.

Does the blurring of policy and ideological lines represent increasing policy maturity, the increasing cognitive complexity of the candidates, or strategic manipulation in the service of personal ambition? It is likely that all of these elements play some role. However, the effect of this trend has been to deprive voters of a useful, rough-and-ready calculus by which to evaluate presidential candidates.

The Increasing Importance of Leaders

Greenstein (1969), in his seminal work on the logic of inquiry in the personality-and-politics field, notes that at least two distinct questions can be raised regarding the impact of political leaders. One is the question of "action dispensability" (Greenstein 1969, 40–46). It asks, in essence: Do the personal characteristics of the leader help us to explain a leader's behavior? To the extent that the personal characteristics of a president— his skills and limitations, leadership style, and quality of judgment—are important elements of presidential performance, the answer must be a qualified yes. However, to give such an answer simply leads to the next step, which is to specify which characteristics shape which performance-related behaviors.

Greenstein (1969, 46–57) notes also that even if the first question is answered in the affirmative, there is a further and different question that can be asked: whether or not individual leaders (presidents) make much difference. This is question of "actor dispensability."

The extent to which leaders affect events has been framed by two contrasting views. The first is found in its purest form in the "great man" theory of political leadership (Carlyle 1907). In the view of Carlyle, the great leader is the prime mover of history. The great leader does not merely shape events; he is responsible for them. Hook (1955) accepts this view but distinguishes between "eventful man" and "event-making man." It is the latter who is responsible for major turns of history. As an example, Hook notes, "If Lenin had not been on the scene, not a single revolutionary leader could have substituted for him" (1955, 209).

The alternative view sees leaders as fundamentally constrained, the range of their impact limited. The reasons put forward for the "inherent constraint" seen to characterize leaders are varied. For classical and neo-Marxists, the levers of social causality are to be found in "historical and material forces." Large-scale social trends and long-term institutional dynamics are viewed as providing a very limited context in which leaders may maneuver.

A contemporary variation on this view is found in the idea that the size and complexity of social forces have grown past their ability to be mastered. In this view, too, leaders work at the margins of causality. Their chief role is to buffer change, but certainly not to shape or direct it.

Both the theory of inherent constraint and the "great man" theory of leadership in reality share a common view. Each equates leadership impact with effecting *major* political or historical transformations (as Hook argued for Lenin and the Russian Revolution). By doing so, each denies the importance of any but the most unusual and historically rare examples of leadership importance. The common error of both theories is to equate importance with transforming impact.

The "great man" and "inherent constraint" theories of leadership frame the boundaries of the attempt to gauge leaders' impact. However, they do not provide more than very general parameters for answering the question. Do material facts constrain leaders? Of course they do. Do great men make unique and important contributions to historical outcomes? Allowing for the counterfactual nature of the question, the answer is still best given in the affirmative.

The importance of presidents and leaders cannot rest solely on a "great man" theory of leadership since there are many more presidents and leaders than there are great men, yet their impact is substantial. Even the decisions of "reactive" presidents can have substantial impact. Another framework for assessing the importance and impact of leaders is clearly needed.

Greenstein (1969, 41) suggests that instead of asking the question "Do leaders matter?" we ask under what circumstances they might matter. He lists a number of such circumstances, among them location in the power hierarchy (the higher the more impact), the degree of discretion the leader has, and so on. Greenstein lists ten circumstances that tend to heighten the impact of the leader, and almost all characterize the office of the president. These factors help us to conceptualize the potential impact of the modern president. In the discussion that follows, some of the specific manifestations of these factors are further analyzed.

Social-forces theorists are correct in one regard. Modern industrial societies are structurally highly articulated. Therefore they tend to generate extremely complex social, economic, technical, and political processes. The "inherent constraint" theorists correctly note that such complexity can inhibit presidential impact.

However, social-forces theorists have failed to consider the other obvious implication of their analyses. In addition to complicating the tasks of presidents, such factors have increased the potential impact of leaders. The importance of political leaders and their leadership may be viewed as resting on three essential characteristics of modern industrial societies: decision centrality, the extension of public-sphere responsibilities, and structural amplification. Let us briefly examine each of these.

Decision centrality is a modern manifestation of the traditional division and specialization of labor. All societies develop a division of labor. Modern industrial societies in general and political processes in particular are no exception to this rule. In democracies, citizen concerns and wishes weigh heavily on the direction and boundaries of public policies. But given the number, scope, importance, and timing of policy issues, no society can afford to wait for the results of periodic elections to take action. Because of this, leadership roles have become institutionalized at the center of the decision process. This means simply that one way to conceptualize the work of political leaders in a democracy is that they are persons empowered by citizens to decide. Former New York governor Mario Cuomo once commented that he could spend every hour of every day making important decisions if he wished (*New York Times,* 14 March 1983, B2). I argue in chapter 8 that the centrality of decision making as a key specialization in the political division of labor makes a presidential candidate's judgment a crucial element of his psychological suitability.

The second factor that has increased the importance of leaders and their judgment and leadership is the expansion of their public responsibilities. In part this is another result of increasing national and international complexity. Government, not the individual citizen or even groups of citizen, has become the most potent level at which to organize responses to this trend. This means higher levels of citizen demands for some government activity, which in turn requires more of leaders. For example, since the 1940s the U.S. government and, especially, the president have become increasingly responsible for national economic well-being. The result has been a proliferation of government agencies and units designed and charged with carrying out economic mandates. They, in turn, have become specialized, amplified their own mandates and procedures, and thus created new institutional sources by which leaders may have impact.

The same expansion of governmental activities can be seen in almost all areas of domestic life. The government is now deeply involved in programs for health, education, crime prevention and response, and the environment, as well as a wide range of social welfare programs, among others. Each of these involvements has spawned its own institutional mandates.

One corollary of all this development is the need for ever more decisions about an increasing array of subjects. The tasks of supervising, coordinating, and leading these efforts and the decisions they generate have become the responsibility of political leaders. More particularly, they have become the responsibility of those in positions of discretionary executive power and authority, such as that of president.

A last factor that increases the importance of leaders is structural amplification. One by-product of the articulation of hierarchical structures is that leaders' preferences are elaborated, worked through, and carried out by the activation of powerful institutional structures with enormous resources at their command. During the Vietnam War, Lyndon Johnson was able to direct some of the daily bombing missions of U.S. forces in Southeast Asia.

The implementation of presidential decisions no longer travels slowly. Presidents do not lack authority and resources to carry their decisions out. Nor are they deterred by distance. Traditional impediments to leadership impact are eroding, and structural articulation, rather than impeding leadership impact, amplifies it.

The Emergence of a Framework for Analysis

The factors that have been discussed to this point—historically relevant experience, the decline of policy optimism, the blurring of ideological and policy arguments, and the increasing importance of leaders—are all important elements in the rise of concern with issues of psychological suitability. However, assessing the psychological suitability and performance of presidential candidates also requires a theoretical framework of psychological functioning, which could be linked with a specification of particular role requirements in a democracy.

Such a framework would need to be able to encompass major aspects of psychological functioning such as motivation, affect, and cognitive functioning. It would also need to suggest ways to arrange these elements into a integrated explanatory system that includes consideration of developmental issues. Such a theory would have to be able to encompass "normal" as well as atypical functioning. Further, the framework and its elements should be capable of being disaggregated so that the contribution of the individual parts to specific areas of performance can be ascertained.

There are many branches of psychology whose frameworks and observations are relevant to assessing psychological suitability and presidential performance. However, the most comprehensive framework of individual psychological functioning remains psychoanalytic theory, broadly conceived.[7] Freud believed from the first that psychoanalytic theory was a general theory of psychological functioning and not a specialized theory of impairment. The reason for this view was Freud's belief that unconscious motivation and conflict, defense mechanisms, and the impact of early on later experience were universal.

Freud's associates (Jung, Alfred Adler, Karl Abraham, and others) and successors (Harry Sullivan, K. Horney, D. W. Winnicott, Michael Balint, H. Kohut, and others) have accepted this basic framework, even as they have elaborated and modified aspects of the theory. The contemporary result is a modified but vastly more robust psychoanalytic framework. It is a framework with which one can now address issues of adulthood (Erikson 1956), ambition (Kohut 1977), and object and interpersonal relations (Balint 1968). In many respects, psychoanalytic theory today is to Freud what modern flight is to the Wright brothers. In both cases the original genius of discovery is basic to all that followed, but all that has followed is much more than a simple elaboration of early, fundamental insights.

The importance of psychoanalytic theory to the development of concerns with character issues can be directly stated. That theory does not account for the concern. Rather, it has provided a framework in which those concerns can be understood and discussed.

What did it mean when Gary Hart changed his name? What did Edward Kennedy's behavior in response to the tragic death of his car companion signify? What "inner compulsion" led Richard Nixon and Gary Hart to self-destruct? These and a very large number of similar "couch questions" can be framed and answered only in the context of the existence of a theory that purports to be able to do so.

I am not arguing here for the accuracy of many of the analyses proposed in the name of psychoanalytic theory. I suggest only that the raising of such questions owes much to the existence of a framework within which it may be possible to answer them. However, theory alone, while crucial, is not sufficient. What is also needed in assessing psychological suitability is the emergence of a group of practitioners skilled in these theories and willing to apply them to problems of leadership selection and evaluation.

The Emergence of the Media and the Assessment of Psychological Suitability

Given historical experience that character counts, that policy solutions to public problems are problematic, but that leadership is important, and a theory that promises to help citizens understand the relationship between presidential psychology and performance, the only things then lacking are a medium and individuals willing and able to use it to develop that discourse. For better or worse, the media (both broadcast and print) have emerged in presidential campaigns as the primary source of information and analysis of the candidates.

This privileged position, however, has brought with it controversy over the methods, depth, and aims of campaign coverage concerned with character issues. Controversies over reporters' ethics have at times become as intense as the questions they have raised about the candidates. Whether the issue concerns the propriety of candidate "stakeouts" (Gary Hart), making use of information obtained by the "sensational press" (Bill Clinton), shouted questions about adultery, driving away potentially good candidates by scrutiny of their personal lives, or the tendency to present campaign information in the form of sound bites, the general criticism has been that the media have failed to live up to their responsibilities.

Public and Candidate Responses to Issues of Psychological Suitability

Aspiring presidents have recognized that public perception of their characters or personalities can be an important political asset or, alternatively, a dangerous liability. This recognition has in turn generated pressures, not easily resisted, to shape public perception of candidates' personal qualities. The 1972 discussion of the "new Richard Nixon" was clearly designed by his advisers to counter public uneasiness about the old one. Four years later, candidate Jimmy Carter, running against the excesses of former President Nixon, reminded the public that "character was an issue" and directly contrasted his with that of his predecessor. In a revealing postmortem of President Jimmy Carter's unsuccessful campaign for reelection in 1980 against Ronald Reagan, Carter's media adviser and pollster Pat Caddell acknowledged that there was public discontent about President Carter's performance while in office but went on to add, "Our campaign fought hard to keep these feelings out—to keep real events out. We knew we had to win on narrower grounds, on which man had the best character to handle the job" (*New York Times,* 9 November 1980, 36).

In the 1988 presidential election, Democratic Party nominee Michael Dukakis's disavowal of ideology invited the public to look more closely at the personalities of the two major party candidates. Susan Estrich, Dukakis's campaign adviser, is quoted by Elizabeth Drew (*New Yorker,* 4 July 1988, 71) as noting, "Ultimately, most presidential campaigns are about character, broadly defined; they are a choice between two men, and which one the voters decide to trust with their future."

At the same time, aspiring presidents have used character issues against each other, heightening public awareness and reinforcing their importance. Thus, in the presidential campaign of 1984, the eventual Democratic Party nominee, Walter Mondale, deflected a serious challenge from then rival Senator Gary Hart by criticizing Hart for being a "coldly intellectual man who would bring an unfair, regressive approach to the problems of the common people" (*New York Times,* 6 March 1984, 1). A few days later, Mondale attacked him as an "opportunist and divider" (*New York Times,* 18 March 1984, 24). During the campaign itself, Mondale criticized President Reagan's lack of involvement in the office, not only accusing him of not applying himself but also questioning his capacity to understand and act on complicated issues (*New York Times,* 10 February 1984, 18).

As concern with the issue of character has intensified, the questions asked of candidates have broadened in scope. Areas of personal and family privacy have correspondingly receded. During the 1988 campaign, the early front-runner for the Democratic Party's nomination, Gary Hart, was forced to drop out of the race when it was revealed that although married, he had spent the night with another woman. In the wake of that revelation and the candidate's denial of wrongdoing, reporters were soon asking him directly whether he had ever committed adultery. At the time the question prompted fierce debate among journalists and political leaders, but four years later, in 1992, it was asked again of Bill Clinton, this time during a nationally televised news show with his wife at his side. The boundaries separating private from public are becoming increasingly permeable for political leaders.

Central to these character questions is the assumption that such information tells us something significant about candidates and their possible performance as president. However, it is by no means clear that the media reporting of character is necessarily revealing of what such reports presume to show. Nor is it always clear that the character signs uncovered are necessarily related to the capacity to govern wisely or well in the way it is assumed.

Consider this in regard to the public display of emotion by political leaders. In the 1972 presidential campaign, Senator Edmund Muskie responded to a scurrilous editorial attack on his wife, Jane, in a speech in front of the New Hampshire newspaper that had published it. While delivering the speech, his voice choked and he appeared to be in tears. Publicly showing such relatively deep emotions provoked considerable comment and concern and was seen by some as a sign of potential weakness in the face of tough circumstances. After all, the reasoning went, if a candidate was moved to tears by a newspaper editorial, what would he do when the going really got tough?

In contrast, consider President Reagan's very emotional speech at a military base on the day a number of servicemen killed in an airplane crash were brought home. The president also seemed clearly upset by the occasion; his voice choked several times, and he could be seen brushing away tears. Yet this public display provoked no such controversy. As the search for character signs, both public and hidden, continues, we are still left with the very good point raised by one member of Congress, who said, "If you ask the direct question: 'Are you gay?' the answer is yes. So what?" (*New York Times,* 31 May 1987, 22).

A theory of psychological suitability must provide some guidance by which the "So what?" question can be answered. This has become an urgent task, given the increasing importance of such questions. In the chapters that follow, we examine in greater detail the range of issues that arises in trying to develop such a theory.

The Emergence of the Psychological Presidency

All of the factors discussed so far—the realization that leaders count, the decline of policy optimism, the blurring of policy and ideological lines, and the corresponding increase in leadership responsibility and impact—have played roles in the increasing public concern with issues of psychological suitability. This concern has focused attention on, even as it has fueled, the development of the "psychological presidency."

The modern presidency increasingly requires that the aspiring president define not only his political direction but his political self. In doing so, he must also establish a solid connection with the public. This requirement is not based on the idea of some mythical union of leaders and "the people." It stems instead from the political need in contemporary American democracy for citizens to be able to trust the competence, good judgment, and integrity of their president. If citizens cannot realistically hope that their presidents can fully solve complex social and political problems, they can at least expect that a candidate will have the necessary emotional, cognitive, and character skills to enable him to accomplish some effective policy results and avoid disastrous policy mistakes.

TWO

Assessing the Psychological Suitability of Presidential Candidates: Ethical and Theoretical Dilemmas

In this chapter, I explore the ethical and practical concerns raised by the application of psychoanalytic theory to a presidential campaign. Can a theory that owes its origins to an attempt to address issues of psychological conflict be a suitable vehicle for studying in individuals those capacities which are substantial enough to propel them to the highest levels of political accomplishment? Are there enough data, of the kind necessary to such analyses, to make them? If such analyses could be made, should they? In making such analyses, is the analyst violating ethical standards? Does he or she violate an individual's right to privacy?

The discussion of these and other basic ethical and theoretical issues that arise in utilizing psychoanalytic theory to assess the psychological suitability of leaders is meant to set the stage for the more specific analyses that follow in succeeding chapters.

Some Ethical Dilemmas in Assessing
Psychological Suitability

Attempts to assess the psychological suitability of presidential candidates raise a number of ethical and theoretical questions. Is it legitimate to undertake a psychological analysis of a person who might become president? If so, on what grounds can it be justified? And what of the evidence used to support such analyses, even if they are deemed legitimate? Assessing presidential psychology at a distance is a difficult undertaking, one made no less so by candidates (and their advisers) having a strong, vested interest in presenting themselves as they would like to be seen, which is not necessarily as they are.

The Issues of Privacy, Confidentiality, and Harm

The concern with privacy issues arose with the first publication of psychoanalytic case studies. The issue actually reflects two related concerns, with confidentiality and with harm. The first arises from the fact that, in treatment, a person, relying on the trust established with the analyst, reveals aspects of his or her experience and inner world of the most private and often intimate nature. A further aspect of this relationship is that the patient, in revealing these personal aspects, learns (in the process of working through these experiences with the analyst) even more and perhaps deeper "truths" about his or her life and experiences.

The issue of harm arises out of the level of intimacy and revelation involved in this process. The analyst knows much about the patient, often more at a particular time than the patient might know about him- or herself. Such information must be handled carefully since revealing or learning such information often increases the patient's vulnerability. Such information is often emotionally charged and could cause great pain if not handled carefully or if revealed to others.

Freud was not insensitive to the privacy issues he raised in connection with Prince's analysis of Roosevelt. He wrote, "It becomes the physician's duty to publish what he believes he knows . . . and it becomes a disgraceful piece of cowardice . . . to neglect doing so, as long as he can avoid causing direct personal injury to the individual patient involved" (Freud 1905, 8). How is one to avoid harming the patient?

In presenting Dora, his first case history, Freud took a number of steps. He disguised the names of the persons involved and the actual physical locations of the scenes he reported, didn't tell other physicians of the treatment, and waited four years to publish his paper, by which time the patient's interest in the matters he discussed would have grown faint (Freud 1905, 8). Still, he recognized that publishing the case was "bound to involve the revelation of . . . intimacies and the betrayal of . . . secrets" (Freud 1905, 8). Moreover, he acknowledged that "it is certain that the patients would never have spoken if it had occurred to them that their admissions might possibly have been put to scientific uses."

How did he justify the publication of their work together, given these facts? Freud (1905, 8) wrote that "the physicians have taken on themselves not only duties towards the individual patient, but towards science as well; and his duties towards science mean ultimately nothing more than his duties towards the many other patients who are suffering or will some day suffer from the same disorder." In short, the physician had a responsibility to build knowledge, especially if it might be helpful to others, either to alleviate or to avoid suffering.

Still, Freud recognized that there was a danger that his former patient might one day see what he had written. However, he was prepared to address the issue of harm directly. He wrote, "If her own case history should accidentally fall into her hands . . . she will learn nothing from it that she does not already know; and she may ask herself who beside her could discover from it that she is the subject of the paper" (Freud 1905, 9).

Curiously, given his treatment of information gained in Dora's analysis, Freud extended the zone of privacy in his work on Woodrow Wilson. He wrote, "To publish such a study of deep psychic mechanisms and to expose them to public curiosity so long as the individual lives is certainly inadmissible" (Freud and Bullitt 1966, xvi). Bullitt added (1966, ix) that he and Freud had agreed "that it would be courteous to refrain from publishing the book so long as the second Mrs. Woodrow Wilson lived."

Let us turn now to these issues as they have manifested themselves in the debates over the psychological assessment of presidential candidates.

Should Psychological Assessments of Presidential Candidates Be Undertaken?

Is it legitimate to introduce psychologically grounded theories into public debate before they have been sufficiently validated to serve as a useful guide? Some worry that the introduction of such theories may be premature (George 1974a, 239) and thus, in some ways, ultimately harmful to the purpose for which they are put forward, namely, the selection of better qualified candidates. Others (Barber [1972] 1992a) are willing to incur that risk for what they see as the potential benefits.

This debate within the academic fields of political psychology and presidential leadership has its counterpart in the public domain. Some have argued that any behavior, past or present, no matter how private or personal, should be part of the public record if a person chooses to become president. In this view, there is no "zone of privacy" for a presidential candidate and his family. For others, there are certain areas of privacy that candidates should not forfeit by running for public office, even the presidency.

There are at least three reasons why it might be questionable to introduce unfinished theories into the political arena. The first is that they might cause (emotional) harm to a presidential candidate. The second is that they might result in public confusion or error. The third is that they might be used either by a candidate's opponents or, should that candidate become president, by his enemies (including those in the international arena).

Let us first turn to the issue of harm. A presidential candidate is not a patient and therefore is not subject to therapeutic safeguards of confidentiality and disclosure. However, this fact alone does not resolve the dilemma.

In undertaking a psychologically informed analysis of a living public figure, most often without his consent, one assumes certain responsibilities toward that person. In many cases, the psychologically trained analyst can discern patterns of functioning and their causes that an individual either does not wish or is unable to recognize.[1] Seeing these analyses may cause psychological discomfort and may also cause political harm.

Matters are further complicated by the fact that the analyst, as scholar, has obligations to the academic community also. Just as Freud noted the responsibility he had as a physician to building understanding for the purpose of helping others, so the scholar can claim a parallel set of obligations. Among them is the responsibility to state, directly and forthrightly, the results of research along with their theoretical, empirical bases, as well as the logic by which the argument proceeded. It is only by doing so that others may review and evaluate it.

One might add to this mix the scholar's public responsibilities. A substantial argument could made for the position that the analyst-scholar also has some responsibility to bring before the public information that is relevant to its legitimate concerns. The public wants to have and indeed, it can be easily argued, would benefit from having individuals in high public office who do not suffer from any significant impairments. Taking this argument one step further, the public benefits from having better, more able leaders in office. Analyses that increase the likelihood of this occurring are therefore desirable on public interest grounds. As the Group for the Advancement of Psychiatry APA Task Force Report noted, "Obviously, this argument is not devoid of cogency" (1973, 11).

From this perspective, the fact that candidates may not wish to hear what their behavior leads us to say is somewhat beside the point. Still, it cannot be denied that some analyses may cause a candidate pain and possibly political harm. It is also possible that such analyses, especially those which pinpoint areas of vulnerability that might find expression in presidential performance, could wind up causing some harm to the public interest (GAP 1973, 10). This is not a point to be dismissed lightly.

Balanced against these aspects of potential harm are several other factors. The most frequent assertion made in connection with these issues is that candidates know that in becoming candidates they agree to be examined. No candidate can expect that his psychology will be exempt.

This argument does not depend on the view that privacy is not a normal or reasonable expectation for the famous or powerful.[2] Nor does it depend on the view that having sought the presidency, candidates can hardly complain if the public wishes to know more than they might wish to present. It is based on the assumption that candidates know that such analyses are very likely to be undertaken and put themselves forward nonetheless. This can be construed as reluctant but nonetheless informed consent.

Second, candidates lend ethical legitimacy to the analysis of suitability by their own behavior. When Gary Hart invited reporters to follow him if they believed the stories about his womanizing, he was engaging in a most common form of behavior among presidential candidates—inviting others to see him as he wished to present himself. As long as candidates construct personas whose purpose is to present the candidates in the best possible light, it can be argued that scholars and reporters have an affirmative responsibility to establish the degree of connection that actually exists between these campaign constructions and the real persons.

There is another aspect of the concern with harm that is associated with this issue. Criticisms of suitability analysis assume that it presents novel information that may cause damage to the candidate. Yet as was noted in the introduction, those who are close to the candidate often have a very good understanding of his strengths and weaknesses and construct a persona to accentuate the former and cover over the latter. The information put forward by most suitability analyses that are done "at a distance" is, to paraphrase Freud's words regarding Dora, unlikely to be news. The difference is that the candidate and his staff are often well enough aware of these factors to take steps to conceal them. Under these circumstances, the harm of knowledge—or more precisely, the lack of it—falls disproportionately on the public.

Why, if at all, does the public have a right to know about a candidate's "private life"? One answer to that question is based on theory of informed consent. The political legitimacy of those in power rests on the public having entered into a realistic and informed "social contract" with the leader, in which public sovereignty is temporarily ceded to the leaders on the basis of understandings and expectations that he is who he presents himself as being. The public therefore has not only the right to know but the need. After all, how else will citizens be able to make the kinds of informed judgments that should underlie their consent?

The public's right to know, however, is predicated on a more basic relationship—that of the association between a person's psychological characteristics and his performance as president. The "social contract" justification for knowing more about a leader's private life stems from its relevance to his enacting his public responsibilities and not to some inherent right to any knowledge about a leader. Therefore an official's private life becomes relevant *to the extent* that it can be shown that some aspects of a person's private behavior are relevant to his performance as a public official or leader.[3]

When does an individual's private life become relevant to public performance? The question actually has two distinct dimensions. The first refers to the circumstances under which personal characteristics become relevant. These circumstances help establish the rationale for examining particular personal characteristics. The second refers to the specific elements of a leader's private life that are actually relevant to his performance. In the section that follows I take up the first of these issues, and I leave the second until I present the framework for analyzing character and presidential performance in chapters 7 and 8.

The Public's Right to Know: Some Threshold Criteria

One question that arises in connection with privacy issues and those in public and political roles is whether the same standards should apply to all. If it is legitimate to look closely at the private lives of presidential candidates and presidents, shouldn't every other person in a position of power be held to the same standard? I suggest the answer is no, for the following reasons.

There are at least three usually related circumstances in which the question of personal characteristics becomes relevant to the process of leadership selection more generally. The first threshold is reached when a person aspires to a position of substantial power and, consequently, the capacity for harm is great. I refer to this as the *power potential* of the position. The second threshold is reached when a person occupies a position in which he or she can independently initiate, carry through, or decide policy questions. I refer to this as the *discretionary potential* of the position. The third threshold is reached when the nature of the position specifically requires, as a basis for adequate performance, skills and capacities that can be demonstrably related to the individual's psychology as well as his public skills. I refer to this as the *self-enactment potential* of the position.

In many cases the three thresholds appear to be related. By most of the measures we will examine, the presidency stands at one end of the continuum on which all three thresholds are reached. However, this is not the case for all political roles and positions. In some cases, having high power potential does not necessarily mean that the person has discretionary power. Let us examine each of these threshold criteria in turn.

The first threshold is related to the power potential of the position. What is meant by this can be ascertained by answering a series of questions: What is the latitude or scope of the decision arena? Does the position entail responsibility for a limited area of public life, or are the areas of responsibility extensive? What are the resources at the disposal of the person who occupies the office or role? The president, of course, has ultimate executive responsibility for an enormous range of aspects of public life, coupled with substantial organizational and structural resources through which to carry out his decisions.[4]

The second threshold requires us to examine power discretion. To do so, we must look at not only the extensiveness of the areas of public life affected by a particular role and the resources that accompany it but whether and to what degree power is shared. While in the federal system no political power is absolute, there remain substantial differences in the degree of discretion afforded particular positions.[5]

Third, a threshold has been reached when the requirements for performance in the role are specifically and directly related to a range of personal characteristics of the individual. It is true that all behavior is to some degree a function of, and reflects upon, an individual's personal characteristics, but there are important differences of degree.[6]

Some roles, like that of governor or president, are complex not only because of their power potential and discretion but because they encompass a range of "definition" possibilities. Presidents, for example, may choose from among many potential presidential roles, many or all of which would be legitimate enactments. A political role or position whose enactment is not severely circumscribed and that encompasses a wide range of role definition possibilities would generally engage a wider spectrum of personal characteristics and would thus reach our third criterion, the leadership enactment threshold.

Some Guidelines for the Assessment of Psychological Suitability

Resolving the conflicting responsibilities involved in assessing presidential candidates is, in the words of the GAP Task Force Report (1973, 11), "complex . . . and, indeed, may not be answerable in a categorical way." Nonetheless, it would be useful to develop some boundaries for inquiries into presidential psychology. It is with this limited purpose in mind that I suggest that, in cases where recognized individuals are the focus of much (or all) of the analysis, those who undertake the analysis should carefully consider six important issues: (1) the issue of disciplinary grounding, (2) the issue of appropriate training, (3) the theoretical rationale for the analysis, (4) issues of inference construction and the analyst's own stance toward the material, (5) the issue of tact, and (6) the issue of scope.

The Issue of Disciplinary Grounding

A cautionary requirement for any analysis is that it be theoretically clear and well grounded in the discipline(s) on which it draws. In the present case the disciplines are political science, political psychology, and psychoanalytic theory (broadly defined). Disciplinary grounding is a basic requirement for sound scholarship of any kind, but in this case the importance increases because of the nature of the data that will be examined.

Of necessity, this book requires some analysis of individual psychology, and in some cases it entails the psychological analysis of behavior that would ordinarily be labeled private or personal. A requirement that the analyst theoretically justify a focus on any set of private or personal behaviors helps (but does not guarantee) a distinction between the relevant and the merely sensational.

As an example of the importance of theoretical explicitness, consider the debates about candidates' sex lives and their relevance to questions of fitness. Does the possibility that President Clinton had an affair bear on his suitability for office, and if so, how are we to judge the relationships that we now know President Kennedy had? Some dismiss such concerns as irrelevant, while others view them as somehow deeply revealing. Neither is necessarily the case, and here, as elsewhere, theory can help us. In this analysis we examine some case materials in which the question of extramarital relationships plays a role; however, sex is rarely, if ever, the primary issue. Sex becomes an issue because of the fact that relationships, extramarital or otherwise, rarely occur in a psychological vacuum. It is not sex per se that interests the analyst of psychological suitability. It is the meaning of a candidate's behavior in the context of a package or pattern of behavior.

There are many relevant and important questions that can be asked of presidential candidates about such relationships, and an interest in sex per se is the least important aspect of these. Is the relationship singular or one of many? Is it recent or long-term? Was there an unwarranted expectation of keeping the relationship hidden? Has it involved a public deception? Is it at variance with the person the candidate presents himself to be? Is it part of a character pattern whose manifestations can be found in other areas of the candidate's behavior, or do other character elements counterbalance whatever impact such relations have?[7] Answers to these questions and others that will be asked in the course of the analysis presented in this book can reveal important aspects of a candidate's psychology. However, it is important that such facts, if substantiated, be required to serve theoretical purposes.

The ability to require facts to serve theoretical purposes is an important basis of progress in any field. It reflects in part the accumulated theoretical knowledge in a field. However, it also reflects the analyst's familiarity with that knowledge.

The Issue of Appropriate Training

As noted, the psychological analysis of political leaders and leadership has benefited from the extraordinary accomplishments of some of its early pioneers such as Lasswell, the Georges, Erikson, and others. But it has also suffered from the hasty, ill-advised, and at once too shallow and too deep analyses of less careful, less principled, and less knowledgeable analysts. Given the complexity of character and psychological functioning generally and, in particular, in relation to leadership performance, it does not seem too stringent to suggest that persons who undertake such analyses be comprehensively trained in the disciplines they purport to represent.

Reading Freud alone no more prepares one to undertake a psychoanalytically informed analysis of leaders at a distance than being able to read musical notes prepares one to conduct a symphony. Early pioneers in the field of political psychology received their training in idiosyncratic ways but were serious about receiving it. Harold Lasswell went to Europe and studied with members of Freud's circle. Alexander George made use of the proximity of the Department of Psychiatry at Stanford, Arnold Rogow undertook a full training analysis at the New York Psychoanalytic Society, and so on. There are now many more and varied opportunities (Sears and

Funk 1991; Krosnick and Hermann 1993) to receive the training appropriate to the sophisticated use of the theories involved in the psychological study of politics, whether they be psychoanalytic, cognitive, or of some other branch of psychology. Since there is no lack of real training opportunities, there seems less reason than ever for analyses in this field to be made without it.

In my view, only scholars who have been thoroughly trained in both the uses and the limitations of the theories they use and have had direct and supervised practical experience with applying them should put forward such analyses. Even then, I would argue, one should be highly sensitive to issues 3 through 6, below.

The Theoretical Rationale for Analysis

Clearly, one responsibility of the analyst involves the rationale for analysis. At this stage of our knowledge, the focus must be on explicating and developing the theoretical linkages between character elements and presidential performance. Character is a complex entity, and its elements can be assembled in numerous ways. Moreover, the ways in which various character elements and packages play out in presidential performance are not well understood, in part because neither character nor presidential performance has been clearly specified theoretically.

Given this, the most reasonable expectation from such a study would not be a validated theory of character and presidential performance; nor is the purpose of this study to construct a typology into which presidential candidates and presidents might be placed. Rather, my purpose is to develop a theoretically grounded and coherent set of relationships between character and presidential performance, along with some specifications of the nature, circumstances, and parameters of their operation.

The Issues of Inference Construction and the Analyst's Own Stance toward the Material

Psychological analysis involves inferences about behavior. This being true, explicitness about the process of inference construction is critical. Inferences begin with a pattern of facts. The idea of a pattern of facts is important because facts may have different meanings depending on their sequence and circumstances. The arrangement of facts into a context of theoretical validation is therefore a complex process in which there are many potential pitfalls.

At least since Freud's analysis of Woodrow Wilson, it has been clear that the analyst's political preferences and views can play an important and distorting role in assessing psychological suitability if care is not taken.[8] This can happen because the analyst admires, dislikes, or has some other set of feelings about his subject. Does an analyst favor activist presidents, liberal or conservative values? Does a particular candidate or president anger, excite, or disappoint the analyst?

In assembling a psychologically framed analysis of individual candidates or presidents, a political psychologist's stance toward his or her subject is a potential source of both information and, if one is not careful, bias. Presidential elections are highly charged emotional events from which an analyst cannot fully remove him- or herself. Difficulties in analysis can arise from the direct and obvious distortions that often accompany personal preferences. But they can also arise in more subtle ways when the analyst puts together the facts in a framework of analysis.

The analyst, especially one who makes use of and is trained in psychoanalytic psychology, has a particular obligation to be clear in these matters. No analyst can avoid personal responses to the materials with which he or she constructs an analysis, but one can try to be as explicit as possible. In that explicitness lies at least a partial solution to unintended or, worse, systematic bias.

In the end, of course, the analyst's stance toward the subject, examined or not, must stand the scrutiny of others. Do the frames of analysis put forward appear to cover the most important aspects of what needs to be explained psychologically? Is the evidence for putting forward those categories of analysis persuasive? And finally, are the implications drawn regarding these characteristics found in the real world of the president's actual behavior? These questions, not the correctness of the analyst's personal views, are what must ultimately be primary.

Does this mean that everyone who undertakes such analyses should himself or herself be psychoanalyzed? Not really; but it does require that the analyst be clear that there is a problem here and that he or she take direct, self-conscious steps to examine the analysis with these problems in mind.

The Issue of Tact

Freud and those analysts who followed gave a great deal of attention to the issue of tact. In psychotherapeutic analysis tact is a matter not of politeness but of technique. The reason is straightforward.

Much psychoanalytic psychotherapy consists of assisting the patient to learn about him- or herself.[9] This is often not an easy experience. In therapy, patients must eventually face their losses and disappointments. Among these are errors of judgment or action that have caused oneself or others harm. Mistakes are often difficult to acknowledge; avoidable mistakes, even more so. In the therapeutic process, individuals often come to see that what looked inevitable at the time was in fact a matter of choice—the patient's choice.

After an initial period of exploration, the analyst can often develop a theoretically informed sense of things about the patient that the patient does not yet realize or cannot yet acknowledge. There are many reasons why such information may be difficult for the patient to accept. In most cases, the process of self-understanding and acceptance is neither quick nor easy.

This being the case, the analyst is faced with a dilemma. He often knows more at any particular point than he can tell. However, successful treatment depends on the ability of the patient and therapist together to face the patient's life as clearly and forthrightly as possible. The answer to this dilemma is found in the therapist's approach to interventions, be they interpretations, clarifications, or simply framing the issues.

Most therapists rarely make direct, authoritative statements. They often rely on statements that are phrased in a conditional or tentative manner.[10] For example, the analyst may say, "I have the sense that . . . ," or "You seem to think that . . . ," or "I wonder if it's possible that you . . . ," and so on. There is more to this approach than a pro forma acknowledgment of uncertainty or professional modesty. Rather, it reflects the understanding that casting analytic interventions in a directly authoritative way runs several risks.[11] Among the most important for our discussion here is the risk that even if the intervention is factually correct, it will be too much for the patient to acknowledge and integrate. The clinical and therapeutic responsibility to "tell the truth" is essential to any successful therapy, but working up to understanding, accepting, and integrating these truths is a large and important part of that process.

In undertaking the psychologically informed analysis of presidential candidates, one is not conducting therapy. Nonetheless, I believe that the analytic emphasis on tact is worth keeping firmly in mind. In the end, one cannot be deterred from putting forward the results of this kind of analysis for scrutiny by others. However, one must work to find a way to do so that recognizes and respects the basic worth of most of these individuals without overlooking either their strengths or their limitations.

Some of the five issues discussed thus far can be handled by the traditional tools of scholarship: being explicit about one's theoretical stance and its rationale, being clear in setting forth the basis of one's analyses, considering the different levels at which the psychological process can play out in the arena of presidential performance, and considering alternative explanations of the relationships that appear. The analyst must also make use of the methods available to him for verification and theoretical validation, including cross-checking, plausibility, consistency, and the efficacy of alternative explanations. These are the tools of any scholar, and what all of these approaches share is a concern to be explicit in one's formulations and theoretical constructions. The analyst working in this area has a special obligation to be very clear about his own stance toward the facts that he finds and assembles.

The Issue of Scope

When critics or advocates discuss psychological assessments of presidential candidates, they are referring to a specific form of analysis. The analysis examines an individual's public, observable behavior, often, but not always, in a political context. The analyst then organizes this behavior into discernible and theoretically justifiable clusters and attempts to provide explanations for these patterns and their interrelationships. The patterns are accounted for by intrapsychic or interpersonal psychological dispositions. Most often these patterns are not directly linked to various developmental experiences, although soft psychological inferences from a candidate's early life may arise from time to time.

While it is true that almost all applications of psychological assessments of presidential candidates make use of this general model, they vary in important particulars. First, some assessments focus on one or a few traits, while others attempt a more comprehensive picture of a candidate's psychology.[12]

Second, assessments differ with regard to the specific linkages that are drawn between aspects of a candidate's psychology and their implications for presidential performance. The failure to be clear about such relationships has resulted in a focus on candidate missteps or isolated psychological elements. In the 1988 presidential campaign, Republican candidate George Romney misspoke and said that he had been "brainwashed" when asked to explain his former support for an unpopular war; he was immediately dismissed as a serious candidate.

Third, explanations differ with regard to the use they make of uncon-

scious motivations to explain a candidate's behavior. By definition, unconscious motivation is not known to the person motivated by it. Therefore,
the use of such a level of analysis raises both ethical and theoretical issues.

Last, explanations differ in the extent to which behaviors are accounted
for by early childhood experience. Such attributions raise related issues of
both evidence and inference. Obviously, the farther back in time one goes
to provide a foundation for one's observations, the greater the difficulty of
obtaining evidence and the longer the causal chain that has been developed.

Psychologically informed analyses are on firmer ground the more directly they are tied to the two more public and accessible levels of analysis—phenomenology and dynamics (see pp. 62–65 below). Persons assessing psychological suitability do not have access to the kind of
information necessary to make any more than the most speculative formulations about unconscious motivation. Nor, as I suggest below, is such a
level of analysis necessary for the purpose for which it is developed. There
are, in most cases, enough public data to make relatively informed analyses
without resorting to a level of psychological functioning to which the
analyst, except in extreme cases, does not have access. The same is true for
analyses that lay claim to superior insight into early developmental experiences and their possible effect on presidential behavior with little data.

General Theoretical Issues in the Assessment of Psychological Suitability

The attempt to apply psychological (and especially psychoanalytic) theories
of character to presidential performance raises a number of theoretical
questions. Some of these questions do not arise solely in connection with
assessing psychological suitability. They are more generally connected with
social science research. Other questions, however, are either particular to
this effort or represent general social science questions that take a specific
form in this arena. In this section, I focus on questions that are in some
ways particular to developing theories that link character to presidential
performance.

The Level-of-Analysis Problem

When social scientists speak of the level-of-analysis problem, they generally refer to the difficulties involved in moving up from the individual
through the small group and collective (mass) levels of analysis (Singer
1968; see also Smelser 1968). However, in studies of political leaders there
is a level-of-analysis problem of a different but no less difficult type.

Two frequent, related, but erroneous assumptions about the psychoanalytically informed analysis of presidents should be addressed at the outset. The first is that it is deep levels of psychological analysis that justify the use of psychological and especially psychoanalytically informed analyses of presidential behavior. The second is that psychoanalytically oriented analysts are particularly able to tap the deepest layers of presidential psychology.

Recall Greenstein's (1969) distinctions between three levels of analysis: phenomenology, dynamics, and development. The first consists of the facts: *(a)* "as they are," *(b)* as they are seen, and *(c)* as they are organized. It is clear that theory plays some role in this process, especially with regard to those facts *(b* and *c)* that require some sorting or construction exercise on the part of the analyst.

The second, the dynamic level, consists of theoretically informed hypotheses or tentative explanations that try to account for the facts as they have been seen and constructed. The third, the developmental level, seeks to account both for the origin and evolution of the characteristics that are put forward to explain the pattern of facts and for their social and psychological explanations.

The first level of analysis is the foundation for the others. Therefore, the analyst must sample a wide range of behavior, across similar and different circumstances. However, it is only when the range of behavior is clear and well documented that one can plausibly begin the next stage, which is to examine and consider theories that account for it.

As George and George (1956, 34) have pointed out, the first two levels of analysis (phenomenology and dynamics) can, strictly speaking, stand or fall on their own and do not depend on the third. That is, when one can document repeated patterns in a candidate's or president's behavior and authoritatively link that behavioral pattern to a set of theoretically grounded psychological patterns, one does not necessarily need to delve into the specific impact and meaning of earlier developmental events.

When the first and second levels of analysis have been substantially examined, one can begin the third and, in some ways, most difficult level of analysis. The task of developmental analysis is to trace the paths through which these psychological patterns developed. This is ordinarily an extremely difficult undertaking, for a number of reasons.

One problem is the availability of reliable data. A president's or candidate's own reconstruction of his developmental history is fraught with many dangers. He (like anyone else) may not remember, may not choose to remember, or, more likely, may choose to remember things in particular ways for personal or political reasons.

Firsthand accounts by others of a candidate's or president's early experiences are subject to the same cautionary concerns. This may be particularly true of parents or friends, who may wish to shield the president emotionally or politically. Relying on biographers does not solve the problem because they must often rely on their subject, intimates of their subject, friends (or enemies), or relative outsiders for information. The first three are all subject to the concerns noted above (or in the case of enemies, to a desire to harm), while the last group may lack enough access to be informative.

The fact that the kinds of data that would be truly useful for developmental reconstructions of presidential life histories are exceedingly difficult to obtain creates a formidable, but not insurmountable, barrier to such attempts. Early first-person materials such as letters, diaries, or contemporaneous reports are obviously helpful. In most cases, though, evidence from early periods of a president's life is likely to be somewhat fragmentary, especially when considered from the vantage point of the information available in the psychotherapeutic process.

Even in a psychotherapeutic context where such information is most directly and repeatedly available, the fact that one or more events happened does not automatically bestow on them causal significance. Many political leaders—and members of the public, for that matter—have experienced emotionally distant fathers (or mothers), but those experiences do not result in uniform outcomes. Along with knowing that events have happened, it is important to understand what their meaning was to the person involved, the ongoing context in which they occurred, as well as any offsetting factors that may be relevant.

In psychoanalytic psychotherapy, the meaning of these early experiences is varied and complex. They emerge with some clarity, if at all, only after a period of sustained analysis and reflection on them, often from a number of vantage points. Through this process the meaning of these experiences *to the patient* gradually becomes clear, as does their role in his or her development and the ways in which they have become a part of, but not synonymous with, adult behavior.

In the absence of any real capacity to meticulously trace events and their meanings, genetic reconstructions are likely, of necessity, to be somewhat provisional. For these reasons, political psychology theory cannot offer a certified analysis of the deep motivations of a presidential candidate or president. Nor can such analyses specify with great certainty the psychological paths by which character develops and has been translated into actions.[13]

As I noted in the Introduction, in the context of discovery (not valida-tion) at this stage of inquiry, extensive analyses of early experiences of the candidates I analyze here would be premature and not directly relevant to my purposes. One must first develop the phenomenological and dynamic levels of analysis before plunging into the depths of developmental history and its meaning.

Constructing Psychological Understandings

If political psychology cannot necessarily provide validated deep analyses of the sources and development of presidential behavior, what can it provide? One answer is that a psychologically informed analysis of a candi-date's behavior sensitizes us to the meaning of the behavior we observe and allows us to put forward some hypotheses about the relationships of behav-iors with one another and with other clusters of action. Thus, we may provide important clues for developmental analyses and even the basis by which deeper levels of psychological functioning are approached.

There is a theoretical and conceptual paradox in such work. Evidence of any intrapsychological element, including character and personality, is found in behavior, but it is also behavior that we seek to understand and explain. The analyst obviously cannot use a particular behavior both to extract by inference and to cross-validate an element that is then used to explain that same behavior. What the analyst does in these circumstances is examine a range of behaviors in order to strengthen his or her psychological inferences. These behaviors must then be cross-validated by reference both to other psychological characteristics that there is theoretical reason to assume are related and to behaviors other than those used for the original inferences.

While a psychoanalytic perspective is no guarantee of sound, behavior-ally significant developmental, dynamic, or phenomenological explana-tions, one can carry caution too far. The psychoanalytically trained observer of candidates and presidents can often find some insight into the meaning and impact of events, both contemporaneous and historical. He or she does so by observing behavior in a variety of contexts to gain some understand-ing of the person's most important behavioral preferences and then seeking out clues to the pattern of such behaviors. These patterns, which form the basis of psychological inference, in turn need to be tested against other, different behaviors (for consistency with theoretical understanding) and in relation to an understanding of the contexts in which these behaviors took place.

An example drawn from the 1992 presidential campaign will perhaps make these points clear. During the 1992 presidential campaign, there were several stories concerning then-candidate Clinton's temper and outbursts of anger. Berke (1992a, A14) notes that during one campaign stop Clinton, unaware that the microphone he was standing near was on, lashed out at Jesse Jackson saying he was "back-stabbing" him, after erroneously being told that Jackson had endorsed Senator Tom Harkin (a rival for the nomination).

When the press raised the issue of his draft record, Clinton responded with an angry diatribe against the press and their "blood lust." Mark Miller, a reporter for *Newsweek* who was granted extraordinary access to the inner workings of the Clinton campaign (thanks to the permission of the candidate himself), reported that when Bush ads suggested Clinton's economic package would mean higher taxes for everyone who made over $36,000, Clinton blew up (*Newsweek* [December 1992], 3). Miller quotes Clinton as saying, "I want to put a fist halfway down their throats on this. I don't want subtlety. I want their teeth on the sidewalk" (*Newsweek* [December 1992], 81). *The Economist* noted in an editorial that Clinton "gets angry (and when angry loses his temper) often. . . . One of his closest advisors recalls that Mr. Clinton loses his temper with his staff five to ten times a day, more during those days in the last week of the campaign" (1992, 38). When Clinton became president-elect and was confronted by several reporters at a golf course where he was playing, he lost his temper, cursing and complaining loudly to the club manager (Kelly 1992f, A28). And since Clinton has become president, there have been numerous public examples of his anger at the press—for example, at his press conference announcing the appointment of Ruth Bader Ginsberg to the Supreme Court and in his famous interview in *Rolling Stone* magazine (Wenner and Greider 1993), where he exploded in response to an interviewer's question.

At a minimum, the cumulative impact of these (and similar) reports suggests that anger is an element in Clinton's psychology that needs to be addressed. Even if one of these items were to prove not wholly and fully accurate, the number of such items, their consistency, and the fact that they have been reported from different sources on different occasions (some "behind the scenes," some public) add confidence to the view that there is something to be examined. Moreover, it is an element that runs counter to the candidate's "presentation of self in political life," that is, it is not the official, preferred view of President Clinton.

The point of these observations (and similar illustrations that could be brought forward) is not to suggest that President Clinton is an ogre. However, they do suggest that the picture of a folksy, empathetic president who is always eager to please does not present a full or comprehensive portrait. More to the point, they present the analyst with a set of theoretical questions.

These behaviors run counter to other conventional explanations of Clinton's character and leadership style, most particularly his frequently commented-on need to be liked. The question, of course, is why an individual who supposedly has such a high need to be liked engages in behavior that seems likely to produce the opposite effect. Is it the frustration of office? Is the candidate (or president) an angry man, and if so, why? Is there a particular relationship between his outbursts of anger and the specific circumstances that trigger it? (I put forward a provisional explanation of this set of data in chapter 11).

Assume for a moment that anger is indeed a variable to be understood and explained. How, then, would one approach this task? A somewhat heavy-handed approach would be to trace the current anger directly back to childhood experiences. In Clinton's case (as with most others), one could doubtless find many explanatory candidates for his anger among his early experiences: Clinton's biological father died before he was born, his mother left him in the care of her mother and father for several years while she moved to New Orleans to study to become a nurse-anesthetist, and so on.

The point is not that none of these events had any impact. It would be highly unusual if they didn't. The points are that (1) anger may be one but is by no means the only outcome of such experiences, and (2) even if anger is one important outcome, the analyst must still explain how this outcome is represented, along with others, in an individual's adult character and other psychological structures. In others words, a dynamic theoretical explanation of an element of a candidate's or president's behavior and an accounting of its origins are separate enterprises. One has not provided a dynamic explanation of an adult characteristic by giving an accounting of its origins.

Consider the characterological element of ambition. An analyst has not completed his task when he is able to bring forward enough evidence to support the existence of high (or low) ambition in a candidate (or president). Many questions important for addressing the role this element plays in presidential performance remain. For example, how is ambition connected with the individual's sense of accomplishment? Is it uniform across circumstances? If not, what accounts for differences? With what other psychological and behavioral elements does it appear to be associated?

Such data help us further to clarify and understand behavioral elements that manifest themselves on observation. High levels of ambition, for example, can spring from a number of psychological sources, including the wish to achieve, the wish to bolster one's sense of self-worth in the face of doubts expressed by others, the wish to please a demanding parent. Examining the contemporaneous dynamics of such an element (with what other elements it is associated, when, and why) can help us in distinguishing its origins as well as in clarifying its theoretical dynamics.

Drawing the Line: The Dilemmas of Error and Risk

There is a fundamental dilemma involved in attempting to develop a framework for the analysis of psychological suitability that should be acknowledged at the outset. The framework, at its best, may sharpen the analysis of psychological suitability. However, it does so, if at all, in the context of a set of probabilities, not certainties. The contribution of even a successful analysis of psychological suitability would not guarantee the selection of superior presidents. Rather, it would lie in reducing the risk of making one of two fundamental predictive errors.

In statistical analysis (Blalock 1960, 93–94), this dilemma is referred to in the context of Type I or Type II errors. In the first type a person rejects as untrue something that actually is true (in this case, a candidate would be a good president but is inappropriately rejected). In Type II error something is accepted when it should be rejected (e.g., a person who would make a poor president and ought to be rejected is actually selected).

In probability analysis, the question concerns what level of risk is associated with the likelihood of making each kind of error and how we calculate that likelihood. In presidential campaigns, the questions are more difficult since we cannot rely on well-refined models of probability. What constitutes a major reason to reject a candidate and which reasons are relatively minor are still, in many cases, unclear but are at the heart of the analysis of psychological suitability.

The public, analysts, and commentators have searched for clues that can provide insight into the psychology of presidential candidates, frequently without success. The fact that presidential candidate Edmund Muskie became choked with emotion in public in the 1968 campaign derailed his bid for the presidency. In the 1988 presidential campaign, much was made of the fact that one candidate, Gary Hart, changed the way he signed his name. Were these facts important? They were thought so at the time. A framework for the analysis of psychological suitability might provide a way to answer such questions.

Aside from the question of Type I and II errors, the analysis of psychological suitability must deal with the "general rule of composite characteristics." The term *psychological suitability,* like all terms that deal with assessment, must have some way of incorporating the fact that individuals rarely come in neat diagnostic categories. This may be especially true of persons with the requisite talents and skills to make it to a presidential campaign.

The general rule of composite characteristics is that psychological assets and limitations come in combinations or packages. Any analysis of psychological suitability must pay attention to this basic fact. Consider in this regard two presidents, Lyndon Johnson and Richard Nixon.

Lyndon Johnson is widely credited with being an extremely effective master of the legislative process. The "Johnson treatment," a mixture of flattery, pressure, and, when all else failed, the threat of severe sanctions generally won him high marks as a legislative leader. The same skills were instrumental in passing much of his "Great Society" legislation.

Could the country have obtained the Great Society programs without Johnson's ability to manipulate and dominate Congress? Perhaps not. Were the same tendencies toward manipulation to accomplish purposes evident in Johnson's handling of the Vietnam War? I think a reasonable argument can be made that they were.

It is equally clear that Richard Nixon was an accomplished and skilled leader in many respects. He is generally acknowledged to have been an intelligent and involved president whose administration produced some notable and significant policy accomplishments. His opening to China is generally considered a masterful stroke of diplomacy, and historical assessments will also have to consider such successes as his strategic agreement with the Soviet Union on ballistic missiles.

Yet against this record of accomplishment one must also consider the intimate and deeply disturbing view of the Nixon presidency provided by the Watergate tapes. The tapes portray a bitter, indecisive, occasionally inarticulate, and even coarse man at the center of power, arguing after his landslide election that "we have no friends." Is it possible to have a tough, realpolitik view of international relations that results in treaties with opponents based on mutual self-interest without, at the same time, having a view that there are no "real" friends in politics and that one's domestic enemies must also be manipulated and even punished to bring them into line?

When he was caught in several lies surrounding his pursuit of an extra-marital affair during the 1988 presidential campaign, Gary Hart defended himself by saying, "We are all sinners." While this may be true as a matter of theology and may even be statistically accurate, for the political psychologist interested in issues of psychological suitability it is beside the point. It is the specific nature of the flaws or strengths and their relationship both to other aspects of psychological functioning and to the requirements for successful accomplishment that constitute the central issue for psychological suitability. The analysis presented here aspires to help develop a framework in which questions of composite functioning can usefully be addressed.

Conclusion

There are risks in introducing theories of candidate psychology and presidential performance into presidential campaigns. Profiles of particular candidates may confuse or mislead the public. The public may not fully understand that such analyses are tentative, based on somewhat broad and nonspecific framing of characteristics, or may simply be in error.

Yet there are also risks in not attempting such analyses. The chief risk is that the public will not have available to it information that is demonstrably important. Worse, without such inquiries candidates will be more able to define themselves as they wish to appear, without much worry about the public learning more of who they really are.

There is also another risk in introducing unproved theories into the public domain. Such analyses may wrongly or prematurely typecast candidates. Yet theories of what it takes to convince the public that a candidate is a superior choice on the grounds of his character and abilities are already a major focus of presidential contenders. Suggesting in these circumstances that political psychologists cease their efforts is a little like trying to resolve a war by calling on one side to lay down its arms.

Moreover, there seems no reasonable way to develop and evaluate theories of character and presidential performance without drawing on the actual political context they are meant to explain. The subject matter of these efforts is character, judgment, and leadership. The task is to better understand what information best serves the public's choice among candidates. This, in turn, requires some attention to the relationship between campaigns and presidential performance. To some degree, the analyst by necessity is drawn into a public context because the material he bases his work on must also draw from that context.

Ultimately, of course, questions of psychological suitability are settled politically. The ultimate judgment regarding a candidate's viability, psychologically or otherwise, is reserved in this political system to the public. Attempts to develop a clearer understanding of the relationship between a particular presidential candidate's psychology and his capacity for effective performance should therefore be viewed as a supplement to and not a substitute for such judgments.

What, then, can one hope to accomplish in developing a framework for the analysis of psychological suitability? Such a framework at its best may accomplish four things: It may help identify the elements that are important to consider in assessing character, presidential performance, and their relationships. It could make, at the minimum, a plausible (and at the maximum, a persuasive) case for why it is important to consider these elements, including a demonstration of their behavioral and political implications. Third, it may provide some theoretical and conceptual tools for obtaining the information relevant to making such analyses. Finally, it could provide illustrations that, in turn, offer some basis for judging the usefulness of the framework, as well as laying the basis for improving it.

PART II

*Assessing the Psychological Health of
Presidential Candidates*

THREE

Psychological Health and
Presidential Performance:
A Foundation for the Assessment of
Psychological Suitability?

U ntil character issues became prominent, traditional
concerns regarding psychological suitability focused
on whether a candidate was or might become "mentally ill." [1] This concern
did not originate in any general interest with the psychological functioning
of presidents or candidates per se. Rather, it reflected a more limited,
specific worry that a president might become sufficiently impaired psychologically to begin a nuclear exchange.

The demise of the Soviet Union has dramatically decreased the chances
of nuclear confrontation between the two superpowers. This, in turn, has
lessened concern [2] about a "Dr. Strangelove" scenario in which a psychotically impaired president triggers a nuclear exchange. Consequently, the
"mental health" of presidential candidates and presidents is a subject less
frequently discussed than its importance merits.

This lack of concern is unfortunate. The issues raised by concerns
reflected in analyses of the "mental health of our leaders" have not disap-
peared with the end of the cold war. Indeed, I argue that the very structure
and nature of the presidency, as it has evolved, make it likely that optimal
psychological functioning cannot always be assumed.

Moreover, some evidence suggests there is little reason to be sanguine
about the psychological well-being of candidates or presidents on the basis
of past historical experience. There have been a number of serious questions
raised about the psychological suitability of presidential candidates, and
even of sitting presidents, during the past two decades. In at least two cases

such concerns appear to have led to concrete steps of prevention or assessment.

In this chapter, I first focus on the conceptual and theoretical questions involved in the issue of impaired or adequate psychological functioning. I do so in order to address some of the confusions and difficulties that ordinarily attend discussions of psychological suitability in the presidency from this perspective. We must therefore directly confront some of the most difficult and controversial issues in clinical psychology and psychiatry. Is there such a thing as "mental illness," and if so, of what does it consist? What exactly is "mental health?"[3] Is it synonymous with normality or with rationality? Not surprisingly, the application of these same issues has proved difficult in the arena of political leadership. In politics generally, and in the case of presidential candidates and other leaders in particular, one may ask, with Galyin (1973, 57), "What's normal?"

In this chapter, I first examine the concept of mental health as a tool for the psychological evaluation of presidential suitability and performance. I examine whether there is such an entity as mental health and, if so, what the criteria are for evaluating and applying it. Second, I explore the relationship of "mental health" to the concept of normality, both as it is formulated in clinical settings and as further complexities are introduced in its application to the political arena. Third, I take up the issues involved in trying to apply these concepts to the arena of presidential performance. Fourth, I examine the consequences for our understanding of psychological suitability in cases where patterns of behavior, even those damaging to the individual and others, are so widespread that they are taken for granted. This is a social pattern defect, and I explore the extent to which political ambition qualifies as such a defect in American political culture. Finally, I examine the question of "what's normal" when assessing the psychology of high-level political leaders such as the president. Can or should such individuals be evaluated by the same standards as ordinary people?

Mental Health and Psychological Suitability

What role, if any, should questions of mental health play in the assessment of psychological suitability? To answer this question we must begin with two others: Is there such a thing as mental health? If so, of what does it consist?

The answers to these questions are not as obvious as it may intuitively seem. The concept of mental health is difficult to define. For some, mental health denotes the absence of a severe impairment. For others, it implies more than just the absence of mental disease; it implies that one is fully functioning and making the best use of one's abilities.

Some argue that there really is no such thing as "mental health," as generally understood. That is the position of Thomas Szasz (1960), whose well-known argument is that "mental illness" is a myth. Szasz's view is that assessments of mental health owe more to a psychiatrist's personal values than to an individual's psychological functioning.

It can be argued that Szasz's critique of the medical model that underlies most professional understandings of the term *mental health* is somewhat dated. However, I suggest that Szasz's position is not so much dated as erroneous. Moreover, it is important to our work here to explain why.

Szasz's critique of the medical model attacks the assumptions of the model at its core. If Szasz is correct, then concerns about the mental health of our leaders are simply a matter of misplaced personal values being inappropriately transposed to the political system. To evaluate Szasz's arguments carefully, we must first explicate the target of his analysis, this most basic model of psychological functioning in clinical practice, the "medical model."[4]

As its name implies, this model assumes that mental health and illness are analogous to their physical counterparts. Involved are at least four distinct propositions. First, the medical model assumes that physical and mental (psychological) concepts of disease are essentially analogous and that we therefore can understand mental illness in much the same way as we understand physical illness. Second, the medical model assumes that valid information does exist regarding the nature of mental illness and that mastery of this knowledge is essential to correct diagnosis, understanding, and treatment. Third is the view that such technical and specialized knowledge should and can be used only by properly trained clinicians. Fourth, the medical model assumes that once someone is diagnosed as "ill" by a properly certified expert, the person so designated enters an altered social state that changes his network of social obligations, responsibilities, and privileges; the person is no longer considered fully responsible for his or her own behavior. The diagnosed person therefore is subject to greater control by those (who because of position or training) deemed better able to take responsibility.

Szasz bases his objections on two fundamental points. First, he argues that the medical model requires that mental illness, like physical illness, be ultimately traceable to some physiological deficiency. Szasz grants the existence of mental illness to a disease of the brain, not of the mind,[5] in the same way that physical symptoms reflect disturbances of interior organic systems. This view is shared by many psychiatrists who believe that mental illness will ultimately be found to be biological in origin and that mental illness will ultimately be curable through psychopharmacology.

Szasz's second and stronger point is that evaluations of mental health symptoms involve some judgment on the part of those making the diagno-sis and that these are substantially different from the judgments made regarding physical symptoms. According to Szasz,

The concept of illness, whether bodily or mental, *implies deviation from some clearly defined norm*. In the case of physical illness, the norm is the structural and functional integrity of the human body. Thus, although the desirability of physical health as such is an ethical value, what health *is* can be stated in anatomical or physiological terms. What is the norm deviation from which is regarded as mental illness? This question cannot be easily answered. But whatever this norm might be, we can be certain of only one thing: namely that it is a norm which must be stated in terms of *psycho-social, ethical,* or *legal* concepts. (1960, 114, emphasis in original)

Szasz goes on to argue that the discipline of psychiatry is more closely tied to ethics than to medicine. The reason is that mental illness refers in practice to "problems in living" and not of physiology and that such problems can be analyzed only within a social and ethical framework. The consequence of this requirement, in his view, is that judgments of mental illness are inevitably biased by the personal values of the individual making them, as well as by the more general values of the society to which the evaluator belongs.

Szasz's position has implications for understanding psychological suitabil-ity, viewed both as emotional and psychological well-being and as a set of characterological-political elements. If, as he argues, clinical judgments are based in essence on personal values, then emotional and psychological well-being as an aspect of psychological suitability merely reflects the analyst's personal preferences, in which case one set of preferences should be as viable as another. Character-based assessments of psychological suitability in this case are also suspect, on the same grounds. If Szasz is correct, having psychologically trained analysts involved in assessing such suitability assigns too much importance and political weight to personal values, without any scientific grounds for doing so. It is therefore of some importance to examine Szasz's argument more closely.

The first of Szasz's arguments refers to the ultimate referents or sources of the phenomenon characterized as *mental illness*. Szasz would accept the term if it could ultimately be shown to refer to some physical lesion in the brain, a position that denies ontological status to anything incapable of physical reference. The problem is that, on these restricted grounds, any discussion of physical disease would be ruled out as well.[6]

The real question here is not whether mental illness has some concrete physiological location (which it may ultimately be found to have but which is, in any case, beside the point in this argument) but whether it is legitimate and useful to extend the term to cover impairments for which there is no known physiological cause or site. If the construct cannot be legitimately extended to cover psychologically based and operative dynamics, it makes no sense to analyze and develop a theory of psychological suitability or to apply relevant clinical psychoanalytic theory to presidential candidates and performance.

There is, however, reason to believe that such extensions are legitimate[7] and that the political application thereof is possible. Margolis (1966, 73) points out that the line between physical and mental illness is not as sharp as Szasz would like to have us believe. Margolis mentions psychosomatic and hysterical conversions as two illustrations of a class of impairments of functioning that present concrete physical symptoms but that do not have concrete organic or neurological causes.

It is clear from this that it is not only the capacity to locate specific causes which permits us to refer to something as an illness but also the effects produced by the element. The history of medical science is replete with illustrations of diseases that were recognized as such (e.g., polio) well before any particular physiological origin was uncovered. According to this line of argument, it is the *pattern of illness,* not the cause, that supports application of the concept of disease.

Szasz notes another problem relevant to our concerns. He observes that one difference between physical and mental illness is that in the former the disturbance is referenced by signs or symptoms (e.g., fever, pain). However, in the latter we refer "to a person's communications about himself, others and the world around him" (Szasz 1960, 114). Szasz argues that the former are more *public* than the latter, which he terms *private,* a somewhat curious understanding of the two terms. There appears to be no a priori reason to confer a different status to "communications about himself" from that of any other signs or symptoms. It is true that persons other than professionals enter into evaluations of mental health symptoms (or communications). However, this by itself is neither a necessary nor a sufficient reason to call for abandonment of diagnosis.

Indeed, Szasz is perfectly willing to continue such characterizations as long as they are termed *problems in living,* rather than *mental illness.* But to the extent that the former refer to the same set of "symptoms" as the latter, it is hard to see just what is accomplished by the change. It is also, of course, perfectly plausible and logically consistent to say that someone is having "problems in living" and to characterize that as an illness, remaining within the boundaries of the medical model.

Mental Health and Normality in the Assessment of Psychological Suitability

It is Szasz's second set of contentions about the normative basis of clinical judgments, rather than his first dealing with psychological sites that is more troublesome. The concept of illness, whether physical or mental, implies deviation from a norm. The crucial question is which norm.

Szasz argues that beyond the problem of linguistic designation is even a more basic problem, namely, that clinical judgments ultimately rest on psychosocial, ethical, or legal norms. In essence, he argues that "the judgment entails . . . a covert matching of the patient's ideas, concepts and beliefs with those of the observer and the society in which they live" (Szasz 1960, 114). If this matching can be shown to consist of ill-conceived, inappropriate, or invalid reflections of the phenomenon it purportedly clarifies, then any judgments based on the matching must clearly be called into question. If Szasz is correct, there is little value in attempting to develop criteria of psychological suitability since whatever criteria are put forward will simply be a reflection of the theorist's personal values.

There are several ways in which the concept of normality is used within the context of discussions of mental health. The first and most frequent use of the term refers to a statistical norm. In this formulation normality is defined in part by occurrence; but such a formulation quickly runs into well-known problems, the most immediate of which springs from the inappropriateness of equating statistical frequency with "health." Tooth decay, for example, is widely prevalent in our society and in that statistical sense might be considered normal; however, one would hardly wish to argue that it is healthy.[8]

Similar problems arise when we consider psychological processes and individual behavior from the standpoint of statistical frequency. Narcissism, the operation of defensive mechanisms, and unconscious processes are examples of psychological conditions that are considered almost universal, but clinicians would not necessarily conclude that every manifestation of these psychological elements should automatically be considered as healthy. The issue, of course, is one of degree.[9]

The appropriateness of using normality to signify the emotional and psychological basis of presidential suitability is further compromised when we consider the variations that occur cross-culturally in "normal behavior." As Karen Horney (1937, 15) pointed out many years ago, "The conception of what is normal varies not only with the culture but also within the same culture, in the course of time." To cite one of numerous examples that could be given, anthropologist Ruth Benedict found that the Kwakiutl Indians of British Columbia engage in behavior that is, "by our standards, paranoid and megalomaniacal. Their world view is similar to a delusion of grandeur in our culture" (1934; quoted in Jahoda 1958, 12).

Visions, communications with deceased ancestors, and trance states are only some of the behaviors that are treated routinely in some cultures but that would be considered evidence of gross disturbance in ours. One implication is that we cannot assume that a particular behavior reflects a similar meaning in different contexts or the same underlying etiology. As Jahoda (1958, 12) put it, "Similarities in symptoms must not be mistaken for identical disturbances in functions." This point certainly seems to mitigate against the development, at least at present, of a universal set of criteria with which to make cross-cultural judgments of mental health or illness.[10]

The Role of Norms in Clinical Evaluations

Problems with statistical and other concepts of normality and their equation by some with "health" make clear that Szasz's criticisms of clinical judgments are not without some foundation. He is certainly correct in stating that such judgments are related to the social system in which they take place, but I think he errs in the implications he draws from this association. Szasz argues that a crucial matching occurs between the patient's behaviors and psychosocial, ethical, and legal norms. He maintains that the personal values of the psychiatrist enter into the analysis at this step, implying that psychiatrists take societal norms as their criteria for health. Szasz is correct in arguing that a matching does take place, but it is not necessarily the matching he describes.

The psychosocial, ethical, and legal norms to which Szasz refers can actually enter into the assessment in several different ways. One of these could be by simply adapting social norms as valuative criteria, which is the role that Szasz proposes for them. But they can also be used in another way.

They can be used as an existing set of external reference points by which the analyst assesses aspects of behavior. Knowledge of cultural rituals, social situations, and the aspects of the patient's reality world is an important contextual dimension of the interpretative process. Thus, knowledge and understanding of social processes, far from being an impediment to accurate assessment, may be a precondition for it. In this instance, social norms and processes are important not because the analyst believes they embody wisdom or health but because they provide data as to how the individual responds to a specified set of circumstances.

To say that a psychiatrist's (or a political psychologist's or other psychologically trained observer's) personal values enter into the diagnostic process is immediately to invite the argument that values reflect mere preferences, none of which can be distinguished on the basis of any "scientific" standard. No one would deny that personal values (the wish to help is an obvious one for clinicians) can and do enter into clinical decisions, but it would be a mistake to assume that the latter can be reduced to the former.

When we say that someone has personal values, we refer to preferences that have no other ultimate rationale than their selection by the individual concerned. I can value truth above beauty and rest content that my personal preference is both a necessary and sufficient justification in some circumstances. Clinical judgments, by contrast, rest on public theories of psychological functioning that are subject to professional scrutiny and debate and become modified in the light of theoretical developments and clinical experience. Clinical propositions involve a respect for established functional relationships. They also involve an appreciation that behaviors have multiple causes and that adequate functioning may take place within a fairly wide range of behavior.

Ultimately, of course, diagnosis must reflect a comparison between a present state and some criterion state. Szasz repeatedly argues that such states are ultimately psychosocial, ethical, or legal,[11] as if this statement by itself constituted an irremediable indictment. Yet each of these states operates differently in the process of assessment and, accordingly, lays claim to different levels of legitimacy.

A case can be made that ethical norms inform clinical judgments. Simply stated, ethical norms involve a web of obligations and responsibilities that arise in human relationships. But again, clinical judgment in these areas rests not on whether the person who may violate these norms is right or wrong but on what psychological pattern they belong to and on whether the patient is able to see, weigh, and act on this set of mutual responsibilities and obligations. The consistent failure to do so, or the clear inability to ever take the role of others, may reflect developmental and interpersonal difficulties, as well as unethical behavior according to some personal or public standard. Recognizing that behavior can be seen in terms of the violating standards does not negate their clinical importance.

It is the first norm, the psychosocial, that is clearly the most relevant of the three for clinical assessment. By grouping all three together, Szasz promotes the impression that they are all equally relevant—and suspect. Yet of the three, only the first is clearly and unequivocally related to general psychiatric assessment through clinical theory and training. The distinction is a simple but crucial one.

Professionally, a clinician may value, say, greater autonomy for a patient, but that value is not the result of personal preference alone; it has its origins in a vast array of data (in this case, clinical, social-psychological, and experimental) which support the proposition that the experience of autonomy is preferred by individuals and is empirically associated with a variety of positive outcomes. The data, of course, may be contested; there may be alternative or additional factors involved, and one can never be totally certain that one has found invariant truth, but this is quite far from the category of mere preference.

Agreeing that psychosocial norms are important in the clinical assessment of psychological functioning provides only the legitimizing of an approach or framework, not a set of answers. It is still necessary to establish the specific clinical norms that are relevant, the basis upon which these norms are selected, and the consequences of doing so. This task is decidedly more advanced in the case of physical health than it is for psychological health.

The Mental Health of Presidents: Global Well-Being or Functional Impairment?

When physicians address the concept of the normal in physical health, they do so in accordance with a well-grounded functional perspective. Some years ago, C. D. King (1945) pointed out that "the normal . . . is objectively, and properly, to be defined as that which functions in accordance with its design." The problem, as the author was quick to point out, is that frequently in behavior disorders (and, one would add, so-called normal behaviors), "we do not know what design or function a certain behavior pattern serves." Behaviors serve many purposes, not all of them evident to the observer or even to the person engaging in them.

Another approach has been to try to develop and refine overall assessments of psychological performance and well-being. Erikson reports (1980, 102) that Freud was once asked what he thought a normal person should do well, and Freud simply said, "Lieben and Arbeiten" (to love and to work). Erikson himself (1980, 51–107) has characterized the healthy personality as one that has successfully passed through a series of psychosocial crises and whose end result is the capacity for intimacy and generativity and the accompanying sense of ego identity and integrity.

Could these more global assessments be used to make judgments of psychological suitability in the political arena? To a limited degree, yes. There are, however, at least two drawbacks to such theories being used by themselves for application to this question. The first is that such theories provide a somewhat general basis for understanding adequate psychological functioning, and it is not clear how they would fare as criteria for suitability in the political arena. A second problem with these models of adequate and healthy functioning is that they represent a state toward which many aspire but which is not easily or ordinarily reached. One implication of the fact that psychological conflicts are ubiquitous is that most, if not all, people function at less than optimal levels. Unless we expect that the end result of developing models of psychological suitability for presidential candidates will only be the selection of presidents without functional difficulties, it will still be useful and important to have a firm grasp of both the functional and the general aspects of psychological health.

Moreover, psychological suitability sometimes requires of presidents traits that are often not seen in a positive light. A president on occasion must be tough and, with certain enemies, even ruthless. He must on occasion be stubborn in defending his point of view. How one can build these elements into a model of suitability is a matter I take up in chapters 7 and 8.

How, then, should the problem of defining psychological health be approached? One promising idea is contained in an observation by Moore (1975, 1490). In discussing the appropriateness of terming hysteria as "illness," he notes:

> The activities for which one is incapacitated by a paralyzed arm differ not a whit, no matter if the paralysis is anatomical or hysterical. In either case, one cannot, for example, play baseball or tend after one's father effectively, etc. . . . Being in a state properly called "ill," then, does not depend on one's knowing, or even . . . of there being, any particular physiological condition. It depends on one's being in a state characterized

(roughly) by pain, incapacitation, and the prospect of a hastened death. There is nothing mythical about such states, whether they be due to a broken leg or a broken home.

What is useful about Moore's observation is not the specific criteria he offers but the fact *that* he offers them.[12] When Moore notes three possible criteria (death, pain, and incapacitation), he has put forward behaviorally observable measures by which to make an assessment. Moore's approach is in keeping with trends in clinical psychiatry over the past decade.

That approach, in a word, is specification. One of the important differences between the first and fourth editions of the *Diagnostic and Statistical Manual of Mental Disorders* (*DSM-IV;* APA 1994) is that in each successive edition, the syndromes of disorders have been theoretically and empirically refined, and in the process, the indicators of such disorders have been further specified. They were refined through a process by which multiple groups conducted and updated comprehensive literature reviews, performed reanalyses of published empirical data when questions arose, and conducted extensive field trials (APA 1994, xvii–xx). Their criterion (APA 1994, xxi) is that each disorder be capable of

a clinically significant behavioral or psychological syndrome or pattern that occurs in an individual and that is associated with present distress (e.g., a painful symptom) or disability (i.e., impairment in one or more important areas of functioning) or with an increased risk of suffering death, pain, disability, or an important loss of freedom. In addition, this syndrome or pattern must not be an expectable and culturally sanctioned response to a particular event, for example, the death of a loved one. Whatever its original cause, it must currently be considered a manifestation of a behavioral, psychological, or biological dysfunction in the individual.

The criterion of dysfunction or impairment is central to this diagnostic enterprise. The *DSM-IV* makes every effort to link its categories to "significant distress or impairment in social, occupational, and other important areas of functioning" (APA 1994, 7). A legitimate question arises as to how one knows that there is an impairment, especially in the many cases when the person him- or herself doesn't see that there is anything wrong.

There are several ways to answer this objection. One is to refer to the wide body of clinical studies which support the proposition that when individuals have been in treatment and are able to understand the costs of their behavior to themselves and others and to exert more control over it (which is to say that one can choose to do otherwise), they do. To take but one clinical example, a person who has multiple and indiscriminate short-term sexual relationships may indeed see nothing wrong with the behavior. But numerous behavioral and clinical studies show that individuals pay a price in intimacy, in the capacity to make real emotional connections with others and, in turn, to be sustained by those connections. Moreover, such studies also support the contention that people who are able to make meaningful emotional connections with others feel better emotionally, are more able to endure stress, and are less emotionally constricted.

One might argue, as does Szasz, that these are nothing more than the clinicians' personal values, but this would miss an important point. These are empirical clinical relationships. One can argue that intimacy is not necessarily a good to be sought after, but that is not the same as saying there is no empirical relationship, say, between the capacity for intimacy and the likelihood that the individual will feel more satisfied with his or her life.

Translating the American Psychiatric Association (APA) criteria directly into the political leadership arena would present some difficulties. The APA suggest as criteria: (1) present distress (e.g., a painful symptom), (2) a disability (i.e., impairment in one or more important areas of functioning), (3) an increased risk of suffering death, pain, or disability, and (4) an important loss of freedom. Of the four, the second and fourth seem the most potentially promising for use in the political area.[13]

What is needed is the political-psychology-of-leadership equivalent to the studies which show that factors *a, b,* and *c,* either together or individually, are associated with outcome *x.* Do studies show that the failure seriously to consider a variety of alternatives has an adverse impact on the quality of a decision? Generally they do (George 1974b; Janis and Mann 1977). Do studies show that going public is an important strategy for presidents to build support and thus legitimacy for their policies? Again, generally they do (Kernell 1986; Rose 1988).

My point here is that if we can firmly identify the tasks of presidential leadership, we then can begin to specify the ways in which such tasks can be either facilitated or inhibited. It will then be possible to get a more clearly empirical standard by which to judge not only if there is a real or potential impairment in this function area but also some idea of its degree.

The *DSM-IV* is able to specify the severity of the impairment in part because it has accumulated substantial research on the range of ways in which difficulties can manifest themselves in particular function areas. Thus the term *mild* (APA 1994, 2) is used to denote few, if any, symptoms used to make the diagnosis, and symptoms that are present result in no more than minor impairment in social or occupational functioning. The term *severe* requires the manifestation of many symptoms, the presence of several symptoms that are particularly severe, or symptoms that result in marked impairment in social or occupational functioning.

What clinical psychiatry has achieved in its domains that political psychology has not to this point is (1) an agreed-upon range of manifestations of important leadership functions and (2) a consensus regarding the range of elements that affect more and less desirable outcomes. It is likely that the development of such information in political psychology is many years down the road. What is important here is not that this information is not currently available but that there is a model and a strategy that can be followed, and that collective understandings reached over time can become the basis for making distinctions about impairments of function.

The model of impairments developed in clinical psychiatry can serve another function for our efforts here. In detailing some of the behavioral manifestations of certain character and personality disorders, it sensitizes us to what is dysfunctional and why it is considered so. Such help may be useful in trying to ascertain why a candidate who has relationships with numerous women other than his wife may be less psychologically desirable than one who doesn't.

Notice, I have phased this in the conditional. The reason is that "assessing whether [a diagnostic criterion] is met, especially in terms of role function, is inherently a difficult clinical judgment" (APA 1994, 7). Again, here as elsewhere, the clinically oriented scholar must rely on the traditional sources of theoretical validity. These are the use of multiple data sources, the consideration of alternative or additional explanations, and specific attention to covariation of factors with outcomes.

Political Ambition: A Case of a Culturally Patterned Defect?

The issue of attempting to analyze psychological suitability from the perspective of normality, even within one culture, raises other issues that are relevant to our concerns in this work. One is the problem of the *culturally patterned defect*. I define that term as a pattern of behavior, and its underlying psychology, that is so widespread that its presence hardly causes discussion.[14] It can also occur when there is a general cultural or political "taboo" that keeps an element out of public discourse. In these respects, culturally patterned defects can often become empirically invisible.

One difficulty in uncovering cultural assumptions that may lead to deficiencies in political process or outcomes is that ordinary behavior rarely merits comment, much less analysis. It is always easier to examine the ways in which cultural ideals inhibit examination in other cultures than it is for our own. When Jahoda (1958, 15–16) points out that the failure to distinguish between the statistical and normative aspects of normality "lead[s] us back into an extreme cultural relativism according to which the storm trooper . . . must be considered the prototype of integrative adjustment in Nazi culture," we immediately understand the point. But it is less clear when we examine the assumptions of our own political culture. One consequence of the internalization of one's own culture is that one does not ordinarily recognize that a "given" frame of reference shapes the perception of problems and their evaluation.

In this section I suggest that political ambition in American culture may well be such a culturally patterned defect. (There could, of course, be others also.) Ambition is most often discussed publicly when questions are raised about whether presidential candidates really have enough "fire in their bellies" or whether they "really want it [the presidency]." Often these questions are raised of candidates who are deemed not sufficiently motivated, aggressive, or assertive in the view of those who cover presidential campaigns.

The drive to "do what it takes" is both demanded as a test of presidential character and judged to be a suspect presidential characteristic. When George Bush said, during an interview with David Frost, that he would "do what it takes" to win the 1992 presidential election, the remark was viewed by some as indicating Bush's willingness to engage in questionable tactics, including attacks on his opponent, although it might have referred to his dislike of campaigning rather than governing. In contemporary American politics strong ambition is fused, for both strategic and psychological reasons, with other motivations, and as a result, the public and the media alike routinely lose sight of the great drive and ambition necessary to gain high public office and rarely discuss their implications for presidential performance.

The functioning of ambition in presidential candidates, and leaders more generally, is complex. Ambition is a key psychological variable that is deeply embedded in an individual's character structure and has enormous implications for presidential performance, yet there is little public discussion of this critical aspect of psychological suitability. The reasons are not hard to discern.

Presidential candidates are hardly likely to say that they are putting forward policies for reasons other than those of the public interest, so it is difficult, if not impossible, to distinguish personal and policy ambition from policy statements. Second, most presidential candidates do have real policy preferences, so it will be hard to distinguish personal and policy ambition from policy preferences, especially strongly held ones. Third, many political leaders appear to combine personal and policy ambition. It is a relatively rare leader who consciously and cynically presents a policy front that has no basis in personal policy beliefs or approaches. For all these reasons, developing ways to distinguish ambition that is in the service of political and policy views and vice versa is an important task for the assessment of psychological suitability.[15]

The dilemma of strong ambition is that it is both necessary and potentially dangerous for political leaders. Without ambition, the long hours, great uncertainties, high risks, and mixed rewards in political life would hardly seem worthwhile. The strong, and perhaps enormous, political ambition that is now necessary to reach the upper levels of political leadership in the United States is most certainly necessary to become president. No one reaches the presidency without an enormous investment of time, energy, and substantial psychological resources. Even Ronald Reagan, whom Barber characterizes (1992a, 227) as a passive investor in exercising power in the presidency (and this would appear to be borne out by the Tower Commission Report on the Iran-Contra affair), nonetheless undertook a grueling campaign for the office, that required enormous personal and political effort.[16]

The very great degree of effort necessary to obtain powerful political positions almost guarantees that persons of small or more evenly balanced levels of ambition will not make the attempt. There is nothing necessarily sinister about presidential candidates or leaders satisfying their needs for accomplishment and recognition through their political activities. The problem emerges when a leader's ambition is, to a substantial degree, a compensation for poor self-development, so that policy accomplishments are secondary to the main object of success, which is to make up for the leader's psychological deficits.

Judgments regarding the appropriateness of politically motivating drives such as ambition must also be viewed against the background of the requirements for obtaining and keeping positions in contemporary politics. Ambition is only one of the traits affected by the nature of the contemporary political process, which acts as both an impetus and a barrier for certain kinds of persons in the recruitment process. Another personal psychological trait, made relevant by the increasing importance of television and the decline of more conventional sources of information about candidates, is the capacity to skillfully portray oneself in a way that is congruent with public moods and concerns. The capacity to project reassurance, competence, or whatever else is called for is clearly an important component of leadership in large industrialized societies, but it raises delicate issues of integrity, authenticity, and, not incidentally, informed consent and accountability.

One implication of these considerations is that the analysis of psychological suitability for political roles cannot focus solely on individual characteristics, as important as these are. Rather, consideration must also be given to the ways in which citizen needs and expectations shape the recruitment, selection, and evaluation process.

Are High-Level Political Leaders "Normal"?

Before concerning ourselves with the implications of high-level leaders becoming impaired before or after obtaining office, we must address a prior set of questions. The percentage of any population that aspires to high political office is, statistically, exceedingly small. The percentage of those who aspire to such offices *and* obtain them is smaller still. Success in reaching the upper echelons of political power requires extraordinary levels of energy, commitment, and skill. Those who succeed are, by definition, not ordinary people in any statistical understanding of the term. However, if they are not "normal," the question arises of whether it is possible to evaluate them by ordinary standards and, even if it should be possible, whether it would be appropriate.

If high-level political leaders are characterized by much higher levels of energy, commitment, and skill than the average person has, is it not appropriate to expect behavior that would for others in different circumstances be considered questionable or dysfunctional? Are not the very high levels of ambition, commitment, and skill that get persons into positions of leadership likely to result in eccentricities and abnormalities? In short, do such leaders gain office and perform well *in spite of* or *because of* their larger-than-ordinary-life characteristics?

We can actually distinguish five specific versions of these arguments. For some, a degree of psychological impairment in high office is simply a fact of life (Torre 1968; Kantor and Herron 1968). Hutschnecker (1974, 45) notes that "if we rule out the neurotic leader, we would rule out every man." The reason is simple. Decades of psychoanalytically framed analyses have suggested that, to some degree, unconscious conflict results from the vicissitudes of developmental experience. Moreover, Lasswell (1930, 27) and others have reminded us that the line between mental health and illness is a gradient, not an abyss. However, this raises a difficulty. As Gaylin asks in his discussion of "what's normal" (1973, 56), "Very well, then, if everyone is a little sick . . . should we worry about the potential impact of mental illness on a man in authority?"

Others see this issue somewhat differently. For them, the ubiquity of psychological conflicts and other impairments is not a fact of emotional life but perhaps is politically desirable. A group of psychiatrists studying the problem of "the VIP with psychiatric impairment" (GAP 1973, 19) has even suggested that "a degree of aberrant behavior in the leader may be helpful." The psychiatrist Fieve notes that "anyone who has the drive and stamina to survive in American politics has to be a little manic" (1975, 136) and that, in the future, "people with moodswings may even be sought after for positions of leadership" (1975, 144).

A third view of this issue sees psychological impairments as necessary correlates to the characteristics that brought the leader into power in the first place. To quote the late Kurt Lewin, "The same heat which melts the butter, fries the egg." If we want leaders who are big enough to fulfill the enormous responsibilities we place on them, we must be prepared to understand and tolerate their dysfunctions and excesses.

Gaylin (1973, 57) notes, "The ambition for office is often combined with the same grandiosity, competitiveness, and narcissism that is characteristic of the paranoid personality." According to Fieve (1975, 138–39),

The problem can be stated simply. Many people in high office have a tendency towards moodswings, since their manic energy has helped get them there in the first place. Once they are in office their emotional make up and mood often shift cyclically. At some point, although not necessarily so, their judgment may become impaired, and in times of extreme depression and extreme mania the distortions in judgment may be severe. . . . For a person in a position of power, particularly political power, this can be dangerous . . . his relative freedom to do what he wants, coupled with his extraordinary power to enforce his will, *make hypomania in high office a potentially dangerous situation, as well as an asset.* (Emphasis mine)

A fourth view is that positions of high power potentiality tend to attract unusual and, in some cases, psychologically deviant individuals. Gilbert's (1950) study of Nazi elites suggests that psychopathological attributes may be highly correlated with upward political mobility in regimes that make use of such persons for purposes of social control. Tucker (1965) has suggested that totalitarian systems, especially those that can be characterized as "fighting organizations," tend to recruit persons with psychopathological tendencies into their leadership ranks. And two recent psychological examinations of Saddam Hussein (Post [1991] has argued the existence of what he terms *malignant narcissism,* and Renshon [1993b] has examined the trait of ruthlessness) suggest that these attributes have been instrumental in that leader's gaining and maintaining of power.

Finally, there is the view that what might otherwise be considered deficiencies are not only the unavoidable by-products of other, more desirable traits but the necessary (though insufficient) basis of the leader's "greatness" or capacity for it. Erikson, whose writings in the field of psychohistory are usually considered a model of probity and balance, makes this point explicitly. He writes, "In recorded history, some such leaders are recorded as 'great'; they, it seems, are able, out of the deepest personal conflicts, to derive the energy which meets their period's specific needfulness for a resynthesis of the world image" (1980, 167). In other words, one element that makes a political leader great is not the absence of deep psychological conflicts but their very existence. Greatness comes when the leader is able to harness and direct those conflicts in ways that resonate in relation to felt but unmet needs of the time. Martin Luther is clearly an example of this kind of relationship, in Erikson's view. Luther's personal identity crisis overlapped with and gave voice to a wider religious malaise.

These questions cannot be settled in an a priori way. Only detailed case studies will reveal whether leaders perform well because of their excesses and dysfunctions or in spite of them. Still, several observations can be made about these different views.

The first argument jumps from the position that some degree of functional impairment is universal to the conclusion that there are no relevant or discernible differences. In this view, the fact that everyone has some unconscious conflicts (or other difficulties) leads to a position of accepting any manifestation of such dysfunctions. Yet, clearly, there are some difficulties that are more tolerable than others when considering suitability for political roles like the presidency. For example, a strict superego (conscience) is the result of internalized unrealistic or harsh standards of conduct for oneself or others. It is certainly an example of a psychological difficulty. However, we might well prefer a president with a strict superego to one who is too lenient or, worse yet, who can justify any means to accomplish his purposes.

The second and third views argue that what might in other circum-stances be considered psychologically suspect may, in politics, be either desirable or at least unavoidable. This argument makes some sense. Cer-tainly, to take ambition as an example, it is unlikely that in the last two decades one would strive for, much less obtain, the highest reaches of political power without substantial ambition. But the question is not whether substantial levels of ambition are necessary to achieve the presi-dency or another high political office and thus are "desirable." Nor is the question whether ambition is connected with other useful traits, such as the desire to accomplish purposes. For both questions we might put forward a qualified yes. The question is whether strong ambition (for example) must *of necessity* be linked with the kinds of behavior that are likely to be damaging to that person and his performance. Put another way, the ques-tion is whether all ambitious persons are the same.

Lasswell (1930; 1948) thought not. He distinguished two general types of political leaders, "political man" and "democratic characters." The former, Lasswell wrote, was motivated toward the pursuit of power to overcome low estimates of the self. The latter was also motivated by seeking power, but power was one of several values.

Lasswell's formulation suggests that power seeking in and of itself is not enough for us to make a judgment. Politics is an arena of power, and those who aren't motivated to getting and using it will ordinarily gravitate toward some other line of work. Moreover, if they do wind up in politics and in high office, they are unlikely to behave in a way that concerns us due to their excesses but rather due to their disinclination to make good use of the power available to them for legitimate and important public purposes.

The question that arises from these two points of view, therefore, is not whether some substantial level of ambition for political power is likely. It is. Nor is the question whether substantial levels of ambition can be associated with personal and political excess. They can. Rather, we need to frame the question in a more empirical, contingent way. Can we distin-guish those other psychological elements in a person's character and per-sonality structure that make strong ambition dangerous, as well as those that moderate it?

The fourth point of view suggests that in certain kinds of political systems, pathological personality traits or organizations may be necessary in order to obtain and survive in power. Most of the studies of this set of circumstances that have been done concentrate on systems with underde-veloped institutional mechanisms of limiting executive power (e.g., Nazi

Germany, the former Soviet Union, Iraq). It is tempting, therefore, to believe that "it can't happen here." Yet if my argument about ambition being a "culturally patterned defect" is accurate, it is possible that even stable democratic systems may have recruitment patterns into high office that are in need of monitoring.

Lastly, let us examine the view that deep and pervasive psychological conflicts are a necessary component of "great" political leaders. If Erikson is correct, then greatness is in part a function of the leader's capacity to give voice to and help resolve great unanswered public questions. These circumstances seem historically to be relatively rare. They come at time when the major social, religious, or political paradigms have lost power and legitimacy. Most leaders, including presidents, are, after all, not seen as "great men," nor do they have to be. Circumstances in this country, at least, are such that truly societywide crises are not an ordinary state of affairs. Yet to meet crises, presidents may indeed stretch the bounds of the permissible. Abraham Lincoln did in dealing with the Civil War, and so did Franklin Roosevelt in dealing with the country's economic collapse. Their capacity and willingness to do so, which might, under ordinary circumstances, be seen as destructive, came to be seen in the circumstances that they faced as necessary and even desirable. However, a focus on such relatively rare situations stands in danger of confusing the most extraordinary circumstances with the most typical.

There is one last sense in which deep conflict and emotional distress may play a facilitating role for leaders, not only in times of great national crisis but in more ordinary times. It is sometimes the case that a leader who has experienced great conflict, suffered great loss, or survived other difficult times may be better able to empathize with those who have similarly suffered. In such circumstances, the leader may find that his quest for political purpose may be modified somewhat by his appreciation of the emotional consequences of his plans for others.

Levitt and Rubenstein argue (1970, 183), "If normality is a quality that cannot be clearly defined by behavioral scientists, it may have limited utility in assessing a man's suitability for political office." I agree. As the above analysis suggests, raising the question of normality in connection with attempts to assess psychological suitability is likely to be somewhat misleading and perhaps beside the point. Normality, however, in the generally understood statistical and theoretical senses of the term, is not really the issue. Even if it turns out to be the case empirically that presidential candidates differ from ordinary citizens with regard to such characteristics as ambition and commitment, we have gained little in "proving" that they are different, and thus not normal in the statistical or normative sense of the word. The real issue is whether a candidate's psychological functioning is incompatible with or likely to compromise his performance of presidential responsibilities.

Yet, given that the concept of normality is not likely to prove helpful in assessing candidates' psychological suitability, is there still cause to be concerned about these issues? Gaylin (1973, 56) asks,

If everyone is a little sick, if nobody is really sick, if no one knows what mental illness is anyhow, and if popular judgments tend to be based on unfounded assumptions . . . should we worry about the potential impact of mental illness on a man in authority? *I believe, in spite of all the ambiguities and confusions, that we certainly should.* (Emphasis mine)

In the next chapter, I try to explain why.

F O U R

Is the Psychological Impairment of Presidents Still a Relevant Concern?

How much concern should we have regarding psychological impairment of our political leaders? Kearns (1976, 317–18) has argued that

> no matter how well a polity's institutions are designed, its leaders are subject to lapses from rational functional behavior. Every society learns to live with a certain amount of irrational behavior at the top, but lest the irrationality feed upon itself and lead to general decay, the polity must have the capacity to marshal forces that influence or compel the faltering actors to revert to the behavior that is required if the polity is to function properly.

A study group of psychiatrists, convened by the American Psychiatric Association, who examined the problem noted that "examples of VIPs who have remained or have been retained in office despite gross impairment can be drawn from government, the military, the judiciary, industry, the church—in fact from every area of public life" (GAP 1973, 33). Moreover, they note, "History is replete with examples of mentally impaired VIPs" (GAP 1973, 22). The Group for the Advancement of Psychiatry (GAP) study mentions and presents brief case summaries of VIPs who have experienced substantial psychological impairment at some point in their public lives because of physical factors, emotional factors, or some combination of the two. Included in their list are King George III of England, Ludwig II of Bavaria, Paul von Hindenburg, Woodrow Wilson, Franklin D. Roosevelt, Benito Mussolini, Earl K. Long, and James Forrestal.

Other psychiatrists who have examined this problem have mentioned the names of Adolf Hitler, Joseph Stalin, and Abraham Lincoln (Gaylin 1973, 54). Fieve (1975), a psychiatrist who pioneered the use of lithium to treat mood disorders, has argued that Abraham Lincoln, Theodore Roosevelt, Winston Churchill, and Thomas Eagleton all suffered from substantial bipolar disorders in which periods of heightened levels of activity alternated with periods of depression.

These examples, case vignettes, and the more detailed case studies of these individuals that can be found elsewhere (e.g., Henry 1970) establish only that leaders with substantial levels of psychological impairment have been in positions of political power. However, these materials don't tell us how frequently severe impairment in political positions occurs. An argument might be made, therefore, that while it can happen, we are still uncertain as to how much we should worry about the issue.

One approach to this issue is to examine the kinds of disturbances that are most worrisome and then analyze the extent to which such elements are either compatible or incompatible with the skills required to gain and keep political power. This is the approach that I have adapted for the most part in this and the succeeding chapters in Part 2. There is, however, another approach by which we might throw some light on this problem, that is, to ask how frequently impairment in high office has occurred. After all, it might be argued that something which has rarely happened hardly merits our concern, much less our attention.

In typical epidemiological studies, a syndrome is broken down into constituent psychological or behavioral parts, empirical indicators of these manifestations suitable for this kind of format are designed, and a random sample is selected and questioned regarding the problem at hand. Leaving aside the formidable problems of specifying syndromes and generating valid indicators, we simply do not have this kind of comprehensive data available regarding impairment in leaders, nor are we ever likely to obtain it. There is, however, another approach. One could survey historical records to see to what extent severe impairment among political leaders has been a problem. The eccentricities and excesses of political leaders have always been fertile ground for the merely curious as well as for the concerned, and there are several works that survey the politically influential from this perspective.

There are some cautions to be noted in connection with this approach, some of which may be suggested by the titles of some inquiries. For example, T. F. Thiselton's *Royalty in All Ages: The Amusements, Eccentrici-*

ties, Accomplishments, Superstitions and Frolics of Kings and Queens of Europe (1903) and Angelo S. Rappoport's *Mad Majesties: or Raving Rulers and Submissive Subjects* (1910) both suggest the reader approach the sources with some caution. While works such as these contain potentially useful information, they suffer from a preoccupation with the bizarre and sensational, a drawback suggested by their titles and by those of other books written by these authors.[1] Ultimately, however, the most fatal flaw of these books is the lack of theory.

A partial resolution to this problem was offered by psychoanalytic theory. A number of more sophisticated investigations of historical incidents of severe impairment in leaders were undertaken. One result of these efforts is that we now have available several detailed case studies of such events.[2] While such studies are an invaluable addition to our understanding of this area, they still do not provide the perspective of, or constitute by themselves, a comprehensive epidemiological survey undertaken by researchers versed in both psychological and political theory.

In the early 1960s, however, just such a survey was attempted by the late Robert L. Noland, a professor of psychology at the University of Dayton. Using a wide variety of primary and secondary sources, covering non-Western as well as Western nations, and going back at least four centuries (Noland 1966, 232), he found that "at least seventy-five chiefs of state have led their countries, actually or symbolically, for a total of several centuries, while suffering from severe mental disturbances." Noland (1966, 232–33) concludes, "There is little reason to assume that we could never be faced with a similar problem in the United States."

This conclusion and the data that give rise to it[3] suggest several points that require mention. The "severe mental disturbances" that Noland records from his historical sources consist of several kinds of maladies. Grouped together are rulers who were congenital imbeciles or feeble-minded, and those judged mentally unstable or "insane." The latter is by far the most frequent category but still leaves unanswered exactly what is meant by the term *insane*. Many historical accounts are clearer in their characterizations than in their descriptions of the behavior that gave rise to them.

Even considering these cautions, however, there are several reasons to believe that Noland's data underreport the problem. First, and perhaps most important, these data were collected only for chiefs of state, not for the wide range of other public officials who form part of the potential sampling of the universe of political leadership. Second, major contemporary clinical entities such as severe character disorders, narcissistic or borderline character structures, and manic-depressive psychoses are little in evidence in the available historical records, although certainly present (if not prevalent) today. It is possible, of course, that such entities did not exist prior to their "discovery," but not very plausible.[4] Finally, Noland's published data were preliminary, and in going over his notes and references for the basic data, I found instances of rulers characterized by their contemporaries as severely impaired that were not included in his published account. On all of these grounds, and given the cloak of secrecy surrounding such issues, it is very plausible that these data underreport the incidence of the problem. The question remains, however, just what implications, if any, we may draw from such a study for the problem raised at the beginning of this chapter.

Do these limited data prove that severe impairment is a substantial historical problem and therefore of direct and immediate importance to us now? Of course not.[5] However, they do suggest points worth considering.

First, on their face, such data suggest that historically, by any reasonable measure, the severe impairment problem is not a unique event or a historical curiosity. It is certainly true that the strengthening of institutional structures, at least in democracies, has mitigated the problems brought about by reliance on heredity or divine right, but not all of Noland's sample fit those categories. Second, the length of time such rulers were in power and the number of people over whom they ruled are not inconsequential from the standpoint of beginning to gauge the social and political impact of such experiences.

It could be reasonably argued that concern with *incidence* of severe impairment in leaders is really beside the point, since such an approach equates importance with frequency. This is clearly a dubious assumption in cases where even one occurrence is cause for alarm. Cataclysmic events such as nuclear wars, holocausts, and reigns of terror may be historically infrequent, but are no less important or transformational for their infrequency.

The issue of importance, defined apart from frequency, goes beyond the possibility of nuclear annihilation, although this is undoubtedly its single most important illustrative event. Leaving aside nuclear weaponry, modern technology and social complexity have transformed the power of political leaders. As I argued in chapter 1, instantaneous communication, access to and control of vast human and material resources, and the interdependency (and thus vulnerability) of contemporary social structures have amplified the already formidable institutionally based power of those who determine and carry out public policy.

Moreover, as the arenas covered by political decisions have expanded, the number of people who are affected by such decisions has increased. It follows that arguments in favor of examining the psychological functioning of political leaders and the quality of the decisions they make need not rest solely on either incidence or the possibility for catastrophe, as important as we may agree these are. Rather, a more general approach begins with the "potential for effect" inherent in the exercise of policymaking in contemporary societies and draws its formulations of importance in part from these calculations.

The Mental Health of Presidents

Historical surveys of impaired VIPs give us some sense of the frequency of the problem worldwide. However, in this analysis we focus on presidents and presidential candidates in the United States. Therefore, the question naturally arises of whether there is any evidence closer to home that these issues should concern us.

Arthur Schlesinger, Jr. (1974), a critic of psychiatric solutions to the problem, argues that we should be concerned with impairment among our own leaders. Writing after the flawed presidencies of Lyndon Johnson and Richard Nixon, he notes:

We are all disconcerted, to put it mildly, by the awareness of the acute vulnerability of our civilization to the unconscious wishes, drives, and obsessions of a few persons possessing vast power. Nor can we any longer comfortably regard this vulnerability as a problem peculiar to dictatorships across the seas. As our own political order has increasingly concentrated power in the presidency, and as Presidents have begun to break out of the constitutional system of accountability, in recent years we Americans have lived more than ever before at the mercy of presidential caprice and compulsion. . . . We have . . . in quick succession elected the two most capricious and compulsive Presidents we have ever had. (1974, 10–11)

The problem may be, as George Reedy (a former White House aide) noted some time ago (1970, 168), that "a highly irrational personality, who might be medically certifiable for treatment, could take over the White House and the event never be known with any degree of assurance." How realistic is Reedy's concern?

Consider that in 1972 the Democratic Party selected as its vice presidential candidate a person who had been hospitalized several times for severe depressive episodes. Many commentators at the time argued that Senator Thomas Eagleton was a victim whose only difficulty was having sought treatment for a common psychological occurrence, depression. I argue that the available data suggest that concerns were justifiable.

The Eagleton episode casts doubt on the belief that substantial psychological impairments always result in behavior that is observably bizarre. This is a basic assumption of the "structural barrier" argument, that is, that impairments will be obvious over time and that persons thus affected will be screened out of political contention. Often, as we will see with the case study of Thomas Eagleton in chapter 6, they are not. Even close associates of a political leader may suspect but not really fully appreciate the degree of impairment that may be present.

In late 1973, as Richard Nixon's presidency began to unravel, there was concern among some presidential advisers that they were managing an "unstable personality" (White 1975, 13), whose behavior toward the end of his presidency was "increasingly erratic" (White 1975, 9). White further reports (1975, 22–23) that, during this period, Secretary of Defense James Schlesinger directed all military commands not to accept any orders from the White House without his personal countersignature. At one point, during a press conference, a reporter asked President Nixon how he was holding up, which appeared to be a not-too-thinly veiled reference to his emotional state. In addition, John Herbers (1973, A36) reported, "Some members of Congress have been consulting medical authorities on their opinions as to Mr. Nixon's health and the possibility that the President's decisionmaking ability might be impaired in the months ahead."

In 1988, two reporters (Mayer and McManus 1988) published a book that raised the issue of President Reagan's psychological competence. They reported that many White House staff members were alarmed by what they saw as Ronald Reagan's detachment from the responsibilities of office. Among their concerns was the practice of having the president's signature signed by aides. James M. Cannon, who served in the White House as an adviser to Chief of Staff Howard H. Baker, Jr., and prepared for Baker a report on White House operations, confirmed to reporters (Roberts 1988b; see also Roberts 1988a) that he had seen a "serious document" on which President Reagan's initials had been signed by someone else. He also confirmed that he drafted a memorandum for Baker suggesting that they consider invoking the Twenty-fifth Amendment to the Constitution transferring power to the vice president. According to this account, the suggestion was dropped when he and Baker visited with the president and found him "the same guy he had always been."

In that same year, direct allegations concerning Lyndon Johnson's psychological stability were made by a former close aide in a book. The aide, Richard N. Goodwin (1988a; see also 1988b, 35), reached the conclusion that Johnson experienced "certain episodes of . . . paranoid behavior" as he struggled with public and internal dissent to his Vietnam policies. Goodwin argued that by 1965, Johnson had "taken a huge leap into unreason . . . almost frighteningly different from anything I had observed before" (1988b, 35).

The descriptions of Johnson's behavior reported by Goodwin were in accord with clinical descriptions of that behavior. The same behavior had also been publicly reported (see Kearns 1976). Goodwin reports that he and then–presidential staff member Bill Moyers were so alarmed by Johnson's behavior that they both independently consulted psychiatrists.

Other Johnson aides have disputed this contention (Weaver 1988). One basis of their disclaimers has been that Johnson's views toward his critics were well known and a natural result of intense political differences. Essentially, they accept the description of Johnson's behavior but dispute its meaning.

The Severely Impaired Leader: Changing Understandings

As noted, the most persistent formulation raised by persons concerned with psychological suitability for public office is the problem of a psychotic leader. In informal discussions it takes the form of worrying about leaders who must be chased around with nets or who might experience "mental breakdowns." In professional discourse, it entails a concern with various forms of psychotic impairment.[6] On the face of things, such concerns seem rather straightforward and their implications even more so.

Two primary indicators of psychotic-level impairment are a substantial break with reality and the presence of substantially disorganized behaviors. In many (but not all) cases, the former consists of delusions, hallucinations, and substantial loosening of associations, coupled with (logical) incoherence (APA [1980] 1994). These represent impairments of perception, experience, and thought. It is this set of symptoms that many persons have in mind when they express concern about the "mental health" of political leaders, and it is not difficult to see why. A person severely impaired in any one of these three basic areas of psychological functioning would be unable to perform the basic tasks of executive political leadership adequately.

Three assumptions are often made about the behaviors that constitute psychotic-level impairment. First, it is assumed that these behaviors are very dramatic and therefore are easily recognizable for what they are. The deranged person talking to himself, often with a wild look in his eye, is probably the general lay conception (not altogether in error) of such disturbances. Second, it is assumed that psychotic behavior is a condition marked by pervasive functional deterioration. A person with psychotic-level impairments will be unable to function in a variety of normal or even elementary situations. A corollary of this assumption is that there is often some degree of accumulated deficit associated with such levels of impairment; it is not only that psychotic-level impairment leads to wide areas of functional inability in the present but that such a person does not develop his skills, capacity to understand, or ability to navigate the complex psychological and social currents of modern societies over time. Third, it is assumed that psychosis, as described, in terms of substantial reality breaks and disorganized behavior, exhausts the conceptual limits of the term *severe impairment*.

To some degree, these factors are interrelated. The newer understandings of character and personality organization that we discuss as the third of these factors clearly have implications for the first question we address (that is, whether severe impairment is always recognizable as such). However, for purposes of analysis, we will examine each in turn.

It must be noted that the accuracy of each of these assumptions has enormously important implications for evaluating the efficacy of the Twenty-fifth Amendment, especially Section 4, which deals with the involuntary removal of a sitting president on grounds of impairment.[7] If severe psychological impairment does not necessarily result in dramatic, easily observed and understood behavior; if it is not a condition necessarily characterized by pervasive functional deterioration; and if it can sometimes be accompanied by behavior that is not only considered normal but highly adequate, then the basis for any confidence in that part of the amendment to work rests on thin ice indeed. And that is precisely what my analysis suggests.

Is Severe Impairment Always Recognizable for What It Is?

Let us first turn to what is perhaps the most basic assumption—that psychotic symptoms of the kind already noted can be easily recognized for what they are. In many cases it is probable that they can be. Even untrained laypersons can recognize dramatic, bizarre symptoms such as hallucinations or broken logic. The problem, unfortunately, goes beyond these.

Psychosis is a process, and in many cases the early symptoms are not seen for what they are. Arnold Rogow's (1963) carefully documented political biography of former secretary of defense James Forrestal makes this point very clearly. Forrestal, within a short time of his retirement from public office, became extremely depressed, suffered from auditory hallucinations and delusion, and subsequently committed suicide while under psychiatric care at Bethesda Naval Hospital (Rogow 1963, chap. 1).

The very first reactions to the onset of Forrestal's symptoms were mistaken. Rogow writes (1963, 342):

Most of those among his friends and associates who were aware that Forrestal was suffering from extreme physical and nervous exhaustion, that he had lost a good deal of weight during the preceding months, and that he more and more frequently was experiencing moods of deep depression, were convinced that he required nothing more than a extensive period of rest and relaxation.

The more manifest symptoms that something was wrong did not appear until well after the onset of the disorder.

Rogow relates (1963, 4) that when aides entered Forrestal's room after his last afternoon of farewell speeches on March 19, he was seated at his desk, hat on, staring at a blank wall, and was unable to respond appropriately to expressions of concern. After that, dramatic symptoms came on more rapidly. These included a suicide attempt and a belief that metal sockets used to hold beach umbrellas had been wired to transmit sound and that his conversations on the beach were being recorded (Rogow 1963, 6).

Well before these dramatic events, there had been more subtle signs. Rogow notes (1963, 342), "Although some friends and associates suspected he was ill late in 1948, it does not appear that they urged him to consult a psychiatrist, much less enter a rest home or private sanitarium." There are several reasons that can account for the failure to appreciate the real significance of what they saw, reasons as relevant today as they were then.

First, the persons involved had neither professional knowledge nor training. Second, they had very plausible alternative explanations, in this case, overwork and fatigue. Third, they were operating in the context of what Rogow has termed the "mental health mythology of official Washington" (1963, 344). This mythology reflects the assumption that while ordinary persons become ill, VIPs do not—in short, that "it can't happen here." Given this belief, one would hardly notice what one assumes does not occur.

In cases of both psychological and physical impairment in high-level political leaders, a further complication often develops: that is, the persons with the most direct access to the leader are those with the most emotional and political investment in continuing his leadership role. There is nothing necessarily sinister implied by this, only that individual loyalty, a lengthy or intense period of association, and enjoyment of one's position may lead those in a position to know about symptoms of impairment to underplay or otherwise misperceive such information.

Constraints in the political system operate against the identification and acknowledgment of such problems. One result is that when an incidence of mental impairment occurs, it is handled with extreme caution by those who might experience or observe the behaviors. The Forrestal case provides some evidence of the personal and political factors that surround the knowledge of such incidents.

For example, the decision to admit Forrestal to Bethesda Naval Hospital rather than to the Menninger Foundation in Topeka, Kansas, was based in part on the desire to keep the nature of Forrestal's condition secret from the general public (Rogow 1963, 8). It was felt that since Bethesda was a general hospital, secrecy would be easier to accomplish than were he in the Menninger Foundation, which was solely concerned with "mental illness." While there were other, persuasive reasons for treating Forrestal at Bethesda, it is clear from this and other cases that concern over public reaction plays an important role in consideration of what should be done, as well as of what is disclosed.

For sitting officials, the reason for such concern seems obvious. Questions of psychological functioning are bound to raise public anxiety about the direction and management of public affairs. Even, as in the case of Forrestal, when the impairment becomes obvious after the official has left office, its existence still raises questions about the conduct of affairs while the person had responsibility. Rogow writes (1963, 345) that official Washington was very sensitive to the implications of Forrestal's illness, fearing that the Russians would use it for propaganda purposes — which they did.

There are also important considerations of individual and family privacy in cases involving psychological impairment. Especially in cases of severe impairment, there is an understandable reluctance on the part of family members and friends to elaborate details of what is surely a painful and disruptive experience for all involved. Although there are legitimate questions regarding the weight that should be accorded such considerations in the case of public officials, the wish to deal with such difficulties privately, without the increased tension brought about by public scrutiny, is understandable. But the net result is that such incidents are shrouded in secrecy.

Even when associates suspect there is something wrong with a public official, factors can operate to delay or inhibit their assessments. Chief among such is the issue of "alternative explanations," already mentioned briefly. Consider the issue of Ronald Reagan's detachment from the responsibilities of his office, which set into motion the events described in the first section of this chapter. What is one to make of this "management style"? Is a detached management style a serious psychological suitability issue, or is it primarily a political suitability issue? Clearly, such a style reflects a degree of psychological detachment, and this can certainly lead to political difficulties. Recall that the Tower Commission Report investigating White House operations after the Iran-Contra scandal concluded that Reagan's lax management style had been a facilitating factor in the affair. However, to make a serious judgment about this issue, one would need to know the individual's previous level of detachment (baseline data) and how it manifests itself (whether it reflects some limited or more substantial psychological disengagement).

When Reagan's newly appointed chief of staff Howard Baker reported that he found the president "exactly the same guy he had always been," Baker did not fully settle the question of whether the degree of Reagan's detachment should have been a matter of serious concern. The chief of staff's evaluation merely alerts us to the fact that expectations can play a crucial role in making such lay assessments.

This issue also arises in the concerns Goodwin raised about Lyndon Johnson's "paranoia." Johnson's preoccupation with enemies during the Vietnam War is well known and documented. Kearns, Johnson's biographer, notes that at the time the president's Vietnam policies had begun to unravel and that "suspicion of motive became his chief instrument in discrediting critics" (1976, 313).

Finally in this connection, consider the concerns raised about Richard Nixon's mental health as the Watergate affair began to unravel his presidency. What follows (see Herbers 1973) is a list of behaviors that were noted by observers and were part of discussions of Nixon's emotional state. I divide the list into two parts, the first having to do with policy and political issues, the second dealing with the president's personal behavior.

In the first area the list includes Nixon's public dismissal of special

Watergate prosecutor Archibald Cox, an alert of American nuclear forces during a Middle East crisis (which some thought an overreaction), confusion in the administration's view of that summer's energy shortage, and the disclosure of conversations missing from the Watergate tapes. On the second, more personal behavioral level, the list includes alternating bursts of secluded brooding and public appearances; a puffy face; occasional stumbling over words; gestures that seemed to be animated and jerky; a tendency to ramble; good humor and high spirits that seemed, given the circumstances, like artificial gaiety; and, at times, undue irritation and fatigue.

To add to the difficulties, Herbers notes:

Signs of his actions are cited *both as signs of deterioration and normality, depending on the point of view being argued*—his private bursts of anger at his critics; his shoving of Mr. Ziegler [a close aide] in public in New Orleans last summer; his distrust of the special prosecutor's office; his restlessness that has kept him constantly moving to his Camp David retreat in Maryland or his Florida and California homes; his difficulties in getting out of bed some mornings and his playing the piano alone late at night, habits that Julie Eisenhower recently attributed to her father, in the course of defending him. (1973, A36; emphasis mine)

It seems clear from the examples of presidents Reagan, Johnson, and Nixon that there is no shortage of behavioral data. The two major problems involve the meaning of the behavior and what one wishes or thinks appropriate to do about it. Neither question is easily resolved. One might prefer a more hands-on management style, for example, but the difference between a detached management style and an abdication of responsibilities, except in extreme cases of withdrawal, is largely a matter of degree, interpretation, and expectations. One might argue that a more involved management style is preferable on empirical grounds, that it provides firmer guidance and stability in matters of governance. But is this a matter to be raised *after* a president assumes office?

Or consider the concerns that Johnson, and for that matter, Nixon, were suspicious about their respective opponents to the point of clinical paranoia. How much of some behavior can be attributed to normal, and perhaps understandable, reactions to intense criticism? How much suspicion of critics—that they overstate their case, that they have a particular agenda they want to forward, or that they don't like the president or his politics—is justified? Perhaps many or all of these considerations frame the critics' views. Should a president be considered paranoid because he believes what might to some degree be true—that his implacable critics would like to do away with his policies, as well as him (if not now, then in the next election)?

Severe Psychological Impairment: Episodic or Continuous?

A second assumption regarding psychotic behavior is that psychosis affects all sectors of the personality. Accordingly, in this formulation, psychosis (as an extreme impairment) in a political leader would be easily recognizable because of its debilitating effect, which would be manifest in all aspects of behavior. It is this point that stands behind the importance of "grossly disorganized behavior" as a behavioral criterion for the diagnostic category of psychosis.

Like the first assumption, this one has elements of accuracy. Many psychotic syndromes are characterized by pervasive disorganization of the personality structure, and their impact on numerous areas of functioning is obvious. It is this feature that has led some political psychologists to propose the "structural barriers argument" (examined at some length in chapter 6), which argues that institutions serve as effective guards against such people reaching high office. However, there are also a number of psychotic disorders that do not manifest themselves in such debilitation in the whole structure. Impairments, although severe, may be seen in these cases only in certain, limited sectors of performance.

Freud's (1911) analysis of Schreber makes this point very clearly. Schreber was a German public official (judge of the lower court) who published an autobiographical account of his illness (which included a fully obvious delusional system that Freud then analyzed). Schreber himself petitioned the court for a return of his civil liberties, arguing that although he admittedly had delusional beliefs, they were circumscribed and did not affect his behavior in any aspect of civilized behavior. He produced extensive evidence to that point and was successful in his petition. In this case, a circumscribed but severely disturbed aspect of the thought process and the intrapsychic structures that support it coexisted with more developed aspects of internal structure and behavior. Somewhat paradoxically, therefore, it would have been quite possible at points to have had a completely "normal" conversation with Schreber, as long as one avoided the area of the delusional system.

A similar "limited psychotic" condition can be seen in the case of severe paranoid personalities. Clinically, such individuals have many of their basic thought processes intact. They can perceive, albeit in a slanted way. They can process information, project and consider possible futures, and make intelligent plans to deal with them. The problem is that their paranoid ideational structure frames their characterological psychology.

To the outside world, such persons may just appear highly suspicious, and they may even learn to cover the depth of their certainty with a socially acceptable facade of just being careful. It is also possible that they would find additional cover in professions where suspicion is either well grounded or expected. Recall that those who rejected Goodwin's view of Johnson's behavior as paranoid, did so in part because they considered the president's behavior to be a normal, expectable outcome of strong policy disagreements.

The point here is that even though psychosis can present itself in the form of severely disturbed functioning, parts of the personality structure can remain intact. Thus, it does not follow that because persons are disturbed they are totally unable to function. Recall also that the behavior Goodwin described as consistent with what he (and the psychiatrist he consulted) understood to be paranoid was not evident in every circumstance and issue. Goodwin (1988b, 42) notes Johnson's leap into unreason but also cautions that it did not occur "on every subject, and certainly not all the time; it was during this same period that Johnson was skillfully crafting some of the greatest triumphs of his Great Society." Critics of Goodwin's view include Jack Valenti, who worked as Johnson's speechwriter and later noted (1988, 8) that Goodwin failed

to square his later version of a President gone berserk in the Spring and Summer of 1965 with the exhibition at the *very same time* of disciplined, thoughtful, persistent, intellectual, irresistible Presidential powers of persuasion that convinced a sometimes-reluctant Congress to pass the Voting Rights Act of 1965, The Elementary and Secondary Education Act, Medicare and an avalanche of legislative triumphs.

This bifurcation of capacity would not seem extraordinary to a clinician. Many of the major psychiatric impairments are now understood to have episodic as well as chronic aspects. Persons may have episodes or periods of impairment but otherwise function adequately, if not well. Moreover, Johnson's vulnerabilities, like his successes, may well have been contextually specific. In areas in which he usually did well, he continued to function well. In areas where he ran into setbacks and frustrations, in which he was unable to succeed using his traditional methods, his emotional vulnerabilities increased.

Continuity of disturbed behavior, therefore, is not the only solid indicator of severity, nor can it be viewed as an invariant guide. These points suggest that even the symptoms of severe impairment do not manifest themselves uniformly. Given this variability of the clinical picture, even for severely disturbed behavior it is not implausible that some kinds of impairments may very well not be screened out of the political system by the present, informal methods.

Is the Traditional Concern with Psychosis the Only Relevant Concern?

Finally, I want to examine the third assumption that is frequently made in discussions of psychiatric impairment among political leaders, namely, that classical psychotic conditions exhaust the conceptual domain of what we should be worried about. The early psychoanalytic formulations of character and psychological functioning were derived from Freud's structural theory. According to that view, character was the result of the inevitable conflict among wishes, reality, and conscience. However, for the most part, the character structures that Freud, O. Fenichel, and others described were of the type that functioned relatively well. Being obsessive-compulsive, for example, may circumscribe a person's availability for experience or limit the range of personal expression or creativity, but it doesn't ordinarily incapacitate people. So, too, those "racked by success" may have diminished ambitions and accomplishments, but they are able to function adequately within their roles and relationships.

These individuals began to stand in stark contrast to another series of character types that was first noticed by a few analysts in the 1940s (e.g., Cleckley [1941] 1976; Deutsch 1942). These analysts reported treating persons who appeared on casual inspection as successful members of the community, as able lawyers, executives, and physicians, but did not succeed in the sense of finding satisfaction or fulfillment in their accomplishments. Cleckely, among the first to notice this group, titled his study *The Mask of Sanity,* reflecting the then-anomalous finding that there were persons who appeared to be functioning well, even very well on a surface, conventional level, but who on closer clinical observation were seen to have areas of deep psychological disturbance, which manifested itself in unstable behavior. Subsequent clinical studies of these individuals, variously labeled borderline, narcissistic, or psychotic character types, have confirmed that such types reveal a wide range of psychological functioning.

The traditional continuum of psychological functioning was distinguished only by the normal person, the neurotic, and the psychotic. The neurotic was characterized by psychological conflicts (manifested in symptoms) that interfered with but did not preclude a substantial degree of "normal" functioning. Psychotic personalities, in contrast, were not able to function in the normal range because of more substantial impairments in their psychological capacities.

The developing understanding of borderline and narcissistic character types has forced a modification of this three-part continuum. Clinical researchers have tended to insert these character disturbances on the continuum between the neurotic and psychotic (Meissner 1984; Chessick 1985; Stone 1986). As a general rule, there is considerable clinical consensus that narcissistic character processes represent a stronger and more integrated psychological structure than do borderline personality organizations.

Borderline disturbances are considered more severe because they often entail distorted thinking and fragmentation of the sense of self-cohesion (Meissner 1984, 96), two clear signs of severe impairment. Narcissistic disturbances, in contrast, are "more concerned with self-esteem than with self-cohesion" (Meissner l984, 133) and tend to be located diagnostically closer to neurotic functioning on the mental health continuum. Yet both borderline and narcissistic personality organizations can be differentiated from severely deteriorated psychological functioning (psychosis).

For example, although borderline personality organization is generally associated with substantial difficulties in psychological functioning, somewhat adequate capacity to see reality clearly may be present, although limited. Alternatively, the borderline patient may exhibit strong tendencies toward the expression of self-destructive impulses, which may be reflected in violent or other uncontrollable behavior. Even so, the borderline patient may occasionally be psychologically organized enough to operate "in society."

In these characteristics, borderline personality organizations differ from those of the delusional psychotic, for whom psychological organization operates at such a low level that he or she is not able to function in society. And, in turn, both types need to be distinguished from the functioning of the "average person," who, while having areas of psychological conflict or limitation, is nonetheless generally able to function and even to function well.

As may be apparent, these newer theoretical understandings of character and personality organization represent a major complication in efforts to assess psychological suitability. It is now clear that substantial talents may coexist with substantial characterological and emotional impairments. Indeed, some of the characteristics of persons with these types of character organizations may facilitate, rather than impede, reaching high-level positions, including high-level political positions. The application of intelligence to getting what one wants is one hallmark of the narcissist and borderline character type, a trait that leads some persons of this type to be substantial achievers. However, such a person, even one with considerable political talents, may well be unable fully to accomplish what successful presidential performance requires. For example, one characteristic of narcissistic and borderline character types is that they frequently don't care much about others, as long as they gain gratification. They may promise others much, and others may rest their hopes upon those words, but ultimately these character types care mostly about themselves.

Either way, Post appears correct in concluding his major review of these character types by noting, "Given the frequency with which political figures with significant narcissistic personality features occupy positions of power, familiarity with the psychology of narcissism is essential for scholars" (1993, 119–20). We will examine these issues in two of the case studies in Part 3 of this book, dealing with the issue of character.

Is Rationality Enough?

Most discussions of presidential performance assume, but rarely analyze, the importance of rationality. On its face, a demand that presidents behave and think rationally seems reasonable enough. Presidents must be logical, coherent, and appropriate in their thinking in order to carry out their responsibilities. However, many discussions of psychological suitability that focus on emotional stability tend to treat mental heath and rationality as roughly synonymous. They are not. Moreover, when one moves away from the most extreme examples of psychological impairment, the practicality as well as the virtue of rationality are by no means a given.

What exactly is meant by *rationality?* Let us begin with the most extreme opposite case—that of the irrationality of the psychotic. Perhaps the cardinal distinguishing feature of psychotic behavior is the loss of the capacity to perceive and test reality. In the most acute cases, the manifestations of this loss are quite obvious, as when former secretary of defense Forrestal claimed that the Russians had wired his golf clubs to operate as radio transmitters. So, too, auditory and visual hallucinations, the failure to contain fantasy and wishes, and the confusion of these with actual events taking place externally all reflect a disintegration of the normal structures of perception and integration. These psychotic manifestations reflect not only a failure to distinguish inner and outer realities but also a loss of understanding that it is necessary to do so. The psychotic person not only has "strange thoughts," which by itself would not be definitive for diagnosis, but often fails to appreciate their strangeness or to take any steps to ascertain their appropriateness.

The term *reality testing,* then, refers to a person's ability to distinguish external from internal reality, to know when to have doubts about the relationship of the two, to have some psychological capacity and mechanisms for testing the relative contributions of each, and to act, to some degree, accordingly. All of this requires the coordination and integration of a number of psychological processes whose successful operation is by no means certain, even given general psychological and emotional well-being.

The "rational actor" in these respects seems the antithesis of the psychotic. The emphasis on rationality may be found in many analyses of political decision making (e.g., Allison 1971, 32–35; Paige 1968). In these analyses, rationality is assumed to be synonymous with the capacity to calculate and behave in a self-interested way. In the rational-actor model, according to a familiar litany, the decision maker considers all relevant values at stake, compares all possible responses in terms of their costs and benefits, and selects the option that maximizes the values most crucial to him or her. Where the psychotic cannot distinguish between internal and external reality, a rational actor perceives external contexts in a highly accurate, albeit limited, way. The rational actor must be keenly aware of contextual complexity in order to calculate the best strategic behavior to further his or her goals. Moreover, he or she must be in tune with the motives (and possible behaviors) of others, so that possible obstacles to achieving these goals can be avoided or overcome.

Criticisms of the application of the model to describe how persons actually behave have concentrated on two major points. First, as Simon (1957) pointed out, individuals do not always attempt to maximize particular values. They may, on occasion or as a matter of orientation, prefer to "satisfice," that is, to be satisfied with less than maximum amounts. A second and more general criticism has been leveled at the assumption of comprehensive rationality. In this view, models of decision making, which ascribe to individuals the rationality described above, err in overestimating the many ways in which cognitive limitations and information slippage keep individuals from being thoroughly rational. There are many limitations to an individual's capacity to perceive external (and internal, for that matter) reality clearly and accurately (George 1980).

Perception can be affected by an individual's motivations, anxieties, or other feelings, which in turn can be affected by an individual's values, beliefs, and attribution errors. And of course, external (and internal) reality presents multiple and frequently conflicting indicators of what is occurring. From these perspectives, the comprehensive model is an "ideal type" and the model of bounded rationality (March 1978) is closer to reflecting the actual constraints under which individuals, including presidents, operate.

The model of the rational actor appears to have been the foundation for concerns regarding the president's mental health. The more a president acted like and gave evidence of being a rational actor, the less concern there was about his mental health. The more a president (or a candidate) failed to approximate this ideal, the more his rationality and, by extension, his mental health was questioned.

There are several flaws in equating rationality and good psychological functioning, even at the extreme ends of the continuum. At the extreme irrational end of the continuum, such a model underestimates the degree to which psychotic persons are able accurately to perceive extremely subtle aspects of their environment. In a classic experiment (Rosenhan 1973) in which "pseudopatients" were introduced into a variety of psychiatric hospitals to see whether admitting or other hospital staff could really discern "mental illness," it was actually the hospital patients who voiced the first skepticism that these persons were "real" patients.[8]

The view that "psychotic" equals "irrational" may also underestimate the extent to which the irrational behavior may be rational from the perspective of the person undertaking it. This happens even in persons with higher levels of psychological functioning. The logic of the behavior may not be clear to others, but it is not necessarily blind or purposeless.

Let us now briefly examine the other end of the continuum. Can we at least favor a president who can closely approach the requirements of the rational actor model, even if he can't fully live up to them? Perhaps. However, to do so we would need to be convinced that strategic calculation, which is the foundation of the conceptualization of rationality, represents the best method of decision making. Secondarily, we would have to be convinced that the use of such a calculus necessarily reflects characterological soundness. I suggest that rationality may not be a suitable criterion for mental health or, more importantly, a useful model of psychological suitability for presidential candidates. Rationality may actually prove to be a minimum and somewhat flawed criterion of psychological suitability.

The problem is not only that requirements of the model are frequently impossible or unlikely to be carried out but that there are serious questions as to whether they should be. For the rational actor, whether he or she maximizes or "satisfices," the primary perspective is still self-centered and the chief criterion remains self-interest. This egocentric calculus obviously affects the perception of problems and the weighing of data connected with making decisions about them. Factoring in others' interests, in the event that they are considered, does not solve this problem. In effect, one is asking the rational actor in these circumstances to play the role of devil's advocate for the interests of others and in opposition to his own. Others' interests are unlikely to receive equivalent status.

Kinder variants of the model require that the decision maker put himself in the shoes of the other person by asking, "How would I behave in similar circumstances?" This is simply a bootlegged variation of an egocentric calculus. How the individual would behave in such a situation is beside the point, since such a calculus assumes that the other person is very much like the person trying to figure him out. This kind of question often reflects what I term a *strategic empathy,* whose basic logic is as follows: How can I understand the other person and his or her views so that I can better anticipate them and accomplish my own purposes?

Moreover, the assumption that other interests, if considered, can or should be bartered may reflect a lack of understanding of others and a shallow affected attachment to them, as well as a disregard for their legitimate role in the policymaking process. A real ability to "put oneself in the place of others" is a key dimension of successful political decision making, especially in a democracy. Not only is this empathetic capacity important for considering various views in the domestic policymaking process, but it has also been shown to be a key aspect of successfully working through at least one major power confrontation that might have ended, but did not end, in thermonuclear war. Janis's (1989, 133–58) analysis of the Cuban missile crisis, which he counts among his illustrations of successful policy process, stresses the way in which John F. Kennedy and his advisers explicitly considered the position of their adversary Nikita Khrushchev. What Janis calls the use of nonhumiliation developed out of the realization that even though the Soviet leader had been dangerously provocative in attempting to introduce offensive nuclear missiles into Cuba, it was important to consider responding in the context of *his* concerns, including the likely existence of competing factions in the Soviet leadership structure at the time and Khrushchev's position in relation to them after having undertaken this action.

This illustration points beyond the importance of empathy to the more general question of the role of affect in effective decision making. Models of rationality, whether comprehensive or bounded, eschew any role for affect, leaving the impression that the two are incompatible. By focusing on a limited view of rationality, we have limited our understanding of the process, and worse, efforts to improve the quality of decision making have neglected this important element.

There is finally the question of whether more rationality is what is truly needed in political decision making. To ask our political leaders to be ever more *rational,* in the limited sense of that term, may be asking of them not only the improbable but in many cases the unnecessary. Shrewd calculation of self-interest among political leaders is already very much in evidence; we certainly don't appear to suffer from a surfeit.

The question before us is this: If comprehensive rationality is an ideal model that doesn't empirically describe how individuals can and do operate in the real world, on what basis, if at all, are we able to make distinctions between more and "better" rationality? I argue that, given the empirical support for the bounded rationality model, political scientists and others who study presidential decision making must reframe their focus. If presidents cannot be expected to display comprehensive rationality, we need to have another conceptual tool by which to judge their capacities. I argue in chapter 8 that this theoretical tool is the concept of *judgment.* The concept of judgment leads us to inquire how clearly the president perceives the real issues at hand, how well he makes use of the data made available to him (whatever his method of information search and external evaluation), and how well he is able to weigh and adequately resolve the conflicting interests (including his own self-interest and the interests of others) with the need and capacity to accomplish public purposes.

These are complex calculations, insufficiently encompassed by the focus on rationality. *What presidents require is not more rationality but better judgment.* It is judgment, not rationality, that promises to provide insight into the making of high-quality decisions, especially given the limitations of any president's capacity to live up to the assumptions of the rational-actor model. If, as will be argued, decision making should occupy a central role in any theory of presidential performance, it is important that the concern with a president's rationality not obscure the larger issue of his judgment.

The White House: Deterrent to or Facilitator of Psychological Excess?

Does the president have too much or too little power? Does he have any real power at all? Neustadt's famous argument is that a president has only the power to persuade. Neustadt argues that the presidential ability to command is limited and the exception, not the rule.

Occupants of the White House echo this view. They often complain about the constraints imposed on them by the need to deal with a multitude of complex problems not of their choosing or making. They complain that they are hampered in addressing these problems by the separation of powers, an often reluctant and fractious Congress, a foot-dragging bureaucracy, courts that are top-heavy with appointments made by a president's predecessors, a White House press corps that seems to show little awe of presidents and their prerogatives, and a public that is increasingly willing to challenge a president, given an opportunity.

To some degree, this view is accurate. Multiple institutional centers of power and the norm of accountability do inhibit excesses found in countries without such safeguards. In the United States, for example, systematic and violent repression of political opposition is something read about in news reports of other countries.

It is tempting to conclude from this that presidents are inhibited for the most part from attempting or, if tempted, from persisting in behavior that reflects a lack of prudence or judgment. Yet there are reasons to believe that while Americans are protected from the worst forms of excess, they are not necessarily protected from excess itself. Schlesinger (1974), for example, notes the gradual erosion of alternative centers of institutional power vis-à-vis the president during the late 1960s and early 1970s. He considers that this became especially notable in foreign affairs but was not limited to it. He then argues, central to our concerns, that the erosion of alternative centers of power has had an unfortunate effect on the psychology of recruitment into the presidency. Schlesinger suggests that "as foreign policy tempted Presidents to break out of the system of accountability, the presidency naturally began to attract personalities on whom accountability exacted an intolerable psychological toll" (1974, 15).

Schlesinger's argument is an interesting one. Traditionally, political psychologists have assumed, on the basis of some empirical evidence (cf. Browning and Jacob 1964), that positions with a high power potential would attract candidates who sought out power potential. Certainly, the presidency is an office with an enormous potential for the occupant to influence national and international politics, even history.

Not surprisingly, there is evidence from at least two sources that individuals who seek the presidency have high levels of ambition as well as of emotional and physical commitment. The first line of evidence comes from the enormous commitment of time, energy, and an individual's life that becoming a presidential candidate entails. The quest for a nomination that will not happen for four years often begins immediately after the November presidential election, and occasionally before.

The second piece of evidence comes from those who could have but did not seek the office. In 1974, Walter Mondale refused to seek the Democratic Party's nomination because he "did not want to spend two years sleeping in a Holiday Inn," and because he "lacked the overwhelming desire to be president which is essential for the kind of campaign that is required" (quoted in Clymer 1987, 2). Later, in reflecting on his losing effort in 1984, Mondale counseled other presidential candidates about how difficult the process is and about the need to "first decide they'd be a good and strong candidate, *be convinced of it,* and then *put everything off in their minds except seeking the Presidency*" (quoted in Weinraub 1987, B5; emphasis added).

Such conviction and single-minded determination have benefits and liabilities. They certainly allow the candidate to mobilize for a long, demanding, and ultimately zero-sum contest. There is, after all, only one president elected at a time. But the same traits can also lead to exactly the kind of overstepping that Schlesinger has written about with concern.

Schlesinger sees the antidote to presidential excess as more institutional responsibility. In this view he is surely correct, but even so, one wonders whether systems of accountability, even the more robust ones, can fully compensate for the institutionalization of presidential power and the remarkable degree to which the office magnifies the psychology of its occupant.

Does the office magnify the president's psychology? As Schlesinger notes (1973, 217), "The Presidency is so particularly personal an institution and . . . the psychic drives of the man who sits in the Oval Office . . . fundamentally affect the impact of each particular Presidency." Elsewhere he notes that "every President reconstructs the White House to meet his own psychological needs" (1973, 218). George Reedy (1970), a close adviser to Lyndon Johnson and observer of presidents for thirty years, provides another insider view. He notes that "the office neither elevates or degrades a man. What it does is to provide a stage upon which all of his personality traits are magnified" (1970, 18–19).

Why do a president's personality traits become magnified? Reedy offers at least three important reasons. First, "in the White House character and personality are extremely important because there are no other limitations that govern a man's conduct. Restraint must come from within the presidential soul and prudence from within the presidential mind" (Reedy 1970, 20). A second reason is that

the atmosphere of the White House is a heady one. . . . Furthermore the President would have to be a dull clod indeed to regard himself without a feeling of awe. The atmosphere in the White House is calculated to instill in any man a sense of destiny. He literally walks in the footsteps of hallowed figures—of Jefferson, of Jackson, of Lincoln. (Reedy 1970, 15)

But the problem is not only the legacy of the past as it affects the president but also his present. A third reason that Reedy notes (1970, 16) is that a president becomes a personification of the people, "and Presidents cannot escape the process. . . . The President becomes the nation, and when he is insulted, the nation is insulted; when he has a dream, the nation has a dream."

As if all these elements were not enough, Reedy observes that

there is built into the presidency a series of devices that tend to remove the occupant from all of the forces which require most men to rub up against the hard facts of life on a daily basis. The life of the White House is . . . designed for one purpose and one purpose only—to serve the material needs and the desires of a single man. (1970, 4)

Reedy relates that a president is treated "with all the reverence due a monarch" (1970, 4). Somewhat later he notes, "A president moves through his days surrounded by literally hundreds of people whose relationship to him is that of a doting mother to a spoiled child" (1970, 23). The view that the president is grappling with critical matters and must be protected, if at all possible, from every conceivable distraction leads to a situation that encourages "his most outrageous expressions, for pampering his most childish tantrums, for *fostering his most arrogant actions*. . . . It serves to create an environment in which no man can live for any considerable . . . time and retain his psychological balance" (Reedy 1970, 22–23; emphasis mine).

One occupant of the White House noted, "There can be no question that the White House can and does become your world. You're absolutely protected. Every need is provided for . . . it's almost a princely existence" (quoted in Wayne 1977, 24).

Is this a president speaking? No, actually it's merely a member of the president's staff, a somewhat mid-level aide, speaking of his experience at the center of political power in Washington, D.C. If a mid-level presidential aide can feel like a prince, an imperial (and somewhat imperious) psychology is not a remote possibility.

Mental Health and the Psychological Suitability of Presidential Candidates: A Still-Relevant but Limited Criterion

I have tried to suggest in this chapter why concerns with the "mental health" and possible psychological impairment of presidential candidates are still legitimate. There are serious questions about whether the common assumptions regarding psychosis are accurate. Many severe psychological disturbances do not result in obviously bizarre behavior, nor do their manifestations necessarily appear continuously. Moreover disturbed behavior may not be recognized for what it is—or isn't. These problems are compounded by the fact that persons with more than moderate degrees of psychological impairment can often present a clinical picture that includes some (and on occasion, substantial) personality strengths. As if this didn't make the task difficult enough, some personality pathologies, such as those of narcissistic and borderline character disorders, may be found in persons whose traits make them more attractive (on the surface) as candidates for high office.

If such problems are still very relevant, what can we do about them? There are substantial practical difficulties in discerning impairment among presidents and especially among presidential candidates. The assessment of *mental health* (if clinically based and defined) must be very heavily anchored in a highly specialized set of observations and data. Except in the case of clearly psychotic behavior, the clinical assessment of *psychological impairment* (a term I prefer to *mental health*) is difficult to perform at a distance, at one point in time, or on the basis of one form of data.

In formal, clinical settings, the assessment of impairment relies on a number of modalities including projective, objective, and behavioral tests, along with observations of verbal and motor functions in natural and specialized settings. It also relies heavily on ongoing clinical interviews, an extremely powerful observational and data-gathering technique in itself. It remains to be seen whether more informal methods of assessment can be useful or even suggestive.

The focus on mental health as a key dimension of psychological suitability for presidential candidates raises an important but limited set of questions. Mental health, as it is usually conceptualized primarily in terms of rationality, is certainly a basic but, in many ways, modest requirement. Of course it is wise to elect presidents who are "rational," but that does not ordinarily take us very far down the path of assessing presidential performance.

It is not enough to assess that someone is generally "mentally healthy" and infer that he therefore is psychologically suited to become president. Indeed, the somewhat paradoxical possibility exists that a president could be psychologically healthy, and politically disastrous. The reason behind this apparent paradox does not lie in the fact that even healthy presidents are not perfect (although this is certainly true). It lies rather in the fact that an individual can be rational, function adequately in social roles, and still have a pathological personality and character structure.

The existence of a "culturally patterned defect" further complicates these issues. In some political systems, traits that would be seen by us as undesirable are actually functional. Also, it is possible that our system tends to reward powerful motivations such as ambition because they are often connected with such culturally desirable values as achievement. Ambition may be one illustration of a socially patterned defect in American political culture.

Focusing exclusively on a president's mental health and defining that in terms of rationality neglects a great deal of presidential performance that lies outside of the need for the president to be rational. It is clear why a psychotically impaired candidate would make a poor president, but this is the start of a useful analysis and not its conclusion.

Over the last two decades, there have certainly been many mistakes made in domestic and foreign policy, and even some major policy fiascoes. However, it is not clear that the leadership failures of the Johnson, Nixon, and Carter administrations have as much to do with overall mental health as they do with specific character and personality issues. It is not the presidential candidate who makes an error and accepts responsibility that we need to worry about but the shrewd calculations of candidates who would stop at little to achieve their goals. Psychological impairment, sometimes of a substantial degree, may be found not so much in the raving of a lunatic as in a president overconfident of his own correctness.

F I V E

Assessment at a Distance:
A Cautionary Case Study of the
1964 Presidential Campaign

The 1964 election signified the first time in a modern presidential campaign that the mental health of a candidate became a major campaign issue. During the campaign, the Republican candidate's emotional stability and suitability for the presidency were questioned publicly as a campaign issue by his opponent. Was the Republican candidate, Senator Barry Goldwater, emotionally stable enough, Lyndon Johnson (the Democratic candidate) asked, to be in control of the country's nuclear weapons?

This presidential campaign is also notable for another reason central to our concerns. During the campaign, a unique psychiatric survey was conducted. In the summer of 1964, the mass-circulation magazine *FACT* sent a letter and a questionnaire to 12,356 psychiatrists, all members of the American Psychiatric Association, and asked them to provide their professional assessment of the mental health and psychological suitability of Barry Goldwater for president. Results of this survey were published in two lengthy articles in the September/October issue of *FACT,* shortly before the election.

Democratic Party nominee Lyndon Johnson won the election by a large margin. Whether this survey and the resulting published psychiatric profile had any direct, independent effects on the election outcome is questionable. Our point here is not to argue that it did. Rather, our interest is in what the psychiatric survey and resulting profile reveal about psychological suitability as a criterion for the presidency and its assessment during a campaign. My analysis does not focus on the campaign itself or on the calculations that led to the decision to make psychological suitability an issue. Rather, I focus on three areas central to our concerns.[1]

First, I analyze the content of the responses to the questionnaire for what they suggest about issues of validity and reliability in psychological assessments of presidential candidates. Second, because the *FACT* survey was conducted during a presidential election campaign, it allows us to gauge the effect of the campaign on the assessment. My analysis of how issues of psychological suitability got played out during an election campaign suggests some inherent dangers present in that process; hence the title of this chapter.

Third, the survey and its results are interesting because they may provide some general, though still useful, observations regarding psychological suitability for high public office. The survey, despite its numerous methodological flaws, is still the only published record of psychiatric observation on the issue of the psychological suitability of a presidential candidate. The respondents were individuals trained and experienced in the observation and psychological analysis of individual behavior (although not necessarily in presidential politics). Therefore, their thinking, even if collectively flawed, may inform or stimulate ours.

The Psychiatric Assessment of Barry Goldwater

In 1964 the Republican Party nominated Barry Goldwater, U.S. senator from Arizona, as its presidential candidate. Senator Goldwater had established himself as a leading spokesman for the conservative wing of his party. He espoused strong views on reducing government involvement in the lives of its citizens and equally strong views on the importance of a strong national defense and tough international stance vis-à-vis the Soviet Union. In part because of these views and in part because of some campaign statements, Senator Goldwater was considered in some quarters as a political "extremist." During his nomination acceptance speech, he stated that "extremism in the pursuit of liberty is no vice," which became a frequently repeated quote that appeared to support his critics' contention.

His opponent in the election, Lyndon Johnson, used this perception in two ways. First, he used it to raise concern over American involvement in Southeast Asia, in particular, Vietnam. Johnson presented himself as the "peace candidate," in contrast to the "hawkish" Goldwater. Second, Johnson's campaign explicitly raised the issue of Senator Goldwater's emotional stability and therefore of his suitability as a potential commander in chief with control over nuclear weapons.

A famous Democratic Party television spot showed a little girl picking flowers in a field, while in the background a countdown proceeded. When the count reached zero, the little girl was replaced with an expanding mushroom cloud from a nuclear explosion, followed by the message "Vote Democratic" superimposed on the screen. This very pointed political commercial was withdrawn after vigorous complaints from the opposition, but the point had been made.

FACT's psychiatric survey was conducted in the summer of 1964, and the results were presented in the September/October issue of the magazine. The first article relating the results was written by Warren Boroson and was titled, "What Psychiatrists Say about Goldwater." It essentially consisted of quotes from psychiatrists who had answered the survey. The second article was written by the magazine's editor and publisher, Ralph Ginzburg, and was titled, "Goldwater: The Man and the Menace." It is the second article that presents the rationale for the survey and attempts to place its results in a more general clinical and political context, and for these reasons it deserves our initial attention.

The article begins with an assertion by Ginzburg (1964, 3) that in considering Goldwater for the presidency, Americans may be electing a man "whose personality traits are reminiscent of Forrestal's and McCarthy's." It is for this reason, Ginzburg asserts, that a psychiatric evaluation of Goldwater is so crucial. The article goes on to claim (1964, 3) that "Mr. Goldwater's illness is not just an emotional maladjustment, or a mild neurosis, or a queerness," but rather that he shows "unmistakable signs of paranoia." Having already provided a preliminary diagnosis, the article then asks whether it is possible "to determine conclusively, without a psychiatric interview, on the basis of what is known about him, whether Goldwater is a paranoid."

It is an important and basic question, but one that is not addressed by the Ginzburg article. Instead, the article notes that presidential candidates are now routinely given wide coverage by the press and other media and that, in addition, there are numerous interviews with candidates and observations by both friends and enemies. From all of these, Ginzburg concludes, "a comprehensive psychiatric portrait definitely does emerge" (1964, 3).

With this as a preamble, the article continues by drawing a psychological sketch taken extensively from six published biographies. In reviewing Goldwater's childhood and subsequent life up to his nomination for the presidency, the article stresses several points that are presumed to have a bearing on his psychological fitness for office.[2] First, it alleges that Goldwater had a cold and distant relationship with his father, who is presented as being somewhat effete. In contrast, the article suggests, Goldwater seems to have maintained a very close relationship with his mother, who is presented as being extremely dynamic and somewhat masculine.

The article goes on to assert that as a child Goldwater developed a taste for sadistic practical jokes and cruel pranks, a characteristic that Ginzburg describes as indicative of an "anal character." Another point developed at some length is Goldwater's "preoccupation" with manhood and masculinity, which the article asserts is frequently expressed as a feeling that others have betrayed him. This behavior, Ginzburg notes, is "typical of the paranoiac" (1964, 4). Finally, the article reports that on at least two separate occasions Goldwater suffered "nervous breakdowns" when faced with highly stressful work situations.

The importance of these assertions is not found in their accuracy. One measure of the article's accuracy is that Goldwater filed a suit against the editor and his magazine for libel and won. Given court rulings on First Amendment protection for authors and magazines in these circumstances, it was no small accomplishment for a public figure to win such a lawsuit.

However, even if some of the assertions had been accurate, they would have remained, from a clinical perspective, non sequiturs. A number of presidents have had difficult fathers who could be characterized as emotionally distant, for example John F. Kennedy and Woodrow Wilson, who are considered by many to have been adequate or better presidents. Or consider the article's innuendo regarding Goldwater's relationship with a dynamic, somewhat "masculine" mother. Again, one can think of several presidents whose mothers were dynamic and did not accept conventions about appropriate feminine behavior, among them Franklin D. Roosevelt, Jimmy Carter, and Bill Clinton. One would certainly not wish to have judged these presidents on such a criterion.

The function of the first article's very loose profile is to set the stage for the results of the survey and provide a rationale for the diagnosis that has already been put forward. It is also worth noting that some of the unsubstantiated assertions of the article, in particular the claim that Goldwater had suffered two "nervous breakdowns," had made their way into the questionnaire itself. The heart of the article, however, concerns the survey and its results, and it is to these that we now turn.

A Note on Method

The first article regarding *FACT*'s psychiatric survey informs the reader that on July 23, 1964, one week after Barry Goldwater was nominated for the presidency, *FACT* sent a questionnaire to more than twelve thousand psychiatrists asking, "Do you believe Barry Goldwater is psychologically fit to be President of the United States?" According to the magazine, the survey was sent out to all 12,356 members of the American Psychiatric Association but only 2,419 members responded. This gives a response rate of only about 19.5 percent.[3]

Overall, the low response rate suggests that those who did respond may well have been atypical in some way (motivation and investment in the issue are clearly two strong possibilities), compared to those who did not respond. The most comforting explanation of the low response rate is good collective judgment, but timing may have also played a role. The survey was sent on July 23, very close to the month of August when many psychiatrists and members of the analytic community are on vacation.

In this regard, it must also be noted that the survey was received and "analyzed" in time to be written up in a magazine that hit the newsstands with its September/October issue. There was clearly no time for a follow-up, as is typically done, and the short time between the sending of the survey and its publication is of itself a cause for concern. But issues surrounding response rates are only the beginning of the survey's major flaws.

According to Rogow (1970, 125–27), the question of Goldwater's fitness was asked in a cover letter[4] accompanying the questionnaire, which consisted of a form on which the respondent could check the appropriate box as to whether Goldwater "was stable enough to serve as President." In case respondents missed the point, the cover letter also asked them to consider whether Goldwater "was prone to aggressive behavior and destructiveness" and whether "he seem[s] callous to the downtrodden and needy." Finally, in what appears to be a complete abandonment of the principle of neutrally phrased or balanced survey questions, the letter asked respondents whether they could "offer any explanation of his public temper tantrums and his occasional outbursts of profanity" and whether they thought "that his having had two nervous breakdowns has any bearing on his fitness to govern the country." The latter, of course, was presented as if it were a certified fact.

These additional questions were not reported in the text of the article, which made reference only to the general psychological fitness question.

The article did note, however, that the questionnaire had left room for comments and reported that "over a quarter of a million words of professional opinion were received." In the magazine's view, that constituted "the most intensive character analysis ever made of a living human being" (Boroson 1964, 24). What the article did not report, and what emerged only in the context of Senator Goldwater's successful legal suit, was that Ginzburg had in some instances printed misleading versions of respondents' statements. He had, for example, "omitted qualifying phrases, and had blended the comments of several respondents together, essentially rewriting and editing as he saw fit" (Curran 1969, 2270).

Ginzburg's readers also were not informed that the survey had been repudiated by every major professional organization associated with psychiatry. The American Psychiatric Association, for example, issued a statement (Kohut 1965, 450) expressing concern about the use of such "unverified impressions" and went on to note:

It is understandable that some members of the professions dealing with mental illness might wish—out of a sense of social responsibility—to share their knowledge with the public in order to make a contribution to one of the most important activities in a democracy: the choice of a leader. However, professional judgments regarding the mental stability of any person have to be based on carefully evaluated psychological data which must be secured through a detailed review of the life history and a thorough clinical evaluation. Such information is most reliable when obtained through a therapeutic relationship.

It is worth observing here that Kohut's statement as president of the American Psychiatric Association appears implicitly to accept the legitimacy of psychiatrists making psychological assessments in the political arena, albeit only after detailed review of the subject's life history and a thorough clinical evaluation. The fact that such data are "most reliably obtained" in a therapeutic relationship does not appear totally to preclude such assessments on the part of psychiatrists but rather to limit severely the circumstances in which the assessments could be judged authoritative.

Other professional organizations were equally critical of the survey. The American Medical Association referred to the incident as a case of "yellow journalism" (*New York Times*, 5 May 1968, 62). The editor of the *American Journal of Psychiatry* (Barton 1968, 140) characterized the incident as "shocking" and went on to suggest that if there were any psychiatrists who really believed that their diagnostic labels, sent by mail, had any scientific validity, "it behooves their peers to find some effective way of disabusing them."

These criticisms go to the heart of the diagnostic process and raise questions of theory as well as method. It is to these questions and their implications for assessing political leaders psychologically that I now turn. In doing so, I underscore that the results of this survey cannot be considered to be methodologically sound from either a clinical or a survey perspective. My analysis of the survey's results therefore is not and could not be directed toward revealing anything about the ostensible object of the survey, Barry Goldwater. Rather, my point is to analyze what the results of this psychiatric evaluation reveal about the process of psychiatric evaluation in a political context.

Assessing the Mental Health of a Presidential Candidate

The Boroson article containing the psychiatric evaluations begins by noting (1964, 24), in boldface type, that 1,189 psychiatrists said that the Republican candidate was not psychologically fit to be president, while only 657 respondents thought that he was fit. On face value, these figures would seem to indicate substantial clinical agreement (about 65 percent) among those who responded to the question. However, an analysis of the elicited "comments" quickly dispels the appearance of diagnostic consensus.

Among the most immediately striking aspects of the printed comments is the very wide range of diagnostic conclusions reached. One psychiatrist wrote, "There is no doubt that Mr. Barry Goldwater is 'mentally de- ranged' " (Boroson 1964, 54). Another felt Goldwater was "intellectually honest, reliable, consistent and emotionally mature" (1964, 62). One re- spondent believed that the candidate was "grossly psychotic" (1964, 63), while another believed him to be "exceptionally well-adjusted" (1964, 54). The wide range of conclusions regarding the general level of Senator Goldwater's mental health is matched by the equally wide range of specific diagnostic assessments made at the level of clinical conceptualization.

In a clinical context, diagnosis serves several functions. The ability to organize "symptoms" into a coherent pattern and to place this pattern into a diagnostic framework reflects on both the skill of the clinician and the soundness of the framework. In the best of circumstances, a skilled clinician using a well-established and valid framework would be able to place a patient's symptoms into a theoretical framework that provides both under- standing and a guide to treatment.

It is important to keep in mind that the respondents were being asked to make a "psychiatric" assessment of someone's "mental health." A *psychiatric* assessment, the purpose of which is to obtain a clinical picture of someone's mental health, is not synonymous with a *psychological* assessment of certain kinds of personality or character trends. In the former, the question of the adequacy of basic psychological functioning is primary. At its most basic level, such an inquiry might seek to establish whether a person is oriented in time and space as well as logical and appropriate in his or her thinking.

A thorough, well-conducted mental-status diagnostic interview may establish a substantial amount of useful and accurate information about the psychological functioning of an individual. Certainly, it can establish whether and to what degree an individual is correctly oriented in time, space, and sequential logic. A skilled clinical interviewer can also gain substantial insight into an individual's typical defenses and ability to handle confrontation or sensitive subjects. However, the point here is not the diagnostic efficacy of such interviews but the need for them. When Kohut, criticizing the *FACT* survey, notes that such information is more reliable when obtained through a therapeutic relationship, he is underscoring the role of an ongoing, intense relationship between patient and therapist as an important source of data collection and refinement.

The respondents to the *FACT* survey all based their observations on the same public data, and while there is some level of diagnostic agreement among the respondents, there is also considerable variation. By far the most frequent diagnosis presented (Boroson 1964, 21 and passim) is that of a "paranoid personality," which is mentioned at least twenty times. This represents a consensus rate of about 12 percent (given the 163 comments that appear). Of course, given what is now known about the heavy editorial hand exercised by the publisher, we cannot assume that these numbers represent actual independent comments.

We must also note that while there is a "modal" diagnosis, it is by no means the only one. One respondent characterized Goldwater as a "compensated schizophrenic" (Boroson 1964, 26), while another felt that he had "a narcissistic character disorder with not-too-latent paranoid elements" (1964, 26). Yet another mentioned the presence of a "severe obsessive-compulsive neurosis" (1964, 37), while one respondent wrote, "My main concern regarding Goldwater is how suicidal is he?" (1964, 40).

Problems in the Assessment Process

It is not enough for our purposes to note the *FACT* survey's relatively low level of diagnostic consensus, or the wide diagnostic variability. It is also important to try and understand why this occurred. In this section and the one that follows, we examine three major difficulties: a mismatch between the level of inference and the data that are used to support it, the complexities of diagnostic entities, and the countertransferential inducements of a contested political campaign.

The first answer to why such a broad diagnostic variability is evident in the Goldwater article begins with an examination of the distinction between the level of analysis employed in the diagnostic descriptions (including the genetic reconstructions and the explication of psychological dynamics) and the nature of the data from which the descriptions are drawn. Greenstein (1969, 65–68; see also Lasswell 1968) distinguishes three levels of psychological data: phenomenology, dynamics, and genesis. The first refers to the observable behavioral characteristics of the person, the second to the dynamic underpinnings of those characteristics (how and why they fit together); the third addresses the question of how these dynamics came into existence.

Genetic reconstructions, which trace the impact of early experience on later behavior, must rest on the meticulous tracing of developmental patterns. Moreover, as noted in the Introduction, in a psychotherapeutic context, the fact that one or more events happened does not automatically bestow causal significance on them. Many political leaders, and members of the public, for that matter, have experienced emotionally distant fathers (or mothers), but those experiences did not result in uniform outcomes.

Along with knowing that events have happened, it is important to understand their significance to the person involved, as well as any other factors that may be relevant. Such information is the foundation of a genetic reconstruction that is useful for clinical intervention. Such data, however, are exceedingly difficult to obtain outside of a therapeutic setting, and this difficulty creates a formidable (but not insurmountable) barrier to attempts outside that context. In the absence of meticulous tracing of events and their meaning, genetic reconstructions are likely to be speculative at best.

Examination of the *FACT* article reveals a level of genetic reconstruction that more closely resembles parody than it does analysis. Throughout, there are numerous examples of the tendency to leap directly from individual, social-level childhood facts to adult characteristics. The assumption in the analysis appears to be that the former carry a particular and specific psychological import.

An example of this is the use (for purposes of genetic reconstruction) that is made of the fact that Goldwater's parents had different religions.

One respondent noted that Goldwater's "mental instability stems from the fact that his father was a Jew while his mother was a Protestant" (Boroson 1964, 31). Another suggested that Goldwater's "ambitions and temper are explained by the fact that in his private life he has suffered from the consequences of a mixed religious background" (1964, 34). Yet another wondered "if Goldwater's position on human rights isn't a strong denial of that minority part of his ancestry, the Jewish part" (1964, 48). One should note here the diversity of outcomes that are presumed to be related to the religious identification of Goldwater's parents.

These quotes underscore the inferential difficulties involved in such leaps. For example, the mere fact that Goldwater's parents had different religious identifications doesn't tell us very much. Among the other important things we would like to know in order to make some assessment are the nature of the religious beliefs and how strongly they were held by each parent, what decisions were made about religious upbringing by his parents, and above all what effect, if any, each of these had on Goldwater's experience and psychological development as a child and young adult.

These questions are not raised or addressed. Had they at least been raised, it is possible that they might have been answered. Answers to these questions were not beyond knowing in the absence of a prolonged diagnostic relationship. Yet without more detailed information about these issues, no reasonable conclusions can be drawn from the relatively shallow fact that Goldwater had a mixed religious heritage.

The genetic explanations offered suffered from a paucity of data on issues that were directly relevant to the explanations' plausibility. But what of the variability in diagnostic assessment? Is that, too, a function of the lack of relevant data?

To some degree the answer must be yes. Consider the diagnosis of narcissistic character disorder that appears in the survey. Such a diagnosis, in its clinical (not its cultural) meaning, requires a fairly detailed knowledge of a person's intrapsychic functioning and interpersonal relationships. Clinical descriptions of this character type include shallow and exploitative interpersonal relationships, in which other persons are used to reinforce the narcissist's grandiose (but ultimately brittle) sense of self. Information about a political leader's interpersonal relationships is important[5] and is available to some degree. However, information about Goldwater's friendships, work relationships with peers and subordinates, and more intimate relations was not sought out or made part of the public record at that time and was never mentioned in the course of the diagnostic discussions appearing in the article.

The failure to explore characteristics that have achieved some clinical consensus for purposes of diagnosis underscores another, more difficult issue inherent in the psychiatric assessment of political leaders, namely, the complex nature of diagnostic entities themselves. A first problem, familiar in medicine, is that many diagnostic facts are compatible with more than one diagnostic category. For example, a cough can be part of diverse disease syndromes, signifying a cold or a lung tumor.

In psychiatric assessment, the same flexibility of a symptom's meaning is evident. So, for example, paranoid trends in the personality do not necessarily signal the presence of a paranoid character. The latter may or may not be accompanied by a flight of ideas, interior logic (meanings and connections that are not generally shared), or nonsequential reasoning, all of which may indicate a major thought disturbance.

Going one step further, clinical entities can frequently present a mixed symptom picture. It is for this reason that the third edition of the *Diagnostic and Statistic Manual of Mental Disorders (DSM-III)* cautions: "Many individuals exhibit features that are not limited to a single Personality Disorder. . . . There is great variability" (APA 1980, 306–7). A further reflection of this fact is that the *DSM-III* contains the category "Mixed Personality Disorder," which is used when "the individual has a Personality Disorder that involves features from several of the specific Personality Disorders, but does not meet the criteria for any one Personality Disorder" (APA 1980, 330). It may even be the case that, as with the borderline diagnostic category, "no single feature is invariably present" (APA 1980, 321).

Diagnostic complexity would appear then to be a second major source of variability, which, when coupled with the paucity of relevant diagnostic data, would seem to go some distance in explaining the poor overall performance of the *FACT* survey's psychiatric evaluators.[6] The operation of these factors raises serious questions about the level of adequacy possible in making even objective and informed evaluations of candidates for high public office. But there is another important consideration here: that the evaluations were made *during* a presidential campaign.

The Politics of Diagnosis

Ordinarily, politics is very far removed from the psychotherapeutic context. It would not be extraordinary for someone to be in treatment for an extended period of time and not discuss his political beliefs, values, or relations to political events. In part, this has to do with the remoteness of politics to everyday concerns for many people. But even if some political subjects were brought up, it is not likely that they would receive more than passing attention. From the standpoint of psychoanalytic psychotherapy, the major focus is on the treatment of intrapsychic and interpersonal difficulties, not the discussion of political or social events.[7]

The entry of psychiatrists and psychiatric theory into the political arena fundamentally alters the relationship between the two. What is peripheral in the traditional relationship becomes central in the new one, and as a result, analytic processes (observation, formulation, intervention, and evaluation) are changed and, in some ways, transformed.[8] Not surprisingly, under these circumstances psychiatric and political evaluations frequently merge.

In 1964, Goldwater was perceived as a hard-liner in foreign affairs and a very right-of-center social conservative in domestic policy. In reviewing the political preferences of psychiatrists (the very group that had evaluated Goldwater) and other mental health professionals, Rogow notes that "they are strong supporters of peace, integration and the welfare state" and concludes that it was "inevitable that Goldwater . . . would be disliked by a number of psychiatrists, some of whom were not hesitant to translate their dislike into the language of the consulting room" (1970, 129).

Evidence of this position is not difficult to obtain. A number of the responding psychiatrists linked psychiatric and political assessments. One psychiatrist, for example, assessed the senator as having a "brittle, rigid personality structure . . . capable of either shattering like a crystal glass or bolstering itself by the assumption of a paranoid stance of more power over others" (Boroson 1964, 24). The very next sentence links this assessment with Goldwater's conservative philosophy: "In his book *The Conscience of a Conservative,* his position is one of anachronistic authoritarianism, using the Constitution in a litigious way. . . . He seems unaware that modern nationwide transportation and communication have increased identification of the population with the nation as a whole—rather than the states."

Another respondent explicitly linked Goldwater's rejection of a major federal government role in domestic policy to the candidate's sense of inferiority, stating that "Goldwater's insecurity and feelings of inadequacy cause him to reject all changes and to resent what he considers to be excessive power by the Federal government. His rejection, may in fact, reflect a threat by a father-image, namely someone [the federal government] who is stronger than he, more masculine and more cultured" (Boroson 1964, 30).

Finally, one responding psychiatrist notes Goldwater's "paranoid and omnipotent tendencies" (Boroson 1964, 26) and then goes on to say that electing Goldwater would "represent a reversal of our progressive politics and our optimistic openhandedness which has made our country the hope and the leader of all new nations and oppressed groups," a reversal that the respondent is clearly against.

These quotes support Rogow's argument about the link between left-of-center political philosophies and the evaluations of Goldwater's psychiatric unsuitability for the presidency. The problem with this analysis is it omits the fact that the linkage between political philosophy and psychiatric evaluations took place at both ends of the political spectrum.

Among the respondents who considered Goldwater psychologically fit to become president, almost a dozen linked psychiatric health with conservative politics. For example, one respondent wrote, "In my opinion Senator Goldwater is a highly-motivated patriotic American. I feel he is a mature, emotionally stable individual who is eminently qualified to hold the office of President . . . and to lead the fight against socialism and the forces of the far left, which seem so strongly entrenched in our present government" (Boroson 1964, 63). Another respondent presents us with a mixed political and psychiatric syllogism of curious logic (1964, 42): "We have long needed the opportunity for the public to choose between conservatism and modern socialism. Barry Goldwater's candidacy offers this choice. He is a sane man."

Finally, another respondent presents a political/psychiatric mélange (Boroson 1964, 33): "Goldwater is less temperamental, less vindictive, more pro-freedom, and pro-integration than Johnson ever was or could be. Can pro-Americanism, anti-communism and pro-individual freedom and initiative really be as terrible as the communication media would have us believe? Yes, I believe that Barry Goldwater is psychologically fit to serve as President."

It is clear from examples on both sides of the political spectrum that clinical and political analysis became fused for both groups. Obviously, the fusion cannot simply be a matter of the left-of-political-center proclivities of psychiatrists as a group, or even of this particular set of respondents. We must search elsewhere for an underlying explanation.

The answer lies, I believe, in the emotional pull of political campaigns, especially those for high office, in which clear and somewhat dramatic differences appear to separate the candidates. The concept of emotional pull, or in more clinical terms, *transference* and *countertransference,* is not a novel idea in psychoanalytic theory. Practitioners have long been aware that patients can trigger certain psychological responses in them, and the question then becomes how much of the analyst's response is a function of what the patient induced and how much owes more to the analyst's personal history than to anything the patient triggered (Kernberg 1975; Grey and Fiscalini 1987).

There can be little doubt that Goldwater and the questions about him raised strong feelings on the part of the respondents. Responding to the questionnaire itself was an indication of intense feelings, not only in the minimal sense of taking the time to do it but in the more important sense of violating a consensual professional norm. One does not ordinarily make professional psychiatric assessments of strangers, even if they are public figures.

Furthermore, the tone and substance of many comments clearly indicate that Senator Goldwater had aroused strong feelings among the respondents. In a clinical setting, when being with a patient results in strong feelings it is natural for an experienced analyst to consider the issues of countertransference. Here, among those who responded, this consideration clearly did not arise.

The Goldwater questionnaire raises serious questions about the capacity of psychological assessments of political leaders to be fair and objective when undertaken during a strongly contested political campaign. At a minimum, I would argue that there should be an expectation and presumption that "neutrality" and "objectivity" are not a routine matter in these circumstances. More specifically, persons attempting these kinds of assessments must be particularly aware of their own reactions to the candidate and to characteristics that they favor or dislike. This would hold true for persons on both ends of the ideological continuum.

Finally, this particular case suggests something about the timing of such assessments in presidential and other political campaigns. From the standpoint of intensity of affect and the issue of countertransference, clearly the worst time to make such assessments is during the final stage of the campaign process. It is then that the emotional currents are most intense because the field has been pared, the issues have been defined, and the actual decision and its consequences are imminent. It would be more prudent to carry out psychological assessments before, rather than during, political campaigns.

Some Perspectives on the Issue of Psychological Suitability and Presidential Performance

The method and results of this survey have illuminated a number of problems that can arise in assessing the psychological functioning of persons aspiring to the presidency, but there is a further set of questions that can be asked, with some profit, of this material. The survey, in spite of its numerous faults, is the only available published survey of psychiatrists speaking directly to the issue of psychological suitability for leadership roles. As such, it may offer useful observations on this issue,[9] even if its specific assessments of Senator Goldwater are problematic.

Two immediate caveats should be kept in mind. Psychiatry is a profession of medical doctors who, for the most part, view their task as the diagnosis and treatment of *mental illness*. There is a danger, therefore, that their observations may be weighted in the direction of pathology. Moreover, it remains an open question whether adequate psychological functioning is best conceptualized solely, or even primarily, as the absence of impairment or conflict.

It should also be understood that although the observations of this sample of psychiatrists as experts in intrapsychic and interpersonal processes are reported and discussed, no assumption is made that such expertise or persons have a preeminent role in defining and answering questions of psychological suitability and presidential performance.[10] Moreover, the concept of psychological suitability covers a broader range of issues than the traditional concern with the mental health of presidential candidates or presidents.

The distinction between a "mental health" definition of psychological suitability and one based on more extended psychological criteria is captured by a respondent in the survey (Boroson 1964, 36–37) who noted that Goldwater "is immature and too impulsive to properly handle the important office of the President. . . . Nevertheless, he is of sound mind and in full possession of his faculties." This respondent, having clearly drawn such a distinction, goes on to say that because he is in "full possession of his faculties," he "therefore is psychologically fit to serve as President."

My own view differs. As I noted in the Introduction, I believe that psychological suitability reflects a relationship between performance tasks and a person's characteristics and capacities relevant to performing them. A person could well be "mentally healthy" but still have psychological characteristics that would cause difficulties (some serious) in the exercise of political power. The concept of psychological suitability therefore requires an understanding of psychological as well as political processes and the link between them.

The data we will examine in this section are much more oriented toward psychological than toward political processes. With few exceptions, respondents had little to say about the specific nature of presidential work and therefore made few explicit linkages between the two domains. Nevertheless, by extrapolating from their assessments we can at least make some preliminary comments about the relationships between the political and the psychological. For the purposes of this discussion, I group their remarks into four categories: character, temperament, cognition, and politics.

Character

The published survey results make clear that character and psychological suitability were linked, in the minds of psychiatrists at least, long before Gary Hart became a household name. However, from the excerpts of responses that follow we can discern signs of several difficulties: (1) in conceptualizing character, (2) in clearly specifying the relationship between the observed behavior and a model of character functioning, (3) in considering alternative explanations of the behavior that served as evidence of a character deficit, and (4) in specifying the concrete political implications of a particular character element.

In keeping with the survey's emphasis on psychopathology, many of the respondents discussed the linkage between character and leadership solely in terms of "character defects." Typical was a respondent who considered Goldwater's characterization of Lyndon Johnson as a "phony" and his later willingness to meet with Johnson personally to be an indication of such a defect (Boroson 1964, 30). The observer seems to equate a lack of consistency in this one instance with a lack of integrity.

One problem here is that even if the behavior described is accurate, it is not clear whether it is a single, discrete behavior or part of a pattern. This is a major problem in using a single item or event to show a particular character structure or style. From a single item, one can never be certain whether one is observing a random element, a part of a trend, or a part of a pattern. Only other, similar (or dissimilar) data points can help resolve this issue.

There is also the problem of alternative explanations for a behavior. Goldwater's willingness to meet with Johnson might be attributed to a lack of either consistency or integrity (it is not clear that the two are always synonymous, since one can be inconsistent without necessarily lacking integrity); however, it is also possible that the meeting represents an adherence to a political norm (one doesn't refuse to meet with an opponent, even an opponent one personally dislikes, in the context of a presidential campaign). Or it might reflect a capacity to forgive. In retrospect, given Lyndon Johnson's duplicitous behavior once elected, one is moved to question whether Goldwater's characterization of Johnson doesn't reflect a good sense of his opponent rather than a character flaw.

My point here is that a single item of data by itself is rarely definitive and may well be misleading. That is why analysts speak repeatedly of searching for patterns. It is a point that needs to be kept in mind when analyzing character issues.

Another problem in this area arises from the substitution of character labels for substantive analysis. One respondent, for example, diagnosed a "narcissistic character disorder" partially on the basis of Goldwater's inability to "dissociate himself from . . . extremists" (Boroson 1964, 24, 26). Another characterized the senator as "authoritarian, megalomaniac, grandiose, basically narcissistic . . . (and like Senator Joseph McCarthy) a slowing decompensating paranoid schizophrenic" (1964, 41).

The use of clinical terms can convey useful information. However, they cannot be a substitute for making explicit the logic of linking particular behaviors to particular character syndromes, on the one hand, and to the political performance implications of character elements, on the other. In other words, to characterize someone as "narcissistic" means that they are overly self-interested. However, not all self-interested behavior qualifies as narcissistic. In addition, the term *narcissistic character disorder* carries with it a range of specific manifestations that can only with the greatest difficulty be stretched to include the failure to disassociate oneself from "extremists" (a word I put in quotes because it is unclear who the author has in mind and why he places them in that category).

In short, clinical labels are no substitute for clinical diagnosis and analysis.

Temperament

The concept of temperament has not been widely used in the study of political psychology. One reason is that it represents a partially biologically based variable in a field whose major developmental paradigm to date has focused on socialized or learned behavior. Nor has temperament been widely used in the analysis of political leaders, although other biologically based variables, such as energy levels, have been noted by scholars (Hermann 1986) and by leaders themselves as having an important impact on performance.

A useful starting point for a definition is Allport's early (1937, 54) view of temperament as "the characteristic phenomena of an individual's emotional nature, including his susceptibility to emotional stimulation, his customary strength and speed of response, [and] the quality of his prevailing mood, and all peculiarities of fluctuation and intensity in mood." Allport viewed temperament as "dependent upon constitutional make-up and therefore largely hereditary in origin." This is not central to our concerns here. One could take the position that temperament is constitutionally based without subscribing to the view that it is unconnected to other, more psychological variables (for example, character) or impervious to cultural, social, and personal experience. Temperament is a psychological as well as a biological variable.

This is also the view of Shapiro (1965), who makes clear that cognitive style is deeply embedded in character structure as well as in the world of behavior. He notes, for example, that impulsive action is characterized by a relatively short period between thought and action, is abrupt and discontinuous in relation to normal activity, and is unplanned. The nature of these actions reflects a short-circuiting of the process by which whims are usually translated into action.

In nonimpulsive persons, the whim is the beginning of a complex process that involves the relation of the whim to longer-standing needs, goals, and values, which results in either its integration into these systems or a loss of interest in its attractiveness. It is this process of elaboration and integration of the whim into the structure of the person's interests, values, and so forth that gets short-circuited in the impulsive style. For this reason, impulsive behavior reflects not only faulty judgment (a comment on the adequacy of cognitive processes and evaluation functions) but also a lack of a stable system of motivation structures.

One useful political application of the term *temperament* is found in the concept *judicial temperament*. This phrase links a particular set of psychological characteristics with at least an implicit theory of the requirements for adequate performance within a particular role. That concept is used both by judicial screening committees to select new judges and by oversight committees who function to evaluate and monitor judicial conduct on the bench.

The concept's use in both instances is connected to demeanor as well as to comportment. A judge, for example, may have strong feelings about a matter, but yelling at participating parties is considered inappropriate. The concept goes beyond a concern with appearance, however. An essential dimension of due process is a hearing before a fair and impartial judge, but a judge's decisions are made in a highly contentious atmosphere where either side may, as part of its strategy or simply through frustration, provoke a decision that either favors its client or may become the basis of reversible error. The ability to withstand such pressures, indeed, to remain calm and focused in a context of high emotion and important stakes, speaks directly to the kinds of concerns raised by Allport's definition and our concerns here.

In the context of the assessment of Barry Goldwater, a number of respondents mentioned a concern with what they saw as the senator's impulsiveness. One respondent noted the candidate's "outbursts" and, because of them, did not think the candidate was "sufficiently stable to serve as President" (Boroson 1964, 30), a clear "mental health" linkage. Another respondent, however, while also noting that the candidate was "too impulsive to properly handle the important office of President," nonetheless concluded that the candidate was "of sound mind and in possession of all his faculties and therefore is psychologically fit to serve as President" (1964, 36). For this respondent, psychological fitness is more narrowly viewed, in somewhat clinically vague terms (e.g., "sound mind," "in possession of all his faculties"), even though being impulsive is deemed sufficient in the first sentence to disqualify the candidate from holding the office.

Others were willing to make direct links between impulsive behavior, the nature of the presidency, and the issue of psychological suitability. One respondent noted Goldwater's "wildly inconsistent statements on vital issues, [and] impulsive outbursts" (Boroson 1964, 28). These were both linked with a concern for the candidate's "mental stability," which in turn was directly related to a concern that he might initiate a nuclear war. Another respondent worried that "likelihood of his being impulsive would create a constant state of tension and apprehension" (1964, 39). In this psychiatrist's view, the rise in public tension is an issue somewhat separate from the concern with nuclear war, and the assessment recalls Lasswell's (1930, 197) early suggestion that one function of political leadership was the management of public tensions.

Summing up both sets of political implications of being impulsive, a distinguished clinician and researcher is quoted as saying:

I know nothing about Senator Goldwater except his public utterances, but their often ill-considered, impulsive quality is, in my mind, sufficient to disqualify him from the presidency. . . . The President is the world's most powerful leader and his lightest words are carefully weighed everywhere. Rash threats, even if subsequently modified or retracted, made by a President would greatly heighten anxiety among both friends and foes, thereby increasing the probability of errors of judgment and rash acts that could start a nuclear holocaust. (Boroson 1964, 31)

Cognition

The analysis of cognition involves at least two distinct sets of phenomena. One focuses on content, the other on process. The first would involve candidate assessment, leading to an examination of the candidate's political philosophy, beliefs, and policy stands. The second leads to questions concerning how the leader perceives, frames, and processes information.

The analysis of cognitive processes is an important element of psychological suitability. There are several ways to conceptualize cognitive processes. Recent research in this area has examined cognitive complexity (Tetlock 1984), the frames or schemata used to store information (Fiske and Linville 1980), and the decision rules, or heuristics, used in making judgments (Tversky and Kahneman 1981). All of these dimensions are elements of cognitive style.

Perceiving, framing, and processing information are not affective or neutral activities. These cognitive activities also have their own developmental history. Cognitive style therefore is not simply a matter of perceptual whim. On the contrary, like temperament, it is embedded in a complex set of psychological structures and processes.

One can conceptually distinguish perceiving from the processes through which perception proceeds. One can, for example, distinguish persons who tend to pay more attention to detail from those who tend to organize perceptions into wholes. Early research on "differentiation" (Witkin 1940) empirically distinguished those who were more likely to respond to the external stimulus properties of an object (field dependent) from those who did not (field independent). Or one can examine the nature, number, complexity, and interrelatedness of cognitive elements. Finally, one can examine the steps that are taken in reaching judgments.

Almost all the comments in the *FACT* survey in this area were focused on the issue of cognitive complexity. A large number of comments emphasized what was perceived as the tendency of the candidate toward "black or white thinking."[11] A typical comment noted that the candidate "seemed to need a single black or white answer" and further observed the tendency to "portray people as either 'good' or 'bad' [which] makes for . . . poor government" (Boroson 1964, 27). Another respondent noted that "everything [has] to fall on one side or the other of the unwavering line dividing black from white, right from wrong, good from evil" (1964, 35).

A clear implication of such criticisms is that more cognitive complexity leads to better political decisions, and while there is no research to directly support or refute this contention, it is worth examining more closely. The logic of such an argument is that solving complex problems requires complex understandings. Complex problems are not solved by simple solutions or the thinking that generates them. This formulation has intuitive appeal. However, that appeal is in some respects deceptive.

The actual number of elements in a belief system is one, but not the only, aspect of complexity. Numbers of elements alone do not guarantee conceptual sophistication or adequacy. Cognition can be complicated without necessarily being competent. Obsessive persons, for example, often have very complicated cognition, as do those with paranoid trends in their personalities. Moreover, not only do both types have large numbers of elements but the elements are integrated, another "positive" sign for some decision analysts. Yet I don't think that one would wish to conclude that such persons necessarily represent high-quality decision making. This is one reason why I have suggested we focus on judgment.

There is a further problem with emphasizing cognitive complexity as a crucial aspect of psychological suitability, namely, that high-quality decisions in a democracy have a political as well as a policy dimension. Considered solely on its merits, an effective policy solution may not be politically adequate, possible, or even desirable. We could, for example, end poverty quickly by legislating a government-advanced earned income tax credit that would guarantee every person a minimum income of $25,000 per year and be financed by strict progressive taxation.

High-quality presidential decision making is a matter of feasibility (George 1980) as well as technical virtue or cognitive complexity. The best decision may turn out to be one that combines policy requirements and legitimate political considerations, rather than relying on one or the other. There are also links between leadership, decision making, and the public's response to both. President Carter was, by many accounts, a complex policy thinker but was unable to translate this sophistication into public understanding and political support (Buchanan 1987). Ronald Reagan, by contrast, whom few have characterized as a complex or deep policy thinker, was able to generate wide public support and accomplish much of his policy agenda.

Decisions not only solve policy problems but affect the public's sense of how things are going. This is not solely a matter of the technical adequacy of the decision or the degree of complexity that went into making it. The public is often moved by how they see decisions being made as well as by the content of decisions. Leaders who project a sense of confidence, capacity, and conviction may well offer adequate or even only plausible policy solutions successfully.

Politics

It should be clear from our examination of character, temperament, and cognition, as well as our discussion of diagnosis, that political criteria are an important dimension of the views expressed in the *FACT* sample regarding psychological suitability. The clearest linkage relates a leader being impulsive with a potentially damaging impact in international tensions, possibly leading to the inadvertent outbreak of war.

What is interesting about this linkage is that it explicitly substitutes a political for a psychological criterion. Impulsiveness calls into question suitability not because it is by itself pathological (i.e., a necessary indicator of "mental illness") but rather because of its political consequences. Interestingly, political criteria were not limited to concerns about the inadvertent outbreak of war.

One respondent wrote that the candidate "appealed to the unconscious sadism and hostility in the average human being [and] to all the delinquent tendencies in the citizens of the United States: bigotry, hatred, etc." and went on to compare Goldwater to Hitler (Boroson 1964, 28). Another respondent wrote that "he appeals to the *worst* of our people" (1964, 29), while yet another pointed out that "history is filled with unstable leaders . . . who for a time are able to mobilize the primitive hate and destruction that resides in some form in all human beings" (1964, 39). Finally, one respondent made the most explicit linkage between psychological suitability and the (perceived) impact of the candidate on public sentiment in noting, "I do not believe that Barry Goldwater is psychologically fit to serve as President of the United States because, wittingly or unwittingly, he tends to bring out the latent paranoid tendencies which exist in a rather large percentage of the population" (1964, 49).

The attempt to judge the relationship between a candidate and the kinds of appeals being made to the public is not a trivial concern. George Bush's campaign use of Willy Horton was widely criticized as appealing to racial fears and antagonisms. And we can see from the most extreme examples (e.g., Hitler's Germany, Khomeini's Iran) that leaders can allow and even encourage the expression of rage and aggression against socially sanctioned targets. A leader who condemns "welfare cheats," "pointy-headed liberals," or "right-wingers" (three terms in frequent use over the past few decades) invites their membership in an out-group for whom the ordinary courtesies of democratic process may not need to be applied.

What, then, is one to make of the candidacy of Ronald Reagan, who was strongly supported by right-of-center political groups? One may gain some appreciation of the difficulties of applying this criterion by asking whether Reagan should not have been allowed to run in 1980 and 1984 because he was supported by strongly ideological right-of-center groups. We easily (and correctly) reject such an idea as antithetical to democratic principles. Therefore, while the concern expressed regarding the nature of a candidate's appeals is legitimate, it would appear that the means are not at hand to use this criterion to make the judgments necessary regarding psychological suitability.

In short, while political criteria for psychological suitability may be important, it is not likely that the particular ones expressed by respondents in this survey will be very helpful. I suggest others in chapter 8.

Conclusion

The *FACT* survey and its analysis may perhaps be most usefully viewed as a cautionary case study. Certainly, the survey's usefulness does not stem from its scientific validity as a survey of psychiatric views of the candidate. Nonetheless, in an age of increasing attempts to assess the psychological suitability of candidates, it does serve to underscore some important points.

For one thing, diagnosis itself is a very complicated process. This is even more the case when the terms used are transplanted from the clinical into the political arena. The problems of transferring models from one context to another include the lack of ongoing personal contact with the person under assessment, the difficulty of making consensually validated diagnoses, the tendency to make "deep" developmental interpretations with insufficient data, and the contamination of diagnostic assessments by political ideologies.

However, the survey, despite its lack of scientific validity, does help shed some light on the question of psychological suitability. It is of interest that character emerged as an important dimension of analysis in this survey long before character issues became important. A concern with character is not the same as having a politically relevant theory of character functioning, but its presence nonetheless gives support to those who believe it to be important.

Temperament also emerged as a potentially important consideration. It has not yet received sufficient attention in analyses of presidential leadership or psychological suitability, and it merits more.

Cognitive functioning likewise emerged as a potentially useful variable in assessing psychological suitability. However, defining suitability in terms of complexity alone would appear problematic. Linking the importance of cognitive processes to issues of suitability will require theorists to cast a wider intellectual net. As an example, one will have to ask whether certain kinds of information-processing routines are more or less suited for presidential and other top leadership roles. To date, no single cognitive style has emerged as superior for political decision making, although more or less adequate decision making routines have been identified (Janis 1989; George 1980).

In each of the areas of psychological functioning examined, another point clearly emerges. The psychological domains of character, cognition, and temperament are not independent of one another. Rather, they are connected in ways that need to be analyzed if any useful conceptualization of psychological suitability is to be developed. It follows that there is a need for *composite* conceptualizations of psychological suitability. That is, no single psychological factor (character, temperament, cognition, etc.) is likely, except in extreme circumstances, to be causally definitive.

Moreover, even the complex composite formulation of suitability will need to be directly linked with political performance criteria. Psychology alone is not enough. Psychological suitability must ultimately be considered in conjunction with political suitability, not as a substitute for it.

S I X

Psychological Health in the 1972 Presidential Election: The Case of Thomas F. Eagleton

In 1972, the Democratic Party nominated as its vice presidential candidate Thomas F. Eagleton, then the junior U.S. senator from Missouri. Shortly after his nomination, the public learned that Senator Eagleton had been hospitalized three times, twice for lengthy periods, for depression. Furthermore, the media revealed that on several occasions during these hospitalizations he had been given shock treatments. In the face of mounting public and professional opposition, Eagleton was forced to give up his candidacy.

In the 1988 presidential campaign, rumors were spread by an extremist group that the Democratic Party presidential nominee, Michael Dukakis, had been treated by a psychiatrist for depression.[1] Most commentary noted that seeking professional psychological help was, for a political leader, the "kiss of death" (*New York Times*, 9 August 1988, A23). In an editorial on the subject, the *New York Times* declared that "it would have been no disgrace if he [Dukakis] had sought psychiatric help—as it is for the millions of Americans who have done so" and closed by noting, "It's time at last to break the psychological barrier" (5 August 1988, A24).

A number of commentators compared the Dukakis case to the Eagleton case. Observers noted that both Dukakis and Eagleton had questions raised about their psychological suitability for the presidency because of allegations that they had suffered from depression and had received professional psychological treatment. They further noted that Dukakis could hardly be blamed for being sensitive to the issue, since "it had been only sixteen years ago, after all, that the revelation that Senator Thomas Eagleton of Missouri had undergone electroshock therapy for depression had cost him the Vice-Presidential spot on the Democratic ticket. It is not at all clear just how mature the American electorate has become on this issue" (*New York Times,* 5 August 1988, A24).

The clear implication of this statement is that depression should not necessarily be a barrier to high elective office and that had the American public been more "mature," Eagleton would not have been forced off the Democratic ticket. This was not an idiosyncratic position. One reporter noted that we should "consider what has happened to other aspirants for high office who have submitted to the politically deadly, if often emotionally healing 'kiss' of therapeutic help. The most vivid instance was of course, when reporters . . . uncovered evidence of . . . Thomas Eagleton's hospitalizations for depression . . . it drove a final nail into the coffin for his quest for high office" (*New York Times,* 8 August 1988, A23).

The author of this news analysis went on to lament the fact that the public and press often persecute candidates who seek psychiatric help and expressed the wish that "news organizations would do much more to put such stories into context than they did in 1972 (with Eagleton) or today." Here again, the implication is that a more balanced account of Eagleton's treatment for depression might have resulted in his not being forced off the ticket.

The Eagleton case is the first publicly documented and acknowledged case of a candidate for the highest level of public office having been diagnosed and treated for "mental illness." As such, it allows us to analyze some aspects of the concerns about the psychological health of a top-level official who might well become president or aspire to. More specifically, the Eagleton case provides an important opportunity to explore at least five major issues regarding psychological suitability as defined in terms of psychological health.

The first is the problem of "composite characteristics." Thomas Eagleton had served as a senator for many years before his nomination (and resignation) as vice presidential candidate and did so again for many years afterward. Was it fair to be concerned about his emotional stability when, according to some, he had already demonstrated his abilities in the office of U.S. senator without incident? How was it possible for someone to serve so well and be psychologically unsuitable? Can one be politically able and psychologically unsuitable?

A second issue has to do with the diagnosis itself. Eagleton has been diagnosed as suffering from depression. Was the medical diagnosis the real problem, or was the actual problem more political? Eagleton's diagnosis of depression raises the issue of whether a presidential candidate (or president) can have episodes of depression or other psychological difficulties and still be perceived as an adequate, even an effective president.

A third important issue that arises in connection with the Eagleton case is the debate on whether structural barriers are sufficient to keep those with substantial (and relevant) impairments out of high-level public office. Lasswell (1964) argued that structural barriers were sufficient to keep such individuals out of high public office. Others, such as Albert Deutsch in an address to the American Psychiatric Association (quoted in Rogow 1963, 44), were less sanguine.

On its face, the uncovering of Eagleton's history of depression and his forced departure from the Democratic ticket can be viewed as supporting the structural barriers argument. Leaving aside the question of whether Eagleton should have been forced off the ticket because of his previous psychiatric treatment, proponents of the structural barriers argument can take comfort that the system apparently worked. However, a close analysis of the presidential campaign of 1972 presents serious challenges to that view.

Fourth, the Eagleton case allows us to examine more closely the argument over whether some forms of psychological peculiarities are not only a requirement of high political office (e.g., intense ambition) but a help. As noted in chapter 4, some have suggested that great political leaders are not "normal." Others have gone so far as to suggest that some degree of abnormality may be a prerequisite for "greatness."

Last, we can examine the Eagleton case with a view toward understanding the process that led to Eagleton's selection. Why did that process fail to uncover such damaging and important information? How did this information emerge? What if anything did the information about Eagleton suggest regarding the issue of psychological suitability for the presidency?

The Structural Barriers Argument

The psychotic-leader case envisions a person seeking or achieving political power who displays signs of severe emotional disturbance. Leaving aside the historical data compiled by Noland (1966), there are contemporary examples of leaders who, though evidencing clear signs of psychological impairment, have obtained political power. For example, Joseph Stalin clearly exhibited paranoid belief systems, although one has to ask whether such beliefs were not functional and, to some degree, based in the reality of the political system in which Stalin came to power and that he so dramatically helped to mold. Adolf Hitler is another frequently cited example of a severely disturbed leader (he is diagnosed as either psychotic or borderline; see Waite 1977).

Critics of concerns over the possibility of a psychotic-leader scenario, while not denying that such cases have occurred elsewhere, argue essentially that it is unlikely to happen in the United States, for structural reasons. Harold Lasswell (1964, 223) argued that severely disturbed candidates for political leadership roles are likely to be shunted to the margins of social and political power because they lack the skills successfully to negotiate the nomination process in our political culture. Robins (1977b, 53) agrees and argues that "pathological deviants tend to be recruited outside of normal institutional patterns" and that, for the most part, "political systems operate well to screen or select out deviants." Finally, Willard Gaylin (1973, 57), in questioning the need for or usefulness of formal psychological screening of those who aspire to political office, argues that such a mechanism would "obviously protect from having some deteriorated psychotic run for office. But this is not a likely possibility—serious schizophrenias commonly become apparent so early in life that they preclude the opportunity."

What these critics have in mind (and Gaylin is explicit on this point) is a particular form of psychological disturbance that manifests itself in gross impairments in secondary processes (those concerned with accurate assessment of external realities, developing coherent systems of thought and understanding, etc.). Persons suffering from this form of psychological impairment also generally fail to develop the capacities that underlie the traits of sociability which are frequently discussed as part of a leader's set of needed skills (Milbrath and Goel 1977). The schizophrenic's delusions, interior logic, and heavily symbolic and condensed thinking (Arieti 1974, chaps. 5, 16) all support the structural barriers argument to a large degree. The problem is that while "deteriorated psychotics" may be kept at the margins of power, schizophrenia is not necessarily the only, or even the most appropriate, cause for concern.

The structural barriers argument does not rely solely on the obvious intrapsychic and interpersonal deficiencies of individuals with severe disorders. In addition, there is an implicit, but nonetheless important, aspect of political structure and process invoked in this argument, namely, the "informal" assessments made over time by numerous people in the course of an individual's career. Discussions of severely disturbed persons reaching high office correctly assume that most high leadership positions are the culmination of a political career, not its beginning.

This point is important because it means that by the time a person has gathered enough of the necessary resources to try to obtain high office (money, staff, etc.), he will have dealt with numerous peers and colleagues, potential supporters, members of the press, and critics. The potential leader will most frequently have already held some position of power and will therefore have left behind a record of performance. Let us now consider how these barriers worked or failed to work in the case of Eagleton.

The Context of Eagleton's Selection

Many of the events surrounding the selection of Eagleton as the Democratic Party's vice presidential nominee are still a matter of contention. The principals and their staffs do not agree on many of the crucial events that led up to the crisis or on what happened afterward. Even so basic an issue as the effect of the disclosures of Eagleton's hospitalizations on the McGovern campaign are a matter of dispute. It will be recalled that the McGovern team lost to the Republican Party ticket, headed by Richard M. Nixon, by an overwhelming margin. McGovern (1977, 191), breaking his silence on these events five years after they occurred, believed they destroyed his candidacy:

> The Eagleton affair destroyed any chance I had of being elected President in 1972. Perhaps neither I nor any other Democratic candidate could have defeated Nixon in 1972, but the heretofore publicly concealed mental illness of Eagleton, my handling of the problem, and the press reaction combined to give Nixon not only his expected victory, but a landslide.

Eagleton, by contrast, in a postelection interview, described his troubles during the campaign and their effect as "no more than one rock in a landslide" (quoted in McGovern 1977, 216). Fortunately, the main outlines of what occurred are documented,[2] and our purpose in any event is not to reconstruct exact historical truth regarding private conversations about which the participants disagree but rather to assess these events from the perspective of issues of psychological suitability.

As background to these events, some brief historical information may be useful. In 1968, President Lyndon Johnson announced that he would not seek reelection. His decision reflected an assessment of the intense opposition that his Vietnam policy and his handling of questions concerning it had generated. In 1968, Johnson's vice president, Hubert Humphrey, ran against the Republican presidential candidate, Richard M. Nixon, and lost.

The year 1972, therefore, found the Democratic Party facing an incumbent president with many aspiring candidates but no clear standard-bearer. Among those contending for the nomination were Rubin Askew, George McGovern, Hubert Humphrey, John Lindsay, and George Wallace. Although Edmund Muskie, a senator from Maine, was considered by some to be a front-runner very early in the campaign, his candidacy faltered badly before the first primary was held in New Hampshire. The incident that caused his candidacy to falter is worth recounting briefly, given our concerns in this analysis.

William Loab, publisher of the *Manchester Union Leader,* a conservative New Hampshire newspaper, printed a series of personal attacks on Muskie's wife, Jane, in late February and followed these with the publication of a spurious letter signed with her name. Muskie flew to Manchester and, at a rally outside the newspaper's offices, made an emotional speech defending his wife and attacking the publisher for having printed such scurrilous attacks. According to Muskie, he was "choked over his anger" at the attack. The televised news coverage of that event showed Muskie standing on top of a flatbed truck delivering his speech, evidently in emotional distress, appearing to be in tears. Thereafter Muskie's support evaporated, and his candidacy was effectively ended. Of this incident Muskie later said, "It changed peoples' minds about me, of what kind of guy I was. . . . They were looking for a strong steady man, and here I was weak" (quoted in White 1973, 105–6).

After this incident, the remaining contenders split the primary votes in so many ways that no single candidate established a clear numerical edge or succeeded to string together enough primary victories. This indecisive pattern continued until George McGovern's "insurgent" campaign began to take hold. White (1973, 125) characterized McGovern's campaign as "a national mobilization of irregulars—a masterpiece of partisan warfare . . . [that] would go down as a classic in American political history."

These "irregulars" were students, blacks, women, and other nonmembers of the traditional party power structure. Aided by changes in the party rules governing the nomination process and building on discontent with "politics as usual," these activists put together a series of dramatic wins, first in Wisconsin and then in Massachusetts and Nebraska. McGovern then carried California on June 6 (with its winner-take-all rules for electing delegates to the nominating convention) and won in New York on June

20. McGovern now had almost, but not quite, enough committed delegates to win the nomination.

What followed was a complex and tricky set of maneuvers by party regulars, revolving around challenges to certain nominating rules, intended to deny the nomination to McGovern. The party's committee on platforms, rules, and credentials met in Washington soon after McGovern's win in New York and was to forward its decision to the party just ten days before the start of the convention. At those meetings, party regulars joined together in a last-minute attempt to deprive McGovern of the nomination by challenging the party's winner-take-all rules for the California primary.

McGovern suggests that this last-minute attack and the failure of party regulars to rally behind his candidacy placed him under the enormous time pressures that led directly to his own failure and that of his staff thoroughly to address the question of a suitable vice presidential running mate. According to McGovern (1977, 195):

> The history of 1972 might have been significantly different if Ed Muskie had endorsed me on June 9 [after the California primary]. That would have killed the possibility of the California challenge and ended the Democratic in-fighting. . . . Instead, the McGovern campaign was forced to devote the next thirty days to an exhausting effort to nail down the New York primary, convert uncommitted delegates, and keep the California delegates we had already won in that primary.

The Selection of Thomas Eagleton

McGovern's staff did not assemble to discuss vice presidential candidates until the morning of July 14. This was three days after the convention had started and the morning after the roll-call vote had finally given McGovern the nomination. A slightly different view of the time constraints McGovern was operating under is suggested by White's account and his observation that "in the first night of action, Monday [July 11], the proceedings had been quite clear. McGovern had won California, had eliminated Mayor Daley [and thus won the challenge made to the Illinois vote], the nomination was his for the asking" (1973, 238).

According to White's account, the nomination was fairly well settled by Tuesday, July 12, at which time both Hubert Humphrey and Edmund Muskie withdrew their names from consideration. Given this view, it might be asked what was being done by McGovern and his staff on that Tuesday and the following Wednesday. The answer appears to be that they spent those two days meeting and dealing with the various constituencies that had supported McGovern's campaign. Antiwar activists, homosexuals, women, and others presented their views and their demands publicly, and many of these same persons demanded and received access to the candidate and his staff.

One effect on McGovern of the energy and attention committed first to securing and then to holding the nomination, as well as to responding to and containing his own activist followers (who would, after all, be needed in the general campaign), was physical exhaustion and emotional fatigue. While physical and emotional fatigue were not the only reasons that Eagleton was selected, there is little doubt that they played an important role. By all accounts, it was an exhausted group that met Thursday morning to consider McGovern's vice presidential choices.

The fatigue and exhaustion brought on by having to deal with attempts to deny him lawfully won delegates form the central part of McGovern's view of why his vice presidential selection process faltered after getting such a late start. In fact, there is evidence that the problem had been given some attention prior to the convention. McGovern notes in his autobiography, "I had decided long before that if I won the nomination, I would press Ted Kennedy to be my running mate" (1977, 193). He also notes (1977, 195–96) that he and his campaign manager, Gary Hart, met in early July, shortly before the convention, to discuss possible candidates, although both were still preoccupied with the delegate challenges. McGovern also mentions that two of his aides wrote a long memorandum—which, McGovern writes, he never saw—to Gary Hart at the time of the California primary, during a systematic, serious consideration of possible running mates.

In addition, the wording of McGovern's autobiography (1977, 194) suggests that possible running mates were being considered with some seriousness before the nominating convention. He notes that Governor Rubin Askew sent an aide to his headquarters before the convention to say that Askew did not feel he could give up the governorship of Florida after having served only two years. This response would appear to be an answer to an offer. And McGovern writes that he was running into opposition to Leonard Woodcock (head of the United Auto Workers union) from some labor leaders, and that Senator Abe Ribicoff told him that under no circumstances would he accept the vice presidency because of his real love of the Senate. McGovern then notes that he didn't feel any concern about these developments because there were still many good alternatives available.

The weight of these data suggests that there was at least preliminary—and more likely, serious—consideration of vice presidential choices well before the Thursday morning that McGovern and his staff met to continue the selection process. It is also worth noting, in view of one of the assumptions of the structural barriers theory, the process that was used. Someone's name was raised and checks were made with various constituencies to gauge their reactions. The thrust of these inquiries seems to have been political acceptability and the potential of the person to add political strength to the party ticket, rather than concerns about the character and psychological suitability of the potential candidate for the second highest office in the nation.

One of the ironies here is that a campaign built on opposition to "politics as usual" and committed to real social change faltered because it used the time-tested practices of the groups it had fought against in the selection of its vice presidential candidate. The persons who were considered had all been active and successful in public life for many years. This was apparently assumed to be prima facie and sufficient evidence of their general suitability. Questions about psychological suitability appear never to have been raised.

Under the new party rules governing the convention, McGovern's vice presidential nominee was due by 4 p.m. on that Thursday afternoon. McGovern writes that he asked a small group of advisers to meet that morning and bring him a list of possible candidates. By his own account, then, after having experienced at least three declines of or other difficulties with his offers for the vice presidential spot before the convention (Askew, Ribicoff, and Woodcock), McGovern had left himself less than seven hours to find, check, and deliver to the convention his choice for this important position.

The list that was brought to him included Mayor Kevin White of Boston, Senator Walter Mondale, Senator Abe Ribicoff, Governor Pat Lucy, Sargent Shriver, Larry O'Brian, and Senator Thomas Eagleton. McGovern has characterized the submission of White and Eagleton as a surprise to him, but writes that he did include them while spending the next hour checking out the list "with a broad cross-section of Democratic leaders" and notes that "many of them gave the highest marks to Mondale, White and Eagleton" (1977, 197). McGovern does not mention exactly what he discussed with this cross-section of leaders or who, specifically, they were, but it seems clear that his point here is to underscore that none of the people he talked with raised any issue about Eagleton at the time. If this is accurate, and there is no indication to the contrary, it means that Eagleton's peers and colleagues were either unaware of his medical history or unconcerned by it. Neither is a particularly reassuring conclusion for proponents of the structural barriers argument.

McGovern writes that at about 1:30 P.M., he invited "a large group of colleagues to gather and decided to make the first offer to Mondale." Mondale declined the offer but, when asked for his opinion regarding the others, strongly endorsed Eagleton. McGovern apparently did not act on Mondale's recommendation at that time, instead calling Kevin White (the mayor of Boston) to ask about his interest in the position, from whom McGovern got a very positive reply. After telling White that he would get back to him after checking his name with others (one wonders why this was not done before the call), McGovern writes, he called Ted Kennedy, who apparently expressed some reservations regarding White. This prompted McGovern to ask Kennedy to reconsider his earlier (preconvention) refusal to consider the second spot. Kennedy promised to give the matter some thought and to get back to McGovern in half an hour, since there was by this time only an hour and a half until the 4 P.M. deadline.

Others who were present remember a somewhat more confused session. Frank Mankiewicz, a senior adviser to McGovern's campaign, is quoted (in White 1973, 258) as saying that when he arrived at the suite that afternoon, there were close to twenty-four people already there, with people popping in as the meeting progressed. White notes that at one point this group had some forty-five names under consideration. Ted Van Dyke, another key McGovern aide, is quoted by White (1973, 259) as later characterizing the discussions as "frivolous."

Perhaps this is a suitable place to pause and consider some aspects of the decision-making process as it has emerged from the information so far. To begin with, it seems clear that the McGovern campaign was forced to spend time and energy fighting for the nomination right up to the convention, although it appears that McGovern actually had the nomination nearly locked up after the California and Illinois challenges had been beaten back on Monday. If this is accurate, it means that McGovern's Thursday morning meeting to seriously consider vice presidential running mates could have taken place two days earlier than it did. This, in turn, would have alleviated the time pressures that contributed to the failure of the process to produce a good decision.

It also seems clear, from McGovern's own account, that he and his aides had begun the search well in advance of the convention but had failed to coordinate their efforts. This is suggested by the detailed memo, written by McGovern's aides to campaign manager Gary Hart, on the very subject of setting up a serious, systematic assessment of possible running mates, which was never acted upon.

When we turn to the decision-making group that actually did assemble Thursday morning, several aspects stand out. For one thing, the size of the group was extremely large. Research suggests that the optimum size of a decision-making group is in the area of ten to twelve persons (George 1980, 22–30). If the group is smaller, there is the danger that important positions will not be adequately represented or expressed. If the group is much larger, there may be too much information to process effectively. That the latter may well have happened is suggested by the information that at one point the group was struggling to assess forty-five people. Even if the number had been half that size, it still would have presented the group with a formidable task.

Another notable feature of the group, described by various participants, is its collective emotional state. McGovern and others mention the fatigue that everyone felt after the long campaign for the nomination, coupled with the need to deal with last-minute challenges to their victories in California and Illinois. Fatigue, of course, does not facilitate effective deliberation (Hermann 1979).

However, another factor not prominently mentioned by the participants but which must have played a role is that of euphoria. The group that assembled Thursday morning did so as winners of the nomination for the highest office in American politics. They had achieved a come-from-behind victory and had fought and beaten the party "regulars." It seems quite clear that the process resulted in some degree of exhaustion, but it is likely that it also resulted in some degree of exaltation. The likely result of exhaustion coupled with exaltation is a form of giddiness, which may help to account for the large number of names considered and the characterization of the process by one key aide as "frivolous."

A last set of not unrelated factors are those concerned with criteria. None of the persons assembled had established working relationships with most of the persons being considered. This meant that, in large part, the group decision process was dependent on the assessments of others. From the descriptions of the process, one after another possible running mate was brought up only to be knocked down — White because of Kennedy's reservations, Larry O'Brian because he would be seen as too partisan, and so forth.

In this regard, of course, the McGovern group process is probably indistinguishable from those that preceded it in other elections. However, this can give little comfort to those who believe there should be additional, not necessarily strictly political, criteria. It is not surprising that recent considerations for such positions have included more detailed questions concerning whether the potential candidate has any "skeletons in the closet," but this would appear to be another dimension of tapping potential political, not psychological, suitability. Given the time pressures on the McGovern group and the difficulty of finding a candidate acceptable to them, as well as influential to others, it is not surprising that the decision emphasis turned from political suitability to availability.

When, after all the other possibilities for running mates had fallen through for one reason or another, McGovern turned to his old Senate friend Gaylord Nelson, it took some time to reach Nelson in Washington, and the potential candidate once again reluctantly declined. But like Kennedy and Mondale, Nelson went on to recommend favorably Thomas Eagleton. With time and possibilities almost exhausted, McGovern placed the call to Eagleton's suite.

The Politics of Deception: Eagleton's Hidden Mental Health History

That call and its aftermath have continued to be surrounded by heated controversy. What is uncontested is that McGovern placed the call to Eagleton and asked him to be his running mate, and that Eagleton responded, "Before you change your mind, I . . . accept." McGovern then said he was turning Eagleton over to one of his chief aides, Frank Mankiewicz, to work out some of the details. What happened thereafter became a matter of bitter debate between the McGovern and Eagleton camps and may never be fully resolved.

According to Mankiewicz,[3] he began by breaking a few details to the press and then posed a series of very specific questions to Eagleton along the following lines: Is there anything in the past we ought to know? Is there anything that could damage or compromise the ticket? Do you have any booze, dame, or college escapades that we should know about? Didn't you once get disciplined in prep school for peeing on the parade grounds? Have you had any law partners or political associates who might be an embarrassment? After a few more questions of this type, Mankiewicz recalls ending with the question: Is there anything at all for which you consider yourself blameless but which could be misconstrued to damage the ticket? To this and all the previous questions, Mankiewicz says, Eagleton replied either "no" or "nothing at all."

Eagleton, in contrast, remembers only that Mankiewicz asked one question, "Do you have any old skeletons hanging around in your closet?" To this question, he replied no. Bob Hardy, a news director at CBS's station KMOX in St. Louis, was in Eagleton's suite at the time and turned on his tape recorder a second or two after Eagleton began talking with McGovern. His tape shows that the McGovern–Eagleton conversation lasted about thirty-two seconds before McGovern turned over the phone to Mankiewicz. The Eagleton–Mankiewicz segment on the tape runs for just twenty-nine seconds, seemingly not enough time for Mankiewicz to have asked all the questions he recalls having put to Eagleton. Still, whether Eagleton is more accurate than Mankiewicz in his recall of the conversation is somewhat beside the point, given subsequent events.

Mankiewicz regrets not having asked Eagleton directly about his health, but even if he had asked only the one question that Eagleton recalls, the meaning of the question and the concerns that lay behind it are hardly subject to misinterpretation. Yet in spite of Eagleton's direct denial that he had any skeletons in his closet, twelve days later he announced to a startled news conference that he had been hospitalized three times for "nervous exhaustion and fatigue." In response to reporters' questions after his statement, he revealed that he had "undergone psychological counseling and shock treatments on two of the three occasions" (*New York Times*, 26 July 1972, 1).

Before analyzing the exact nature of what Eagleton revealed regarding his medical history and its implications for questions of psychological suitability, there are other, prior questions that need to be addressed in view of the structural barriers argument that we have been discussing. Eagleton had been hospitalized three times during the course of a highly visible career in public service. His rise in politics was rapid and dramatic. He was circuit attorney in 1956 at the age of twenty-seven, state attorney general in 1960 at the age of thirty-one, lieutenant governor in 1964 at the age of thirty-five, and U.S. senator in 1967 at the age of thirty-eight. Yet the information about his medical history did not become public knowledge until Eagleton was selected as a vice presidential candidate, twelve years after his first hospitalization.

Given the hiatus between Eagleton's hospitalizations and their revelation during the 1972 campaign, a number of questions emerge: Did the system work? That is, are the proponents of the structural barriers argument proven correct by the fact that Eagleton's medical history was revealed? More concretely, there is the question surrounding the information itself: Was that information hidden from the public? George McGovern's view, as written in his autobiography (1977, 199), is that "Eagleton's history of mental illness and electric shock treatment was a chapter in his life carefully hidden from the people of Missouri. Even veteran political reporters knew nothing of it." However, at the time that the Eagleton story broke, veteran *New York Times* correspondent James M. Naughton filed a story captioned, "Eagleton Illness Known to Associates." That story (*New York Times,* 26 July 1972, 20) reported, "Members of Congress and Missouri politicians said that Mr. Eagleton's history of treatment for what the Senator described as nervous exhaustion was well known in political circles in his home state and among some associates on Capitol Hill." The story went on to quote one senior staff member to a U.S. senator as saying, "It was no secret at all that he had suffered nervous breakdowns."

Eagleton's wife, Barbara, took the same position in a published interview (1972, 155), noting that in discussions with her husband about this issue before the invitation to become the nominee, "the health matter did not loom large . . . because it was so long ago and it's not uncommon knowledge in St. Louis." If this is true, then it raises the question of why this information had not surfaced before in any of Eagleton's campaigns. Was it considered too personal? Was there some informal agreement among reporters and/or opponents that this was not the kind of thing you made an issue? The answers to these questions lie in a twisting tale of rumor, euphemism, wishful thinking, and outright deception.

There is some evidence[4] that rumors concerning some kind of health difficulty began to appear before that fateful two weeks after the nomination had been announced. Miller (1972, 30A) reports that six weeks before the Democratic Party convention, an aide to McGovern approached a high aide in the almost moribund Muskie campaign, seeking an endorsement. During this conversation, Eagleton's name was mentioned as a possible running mate for McGovern, and the Muskie aide replied that his camp would have no objections but that he had heard that Eagleton had some health problems in the past.

Miller also reports that during an interview with Rick Stearns, a key McGovern aide, that took place around the time of the California challenge (which would place it shortly before the start of the convention), he mentioned that "around Missouri there are strong rumors of alcoholism or mental illness in his [Eagleton's] background, but they haven't been documented." When Eagleton ran for the U.S. Senate in 1968, Miller, then Midwest bureau chief for *Time* magazine, had sent reporter Jonathan Larson to cover the race and look into these rumors. Larson confirmed that there were indeed rumors of a serious drinking problem as well as electro-shock treatment for mental illness. But, the report continued (quoted in Miller 1972, 30A), "these stories could not be documented, might not be true, and had certainly not prevented the attractive St. Louis attorney from making a meteoric rise in Missouri politics." The unused report was then put away in Eagleton's biographical folder in *Time*'s New York reference library.

According to Miller, these rumors surfaced again the day that McGovern's large group met to consider possible running mates. When Eagleton's name came up, Stearns says he mentioned that he had been told by a reporter that there were rumors of "alcoholism or mental illness in his background," and apparently several others present recalled hearing that Eagleton had some sort of drinking problem. Another McGovern staffer, Gordon Weil, went off to check on these rumors regarding Eagleton, as well as on another possible candidate's marital difficulties.

In checking on these stories, Weil says that he spoke to one reporter from St. Louis who told him that Eagleton suffered from a stomach problem that made him appear somewhat drunk when he had taken only a drink or two. Weil further recalls being told by another source that there were some rumors that Eagleton had been hospitalized, but Weil gained the impression from the conversation that it was for the kind of ailment described by his previous source. Weil then presented the results of his checks to the group, focusing on the alcohol ingestion problem, and mentioned that there were indications that Eagleton had been hospitalized but these may have been in connection with the alcohol ingestion problem. Viorst (1973, 62) adds that Weil also mentioned to the group that Eagleton had run four tough, state-wide campaigns and that if there had been any substance to the rumors of alcoholism or mental illness, it was unlikely that they would have remained hidden. In retrospect, it is clear they did.

The response of the group, including McGovern, according to Weil (quoted in Miller 1972), was "a general feeling of that's not good, but is nothing serious and we can live with it." Now, it should be recalled that this is Weil's reconstruction, after the fiasco had already unfolded and McGovern's candidacy had been dealt a major blow by it. However, Miller's implied criticism of Weil's failure to ask the relevant questions directly of Eagleton's staff seems misplaced,[5] since subsequent events suggest that no more forthcoming information would have been obtained by doing so at that time.

Weil has suggested that the stories of an alcohol ingestion problem were planted to throw off investigators. Perhaps he is right. However, the number of times they surfaced in connection with discussions of Eagleton suggests that the rumors of an alcohol problem were fairly widespread. In the absence of concrete information about Eagleton's psychological problems, it is not surprising that the stories about his problems with alcohol became confounded with rumors regarding his mental state.

Weil's later suspicions are bolstered somewhat by how Eagleton's hospitalizations were actually treated by Eagleton and his staff at the time that they occurred. During his first hospitalization, Eagleton's father released a story to the newspapers that his son had entered Barnes Hospital because of "a virus . . . complicated by hard work at his successful campaign for the office of Attorney General" (Viorst 1973, 142). According to a report in *Time* magazine (7 August 1972, 15), when Eagleton was hospitalized the second time at the Mayo Clinic in 1964, his office gave out the story that he had been hospitalized for a stomach ailment. When he returned to the clinic in 1966, his law office issued a statement that he had entered Johns Hopkins Hospital in Baltimore for gastric tests. The *Time* story goes on to quote Eagleton as admitting these stories were "a ploy, because when you need rest, you need rest from the press."

The clear and obvious attempt to hide the real nature of these hospitalizations from the press and the public also contradicts another Eagleton contention regarding his failure to respond to Mankiewicz's inquiry about skeletons in his closet. According to Eagleton, quoted in an interview conducted by two *Time* reporters (*Time*, 7 August 1972, 14), he didn't respond to that question with information about his psychological difficulties because

I have never viewed these hospitalizations in terms of being skeletons. I view skeletons as something you've done that is sinister, corrupt, filthy. . . . I very quickly said no. . . . If I were asked the same question today under the same circumstances, I would give the same answer. You can call it nitpicking if you like. I don't. . . . There is nothing dirty or corrupt or evil about the fact that I had voluntarily gone into a hospital.

Actually, this is less a case of nit-picking than a somewhat disingenuous form of "psycho-logic" (skeleton = sinister; hospitalization for psychological problems ≠ sinister; therefore, hospitalizations ≠ skeletons). In another interview with Mel Elfin, *Newsweek*'s Washington bureau chief (published 7 August 1972, 17–19), Eagleton insisted, "It never crossed my mind that day or even the next day about the calculated risks I was taking" (Eagleton 1972b, 19). But this contention is directly contradicted by Eagleton's revelation earlier in the same interview that he had discussed his medical history before the convention with his wife, Barbara. As Eagleton recounts:

> When we got to Miami Beach, Barbara and I discussed the possibility of my being chosen as McGovern's No. 2, and she said: "Tom, you realize you are running the risk that if you go into a national campaign that there will be a public disclosure of your hospitalization." And I replied: "Yes, I realize that. It's quite probable in fact. . . ." The . . . things that went through my mind about the hospital experience were that I would take a calculated risk that the story would not leak out, at least in the form it ultimately did. I thought it would be a general story that I had once suffered from a fatigue problem.

In the end, Eagleton's medical history became public via a very circuitous route. An anonymous informant called the *Detroit Free Press* and relayed the information that Eagleton had been hospitalized for depression and given shock treatments. He gave the name of the hospital, the name of one member of the treatment team, and approximate dates. A reporter for the Knight newspaper chain (which owned the *Free Press*) was in St. Louis to do a background story on Eagleton and pulled out the clippings regarding Eagleton's hospitalization for undefined stomach ailments. Those dates coincided with the dates that had been given by the anonymous caller, and the reporter began to check further, tracking down the doctor who had been mentioned.

The doctor would not comment, but from his nervousness and evasiveness the reporter was convinced there was some truth to the caller's information and began checking further. At the same time, an anonymous caller phoned McGovern headquarters and gave the same information and further indicated that the Knight newspapers were on the story. When the news reporter presented the McGovern campaign with a two-page memo outlining what he had found (which was sufficiently accurate), the campaign was faced with either having the newspaper break the story or going public themselves. McGovern decided the best way to deal with the story, especially in view of his belief that it was a closed chapter in Eagleton's life, was to get the story out and behind them and to go on from there. In retrospect, it is clear that McGovern greatly misjudged the seriousness of the issue. Eagleton was forced to resign as vice presidential nominee, but not without having inflicted severe damage on the McGovern candidacy.

The Question of Motivation: A Question of Character

It seems clear from Eagleton's own words that he was aware he was withholding relevant, important information from the McGovern group when he answered no to the question(s) put to him by Mankiewicz. It is worth asking why he did so. I suggest here that the unfolding of this incident raises questions about psychological suitability not only from the standpoint of "mental health" but also from the standpoint of character.

A plausible interpretation of Eagleton's behavior during this period is that it represents a triumph of ambition over rectitude. In the general sense this is no doubt partially accurate, but it is important to raise and try to answer more specific questions about the nature of that ambition. Was Eagleton's ambition a quest for political power, which he ruthlessly pursued at all costs? Or was there another, underlying pattern to this ambition?

About the intense quality of Eagleton's drive for political office there would appear to be little doubt. Eagleton, appearing before a news conference to announce that he had been hospitalized three times, said of himself, "I am still an intense person, I still push myself very hard" (transcript of Eagleton news conference, *New York Times,* 26 July 1972, 20).[6] Another indication of the intensity of Eagleton's drive for high office, as well as a revealing insight into the motivations underlying it, is found in the *Newsweek* interview (Eagleton 1972b, 19). In discussing why he didn't say anything about his medical history, Eagleton said:

> You just have to understand what that phone call meant to me. . . . I have made politics more than a career. It is my whole life's blood. I eat politics. I sleep it. I breathe it. I'm all consumed by it. I don't play golf. I don't play much bridge any more. I don't play gin rummy any more. I don't putter around the house on weekends. . . . And so there I was, a guy whose entire life was politics, and I had become the Vice Presidential nominee.

If, as Freud commented, good mental health consists of the ability to love and work, the portrait that emerges from these remarks is of a man who had become remarkably specialized in the latter. The words are extremely honest and revealing. They suggest a person who has poured his life energy into his career, giving up in the process recreation ("I don't play bridge," etc.) and leisure time with his family ("I don't putter around the house").

Eagleton's observation that politics is more than a career, and that he is consumed by it, is stark testimony to the power of the drive. But these revelations in themselves do not reveal why such drives are so powerful.

Although an analysis here must be suggestive, not definitive, I suggest there appears to be some evidence here to support the contentions of Lasswell (1948) and others (George and George 1956; Barber 1992a) that intense drives for power can often be related to issues of self-esteem.

In the same *Newsweek* interview quoted above, Eagleton went on to say, after describing how important politics was to him:

And furthermore, I had done it on my own. Heretofore, I had a very strong father to help, a father who had been a tremendous influence on my life. I had my father's financial help as well as his very strong moral and political help. . . . I take enormous pride in the fact that I earned this entirely myself without him. I made it on my own. I worked very hard and I got it. That means an awful lot to me.

There are a number of themes that might be seen in this excerpt. One might note an element of Oedipal conflict, in which the son tries to outdo and replace the father. But the overwhelming emphasis of these remarks is the theme of having accomplished something for oneself on one's own. Adult development theorists have talked about this stage of development in terms of the process of becoming one's own man (Levinson 1978, 202–4). While such striving may be to some degree compensatory for past deficits in self-esteem (as well as in the sense of competence and personal control, two other aspects of the pattern of political motivation and performance that have not received wide attention), it appears too general a stage phenomenon to be only that.

In Eagleton's case we note that this stage may well have been somewhat delayed. The invitation to become McGovern's vice presidential candidate was clearly a significant event for Eagleton. It is this office that he sees himself as having obtained on his own. One problem may have been that he was forty-two years old when the event occurred, whereas adult development theorists talk of the stage of becoming one's own man as more typically occurring in one's late twenties and early thirties. That there may have been some self-esteem problems accompanying this assertion of independence and competence is suggested by Eagleton's description of his state of mind when he received the call from McGovern (Eagleton 1972b, 18):

What was going through my mind in those five seconds. Well, I'll be very candid. I wasn't thinking about this emotional business and the periods in the hospital. The thought in my mind was that here I was talking to the Democratic nominee for President who was asking me—Tom Who?—to be his running mate. So I said I was "flabbergasted" because I was.

This passage suggests the somewhat paradoxical view of a person who has achieved enormous success in his chosen profession by any conventional standard, yet retains a sense of himself as a nobody ("Tom Who?"). The sense of being flabbergasted, as opposed to surprised or pleased, suggests a deep conviction of either unworthiness (nobody would want to choose me) or unlikeliness (even though I am good enough, no one has noticed). The precise nature of the underlying dynamic at work here can't be revealed by our data. What we are able to suggest is that the hypothesis of damaged self-esteem underlying intense political ambition does find support in the specific case of Eagleton, but it is not the whole story.

Self-esteem is also closely connected with accomplishment being rewarded by significant others, and here it seems that Eagleton's intense desire for the vice presidency, and the recognition of himself and his talents that it reflected, represent a normal, if somewhat delayed, event in adult life histories. These observations are not presented as a defense of the deception that occurred but rather as a background to understanding why they occurred.

The Question of Mental Health and Psychological Suitability for High Office

Among the most complex and difficult questions raised by the Eagleton affair are those concerned with the relationship of psychological health to psychological suitability for high public office. The Eagleton case provides an opportunity to examine a number of assumptions about political roles and their prerequisites, the nature of mental illness in relation to the performance of political roles, and, of course, the structural barriers hypothesis.

We might well begin with the actual information that Eagleton revealed about himself at the news conference on July 25, 1972. Eagleton began the press conference by revealing that "on three occasions I have voluntarily gone into hospitals as a result of nervous exhaustion and fatigue." He noted that after his campaign for state attorney general, "I did experience exhaustion and fatigue. I was on my own admission hospitalized at Barnes Hospital in St. Louis. The period of that hospitalization was . . . probably four weeks." He then described his second hospitalization as being

four days in length. I went to the Mayo Clinic . . . between Christmas, December 25, 1964 and New Year's Day, January 1, 1965 . . . for physical examination. Part of the manifestation of my fatigue and exhaustion relates to the stomach. I'm like the fellow on the Alka Seltzer ad who says I can't believe I ate the whole thing. But I do get, when I do overwork and tire myself, kind of a nervous stomach situation.

He then went on to describe his third hospitalization as having occurred in "middle or late September of 1966 when I once again went back to [the] Mayo Clinic, once again for fatigue and exhaustion. The length of that stay was . . . approximately three weeks." (Note: the dates given by the Mayo Clinic for that stay were September 20–October 21; *New York Times,* 26 July 1972, 20.)

After Eagleton had made his statement, he took questions from reporters. Among the most important for our concerns here are the following:

Q: At the risk of being indelicate, did you find during these periods of exhaustion that it affected your ability to make rational judgments?
A: No, I was in a position to make rational judgments and decisions. I was depressed. My spirits were depressed. This was one of the manifestations . . . of the exhaustion and fatigue.
Q: During these periods did you receive any psychiatric help?
A: Yes, I did.
Q: Can you tell us what kind of psychiatric treatment you received?
A: Counseling from a psychiatrist, including electric-shock treatment.
Q: Any drugs?
A: Sleeping pills.
Q: Was the electric-shock treatment at all three hospitals?
A: No, Barnes in 1960 and Mayo in 1966, not at Mayo in 1964.

Several days later, appearing on CBS's *Face the Nation* (July 30, 1972), Eagleton responded to questions from reporters concerning possible alcohol problems, which he strenuously denied. He also responded to questions concerning his use of medication as follows (Eagleton 1972a, 243):

Q: Well, now, people who are under a lot of tension, like you, frequently in this city, as in other cities, resort to something—a drink now and then or a tranquilizer or a sleeping pill. What do you do to combat the tension?
A: Well, I—I said in answer to a question, I forget what city, did I ever take a tranquilizer—I said yes, occasionally. The last time I had one was three or four weeks ago. This week would've been a good one to take one, but I didn't have any to take.
Q: Now the stress, the additional stress you've been under—this has not resulted in—you haven't taken any tranquilizers?

A: No, nor sleeping pills. No.

Q: Have you recalled since—although it's one of those details . . . the name of that tranquilizer?

A: No, I—I'm not ducking you. I said it was a blue pill, but I haven't— I didn't look at the pill or anything to see what the name—I don't remember the name.

The information contained in these public forums is clinically sketchy and raises more questions than are answered. The first set of questions concerns the actual nature of the clinical diagnosis. Eagleton's characterizations of his hospitalizations as being for "nervous exhaustion and fatigue" are lay terms or, in this case more likely, political euphemisms. The importance of the diagnosis is *not* that the diagnosis by itself reveals all that is significant about psychological functioning but that it places that functioning in an empirically based, clinical domain. Placing it in this context is helpful in making assessments of both the nature of the problem and its severity. It is for this reason that general statements made at the time of the Eagleton affair about depression (see, for example, *Time,* 14 August 1972, 41) or its prevalence in the general population—estimated to affect between four and eight million Americans—are somewhat beside the point. Depression is a class of disorders that covers a wide range of symptoms and severity (APA 1980, 205–24, 299–302), and in the case we are considering, the matter at issue is the *specific* manifestations of Eagleton's depression.

So while it is clear that depression was a major element in Eagleton's difficulties, it is not clear what kind of depression, and that is important information. Eagleton's view was that his depression was a by-product of exhaustion and fatigue brought on by overwork. That would make it appear more like a reactive than an endogenous depression.[7] When this is the case, one attempts to deal with the stressor connected with the onset of the difficulty—in Eagleton's case, if the causal arrows did run in that direction, with overwork. If Eagleton's depressions were a reaction to overwork, his reassurances that now "I pace myself a great deal better than I did in earlier years . . . [and] to date—I've experienced good, solid, sound health" would be more convincing. If, however, the causal arrows went the other way and the onset of depression *resulted in* the feelings of exhaustion, pacing one's activity might not be so helpful in terms of prevention.

There is yet another possibility that was not publicly discussed at the time but seems from other data to be at least a strong possibility, namely, some form of bipolar or cyclothymic affective disorder (the severity of the symptoms is greater in the first), in which periods of intense, manic activity alternate with periods of depression. Eagleton's history of intense investment and involvement in political activities and his descriptions of himself in that regard, coupled with his hospitalizations, are consistent with that possibility.

I repeat that my point here is not to provide a correct diagnosis for Eagleton. That would not be possible without access to medical records that, for obvious reasons of confidentiality, have never been made public. Rather, my point is to underscore that such information is relevant if one is to make some assessment of suitability.

In the absence of any specific diagnostic knowledge, the important matter of the severity of Eagleton's difficulties is also open to question. In the *Newsweek* interview Eagleton attributed his reluctance to make public his medical history in part to his specific treatment. According to Eagleton (1972b, 17), "Electric shock is simply something you don't go around talking about at cocktail parties. . . . I therefore preferred to keep [it] in the background because I didn't think many people would understand." Willard Gaylin, a psychiatrist, has pointed out that there is a paradox in public perceptions of illness and treatment. Gaylin notes:

The public shows a bias for physical symptoms of mental illness. For some reason migraine headaches, irritable colon, etc., seem more respectable than phobia, obsession and ticks. . . . While there is greater respect for physical rather than psychological symptoms the reverse seems true for attitudes towards treatment. Here it is the physical that seems more ominous. Someone who has had "shock treatment" . . . is usually seen as much sicker than a mental patient who has not. This is unfortunate. (1973, 56)

Gaylin's observation about the confounding of symptoms and severity would appear, at first glance, to support Eagleton's contention that there is nothing to be inferred about the severity of his illness from the treatment he received. As Eagleton put it in response to a question posed at the news conference about the shock treatments, "At that time, it was part of the prescribed treatment for one who is suffering from nervous exhaustion and fatigue and manifestations of depression." The phrases "at that time," and "was part of the prescribed treatment" convey the impression that shock therapy was routine for conditions like those suffered by Eagleton. Unfortunately, this is not true.

Gaylin (1973, 56), while noting that electroshock therapy "became a convenient way of treating large groups of people when the psychiatrist is overworked or overambitious," also notes that "most therapists who believe in active psychotherapy reserve shock treatments for patients who on the whole would be considered more seriously ill." This view is seconded by Perry C. Talkington, former president of the American Psychiatric Association, in an interview (*U.S. News and World Report,* 7 August 1972, 17):

Q: What is it [electroshock therapy] used for?
A: It is used to cure deep depressions when other forms of treatment— chemotherapy, psychotherapy, or combinations of these two—are not effective, or when, from the patient's point of view, it would take too long. It is a last resort.

These are rather strong words to be used in public under the circumstances by the president of a major medical association. At a minimum, they would certainly appear to lend credence to those who expressed concern about Eagleton's capacity to meet the responsibilities of high executive political office. Another indication of the realistic basis of these concerns comes from McGovern's account of his discussions with Eagleton's doctors, reported five years after the events (1977, 214–15).

It will be recalled that what McGovern knew of Eagleton's medical history came either from Eagleton's staff or from Eagleton himself, who said he had not ever seen his actual medical records (which would not necessarily be unusual).[8] McGovern writes that on Thursday, July 20, 1972, seventeen days after his staff first learned about Eagleton's illness, Eagleton, his aide Doug Bennet, Mankiewicz, and Hart met to discuss the senator's medical history. At this meeting, Eagleton promised to get his medical records, a promise that McGovern says Eagleton repeated to him when they met the following Monday (Eagleton denies having promised this).

When these records still had not appeared by the end of the week, McGovern began to get more concerned and called two nationally prominent psychiatrists for their views (McGovern 1977, 210–11). The first, Wilfred Abse of the University of Virginia, said, "There is no way to predict with any certainty the future behavior of a person with [Eagleton's] mental history," and suggested that Eagleton should leave the ticket rather than risk the possibility of a recurrence while in office. The other, Karl Menninger, who had campaigned for years to increase public awareness and tolerance of mental health issues, concluded their discussion by saying, "As for the interest of the nation, however, you can afford no risks, and I would therefore hope that you would ask Mr. Eagleton to step down."

On Monday, July 31, 1972, more than two weeks after the problems with Eagleton's medical history had surfaced, McGovern finally spoke by phone with two of the doctors who had treated Eagleton during his hospitalizations. McGovern reports that at first the doctors were reluctant to make specific predictions about Eagleton, but that they

> finally offered details of Eagleton's medical history, which I thought raised serious doubts about his capacity to carry the burdens and responsibilities of the Presidency. . . . When I asked him [the first doctor] what the risks would be should Tom have to take over the Presidency, he said, "I don't like to think about that prospect." He then added that the danger of recurrence was always present and that such persons ordinarily experience more difficulty as they get older. In responding to the same question, the other doctor said he was surprised Eagleton had been able to withstand his duties in the Senate and the first week of the controversy surrounding his Vice-Presidential candidacy. Perhaps he could stand up to an even greater test, but "that would make me most uncomfortable," the doctor said. (1977, 215)

These revelations underscore the point I wish to make here, that whatever else may have been involved in the public's concern about Eagleton (the shock treatments, the fact that he had been to a hospital, misleading McGovern, etc.), his capacity and suitability were real issues of public concern. But having indicated there was cause for concern on these grounds, we are still left with the question of the actual nature of the problems that might have arisen given Eagleton's medical history, and it is to these questions that we now turn.

To begin, we must consider the presidency as the center and, in some national security areas, the apex of the political decision-making process in this country. The first question that must be asked concerns the effects of a lengthy removal of the president, say, for one or two periods of the length that Eagleton was hospitalized. Simply stating the problem immediately suggests one appropriate response, namely, that other things being equal, we would prefer that it not happen. No president in modern history has been incapacitated for that lengthy a period.

A critic might respond to this concern by arguing that this line of thought is based on the assumption that the difficulties would reoccur. There is, of course, no certainty that they would. However, in this regard one would need to take into account the fact that Eagleton had three hospitalizations, which indicates that the problems had reoccurred in the past. These considerations are further complicated by the fact that the course of major affective disorders varies over the life cycle. Some individuals "have episodes separated by many years of normal functioning; others have clusters of episodes; and still others have an increased frequency of episodes as they grow older" (APA 1980, 216). We would certainly wish to know more about the past and probable patterns of the difficulties.

This leads to a second possible caveat: the concern that such a person might miss too much time or not be available at a crucial time. That response would argue that this is not solely a problem in the Eagleton case but is an ever-present danger for all political leaders, because political leaders have and do become physically ill while serving in office. In this view, incapacity and the resultant inability to meet the obligations of the office are an inherent risk in the selection of any person.

This of course is true. No political leader is guaranteed perfect health while in office, and we have had a number of presidents who have been physically incapacitated while serving. However, one might wish to draw distinctions among levels of risk and between those potential incapacities with which a person enters office and those that develop afterward. No known medical assessments can predict the latter, but this does not mean we might not wish to make some judgments about the former.

Imagine a presidential aspirant with a progressive neurological impair-ment or a tumor that has metastasized. Would it be reasonable to argue that these impairments have no bearing on capacity to carry out the responsibilities of office or that such information is not relevant to the ultimate political judgment that citizens make in an election? Whether Eagleton's depressions would be likely to reoccur is a question about which there could have been legitimate debate, but it is difficult to argue that the question is irrelevant to his possible performance in office. Given this, the public surely had a right to know and make its own determination of the risks it was willing to accept.

In making the analogy to a major physical illness, our argument suggests that Eagleton's depressions could well have had a negative effect on his ability to carry out the responsibilities of his office, beyond the question of his being absent from office. What evidence is there for this? Eagleton, when asked during his news conference whether his judgment was affected during these periods of "exhaustion," replied, "No. I was in a position to make rational judgments and decisions."

Eagleton's recollection of his capacity, however, may not be accurate. Without access to records, we can only speculate, but it is known that clinically, major depressive episodes manifest themselves (APA 1980, 211) in feelings of inadequacy, decreased attention span, an inability to concen-trate and think clearly, as well as pessimistic attitudes toward the future and brooding over past events. (For purposes of this analysis, we have not included some of the more severe symptoms that can accompany these episodes, such as delusions and suicidal ideas or intent.) It would seem extremely unlikely that severe depressive episodes, requiring extended hospitalizations and electroshock treatment, would not have included most or all of these manifestations.

It also seems obvious that each of these symptoms would have an adverse affect on decision making. Feelings of inadequacy would affect the individual's competence and capacity to make good decisions. A decreased attention span and ability to think clearly would also not bode well for making decisions, and a sense of pessimism about outcomes would be very damaging to conducting an effective search for and appraisals of decision alternatives (Janis and Mann 1977). And these symptoms are not the only manifestations of severe depressive episodes, only the most common.

These are possible intrusions on decision-making capacity, which, I argue in chapter 8, are a core feature of presidential performance. They represent one area of concern, but there is another. There is some evidence that depressive episodes like Eagleton's are actually one part of a cycle in which extreme and concentrated activity alternates with periods of depression.

This reoccurring cycle is called bipolar disorder. During the high-activity, or manic, phase of the disorder, an individual may experience an upsurge in activity and a decreased need for sleep, becoming intensely involved in wide range of activities. He or she may have a continuous flow of ideas without, however, stopping to follow through on them. In the cycle's most acute form, these manic phases may cause a person to become psychologically disorganized and to exhibit bizarre behavior, such as passing out advice and money to strangers. The rapid flow of ideas may pass the point of creativity and become disorganized and incoherent. In contrast, in the cycle's more moderate forms, such manic states can be periods of increased energy and creativity that can make contributions to society. The manic politician may prove very productive, introducing numerous legislative bills, and may become deeply involved in various activities.

Manic episodes characteristically include an inflated sense of self-esteem, ranging from uncritical acceptance of one's own abilities to marked grandiosity. Coupled with this are an inappropriate sense of optimism regarding the outcomes of the manic's own activities and a somewhat disturbing loosening of the sense of interpersonal and social responsibility (after all, if one is special, the normal rules of conduct need not apply). One very telling example of the dangers of this kind of state can be found in the *Newsweek* interview with Eagleton, when he is discussing his reasons for not telling McGovern about his medical history. He began by telling the reporter, "You have to understand what that phone call [from McGovern] meant to me" (Eagleton 1972b, 19). He then went on to detail how important his political career was to him ("I eat politics. I sleep it," etc.) and concluded:

So there I was, a guy whose entire life was politics and I had become the Vice-Presidential nominee. . . . So I was euphoric. I took calculated risks. I misjudged a lot of things. But I was happy, so very happy. . . . I never thought there would be headlines reading: "Eagleton Future in Doubt." I didn't think it [his medical history] was going to be that big. Frankly, I made a mistake.

Eagleton's personal strengths (his intelligence, charm, hard work) coupled with his intense determination, ambition, depressions, and manic phases underscore the fact that all of these different characteristics can find expression in complex combinations of affect, thought, and behavior. Recall that Fieve (1975, 138–39) argued that

many people in high office have a tendency towards mood swings, since their manic energy has helped get them there in the first place. Once in office, their emotional makeup and mood often shift cyclically. At some point, although not necessarily so, their judgments may become impaired, and in times of extreme depression and extreme mania the distortions in judgment may be severe. . . . For a person in a position of power, particularly political power, this can be dangerous. The social responsibility of the politician and his relative freedom to do what he wants, coupled with his extraordinary power to force his will, makes hypomania in high office a potentially dangerous situation, as well as an asset.

Fieve then goes on to ask a most crucial question: Should such a person, "simply because of the possibility that he may at times have impaired judgment . . . be disqualified from public office in spite of frequent periods of hypercompetency and outstanding performance?" Fieve apparently thinks not, since he ends his chapter by pointing out that at some future time, when we better understand the contributions that such persons can and do make to society, "people with mood swings may even be sought out for positions of leadership" (1975, 144).

This may be, perhaps, but I am not immediately persuaded. Clearly, a number of factors would have to be taken into account, among them the nature and severity of the mood shifts and the nature of the political position. Many of Eagleton's colleagues pointed out in his defense that he was a very able legislator. There is every reason to believe this was true, and so it raises the question of why, if he was "well enough" to serve effectively in that position, he wasn't similarly suited for the vice presidency. The direct answer is that the political roles are very different, emphasizing different skills. A senator is one of one hundred involved in a collective decision-making process. A president in many important instances is the single, ultimate decision maker. The damage that could be done with the impaired judgment that frequently accompanies manic-depressive syndromes is of a much greater range and magnitude than can be done by such a person, even in acute phases, in a legislative role.

Fieve (1975, 136) has argued that "hypomanic politicians are tireless campaigners, charismatic leaders, indefatigable organizers . . . [and] are particularly suited to the lifestyle of the Senate or House." These observations may well be true, but they do not preclude extreme concern over the consequences of having such persons in executive political positions, especially the presidency.

Conclusion

I began this case study by pointing out that the Eagleton affair was among the few documented cases of a public figure with a certifiable psychological impairment whose condition and history became somewhat public. As such, it affords us an opportunity to assess the adequacy of the structural barriers theory, which suggests that persons with substantial psychological impairments are precluded from occupying high office because *(a)* they lack the skills necessary to navigate the access routes to political power in our society or *(b)* they will be judged inadequate by working colleagues, the press, or others who might be in a position to restrain any political progress they might make. It also allows us to examine some of the issues that arise in connection with questions of psychological suitability for high political office.

In fact, the Eagleton case suggests the two sets of considerations are interconnected. Turning first to the structural barriers argument, it seems clear that the evidence in support of the theory is mixed. The reasons for this are related to the nature of Eagleton's ailments and positions. The structural barriers theory is based on a particular set of disturbances being screened out in political leadership roles. The psychotic fanatic with delusions (whether of persecution, thought broadcasting, thought insertion, or something other) will demonstrate questionable emotional stability and rationality. The kinds of symptoms associated with those disturbances are manifestly evident and clearly indicative of a psychological disorder. Such individuals also really do lack the skills necessary to organize, build, and maintain support in stable structural climates.

But the Eagleton experience supports my suggestion in chapter 3 that the psychotic-leader scenario envisioned by that argument is much too narrow a slice of the problem. The Eagleton case suggests that a leader can have major psychological difficulties, yet obtain and keep high public office. One reason for this has to do with the nature of psychological difficulties, namely, that only in unusual cases are they *the* defining characteristic of the person's functioning.

In the Eagleton case, there seems little doubt that there were periods of substantial psychological difficulty, but they were episodic. Another factor to consider here is that Eagleton's difficulties coexisted with some substantial personal abilities. He was intelligent, personable, and hard-working, all qualities that would lend themselves to success in political life.

A third complication suggested by this case is that the very qualities that help facilitate political success may also, on occasion, become extremely problematic. This difficulty presents itself in two forms: in questions of suitability from the standpoint of mental health and from the standpoint of character. In the first, we have to ask whether Eagleton's intense level of activity, which in many ways is functional for an upwardly mobile political leader, is not in itself a cause for concern (as per our discussion of manic symptoms above). In the second instance we are concerned about character, not overall psychological functioning. Here we are led to ask whether Eagleton's intense drive to obtain political office does not reveal a problem with self-regard and, further, whether that very strong need for affirmation had the effect of leading Eagleton into some very questionable acts (for example, his failure to respond adequately to the question[s] put to him by Mankiewicz about his past).

When we turn to the argument that severe psychological difficulties will be a bar to political advancement because of the observations of colleagues, the press, and others, it is difficult to make a definitive, unequivocal judgment. On the one hand, it seems clear that Eagleton was effectively able to hide the real nature of his hospitalizations, even though he was the subject of numerous newspaper articles, interviews, and other coverage as he rose higher and higher in the political structure. And this applied to three periods of hospitalization, two of which were a month or more in duration.

On the other hand, one could suggest with some truth that the whole

Eagleton experience, coupled with a new, more assertive investigative tone to reporting on political candidates, has made another such cover-up more difficult. But what if Eagleton had not been treated at a hospital and therefore had not been out of public view for such long periods? In the end, it should be recalled, it was an anonymous call to a newspaper that started the chain of events leading to the disclosure of Eagleton's medical history and his subsequent resignation as a vice presidential candidate. One could argue that ultimately the system envisioned by the structural barriers theory did work, but an anonymous phone call seems a slender thread on which to hang one's confidence, much less the risk to this republic.

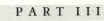

PART III

*Character and Presidential
Performance: Theory and Assessment*

SEVEN

Toward a Framework for Analyzing Presidential Performance: Some Observations on a Theory of Character

The need for criteria by which to assess presidential candidates has become pressing as character has assumed increasing importance. The American public now routinely evaluates leaders on their "integrity," "leadership," and even "intelligence" (Markus 1982; Kenney and Rice 1988; Miller, Wattenberg, and Malanchuk 1986; Krosnick and Kinder 1990). The use of traits to evaluate presidential candidates has much to recommend it. Traits are distinct and specific and, from the standpoint of assessment, seem amenable to measurement at a distance. We can generally tell if a candidate appears well informed, at ease under pressure, or charismatic.

Moreover, in some instances it is easy to see the connection between a particular trait and desirable political skills. It is easy to see why a candidate's integrity is important, given that citizens are often asked to accept a president's statements about policy actions and the reasons for it. So, too, a concern with a candidate's intelligence would seem to be related, if not always directly, to an ability to grasp and perhaps resolve complex public problems.

However, as intuitively appealing as trait evaluations might be, there are a number of substantial problems in using them as the primary tool of candidate assessment. The first is that it is sometimes unclear what these trait categories mean. Consider the trait of intelligence: Is intelligence synonymous with that generalized ability which is purported to be measured by IQ? Sternberg (1979) has suggested a number of different types of intelligence, several of which might well have implications for a leader's decision-making skills. A singular focus on intelligence as IQ may obscure the other personal or cognitive skills that might inform skillful presidential decision making or judgment.

Second, trait-based evaluations often fail to address the relationships between and among trait categories. For example, while a high level of intelligence in a leadership role is often a virtue, it is not necessarily so. It would make things much easier if very intelligent candidates were always, say, compassionate and honest. But this isn't always the case. Intelligence, even when it is a virtue, must be considered in relation to other parts of the candidate's psychology.

Third, trait-based evaluations assume that the effect of a trait is equally important across situations. There are many complex reasons that a trait may not operate similarly across situations. A specific situation may call for the suppression of a characteristic rather than its expression. For political or other strategic reasons, a presidential candidate or president may choose to show less of a trait such as intelligence or ambition. Moreover, some situations tend to elicit the expression of certain traits while others do not. A president may become more rigid when his competence rather than his policies are questioned.

Fourth, trait-based evaluations do not take up the question of how a particular trait fits into other aspects of psychological or political functioning. Even assuming that it is intelligence (as measured by the generally understood concept of IQ) that presidential candidates (and presidents) ought to have more of, one cannot discount the role that character plays in its expression. Many presidential candidates and presidents who would uniformly rate high on intelligence nonetheless make remarkable errors of judgment, as Gary Hart did in 1988 (see chapter 9) and Bill Clinton did in 1992 (see chapters 10 and 11).

Fifth, and a corollary of the preceding point, is that trait-based evaluations are not helpful in choosing among characteristics, except in obvious cases. Of course it is better to have an intelligent candidate than a dumb one. But whether intelligence in a presidential candidate is more important than political leadership is a question that trait-based evaluations have difficulty in addressing.

Sixth, trait-based evaluations do not address the very important question of *when* relationships among traits should be weighed differently. Are there circumstances in which integrity is more important than intelligence? Almost certainly there are many. This is not an ethereal question. Nor is it necessarily a matter of values. Without a theory of the nature of presidential performance, it is difficult to conclude whether a particular trait is relevant. Specifying a trait is the first step in examining its contribution to presidential performance (e.g., smart is better than dumb), not the last.

To raise this issue is to point to the seventh, and in some ways most important, limitation of trait-based evaluations: they fail to build a more comprehensive and theoretical view of psychological functioning and presidential performance. There are some traits that it is important for a president to possess; there are others for which he need only be capable. Trait-based evaluations fail to distinguish these or to make clear the circumstances in which a trait might be crucial or merely preferred. In short, trait-based evaluations are not necessarily wrong, just ad hoc.

The public, of course, is not interested in personality theory per se, nor should it be. It is concerned with finding a basis for selecting better presidents. If trait-based evaluations represent a step toward that goal, what further steps might be taken?

One further useful step would be to develop a more substantial understanding of character and how it functions in presidential performance. Is there a specific "presidential character" congruent with the exercise of power in a democratic system? If there is, what are its elements, and how well do presidential campaigns allow us to view them in action?

In this chapter I examine the analysis of character as it has developed in psychoanalytic theory. I then develop a framework for the analysis of character that centers on three core psychological elements: the domains of *ambition, integrity,* and *relatedness.* I argue that these three character elements are at the core of presidential and, more generally, leadership performance.[1]

The Nature of Character: Early Formulations

The term *character* is derived from the Greek word χαρακτηρ, which means "engraving." Allport, in his classic work on personality theory (1937, chap. 1), defined it as "a person's patterns of traits or his lifestyle." He distinguished the term *character* from *personality.* According to Allport (1937), personality denotes "appearance, visible behavior, surface quality," while character implies "deep (perhaps inborn), fixed and basic structure."[2]

Allport's formulation parallels general public understanding of character. In recent political campaigns, the public has searched for clues to the more basic, enduring characteristics of each presidential candidate. It does so not on the basis of sophisticated personality theories but rather with an experience-based and intuitive sense of which traits are important. However, even if the public wanted more sophisticated and complex theories of character and turned to analytic theory, it would receive limited help. The concept of character in psychoanalytic psychology has developed slowly (Baudry 1984), and in directions dictated by clinical concerns.[3]

Early theoretical formulations of character focused on several interrelated psychological traits bound together to form a behavior syndrome. For example, in the "compulsive" character type (Fenichel 1945, 463–540), traits such as cleanliness, stubbornness, and parsimony were bound together psychologically by the anxiety accompanying loss of control (over impulses) to produce a persisting pattern of behavior. More than forty years later, Baudry reaffirmed that character refers to "the broadest grouping of stable, typical traits by which we recognize a particular person. Our concept of character is made necessary because we find in individuals reoccurring clusters of traits with a degree of consistency suggesting that some underlying principles govern the selection, ordering and relations of these traits to one another" (1989, 656).

The early understanding of character reflected several basic clinical observations. First, character was clinically observed to be involved in important areas of the individual's psychological and social functioning. Second, the psychological elements of character and their operation resulted in observable, consistent patterns. A person who spoke in measured tones, used precise words, was meticulous about arriving on time for therapy sessions, and perceived the world in detailed terms was not likely to be given to wild displays of public emotion. Third, character, being basic to psychological functioning, was present in a variety of situations.[4]

These general formulations of character, while helpful, also highlight several shortcomings. For one thing, they are almost exclusively clinically derived and oriented. The observational and theoretical focus on obsessive character runs the danger of confounding "*some* character types met in *psycho-analytic work*" (Freud 1916a; emphasis mine) with character operation in general. Other, more general models of character development and functioning are needed to supplement the clinical observations based on psychoanalytic patients.

As noted in chapter 3, recent psychoanalytic theories of character have attempted to redress this problem by expanding the list of character syndromes and disorders.[5] However, while the number of clinically defined character types has increased, the theoretical understanding of character itself is still based on the same premises. Recent models of character functioning and development, like their predecessors, are substantially derived from clinical practice. That such models concentrate on difficulties and disturbances is in keeping with the theoretical needs, as well as the observational realities, of clinical practice.[6] As general models, however, they are not always helpful in understanding adequate or effective character functioning.

The view of character as essentially the sum of a person's defensive mechanisms or his or her deficient resolution of psychological or developmental dilemmas is unsatisfactory for at least four reasons. First, it is not clear that character is always defensive in operation. In clinical practice, as in real life, individuals do not typically function at the lowest common denominator of their psychological organization. Barber's (1992a) model of "presidential character," for example, which he notes grows out of the "psychology of adaptation," reflects this. And surely his active-positive character type is an example of a substantially nondefensive character type in operation.

Second, the "character as defense" formulation tends to reflect a static view of character development. Traditional psychoanalytic formulations of character tend to stress the early and enduring nature of character without giving much attention to the ways in which it can develop after childhood and through adulthood. A person at forty has many more skills and resources with which to modify character styles than does a child. Many people are able to gain some appreciation of their patterns of behavior outside of a therapeutic context, by virtue of time, accumulated experience, and the empathic appraisal of oneself by others.

Third, the traditional psychoanalytic formulation of character focuses on some important aspects of its operating dynamics, for example, its pervasiveness across time and situation. However, such formulations do not adequately distinguish character from other, less fundamental psychological characteristics such as beliefs or even attitudes.

Even if these difficulties were overcome, there would remain a fourth and, for our purposes, critical difficulty. Present psychoanalytic models of character do not provide a useful guide for the analysis of character in our political leaders because they are primarily geared to explaining deficiencies and disruptions of psychological functioning. An empirically based fact of political life is that many, if not most, candidates for the presidency have substantial character strengths and skills.

Clinicians concerned with psychological functioning are interested in character theories in connection with their therapeutic interventions. They are interested in cures, not politics. Not surprisingly, they have not focused on the applications of their theories to presidential leadership.

At the same time, the psychological analysis of political leaders has gone well beyond an early concern with whether or not leaders have unconscious conflicts. Like everyone else, they do. As George points out (1980, 6), one has not learned anything extraordinary when one can point out the existence of defense mechanisms in a political leader. The assessment of psychological suitability requires models that reflect the mix of skills and difficulties that characterizes most leaders.[7] To develop these models, it is necessary to formulate the core components of character and their operation in a way that does not wholly rely on traditional psychoanalytic metapsychology. It is to this task that I turn in the following sections.

Toward a Theory of Character

How, then, can we conceptualize character? We begin by pointing out that character differs from other psychological features in that it is pervasive not only across time and circumstance but *across personality itself*. Beliefs, attitudes, and even neuroses typically represent only small parts of the total personality system. Each may be relevant to and therefore engaged only in limited areas of functioning.

Character, in contrast, stands at the core of the personality system and is the basic foundation upon which personality structures develop and operate. Character shapes beliefs, information processing, and, ultimately, styles of behavior. It is therefore deeply embedded in the most basic and important foundation of psychological functioning.

These introductory comments tell us something about the general nature of character, but they do not precisely suggest the elements of which it consists. Nor do they reveal much about the development of character. Both issues need to be addressed, even if briefly, to lay a firm foundation for our discussion of character and presidential performance.

What is character, and how exactly does it develop? One clue is found in Barber's apt observation (1992a, 4) that character reflects "a person's approach to experience." Barber's observation is in accord with clinical evidence. However, one must ask a further question: What accounts for a particular "approach to experience"?

The phrase "approach to experience" suggests lessons learned and applied. The question is: Which lessons? Character development is clearly anchored in experience, but of what kind? The answer I propose begins with the early *and continuing* interplay between a person's psychological aspirations (the things they want, need, or wish) on the one hand and the reception of those desires and needs in the world on the other.[8] The experiences that arise from this interplay frame what I refer to as the *basic developmental dilemma.*

The basic developmental dilemma can be simply stated: Life does not always provide satisfaction. There is always a gap between what individuals need or want and what they receive. Even persons born into comfortable economic, political, and psychological circumstances experience empathetic lapses from others (be they parents, friends, teachers) on occasion. These lapses need not be crippling to shape an individual's developmental path. Often the lapses are the result of others' characters and thus more systematic than random.

Deprivation in the general sense, when it is not substantial or overwhelming, is not the major issue in ordinary character development, since it is, to some extent, inevitable. Nor is the balance between deprivations and satisfactions the whole story, although that relationship is surely important. Rather, the key questions are: (1) What characterological, cognitive, and interpersonal capacities are available to the individual to deal with the basic developmental dilemma? (2) How responsive to those capacities are the environments in which the person finds himself? (3) What strategies, if any, does the individual develop to address any differences between the first two?

From this perspective, we can say that character is the result of a person's attempt to harness his or her abilities and skills in the service of self-development and life satisfaction. It reflects the person's best attempt[9] to navigate the course of life, resolving, to the extent possible, the basic developmental dilemma. The consolidation of an adequate, stable character structure is a by-product of this necessary task and builds on an individual's characterological, cognitive, and interpersonal skills.

The Three Foundations of Character: Ambition, Character Integrity, and Relatedness

The fact that each individual comes into a world in which wishes are tempered by reality helps us to understand how and why character develops. But it does not tell us what psychological elements constitute character or what their relationships to one another are. I argue that the capacity to successfully construct a life that can satisfy one's basic aspirations and needs rests on a set of three core psychological structures, which form the foundation of character and its development.

The three structures I suggest are ambition, character integrity, and relatedness, and in the following material I explicate and trace some of their dynamic implications. A schematic representation of the character elements and their relationships and implications is contained in Appendix 2.

The Domain of Ambition

The first character domain is that of purposeful initiative, action, and capacity. This is the sphere of ambition. The basic concerns in this domain are the capacity, desire, and ability to invest oneself for the accomplishment of one's immediate and life purposes. A consolidated sphere of ambition gives rise to a sense of personal effective capacity.[10] It reflects the development and consolidation of a set of skills that can be successfully engaged in the pursuit and accomplishment of one's goals and the realization of one's values.

Kohut (1971; 1977) reminds us that ambition, the sibling of what he calls "healthy narcissism," is, along with ideals and the talent to achieve them, one foundation of a well-realized life. Without ambition there is no achievement, and without achievement there is little basis on which to consolidate self-regard. This being the case, the neglect of this core motivational element carries with it substantial theoretical and explanatory costs.

What theoretical advantages accrue to political and, especially, presidential psychology by examining ambition more closely? First, a focus on ambition allows us to examine one important motivational element that appears to be a prerequisite for reaching high public office. It also appears to be related to performance in it. Whether the presidential candidate is an active-negative (in Barber's terms) who amasses power because he is driven by low self-esteem or is more oriented to achievement, ambition is the underlying, common element.

Second, ambition helps us to focus on a basic dilemma in presidential recruitment: that achieving high office, especially the presidency, requires an enormous investment of time, energy, and oneself. Even those who, like Ronald Reagan, may approach the presidency in a relatively detached manner *after* they are elected still make substantial personal and professional investments of their time and energy to gain office. How do we account for this? An answer must surely include an account of the role of substantial levels of ambition.

A word of caution is necessary regarding the analysis of ambition. In both academic and ordinary discourse, ambition carries with it negative connotations. To be characterized as ambitious is to be labeled as essentially self-serving, unmindful of others, and manipulative. A similarly negative connotation is evident in studies of presidents and other leaders whose ambition has primarily been in the service of compulsively accumulating power. The dilemma for psychological studies of presidential behavior is that ambition is clearly suspect but also clearly necessary. What is very much needed is some theoretical way to distinguish different kinds of ambition.

In Kohut's theory, ambition, even substantial ambition, is not problematic. On the contrary, for Kohut a substantial lack of ambition would denote a developmental arrest. Childhood grandiosity is the foundation of adult ambition. As long as it is gradually and successfully modulated by empathetically attuned others and "optimally frustrating" experience, ambition does not run the risk of careening out of control and interfering with judgment and behavior (Kohut 1971, 8–9, 107).

Kohut (1977, 123) notes that both too little and too much ambition are brought about by empathetic failures by parents. In the former case, the parent fails to respond positively to the child's budding grandiosity, causing it to falter. This undermines the development of healthy narcissism, which is a foundation of ambition.

In the case of too much ambition, childhood grandiosity is reinforced, rather than modulated, by empathetically unattuned others. In this case, one or both parents overstimulate the child's "grandiose self," reinforcing unbounded expectations. The parent seemingly gives love without limits to the child, reinforcing the sense of specialness and entitlement.

Kohut attributes most of the sources of difficulty in the sphere of ambition to parental failures of empathy in one direction or another. However, external circumstances can also play a reinforcing role. For example, being a "big fish in a small pond" may facilitate ambition. In these circumstances, the developing child may experience relatively easy success (compared to others whose achievements come less easily), which reinforces rather than modulates expectations of getting what one wants.

Interpersonal relationships beyond those with one's parents may also play a role. A child who is smart and otherwise talented and who is also outgoing, friendly, and able to make connections with others will generally achieve substantial "popularity." In such cases, there is a danger that idealization by others may reinforce rather than modify the individual's self-idealization. This, in turn, may reinforce rather than moderate the child's grandiosity.

What can make ambition problematic is its relationship to other characterological elements, such as one's view of and confidence in oneself or one's relationship to others. In short, we must look to a constellation of characterological elements, rather than to a single one, to help distinguish between productive and problematic ambition.

The Domain of Character Integrity

The second character domain is that of ideals and the capacity to realize them. It is the sphere of character integrity, in which ideals are developed, refined, and integrated into the character structure by the individual's fidelity to them. The result of a well-developed and substantially realized set of ideals and values is a consolidated[11] personal identity and sense of self-esteem.

Ideals can falter at any of three points. A person may never develop ideals that go beyond securing what they want. Or a person may never be able to resolve the many conflicts that occur among ideals, to come to a resolution which provides a sense that there is a basic integrity connected to one's fundamental ideals, aspirations, and unfolding identity. Or a person may have developed and refined his or her ideals and values but lack the capacity to realize them in a manner that maintains fidelity to them. A developmental failure at any of these stages compromises a person's sense of having purpose guided by ideals and not solely by self-interest. Failure to consolidate one's ideals also undermines the development of a sense of authenticity and self-esteem. One can always justify self-interest to oneself. However, it is a measure of the power and importance of ideals that the selfish often feel obligated to provide some less self-referential reasons (to themselves as well as others) for their behavior.

The development of a consolidated identity in adulthood is a process in which each of these separate elements plays an important role. The first step is the development of ideals. Ideals come primarily, but not exclusively, from parents and the other early models who try to guide and help us. They develop from what individuals see, what they are told, and what they experience (these may often not be synonymous). In favorable circumstances, they provide the foundation to develop the ethical frameworks within which one's ambitions can be pursued.

Early ideals are somewhat abstract and often grandiose—that is, they incorporate levels of virtue and even perfection most often found in how others would like (or like us) to be but are not. Moreover, there are a number of ideals by which one might be guided, not all of which are easily reconciled. Therefore, it is not necessarily a criticism to say that fully realized ideals in adulthood are often a modified version of their childhood counterparts.

How do the different ideals by which one might live become refined and consolidated? They do so in part through the process of addressing, with the help of others, the dilemma of translating ideals into values[12] that may adequately address the circumstances which must be faced, but that also reflect who one is and wishes to be. Erikson (1980) nicely captures this particular aspect of ideals and their refinement in his observations on the difference between *ego identity* and *ego ideal*. He notes that the former

can be said to be characterized by the more or less *actually obtained but forever to be revised* sense of the reality of the self within social reality; while the imagery of the ego ideal could be said to represent a set of *to-be-strived-for but forever-not-quite obtainable ideal* goals for the self. (1980, 160)

Finally, having developed a set of ideals and refined them in a way that does justice to the person an individual feels comfortable with and aspires to be, there remains the step of actually living by them. Ideals, even refined ones, are not always easy to live by. Circumstances may make it difficult to enact ideals without severe or substantial penalties. Others with different views of what ought to be done can fairly ask for a consideration of their point of view. However, as difficult as it may be in many circumstances, it is crucial to the consolidation of one's ideals into one's identity to try to live by them. This does not require perfect virtue or total fidelity regardless of circumstances. An analyst who values truth must also, at the same time, respect his patient's vulnerabilities.

From the psychological perspective, what does it take to live in accordance with one's ideals and values? First, it requires a capacity to endure loss. Choosing to live as fully as possible by one's ideals must be governed by the realization and acceptance of the fact that, on occasion, to do so may prove costly to ambitions. Second, one must be able to endure conflict and a degree of separateness from others. This is especially important for those in high political office, since much of what they do requires decisions that make some people unhappy.

It is perhaps clearer now why the concept of integrity is so important to an understanding of character and why it has played such a crucial role in evaluations of presidential candidates. Character integrity does not just involve a candidate's public identification of himself with the virtues and ideals that most would find laudable. No one would expect a candidate to say otherwise. Rather, the question of whether and to what extent integrity exists requires confirmation by an examination of behavior, over time and through difficult circumstances, to see how a candidate or president has handled the complex dilemmas involving ambition and ideals. The development of integrity suggests the candidate has integrated his basic psychological motivations, skills, and ideals into an authentic, coherent, and consistent sense of who he is and what he stands for. It follows that there is little substantial difference between the person he sees himself to be and would like to be seen as and the person that he really appears to be.

What is the relationship between the spheres of ambition and integrity? Is ambition incompatible with the respectful (of self and others) pursuit of ideals? Traditionally, political psychology theory has viewed strong ambition as underlying extreme power motivation and antidemocratic tendencies (see Lasswell 1930, 1948; George and George 1956, for early but still representative views). Indeed, this model has fit some presidents. The question is: Does it fit all?

The psychoanalytic theory of the self suggests that it doesn't. Kohut (1971, 248) notes that ambition in the pursuit of ideals, many of which are socially valuable, is an integral part of the development of a strong and favorable sense of self. In other words, we need to distinguish between ambition in the service of realizing ideals and ideals that are primarily in the service of ambition.

Personas and Identity: The Crucible of Character Integrity

The rise of persona construction in presidential campaigns makes it important to distinguish between persona and identity and to examine the role of integrity in that relationship. Identity reflects the confluence of a person's needs and motives, skills, experiences, values, and understandings. It is a constellation of motivational, emotional, and cognitive (psychological) structures that become bound together in the course of an individual's particular developmental history. Psychologically, the presence of a firm personal identity reflects a certain level of developmental accomplishment. It reflects the fact that a candidate has been able productively to combine his ambitions, skills, and style. He has consolidated his capacity for and enactment of integrity.

Political identity represents a candidate's (at least partially) successful attempt to combine his or her particular cognitive capacities, characterological strengths, values, and interpersonal skills in a political role that makes use of and allows for their development. Like personal identity, which develops out of the integration of ambition and ideals, the development of a firmly grounded political identity represents an important psychological accomplishment. It reflects the fact that the candidate has developed a public role that honestly allows personal ambitions, skills, understandings, and style to find expression in a manner that satisfies not only the leader but also his public. The failure to develop a strong sense of either personal or political identity therefore is cause for concern not only on psychological grounds but also on political ones.

A solid political identity is necessary for effective political leadership in general and for effective presidential performance in particular. The presidential candidate with an established political identity stands for particular personal, political, and interpersonal values and has also established a style of pursuing them. A candidate's political identity has its roots in personal identity and values but develops as the individual engages the public issues that are part of his political coming of age and those issues that help to define his political maturity. A firmly developed political identity also plays a role in a candidate's connection with the public, allowing the electorate to define and understand what the candidate is likely to do and where he is likely to lead them. The candidate asks the public to take him as he appears, because how he appears, for the most part, reflects who he is.

Personas, by contrast, are constructions that are often developed to present the candidate as he wishes to appear. Allport (1937, chap. 1) noted that the term *persona* in Latin originally meant "mask." Many presidential candidates have attempted to substitute political personas for political identity.

There are varied reasons why candidates (and presidents) adopt personas. Often they use personas to reframe circumstances. Candidate Bill Clinton's self-described persona as the "comeback kid," after placing second in the New Hampshire primary, was a deft twist. It built on something he had accomplished and reframed it in a way that allowed a second-place finish to look like a victory.

Personas can be used to generate political support or as a tool of political leadership. President Eisenhower's persona as a genial, not quite hands-on president apparently masked a clear and incisive mind that was very much concerned with specifics of presidential decision making. Eisenhower's "hidden-hand presidency" (Greenstein 1982) allowed him to do the hard work of presidential leadership and decision making while giving the impression that not much urgency affected his day-to-day routine. In a sense, by not going public Eisenhower was able to govern with a freer hand.

The difference between the public persona and the "real" president behind it is a matter of concern and importance. Persona can have roots in the individual's sphere of identity. However, a candidate (and president) can also develop a persona whose essential purpose is to satisfy his personal and public ambition.

What is the difference between these types of personas, and more importantly, how can one distinguish? One clue lies in the solidity of a coherent, stable, identifiable, and authentic political identity. Eisenhower appears to have used his public persona both to reassure the public and to provide room for himself politically. His political identity, however, was well established and authentically represented many of his personal and political values, including a tendency to value accomplishment over getting public credit.

One way to distinguish between personas linked to identity and those linked primarily to ambition is to be found in the degree of consolidation of and the authenticity of the link between the personal and political identities. The ability to develop multiple (and divergent) personas in response to the press of circumstances is, in the view of some authors, a reflection of a "post-modern identity" (Gergen 1991). To the public, however, it raises the suspicion that at the core of these various personas is a person whose only consistency is his attempt to manipulate perception in the service of ambition.

The use of the word *new* before a candidate's (or president's) name (e.g., the "new" Richard Nixon in 1972 and the "new" Ronald Reagan in 1984) invites the assumption that the leader has learned something important from experience and will now be appreciably different. This often proves not to be the case, and the reason is simple: it is hard to be a "new person" after so many years of being the "old" one.

The Domain of Relatedness

The third basic character domain concerns one's basic stance toward relationships with others. This is the relational sphere. In this sphere is a continuum of interpersonal relationships and the psychology that shapes each. They range from antagonistic, unfriendly relationships at one pole, through various kinds of friendships, to intimate relationships anchoring the other pole.

It is tempting to think of character (like ambition and authentic, well-realized ideals) as solely the reflection of intrapsychic factors. But clinical psychoanalytic theory has long understood otherwise. Freud realized early in his clinical studies that what is today termed *object relations* (Greenberg and Mitchell 1983; see also Bowlby 1969) was a necessary part of human development. In 1921 he pointed out:

The contrast between individual psychology and social or group psychology, which at first glance may seem to be full of significance, loses a great deal of its sharpness when it is examined more closely. . . . In the individual's mental life someone else is invariably involved, as a model, as an object, as a helper, as an opponent: and so from the very first individual psychology . . . is at the same time social psychology as well. (*S.E.* 18: 69)

Horney (1937) theorized that individuals, because of early experience, develop an interpersonal tendency to move either toward, away from, or against people. In the first, an individual reaches out toward others, gaining psychologically from relationships. In the second, the individual moves away from relationships, either because they are less important than other needs (like those for autonomy or solitude [Storr 1990]) or because of disappointments. In the third, the individual wants contact but engages others in a way that ensures distance and not intimacy or friendship. Each of these general orientations toward relationships is accompanied by a specific constellation of personal needs and skills. More recently, Kohut's (1971, 3–6) concept of a "selfobject" and the clinical work that has followed it (Goldberg 1988; Wolf 1988) have confirmed the basic insight of the importance of the role of others in the development of an individual's character structure and operation.

The successful development of the characterological elements discussed above (ambition and ideals) rests on productive experiences in establishing a variety of interpersonal relationships. Character integrity, for example, is involved with domain of relatedness in two direct ways. First, ideals develop out of relationships with and the incorporation of our experiences with others (parents, siblings, mentors, friends, and even those who may not care for or who dislike us). Second, our sense of self is intimately tied to our relationships with significant others, ranging from the intimacy of parent and family bonds to the other important relationships that develop as a person matures. Harry Stack Sullivan (1953) viewed the self as the "sum of reflected appraisals." His point was that how others see us has much to do with how we experience ourselves. Our view of ourselves is unlikely to be a simple sum of what others think, since some views are clearly more important than others. However, the basic point is well taken. Making interpersonal connections, sustaining them, and being nurtured by them are basic building blocks of character. Character and its intrapsychic elements have an interpersonal, relational dimension.

A capacity for interpersonal connectedness is clearly related to the other two character elements we have discussed. Others' emotional responsiveness is instrumental in the development of ideals and important in the process of refining and consolidating them. The sense of effective capacity, which springs from experience in realizing one's ambitions, has a direct interpersonal component. Whether one is in competition with others, working in cooperation with others to achieve common purposes, or simply measuring one's accomplishments by reference to others (in the intrapsychic or external world), other persons are inevitably involved.

Primary Consequence of Character: Character Style

Character forms the foundation and basis of a person's overall psychological functioning. However, the configuration of the three basic character elements has implications for the larger personality structure of the individual. They are related to the development of a stable set of psychological orientations that I term *character style*.[13] Character style develops out of the specific ways in which the three basic character elements have come together and become linked with the individual's personal skills and resources. Style is the operational enactment of character.

The set of skills and capacities a person has and can develop influences the extent to which his or her needs are likely to be met. But it also influences *how* one attempts to get those needs gratified. Just as a person develops characteristic approaches to experience, a person also develops a *character style,* which consists of the ways in which that particular person's strengths and limitations become integrated into patterns of behavior meant to navigate the basic developmental dilemma. Character style is the mediator between character and the external world.

Character style develops along with character itself. This makes some sense, since character style reflects the ways in which a person attempts to address and resolve the basic developmental dilemma. The use of the term *character style* carries the implication that character can, and does to some degree, develop. It is not static.

What implications does this formulation have for assessing the character of presidential candidates? Two come immediately to mind. One mistake that is often made in analyzing the character of presidents is to assume that because character develops early in a person's life history and lies "deeper" in the personality structure, its operation in adulthood will be primitive too. It is true that by the time a person reaches mid-adulthood, basic character elements have been established, elaborated, and in most cases consolidated. Therefore, by the time a president is ready to enter office, he does so either with a stable, consolidated sense of self-regard and identity or without such a sense.

However, it would be a mistake to look for simple repetitions of childhood patterns in presidential candidates. By the time individuals reach adulthood, they have had ample opportunity to develop more fully a range of skills that in turn will affect their capacity for accomplishment. Most political leadership positions involve a large number of opportunities to specialize; indeed, they require some specialization. It is quite possible for most people to find some areas within complex role structures to express their skills as well as their needs.

There is, therefore, often an evolution of psychological constellations over the political leader's life history (Renshon 1989b, 258). Needs themselves develop in some respects over time. The need for reassurance, for example, is not the same at six as it is at forty. So, too, in adulthood, the sense that one is a good enough person rests on a very complex set of sometimes conflicting feelings and responsibilities that go well beyond the child's concern with whether something is "good" or "bad."[14]

The particular character style that evolves will be shaped by the capacities and skills that the person possesses, as well as their success, given the particular circumstances of an individual's socialization. Intelligence may be strongly valued in one family, charm in another. Once a particular mix of skill, circumstance, and need has produced a more or less satisfactory "solution" of the basic developmental dilemma, it tends to become integrated, reinforced (since it does bring some degree of "success"), and therefore persistent.

Individuals vary in their genetic and psychological endowment and hence in the capacity to specialize in one or another way. There are limits to the extent that people who are inclined to move more away from than toward others can develop charm. However, for analytical purposes we can distinguish three sets or categories of endowed or developing skill areas. They are capacities that develop in the cognitive/creative domain, in the interpersonal domain, and in the characterological domain.

The cognitive skill domain is the arena of thought, broadly defined. Interpersonal skills include empathy, identification, and other forms of emotional connectedness that facilitate relatedness. Finally, characterological strengths refer to the capacities to commit oneself to one's purposes, to endure frustration, and to maintain determination. These elements underlie the capacity for self-reliant, autonomous functioning.

One way to examine the aspects of character style is to consider them as being located on three continua. The cognitive style continuum would be arrayed along an axis anchored at one end by strong analyzing, synthesizing, and integrating abilities. The other end of the continuum would be anchored by the tendency to see things in broad analytical, sharply differentiated categories. I conceptualize this continuum as that of *analytical versus global*.

The interpersonal style continuum would be anchored on one end by a tendency to move toward people and try to develop and maintain close connections. At the other end would be those characterized by moving away from close interpersonal connections. I conceptualize the interpersonal continuum as that of moving *toward versus away from people*.

The characterological style continuum would be anchored on one end by a tendency to rely on oneself and to take on and persist in independent action. At the other end of the continuum would be those who hesitate to take on individual initiatives that are not sanctioned or approved by important others. I conceptualize the characterological domain as that of being *autonomous versus dependent*.

Individuals located further toward the autonomy pole are more likely to be able to accomplish their purposes, even if the odds seem high. They are therefore more likely to move directly toward goals, bolstered by a secure sense of what their personal and professional goals are, as these are shaped by well-considered and strongly held values. Such persons are likely to be more persistent and also more resilient, able to tolerate setbacks and disagreements.

Character Style and Presidential Performance

The analytic utility of character style lies in its ability to uncover differences and point to patterns. Not every person (or president) possesses strong or superior analytical or other cognitive skills. Not every person (or president) has good interpersonal and relational skills. Not all persons (or presidents) are equally secure (a consequence of consolidated character elements) or able to be self-reliant.

Barber (1992a, 5–6; see also George's [1975, 243] consideration of Barber's use of style) is one of the few political psychologists to take seriously the importance of style. He defines style as a president's relative emphasis from among the tasks that he sees each president as having to do. These tasks are rhetoric, interpersonal relations, and homework. The first has to do with communicating to others in order to educate and mobilize them. The second has to do with dealing face to face with other politicians and others in small groups to accomplish his purposes. The third involves the management of "the endless flow of details that come across his desk."

Style, as Barber conceives it, is therefore synonymous with the defining elements of presidential performance. I argue in the next chapter for a different set of defining characteristics of presidential performance. Here, though, I want to point out another difference between my conception of style and Barber's.

Barber's concept of style is largely divorced from his discussion of character. That is, there is no particular linkage between character, as Barber defines it in terms of his theory of presidential character, and the stylistic emphasis a president may choose to make. An active-positive president like Kennedy may choose to emphasize rhetoric, but so may a passive-positive president like Ronald Reagan.

How are the character styles that individuals develop related to presidential performance? We can distinguish a number of ways. It is a very rare for a successful presidential candidate or president not to have substantially developed at least one of the stylistic elements. Some potential presidents fully develop only one; they are character-style specialists. I suggest that most successful and effective presidents have developed at least two and often all three of the character-style elements discussed in the previous section.

We can examine the effects of character style on presidential performance by concentrating on the particular skill or capacity area(s) that a candidate reveals. In this section, I briefly outline some connections among character, character style, and presidential performance. I begin with a brief discussion of each character-style element (interpersonal, characterological, and cognitive) in relation to presidential performance.

One aspect of character style that is very relevant to presidential performance is that connected to relationships. The importance of a president's relationships has been recognized to some degree in previous research. Neustadt's (1990) argument that the essence of presidential power lies in persuasion underscores the importance of interpersonal relationships.

Similarly, recent analyses of Ronald Reagan's political success (Jones 1988) suggest that it was related to the Reagan administration's ability to develop and maintain good working relationships with key Washington power centers. The failure to accomplish this is frequently suggested as one reason that the Carter presidency floundered (Buchanan 1987). In terms of our previous discussion, successful presidents move (primarily, but not always) toward people, not away from or against them.

Among the important psychological components of interpersonal skills are the capacities for emotional attunement and sensitivity to others, which are the building blocks of the capacity to connect with others. Persons who develop these capacities are readily able to form relationships and to work well with others. Presidents with this character style tend to emphasize their interpersonal relationships in politics and are good coalition builders. George Bush appeared to illustrate this style during the Gulf War (Wayne 1993), as did Bill Clinton in winning the 1992 presidential election.

The second area, characterological strengths, refers to those aspects of the self, originating in the successful development of the three character elements (ambition, integrity, and relatedness), that help individuals overcome the inevitable setbacks that occur as they make their way in the world. They include, as noted, the ability to persist in moving toward one's goals when faced with setbacks and adversity. Barber's (1992a, 140, 142) observations on Richard Nixon's fighting style and fierce determination appear to place the former president in this category. Bill Clinton's ability to persist, despite a number of setbacks, during the 1992 presidential primaries and the general election would also seem to place him in this category (Renshon 1993b). Candidates and presidents with this style tend to be more autonomous than dependent.

The last set of skills that are instrumental in developing a character style rests on strong analytic capacities. The emphasis in this style is on analysis. A person with these skills may not be attuned so much to persons as to problems. They are skillful problem solvers, able to abstract, conceptualize, and analyze. When these skills are not combined with interpersonal strengths, the person may find himself somewhat ill equipped for political life, which, after all, requires the solution of problems within a context of relationships with others.

Kellerman (1983b) notes that Jimmy Carter was an able decision maker who had difficulty with the interpersonal aspects of exercising power because he was somewhat introverted. Barber (1992a) notes that Nixon emphasized homework, an important part of making decisions, yet he lacked the interpersonal skills to develop collaborative political leadership, also an important skill in presidential performance. In presidential campaigns, the failure to combine an ability to connect emotionally with people and analytic skills can get a candidate into severe trouble. Michael Dukakis, when asked during a presidential debate how he would respond to a criminal who attacked his wife, gave an answer that reflected his understanding of due process but left unaddressed the feelings of hurt, anger, and (perhaps) revenge that many might feel (but not act on) upon learning such news.

The Question of Motivation

All three elements of character style raise important questions about the fit between a candidate's style and his potential presidential performance. Does a candidate possess unusual skills of analysis or judgment? Does the candidate exhibit a strong sense of capacity, persistence, and resilience? Which aspects does the candidate combine, and in what degree?

Stopping with that information is a fundamental but common error. It is not enough to know, for example, that a candidate emphasizes an interpersonal (rather than a cognitive/creative or characterological) character style. One also needs to know how the elements of character style are related to the underlying character elements that shape them.

Is the relational style motivated by the hope of being accepted, admired, respected? Is the candidate's intelligence primarily in the service of his personal or political ambitions? Is his persistence driven by the need to be validated? In short, one needs to analyze *how* the candidate's style fits in relation to his overall psychological and behavioral patterns. A major question is whether the candidate's style flows from developed and consolidated characterological elements or whether it operates primarily to help the individual acquire what he does not feel he has and cannot count on getting—in other words, in a compensatory manner.

Consider the skill area of interpersonal relations. It is, as noted above, important to know whether a candidate (or president) has skills in this area. But it is also important to note *how* these skills are used.

Lyndon Johnson is often credited with being a masterful president in this regard. His skills at cajoling, manipulating, flattering, and, where necessary, threatening are legendary. Barber calls this the famous "Johnson Treatment" (see also Evans and Novak 1966, 95–117) and argues that Lyndon Johnson "exemplifies, as no other President in history, an emphasis on personal relations" (1992a, 67). Kearns writes that Johnson obligated his followers by providing them with services or benefits that they desired or needed. But the line between obligation and coercion was often thin. In return for his gifts, Johnson demanded a high measure of gratitude, which could only be acceptably demonstrated by the willingness to follow his lead. . . . These demands for submission invariably worked against him. (1976, 371–72)

There can be no doubt that Johnson had strong interpersonal political skills. But the skills were in the service of an even stronger psychological need, that of getting his own way at whatever cost. The very array of information about the strengths and weaknesses of others and the range of his approaches to them reflect that Johnson had a specialized and well-developed skill. But this is not the whole story. Johnson could be demanding, forceful, and, more than occasionally, personally abusive to those who balked at his wishes. This capacity and the frequency with which these tactics surfaced suggest that the skills were in the service of a very strong psychological motivation to get his way, in some cases at the expense of a respectful stance toward disagreement and at the expense of others' self-esteem.

The problem is further complicated by the fact that we cannot assume that character elements will always appear in such a stark guise. They can also be expressed in unexpected skills. A "narcissistic character" might well ultimately be interested in exploiting people for his own ends but might nonetheless develop gracious social skills.

There are very practical reasons for developing means to mask the operation of certain character elements. These reasons include social acceptability and strategic calculation. One of the problems in assessing the psychological suitability of presidential candidates is that smart and ambitious political leaders can develop masking strategies to cover over or otherwise deflect an appreciation of the role that unwanted character elements might play.

A Further Consequence of Character: Character-Based Beliefs

Beliefs are important in the psychological assessment of presidential candidates. They represent a layer of psychological organization that can exist at a relatively deep level of the personality structure (Renshon 1974; Knutson 1972), that of not fully articulated assumption. Beliefs can be embedded deep in the personality system, but not so deep that the individuals themselves, as well outside observers, are unaware of them. As such, beliefs can operate as a transitional analytic structure between the relatively unconscious and inaccessible parts of an individual's character structure and those that are more directly evident and visible.

Obviously, one must distinguish different types and levels of beliefs. There are the beliefs and belief systems of which political philosophy and ideology are representative. These are usually fairly well articulated and also fairly conscious to individuals, especially if the political domain is especially relevant to them.

But there is a class of beliefs that is not always so fully and explicitly articulated. These beliefs are not unconscious, and if pressed or asked directly, most individuals would be able to articulate them to some degree. They exist and operate primarily at what psychoanalysts would call the preconscious level. I term these *basic character beliefs* because of their assumptive nature.

They develop out of the same experiences that forge character. While the mix of need, skill, and circumstance is developing into a character style, a parallel psychological and cognitive process is occurring. That process consists of the development of beliefs that reflect a person's basic experience and arise out of the attempt to resolve the basic developmental dilemma. These beliefs are *frameworks of assumption*. They are the person's basic view "of the way things are" and, as such, serve as guides for the approach to and interpretation of experience.

Basic beliefs are not representative of the range of possible experience available to the ordinary person. Rather, they are representative of a person's own *particular experiences* and are therefore, in important ways, unique. They are not true or false in the conventional sense of being empirically verifiable. They are, rather, the person's *standard operating interpretations* of actual and potential experience, derived from expectations that are based, in turn, on assumption. Character beliefs are the cognitive expressions of character and the handmaidens of style.

Each of the three basic character elements discussed above (ambition, integrity, and relatedness) and the character style that an individual develops give rise to a set of related basic beliefs. Among the character beliefs that arise from successful outcomes in the ambition domain is the assumption that initiatives are worth making because experience confirms that success is a product of effort. I term these kinds of assumptions the *mastery beliefs,* and they result in a sense of effective capacity.

Among the character beliefs that arise from the sense of consolidated identity, which is built on a solid foundation of personal and interpersonal ideals and values, and from the experience of responsiveness from those who have helped the individual attain this developmental step is the assumption that one is "good enough" to be connected to others and that others will be responsive in return. I term these kinds of assumptions *relationship beliefs*.

A third major belief set that accompanies character development consists of those that arise out of an individual's consolidation of his ambition, ideals, skills, and style into a package that uniquely defines each person's identity. These beliefs develop as the individual tries to find the fit between his or her character, skills, and aspirations on the one hand and social opportunities on the other. In the process, the individual comes to crystallize not only who he is but what he stands for. These assumptions I term, after Erikson's (1956) designation, *identity beliefs*.

Each of these three sets of character beliefs is important in the president's exercise of his responsibilities in decision making and political leadership. Mastery beliefs are critical to presidential performance because they support the capacity for initiative and persistence. If a president truly believes his actions are not likely to count, he will find little cognitive or motivational basis for the exercise of leadership. Such a person may also have difficulty engaging in the difficult process of reconciling diverse and conflicting alternatives that often characterizes presidential decision making.

Relationship beliefs are crucial to presidential performance in several ways. They help to frame the president's expectations with regard to a key element of presidential leadership: the reactions to his choices from others. Does the president believe that people will be responsive to his honest, straightforward understanding of what they collectively face? Does he believe that responsiveness depends on his presenting things as others would prefer them to be, rather than how they are?

Finally, identity beliefs can be considered the anchor of presidential judgments and leadership. Through often-shifting calculations and fluid situations, through the many interests that must be considered in presidential leadership and decision making, the president requires a core understanding of what he stands for and what he wants. A president who lacks such an understanding or, as is more often the case, has too fluid an understanding will find himself emotionally and politically buffeted by the demands he must confront.

Conclusion

The model of character development put forward here is meant to operate as a framework for the analysis of psychological suitability within one political role, the presidency. The character elements, individual skills, and the character style that develop in each person emerge in a layered pattern. The individual's solution to the basic developmental dilemma results in a functional pattern of psychological elements.

These elements, and the associated patterns that develop from them, are put forward as useful frames for the analysis of the two crucial dimensions of presidential performance, judgment and leadership, which I will discuss in the following chapter. Important questions are whether character or any of its important elements develops, and if so, how and under what circumstances.

The importance of these questions in the context of our discussion lies in two related but distinct aspects of psychological assessment. First, if character is relatively stable, it should provide a fairly reliable set of indicators regarding a candidate's approach to private and public life. To the extent that character is consistent over time, an examination of a presidential candidate's personal and political history can provide more valid and useful data of how he might handle his presidential responsibilities.

The second aspect of assessment concerns a different kind of intervention. Ordinarily, we seek to assess character to estimate the chances of harm or success that might follow from one or another character configuration. But the answers to the questions of whether character develops, as well as how, and under what circumstances may also be used to develop methods or strategies by which character-related elements of presidential performance might be examined with a view toward strengthening virtues and diminishing difficulties. We will take up this question directly in the discussion of the preparation of individuals for political power in Appendix 3.

I have argued here that character does become consolidated and thus stable. That allows the possibility that character will be reflected in publicly observable behavior, presidential and otherwise. But I have also suggested that elements of character can and do develop. The president is not simply a child in man's clothing. The development of cognitive, characterological, and interpersonal skills provides the means by which the ongoing basic developmental dilemma between what one wishes to get and actually receives can be, if not entirely resolved, at least accommodated.

In the next chapter I present a model of character and presidential performance. We will then be in a position to evaluate two recent presidential campaigns, those of 1988 and 1992, in the context of psychological suitability. My purpose is to examine the degree to which the characterological elements put forward here were either evident or observable in those campaigns. We will then be in a firmer position to assess the utility of using these elements in evaluating other campaigns.

E I G H T

Toward a Theory of Character and Presidential Performance

The responsibilities of the presidency have grown dramatically (Rose 1988). In addition to the traditional
constitutional obligations, a large and growing list of presidential duties and
responsibilities has developed (Cronin 1975, 155; Kellerman 1984, 12–16).
The growing number of presidential responsibilities and their complexity
appear to defy efforts either to categorize or to accomplish them. Can we
discern within this widening list a basic and irreducible core of presidential
performance?

It would be helpful to have an answer to this question that would not
depend on specific debates over policies and their effects but would still
allow the appraisal of a president's approach to policy. Also, since policy is
enacted through a political process, it would be useful to focus on a
president's skills in accomplishing his purposes. In short, a useful conceptual
framework for analyzing presidential performance would include a concern
with both policy thinking and political action.

In considering the basic, core responsibilities of presidents, we must
keep in mind two fundamental facts. First, the ultimate responsibility to
decide lies with the president. Second, a president must be able to mobilize
support to carry through his plans. The first point leads us to focus on the
quality of a president's understanding and decision making. It points us
toward the qualities of analysis, temperament, and appraisal that underlie all
of the president's decisions in office. In short, it leads to a consideration of
an individual's personal, policy, and political judgment.

The second fact points to a president's capacity to build support and exercise power and his methods for doing so. In short, it leads us to consider political leadership. Suggesting that judgment and leadership are the basic pillars of presidential performance allows us to ask more precise questions about how character affects them, and it is to these questions that we now turn.[1]

The Role of Judgment in Presidential Decision Making

An emphasis on making decisions as a key ingredient of presidential power is evident in many definitions of politics. Easton (1965) defined the field of politics as being concerned with the "authoritative allocation of scarce resources," in other words, making decisions that stick. Even earlier, Lasswell (1930) proposed that politics be defined as dealing with questions of who gets what, again implying that decisions about these matters are central to the understanding of the field. Indeed, it is hard to escape the underlying importance of making decisions in any account of important presidential responsibilities.

What is new in this formulation is the focus not on decisions per se but on the qualities of judgment that inform them. Presidents are called upon to make a wide variety of decisions. Some function to set the political agenda. Some structure the process of policy debate and resolution. Some serve as the final word on a policy issue.[2] Beyond these variations lies the elusive but crucial domain of presidential perception, inference, and preference.

At the heart of leadership lies choice. And at the heart of choice lies judgment. It is in the realm of judgment that character, experience, and vision intersect with political realities to produce results that are central to assessing presidential performance.

Judgment is a complex but little studied concept, with obvious relevance to presidential performance and candidate evaluations. What is judgment, and how can it be analyzed? What differences are there between flawed judgments and those that appear adequate to the circumstances? Is there such a thing as good judgment? Can we distinguish a set of characteristics that would support the concept of good judgment? Is it a matter of character, situation, or both?

The Nature of Judgment

Any answers to such questions must begin with the nature of judgment itself.[3] We can understand judgment as the quality of analysis, reflection, and, ultimately, insight that informs the making of consequential decisions. Only decisions that pose significant questions and therefore have significant consequences for areas of presidential responsibility raise issues of good or flawed judgment in any fundamental way.

I term these major forks in the decision road *framing decisions*. Framing decisions are crucial because they represent key and sometimes (but not always) starkly contrasting alternatives, each of which will point to a different path, open up some options, close others, and bring about different results. One consequence of emphasizing the relationship of judgment to framing decisions is that it allows us to distinguish the quality of judgment in the making of framing decisions from that of subsequent decisions.[4]

Adequate or even good judgment alone does not guarantee good outcomes. There are at least three important reasons why this might be the case:

1. A framing decision may reflect good judgment, but some of the subsequent decisions that flow from it may be flawed. In making an overall assessment, one would have to balance the judgments that went into making an appropriate framing decision and the nature of the flaws in any decisions that followed from the initial decision during implementation.[5]

2. Judgment is only one part of the process that leads from decisions to results. Good judgments alone, if they are not accompanied by a set of capacities to realize the fruits of one's judgments, will not result in high-quality outcomes. The bridge between high-quality judgments and (the potential for) high-quality outcomes is political skills, the most important of which, I argue, revolves around political leadership.

3. The complex process that leads from presidential judgments to outcomes is not carried out in a contextual vacuum. That process involves other actors, some of whom have considerable resources of their own. Their actions may deflect or even thwart the impact of presidential judgments. The assessment of a judgment's impact therefore has to include not a static world in which judgment proceeds without interference but a world in which others are actively striving to modify or reverse the effects of the president's judgments.

The development of a framework for assessing judgment requires us to focus on four related considerations: the problem itself, the context(s) within which decisions are made, the actual decisions that were made, and the results of those decisions. In analyzing the problem, we must know what fundamental issues it raises. In analyzing domains, one can distinguish domestic from foreign policy spheres (Wildavsky 1987) and then further specify an appropriate placement within those domains for a particular problem (for example, economic interdependence). In analyzing the decisions themselves, we need to understand what factors were weighed (for example, the relative weight given to policy and political concerns)[6] and with what results. And last, in analyzing outcomes we need to appreciate the consequences of the decision.

Judgment Frameworks

Judgment is a joint function of a president's (or leader's) analytical and reflective abilities on the one hand, and the nature of the problem to be faced on the other. Procedural, cognitive, and psychodynamic models of decision making have treated the problem at hand as a given rather than as a variable.[7] The analysis of presidential judgment is concerned with the problem to be addressed in two distinct ways. First, appreciating the nature of a problem is crucial to deciding what is at issue and what solutions are viable. Second, the nature of the problem also has an impact on the understanding and experience that a leader can bring to bear on it. Both are important.

I use the term *judgment framework* to denote the major conceptual organization that a president brings to bear on the analysis of a problem. Judgment frameworks can be conceptualized as *adequate, defective, incomplete,* or *complex.* An adequate framework places the problem into a frame for analysis that correctly, but not necessarily fully, fits the problem at hand. For example, before the collapse of the Soviet Union many international problems could be put into the conceptual category of "superpower conflict" or "East–West tensions." This does not mean that a problem may not have had other dimensions, only that the category selected did indeed fit a major aspect of the problem.

A defective framework for analysis is one that does not provide adequate historical or personal experiential guidance for solutions. It represents an inappropriate assignment of a problem to a framework whose lessons are not generally applicable and that therefore mislead and divert attention from more relevant understanding. Placing U.S.–Japanese economic competition into the framework of "trade wars" may correctly reflect the competitive economic nature of the problem but inappropriately add the model of "war" to what is essentially a developing partnership.

Incomplete frameworks are probably the most prevalent form of heuristic (problem-solving) difficulty. In this case, frameworks for analysis are not necessarily wrong, just deficient. There are several reasons why incomplete frameworks may be used. In some situations and historical periods, models simply may not have been developed and experience-tested. This appears to be the case for foreign policy analysis in the aftermath of the collapse of the Soviet Union. With that collapse, a major—perhaps the major—model for the analysis of foreign policy has been rendered obsolete. The phrase "new world order" states the obvious but gives no clue to the nature of that "world order."

Another frequent cause behind the use of incomplete judgment frameworks is that strong extant frameworks tend to overshadow other possible, even complementary, frameworks. One of the clearest examples of this occurred during the Cuban missile crisis. A reading of the National Security Council (NSC) transcripts (Welch and Blight 1987/88; Tractenberg 1985) reveals that little thought was given to the Cuban view of this crisis at the time it was unfolding.

At a conference held in 1991 that brought together former participants in the Cuban missile crisis (Blight, Lewis, and Welch 1991), General William Y. Smith pointed out that "at that time people . . . dealing with military matters—those at the civilian level and at the military level—*looked at everything primarily through a U.S.–Soviet prism*" (emphasis mine). Arthur Schlesinger, another participant in the events and at the conference, pointed out that "the reduction of a complex triangular crisis to a bilateral conflict between the two super powers . . . reflected . . . unconscious Great Power attitudes towards small states" (Blight, Lewis, and Welch 1991, 197). The use of the great-power conflict lens was not wrong as a judgment framework. However, it tended to obscure other important considerations.

Three Characterological Questions

Can characterological strengths overcome the operation of incomplete judgment frameworks? Preliminary evidence suggests the answer is a qualified yes. The NSC tapes reveal that on the first day, John F. Kennedy was not only surprised but stunned and enraged by what he saw as the audacity of Nikita Khrushchev's move of missiles into Cuba. The first NSC session was given over to Kennedy's assertion that the missiles must go, most likely by military force in the form of an air strike.

It is one reflection of Kennedy's characterological strength that he was able to recover from his shock and anger and harness his determination to respond forcefully to a more constructive and less immediately dangerous set of responses. This is also evident in his openness to information and argument during the process. The level of give-and-take that characterizes these meetings is evident, even if the progression of the argument is not always systematic or sequential.

Complex judgment frameworks usually involve the integration of one or more frameworks into which the problem might productively fit. It is now clear, for example, that a more complex framework for judgment and analysis during the Cuban missile crisis would have been one that included U.S.–Cuba (large power–small state) relationships. Had the executive committee members had that model in their minds, they might have been better able to answer the question "Why would the Soviet Union put missiles in Cuba?" and perhaps had the basis for a settlement of the crisis, a "no-invasion pledge."[8]

Do complex judgment frameworks require an equally complex mind? The ability to hold and synthesize alternative frameworks is partially a reflection of cognitive capacity. Some leaders are able to integrate and hold more information, demonstrating what Suedfeld (1992) has termed *cognitive complexity*. However, it is not clear that cognitive complexity is necessary for high-quality decisions, an issue that Tetlock (1984) raises.

Complex thinking does not necessarily lead to better policy judgment. Obsessive thinkers, for example, usually exhibit highly complex and differentiated thinking. However, such individuals do not as a rule have good judgment. While their thinking may be complex, it often lacks depth, flexibility, and sophistication. It is the latter three qualities, not the first, that help to define the quality of judgment.

What is crucial to good judgment is understanding, not complexity per se. The amount of reflective insight that a president brings to bear on a problem may prove more important than the degree of complexity in his thinking. Reflective insight is only partially and indirectly related to cognitive complexity.

Is good judgment situational? I argue that some basic characterological elements stand at the core of good judgment, which would seem to be an argument in favor of a general characteristic of good (or poor) judgment in presidents and leaders. While this is accurate to some degree, good judgment is also closely connected to particular domains, problems, and the frameworks that have been generated by experience. A president's (or leader's) range and depth of understanding of a problem are related to his experience with (and understanding of) problems of the same sort.[9]

A president may have very good judgment on domestic issues and politics but lack the experiential frame to have equally good judgment on national security or foreign policy issues, and vice versa. Even within one domain, such as international relations, it seems possible for different problems to result in different levels of judgment in response. A president might be very well positioned to exercise good judgment in the areas of international political competition and conflict, but not as well prepared if the international challenge is primarily economic.[10] This is not to contend that good judgments cannot be reached in unfamiliar areas, only that they are facilitated by understanding that has been refined by experience.

The extent to which good judgment is possible in the absence of accumulated experience in a major area is an open question. Certainly, experience is no guarantee of good judgment or of successful presidential performance. For example, in the 1992 presidential election Ross Perot argued that his experience running large corporations and "getting things done" was a sufficient qualification for him to be seriously considered for president. Perhaps; but what experience provides are judgment frameworks developed and refined in the same contexts in which they will be applied. Ross Perot's business experience, however successful and whatever the lessons he learned, would not necessarily prepare him for the political and military complexities of possible military intervention in Bosnia. When experience is lacking, sophisticated judgment frameworks are difficult to develop.

Anticipation versus Prediction

The importance of anticipating consequences raises the question of the degree of foresight that one should expect to inform judgments. Tetlock (1992) argues that the ability to *predict* outcomes is a crucial element of good judgment. This may be too strong a requirement.

Consequences, sometimes unintended and at other times unforeseen, do play a role in assessments of judgment. Good judgment, however, does not require that a president foresee specific consequences that may unfold from a framing decision. To do so would require that a president be able either to read minds or to predict the future. Our current theories, the complexity of events, and past experience do not provide much confidence that we (or a president) can count on this.

In reality, the issue may not be so much the ability of a president to predict outcomes as his capacity to understand and anticipate a *range* of possible or likely consequences. We can expect that a president will appreciate the possible major consequences to flow from a framing decision and act accordingly. Indeed, one way to distinguish good from poor judgment is that in the latter case a president will fail to appreciate what clearly could and should have been known, or will realize it but fail to act accordingly. Good judgment clearly entails the capacity to appreciate and act on probable consequences but also to anticipate possible ones.

Evaluating the Consequences of Judgment

Evaluating the consequences of judgment in policy decision making is perhaps the most controversial and difficult task connected with developing a theory of good policy judgment. This task has proved so conceptually difficult that it has led political psychology theorists to focus on the quality of the decision process[11] rather than to attempt to assess outcomes.[12] But attempting to assess outcomes, while very difficult, is worth the effort. Decisions and the judgments that support them are important because they have effects, not because they were arrived at by a process.

The ultimate test of any judgment is how well it addresses the issue at hand. Of course, most issues raise more than one problem. Alexander George has pointed out (1980, 1) the trade-offs that occur frequently between decision quality and (political) acceptability. The "best" decision may not be politically possible. Often the president is forced to choose between a better and a worse decision rather than between a good and a bad one. Some policy problems appear to have no good solutions (Calabresi and Bobbitt 1979).

Still, an analysis of the quality of decision making that focused on political feasibility alone would leave important unanswered questions. Was the quality of the decision compromised with regard to substance by too much concern with feasibility? Could the commitment of leadership resources and skills have made a different decision more politically feasible? These are difficult questions to answer since they are, to some degree, counterfactual.

Evaluating the quality of a president's judgment is always a complex task, given that policy choices are so varied. Yet while it may sound somewhat strange, this is not an issue that need particularly concern us in presidential campaigns. The reason is that candidates don't make real policy judgments. They are running for office, not already in it. The most a candidate can do is criticize a president who is running for reelection by saying what he would have done or would do differently, but this is hardly the kind of data that allows us to evaluate a candidate's judgment.

Deprived of real case data on a candidate's policy judgments,[13] the press and public focus, not unreasonably, on his personal and political judgment during the campaign. While there are many complexities involved in appraising the judgment of others, it sometimes quite possible to do so. In chapter 6, while examining the quality of judgment exhibited by Thomas Eagleton with regard to his medical history, it did not seem unusually difficult to assess his reasoning and to categorize it as poor judgment. The same can be said for the exploration of Gary Hart's judgment in connection with his failed campaign for the Democratic Party's presidential nomination, which is taken up in the next chapter. What these cases have in common is a clearly sought goal (the nomination), a clear and public set of behaviors that call the goal into question, and, most important, data that allow us to understand the reasoning that went into the behavior.

Character and Judgment

A president's judgment is not primarily an act of cognition or general intelligence, as cognitive models of political decision making suggest. Judgment reflects a blend of intelligence, experience, and insight. It also requires a consolidated set of character elements to withstand the rigors of the decision process.

I defined character in the preceding chapter as an individual's basic psychological stance, along with his capacities and the resultant style that both of these bring to bear on experience. Character at its best reflects a president's sense of himself as an able, honest, and related person. It includes the style that he has developed to engage the world and his beliefs in doing so. His feelings of capacity and worth, and the psychological structures that support them, are linked to skilled judgment in a number of ways. So, too, feelings of inadequacy (or hyperadequacy) or low (or high) self-regard, and the psychological structures in which these are embedded, are linked with poor judgment. We shall explore both of these sets of relationships shortly.

In examining character, we must also be interested in the extent to which a candidate's (or president's) character structure has evolved, consolidated, and integrated the diverse demands with which it must deal.[14] Among these is the capacity to modulate but satisfy basic (developmentally normal and appropriate) wishes for accomplishment and recognition. Mature character consolidation also reflects having satisfactorily resolved sometimes conflicting needs and their resulting dilemmas: interpersonal connectedness versus personal autonomy, approval versus independence, and self-interest versus a concern for others. While poor judgment can result from a failure to respond adequately to threat, it can also occur when a president realizes the risks but because of overconfidence is not deterred. Unbridled ambition and rage (Renshon 1993a) are two other characterological sources of poor judgment. Last, mature character involves having a developed and consolidated personal identity (including ideals and values) that provides the president not only a vehicle for the expression of himself in the world but also an internal compass for the evaluation of policy dilemmas.

Character consolidation reflects relative success in another crucial developmental and functional task—that of making and developing a range of interpersonal relationships. Being able to make emotional connections to others reflects a number of important psychological accomplishments, including a capacity to go beyond self-interest, and provides direct emotional and cognitive experience of the concerns and feelings that others have. This experience is crucial to empathetic understanding, a fundamental element of political empathy and, as I will argue, good policy judgment as well.

Psychological Elements of Good Judgment

While good judgment is to some degree contextually specific, poor judgment tends to be systematic. Good judgment, as noted, is related to the qualities of both analysis and reflection. This distinction underscores the point that good judgment is only partially cognitive.

The model of presidential judgment developed here distinguishes among *analysis, reflection,* and *enactment.* Analysis refers to the capacity to discern the essential nature of problems, the potential avenues of response and their implications, and the method(s) by which responses might be accomplished. Of course, this requires the ability to comprehend and process information, as well as to compare information elements with one another and with other frames of reference. These are ordinarily considered cognitive skills, and to some extent they are. However, they are substantially affected by character.

Reflection refers to the capacity to consider and evaluate analytical information from a series of perspectives. Good judgment requires the ability to place information in a framework that makes intellectual, experiential, and emotional sense not only to the president but to those whom the decisions affect. The reflective dimension of good judgment therefore rests not only on cognitive skills but on the capacity to anchor analysis by frameworks of understanding, evaluation, and action. These frameworks involve the president's own ideals, values, and views; the values and views of other actors involved; and both long- and short-term political and strategic considerations.

Finally, enactment refers to the ability to find and utilize means to implement the results of judgment. The focus here is on the means that are chosen. Are they adequate and appropriate to the task? Does a president (leader) choose to talk, to threaten, to fight? Does he concentrate on one approach or choose a mix? Are there other, less costly means that could accomplish the same ends? These questions are important not only because they bear on the issue of the quality of a president's thought and judgment but also because they reveal something about his character and leadership.

Psychologically, then, good judgment reflects a set of composite skills. Among them are the abilities to:

1. see the framing decision for the crucial choice that it represents;

2. understand the essential elements of a problem and their significance and place the problem within an appropriate judgment framework;

3. consider and reflect on the range of issues and values raised by the situation in order to deal adequately with the various interests (political, social, and psychological) involved;

4. consider and reflect on information that is frequently limited and often discordant;

5. make use of, but not be subservient to, feeling or impulse,[15] including the anxiety generated by uncertainty and high risk;

6. place the above (1–5) in a framework of understanding that adequately assesses the basic nature of the problem and points to a range of responses that preserve and perhaps even advance the values and interests at risk to develop a fitting solution;

7. draw on understanding of the past and present (see point 1) to consider how alternative choices will shape the future (the extrapolation of implications);

8. develop, set in motion, and maintain a series of steps to accomplish purposes consistent with one's understanding of the issues raised and values

at risk. The steps should accomplish these goals with minimal harm if harm proves necessary.

This list includes both analytic and reflective skills. Some of these capacities are clearly cognitive. Others are more clearly affective. Some require the leader to translate effective thought into effective policy. All, however, are to some degree shaped by character. The relationships among them are varied and complex. (These linkages are schematically represented in Appendix 2.) It is to these linkages that we turn in the following sections.

Policy Framing and Analysis: The Role of Character

Good judgment begins with understanding the nature of the problem. Of course, to understand the essential elements of a problem, one must first recognize there is one. Not all leaders are able to do this. Some cannot discern the facts, others discern the facts but decline to accept them, while still others think that there are special reasons why they can afford to ignore them.

At the level of character, the reasons for not being able to grapple with problems can be complex and varied. The inability can originate from either a meager or an inflated sense of capacity and self-regard. Presidents who suffer from the first either can be too inhibited to respond boldly and directly to an issue or prefer optimism over realism. Similarly, the optimistic weighing of sobering information (wishful thinking), a dislike of conflict, a strong sensitivity to criticism, and a strong need to be liked all play inhibiting characterological roles in the failure to meet difficulties directly.

An inflated sense of capacity and self-regard can lead to equally damaging results. The sense that "it can't happen here" can inhibit the accurate appreciation and diagnosis of problems; so, too, can feelings in the president that he possesses unusual competence, invulnerability, and entitlement.[16] These arise from feelings that the leader is special, powerful, and beyond the reach of ordinary circumstances. In such cases a leader may discern the facts but discount their significance because of his special accomplishments, circumstances, and so on.

A second analytic requirement for good judgment is the capacity to "diagnose" a problem. This is a matter not just of being smart in the IQ sense of intelligence but of being able to discern and appreciate the essential issues raised by a problem. This requires the ability to appreciate implications and to extract significance from an incomplete set of facts.

The capacity to understand and diagnose a problem often reflects a president's range of experiences and what he has learned from them. Learning from experience requires that mistakes not be viewed or felt as intolerable indictments of competence and self-respect. Presidents (or leaders) with low self-regard have trouble learning from mistakes precisely because it is so difficult for them to acknowledge their errors without damaging their feelings about themselves. One basic problem that dictators have in this regard is that they are often shielded from the results of their mistakes. Therefore, experiences that might have an ameliorating effect on the leader's policy and decision making do not play that role.

Reflective Skills

Reflective abilities require more of leaders than the capacity to analyze discrete elements. Ultimately, skillful judgment leads to higher-quality decisions because information is assembled into an understanding that both correctly diagnoses the situation and points toward adequate responses. Information alone, however abundant, is not enough.

High-quality decisions require a president to weigh, evaluate, and place into a framework many elements of information, assumption, and analysis. A president must be able to see the ways that parts relate to one another and to larger frames of reference that help give meaning to discrete events. So, too, a president must be able to extrapolate implications from limited data and to anticipate some possible results of various situational elements and actions.

The ability to reflect, to draw on past and present, and to extrapolate from them to possible futures involves several psychological processes. Among the most important is the capacity to hold onto and work with incomplete and often unsettling information while shifting among perspectives. A president must be able to endure uncertainty without needing to overcome anxiety by action.

The president must also enter into a weighing process by which the various factors are accorded importance and then put together into some overall assessment. Obviously, this requires more than a listing of pros and cons. It is not only the facts that must be weighed but also the frames of analysis. Does the president give more or less weight to his own policy ambitions, the policy concerns of others, his standing with the public, his calculations for reelection, or other considerations?

Individuals with tenuously held personal or political identities, or identities that have not yet resolved and incorporated consolidated ideals, would seem to be particularly vulnerable in this process: first, because a firmly rooted personal and political identity can help to anchor and shape this part of the decision process; second, because the lack of a consolidated personal and political identity also has implications for the individual's level of consolidated self-esteem. Those without such an anchor run the risks associated with having too high, too low, or too labile a sense of themselves, and this, in turn, has implications for learning.

Individuals with low self-esteem who also lack a consolidated sense of personal effectiveness often avoid new information.[17] It may present too much of a challenge to existing views, may challenge the individual's ability to make sense of it or to act on it. Inflated self-esteem, in contrast, runs the risk of leading the individual to ignore or downplay important information because it does not fit in with what he already knows to be true or because he overestimates his capacity to overcome its implications.

Last, and perhaps most important, good judgment rests on the president's ability to consider the facts and understandings from the vantage point of his own and others' perspectives. Judgment requires evaluation, but the question is: From what perspective? Facts rarely speak for themselves, and complex situations can be addressed in numerous ways.

Ultimately, myriad facts and alternatives must be filtered to be evaluated, and the most important filter is the president's own set of ideals, values, and personal and political ambitions. A president without a coherent, well-formed, and consolidated personal and political identity is like a ship without a rudder. He runs the danger of drift and being subject to the strongest current, whether internal (psychological) or external (political).

Empathy in Good Judgment

A consolidated sense of self, including the ambitions, ideals, and values that inform it, is an important anchor for exercising good judgment in a complex decision field. But the president acts in a world of others, many of whom may not share his values, views, or perspectives. The president, more than any other political leader must be able to "take the role of other."

Empathy is one of those "virtues" that bears closer examination. It has been put forward, mistakenly in my view, as a foolproof cure for misunderstanding and conflict. In reality, there are strong limits to what empathy can accomplish along these lines. And while presidential empathy with the position of others is an important aspect of good judgment, it does not require of the president that he adopt others' views. Moreover, I argue that empathy is not always what it seems and should not necessarily be taken at face value when it seems to be exhibited by candidates or presidents.

What is empathy? Empathic attunement refers to the capacity to understand another by entering into an appreciation of the other's experiences, feelings, expectations, and perspectives. It is a function of at least partially shared (in the sense of understood and appreciated) perspectives. It is a reflection of a person's ability to make real connections with others — what I have previously termed a *capacity for interpersonal connectedness*.

Why is empathetic attunement important to presidential performance? One set of reasons has to do with the limitations of other alternatives. When weighing policy alternatives and their implications, simple or selfish national or individual self-interest is ultimately a poor criterion for adequate policy. The obvious reason is that both are frequently self-defeating. Treating general policymaking as a zero-sum game in which one's gains must necessarily be at another's expense and every compromise felt as a substantial loss guarantees high levels of conflict, some of it unnecessary and counterproductive.

There are other reasons as well, one of which is political the other more psychological, to focus on the uses of empathy. The political reason derives from the fact that considering the concerns and feelings of others is an important element of political authority in democracies. The voluntary ceding of power to a president is based on the expectation that others will be considered even if an ultimate decision is adverse to one's interests.

At the more psychological level, the capacity for interpersonal connectedness that undergirds empathic attunement has implications for the capacity to exercise good judgment and, as will be argued shortly, for effective political leadership as well. Every policy decision a president makes affects others, and the ability to consider how others might respond helps distinguish effective presidents from their counterparts. I have in mind here not political calculation but considerations of another kind.

Leaders whose ambitions and sense of entitlement lead them to view their actions as inherently justified don't worry much about the real effects of their acts on others. To do so might require them to reconsider their sense of entitlement or moderate their ambitions. It is clearly politically inexpedient to reveal any such feelings, and besides, leaders often want to calculate the effects of what they do for their own political purposes. The result is *strategic empathy*.

Strategic empathy[18] is clearly distinguishable from empathetic attunement. Its basic purpose is advantage rather than understanding. There are several motivational variations of this strategy, each related to the advantages that accrue to an individual. Each reflects a different level of interpersonal connectedness.

One motivation for strategic empathy is to use understanding to get others to do what you want and what they might not necessarily wish to do. Strategic empathy in this instance is a sophisticated form of manipulation for direct gain. The leader who makes use of this form sees others as objects whose primary function is to provide what he wants or needs. There is no real consideration of the other, since to do so might interfere with his or her use.

A second form of strategic empathy shares some aspects of the first but is based on a different type of relationship with others. The leader using this form of strategic empathy begins from narcissistically projected feelings of self-identification with "the people." In these cases, a leader has no real empathetic connection with others apart from his belief that somehow his rule embodies their aspirations and needs.[19] This form of strategic empathy reflects the most severe absence of interpersonal connectedness. In this case individuals are not even considered for what they *might* provide, since the leader already assumes that he has a right to expect that what others have is his.

A last motivational source of strategic empathy is the attempt to please others. Here empathy is put in the service of knowing what others want, so that one can please them and be liked or appreciated in return. The primary motivation in this instance is not so much to take as to receive.

There is a level of connection with others in this case, but it runs counter to good judgment and decision making. The reason is that the leader becomes too attuned to what others say they need (want), without being able to distance himself and perhaps make a decision others may find adverse. Here the need to be accepted or appreciated interferes with the ability to make decisions that may be necessary but disliked.

A president who wants to make effective and feasible policy must be able to enter into the experience of others. How does the leader accomplish the task? It requires more than political calculation or strategic empathy. It requires *realistic empathy*.

This type of empathy begins with the capacity to make real interpersonal connections. This is not a matter of appreciating what "I would do or feel if I were in this situation." That approach presupposes that the other is fundamentally similar to oneself. Rather, realistic empathy involves an attempt to enter into a different frame, one that starts from different assumptions and that may lead to different conclusions.

Realistic empathy is a difficult psychological task for several reasons. It requires a president to "suspend self" and self-interest, if possible, if only for a short period. It also requires that the president enter into a perspective that can frequently be approached by analogy and extrapolation, not by directly similar past experience.[20]

Realistic empathy does not require that a president be bound by the concerns, expectations, experiences, and perspectives of others, only that he really consider them. Ultimately, a president must be guided by his personal and political identity. His values, policy aspirations, and feelings regarding a given policy issue are appropriate and legitimate tools of policy choice. For these tools to be effective, however, they must be present. The ability to follow an analysis to some conclusion requires a coherent political and personal view, if not vision. These come primarily from a strong sense of purpose, direction, and identity.

While the capacity for empathy is related to good judgment, the two are not synonymous. Empathy, like other psychological characteristics, is not without its dangers. Strong empathetic attunement with others can combine with other characterological elements to produce effects that run counter to good judgment. A president can be pulled too much by the emotional weight of an empathetic experience. By many accounts, President Jimmy Carter was extremely preoccupied and distracted by his concerns for the fate of the hostages taken from the American embassy in Iran. While such concern is personally laudable, a preoccupation can have troubling consequences to presidential performance.

A president whose characterological foundation includes low self-esteem or who lacks a consolidated sense of personal effectiveness can be overly dependent on others. Having less confidence in himself, he may become adept at ascertaining what others think or want. Too much empathy also may lead to overvaluation of some concerns and undervaluation of others. Too much focus on the concerns of one person or group may leave other groups relatively underrepresented in the president's thoughts.

Finally, the relentless pursuit of empathy by a president may indicate a defensive reaction to less altruistic feelings such as anger and entitlement. Empathy requires the ability to temporarily suppress feelings of competition and the wish for personal advantage, which are a part of ordinary life. A belief that one must suppress these feelings in favor of always being attuned to the needs of others is not necessarily a desirable psychological trait for a president.

The Capacity to Endure Anxiety and Uncertainty

Major political decisions generate intense emotions as well as calculations. Especially in times of crisis, but otherwise too, a president must control and delay whatever impulses toward premature closure or action may be activated by the circumstances.[21] In the 1990 Persian Gulf War, the pressures on President George Bush included the potential costs of delay, which might have placed the situation beyond even difficult solutions. In 1992, President Bill Clinton's policies initiated to address economic difficulties raised intense emotions of a different kind.

The capacity to persist in trying to find solutions in the face of personal and public anxiety, policy criticism, and demands for action is crucial to carrying out effective policy search procedures. To have this capacity requires that a president have confidence in himself and in his abilities. Why is it preferable to have political leaders with a strong, stable[22] sense of effective capacity and personal confidence in office during times of crisis? One reason, as Janis and Mann (1977) have argued, is that even the best-designed information-producing procedures will not be adequately used in the absence of optimism that a solution can be found. Without hope, purpose falters.

Janis and Mann argue that a strong sense of hope for the ultimate accomplishment of one's goals is crucial for vigilant decision making. Hope reflects a belief that accomplishment is not only possible but plausible. In the absence of a sense of effective capacity, of substantial positive experience in the character domain of ambition, there is little likelihood that hope can be maintained in the face of deep policy dilemmas and their attendant anxiety.

In a decision context characterized by high stakes and conflicting information, the lack of personal confidence can lead to paralysis. Presidents are frequently faced with conflicting views, and often these views are strongly held. The ability to preserve one's options in the face of strong views (that is, to resist pressure) requires either strong views of one's own or the ability to tolerate the pressure of intense efforts at persuasion (or both).

Consider the case of President Warren Harding, who, when faced with an important economic decision, confided to a friend:

John, I can't make a damn thing out of this tax problem. I listen to one side and they seem right, and then God! I talk to the other side and they seem just as right, and there I am where I started. I know somewhere there is a book that would give me the truth, but hell, I couldn't read the book. I know somewhere there is an economist that knows the truth, but I don't know where to find him and haven't the sense to trust him when I do find him. God, what a job. (George 1974b, 187)

A president whose basic character beliefs reflect the assumption that hard effort is worthwhile and whose confidence in his abilities rests on solid ground is not likely to experience the deep doubt and inadequacy reflected in Harding's lament.

Character by itself shapes but does not guarantee positive policy outcomes. A president's skill, judgment, and character are, after all, parts of a complex causal process which includes a number of factors that cannot be fully controlled. Still, other things being equal, I argue that substantially developed character capacities are instrumental, if not necessary, correlates to good judgment. However, it is clear that good judgment is a necessary but insufficient element in presidential performance. Presidents must still put their judgments into action. It is to the last part of the presidential performance equation, political leadership, that we turn in the following sections.

The Nature of Political Leadership

The search for leadership has become increasingly important in presidential campaigns. However, leadership is an ambiguous concept. Its nature remains elusive (see Hermann 1986; Tucker 1981) and its manifestations varied (Greenstein 1982; Destler 1988).

Some associate leadership with charisma—that vaguely defined term that includes the ability to generate political excitement. Others view it as a personal quality, akin to gravitas, that allows the leader to command respect and, above all, compliance. Still others see leadership as the act of faithfully representing constituent views and goals.

Political leadership may involve all of these elements to some degree, but in a democracy it is essentially to be found in the willingness and capacity to direct and exercise power for public purposes. The capacity to do so wisely and well is a key dimension of assessing psychological suitability for the presidency.

Political leadership therefore can be defined in relation to the capacity to act on the implications of one's judgments and achieve results. In that respect, leadership and power share a definition that includes the ability to accomplish purposes. However, political leadership in a democracy requires, where power does not, that a president's judgments not only lead to "fitting solutions" but be publicly understandable and defensible.

Political leadership also requires skills to translate judgment into effective policy. Presidential leadership does not take place in a behavioral vacuum. The personal and political means that a president has at his disposal, and chooses to use, will weigh heavily on the policy ends.

It is important to underscore the means a president selects to exercise leadership. They reveal important information regarding psychological suitability. Even good judgments can be frustrated if the means of their implementation are not productive and appropriate.

Following Neustadt ([1960] 1990), the focus of much presidential scholarship has been on the consensual nature of presidential power. Presidents bargain, they persuade, but they rarely command. There are, however, several drawbacks to this focus.[23] One is that Neustadt's model suggests that presidents and those who observe them look to the short term rather than the long term. Power, after all, is to be found in the daily, almost hourly calculations of the president and those who watch him. The model is not responsible for, but appears to reinforce, recent presidential tendencies to be concerned with how things look rather than how they are and what to do about them.

Absent from the model is a serious consideration of the president's role to educate the public on his view of their needs. Public education is not merely a "textbook" virtue for a president. It has more direct and practical consequences for his ability to lead. Education is part of the basis by which people come to understand their predicaments. It is the basis on which they can begin to understand what can (and cannot) be done about public problems and the consequences of different actions (and inaction). Establishing credibility in these areas is central to establishing trust between the president and the public, a crucial element in presidential leadership and effective performance.

A second drawback to Neustadt's model is that it leaves the impression that presidents can go only as far as they develop their positions through persuasion or agreement. Sperlich noted that one consequence of Neustadt's model is "an unnecessarily sharp restraint in the use command" (1975, 419). The problem here is that few effective presidents rely solely on agreement. To do so would commit them to political and policy passivity.

A third drawback concerns Neustadt's use of the term *persuasion,* in that it misses the extent to which persuasion in practice can look very similar to power in theory. In reality, as Neustadt recognized, presidents with a personal, political, or policy agenda use a very special kind of persuasion, that backed by the threat of sanctions. In its general character and effects, this kind of persuasion is remarkably similar to those definitions of power (e.g., March 1966) that stress the ability to get people to do what they might not otherwise have done.

A fourth drawback to assessing psychological suitability primarily in terms of persuasion and not power is that a very important presidential character domain is lost. How a presidential candidate approaches disagreement, outright opposition, and neutrality to his purposes is a key aspect for understanding how he will handle the realities of the presidency.

The number of cases of actual "commands" in the presidency may be relatively few, as Neustadt argues (1990, 17–28); however, on closer inspection it is somewhat difficult to see why. Command leadership requires that five circumstances be present: (1) that a president's involvement be unambiguous, (2) that his words and therefore his purposes be unambiguous, (3) that his order be widely publicized, (4) that he have all the resources that he needs to carry out his wishes, and (5) that he be seen to have the authority to issue such commands.

Of the five circumstances that favor command, only the third and sometimes, to a lesser extent, the fifth present difficulties. A president can easily become unambiguously involved, and his words may clearly reflect this. The president's position can be widely publicized quite easily. What remains are the questions of authority and resources. Presidential authority is, as Pious (1979) has shown, substantial; it is also, as Schlesinger (1973) has shown, robust. Presidents have wide latitude. A combination of inventive interpretations, willingness to press them, and disinclination on the part of Congress to challenge them on occasion has expanded presidents' command legitimacy over time.

Neustadt's fourth factor is the most problematic, given the constitutional arrangement of shared, overlapping powers to which he has correctly called attention. It is true that presidents cannot expect compliance because they have spoken. However, given that at least three—or more likely, four—of the command prerequisites are generally available to a president, it seems somewhat misleading to focus primarily on influence as the primary tool and consensus as the primary outcome of presidential leadership.

If the president does not exercise raw power and if the concept of persuasion omits too much, how, then, can we characterize the range of the instruments available to and used by presidents to exercise their political leadership? Perhaps a more appropriate descriptive model of what presidents actually do would be a continuum, anchored by *enforceable authority* at one end and *consensual agreement* at the other. *Persuasion* would occupy a midpoint range between the two.

The term *enforceable authority* denotes that not all persuasion has a largely consensual or voluntary element in it. The origins of enforceable authority lie in those larger tracts of presidential authority that have been constitutionally given and/or have developed over time (Pious 1979). There are many tools in this collection. However, what is important is not so much the number but which are selected, how often, and for what purposes. We learn something of psychological importance when focusing on whether or not a president can get along with, bargain with, and influence others and why he does so. Some presidents bargain to avoid hard conflicts. Others depend on influence because they are particularly able to charm. A few get along because they are honest, sincere, and principled. A very few are honest, sincere, principled, and tough.

Each of these approaches to the exercise of power springs from a different configuration of a president's character and psychology. Each package includes the president's basic character elements, beliefs, and character style. The way they come together will help shape a president's approach to the exercise of power. It takes a consolidated sense of capacity (a reflection of ambition) and self-regard (a reflection of personal integrity and identity) for a president to weather critical reactions to his proposals. Too strong a need to be liked may interfere with the ability to take the strong stands required to see one's purposes accomplished. Or an inflated sense of capacity may lead a president to overestimate his abilities and his reach.

The Tasks of Presidential Leadership: Mobilization, Orchestration, and Consolidation

I propose three distinct aspects of presidential and political leadership: mobilization, orchestration, and consolidation. Although they are related, each requires different skills of a president. A skilled political leader will be adept at all three or know enough to authorize others to carry them out. Most effective political leaders have strong skills in at least one of the first two areas; it is very rare for a candidate or president to be an effective leader without one or the other.

The first task, *mobilization,* refers to the president's ability to arouse the public. This presupposes that the president has identified a problem in need of solution and can convey that need to the public. The ability to anticipate potential problems and educate the public regarding them is rare but nonetheless the exemplar of political leadership in the presidency. An approximation of this decisive act of presidential leadership is more likely to occur, as when a particular problem of magnitude looms before the president and the public that is difficult to ignore. An example of this occurred with the domestic economic difficulties that were a campaign issue in the 1992 presidential election.

Mobilization requires that the president himself be invested in solving the problem. One can distinguish here between ritualistic public announcements (the United States should be taking the lead in *x*) and intensely felt and acted-upon commitments to particular policy goals.[24] George Bush's intense diplomatic efforts in response to the invasion of Kuwait and Bill Clinton's investment in pushing his economic policies provide two recent illustrations. Once the emotional investment occurs, the president's ability to mobilize support depends on how clearly he conveys what is at stake, as well as on how much effort he invests in getting results.

The second component of political leadership, *orchestration,* refers to the need to move beyond public arousal, understanding, and support in exercising political power. The effective use of arousal requires that it be *applied* to the achievement of goals. It refers to the ability to shape mobilization in specific, policy-relevant ways. George Bush's effective use of the international community's arousal after the invasion of Kuwait provides an illustration. President Bush proved very adept in using this mobilization to craft specific policies and UN resolutions to further his policy objectives.

The third aspect, *consolidation,* refers to the skills and tasks necessary to preserving a set of supportive relationships and institutionalizing the results of one's policy judgments. Consolidation is a dynamic, not a static, process. It may involve continuing public explanations (education) as a policy dilemma develops. It may also involve recognizing and responding to changes in circumstances among the various partners in the relationship as time progresses and the problem unfolds.

Consolidation involves setting up and into motion policy structures or procedural regimes that solidify the results of the president's policy judgments. This may include the creation of new agencies, working groups, or other institutional forms. Or it might combine these with refocusing the functions or direction of existing policy structures. These methods of consolidation also represent a way in which a president's policy decisions can have an enduring effect. They are, in essence, a legacy of a president's judgment and leadership.

Character and Political Leadership

The basic character elements and their related character styles enter differently into the enactment of the three dimensions of presidential leadership. Ambition and integrity play important roles in all three aspects of political leadership but especially in mobilization and orchestration. All three dimensions of presidential and political leadership require a sense of effective capacity and confidence on the part of a president. In the preceding chapter, I suggested that these two qualities arise out of the successful interplay of ambition and skills, guided by a sense of personal ideals and public values. It takes a solid capacity to achieve results, and self-confidence and optimism to attempt the mobilization and orchestration of purposeful leadership.

Political leadership also takes a considerable ability to make and maintain interpersonal connections, the third element of individual's basic character. Each aspect of political leadership (mobilization, orchestration, and consolidation) involves a president in a variety of relationships. These include, but are not limited to, his immediate staff, other domestic centers of power (Congress, the press, etc.), peers (other heads of governments), independent "colleagues" (the bureaucracies), and of course the public. The president's capacity to form effective working relationships with those with whom he must share power in a democracy is crucial to any administration's success.

This element may easily be obscured during smoothly run political operations. Yet consider for a moment two illustrations in which failures in the area of interpersonal connectedness were instrumental in an administration's undoing. Jimmy Carter came to the White House as an "outsider" and remained one until he was defeated for reelection. The character style that Carter developed[25] was based in large part on self-reliance. This is a perfectly adequate style for many areas, but not for exercising effective political power in a democracy. By most accounts, he was never able to establish working relationships with key members of Congress, the bureaucracy, and other members of the "Washington establishment," and his administration's policy initiatives suffered because of it.

Nor was Carter very successful in establishing connections with the public. His famous "malaise speech," which seemed to blame the public for his administration's problems, did not resonate with the American public at the time it was given. Rather, it resulted in ripples of public anxiety regarding Carter's state of mind. That speech reflected a clear misreading of the public mood and may have been more a function of Carter's feelings than the public's. More than this, it is reflective of a failure to establish a realistic connection with the public.

Difficulties in the area of interpersonal connectedness are not limited to the inability to develop working relationships, as the case of Lyndon Johnson suggests. In many respects, but especially in his mastery of congressional relationships, Johnson stands at the opposite pole from Carter. Yet Johnson's relationships with his advisers, other centers of power (particularly the press and Congress), and, ultimately, the American public were manipulative, contemptuous, and deceptive to a large degree. This approach did bring some measure of policy success, but this character style ultimately led to the unraveling of his administration.

Or consider a third case, that of President Bush mobilizing members of the world community against the Iraqi invasion of Kuwait. By all reports, Bush invested a lot of his time in developing personal relationships with various world leaders. Leaving aside questions of mutual interests, it is clear that these relationships were helpful in Bush's maintenance of the widely based, multinational alliance.[26]

The impact of character on political leadership is not confined to character style in interpersonal relations. It also enters in the form of the character beliefs we have discussed. For example, one essential element of political leadership involves going somewhere, that is, leading in a particular policy or political direction. Both the sense of effective capacity and self-regard and their related character beliefs are crucial to this effort. A strong sense of effective capacity and self-regard allows the president to take the risks (both personal and political) that accompany efforts in political leadership. In the absence of strong expectations that effort is worthwhile, political leadership cannot really emerge. So, too, the president's personal and political identities play an important role in his ability to lead. The president's sense of confidence in himself and his goals, as well as his belief in the essential value of what he is attempting, helps him to persist in the face of the inevitable opposition and apathy that are part of the political process.

Conclusion

The model of character and presidential performance put forward in this chapter is meant to provide a framework by which presidential candidates may be assessed. Judgment and leadership, the two principal elements of presidential performance, can be thought of as distinct but related criteria. A focus on judgment leads to the questions of what the president decided and how he arrived at his conclusion. A focus on leadership leads to the question of how, and by what methods, he will he translate his judgment into action. Decision and action, judgment and leadership—both need to be addressed by any theory of presidential performance.

At present, the most systematic mechanism for assessing these two elements of performance is the election campaign. Is it possible to make any assessment of character and judgment during a presidential campaign? Can we learn anything important about how candidates might handle the tasks of mobilization, orchestration, and consolidation, before they take office? It is to these questions that we turn in the next three chapters.

NINE

Character and Judgment in the 1988 Presidential Campaign: A Case Study of Gary Hart

For a short period during the 1988 presidential campaign, Gary Hart, then senator from Colorado, held a substantial lead in public opinion polls over other Democratic Party candidates. But less than three weeks after the announcement of his candidacy (May 8, 1987), he was forced to withdraw from consideration. Although Hart attempted for a brief period to reenter the presidential race, with limited success, revelations about his personal behavior during the campaign essentially destroyed his candidacy.

The immediate cause of this reversal of political fortune was the discovery that although married, Hart had met, dated, and spent the night with another woman in the middle of the nomination campaign. He had done so after publicly inviting newspaper reporters to follow him if they didn't believe his denials of stories circulating about his extramarital affairs.[1] Thus, although Senator Hart's extramarital relationships were the immediate cause of his political demise, infidelity was by no means the sole issue raised by his behavior.

In this chapter I examine Hart's failed candidacy. I argue that the failure of his candidacy was not directly caused by his extramarital relationship(s). Rather, his candidacy ultimately failed because of deeper questions concerning the three fundamental elements of character I outlined in chapter 7—his ambition, the integrity of his identity, and the nature of his relationships with others. I further argue that his abilities in the two basic domains of presidential performance, judgment and leadership, also came into question as the controversy unfolded.

Hart's failed candidacy allows us to examine in greater depth the ways in which disturbances in the three basic character elements can affect the public's perceptions of a candidate's suitability and, also important for our purposes, a candidate's actual behavior. His candidacy also throws light on those qualities of a candidate that are necessary and those that may only be desirable but not in themselves sufficient. Consider, for example, the question of intelligence, a trait usually seen as a desirable characteristic for presidential candidates. Senator Hart certainly was a candidate with intelligence. One *New York Times* reporter wrote that "Hart is without question one of the most intelligent figures of contemporary American politics" (Dionne 1987, 28). He was also, at the time of the campaign, a man with political experience, charisma, and the ability to inspire loyalty among his followers. Such characteristics are usually associated with success and effectiveness in public life, and indeed, until the time of the presidential campaign, they had been so for Senator Hart. Yet in less than three weeks, Hart's candidacy was destroyed amid charges and countercharges.

The destruction of Hart's candidacy raised questions that still permeate our presidential campaigns. Did the press go beyond the bounds of appropriateness, decency, and privacy in breaking this story? Hart and many commentators said that it had. Was the story of Hart's affair really relevant to assessing his possible performance as president? Hart and others argued it wasn't.

The *New York Times* summary of the story was contained in its headline (10 May 1987, sec. 4, 1) "A Would Be President Fails the Test of 'Character.'" While this may be true as a general description, our interest goes further. What specific aspects of character did Hart lack? Any number of negative character aspects have been proposed, including infidelity, "womanizing," risk taking, poor judgment, differences between his political persona and his real values, as well as possible self-destructiveness. Are these assessments accurate and relevant? These questions are central to dealing with the psychological suitability of presidential candidates. But the Hart case raises larger questions about the process of selection itself.

While many commentators on the Gary Hart episode cast their analysis in terms of the "character issue," not all were convinced such issues were necessarily the most important. Commentator Tom Wicker (*New York Times,* 9 May 1987, A31) complained about the "swamp of pop psychology" surrounding these events. In the process, he took the somewhat paradoxical position that while the character concerns that had been raised were "all very glib, and some of it might even be true," the real question was "not so much Mr. Hart's judgment, as bad as that was, but the judgment of others on what they took to be his behavior." Wicker noted that "no other candidate in either party has yet shown Mr. Hart's scope, depth and intellectual vigor." He then went on to lament the "trivialization" of the campaign process, in which "questions of public policy have further been subordinated to personal matters."

Another commentator, a professor of history at Harvard, agreed with Wicker's analysis, suggesting that the public's concern with character reflected a lack of more important frames of analysis, particularly with regard to the candidates' public philosophies. He noted (*New York Times,* 21 May 1987, A31) that the collapse of the Hart candidacy "is less important for what it tells us about his campaign or the press than for what it reveals about the condition of American public life as a whole: the absence of any meaningful public philosophy capable of mobilizing the electorate behind something more meaningful than 'character.' "

Some saw in the destruction of Senator Hart's candidacy an indictment not so much of the man or even of the public but of the system itself. An editorial in *The Economist* (9 May 1987, 11–12) suggested that one should "blame the candidates, for their shortcomings; blame the press, for exposing them, and more; blame the people, for expecting the impossible which only a freak could deliver." But, the editorial suggested,

above all blame the system. America gets bad Presidents because it gets bad candidates, and it gets bad candidates because they are now chiefly chosen in a series of primary elections in which voters put a premium on superficial qualities televisually conveyed, with little consideration of the qualities needed to run the most powerful country in the world.

I argue that in the 1988 campaign, the system worked, but barely. The evidence suggests that the fault, if any, lies not with the press, the public, or the system. If anything, the problems that Senator Hart revealed during the campaign serve as another warning of how vulnerable the system is to smart (but flawed) leaders.

My analysis is based as far as possible on evidence in the public domain, including the candidate's own publicly recorded statements and reactions.[2] The ability to develop and sustain a plausible analysis of this case, based on this kind of evidence, is of some importance. It tests in a general way whether, on the basis of publicly available information, characteristics of substantial importance about a candidate can be known and publicly understood. In short, can election campaigns serve the vital function of character assessment?

The Character Issue in the Gary Hart Case: Theoretical Considerations

I noted in chapter 3 that beginning in the 1940s, a number of analysts began reporting that they had treated persons who, although they appeared to be functioning well—even very well on a surface, conventional level—were found, upon closer clinical observation, to have areas of deep psychological disturbance that manifested themselves in unstable behavior (Cleckley [1941] 1976). Among these were persons with narcissistic disturbances.

The primary difficulties for such persons lie in the area of self-esteem regulation. Problems in self-esteem regulation can be seen as a by-product of the three character areas basic to presidential performance, the spheres of ambition, integrity, and relatedness. A person who lacks either ambition or the tools with which to fulfill it, for example, will have difficulty experiencing the satisfaction and esteem that derive from accomplishment. A person without strong integrated ideals and the experience of having adhered to them in difficult circumstances will have missed the opportunity to develop the stronger sense of esteem that derives from having done so. Finally, persons whose relationships with others are neither mutual nor satisfactory in other ways are likely to miss the important affirming experiences that facilitate self-esteem.

Persons with narcissistic personality organizations have achieved a somewhat cohesive (unfragmented) sense of self, functional psychological stability, and stable character traits. These appear to be substantial psychological achievements, especially when compared to borderline and psychotic levels of character organization. Certainly this was true of Gary Hart.

Our analytical task here is further complicated by the fact that narcissistic character types and persons with strong narcissistic vulnerabilities present a decidedly mixed picture of psychological functioning. Areas of functional inadequacy or impairment coexist with areas of functional capacity and even strength.[3] Individuals with narcissistic character organizations can be very intelligent, even shrewd, and intensely focused (sometimes to their own detriment), frequently talented, and quite accomplished.

Cleckley's original study included professionally accomplished individuals (doctors, lawyers, executives) and other "successful members of the community,"[4] and there may be a good explanation for this. Masterson (1988, 93) notes:

The successful narcissist . . . must be creative and imaginative, and often quite talented, to develop a lifestyle that will resonate to his grandiose projections of himself and fuel his narcissistic needs. Creating this self-contained system of re-enforcement . . . is a major accomplishment in itself, requiring enormous energy and diligence, and when done well, it too becomes a source of gratification, contributing to the narcissist's grandiose sense of himself.

But these accomplishments also reflect vulnerabilities that make such persons particularly unsuited for positions of power and authority. The *DSM-III* (APA 1980, 315; see also Chessick 1985, 7) notes that persons with a narcissistic personality organization have a highly elevated (grandiose) view of their own importance and specialness (uniqueness). Because of their excessive sense of importance and uniqueness, there is often an accompanying feeling of entitlement, realized in a sense that they deserve special consideration. They frequently exhibit a strong need to be idealized by others and to be *the* object of attention, if not admiration.[5] When they are not sufficiently reinforced in their own somewhat elevated view of themselves, their reactions are strong. Criticism or disappointment tend to elicit marked feelings of rage, contempt, or, occasionally, icy and angry indifference. These traits too could be seen in Hart.

Because of this inflated sense of his or her own talent and accomplishment, and the accompanying sense of entitlement, such a person easily slips into believing that others are there to provide what he or she needs. Having little real interest in knowing what goes on for others, beyond what is necessary to secure his or her own needs, the capacity for empathy does not adequately develop. Interpersonal relationships for such people therefore tend to be shallow and exploitative.[6] As Meissner (1984, 106) points out, "There is often a quality of arrogance or contempt in their relationships with others." At their worst, according to Chessick (1985, 8), "they are haughty, grandiose and controlling, any of which they may show only privately in their relations to others or—to the common misfortune—only when they reach positions of power."

But narcissistic character types may have also developed the language of concern, part of what I referred to in the previous chapter as strategic empathy, especially if their success requires it and even if the capacity for true concern eludes them. In these cases, the one-sided nature of relationships comes through in (large and small) choices that the narcissist makes. Overall the choices reflect self-aggrandizement, frequently at the expense of others. The revealing characteristic is not only that others may be directly used but that they figure so little in the calculations.

The discovery and elaboration of these character types adds a layer of complexity to the traditional psychotic-leader debate, that is, the concern that an extremely disturbed individual might gain access to political power (Lasswell 1964, 223; Tucker 1965, 575–77; Robins 1977a, 14). As suggested in the discussion of the Eagleton case, the structural barriers argument (i.e., that extremely disturbed individuals are not likely to gain political power because they lack the skills to develop and maintain political organization and support) is accurate, but not fully. Therefore, it cannot be persuasively reassuring. If it is true, as Chessick (1985, 8) argues, that "these individuals [narcissistic character types] may obtain high office, and even be elected President of the United States," then surely there is reason for apprehension. In the material that follows, I will try to make clearer why the case of Gary Hart raises exactly this issue.

The 1984 Hart Campaign

Hart's quest for the presidency and his troubles with regard to the character issue did not begin with the 1988 presidential campaign. Rather, they can be traced to the previous presidential campaign in 1984 when he challenged (for a time successfully) Walter Mondale, who eventually went on to become the Democratic Party's presidential nominee.[7]

Walter Mondale was, by all accounts, the front-runner and seemed well on his way to securing the nomination until Hart scored an upset victory in the New Hampshire primary. By accomplishing the unexpected by a clear (39 percent to 29 percent) but far from sweeping vote, Gary Hart emerged as a credible challenger, a role he continued when he won the Maine caucuses in early March. Almost immediately thereafter, questions began to surface about his character.

Some of these questions were raised directly by Mondale as part of an effort to recoup his own sagging campaign. For example, in a campaign speech in Boston, Mondale portrayed Hart as a "coldly intellectual man who would bring an unfair and regressive approach to the problems of common people" (*New York Times,* 6 March 1984, A1). The accusation is interesting for a couple of reasons, in view of subsequent events. First, it raises the issue of emotional distance from others as a characteristic worth examining in presidential candidates. Second, it connects this issue to the question of his capacity for political empathy. It does not necessarily follow that being an intellectual means that one lacks the capacity for emotional closeness, but a lack of the capacity for emotional closeness would indeed raise questions about a person's capacity for political and other forms of empathy.

At the same time that Mondale was making these and related charges,[8] other concerns surfaced. Among them was the fact that Hart had changed his name from Hartpence to Hart in 1961 and that he had, on a number of formal documents, misstated his age by a year (he had given his correct age on other documents); in both cases he had provided differing accounts of why he had done so.[9] No questions were raised by the press about reports of Hart's association with women other than his wife, although it was noted that he and his wife had been separated twice. These early questions were never fully laid to rest and surfaced again in the 1988 campaign. Then, of course, they were overshadowed by the exposure of Hart's extramarital relationships.

Changes in details related to aspects of Hart's personal identity raised questions. Did the name change reflect someone who was uncomfortable with himself? Did Hart's change of penmanship "from a cursive signature which included his middle initial to a modernistic, printed signature almost digital in appearance without a middle initial" (*New York Times,* 24 March 1984, 28) indicate a man trying to change his public persona, his identity, or did it reflect "a style of writing that has the effect of concealment"[10] (Sheehy 1984, 86)? Were his mannerisms adopted from his political heroes Robert Kennedy and John F. Kennedy?[11] And if so, did this mean that his political persona was suspect?

Personal Identity, Political Identity, and Persona

The direct concern expressed in these 1984 questions of Hart's identity is one regarding honesty; there is also an indirect concern about the candidate's authenticity and integrity. A concern with honesty focuses directly on the truth of documented facts (e.g., the problem of different ages) and the plausibility of explanations of discrepancies. The concern with authenticity and integrity looks to larger issues of personal and political identity. It is the latter that stands at the center of Hart's difficulties in 1984. The presidential candidate whose personal and political identities are perceived as too dissimilar raises public concern and the view that he needs to explain. This is what happened to Gary Hart. Some, as noted, tended to see the changes in his name, age, and so forth as an indication of his insincerity and lack of integrity and authenticity. I think not.

Hart grew up in a small town, was raised in a fairly religious (Church of the Nazarene) household, and had a fairly conventional youth. He attended a small religious, and at that time unaccredited college in Oklahoma (Bethany Nazarene College). While at college, he was challenged and stimulated by one of his philosophy professors. He then went on to Yale, first as a divinity student and later as a law student. It was as a law student that he became involved in politics, working first in John F. Kennedy's and Robert Kennedy's campaigns, and then for George McGovern's presidential campaign in 1972.

Hart was elected to the Senate in 1974 and reelected six years later. While there, he developed a reputation as an expert on military affairs but was not a political insider. Gary Hart was not a man whose political style included intense concern with the personal and political relationships that make one an insider. He did not invest his whole life in his political role, preferring instead to preserve a substantial portion of his private life.

It was not only that Hart chose to preserve his private life but the nature of that life that raised questions. Hart's friendship with the actor Warren Beatty, his presence at celebrity parties (like the one where he met Donna Rice), and his presence at private clubs such as the Turnberry in Miami suggest an attraction to the "celebrity life."

Clearly, by mid-adulthood, Hart had accumulated considerable political experience and developed a significant set of political skills. He came a long way from the intellectual and interpersonal world of his childhood, youth, and early adulthood, and a long emotional, psychological, and intellectual distance lies between the young Gary Hartpence and the adult Gary Hart.

One can interpret Hart's name change, altered writing style,[12] and even the development of his political style from his identifications with the Kennedys as an attempt to forge a composite identity, based not on who he was but on the person he had partially become and wanted to be. The uneasiness expressed by some commentators with these changes and with Hart's search for a solid personal identity is understandable, but there is nothing inherently sinister about the unfolding development of an identity, especially if the person cannot easily draw on childhood, adolescent, or early adult sources.

Hart's difficulties here may stem less from inappropriate or inauthentic change in his public identity than from the tension between the requirements of his public identity on the one hand, and the conflict that existed between his original, core identity and the person he had, and wished to, become on the other. He had, according to the theory outlined in chapter 7, failed to reconcile his ambitions with a solid and stable set of ideals. Clearly, the rewards of a fast-moving, celebrity life were attractive to Hart. However, it was not possible for him to reconcile the two strands of his developing identity. One cannot easily be a married man with grown children who aspires to serious public responsibilities and still take young dates on a pleasure craft named Monkey Business.

The Crisis: Hart, Donna Rice, and the Character Issue

Hart's 1988 presidential bid officially began on April 13, 1987, when, with his wife and daughter at his side, he announced his candidacy to become the Democratic Party's presidential nominee. His short speech emphasized the need to "recapture our basic principles, beliefs and values" (*New York Times,* 14 April 1987, A16). The juxtaposition of his wife and children at his side during the announcement and the emphasis on recapturing basic values suggested that the two might be related. Furthermore, during the same speech, Hart declared of himself and other candidates, "Since we are running for the highest and most important office in the land, all of us must try to hold ourselves to the very highest possible standards of integrity and ethics and soundness of judgment" (*Miami Herald,* 8 May 1987, 15A).

A short time later, an article interestingly (given the questions raised in 1984) titled, "The Elusive Front Runner," was published in the Sunday magazine section of the *New York Times* (Dionne 1987). It was in the context of an interview for this article that Hart, responding to questions about his extramarital relationships, issued his famous challenge to the press: "Follow me around. If anyone wants to put a tail on me, go ahead . . . they'd be very bored" (Dionne 1987, 38).

In this interview, Hart stated that he and his wife, Lee, had separated twice and that he had dated but had not tried to hide it. In Hart's view, questions about his extramarital relationships reflected the price he was paying for this honesty. He is reported as saying that his main problem was that "unlike other politicians, he and his wife are honest about the troubles that they've had . . . and again [he] is suffering for his honesty" (Dionne 1987, 36).

It is an interesting view. On the one hand, it builds on some degree of fact, namely, that Hart was more straightforward than was customary at the time in openly alluding to his marital difficulties.[13] On the other hand, it does leave some questions unresolved. In the statement there is a direct implication that Hart saw other women only when he was separated from his wife, but his behavior during the campaign undercuts this assertion.[14] There is also the implication that Hart believes that his straightforwardness marks him as different and better than others ("unlike other politicians"). Furthermore, there is the implication that he is being singled out for especially hostile treatment. This pattern of response reappeared during the unfolding of the crisis.

Ironically, even as the *New York Times* article appeared in print, Hart was confronted by reporters who, following up an anonymous but detailed tip,[15] had tailed a young woman whom he was meeting in Washington, D.C., and with whom he spent the night. While aspects of the story are contested by the participants, the general facts are worth noting. They seem to be as follows.

According to the woman,[16] Donna Rice, she first met Hart at a New Year's Eve party in Aspen, Colorado, given by a well-known singer. They met again in March at a private resort club in Miami Beach. She said that Hart called to invite her to accompany him on a boat trip to Bimini a few days later. She went along with another single woman friend and William Broadhurst, a friend of Senator Hart. This day trip turned into an overnight trip because, they said, by the time they were ready to leave, customs on the island was closed, so they had to stay until the next morning. Subsequent inquiry suggested that boats routinely arrive and leave from Bimini after customs has closed (*New York Times*, 6 May 1987, B9). All involved in the trip denied that Hart and Rice spent the night alone together.

Hart acknowledges calling Rice a number of times after that while he was campaigning.[17] By Donna Rice's account, she came to Washington with her friend, who was being interviewed for a job as a social coordinator for Hart's friend William Broadhurst. Both Broadhurst, who is a contemporary of Hart, and Rice's friend and contemporary Miss Lynn Armandt had accompanied Hart and Rice on the boat trip to Bimini.

As to the weekend in Washington, all agree that Hart was confronted by *Miami Herald* reporters on Saturday morning. The reporters saw Donna Rice enter Gary Hart's townhouse the previous night and did not see her leave. Hart contended that she left by the back door, which the reporters missed. Rice and Hart denied that there was any romantic relationship between them. Different and conflicting accounts of this and other circumstances were given by Hart; his campaign manager, William Dixon; and William Broadhurst.[18]

To put the matter directly, Gary Hart's explanations of his relationship with Donna Rice strain credulity. The sequence and nature of the parties, calls, and meetings between the two by themselves undercut the credibility of the senator's explanation, as do the inconsistencies and contradictions among the several explanations put forward in his defense. To this one can add the story that appeared in the *Washington Post* on December 20, 1987, and which was subsequently confirmed in greater detail (by the *Post*), about a long-term relationship between Hart and another Washington woman. Indeed, Hart's campaign manager was informed by the paper a few days before the senator withdrew from the presidential campaign that it planned to publish the results of its more extensive investigation, including the woman's name (*New York Times,* 9 May 1987, A8).[19] Somewhat later, in another public context, Hart indirectly confirmed the accuracy of the story regarding this relationship.[20]

Hart's explanation asks us to accept that a man who has been called one of the most intelligent in politics, who clearly was aware that his relationships with women had been and were an issue in the campaign, and who had invited reporters to follow him if they didn't believe his denials about "womanizing" would call and invite[21] a young, unmarried woman on several overnight outings, even if accompanied by another, married friend who was himself in the company of a young, unmarried woman, and expect people to believe that these clearly planned outings were totally innocent. Accepting this story would require citizens to believe that Hart was merely naive. But the explanation simply does not appear credible.

Hart's Response to the Unfolding Crisis

Hart's response to this unfolding crisis is of interest to us for two reasons: first, because of the nature of the crisis itself, but second, because of how he responded. At first he denied having any personal relationship with Donna Rice, calling her a "friend of a friend." This is contradicted by his calls to her, both the call to invite her on the boat trip to Bimini and others afterward as he campaigned.

From the start, Hart presented himself as an innocent victim. Campaign aides speculated initially that he had been set up by unnamed others in a bid to destroy his candidacy (*Miami Herald,* 4 May 1987, 10A). At the same time, in an interview with the *Denver Post* that appeared on May 4, 1987, he was quoted as saying that he had been "victimized" by the *Miami Herald* story. In remarks to a group of supporters on the evening of May 5, Hart noted that "it doesn't really matter if the leader is struck down in battle or with a knife in his back, because the cause goes on and the crusade continues" (*New York Times,* 6 May 1987, B8).

On these occasions Hart also raised the issue of the appropriateness and effects of subjecting the private lives of public officials to such intense scrutiny, an issue he continued to raise at numerous points.[22] He warned a reporter in his *Denver Post* interview, "Somebody's got to clean up your profession . . . or it's going to drive anyone that's got an ounce of integrity out [of politics]." At his first public address on May 5 before the Newspaper Publishers Association (Hart 1987a, B8), besides attacking the *Herald* for its "false and misleading" story, Hart denounced "deeply personal questions, asked by total strangers" and said they are "clearly one of the reasons many talented people in this nation opt out of public service." He went on to note that "our whole system is at issue here, not just a candidate or an individual campaign."

In his address to the group, Hart recalled that when he had announced his candidacy for the presidency, he had said that all candidates should be held

to the highest possible standards, of competence to govern, of character, of vision and of leadership. I believe that even more today than I did then. . . . I have always held myself to a high standard of public and private . . . but the events of the past few days have . . . taught me that . . . even the *most commonplace and appropriate behavior* can be misconstrued by some to be improper. That just means I have to raise my own personal standard higher. (Emphasis mine)

Finally, the senator conceded that he had made a mistake by "putting myself into circumstances that could be misconstrued" but denied that he had done anything "immoral."

The next day, at his first full-scale press conference since the story broke, Hart answered a number of very direct and personal questions. Among them were "Do you think adultery is immoral?" ("Yes"), "Have you ever committed adultery?" ("I don't have to answer that question"), and "Do you and your wife have an understanding that it's all right to have sex with others?" ("No, we don't have that kind of understanding"). The directness of the questions angered Hart but also raised questions of their propriety among news commentators and analysts.

At the news conference, Hart again was critical of the *Herald,* accusing the paper of a "tremendous breach in journalistic ethics." He also appealed to the public to see him as a human being who made a mistake—a very serious mistake—but one that "I won't make again." The mistake, according to the senator, was "to get involved in a series of activities over last weekend leading to the conclusion that I was involved with a woman—which I was not." He said that he had not realized how his phone calls, boat rides, and visits with Rice would appear to others. In part this may reflect that he never considered the possibility that others would be in a position to judge his behavior. When asked why he had not realized how his activities would appear, he replied, "I was tired. I didn't think. I just did what seemed to come naturally."

During this period, Hart's public support deteriorated rapidly. On Thursday he flew home with his wife, and his campaign was put on hold. The next day, May 9, in an angry speech consistent with his view that he had done nothing seriously wrong, he withdrew from consideration for the nomination.

The speech itself is rich in images and affect (Hart 1987b, A9). However, several themes stand out. One of them is angry defiance. Hart began by noting that he had intended to read a short, carefully worded statement but had awakened in the middle of the night and said to himself, "Hell no—I'm not going to do that." He said that he was "an angry and defiant man . . . but I don't break and believe me I'm not broken." At one point he said, "I am who I am, take it or leave it." And toward the end he told his audience that he would have been a very good president, "but apparently now, we'll never know." The implication is that they, as well as he, would be sorry.

What stands out equally in the speech, however, is Hart's view of himself as especially able. He noted, "I'm a proud man and I'm proud of what I've accomplished." He went on to say, "I'm pretty happy with who I am, and so are many voters."

Hart's view of his political uniqueness is a another aspect of being especially able. Many of the qualities that the senator saw as making him special also contained not-so-veiled criticisms of his peers and colleagues. For example, he was not like others because "I haven't been very good at playing the political game." Moreover, he hadn't "spent a lot of time and effort trying to create an image." He noted, "With all due respect, most politicians . . . wait to see how political events are breaking before risking their political capital." Hart clearly did not see himself in that category.

Yet in spite of what he saw as his admirable behavior, it appears he felt that he had been singled out for special attention and hostility. In the speech in which he withdrew from contention for the nomination, he noted, "I guess I've become some kind of a rare bird, some extraordinary creature that has to be dissected" (Hart 1987b, A9). That image speaks to

Hart's senses of uniqueness and victimization (or perhaps martyrdom). However, in spite of having endured a process that "reduces the press of this nation to hunters and the presidential candidates to the hunted," Hart proclaimed himself still "an idealist."

The elements of perceiving himself as being uniquely and especially qualified surfaced again when Hart unexpectedly reentered the presidential race in mid-December. Among his reasons for doing so, he said (Hart 1987e, B7), were that "I have a sense of a new direction and a set of new ideas that our country needs and that no one else represents." When discussing his vision while being interviewed a few days later on CBS's *60 Minutes* (Hart 1987f, 5) after reentering the primary race, he compared himself to other Democratic candidates in the following exchange:

> *Hart:* My vision is different. I think it's bigger. The voters have to decide whether it's better.
> *Bradley:* But you think it's better.
> *Hart:* Well, of course I do.

In his December 16 speech marking his return to the primaries (Hart 1987e, B7), Hart noted that he would not have the traditional sources of political strength, "like money, I don't have pollsters or consultants or media advisors or political endorsements. But I have something even better. I have the power of ideas and I can govern this country."

In a December 15 interview on ABC's *Nightline,* he characterized his viewpoint as "unique" (Hart 1987d, 7), a characterization he had made in identical terms in a previous interview on *Nightline* (Hart 1987c, 9), given after he had dropped out of the race. Hart also said, on reentering the race (Hart 1987e, B7), that he "had hoped that his ideas would be adopted and put forward by others . . . but neither of these things has happened." The implication is that he was forced to reenter the race because no other candidate had a vision or program to match his.

Hart's attempt to come to grips with the degree of his personal responsibility for the crisis had only limited success. It will be recalled that the Hart campaign first raised the possibility that Hart had been "set up," presumably to wreck his nomination. Hart had characterized himself that evening as having been "victimized." Thereafter he attacked the *Miami Herald* for its pursuit of the story and questioned the appropriateness of the coverage. A large portion of his May 5, 1987, speech before the Newspaper Publishers Association repeated his charges, but he ended by admitting a mistake. The mistake, however, was not of conduct but of putting himself in circumstances that could be misconstrued, and he denied doing anything immoral. His withdrawal speech of May 9, 1987, contains angry attacks on the press in general and the *Miami Herald* in particular but not one word related to any responsibility on his part for the matter.

In his September 8 interview on *Nightline,* Hart first seemed to accept responsibility, saying, "I assume total responsibility," and arguing that "I have never tried to shift blame away from myself" (Hart 1987c, 3). However, by the end of the interview, his view of the degree of his responsibility had lessened somewhat. He noted that "we've been talking about sin here this evening, I guess that's what it gets down to, not crime but sin" (Hart 1987c, 9).[23] He went on to note, "But the Bible that says that being unfaithful is a sin also says we're all sinners, and that only those who are without sin can cast the first stone, and it says further that one of the greatest sins is to waste God-given talent. I've been given some talents."

Hart's reentry speech contains no discussion of his responsibility for the circumstances that led him to withdraw from the race. In the December *Nightline* interview, he noted with some annoyance, "I've apologized publicly [but] I don't intend to do that for the rest of my life" (Hart 1987d, 11). Moreover, he said, "I could be flip and say I'd like to have the votes of the people in this country who have made a mistake." In that interview Hart said that he should be judged on the whole of his public life, not just one part of it, and that he was "willing to put my performance in public life against almost anyone else."

Of all the rationales that Hart put forward for his behavior, and for being forgiven and forgotten by the public, perhaps the most startling occurred when he discussed his wife's reaction to and support of his getting back in the race. In the December 15 *Nightline* interview (Hart 1987d, 7), when answering a question about his wife's support of his reentry into the race, he asserted, "And she made the decision that the interests of the country rise above her own personal interests." Lest the implication be lost on the public, he raised the point again in an interview on *60 Minutes* (Hart 1987f, 4), where he pointed out that even his wife was able to

detach her relationship to me as a wife from my role as a candidate for Senate or President. And she's said . . . I think this is the best man to govern the country, and she really believes it. I mean . . . she wasn't giving the traditional, spouse message: "Elect my husband because he's a nice guy or a nice father or anything like that." She said, "This man *ought* to be President of the United States." (Emphasis mine)

Clearly, in Hart's view, if his wife thought that his special abilities and uniqueness qualified him for her support in spite of his behavior, others should be equally forgiving.

The Gary Hart Case: An Analysis

In his withdrawal speech, Hart conceded that he had made "some mistakes . . . maybe big mistakes, but not bad mistakes." When he rejoined the presidential campaign in December, he was asked at a forum of Democratic contenders whether voters had the right to consider a candidate's character. He replied that he had been a "sinner" but added, "My religion tells me we are all sinners." He went on to add that "in the past, people who have not led perfect lives have been some of our finest leaders" (*New York Times,* 16 January 1988, A8).

Hart clearly felt that his behavior was absolutely no bar to being, in his words, a "very good President." Others have disagreed, but the basis of these assessments has differed. The exact nature of the issues that are relevant to Hart's behavior and his capacities for political leadership have been debated but not sufficiently analyzed. In the sections that follow, I analyze these issues.

Extramarital Relationships

The first question that arises is whether Gary Hart's marital arrangements were really his (and his wife's) own business. Second, many, including Hart, have pointed out that there have been presidents who have had intimate relationships outside of their marriages yet have been considered good or at least adequate presidents. There is no evidence, it is argued, that their relationships interfered with their leadership. Let us examine these matters more closely.

At the outset, the obvious must be acknowledged and a caution advanced. Affairs occur, and they most certainly occur among political leaders. Analyzing the meaning of such relationships does not commit an observer to any particular moral position on this issue. Moral judgments are a part of the public view of such behavior and citizens are entitled to make them, but they are not the purpose of this analysis.

This having been said, two questions arise: First, are all affairs equal? Second, what is the connection, if any, between such relationships and presidential performance?

Certainly, not all affairs are equal, since they spring from diverse sources and can result in an array of relationships among the parties involved. Spouses have diverse reasons for becoming involved with others, including dissatisfaction with oneself, one's life, or one's partner. Such dissatisfaction can be chronic or episodic, and the search for another relationship similarly so. In politics, as in life more generally, it makes some difference whether such relationships are the norm or the exception, given that they exist at all.

The outside observer must take seriously the psychological discomfort that the felt need to make such choices reflects. The choice to have another relationship reflects a relational impasse in a primary relationship, and it involves emotional losses for the person (man or woman), even if the new relationship is viewed as a form of self-affirmation. Yet for the outside observer, the pattern and context of such relationships are equally important and help to inform the meaning of the relationships. When the person involved aspires to political power, questions and analysis are both necessary and appropriate.

The first distinction that has to be drawn, therefore, appears on the continuum that separates an affair from "womanizing." A single, long-term relationship with another differs significantly from the series of short-term relationships that characterizes womanizing.[24] But what are the differences?

For one thing, development of an alternative or supplementary long-term relationship, though outside of marriage, does reflect some capacity to make and maintain an emotional commitment. It reflects a certain stability of "relational choice" and the accompanying ability to negotiate and maintain a relationship through its considerable vicissitudes. While it certainly supplies emotional gratification and some satisfaction for the individual, the long-term nature of the relationship suggests that it does so to some degree for both parties.

The womanizer, by contrast, selects his partner primarily for his own satisfaction, which is quickly lost, necessitating the search for someone new. Generally, there is little or no emotional investment in the other person, since her purpose is to be not part of a relationship but an object of (brief) desire and satisfaction.

Where is one to put Gary Hart on this continuum? The evidence points away from the single, stable relationship end of the continuum. Not only was the number of relationships documented in 1987 more than one (and there is an open question as to whether one was ended before the other began), but the circumstances and nature of his relationship with Donna Rice point to a basis in Hart's personal satisfaction. By all accounts, Hart's relationship with Rice was not political (she did not reveal much interest in politics) or work-related. Given the context of their meetings, it appears to have been a recreational relationship for Hart, probably tied to his own relaxation and satisfaction.

Yet there is another aspect of such relationships that requires discussion. Affairs out of marriage involve at least three people, so beyond the person's new relationship, there exists the older one. Hart had been honest with the press about his separations from his wife, and one must acknowledge the loss that such separations involved for both persons. Moreover, to acknowledge and share such loss publicly does reflect some degree of courage, even if it may also be a matter of political necessity.

The Harts' relationship, which was discussed at the time by the press and by the senator himself, raises questions that no outside observer can presume to answer fully. It seemed that a reconciliation and perhaps a successful accommodation (for both) had taken place. Certainly, that was the public picture the Harts chose to project as part of the senator's political persona, that of a family man. This public image was used to counter questions about Hart's womanizing.

It is important that the Harts chose to project this persona in the context of a political candidacy and campaign. It was not accidental. The public expects the president to incorporate and display the virtues that it aspires to, including the virtues of family and stable relationships. Hart held himself out as one who possessed these virtues and asked to be accepted as such. So the Harts' linkage of their marital/family relationship with Gary Hart's political persona is one connection between Hart's private and public lives. By making a public statement about themselves as one basis of Hart's candidacy, the Harts legitimized scrutiny.

Thus we have a partial answer to the question of what Hart's relationship with another woman (or any leader's relationship with someone outside his marriage) has to do with his suitability for leadership and power roles. It is not the only answer, however. The Donna Rice episode exposed the fragility of whatever reconciliation and possible accommodation had been made as the basis for the Hart's public stance as a married couple, even as the facts and context surrounding the senator's extramarital relationships raised larger issues of his use and misuse of others.

Judgment

Some commentators looked at Hart's problem as one not of infidelity or character but of judgment. If, as I argued in chapter 8, decision making is central to presidential leadership and, more generally, presidential performance, and if at the heart of decisions lies judgment, this question is crucial. According to one view, by choosing to pursue and meet repeatedly with an attractive, unmarried woman in circumstances that raised unflattering questions about his motives and behavior, Hart showed that he could not be trusted with the depth and maturity of judgment required of a president. In contrast, a *New York Times* editorial took the position, after Hart's relationship with Rice was uncovered, that "the disputed facts are pivotal to the question of Mr. Hart's private morality, but not to a reasonable judgment about his political judgment" (5 May 1987, A34).

In Hart's view he had made a mistake, and he even acknowledged that it was one of bad judgment (Hart 1987c, 9). But his basic view was that his mistake was a small one that needed to be judged against a lifetime of accomplishment (which presumably reflected his good judgment). Moreover, Hart argued, other presidents had been known to have similar relationships and had been good leaders; therefore, his mistake, however unfortunate, was irrelevant to his ability to govern and lead. In Hart's view, his mistake did not mean that he would not be a "very good President."

Before evaluating these claims, I will briefly review those aspects of the theory of judgment developed in the previous chapter that seem particularly relevant to analyzing the question of Hart's suitability. I argued that we can understand judgment as the quality of analysis and reflection that informs the making of consequential decisions.

Good judgment, then, refers to qualities of analysis and reflection that result in a "best-fit" solution to problems which raise important issues and will result in significant consequences. A best-fit solution adequately addresses the basic nature of a significant problem(s) and develops a solution that preserves the most important interests at risk while resulting in minimal harm to the basic interests of those positions or solutions that, though legitimate, differ.

Flawed judgment, by contrast, reflects a response that does not address the basic nature of the problem(s) at hand or does so in a way that causes damage to the basic well-being and interests of the individual, those he represents, or the wider community. Bad judgment frequently results in harm to the well-being and interests of all three.

Good judgment ordinarily takes time as well as capacity. The issue of time arises in two ways: first, in the external, temporal sens enough time to analyze and consider; second, in a more char; way, in the ability to control and delay whatever impulses tov ture closure or action may be activated by the circumstances. The impulse toward self-gratification, for example, must be tempered by the ability and the willingness not only to consider fully the perspectives of others but to consider the implications of action for oneself. The ability to size up circumstances and make adequate, if not good, judgments under time pressures are important components of presidential judgment.

I suggested that judgment entails both analytic and reflective abilities. Analytic abilities includes the capacity to discern the essential nature of problems and the potential avenues of resolution and their implications, as well as a sense of the method(s) by which resolution might be accomplished. Reflective abilities include the capacity to consider (evaluate) analytical information from a series of perspectives. These often include one's own (or others') values and views and both long- and short-term political and strategic considerations. Narcissism interferes with these processes.

Analytic skills are not solely cognitive. They require the ability to appreciate crucial implications and extrapolate significance from an incomplete set of facts. Experience helps in this process, but character, too, plays a role. A preference for optimism over realism may impede judgment.

Motivated avoidance can spring from several sources. Narcissistic compensations such as the sense that "it can't happen here" can inhibit the accurate discerning of problems. Foundations of narcissism include grandiosity, invulnerability, and entitlement, which arise from feelings that the candidate (or president) is special, powerful, and beyond the reach of ordinary circumstances. In such cases a candidate (or president) may discern facts but discount their significance because of his special powers, circumstances, and so on, as Hart did with Donna Rice.

A leader's grandiosity and accompanying sense of invulnerability and entitlement often reflect an underlying masked anxiety or an insufficiently consolidated sense of self-esteem. This anxiety may arise from the direct personal and political implications of events themselves or may be related to the steps that might need to be taken if events are viewed clearly and seriously.

In reality, the analytic skills involved in judgment are part of a constellation of characterological factors that affect whether a leader's judgment is adequate, flawed, or good. The same is true for the reflective aspects of judgment. Good judgment is a combined product of a president's insight and analysis, basic sense of self, and emotional attunement to himself and others.

This last factor, emotional attunement, is an important part of good policy and political judgment. Good problem diagnosis requires a realistic appraisal of the effects of the problem on others. Simple self-calculation is ultimately a poor guide to good political judgment, since sound solutions require a consideration of the concerns of others, even if their preferences cannot be given decisive weight.

With these observations as a framework, let us focus more directly on Gary Hart. Is his behavior a refection of a misjudgment or something more troubling? Did his judgment in this matter reflect in any way on his capacity for presidential leadership, and if so, exactly how?

Let us first turn to the nature of the judgments involved. At the outset, it must be recalled that in 1984 Gary Hart himself had become an issue. It is true that the issue of womanizing was not given as much public attention then as his name change, different statements of his age, and other aspects of his personal and political identity, but it was enough of an issue to be raised in the interview whose publication immediately preceded Hart's difficulties. Moreover, Hart clearly knew it was an issue, which the "if you don't believe me, follow me" remark was meant to address.

There can be no doubt that the stakes were enormous. Hart had spent several years preparing to run for the presidency. He had assembled a team, raised money, drawn a following willing to work for him, and was, by all accounts, the front-runner. Moreover, the stakes involved in his obtaining the presidency were, *in his own view,* enormous. He eventually reentered the campaign because no other candidate had (in his view) the policies and leadership abilities to govern this country well. As a serious, leading, and potentially successful candidate for the presidency, Hart had an important political future, regardless of whether he was elected to the office. One therefore has to count this situation as one in which much was at stake for both Hart and the country.

Hart was under no external time pressures to pursue Rice; indeed, the contrary was true. Hugh Sidney has pointed out (1987, 20) that "sex—real or imagined—is far more hazardous to the political health of a presidential candidate than to a sitting President." He notes that a president is more protected than a candidate, and moreover, a president's record provides much more to judge than a private indiscretion.

An outside observer cannot be fully certain what particular motives were involved in Hart's pursuit of Rice during the campaign. What is important to our analysis is that he did choose to pursue her during his candidacy, despite the questions raised in the past about him and the fact that the personal lives of candidates had come to play an increasingly prominent role in presidential campaigns. I do not care to speculate about Hart's motivations, but we can make inferences and analyze the issues that his behavior raises. There are at least three related to the capacity of good judgment.

The first issue is Hart's contention that he didn't appreciate how his behavior would look to outsiders. If that explanation is not disingenuous, it certainly raises questions about Hart's political judgment. More basically, to accept that he failed to see that arranging meetings with an unmarried woman he met at a party, invited on a boating trip, and so forth, would raise questions is to raise the issue of a substantial failure of reality assessment.

Why did Hart never consider how his behavior would look to others? One possibility is that the behavior was so innocent in his mind that he could not think it would not also be so in others'. This would require him to believe that everyone would appreciate the innocence of the relationship and that he would not be called upon to explain it further. Once the possibility is even considered that one might need to explain one's behavior, the assumption of innocence by itself is not likely to go very far.

It is also possible that Hart never considered how his behavior would look because he didn't sufficiently consider the possibility that he might be called upon to explain it. Feelings of being special and invulnerable often result in a feeling that "it can't happen here." When that occurs, considerations that might be more self-protective are not given serious enough attention. Such feelings are a particularly dangerous illusion for presidents and other high-level political leaders.

The second issue is impulse control. Whatever Hart's motivations for his relationship with Rice, the fact that he was not able to delay consummating them, given the circumstances, is itself important. The fact that a candidate is more vulnerable than a president in such relationships, as suggested by Hugh Sidney, is not presented as an endorsement of such behavior. Rather, it points to the fact that at least some of the satisfactions of the motivations usually involved in such relationships were not beyond Hart's reach had he chosen to wait.

This issue leads directly to the third, which is the disparity between what Hart gained and what he put at risk and ultimately lost as a result of his relationship with Rice. When Hart withdrew from the campaign, he repeated an earlier statement about how much he cared about the country and noted that his candidacy had been about his trying to "change the future and the direction of the country" (Hart 1987c, 9). This is a large and admirable goal, but the very fact that its accomplishment was in reach would seem to dwarf whatever satisfactions could be obtained by a relationship with Rice raises questions.

A first question concerns the adequacy of Hart's calculation regarding risks and rewards. Every political leader's "operational code" (see George 1969) contains some assessment of the nature and calculation of political risk. Leadership decisions of any consequence almost always contain elements of risk. But it is one thing to take risks when they are necessary, and another to take unnecessary risks. Hart's argument that any tendency toward inappropriate risk reflected in this episode would have nothing to do with how he would assess other risks once in office is unconvincing.

Second, the fact that Hart was willing to risk so much of what he and many others had worked so hard to accomplish for the sake of pursuing a relationship with Rice raises the question of just how much weight he gave to the policy goals espoused in his campaign and political career. This is a difficult question, but one that must be asked. A leader ready to abandon the chance to accomplish his adult career goals calls into question his seriousness of purpose, regardless of his intelligence.

Hart did more than risk his own future and the advancement of the political programs and issues that were the basis of his campaign. By his behavior, he also put at risk the trust, faith, and hard work of members of his campaign staff and volunteers who believed in and were committed to him. Hart's exhortation in his withdrawal speech to those who had supported his campaign that they not lose their idealism because of what had happened *to* him and his own view of himself as an idealist are hard to credit in a speech that disowns much personal responsibility.

There are further issues raised by Hart's behavior after the story was uncovered, for example, issues that relate to his continuation of inaccurate statements about the events surrounding the confrontation between himself and reporters at his home in Washington and its aftermath. There also is the issue of his repeated attacks on the press and their behavior, at the same time that his responsibilities in the matter were denied or minimized. There remain further issues surrounding his reentry into the race, the most prominent of which is Hart's view that no other candidate was measuring up to the task, thus literally requiring him to be a candidate again.

There is little reason to examine these issues at great length here. Yet they supplement and do not contradict our understanding of a pattern of behavior already discussed at length. It remains for us to discuss briefly some implications of the Hart case.

Epilogue: Some Implications of the Hart Episode

This study of Gary Hart suggests several cautions. First, it suggests that attractive, articulate, and intelligent candidates may be otherwise psychologically unsuited for high political positions. Elements of ambition and narcissism are probably essential in ample degree for persons to aspire to high political roles, but there are lines, the nature of which we do not yet understand, to be drawn between intense personal and political ambition, narcissistic feelings of worth, and those extreme feelings that wind up creating political and personal disasters.

The lines that need to be understood and drawn here are much more difficult to place than the traditional divisions of behavior along the neurotic–psychotic continuum. Here we face the possibility that the very traits we find attractive in presidential candidates may come in a characterological package that will lead us to regret choosing them.

The Hart case also underscores the point that while a strong sense of self-esteem, capacity, and effectiveness is preferable in presidential candidates (and presidents), it is not necessarily true that more is always better. Indeed, the Hart case underscores a major anomaly in the attempt to analyze characters of some presidential candidates and presidents. What manifests itself publicly as confidence and a strong sense of capacity may in fact be a form of pseudo–self-esteem, in which a *false self* (to use psychoanalyst Helen Deutsch's term) has been constructed by the person to cover vulnerabilities in his sense of adequacy and self-esteem. Such persons, as Gary Hart illustrates, may have enormous energy, intelligence, and political success, but the real foundation of character shows itself in a tendency to flout conventional rules because one is so special as to be exempt from the normal rules of cause and effect.

The process that derailed Hart's candidacy was not pleasant, but it was necessary. Because of it, the country was spared the need to discover whether or not Gary Hart could overcome the difficulties that caused him to squander his personal and political capital as a candidate in the presidency. And once again, as in the Eagleton case, a large and important story began with a disaffected tipster, a fact that only underscores the need for a more systematic and effective method of evaluating presidential candidates.

TEN

Bill Clinton as a Presidential Candidate: What Did the Public Learn?

What can be learned about the character and psychology of candidates in presidential campaigns that has relevance for the elected candidate's performance as president? Do presidential campaigns perform their second major function—that of enlightening the public about the nature of the persons seeking the office, their strengths and limitations? Do campaigns tell us anything important about how the successful candidate, once elected, will govern?

In this chapter I examine the candidacy of William J. Clinton from the perspective of the three basic character elements: ambition, character integrity, and relatedness. I first examine the extent to which it was possible to place Clinton in each of these categories of analysis and on what basis. I also examine the extent to which the campaign offered relevant clues to the two major dimensions of presidential performance examined in chapter 8, judgment and leadership. Finally, I examine the draft controversy that arose during the campaign as a small case study of the way in which Clinton's character elements manifested themselves in a context of crisis for himself and his campaign.[1] In chapter 11, I will analyze Clinton's first two years in office. My purpose there is to analyze the extent to which the information obtained during the campaign regarding these three basic character elements carried over to President Clinton's approach to decision making and leadership.

A Note on the Basic Public Dilemma

I noted in the Introduction that each president is selected in part because he is perceived as the best person to address and resolve what I term the *basic public dilemma*. I defined the basic public dilemma as a fundamental, unresolved question concerning public psychology that faces the president on taking office. It is not a specific question about public policy but rather a matter of the public's psychological connections to its institutions, leaders, and political process. This unresolved public concern underlies and frames more specific policy debates. The basic public dilemma may be fully appreciated by the public or other observers only in retrospect, which may help to explain why the "stock" of some presidents rises or falls well after they have left office.

What is the basic public dilemma that Bill Clinton faced during his candidacy and now faces as president? It is not Bosnia or his policy toward the former Soviet Union. It is not a problem with the deficit, trade, or health care, as important as all of these issues are.

In my view, the basic public dilemma that Clinton faced is one of public trust in public policy. At its base, this dilemma reflects a fundamental public question about whether government policies, even those that are constructive in intent, can be fair in formulation and successful in result. As noted in chapter 1, Americans' belief in the competence and fairness of government has been repeatedly challenged in the last three decades. Policies of government intervention designed to address economic and social imbalances, which on occasion were constructive and even admirable in intent, have often not realized their goals. Moreover, they have often resulted in unanticipated and unsatisfactory consequences. More recent government policies designed to let the market accomplish laudable social purposes have not yet proved adequate to the task, as the persistence of problems with poverty, crime, and the environment attests.

President Clinton campaigned on a platform that stressed government's ability to develop and implement public policies that would be fair to groups across the political spectrum, not just those that have traditionally supported the Democratic party. He promised that his policies would solve old problems while not creating a host of new ones. And he promised that they would do so in a way which the public would understand and support. In short, he promised, in Osborne and Gaebler's (1992) ambitious phrase, to "reinvent government."

The extent to which Clinton is able to do this will depend not only on the policies themselves but also on his character, judgment, and leadership. Let us now assess these elements as they seemed to make themselves known during the 1992 presidential campaign.

The Three Domains of Character as They Emerged during the 1992 Campaign

In chapter 7, I put forward a framework for the analysis of character that consisted of three elements: ambition, character integrity, and relatedness. What are the three core elements of Bill Clinton's character and psychology that correspond to this formulation? I suggest that they are (1) a substantial level of ambition, coupled with the skills to realize it; (2) a substantial level of self-confidence, coupled with a somewhat idealized view of himself; and (3) a movement toward relationships, shaped by a strong need for validation. Each of these elements was evident to some degree during the campaign and, as I will suggest in chapter 11, shaped Clinton's approach to his presidency.

In the following sections, I examine each element as it appeared publicly during the campaign. I begin with the domain of ambition and the skills relevant to its accomplishment. I then move to the domain of character integrity and identity, perhaps the most complex of the three elements in Clinton's case. I examine his level of confidence and his view of himself both politically (as a "New Democrat") and personally. Finally, I move to the character domain of relatedness. I frame these three elements as they present themselves or appear publicly, reserving more dynamic formulations until chapter 11.

The Domain of Ambition

I earlier conceptualized ambition as the desire to accomplish, facilitated by capacity. During the campaign, there could be little mistaking Bill Clinton's substantial level of ambition in this sense. His path from Hope, a small town in rural Arkansas, to 1600 Pennsylvania Avenue in Washington, D.C., is a chronicle of, and a testament to, his personal and political ambitions (Oakley 1994; Maraniss 1995). He was an outstanding student at Hot Springs High School, an accomplished student at Georgetown University, a Rhodes Scholar, and a graduate of Yale Law School. These accomplishments preceded his substantial and upwardly directed political career, which included winning the post of attorney general of Arkansas in 1976 at the age of twenty-nine, becoming the youngest governor in the country in

1978 at the age of thirty-two, and successive reelections to that position in 1982, 1984, 1986, and 1990. He was named co-chair of the National Governors Association in 1986 and chairman of the Democratic Leadership Council in 1990.

Nor was there much doubt about the fact that Clinton had at his disposal enormous energy. There are numerous accounts of Clinton's high levels of activity, beginning with his high school years (Levin 1992, 30–32) and extending through college and both Oxford and Yale Law School. For example, in high school Clinton was involved in numerous extracurricular activities. In addition to compiling a strong academic record, he was a member and/or president of a number of school organizations.[2]

The energy to "fund" his psychological investments was evident during the campaign. Describing Governor Clinton's frenetic schedule during the presidential campaign, Senator David Pryor (1992, xx), a good friend, noted that he has "enormous energy. . . . His schedule defied human tolerance. . . . On February 17, the day before the New Hampshire primary vote, he made 17 stops over the state. At 11:30 that night, schedule completed, he asked, 'Isn't there a bowling alley that's open all night? We need to shake some hands.' "

Ambition is reflected in purposeful action. The realization of ambition, as Kohut reminds us, requires talent and skills. They are its means. Without them, ambition is an empty vessel for accomplishing purposes.

What personal and political skills did Clinton evidence during the campaign? I suggest there were at least three, one primarily cognitive and the other two primarily motivational. They are (1) high-level cognitive capacities, (2) an ability to invest himself in work, and (3) an intense commitment to accomplishment of his purposes.

Clinton's cognitive capacities are clear, both historically and in the campaign. Historically, they are reflected in the list of successful academic and governmental accomplishments previously noted. They were also on display during his campaign. Clinton was able to answer a variety of questions on diverse policy topics with an array of information and a sophisticated appreciation of the issues involved. He clearly had mastered a wide range of information and had also developed meaningful categories in which to organize it.[3]

The second and third characteristics, his ability to invest himself in activity and his commitment to accomplishment, are reflected not only in the history of his academic and political career but in the many other activities he was involved with while doing these things. The same active involvement in a range of activities could be noted for his time at Georgetown, for the time he worked for Senator J. William Fulbright, and throughout his political career in Arkansas.

In these activities Clinton was not only a participant but an invested one. In high school, for example, he not only played in the band but made "all-state," a recognition of talent as well as practice and commitment. Carolyn Staley, a high school friend with whom Clinton practiced for state music competitions, recalls, "We met several times a week at my house to perfect his solo. We never sat around and chatted. The rehearsals were intense. Bill was always serious about his performances and worked hard to win first place" (1993, 36).

At Georgetown, Clinton worked in a student service that greeted new freshmen. The first blind student accepted at the Georgetown University School of Foreign Service recalled how Bill Clinton personally helped him learn his way around campus by guiding him through various routes until he had mastered them (Levin 1992, 46–48). In 1970, Clinton did the same thing when this student came to Oxford as a Rhodes Scholar (Levin 1992, 67–68). This is someone who appears to have joined organizations not for the sake of friendship or membership alone but actually to accomplish things.

The Domain of Character Integrity: Identity and Persona

The second basic element of a president's character, integrity, reflects a dual perspective. First, how does the individual see himself and want to be seen, both politically and personally (self-image)? What is the relationship between the ideals and values that truly define who he is and the person he presents himself to be? Second, has the individual developed a stable, coherent sense of self that anchors a consolidated sense of self-worth? How much and what kind of regard does the individual have for himself?

Where would the evidence available during the campaign allow us to place Bill Clinton in this domain? Let us begin with the question of self-regard. When a strong sense of self-regard is coupled with a strongly positive view of oneself (self-image), one result is a substantial level of personal confidence. There are several strands of evidence to support the view that Clinton has developed extremely high levels of self-confidence. Rudi Moore, Jr., Clinton's campaign manager during his first run for governor and also Governor Clinton's chief of staff during his first term, recalls that Clinton "always had boundless confidence in his ability to forge a consensus and work out any problem" (1993, 92).

Another piece of evidence is his willingness to talk publicly, at length, without notes, on a range of subjects. Clinton was one of the most verbal presidential candidates in modern history. Few candidates have felt so secure talking at length in a variety of settings on so many subjects.

Another way in which Clinton's self-confidence manifested itself publicly was in his ability to weather the multiple crises of his candidacy, beginning with accusations of marital infidelity and avoiding the draft and with his original (although somewhat evasive) answers to the question of whether or not he had ever smoked marijuana. One reporter (Tierney 1992, A20) covering the candidate, in an article titled, "Grace under Pressure? It's Working for Clinton," noted that Clinton's apparent "serenity" in the face of these accusations was an important aspect of his campaign's ability to weather them. A less self-confident and determined candidate, it was reasoned (with some legitimacy), would not have been able to do so.

The other element of this character domain, the integration of Clinton's view of himself and his political identity, is essential to understanding Clinton's psychology. As noted, personal identity reflects a candidate's view of himself, while political identity refers to the individual's presentation of himself to the public as a political actor. The degree of coherence, stability, and authenticity that exists between the two identities helps to define the arena of character integrity.

Clinton's political identity has many aspects (Bennett 1995). Here I focus on Clinton as a "New Democrat." Central to his view of himself, and certainly to his public identity in the 1992 campaign, was his assertion that he would bridge and transcend traditional left–right politics. He saw and presented himself as neither a liberal nor a conservative but rather as a leader who would sit down with all concerned to work out the best solution to public problems, regardless of whether the persons involved were considered left or right of center.

Clinton is quoted in one representative speech to a television audience in Seattle, Washington, and Portland, Oregon, as saying:

My belief is—this may sound naive but it grows out of my own experience, that if you let people who are genuinely affected sit down in groups where all their interests are represented and try to hammer out solutions, you can almost always get a compromise that people feel is the right thing. I don't think there are many people who want to squander the environment of this country and I don't think there are many people who want to shut the economy down. (Ifill 1992e, A11)

In the same article, Clinton is quoted as saying (in a speech to the Urban League, to a largely black audience), "Your plan and my plan . . . do not involve liberal versus conservative, left versus right, big government versus little government. That's a load of bull we've been paralyzed with for too long. Your plan and my plan are about big ideas versus old ideas."

In the introduction to his campaign book (written with Al Gore), Governor Clinton noted that "our policies are neither liberal or conservative, neither Democratic or Republican. They are new. They are different. We are confident that they will work" (1992, viii).

In terms of the basic public dilemma discussed at the start of this chapter, Clinton presented himself as a candidate who would successfully address that dilemma. His policies would move beyond the politics (and policies) that had given rise to this particular dilemma in the first place. In place of policies that proved inadequate, there would be new, smarter solutions. In place of conflict and stalemate, there would be thoughtfully reached agreements that would work.

What of Clinton's view of himself as a individual aspiring to lead? There was evidence in the campaign that Clinton entertained few doubts about his motives, values, and candor. In his responses to the press and others who raised questions about him during the campaign, he presented himself as a man of conviction, determination, integrity, and principle. He presented himself as fair, open, honest, and genuinely interested in and responsive to others' points of view and concerns. Critical to his self-image (as well as to his campaign strategy) was a view of himself as a victim.[4]

When questioned by a college student about a lack of candor in the handling of questions concerning the draft, extramarital relationships, and smoking marijuana as a young adult, Clinton offered a "rambling, insistent defense of his own character," which "at times resembled a tirade" (Ifill 1992d, A21). Governor Clinton is quoted as having made the following points: "There is no trust issue, except the press again trying to make a mountain out of a molehill." "One of the things that amazes me is that if I don't say something they say I'm not being candid, and if I tell the whole truth I'm not being candid."

He attributed to himself the most sincere and best of motives, and errors, when acknowledged, were presented as the result of faulty memory of small details that occurred many years before (in the case of the draft controversy, decades), as misunderstandings that would disappear or be mitigated if people knew more of what he knew, or as attributable to naïveté and inexperience. The last of these is, of course, another way of attributing to oneself good intentions gone awry because of the faults of others.

I don't list his understandings because I believe them wholly untrue. Rather, I note them because they reflect a strong component of *self-idealization*. Most people wish to think well of themselves. However, Bill Clinton appears to have come to believe the *best* of himself and either to avoid or to discount evidence from his behavior that all is not as he believes it to be. Any attention called to a number of discrepancies between his real behavior and his view of it, as was done by the press during the campaign (and first two years of his presidency), was met with denial, exculpatory explanations, mostly long but sometimes short answers that did not deal directly with the point, and, when all else failed, unconcealed frustration and anger.

The Domain of Relatedness: Interpersonal Relations

The third basic dimension of character is a person's stance toward interpersonal relations. In chapter 7 I noted that Horney (1937) theorized that individuals, as a result of early experience, develop an interpersonal style in which they move toward, away from, or against people. On the face of things, it seems clear that Clinton's interpersonal style is a movement toward people. Much has been made of his empathy and natural friendliness, and to a substantial degree (with some caveats to be noted), these characterizations appear accurate.[5]

Much has also been written about Clinton's difficulty in saying no (e.g., Clift 1993) and his eagerness to please (e.g., Klein 1993). Both are often attributed to "Clinton's well-known need to be liked." Indeed, the brief biography of Governor Clinton that appeared on the front page of the *New York Times* on the day of his election was titled, "A Man Who Wants to Be Liked, and Is" (Kelly 1992e). However, at least two theoretical and factual difficulties stand in the way of this argument.

First there is the issue, already noted, of Clinton's very strong sense of self-confidence. Ordinarily, the need to be liked would not be associated with such high levels of personal confidence.[6] Second, the idea of a need to be liked does not fully come to grips with Clinton's frequently observed tendency toward public and private displays of anger. During the nomination campaign, when Clinton was told (erroneously) that Jesse Jackson had come out in support of a party rival, Clinton, who was not aware that he was speaking near an open microphone, angrily denounced Jackson as a "back-stabber" (Berke 1992a, A14). When news reporters followed the president-elect onto a golf course, he lost his temper, cursed them, and complained to the manager of the club (Kelly 1992f).

Nor does the need-to-be-liked theory address another psychological tributary of Clinton's political style—his tendency to build up anger and then lash out against institutions or groups who oppose his policies. The press is one example of such a group, but there are others, including "lobbyists," "special interests," "profiteering drug companies," "greedy doctors," "muscle-bound" labor unions, and so on. Presidents, like others, can be known by and benefit from having certain kinds of enemies. However, for a man who is said to have such a strong need to be liked, the list of enemies is rather long and inclusive and his characterizations often somewhat harsh. Moreover, Clinton's tendency to develop enemies, even if partially for political purposes, runs counter to another important theme that he has often publicly expressed—the need to bring Americans together and stop practicing the politics of division.

Clinton's view of himself as an honorable person hounded by the press and his political opponents was central not only to the survival of his candidacy but to his view of himself. However, his own ambition and behavior were always an unacknowledged subtext in the controversies that gave rise to his feelings. It seems worthwhile, therefore, to explore at some greater length at least one of the "character issues" that arose during the campaign: the draft issue. The allegations, as well as responses to them by Clinton and his campaign, provide a useful set of data through which to examine the interrelated character domains of ambition, integrity, and relatedness.

I selected the draft issue in part because, like the extramarital affair(s) controversy that surrounded Gary Hart, it raised an important and specific set of allegations about Clinton's character and candor. It also arose during the campaign and thus is relevant to our focus on whether campaigns fulfill their function of allowing us to learn important things about the character and psychology of the candidates who would be president. I also chose it because it was the most fully and publicly documented of the controversies surrounding Clinton at the time.[7]

The Draft Controversy as a Crisis of Ambition, Integrity, and Relatedness Issues

The draft issue is complicated, in part because it unfolded over a long period of time, and information that became public at one point left one impression while information that was revealed later left another. Information that emerged months after the story first broke lost some impact because it was not immediately picked up or connected to previous information.[8] Moreover, it was difficult to assign significance in the larger story to individual facts as they were revealed for three reasons: first, because the facts of the unfolding story did appear piecemeal; second, because they emerged in this manner in the middle of a furiously contested presidential campaign, with many other issues vying for public and commentator attention; third, because each disclosure brought forth a round of new explanations and criticisms for the particular item disclosed but no one, overall analysis of the story or its implications.

The draft issue is complex for another reason. It involves a reading of Clinton's behavior and intentions in relationship to the draft during an unpopular and divisive war. However, the importance and interest to us are not to be found solely, or even primarily, in Clinton's behavior at that time, but in his response to this part of his personal history as a political candidate in Arkansas and as a presidential candidate. It is the package of these elements, rather than any single one, that is of interest.

The unfolding events regarding Clinton's relationship to the Vietnam War and the draft were framed for the public, and those who argued over it, by one major question: Did the available evidence indicate that Clinton (who opposed the war, as many of his generation did) was principled in his behavior, at the time and thereafter, with regard to his dilemma of possibly being called for service in a war that he opposed? Clinton argued forcefully that he had been. His critics argued that he had not.

Our interest is related to this concern but goes somewhat beyond it. As I will argue below, some of the questions regarding Clinton's behavior cannot be fully resolved from the available record. However, the record as it developed is useful for our analysis in several ways. Clinton's behavior at the time and his responses as this issue developed do provide some insight into the domains of ambition, integrity, and relatedness.

The Unfolding Draft Controversy

On February 6, 1992, the *Wall Street Journal* published a long article asserting that Clinton had secured a deferment by promising to enroll in the Reserve Officers' Training Corps (ROTC) program at the University of Arkansas but had then reneged on that promise. In response to that article, Clinton said that he had felt that it would be wrong for him to take advantage of the deferment when other young men whom he knew were taking their chances with the draft: "I had high school classmates who were already dead, I decided it was an inappropriate thing to do." Clinton said that if he had ever received special treatment from his draft board, he had never asked for it or known about it; "I certainly had no leverage to get it" (Ifill 1992a, A16).

The same issue had been raised before, in 1978 during Clinton's campaigns for the governorship of Arkansas. At that time, in answer to the charge that he had avoided the draft by securing a deferment on the basis of his assurance that he would enroll in the ROTC program, Clinton said he had received a student deferment as an undergraduate and that he had been eligible for induction while he was a Rhodes Scholar in England but had been fortunate enough never to have received the call. This turned out to be only partially accurate and an extremely limited account.

After the 1992 *Wall Street Journal* article, journalists and others raised questions about Clinton's candor. He responded with complaints about "the obviously well-planned and well-coordinated negative hits" he was forced to endure (Ifill 1992b, A14). In his view, he had told the truth, and questions to the contrary did not arise from his behavior but from the questionable motives of others. Goldman, DeFrank, Miller, Murr, and Mathews describe Clinton's private reaction at the time of the draft controversy as "a sulfurous mixture of anger at the media and pity for himself" and quote him as complaining, "No one has ever been through what I've been through in this thing. *No* one. Nobody's ever had this kind of personal investigation done on them, running for president, by the legitimate media" (1994, 118; emphasis in original).

On February 12, a letter that Clinton wrote to the head of his local draft board, Colonel Eugene Holmes, surfaced. The letter was dated December 3, 1969, two days after Clinton had received a high draft number in the lottery and thus had known he was very unlikely to be called up as a draftee. The letter (written when Clinton was twenty-three years old) is remarkable for the depth of apparent anguish and difficulty in resolving what for Clinton (and for others at the time) was a great personal and political issue.

The issue, as Clinton's letter framed it, was whether he should give up the ROTC slot that had been made available to him and thus make himself liable for the draft and take the risk of serving in a war that he thought was wrong and perhaps illegal. In the end, he wrote that

the decision not to become a resister and the related subject decisions were the most difficult of my life. I decided to accept the draft in spite of my beliefs for one reason: to maintain my viability in the political system. For years I have worked to prepare myself for a political life . . . it is a life I still feel compelled to try to lead. (Clinton 1992, A25)

This part of the letter is revealing of Clinton's determination and political ambition at that relatively early stage of his life. It also appears to contradict his statement, made several days before the letter's publication, in response to the *Wall Street Journal* article, or at least to provide additional reasons for his decision to give up his ROTC deferment. The letter is also of interest for the struggle it portrays between Clinton's ambition and his values and ideals. In the end, as Clinton saw it, his values and ideals won out, and he presented himself for the draft.

Did Clinton Voluntarily Give Up His Deferment?

Several substantial questions remained. Did Clinton notify his draft board *before* receiving his high number in the lottery or *after?* Did he make a principled decision to give up his deferment and put himself at risk for his values? Clinton stressed, both in public (e.g., Ifill 1992b) and in private to his staff (Goldman et al. 1994, 39), that the bottom line was that he had made himself available for the draft.

That specific issue, however, was never fully resolved. Maraniss (1995, 185–203) believes he did, but only after it became very clear that it was unlikely he would ever be called. The analysis I will present shortly calls that conclusion into question. However, what is unambiguous is that the process by which information became available and the veracity of other aspects of Clinton's explanation also became an issue.

Clinton was reclassified 1-A (the highest availability for the draft) after he graduated from Georgetown University in the spring of 1968. He was then twenty-three years old and highly likely to be drafted, because most of the older men eligible for the draft from his district had either satisfied their obligations or been found unqualified. Deferments for students going on to graduate school were no longer allowed.

Nonetheless, Clinton received a special deferment from his draft board to go to Oxford in September 1968 as a Rhodes Scholar. According to draft board records, he took and passed a preinduction physical in England on February 3, 1969. He returned to Arkansas in the summer of 1969 and at that point met with Colonel Holmes, head of the ROTC unit at the University of Arkansas, and was offered a slot in the program. That step removed him from exposure to the draft and allowed him to return to Oxford in September 1969.

But acceptance of the ROTC slot also effectively delayed Clinton's availability for the draft until the summer of 1970, for two reasons. First, draft calls for the rest of the year, announced in September, were low nationally and particularly low for Clinton's draft district (Hot Springs). Second, and more important, President Nixon announced on October 1, 1969, that even students who were called up could finish their year in graduate school.

Clinton was again reclassified 1-A, on October 30, 1969, while in his second year of a two-year program at Oxford. The draft lottery was established on November 26, 1969. In the first lottery drawing on December 1, 1969, Clinton received a high draft number, ensuring that he would not be called in the draft. On December 2, he submitted his application to Yale Law School. His letter withdrawing from his ROTC promise and thanking Colonel Holmes for "saving him from the draft" is dated December 3, 1969.

In the letter to Holmes, Clinton recalls that he wrote a letter dated September 12, 1969, to the chairman of his local draft board, soon after he and Holmes met (during the summer), asking to be let out of his promise to join the ROTC and to be reclassified 1-A. Clinton wrote to Holmes that he never mailed that letter,

> but I did carry it on me every day until I got on the plane to return to England. I didn't mail the letter because I didn't see, in the end, how my going into the army and maybe going to Vietnam would achieve anything except a feeling that I had punished myself and gotten what I deserved. (Clinton 1992, A25)

In response to the February 6 *Wall Street Journal* article (before the February 12 release of his 1969 letter to Colonel Holmes), Clinton recalled having informed Holmes of his decision to withdraw from his ROTC promise in September or early October (Kelly 1992c, A1). Yet it is somewhat unclear, given the December 1969 letter in which Clinton relates writing but not mailing a letter of withdrawal and his conviction that being drafted would serve no purpose, why he would have done this so shortly after having concluded that there was no purpose to be served in doing so.

The phrasing of Clinton's response to the February 6 *Wall Street Journal* article implies that he informed his draft board personally in October 1969 of his decision. However, in an interview with Ted Koppel on *Nightline* (ABC transcript, 12 February 1992, 9), Clinton said that he had asked his stepfather, who had since died, to pass on to Colonel Holmes Clinton's intention to stand for the draft in late September or October. Again, it is unclear why he would do so, after having written a letter withdrawing from his commitment but not having mailed it, since he had come to the conclusion that his induction would serve no purpose.

Clinton was reclassified 1-A on October 30, 1969, an event consistent with his memory that his stepfather told the draft board that Clinton wished to be released from his promise. However, Colonel Holmes and his assistant Colonel Clinton D. Jones said they did not recall hearing from Clinton in October but, rather, after the December lottery, in which Clinton received a high number (Kelly 1992c, A23).

Why would Clinton have been reclassified 1-A in October if he (or his stepfather) had not informed his draft board, as Clinton said? One suggestion comes from the director of the ROTC program, Colonel Holmes. He is quoted in the *Wall Street Journal* (6 February 1992, A16) as saying he was under the impression that Clinton "was going to finish a month or two in England and then come back to the University of Arkansas." Holmes said in that same article that he would not have given Clinton another full-year deferment, since to do so "wouldn't have been ethical."

It is possible that the draft board reclassified Clinton 1-A in October not only in anticipation of his being drafted but more immediately because he failed to be in touch regarding his return to take up the ROTC appointment. In a widely overlooked line in the 1969 letter to Holmes, Clinton stated, "I am sorry to be so long in writing. *I know I promised to let you hear from me at least once a month and from now on you will*" (Clinton 1992, A25; emphasis mine). That letter was written and sent at least four months *after* Clinton had met with Holmes in Arkansas in July 1969 and had secured a deferment. Apparently, Clinton had promised to be in touch with Holmes on a very regular basis and had not done so. It is possible that this failure to contact the colonel was involved in the decision to reclassify Clinton.

Clinton does not mention in this letter that he or his stepfather had contacted Colonel Holmes in October 1969. Before the 1969 letter was released, Clinton insisted that he or his stepfather had been in touch with Holmes by October. Yet his December 3, 1969, letter mentions only the letter Clinton says he wrote but never sent. Clinton's apology for taking so long to write and his acknowledgment that he had not kept his promise to "let you hear from me at least once a month" are inconsistent with the later assertion that he had been in touch with his draft board and with Colonel Holmes in late September or early October.

According to Maraniss (1995, 204), Clinton's letter to Holmes that he was not taking up his ROTC slot came as a surprise to the ROTC staff, which apparently, as of December, was still expecting him. Maraniss quotes Ed Howard, the unit's drill instructor, as saying that "the letter only intensified the anger that the ROTC staff had felt toward Clinton since he had failed to enroll at the Law School." The implications here are that Clinton had been expected to enroll in the University of Arkansas Law School *before* the December 3 letter was received, that he had failed to do so, and that this failure had caused anger in the ROTC's staff. The actual letter regarding his decision not to take up his ROTC appointment was a *later,* additional source of their anger at Clinton.

The fact that Colonel Holmes and members of the ROTC unit were still expecting Clinton to take up his appointment at the University of Arkansas Law School *even after* Clinton was reclassified 1-A is extremely puzzling, if, as Clinton says, they had already been notified by his stepfather in late September or early October that Clinton was withdrawing from his slot in the ROTC program. The issue of whether Clinton notified his draft board before receiving his high number in the lottery, thus making a principled decision to give up his deferment and put himself at risk for his values, or was reclassified is not fully resolved by the public record. Clinton's account is possible but, in a number of respects, questionable.

Did Clinton Ask for and Receive Special Treatment?

Bill Clinton wrote to Colonel Holmes that he had concluded that to go into the army and possibly to Vietnam would serve no purpose except to punish himself. A reasonable question arises: Did others who might similarly have seen little or no purpose in serving in the army and perhaps going to Vietnam also have the opportunity to make the choices Clinton made? In short, did Clinton receive special treatment?

Clinton strongly objected to the *Wall Street Journal* story that accused him of manipulating the draft process to gain a deferment. In response, on February 6, 1992, he strongly argued that he had never received special treatment (Ifill 1992a, A16). He further said that if he had received special treatment, he had never asked for it or known about it. Finally, he said, "I certainly had no leverage to get it."

In April 1992, the *Los Angeles Times* printed excerpts from letters written by Clifford Jackson, a Fulbright scholar at Oxford at the same time that Clinton was there as a Rhodes scholar in 1969, to friends, concerning Bill Clinton. In the excerpts, Jackson described efforts by himself and others to help Clinton avoid the draft (which many were attempting to do at the time). These excerpts described Clinton as "feverishly trying to find a way to avoid entering the army as a drafted private." Jackson's letters further noted that he had "enlisted several of my friends in influential positions, trying to pull strings on Bill's behalf." Kelly noted at the time the excerpts were printed that "Mr. Jackson's assertion that Mr. Clinton arranged a campaign of political influence to secure the delay and the R.O.T.C. slot is unproven and has been denied by Mr. Clinton" (1992c, A1).

Seven months later, on September 2, 1992, the *Los Angeles Times* reported that Clinton's late uncle, Raymond Clinton, had led a successful effort to protect his nephew from being inducted during a ten-month period in 1968 when Bill Clinton was reclassified 1-A. This account was of importance in another respect, since it focused attention on the time of Clinton's first year at Oxford in 1968, well before he had approached Colonel Holmes for the ROTC deferment. The newspaper reported that Clinton's uncle had used his political connections to have an additional slot created in a naval reserve unit, at a time when such slots were no longer normally available to young people in the area. Clinton responded that he had no knowledge of any such efforts, saying, "It's all news to me" and "This is the first I've ever heard of any of this" (Kelly 1992a, A20).

Two days later, on September 4, Clinton acknowledged that he had been told in March 1992 of his uncle's efforts. He was responding at this point to an article that appeared in the *Arkansas Democrat-Gazette* the previous day, which quoted Trice Ellis, Jr., a retired navy commander who had supervised the naval reserve program in Hot Springs, Arkansas, at the time in question. Clinton said, "I did not know about any effort to secure a Naval Reserve assignment before Mr. Ellis mentioned it to me in Hot Springs. There was no way to document or confirm what he told me" (Kelly 1992b, A7).

On a talk show linkup on September 14, Clinton was asked whether there was anything concerning his explanation of the draft that he would do differently now than he had back in 1969 or during the campaign. He replied:

In terms of whether I could have handled it differently during the campaign, I think there's no question about that. You know, I'd like to explain why I didn't do such a good job of it. I didn't go back through all my letters, notes, to try and put this all back together again . . . and I think I was always kind of playing catch up because I gave a lot of answers to questions off the top of my head, halfway on the run when the press would hit me. And you don't remember everything after twenty-three years, every detail and every specific. (Kelly 1992c, A1)

On September 18, Colonel Holmes released a statement and an affidavit (reprinted in its entirety in Brown 1992)[9] concerning his recollection of the events that took place in 1969. Holmes said that he felt Clinton had deceived him about both his views and intentions. Apart from stating the colonel's view of the situation, the affidavit contained no new information, with one exception: a recollection of calls received from Senator J. W. Fulbright.

On September 19, a damaging story (Suro 1992) for Bill Clinton broke. It revealed that he had asked for help from Senator J. W. Fulbright's office (Clinton had worked for Senator Fulbright while in college) to secure Clinton a spot in the ROTC program. The story, acknowledged by Clinton's aides, was based on a sheet of handwritten notes found in the Fulbright archives. The notes refer to Clinton's wish to get an ROTC slot and deferment and contain Colonel Holmes's phone number and the notation "Holmes to call me Wed. 16th." Both Clinton's visit to Fulbright's office at this time and its nature were confirmed by an aide to the senator. This story appeared to contradict all of Clinton's early assertions, namely, that he had not asked anyone for help; that he had not received any help; that if he had received help, he didn't know anything about it; and finally, that he lacked the leverage to get anyone to give him special help.

When the story was first reported in March in the *New York Post,* Clinton campaign spokesperson Max Parker replied, "Governor Clinton says he never asked anyone for help" (Suro 1992). On September 16, before the *New York Times* story came out, Clinton aide Betsey Wright said, "Governor Clinton has no specific recollection of any specific actions" (Suro 1992). The *New York Times* article also reports that Lieutenant Colonel Clinton D. Jones, who served as Holmes's deputy, recalled receiving calls from both Senator Fulbright and Winthrop Rockefeller, then governor of Arkansas, asking if they could do anything to help Clinton. Colonel Holmes, in his affidavit, recalled that the day after speaking with Clinton for two hours at his home, he received calls from the draft board, saying that "it was of interest to Senator's Fulbright's Office that Bill Clinton, a Rhodes Scholar, should be admitted to the ROTC program. I received several such calls. The general message conveyed by the draft board to me was that Senator Fulbright's office was putting pressure on them and they needed my help" (quoted in Brown 1992, 146).

The day after the *New York Times* ran the story about Senator Fulbright's help, Clinton acknowledged his visit to the senator, saying he had gone to Fulbright's office to get information. Clinton said further that "when people ask you about special treatment, they mean did you leverage money or power, or something to get something that other people wouldn't have gotten, and the answer to that is no. But the truth is that the rules themselves wrote in special treatment" (Ifill 1992f, A26). In other words, in Clinton's view he did not get special treatment because that applies to situations in which one must pay (money) or use political power to get it. Moreover, he argued that it was not pressure that got him special treatment, but loopholes already built into the law. It was the law's fault, not his.

Finally, on September 26, an article that appeared in the *Los Angeles Times* reported that Clinton had been the beneficiary in 1969 of efforts by Arkansas Republicans to arrange a meeting for him with Colonel Willard A. Hawkins, the director of the Arkansas Selective Service System. In response, Clinton acknowledged that he might have met with Hawkins but that such a meeting, if it did occur, was part of a routine procedure suggested to him by his local draft board. He is quoted as saying, "They told me what procedures to follow, and I followed their procedures" (Kelly 1992d). It strains credulity to believe that meeting with the head of the state's selective service system at the height of the Vietnam War was "normal procedure" for someone seeking a deferment or that local selective service boards routinely told applicants for such deferments to do so.

Ambition, Ideals, and Clinton's Resolution of Quandaries: An Analysis of the Draft Issue

What does the draft controversy reveal about Bill Clinton's psychology? Does it reveal him to be an unprincipled opportunist? I argue that it doesn't. Does it reveal him to be, as he sees himself, a man of conviction, courage, and principle? Again, I argue that it doesn't. A more accurate portrayal, in my view, begins with seeing Clinton as a man struggling, not always successfully, to reconcile his ambition and his ideals. Let us begin with his ambition.

I noted in chapter 7 that ambition is not in and of itself problematic. It is a primary source of motivation for a range of acts, including accomplishment. So from the standpoint of the model outlined in chapter 7, Clinton's ambitions concerning his political career, as expressed in his December 3, 1969, letter, may be unusual for the degree to which they are articulated but are not a matter of strong concern. They reflect (by themselves, not considering their relationships to the other character domains, integrity and relatedness) a psychological point that Clinton had come to see a goal for himself (in the more technical term used by Erikson (1980), an ego ideal) and a context for the realization of his aspirations.

Recall further that one of the other two domains of character is that of integrity, which includes fidelity to the set of ideals and values that, in the best of circumstances, shape and guide ambition. Here, too, Clinton's 1969 letter to Colonel Holmes displays evidence of Clinton's ideals. He refers in the letter to having had the opportunity, while working in Senator Ful-bright's office, of "working every day against a war I opposed and despised with a depth of feeling I had reserved solely for racism" (Clinton 1992, A25).

There is no reason to doubt the authenticity of these feelings. Carolyn Staley, a high school friend of Clinton, recalls that when she visited him at Georgetown at the time of the riots that erupted after the murder of Dr. Martin Luther King, Jr., she and Clinton drove down to the black area of town to deliver food (Staley 1993). Clinton's ideals were, I believe, authentically felt then, if not always realized.

During the campaign, Clinton pointed to having voluntarily given up his deferment because "he felt a moral obligation to do so," since four of his friends had fought and died in Vietnam (Rosenbaum 1992b, A1). It was the most important, he implied, motivation for his behavior, and Clinton's view of himself as he asked to be seen. It is easy to allege that this was solely a response to the political circumstances in which he found himself when the draft controversy broke. However, it is also quite possible that it represents Clinton's idealized view of his behavior.

If so, this somewhat self-idealized view is at variance with the much more complex picture of his motivations that Clinton presented at the time. In his 1969 letter to Colonel Holmes, he wrote that he had "decided to accept the draft in spite of my beliefs for one reason: to maintain my viability in the political system. For years, I have worked to prepare myself for a political life. . . . It is a life I still feel compelled to try to lead" (Clinton 1992, A25).

Much of the attention that accompanied the release of Clinton's letter to Holmes focused on either Clinton's ambition (his critics) or his principled anguish (his supporters). Both are evident. Clinton's strong interest in a political career at this stage of his life is obvious and, as noted, not necessarily questionable by itself. What is striking is the depth of Clinton's appreciation, at this relatively early stage in his development, of the possible implications of his choices regarding the draft for his future ambitions. It is not the ambition to pursue a political career that draws one's attention here but the keen calculations that accompany it.

Equally important for our analysis is how Clinton attempted to resolve this acute dilemma. He said he was opposed to the war and thought the draft illegitimate. He could have chosen to register his convictions, especially the second, by applying for status as a conscientious objector, as did two of his friends whom Clinton mentions in his letter. He chose not to do so. He could also have become a draft resister. This would have doomed any thought of a political career, as Clinton acknowledges in his letter when discussing his reason for submitting to the draft. So, in the end, he chose not to do so.

Faced with the tension between his desire for a political career, for which, he wrote, he had been preparing himself for years, and submitting to a draft that he thought illegitimate and a war he thought immoral, what did Clinton do? He did what was to become a pattern in his approach to his persona and identity during the campaign, and what became part of an evident pattern in his presidency. He tried to do both.

He chose the ROTC deferment. However, his stated reasons for doing so are instructive. To Colonel Holmes he wrote, "R.O.T.C. was the only way left in which I could possibly, but not positively, avoid both Vietnam and resistance" (Clinton 1992, A25). In other words, Clinton tried to have it both ways.

There is another element of Clinton's letter on which no one has focused, that is, his view of himself as being special and entitled. Clinton wrote in his letter to Holmes that he had decided to agree to join the ROTC unit because he had concluded that he "didn't see, in the end, how my going to the army and maybe going to Vietnam would achieve anything, except a feeling that I had punished myself and gotten what I deserved." The guilt expressed in the last part of that sentence seems fairly obvious, as does its probable source.[10] However, I would call attention to Clinton's view that his going into the army (and perhaps to Vietnam) would serve no purpose other than to punish himself. It is an interesting argument.

Clinton decided, on his own, that no purpose was served by him going into the army. He acted in accordance with that conclusion, and it was clearly part of his justification (to himself as well, at the time) for pursuing his avoidance of the draft. Yet there is an element here of being above and beyond the concerns that might be appropriate for others. He could have chosen to justify his behavior on a number of grounds (fear of harm, saving his abilities to use in another time and place, and so on). Yet everyone else who went into the army might also have voiced the same considerations. For Clinton, the view that he finally came to, namely, that no purpose could be served by his going into the army, was ultimately decisive by his own admission.

There is another, related element that needs to be addressed in this analysis, and that is the character domain of relatedness. There is clear evidence of Clinton's choice of moving toward people. His friendliness and openness are well known. However, the draft incident revealed another, less positive aspect of his approach to interpersonal relations—an ability to tell people what he knows they want to hear, in order to get what he wants.

Clinton met with Colonel Holmes at his home for two hours during the summer of 1969 (as is now known, through the intervention of Senator Fulbright and others). He wrote the December letter in part to thank Holmes for being "so kind and decent to me last summer when I was as low as I have ever been. One thing that made the bond we struck in good faith somewhat palatable was my high regard for you personally" (Clinton 1992, A25).

Clinton speaks of his high regard for Colonel Holmes and their good-faith bond, yet Clinton's good faith is not entirely evident. He acknowledges that "*in retrospect* the admiration might not have been mutual, had you known a little more about me and about my activities" (Clinton 1992, A25; emphasis mine). It is at this point in the letter to Holmes that Clinton reveals his deep feelings about the war and his various antiwar activities.

Toward the end of his letter, Clinton relates to Holmes his reasons for feeling upset at having made the compromise with his views that allowed him to accept the deferment. One of the reasons he gives is that "*I began to think I had deceived you, not by lies—there were none—but by failing to tell you all the things I'm telling you now*" (Clinton 1992, A25; emphasis mine). The phrases "in retrospect" and "I began to think" are interesting, as is Clinton's understanding of the relationship between deception and lies.

In using the two phrases "in retrospect" and "I began to think," Clinton appears to suggest that the idea that he may not have been honest with Colonel Holmes only began to occur to him *after* he had received the deferment. This asks Holmes (and us) to believe that a man who was smart, sophisticated, and prescient enough to realize that his ambitions for office might be damaged many years later by his failure to have served in some capacity in this war would not be aware of the colonel's likely feelings about Clinton's views and activities.[11] It is difficult to credit Clinton with such an obvious lapse of understanding and empathy, given that these characteristics were so much in evidence in other parts of his life.

Clinton's view of deception and lying is also of interest. According to Clinton, he did not say anything that was directly untruthful. Rather, he began to worry that he had deceived Colonel Holmes by "failing to tell you all the things I'm telling you now." In other words, the deception consisted of not telling anything near the full story and of keeping major and relevant elements of his beliefs and activities from the colonel. Clinton began to see, "in retrospect," that if Holmes had known these things, he "*might* have thought me more fit for the draft than for R.O.T.C." (emphasis mine).

A pattern of withholding information that is clearly relevant to the judgments that people will make or are making, especially when that information does not present Clinton in the light in which he wishes to be cast, is evident through this controversy. It is evident in Clinton's behavior toward Colonel Holmes, and it became evident again in his handling of the draft controversy as it evolved. For many years as governor, Clinton gave the same deliberately condensed (and therefore deliberately inaccurate) story to the public regarding the draft.

When the draft story broke in February, Clinton denied that he had deceived Holmes about his intentions; but then his December 3, 1969, letter came to light, and it showed that, by his own admission, he had. Clinton said, too, that he had not asked for or received any special treatment, which also turned out to be inaccurate. He said he had never heard about efforts to secure him a naval reserve slot, and it was revealed that he had been told. He never mentioned—and in fact, denied—having received a draft induction notice, but he had.

The technique that appears to have been followed in the draft case is also interesting. It consisted of *selecting* very small parts of a large set of events. Those parts gave a very distorted and inaccurate picture of the events. The parts were (sometimes, but not always) accurate, as far as they went, but unrepresentative of the whole. The elements selected for public presentation allowed Clinton to present himself in the best light, or at least to interpret his behavior in that manner.

Elements of the story that might have contradicted this somewhat self-idealized view of Clinton's behavior were simply omitted or else interpreted in a way that further stretched the bounds of common understanding. One example of that tactic occurred when Clinton was forced to admit that powerful others, such as Senator Fulbright, had interceded on his behalf. In response Clinton said, "When people ask you about special treatment, they mean did you leverage power or money, or something to get something that other people wouldn't have gotten, and the answer to that [the question of whether that happened] is no" (Ifill 1992f, A1). This statement is reminiscent of Thomas Eagleton's explanation of what he understood the McGovern campaign to be asking him when they inquired about any skeletons in his closet (see chapter 6, p. 161), justifying his evasive and damaging response by equating skeletons with something awful, which Eagleton said he did not believe were descriptions of his hospitalizations.

In other words, by redefining special treatment in a very narrow way (as buying favors with money), Clinton was able to compare himself to the worst possible case and find his behavior acceptable. His definition of special treatment as something that other people wouldn't have gotten allowed him to argue that it was the system's fault for providing loopholes and to imply that they were open for a number of others. This argument appears to have some merit until one asks whether it fully acknowledges the very formidable political power that Clinton was able to bring to bear, through his family, state, and national political connections.

I emphasize the word *selecting* in describing Clinton's technique in this case because it is important to be clear that he had many more facts about his behavior at his disposal than did anyone else. That he chose to present some, and only those that either cast a good light on his behavior or allowed him to do so, reflects the fact that he took some time to think about what he would and would not say. The root of deception in this issue is not, as Clinton framed it in a passive way, that he "failed to tell." Rather, it is that he selected and chose what he would and what he wouldn't say. His deceptions were much more conscious and intentional than he has ever admitted to the public, and perhaps to himself as well.

I want to underscore that Clinton's wish to avoid the draft is and was understandable on a number of grounds, including self-preservation, his real objections to the war, and even his political aspirations. However, he seems not to have been willing to pay the price of his considerations at the time because, as he noted in his letter to Colonel Holmes, he could not have still obtained the ROTC-based draft deferment. However, not paying the price at the time only delayed the reckoning and made him have to scramble even harder to cover his original wish to finesse the conflict and preserve his future options. In short, he was not able to muster the courage of his convictions; he was unable to maintain a commitment to his ideals under difficult circumstances.

Nor had Clinton ever been willing to face up publicly, or even to close aides, to the complex motivational mix of his behaviors. In his eyes he did nothing wrong, was motivated by the highest principles, and acted in accordance with them. Any suggestion by others that many aspects of his behavior in this situation called into question his somewhat idealized view of himself were met by outbursts of anger and self-pity that he was being singled out (another way of viewing oneself as special).

To Harold D. Lasswell's early (1930) dictum that the political man pursues power and rationalizes the results in terms of societal interest, the draft controversy suggests a particular modification in the case of Bill Clinton. Faced with the need to reconcile equally powerful ambitions and ideals and unable to make a principled choice in favor of his ideals, Clinton tried to bypass his dilemma by choosing a path that appeared (to him and, he hoped, to others as well) to offer the possibility of accomplishing both without sacrificing either. In short, he tried to have it both ways. The difficulty, indeed the unlikeliness, of accomplishing this in a specific circumstance (such as the draft situation) led Clinton to a self-idealized view of himself, which must be validated by others.

I think the central emotional issue for Bill Clinton, rather than a need to be liked, is a strong need to be validated, and this need is the key to understanding the third basic element of his character—his stance toward others. The need for validation is reflected in the individual's efforts to be acknowledged for the specific ambitions, skills, and accomplishments that the person views as self-defining and that are therefore central to one's view of oneself. It is important that these specific aspects of oneself be met with appreciation and acknowledgment from important others.[12] Validation and self-regard are closely connected under normal circumstances but are even more critically joined in cases such as Clinton's, where self-regard and idealization are firmly entwined.

Conclusion

The long presidential campaign revealed a great deal about Bill Clinton and, I would argue, about the other candidates as well. The public learned of Clinton's ambition, his energy, and his determination. It learned that he moved toward people and that connections with people were important to him. The public also learned that Clinton had substantial confidence in himself and in his abilities and a view of himself as very decent and honest.

His view of himself as a "New Democrat" (his political identity) was clearly presented.

However, the presidential campaign also revealed some troubling aspects of Clinton's psychology in each of the three major character areas. Clinton's victory in the election allows us to trace the development of all of these issues in the context of governing. It is to that analysis that I turn in the next chapter.

ELEVEN

William J. Clinton as President:
Some Implications of Character
for Presidential Performance

As a presidential candidate, Bill Clinton did not appear hard to place, at least in a preliminary way, in each of the three major characterological categories. He was ambitious and appeared to possess the skills, especially the intelligence, to accomplish his purposes. He showed a capacity to invest himself and an intense commitment to the accomplishment of his purposes. He also exhibited substantial confidence in himself and his abilities. I suggested in the previous chapter that Clinton viewed himself as an honest, open, and caring person. This view was central to his self-image, even though there was substantial evidence during the campaign that he was more complex than he generally allowed others (and perhaps himself) to see or acknowledge.

The second aspect of his identity, his presentation of himself as a New Democrat, was easily seen and had the most important, direct implications for Clinton's ability to address and resolve the basic public dilemma, outlined in brief in the Introduction. Given the obvious difference between presidential campaigns and the responsibilities of actually governing, one could not resolve *before* the election whether, or the extent to which, Clinton's political identity would turn out to be the basis by which he would govern.

Finally, in the domain of relatedness, it was also not difficult to place Clinton. His history as it was available to the public and his behavior during the campaign showed him to be a person who moved toward people. He also appeared to friendly, open, and concerned about the fate of others, although his tendency toward angry outbursts and some of his behavior during the controversies surrounding his candidacy suggested that a more detailed analysis of these matters was warranted.

The draft controversies, and to a lesser extent, the Gennifer Flowers controversy, revealed additional, important details about each of the three character domains. In the areas of ambition and identity (especially self-image), the draft controversy revealed a man in conflict over his substantial ambition and his strong ideals. In attempting to resolve the dilemma between the two, Clinton tried to preserve them both. However, in doing so he chose a path that involved deceiving others, and apparently, to some degree, himself, about his behavior. He continued that pattern during the campaign as he sought to extricate himself from the consequences of attempting to have it both ways.

One could make some suggestions about the ways in which these characteristics might play themselves out in a Clinton presidency, and it is to this and related matters that we turn. In this chapter, I examine more closely the three basic character elements as they have played out in the first two years of the Clinton presidency.[1] I first briefly examine the three character elements as they emerged after Bill Clinton won the election. I then focus on some character-based personality traits of President Clinton and implications for his presidential performance. Finally, I examine some implications of his character and more general (presidency-related) psychology, as well as some dilemmas that flow from his psychology.

The Three Domains of Character as They Emerged after the 1992 Election

The Domain of Ambition

I noted in the previous chapter that during the campaign, Clinton's high levels of activity were clearly observable. What can be said of Clinton's behavior after the election? Consider the following representative story (see also Drew 1994, 90) by a reporter covering President Clinton on his trip to the Group of Seven (G-7) meeting in Tokyo. In discussing why Clinton might well make some small social gaffes, Ifill (1993a, A8) notes:

It's little wonder that the President was feeling silly when you consider his schedule today. Mr. Clinton shuttled from a breakfast and news conference with Boris N. Yeltsin to an announcement with Prime Minister Kiichi Miyazawa. By mid-afternoon he was in South Korea where he met with President Kim Young Sam and appeared before news reporters for the third time today. By this evening he and his wife Hillary were toasting their hosts at a state dinner at the Blue House.

Ifill went on to note that the Clintons planned to meet their daughter, Chelsea, in Hawaii for a brief vacation but did not plan to rest immediately; "unable to resist the chance to shake a few more hands . . . , Mr. Clinton has scheduled a rally in Honolulu for Sunday afternoon."

Other equally tangible reflections of Clinton's postelection ambitions are the numerous domestic legislative initiatives undertaken by his administration in its first year. A partial list would include his stimulus package, reform of the banking system, his "reinventing government" initiative, the family leave policy, a new student loan program, a major health care reform initiative, the North American Free Trade Agreement (NAFTA), a major crime bill, a change in policy regarding homosexuals serving in the military, a national service program, an immunization and vaccination program, a retraining and jobs bill, a deficit reduction plan, and so on.

It is obvious from simply listing administration initiatives that the Clinton agenda was very ambitious, perhaps overly so. What has become clearer is that even those working inside the White House were worried about the number of initiatives and their effect on one another and on Clinton's ability to deliver on them. Books by Bob Woodward and, especially, Elizabeth Drew are replete with quotes from high-ranking Clinton officials who worried about President Clinton taking on too much and more than occasionally advised him that he was doing so. Drew reports:

While the President was fighting for his economic program, he was also trying to get his national service program and his empowerment zone program and a number of other things through Congress. [Secretary of the Treasury Lloyd] Bentsen was so troubled by the overload that in mid-May he told Clinton in a private meeting in the Oval Office, "You have too many issues out there, and the public is losing focus on what you're trying to do." . . . But nothing much changed. (1994, 166)

President Clinton was personally involved in trying to win support for almost all of these initiatives (some more than others). Accounts of his attempt to win passage of his first budget (Woodward 1994) make clear that he was involved in a day-to-day and hour-to-hour, hands-on attempt to acquire the necessary votes. The same pattern was reported by observers of President Clinton's attempt to secure enough votes to pass NAFTA (Drew 1994, 340). As Woodward notes in his description of Clinton, "He had essentially extended the campaign through the first nine months of the presidency taking up the battle with all the urgency of FDR during the depression or a president in war" (1994, 329).

Finally, the same talents and skills that had bolstered Clinton's ambitions during the campaign were also evident after he was elected. His strong cognitive performances were easily observed in such public contexts as the "economic summit" that he chaired in December 1992. Many commentaries at the time noted the mastery displayed by "Professor Clinton" (see Friedman 1992, B12; Rosenbaum 1992a, A1) as he questioned and discoursed at length on complex economic matters. The general impression conveyed by his performance was of a president who not only understood but had mastered the complex interpretations needed to address the increasingly interdependent domestic and international economic systems.

Clinton's press conferences as president also displayed a mastery of detail and subject matter on a wide range of issues. Indeed, after one particularly effective press conference, one of his aides remarked that he ought to do them more often since they showed off his skills to such good advantage.

The Domain of Self-Regard: Postelection

One postelection public indication of Clinton's self-confidence was his performance in addressing a joint session of Congress about his health care plan. This was an important event for President Clinton, and his proposal was delivered in front of a large, nationwide television audience during prime time. When the wrong speech was put into the teleprompter and began to unfold, Clinton did not hesitate. He did not wait until the right speech could be placed in the machine. Rather, he continued and delivered the speech extemporaneously, drawing on his notes. His response to an unexpected technical glitch, which could have been the cause of a major public embarrassment, suggests and reflects a strong sense of confidence.

The Domain of Character Integrity: Self-Image and Political Identity

In chapter 10, I suggested that Bill Clinton had developed a somewhat idealized view of himself. I suggested that it was not that the characteristics which he attributed to himself were not present but rather that they were not the whole story of his behavior. I further suggested that Clinton seemed unaware of the discrepancies that existed between what he thought and how he acted, and that when confronted with them, he reacted with anger and disavowal.

What can be said of Clinton's postelection behavior? Is there any further evidence for this formulation? During the first months of the Clinton presidency, as during the campaign, there were many examples of President Clinton engaging in contradictory behavior (see the discussion in this chapter of "The Wish to Have It Both Ways").

However, two of the most striking pieces of evidence for the formulation advanced in the preceding chapter are contained in a *Rolling Stone* magazine interview. The first emerged when the interviewers asked why, if Clinton supported Jean-Bertrand Aristide's return to Haiti to govern that country, he allowed the Central Intelligence Agency (CIA) to testify before Congress about a very unflattering CIA profile of Aristide:

> *Greider:* But can't you direct the CIA either to shut up or support your policy? In another administration, the director of the agency would have been gone by that evening if he had done that to the President.
>
> *Clinton:* The director didn't exactly do that. The guy who expressed that opinion—or at least revealed the research on which it was based—was a career employee. He did that work in a previous administration under a previous director. Under the rules of Congress, when someone is called to testify and asked their personal opinion, they have to give it.
>
> *Greider:* Yea, but the CIA, come on. They're the last agency to believe in free speech.
>
> *Clinton:* All I'm saying is, consider the flip side. What if the story is, today the President suppressed information from the CIA . . . information that [North Carolina Sen.] Jesse Helms knew about because he's been on the committee.
>
> *Greider:* He had you either way.
>
> *Clinton:* He knew he had me either way. He knew I'd been given this information when I became President. . . . So what was I to do? Try to jam it? Eventually it would have come out. . . . So I reasoned that since I knew it was out there before I took office, and it was a matter of fact, and Congress had a legal right to know it, that rather than gagging this guy or playing games with him, the best thing to do was to let it happen.
>
> *Wenner: What's the most important thing you've learned about yourself since you've become President?*
>
> *Clinton: All the old rules are still the ones that count. I feel better every night when I go home if I've done what I think is right.* (Wenner and Greider 1993, 81; emphasis mine)

There are many interesting aspects to this exchange. The president, in his answer to the question of why he didn't suppress an unfavorable report, essentially said that it wasn't possible to do so since others already knew of it. (He also appears to be arguing to the interviewer that he shouldn't be blamed for failing to suppress information because he had no choice.) One can view this as simply an illustration of "hardball politics" or, alternatively, as reflecting a good grasp of "political reality." However, it also appears to reflect a strong element of expediency. The ethical calculus expressed appears very responsive not to what is right but to how it would look in the morning papers.

The striking aspect of this exchange in view of our formulation about Clinton's somewhat idealized view of himself is that when he was asked what was the most important thing about himself that he had learned in the presidency, he responded about the importance of old, traditional virtues, which, he clearly believes, were reaffirmed in his behavior as president. He then added that he could sleep better knowing he had done what he thought to be right. This, of course, took place immediately after he discussed the most basic kinds of political calculations that went into his decision not to attempt to squelch the damaging profile of Aristide.

President Clinton showed no indication that the two sets of statements, one immediately following the other, might somehow be related. Political expediency was clearly one part of his decision to release the data. So was the fact that others already knew about the study. But having established his decision on these grounds, he appears to have felt a need to cloak it in a more virtuous frame.

One important and related consequence of President Clinton's enormous accomplishments, coupled with his self-idealization, is a belief in his own essential goodness and *correctness*. It is a sense that he has about himself, about what he does, and about what he wishes to accomplish. The importance of maintaining this view of himself is, I believe, at the heart of the third core element of his character, his interpersonal relations, which are organized, in my view, around his need for validation.

Consider in this regard the postelection interview with President Clinton that appeared in *Rolling Stone*. At first, President Clinton's responses to the question posed to him appear to indicate a typical "active-positive" response:

Wenner: Are you having fun?
Clinton: You bet. I like it very much. Not every hour of every day is fun. The country is going through a period of change.

Wenner: But are you having fun in this job?

Clinton: I genuinely enjoy it. (Wenner and Greider 1993, 40)

At the end of the interview, one of the reporters told Clinton of a call he had received from one young person invited to the inaugural ceremonies as one of Clinton's "Faces of Hope." The interviewer told the president that this young man was very dejected and disappointed with Clinton's performance. The interviewer then passed on to Clinton a question from the young man: "Ask him what he's willing to stand up for and die for."

The second reporter describes the subsequent exchange as follows (Wenner and Greider 1993, 81):

Wenner: The President, standing a foot away from Greider, turned and glared at him. Clinton's face reddened, and his voice rose to a furious pitch, as he delivered a scalding rebuke—an angry, emotional presidential encounter, the kind of which few have ever witnessed.

Clinton: But that's the press's fault, too, damn it. I have fought more damn battles here for more things than any President in the last twenty years . . . and have not gotten one damn bit of credit for it from the knee-jerk liberal press, and I am sick and tired of it and you can put that in the damn article. I have fought and fought and fought and fought. I get up here every day, and I work till late at night on everything from national service to the budget to the crime bill and all this stuff, and you guys take it and you say, "Fine, go on to something else, what else can I hit him about?" So if you convince them I don't have any convictions, that's fine, but it's a damn lie. It's a lie. Look what I did. I said the wealthy would have to pay their fair share, and look what we did to the tax system. [Clinton then mentions another accomplishment.] Did I get any credit for it, from you or anyone else? Do I care if I get credit? No. Do I care that man has a false impression of me because of the way this administration has been covered? . . . I have fought my guts out for that guy and if he doesn't know it, it's not all my fault. And you get no credit around here for fighting and bleeding. . . . And if you hold me to an impossible standard and never give us any credit . . . that's exactly what will happen, guys like that will think like that. But it ain't my fault, because we have fought our guts out for 'em.

Here Bill Clinton sounds more like Richard Nixon than John Kennedy, as the whole exchange has a definite "active-negative" cast to it and appears to contradict the earlier assertions of how much President Clinton is enjoying his role. The sense of being "done in" in spite of good deeds, of receiving no acknowledgment for hard—indeed, almost herculean—efforts ("fighting my guts out," "fighting and bleeding"), and of being held to "an impossible standard" (in a sense, being set up by others for failure) are all consistent with the bitter sense of futility ("no matter how much I do, it's never good enough") that pervades active-negative character types.

With regard to political identity, in answer to the question "Who am I?" Clinton has continued to argue that he is an amalgam. During the campaign he said he was a new kind of Democrat, one who is for government programs, but only if they work; he accepts the use of force in international affairs, but only if it is consistent with American ideals; and so on.

Governing, however, requires that choices be made, and the choices, in turn, help to define the relationship between a president's professed and actual political identities. Many of Clinton's social and public policies in his first two years of office (up to the 1994 midterm elections) reflected the traditional policies of the Democratic Party. For example, the stimulus package and large, new government programs in a variety of areas (health, national student service, and others) seem largely in keeping with the traditional Democratic Party focus of activist, interventionist government.

In addition, President Clinton has been extremely sensitive to the traditional Democratic Party constituency politics. There have been programs and policies for labor, racial minorities, homosexuals, women, and so forth. Clinton may be a New Democrat in his mind, but in some important ways he resembles an old one.

President Clinton has, on occasion, been willing to say no to some groups traditionally associated with the Democratic Party. He supported NAFTA in spite of opposition from some labor unions.[2] However, he has more frequently supported labor's agenda. He has canceled the ban preventing the rehiring of air traffic controllers who went on strike, instituted by Ronald Reagan (Bradsher 1993); supported legislation barring companies from replacing union personnel on strike (Kilborn 1993); rescinded an order requiring federal contractors to post notices informing nonunion members they are not obliged to join unions or allow unions to use money collected from them in lieu of dues for union activities (Kelly 1993a); and reversed an order prohibiting federal agencies and contractors from requiring that workers on government projects be union members (Kelly 1993a).

These illustrations suggest that while President Clinton has occasionally been willing to disagree publicly with the traditional allies of the Democratic Party, he has more often supported them. Moreover, on a number of other issues, such as his proposal to lift the ban on homosexuals serving in the military, his lifting of the ban on government support of family planning agencies, and his large-scale government health care program, Clinton has looked very much like a traditional Democrat. The question may not be whether or not President Clinton is a New Democrat, but whether his version of being a New Democrat is significantly different from being an old one.

The Domain of Relatedness: Interpersonal Relations

In the preceding chapter, I noted the importance of interpersonal relations to Bill Clinton. In what ways does this influence his approach to presidential leadership? Several hypotheses can be put forward; one is that President Clinton's need for validation is very closely connected to his intensely personal style of leadership.

It has been and will continue to be a very personal presidency. We can see this in the importance that Clinton attributes to "chemistry" when interviewing potential appointees to the Supreme Court. In his first interview with Judge Stephen Breyer, President Clinton was not able to establish a comfortable, personal connection with the judge, and Breyer was passed over (Drew 1994, 215–17). In contrast, President Clinton told an aide that he "fell in love" with Judge Ruth Bader Ginsburg, whom he did nominate to the Supreme Court (Drew 1994, 217)

We can see it also in President Clinton's love of campaigning. Like other presidents, Clinton seems to thrive on close, personal contact with friendly crowds (Drew 1994, 95). He is a man for whom interpersonal relations and "chemistry" are critical, but his relationships with others are more complex than has generally been acknowledged.

Clinton is, by many accounts, a charming, gregarious, and friendly man. Unlike Gary Hart and Richard Nixon, two men with a tendency toward interpersonal isolation, Clinton is surrounded by a group of admiring friends.[3] Given his concern with validation and his interpersonal skills, this is not surprising.

Further Consequences of Character: Character-Based Personality Traits

Character forms the foundation of a person's overall psychological functioning, and the configuration of the three basic character elements is generally associated with the development of a stable set of psychological orientations. I term these orientations *character-based personality traits,* to underscore the important link between character and personality. These traits are the stable characteristics of the person, which spring from the ways in which the three basic character elements have come together. Character-based personality traits develop out of character but are not synonymous with it.

How are these personality traits, these primary branches of basic character elements, to be understood in the overall psychological structure of the individual? Every individual can be located along a wide-ranging continuum of personality traits. Some traits, however, will play relatively minor roles in an individual's psychological structure. Others will have much more centrality in the person's overall psychological functioning.

The concern of the political psychologist is to identify those character-based personality traits that are more central to the individual and thus potentially more important in understanding that person's approach to experience and behavior. Those traits which arise most *directly* out of the integrated psychological package that reflects the three basic character elements would appear to be a promising area to examine. This approach differs from the "big five" approach (cf. Costa and Widiger 1995; see also chapter 7, note 13 in this volume), which assumes that each of the five basic traits is, important for all individuals.

One can discern several important character-based personality traits in Clinton. Their origins are to be found in his character structure. That structure, it will be recalled, included strong ambition, an apparently strong sense of personal confidence coupled with a substantial level of self-regard (shading over to self-idealization), and an orientation toward people, one primary psychological purpose of which is to secure continued validation for his somewhat idealized view of himself. In the analysis that follows, I examine these personality traits and draw some implications for Clinton's approach to political leadership and the presidency.

Persistence

Persistence refers to the capacity to pursue one's goal consistently and systematically in the face of adversity. Psychologically, it reflects a capacity to tolerate disappointments, frustrations, and setbacks to one's plans and not to be deterred from continuing attempts to achieve them. Persistence is a good example of a character-based personality trait because while it is related to character, it is not synonymous with it.

The capacity to persist is a partial function of the strength of an individual's desire to achieve his or her purposes (ambition). The higher one's ambition, the more likely one is to continue trying to realize it. Persistence is also related to self-regard. Generally, the greater one's self-regard, the more capacity one has to persist. A no less powerful association is to be found in the reverse: namely, the more important success (however defined) becomes to maintaining or validating a person's self-regard and identity, the more determined the person may become to obtain what success provides.

The trait of persistence owes its development both to a person's level of ambition and to experience. It is also related to the range and level of an individual's skills and capacities. The more developed one's skills, the more personal resources one has to bring to bear on achieving one's goals.

Persistence also depends on the level of self-confidence that one has, as well as past levels of success (these two are related). And finally, the capacity for persistence is related to the emotional and (sometimes) material support of others at times of need.

Evidence suggests that President Clinton is both determined and resilient. We know that, as governor and as president, Clinton has had a number of serious setbacks from which he has (at least partially) recovered and gone on to new achievements. This pattern dates back to his high school days.

Clinton's developmental history is quite clear with regard to his ability to recover both personally and professionally from setbacks, some of them quite serious. He has used the "comeback kid" persona quite effectively, especially when he came in second in the 1992 New Hampshire primary. Clinton himself views his determination as a political asset (Blumenthal 1994, 33, 43), which it is.

However, one can note Clinton's ability to recover and still question why he is often in the position of having to do so. Are there some elements or consequences of Clinton's character that continue to get him into both personal and political trouble?

Achievement

Clinton's combination of intense ambition, equally high self-regard, and apparent self-confidence leads him to be very directed toward achievement, but achievement of a particular type. Modest attempts as the basis for achievement are not sufficient. His achievement is self-defined at extremely high levels of attempted accomplishment. One might even use the word *grandiose* to characterize some of his attempts toward achievement.[4] The formulation and successful implementation of *some* major policy initiatives is not enough. Many successes may even be too few, given Clinton's definition of policy success.

Empathy

Many find in Bill Clinton traits that make him an attractive president. He is outgoing and conveys the sense that he cares. He has been compared to an "empath," a species from the *Star Trek: The Next Generation* television show, whose special power lies in being attuned to the emotions of others.

However, there are several reasons to suggest that this characterization is somewhat broadly drawn, and may well be overdrawn. One reason is that the characterization of Clinton as an empath makes no attempt to distinguish between real and strategic empathy and to measure the relative mix of these in this particular individual.

Strategic empathy, as noted in chapter 8, must be carefully distinguished from empathetic attunement. Its primary purpose is advantage rather than understanding. In reality, most persons and presidents combine some aspects of both in their interpersonal relationships.[5] An evaluation of empathy's psychological role and meaning would depend on a range of circumstances and the degree to which it is employed.

Strategic empathy may serve a number of purposes, each of which has a somewhat different implication for understanding a person's interpersonal relationships. One purpose is to get something from others they might not otherwise offer. Strategic empathy in this instance is a sophisticated form of calculation for direct personal gain. A person who makes use of this form sees others essentially as objects whose primary function is to provide what he wants or needs. There is little real consideration of the other, since such consideration might interfere with their use.

Another motivational source of strategic empathy is the wish to receive validation or approval from others. Here empathy is put in the service of knowing what others want so that one can be appreciated for providing it. The primary motivation in this instance is not so much to take as it is to give for the purpose of receiving.

At a theoretical level, it may be prudent to explore these dimensions of strategic empathy in connection with President Clinton. Such an exploration does not begin with the assumption that he is manipulative,[6] only that the view of Clinton as being selflessly attuned to others may be somewhat idealized.

One reason for exploring this concept more closely is that there are clearly areas where Clinton's empathetic attunement does not extend. One

20Blaze

strand of evidence that runs counter to the view of Clinton as wholly empathetic is the number of groups that he has publicly excoriated: "greedy doctors," "muscle-bound" labor unions, and so on. These groups had legitimate concerns about aspects of Clinton's policies, some of which came to be shared by substantial segments of the American public (for example, in the health care debates). It can be suggested that real empathy, as opposed to strategic empathy, would result in an attempt to address these concerns and, if unable to, would at least respect the legitimacy of another's view. A leader's public demonization of those who come to disagree with him may be a useful political tool, but it is not a reflection of empathy.

Another strand of evidence that runs counter to the view of President Clinton's unfailing empathy is his anger. Before his election, as previously noted, there were public signs that Clinton had a temper. What had not been clear during the campaign, but has come into much sharper focus since his election, is the chronic nature of his angry outbursts.

President Clinton is not the only president to have had a temper. Dwight Eisenhower and Lyndon Johnson were well known for theirs. Of interest to us regarding Clinton's temper, however, are the situations that trigger it, its targets, and its chronicity. The frequency of his angry outbursts leads me to characterize them as somewhat chronic. This is an important characteristic of President Clinton's psychology. We cannot cover all of the issues in this context,[7] but there are several important points to note.

Two triggering mechanisms seem primary. The first has emerged publicly, generally when Clinton is challenged about some discrepancy in what he says and does or in connection with his handling of the presidency. I have already noted one example from the *Rolling Stone* interview. Another occurred when President Clinton was asked about the long and winding decision process that resulted in the nomination of Ruth Bader Ginsburg to the Supreme Court. Clinton angrily rejected the question and abruptly terminated the news conference, saying, "I have long since given up the thought that I could disabuse some of you from turning any substantive decision into anything but political process. How you could ask a question like that after the statement she just made is beyond me. Goodbye. Thank you" (transcript, "Remarks on the Nomination of Ruth Bader Ginsburg," 1993, 1082). The question, of course, was not about Justice Ginsburg but about Clinton's decision making.

The second, less public aspect of President Clinton's anger manifests itself in connection with his staff. According to a number of independently confirmed reports, President Clinton is frequently and extremely angry at various members of his staff for (in his view) having failed him. Woodward (1994, 55) reports that during the campaign Clinton was frequently enraged at his assistant George Stephanopoulos. Indeed, Woodward reports that the latter came to feel that it was part of his role to be the target of Clinton's wrath. Commenting on President Clinton's temper, Drew says, "There is a self-indulgence in Clinton's tantrums, an immaturity, a part of him that never grew up and a part—shared by other politicians who took advantage of their power over others—that felt free to chew out aides, who couldn't argue back and weren't likely to quit" (1994, 96). A person with strong empathy for others would be unlikely to do this on a regular basis with those who have invested themselves in his presidency and who are in a dependent position.

The Need to Be Appreciated, Even Admired, as Someone Special

Clinton is a man with strong, analytic capacities and a mastery of facts that comes from decades of immersion in these policy areas, and he wants us to know it. He is a man who believes strongly in his abilities to solve the public's problems, and it is important to him that others know and appreciate what he is doing.

This characteristic is reflected in Clinton's personal and public association with the development of his policies, as well as their implementation. One striking illustration was seen during the economic conference staged by the newly elected president and his staff in December 1992. "Professor" Clinton demonstrated his grasp of policy detail at length, putting his intelligence on display in a setting structured to be supportive of ideas he had presented during the campaign.

When President Clinton does not feel sufficiently validated for his efforts, he validates himself. In such circumstances, he has a strong tendency to say directly how much he has done. For example, at a press conference in which he was asked about his first hundred days in office, President Clinton recited a list of accomplishments and then said, "So I think it's amazing how much has been done. More will be done" (Clinton 1993d, A7). One could translate this as saying that not only had he accomplished an amazing number of things but he would do even more. In another session with reporters, he asked the press to "look [at] what's happened in four months" and then went on to say of his performance, "It's pretty impressive" (Clinton 1993c, A14).

The need for validation requires that one be appreciated. For Clinton to be appreciated, others, especially the public, *must* know all that he is doing. This is one reason Clinton would not find it easy to become, like Eisenhower (see Greenstein 1982), a "hidden-hand" president. Clinton's characterological impulse is to be a most public president.

The view that one is special is not uncommon and, in its milder forms, is the foundation of what Kohut (1977) referred to as normal narcissism. Feeling comfortable with and good about the particular way one's ideals, aspirations, and talents have come together is the foundation for a consolidated sense of self-esteem. The problem begins when the sense of being unique and special in this more modest way begins to shade over into feelings that one is so special that he or she is entitled by virtue of it. One form of this sense of entitlement is the view that the individual should not have to be bound by ordinary rules; he won't have to make the hard choices that confront ordinary people, do the best he can to reach the best choice, and then be able to accept the necessary loss that comes with having to give up something.

The Wish to Have It Both Ways

In discussing Clinton's somewhat idealized view of himself, I noted that he often seems unaware of the discrepancies between what he says and what he does. These came up several times during the campaign and have done so on a number of occasions since he assumed office. The *partial* list (see Renshon 1995; 1996 [in press], for a more complete list) of such discrepancies that follows suggests this is an issue that bears exploration.

In the area of ethics, President Clinton has spoken of his commitment to setting a high moral tone for his administration and to a tough standard of ethics. Yet his administration skirted the laws regulating campaign contributions by inviting big contributors to the Democratic Party to a "breakfast with the president." This plan was dropped after word of it became public (Ifill 1993b).

The president has consistently decried the pernicious role of lobbyists but visited a large fund-raising dinner for lobbyists while not allowing the press to take pictures of him doing so. When criticism of this "stealth visit" mounted, Clinton promised to be more open in the future (*New York Times*, 13 October 1993, 22). Further, Clinton's nominee for secretary of commerce, Ronald Brown, a Democratic Party official with extensive lobbying interests, at one point was set to throw a party for corporate lobbyists, charging ten thousand dollars a person to attend (Labaton 1993a). That party was canceled when criticism mounted (Labaton 1993b).

During the campaign, Bill Clinton presented himself as a middle-class man of the people. He stressed the modest economic circumstances of his childhood (a not fully accurate characterization). However, in this area he seems quite different from Harry Truman (to whom Clinton is sometimes compared), who came from modest origins and remained in touch with them. In his social and personal trajectory, Clinton more clearly resembles Gary Hart. Candidate Clinton went to high-powered retreats (Kelly 1992f) and played golf at an exclusive, all-white country club, and as president he got a two-hundred-dollar haircut (Friedman 1993b) and hobnobs with Hollywood stars (Dowd 1993). The projected image and the reality are quite different.

The point here is not that there are differences between President Clinton's words and behaviors. Few people are totally consistent. Nor is it that there are not some possible, even plausible, explanations for some of these matters. It is the very large number of such discrepancies that draws attention. (I have specifically excluded from this list many substantive differences between words and deeds on policy issues such as homosexuals serving in the military, sending back Haitians who attempt to reach the United States by boat, the ongoing conflict in Bosnia, and so on.)

There is an element in President Clinton of not wishing to—or perhaps, thinking that he does not have to—make the ordinary choices that individuals and presidents do. The analytic point here is that these incidents are numerous. Cumulatively, they give the strong appearance of a president who has difficulty following through on what he said he would do. It further conveys the strong impression of a president who wishes to give the appearance of following through on commitments while acting in a manner that is not wholly consistent with adhering to his commitments. This tendency was evident in connection with Clinton's campaign responses to questions about his draft status in the late 1960s (discussed in chapter 10).

My hypothesis about the dynamic origin of this behavioral tendency is that it lies in the sense of not wanting to be limited in any way, personally or politically. This is an understandable wish. However, in ordinary developmental experience a child's grandiose wish to "have it all" becomes modified by the acceptance and appreciation of realistic limits. The tendency to believe that one can "have it all" or "have it both ways" also could be observed in the 1969 letter that Clinton sent to Colonel Holmes about his draft status, which suggested that Clinton wanted both to have what he wished for (deferment of military service) and to be seen (and see himself) as doing the right thing. In this incident, too, there is the element of doing something publicly for which one would receive credit while taking steps to ensure that one sat-isfies personal, less public-minded motives.

Some Aspects of President Clinton's Leadership Style: Potential Dilemmas

Every president has three mandates: he must address policy issues, make decisions, and invest effort in carrying them through. The first requires us to focus on the president's approach to policy dilemmas. The second points us toward the president's understanding of the issues involved and his judgments about resolving them. The third points us to how a president mobilizes, orchestrates, and consolidates support for his policy decisions. Let us now turn briefly to some potential dilemmas of Clinton's psychology and political style in each of these three areas, beginning with the first of the two essential dimensions of presidential performance identified in chap-ter 8, that of leadership.

Presidential leadership consists of mobilizing others for public purposes. It is the mechanism through which decisions are translated into outcomes. As such, it occupies a crucial role in presidential performance. What can be said to date of trends that have emerged in President Clinton's approach to the problems and opportunities of political leadership?

A Presidency of Substantial Policy Ambition

The Clinton presidency, in its first two years, was a presidency of substantial policy ambition. From the standpoint of political leadership as outlined in chapter 8, Clinton seems to be most comfortable with the initiation and orchestration phases of political leadership. Consolidation and implementation appear to be stressed less and are generally left to others.

This is in keeping with President Clinton's confidence in his abilities, his disinclination to focus for long periods of time, and his orientation toward "getting things done." In the first two years of the Clinton adminis-tration there were a large number of policy initiatives, many of them major and many (but not all) successfully enacted into law. Even after the Republicans swept the House and Senate in the 1994 midterm elections, the Clinton presidency was soon proposing, among other things, an initia-tive to add five billion dollars to the budget of the military, as well as gearing up to take on welfare reform and banning some forms of embryo research with live fetuses. The impulse of the administration appears to remain activist, even if it cannot dominate the political agenda.

An Episodic, Discontinuous Presidency

There has been some evidence to date of a discontinuous, episodic quality to the Clinton presidency. There have been some impressive accomplishments but also some serious setbacks, a number of which are of the administration's own making. Among the pieces of evidence for this characterization are the confusion during the administration's first months in office, including the frustrating and frustrated search for an attorney general and other appointments; policy reversals and retreats; momentum gathered by excellent speeches (such as the president's address to Congress on health care) that then dissipated as no actual policy was presented; and so on.

The high level of policy ambition that characterizes this administration, coupled with President Clinton's firm belief in the correctness of what he sees Americans as needing him to do, is what leads to an episodic, discontinuous presidency. The high level of policy ambition means that often the administration must cope with many—perhaps too many—policy initiatives at the same time. (I take up the implications of this tendency in the section on judgment and decision making below). President Clinton at one point acknowledged this difficulty but then backtracked in favor of continuing his self-imposed fast pace.

The fact that Clinton so firmly believes in the necessity and correctness of his policy undertakings leads him toward action. But this very same set of beliefs leads to the possibility that his many purposes may run into trouble.

The first source of difficulty during the first two years of the Clinton presidency was that the machinery of policy deliberation and public understanding was unable to sustain the pace the administration set. A lack of understanding and comfort with Clinton's policies was one result. Second, the president's conviction that all these policy initiatives must be accomplished quickly raised the concern that there was not enough time for real public consultation and education. Third, the consistent introduction of new initiatives, coupled with the almost continuous refinement of the old ones as they met opposition from one source or another, meant that it was difficult to keep track of all the policies (for the public, the Congress, and the administration) and to follow through on them.

The fast pace of President Clinton's policy initiatives was one strategy for accomplishing rapid social and political change, but in the past Clinton has paid a price for that strategy. During his first term as governor of

Arkansas, the pace of his social and policy agenda cost him reelection. In view of the 1994 midterm election results, he appears in danger of paying that price again.

An Intensely Political Presidency

The Clinton presidency has emerged as a very political one. This almost seems an oxymoron, but it is not. The combination of a large and controversial social policy agenda, the determination to accomplish it, and a style that emphasizes relentless efforts to win people over augurs a presidency in which the public will be consistently lobbied for support of a continuing series of initiatives.

The first and most obvious aspect of President's Clinton's leadership style is that it is framed by the politics of his ambitions. Given the scale of Clinton's policy aspirations, he frequently falls short of them.[8] However, large ambitions that produce modest results do not appear to be what Clinton has in mind for himself or his presidency.[9] The attempt to achieve a lot and settle for substantially less is one possible strategy of policy leadership, but it has costs.

Using a "maximizing" strategy to achieve "satisficing" policy objectives raises at least three issues.[10] First, constructing ambitious, complex policy architecture runs the risk of creating policy structures that will prove unworkable. Such an outcome would cast further doubt on government's ability to solve social problems. Second, a corollary difficulty is that such large-scale policy architecture and concerns about its workability run the risk of increasing public anxiety. Third, large-scale, complex policies generally offer numerous targets for critics. More modest proposals present less numerous targets for concern and disagreement.

A Presidency of Persistence

President Clinton has experienced many setbacks, but experience suggests (and he believes) that planning, the application of intelligence, and sheer determination will eventually accomplish his goals. Clinton is not used to losing or to permanent setbacks; there is always another way to be tried and another day to succeed. His level of energy, coupled with his sense of policy correctness and determination, suggests a strategy of coming back repeatedly to accomplish his purposes until opponents either tire or despair.

The problem with this approach is that it may also exhaust public understanding and patience. It is a strategy that may be effective in the short term to get policies passed, but it runs the risk of not providing a firm foundation for public acceptance. In that regard, President Clinton could be successful in getting one or another of his policies enacted in some form but still unsuccessful in resolving the basic public dilemma that he faces.

Struggles with Trust and Mobilization

It is the basic paradox of short-term policy successes whose pace, subject matter, and methods call into question the larger enterprise that is at the root, in my view, of the poor showing of Clinton's party in the 1994 midterm elections. Yet I suggest that the 1994 election results cannot be adequately explained without examining another important leadership element, that of trust and mobilization.

Effective presidential leadership involves the ability to mobilize others. This, in turn, reflects some relationship between the president and those he wishes to mobilize. Many such relationships are possible, yet not all of them are equally effective.

Presidential leadership involves explanation as well as exhortation. The president must not only have a view of where he wishes to go but a reason for going there and an appreciation, conveyed to those he wishes to lead, of the realistic costs and opportunities involved in doing so. This was part of the promise Clinton made as a New Democrat. The specific policy positions of the administration were meant to reflect not only that they had a plan but that they would be direct and forthright regarding their intentions.

However, in President Clinton's administration there has emerged a willingness to shade meaning and be less than forthright. This came up during the presidential campaign in his evasive answers to questions about the controversies surrounding the draft, Gennifer Flowers, and his use of marijuana. It has surfaced again in his presidency.

There has been a substantial tendency in the Clinton administration to concentrate on appearances, even when an appeal to substance would appear to reflect well on its plans. There has also been a tendency to sell the administration's policies by clever packaging and slogans rather than through frank education. In this section, I explore briefly these two aspects of trust and mobilization.

One problem that seems apparent is the administration's tendency to be fairly loose with its budget figures and estimates. To the extent that trust in government policies is the major public dilemma facing President Clinton, his reoccurring suggestion that major savings would help finance his new programs was bound to generate some skepticism. In announcing his health care proposals, Clinton suggested savings were the means of funding them. In announcing his new welfare reforms in 1994, unspecified large savings were also put forward as the method of funding. A study by a respected non-partisan organization calculated that Clinton had underestimated the cost of his health care program by seventy-eight million dollars. New and dramatic savings were also said to be one result of his "reinventing government" initiative. However, a study by the Congressional Budget Office suggested that the real savings from such a program would be substantially less than those projected by the Clinton administration (Reischauer 1993).

One can argue (correctly) that previous administrations have also supplied misleading cost and savings projections, but this argument misses an important point. Candidate Clinton campaigned against "politics as usual," one aspect of which was not to inform the public fully. Other presidents have paid a price for this strategy, and it has had a damaging effect on the nation's support of government programs.

One can also see these tendencies in the Clinton administration's very strong concern with appearances. For example, the economic conference held shortly before Clinton took office was presented as analogous to a free-ranging seminar, with no question too difficult to ask. Yet the economic views given the most prominence were those already in substantial agreement with Clinton's views. The economic conference was more of a showcase for President Clinton than a real, no-holds-barred debate about the usefulness of alternative economic approaches. Blumenthal (1994, 34) characterized it as "one last campaign stop, a sterile event conducted in the absence of conflict." One might argue that the conference simply reflected that President Clinton knew what he wanted and thought was needed. But if that is the case, to present the conference as a wide-ranging education for the American public was somewhat misleading.

Another example of concentrating on appearances is the tendency to claim more for the results of his policies than is warranted. Again, Clinton is clearly not the first president to do so. However, given the nature of the basic public dilemma that he and his administration faced and his personal problems with issues of honesty and trust, this tendency is an unfortunate choice. The July 1993 economic summit in Tokyo provides a public case in point. The ambiguously worded agreement reached by President Clinton and the Japanese prime minister, Kiichi Miyazawa, at the G-7 summit was hailed by the administration as a "major breakthrough" (Apple 1993). In fact, it was an agreement to hold future talks about trade and appears to have been brought about by the administration's retreat from its publicly stated position of requiring that Japan agree to specific levels of reduction in its trade surplus (Sanger 1993; Pollack 1993). By February 1994, the "breakthrough" based on "mutual understanding" had, in fact, resulted in a total impasse and renewed threats of a trade war (Ifill 1994).

With regard to the tendency to sell policies rather than educate the public, the Clinton presidency has made extensive use of the development of an extremely wide-ranging, but not always effective, public lobbying apparatus. Drew notes:

> The role of [political] consultants in the Clinton Presidency was without precedent. Previous Presidents had pollsters and other outside political advisors, but never before had a group of political consultants played such an integral part in a Presidency. Clinton's consultants were omnipresent, involved in everything from personnel to policymaking to the President's schedule. The consultants—and some members of the President's immediate staff—made a point of saying that they weren't involved in foreign policy matters, but at various times, in various ways, they were. (1994, 124)

By means of such an apparatus, policy issues and positions are fully pre-tested with multiple focus groups, while words and phrases are honed and others deleted. The results are marketed through sophisticated public relations strategies, which include the systematic convening of selected members of the "ordinary public" to whom the president presents the most effective, but not necessarily the most representative, aspects of the policies that are to be "sold." The president's economic stimulus package, his health care proposals (Kelly 1993b), and even the inaugural (Berke 1993b) were carefully scripted public events designed and carried through for political purposes.

All presidents must sell their policies to some degree. However, the student of political leadership must remain alert to the distinctions between *selling* and *educating*. This is a particularly important distinction for President Clinton, given his promise to reinvent government, and the lingering problems of trust with which he began his presidency.

All administrations must educate the public regarding new policies and build support for them. Traditional democratic theory assumed that there was a relationship between the education and support. There seems, however, to be an emphasis in the Clinton administration on selling its policies, as opposed to educating people on the merits and limitations of the alternatives chosen and on the rationale for having done so. This is policy implementation by a focus group, and it does not augur well for President Clinton's attempt to resolve the basic public dilemma.

The hype surrounding the health care proposal and the NAFTA agreement are two large cases in point. President Clinton's ambition to accomplish, coupled with his belief that he knows what should be done and his determination to do it, sometimes appears to lead him to cut corners. Leadership consists of real public education, not selling policies by big concepts like "security" that are not really representative of the range of consequences that a given proposal will entail.

Some Aspects of President Clinton's Decision-Making Style and Judgment: Potential Dilemmas

I have argued that decision making is a fundamental element of any presidency, and President Clinton has the intellectual tools to be a good decision maker. However, as I suggested in my discussion of judgment in chapter 8, cognitive ability alone is not sufficient.

What patterns have emerged in the Clinton presidency in this area? In this section I briefly discuss five: the interrelationship of chemistry and advisers, the impact of ambitious agendas on presidential focus, the influence of President Clinton's view of his own abilities on his judgment, the effect of his dislike of limits, and the efficacy of "yes and" approach to policy solutions.

Chemistry and the Advisory System

One obvious starting point in examining the Clinton presidency with regard to decision making and judgment is Clinton's strong intelligence and his mastery of policy detail. However, his selection of advisers on the basis of "chemistry" (which can be translated as "they get along with me and I with them") runs the risk of giving too much weight in the decision process to concurrence. By all accounts, President Clinton dominates his domestic-policy staff meetings. Blumenthal (1993b, 37) notes that Clinton has "surrounded himself with deferential advisers who are either without national experience or much younger." [11]

Who is knowledgeable enough, strong enough, and secure enough in his or her position to tell Bill Clinton when he's wrong? Al Gore has emerged as one person who does so on occasion, but one person is not enough, and apparently Gore, even while pressing his views, has limits to his insistence (Berke 1994; see also Drew 1994, passim).

Hillary Clinton's role in the White House is substantial and in some respects unprecedented. [12] While various reports suggest she is the more "pragmatic" of the two and leads her husband in that direction, there is an emerging body of substantial evidence to the contrary. It was Mrs. Clinton who championed the large, complex health care proposal that went down to defeat. Evidence from senior advisers who spoke to Drew (1994) suggests that Mrs. Clinton has a very robust view of what the Clintons came to Washington to accomplish. If anything, the evidence suggests that Hillary Clinton reinforces her husband's activist tendencies rather than inhibits them.

The Question of Focus in Relation to Judgment

The matter of whether Hillary Clinton reinforces or inhibits President Clinton's activist tendencies is important in a very basic and direct way in relation to the quality of judgments in the Clinton presidency. Good policy and political judgment requires time, as well as information and perspective. Generally, the more initiatives that a president undertakes, the less time there is to focus on any one of them.

The lack of presidential focus has emerged as a major drawback in President Clinton's decision-making style. Many of the problems in the Clinton White House documented by Drew (1994) and Woodward (1994) grew out of Clinton's and his advisers' attempts to take on too many things. Bruce Lindsey, a senior presidential aide, told Elizabeth Drew that

there are only twenty-four hours in the day, and you should sleep a few of them. You can't be meeting with Boris Yeltsin, reforming health care, and working on campaign reform, lobbying restrictions, education reform, and welfare reform. If you try that you can't be effective on anything. What he's [Clinton] starting to do is to figure out the best use of his time. He would say [the problem] is the way he's been scheduled, *because he never thinks he has taken on too much.* (Quoted in Drew 1994, 134–35; emphasis mine)

The inability to recognize and accept limits that is central to President Clinton's psychology is also central to his presidency. President Clinton is a man of large appetites, which is another way of saying that he dislikes and is uncomfortable with limits. In clinical terms, the idea that one need not take account of or be bound by limits is a reflection of grandiosity.

This characteristic can sometimes be useful in allowing individuals to go beyond what is considered possible, sometimes to very good effect. However, it can also prove very damaging, when it keeps individuals intent on accomplishing all from accomplishing much. It must also be noted here that psychological characteristics like grandiosity must be seriously considered in the context of the setting in which they operate.

I noted in chapter 4 that the White House appeared to be a context where presidential psychology was likely to be magnified, not limited. Clinton's presidency to date gives some added confirmation of this and points to the danger of such elements for adequate presidential performance.

The Dual Role of High Self-Confidence

Self-confidence is crucial to good decision making, because tough problems may seem insoluble and therefore hopeless. However, it is not the case in decision making that the more confident, the better, or the more confident, the higher the quality of the decision. Like other variables, the relationship of confidence to the quality of decision making is curvilinear. Too little confidence can result in the loss of hope, too much can result in the overestimation of one's abilities, the likely results of one's efforts, or both.

With regard to President Clinton, there are signs that his strong self-confidence may have a problematic effect on his judgment. Clinton's strong sense of his own competence runs the danger of becoming overconfidence. One striking example of this occurred in an interview he gave (Clinton 1993a, A10) before his inauguration, regarding the possibility of a new relationship with Saddam Hussein. His comments on the matter reflect a remarkable self-assurance about his ability to change the Iraqi leader and his pattern of behavior:

I think that if he were sitting here on the couch I would further the change in his behavior. You know if he spent half the time, just a half, or even a third of the time worrying about the welfare of his people that he spends worrying about where to place his SAM missiles and whether he can aggravate Bush by violating the cease-fire agreement, what he's going to do with the people who don't agree with him in the South and in Iraq, I think he'd be a stronger leader and be in a lot better shape over the long run. (Emphasis mine)

President Clinton appears to believe that he can personally bring about this change. Moreover, and in keeping with the political skill that Clinton emphasizes, the president believes that he can do so by persuading Hussein that he would be a better leader and be better off if he followed Clinton's advice. The expectation that people can be won over by words is an understandable and plausible premise, given Clinton's experience in the presidential election, but it is a potentially dangerous misapplication in this context.

There is an element of naïveté to be found in Clinton's apparent belief that he would be able to overcome, indeed reverse, the character patterns that have been evident in Hussein's adult career and behavior, and that

Clinton could do so by appealing to what he sees as Hussein's long-term interests. The confidence that Clinton expresses in his ability to bring about such a change is a potential source of difficulty. The potential error of judgment that may await President Clinton, in this and similar cases, is not that he will discount Hussein's shrewdness but that he will overestimate his own potential impact.

Judgment and Risk in the Clinton Presidency

Substantial ambition and high self-confidence combine to push President Clinton toward considerable risk taking. Evidence of his willingness to take large political risks can be found in his handling of his economic package, the NAFTA agreement, and his health care package. Each of these reflected a mix of ambition and self-protective hedging. For example, the budget package proposed in August 1994 called for increased government spending first (that is, during his first term in office) and cuts in government spending to reduce the deficit in 1996 and later (*after* he would stand for reelection). Similarly, the health care program that failed to gain acceptance in 1994 called for major changes and was based on projections of savings that would not be seen for some years after it was to be enacted; in other words, its results, for better or worse, would not have been clear for some years.

President Clinton thus is willing to take both large personal and large political risks.[13] His high levels of self-confidence lead him toward policy initiatives that are sweeping in both their scope and complexity. This means that President Clinton is willing to take a large policy gamble: that the untried policies he proposes will, in fact, work the way he says they will—that they will not result in damaging public consequences and that they will function in a way that is fair.

President Clinton clearly understood he was putting forward a large, complex health care program and overrode a number of his aides' concerns and went ahead anyway. Why? Drew remarks that the answer "probably lay beyond their indulgence of an F.O.B. ["Friend of Bill" Ira Magaziner] in their sense that they were smarter than anyone else. For people who considered themselves masterly politicians with a fine feel for the public, and people who were of considerable political talents, they misjudged probable public reaction" (1994, 305).

As I noted in chapter 8, substantial ambition coupled with strong self-regard, and in this case reinforced by a somewhat idealized sense of one's capacities, can lead to poor judgment. President Clinton not only underestimated the public's response to his health care plan but overestimated his ability to overcome it. Moreover, the method he chose to help him win acceptance of the health care plan, emphasizing security (which became the selling point after polling had indicated it would be effective) instead of dealing directly with the many complex and difficult issues his plan raised, exacerbated the difficulties.

Multiple Agreements and Equivocation: A Dislike of Limits

One aspect of Clinton's decision-making style is his well-documented tendency to convey the impression to each party he talks with that he understands and is in touch with its views (even if the views of the parties he talks with are in strong opposition). A corollary assumption, which Clinton does nothing to dispel, is that he is in agreement with each person's views and will act on that agreement.

This tendency came up several times in the recollections of those who worked for Clinton when he was governor of Arkansas. Stephen Smith, a friend, political adviser, and assistant to Governor Clinton, notes:

> Many times I saw groups that got a full and fair hearing subsequently feel betrayed by a lack of support for favorable action on their request because they assumed that the absence of "no" meant "yes." That happened partially because supplicants for support are always more inclined to hear what they wanted to hear and partially because *they were not explicitly or immediately told what they did not want to hear.* (1993, 14; emphasis mine; see also Moore 1993, 92)

John Brummett, a reporter who covered Clinton's years as governor for the *Arkansas Gazette-Democrat,* recently noted that this same tendency of Clinton's to make everyone think he agreed with him had resulted in an "Arkansas landscape . . . strewn with people who believed Clinton had lied to them, double-crossed them, or left them out to dry" (1994, 71).

Over a decade later, with Clinton in the White House, a senior presidential aide made the following comments to Drew (1994, 241):

> Sometimes when the President says "That's a great idea," or "I really like that," that doesn't mean "Go do it." It means "Let's think about it." He'll [the president] say "That's incredible," or "I really like that, we ought to think about that," and then launch into another subject. You had to edit out the last phrase. . . . It's like a conversation tic, but people hear the part they want to hear.

This behavior has come up several times in his presidency. When his secretary of labor, Robert Reich, suggested that the new Republican Congress more closely examine "corporate welfare," Clinton publicly stated this was a good idea. However, when his secretary of the treasury, Lloyd Bentsen, dismissed the idea, President Clinton backed away from it too. Drew notes, "Everyone has fallen victim to this well-intended equivocation, even [Vice President] Gore and [now former chief of staff Thomas "Mac"] McLarty" (1994, 241).

There are several points worth noting about this tendency, not all of which point in the direction of this trait being, in Drew's words, a "well-intended equivocation." For one thing, in spite of it having caused Clinton, first as governor and then as president, much trouble and bad feelings on the part of the many who misunderstood what they thought they were being clearly told, he has persisted in the practice. It is clear that Clinton is aware of the problems the practice causes, yet he has chosen not to or cannot change this aspect of his style. A legitimate question is why.

It is possible to argue that Clinton continues his equivocations because they bring him the rewards of not telling people what they may not want to hear, thus mitigating their potential political opposition. However, this argument falters when one considers that many come away from the experience angry and perhaps even more in opposition to Clinton than they might have been if they agreed to disagree.

Nor does the contention that Clinton has adopted this style because of a "desire to be liked" (Brummett 1994, 70) make much sense. Leaving individuals with the (erroneous) impression that he agrees with them, only for them to find out shortly afterward that his agreement had no necessary correspondence to his subsequent behavior, is a recipe for anger, not liking. Whatever role a need to be liked may have played in the early stages of this trait, the actual effects of this behavior have been clear for many years. They are unlikely to have been lost on someone who, like Clinton, is said to be so keenly aware of his standing with others.

My hypothesis is that Clinton's tendency to agree with many, opposing positions stems in part from the same dynamic that underlies his difficulty in focusing and his energetic pursuit of his substantial personal and policy ambitions, namely, his dislike of limits and his belief that, in the end, it may be possible not to be bound by them. The dislike of limits is a manifestation of narcissistic entitlement. The narcissistic person refuses to concede that ordinary boundaries apply to him because he is so special.[14]

Resolving Policy Dilemmas: The Problems with a "Yes and" Approach

In the policy arena there are numerous examples of Clinton's "yes and" approach, which is the policy equivalent of wishing to have it both ways.

There are many examples of this, including his stands on defense ("I'm for a strong defense and for cutting it dramatically") and trade ("I'm for free trade, but we must protect vital industries" [Bradsher 1993]).

It is not clear whether this approach is a function of cognitive complexity, political opportunism, an inability to make and be bound by the inevitable limits of decisions, or some of all three. It is possible that Clinton believes he has developed a special and unique synthesis of these opposites. However, it is also possible that Clinton may convince himself that there are more options than really exist or than it is possible to implement.

There are, of course, many reasons why presidents may choose to try to have it both ways. One reason is that it gives them political flexibility in dealing with problems of mobilizing constituents. Another is that it also may give them policy flexibility as they attempt to orchestrate their policy initiatives. It may also be used as a gauge to ascertain responses to one side of an issue or another, or alternatively, it may be used to reassure every side that the president is considering all points of view. I have already noted that Clinton used this approach to political decision making as governor of Arkansas.

However, like other patterns of chosen political behavior, trying to have it both ways may *also* reflect psychological elements operating for the president. A "yes and" view of policy may reflect a certain disinclination to be bound by the need to choose, that is, an inability to recognize and accept limits. Certainly this is one psychological lesson that Clinton could have drawn from his experience of successful accomplishment and overcoming barriers.

A "yes and" approach to policy issues may also reflect the very high and idealized standards that define Clinton's level of "satisfactory accomplishment." When one has an extremely strong sense of self-confidence and a somewhat idealized view of oneself and has committed oneself to large goals, modest accomplishments may be experienced psychologically as substandard performance. Clinton's "yes and" approach seems clearly reflective of his ambitious policy aspirations.

It remains to be seen, given Clinton's dislike of limits and traditional policy categories, whether his policies will really integrate alternative policy ideals in a constructive way. It may be that his policies will ultimately be seen as adopting a "split-the-difference" approach, in which one adopts the symbol and substance of both the liberal and the conservative approach to policy issues and attempts to combine or finesse the two without really integrating them.

Conclusion

In this chapter I addressed the issue of whether and how the three characterological elements, outlined in chapter 7 and in the analysis of Clinton
during the 1992 presidential primary, played themselves out in the first two
years of his presidency. There is evidence—not surprising, if character as a
concept has the causal power so often attributed to it—that there has been
a substantial carryover from the campaign to his presidency. Clinton's
ambition, self-confidence, and somewhat idealized view of himself, as well
as the centrality for him of interpersonal relations, have been as much in
evidence since he began to govern as they were while he was running for
office. On these grounds, it does not seem imprudent to suggest that, at
least for persons like Clinton, with strong characterological elements in
their psychology, it is possible to make preliminary statements of some
validity about them. Whether this would be the case for candidates whose
character elements are more modulated is a question for future analysis.

Moreover, it was also possible, at least in Clinton's case, to suggest the
ways in which these character elements manifested themselves in more
general personality traits, whose importance for his performance in the
presidency it was possible to trace. An examination of Clinton's first two
years in office suggested that the three characterological elements and their
related personality traits could be empirically linked to specific aspects of
the two major dimensions of presidential performance, decision judgment
and political leadership. These central features of any presidency do not
exhaust the important elements of an administration that can be usefully
examined. However, if the Clinton presidency holds up as a model for the
usefulness of their application, they do seem to provide a tool for examining
the center of a presidency and helping us to understand and explain the
factors that contribute to its successes or difficulties.

PART IV

Assessing Psychological Suitability:
The Role of the Press and
Presidential Campaigns

The Private Lives of Public Officials: Observations, Dilemmas, and Guidelines

The 1992 presidential campaign, like its predecessor in 1988, became a forum for the disclosure and discussion of intimate personal information about a presidential candidate. William J. Clinton, the Democratic Party's nominee, was asked to explain an extramarital relationship, his use of drugs, and whether he had manipulated his draft board during the Vietnam War to gain a deferment (Ifill 1992a, A1; Toner 1992a, A25). Like Gary Hart's before him, Bill Clinton's candidacy was damaged, although he eventually won the general election.

As with the Gary Hart episode in 1988, the public and those who comment on the disclosure of personal information were divided. Some commentators considered these matters important (Swift and Finegold 1992, A23). Others did not (Gerzon 1992, A23). The public likewise split both ways.

Bill Clinton's difficulties, like those of Gary Hart before him, raised important questions about the role of personal disclosures during presidential campaigns. What should remain private when a candidate runs for or gains the presidency, and why? Are there areas of private life that should be fundamentally "off limits" to public scrutiny? If so, on what grounds? Where is the appropriate dividing line between the public and private lives of our political leaders?

Other than candidates, the group most on the front lines with this issue is the media. They are accused of hijacking presidential campaigns away from their true purpose, which, in the minds of some, is to concentrate on the issues. Patterson (1993, 16), for example, is not alone in discussing what he sees as the loss of substance in campaigns; he names the culprit directly: "Journalists are the problem here." The problem, however, is not that simple.

Candidates and presidents have added to the difficulties in addressing the public–private issue by routinely attacking the "excesses" of the press, a method of deflecting unflattering stories. For that reason, a discussion of journalists' ethics cannot be adequately understood apart from the role that candidates themselves have played in bringing about the current state of affairs. Misleading, evasive, and otherwise dishonest answers have eroded a basic element of trust that might help to temper an already ambivalent relationship.[1] Meanwhile, the public responds to the complaint that candidates are victims. It dislikes the press for uncovering such information and voices its disgust with character attacks, even as the information shapes their political judgments.

In this chapter, I first examine the nature of privacy and its important functions for individuals and political leaders. I argue that the dilemma of privacy is that it is psychologically necessary for candidates, but that necessity has often been used in an attempt to shield them from unwanted or potentially damaging scrutiny. In making use of the latter, candidates have, ironically, weakened their claims to the former.

I then turn to an examination of the press and trace the changes in reporting of character issues. I analyze the distortions that arise from professional and personal sources. Distortions, however, are not confined to the press. Other professional observers, political scientists and psychologists among them, share in this difficulty. I examine the particular ways in which such problems manifest themselves in professional analysis of presidential politics.

What is needed, of course, is a set of consistent standards by which to judge whether boundaries are or are not being treated appropriately. Accordingly, I examine the arguments that arise from the public's "right to know" and, using the theory developed in chapters 7 and 8, suggest some criteria for evaluating stories or questions that deal with psychological suitability.

The Nature of Privacy

Before trying to ascertain the appropriate boundaries of candidate privacy, it is useful to consider the nature of privacy itself and its functions. Almost every culture distinguishes between those interactions and self-presentations that are considered "public" and those considered "private." Ordinarily we equate "private" with that which takes place when one is alone or when one chooses to share confidential information with others with whom one is intimate (for example, spouses, good friends, etc.). "Private" in that sense assumes limited exposure to those who have been specifically selected to hold and maintain an information boundary.

Sometimes, however, privacy extends even to public acts. People who are caught in public by tragic news, for example, may display their grief publicly, but in some cultures it is still considered intrusive to treat their spontaneous emotional response as a "public" event. Thus, the Japanese news agency that taped and distributed pictures of President Bush's illness during a state dinner in Japan was severely criticized by that government's officials. Japanese government officials argued that showing the tape, even though of a public event, was an invasion of privacy (*New York Times,* 12 January 1992). The point here is that line between public and private is not a given but a social convention.

In our culture, the right to privacy has achieved the status of an important social value. Yet, increasingly, it has to contend with an ethic of disclosure. The "inside story" has long held attraction. As people more often publicly give voice to their angers, their fears, their fantasies, and in some cases material that goes even farther—their behavior—the line between public and private has become increasingly blurred.

At a different level, the role of privacy has a quieter, less contested function. Goffman (1959) pointed out in his classic work that individuals often need semiprivate rehearsal time to practice their public performances. There is nothing inherently sinister in these practice sessions, nor is there any implication of an intent to deceive. Rather, Goffman points out, it is simply that one often tries out new aspects of self and performance in private or semiprivate settings before presenting them "in public."

At a more direct psychological level, privacy and the capacity to be with oneself have developmental and functional significance. Winnicott (1958) and Storr (1990) argue that the capacity to be alone reflects a cohesive sense of self, one that is not so dependent on others. In addition, the capacity to be alone is important for working through the various issues that arise in life. An inner life dominated by external motion is not often conducive to deepening understanding and development.

Both of these elements, the psychological and the sociological, help us to understand the tensions that exist in political life between public and private. For example, "trying out" various aspects of one's political self or testing the relationships between one's personal and political identities must be considered a legitimate part of every presidential candidate's developmental history. The problem with Gary Hart's candidacy was not that he had changed from the young man he had been but that he was not quite sure which of several adulthoods he desired.

Or consider the need for privacy. Spending time alone, away from the responsibilities of office, or striving to do so, is a legitimate need and desire. The question is whether this can be extended to cover certain areas of information.

Privacy and the Presidency

Presidential candidates and presidents do not automatically surrender all their rights to privacy. Nor would it necessarily be in the public interest that they do so. The public and the press need to be sensitive to the fact that presidents and candidates cannot always be "on stage" or "on call." The psychological fact is that presidents and candidates, like the rest of us, need time to be alone and need to have areas of their lives, including personal feelings and views, that are theirs to share or not, as they see fit. This may even extend to some areas of a president's public responsibilities.[2]

Consider the "zone of privacy" issue raised by Hillary Clinton, and Gary Hart before her. It is not necessarily a false issue just because it was also part of a political effort to rescue a damaged candidacy. Hillary Clinton was reported to be furious about leaks alleging that she and the president had fights, and she had every right to be, even if the reports were true (which she denied). Most couples' personal relationships contain areas of strain and areas of pleasure and satisfaction. The general tenor, ebb and flow, and tributaries and eddies of a marital relationship are, under most circumstances, the couple's own business. If total martial harmony was the standard for becoming president, candidates would be in short supply.

However, like most issues in this area, what may appear on first glance to be simple can quickly become more complicated. Consider again Hillary Clinton's complaint about the specific breach of the zone of privacy noted above. On its face, her argument is reasonable and sound. However, the Clintons, like the Harts before them, presented themselves to the public as a family built on a real relationship, not on one constructed for campaign purposes. They acknowledged past difficulties in a nationwide interview, in response to allegations that candidate Clinton had been involved in an extramarital affair. As for Gary Hart, the question was not so much one of sex but of the possible discrepancy between appearance and reality.

The candidates' attempts to manage their public images have played a role in the persistence of these kinds of questions. After Clinton's election, stories (Kelly 1992g) emerged concerning the candidate's so-called General Election Project (which his staff dubbed the "Manhattan Project"). *New York Times* reporter Michael Kelly received a copy of the project report, and its authenticity was verified by campaign strategists. A copy of the interim report of that project can be found in Goldman, DeFrank, Miller, Murr, and Mathews (1994, 657–64). Among the areas covered by the comprehensive blueprint was the public relationship of the Clintons. According to Kelly (1992g, A1), who based his report on the project's memos, the Clinton campaign attempted "one of the most ambitious campaigns of political rehabilitation ever attempted. They proposed the construction of a new image for Mr. and Mrs. Clinton: An honest plain-folks idealist and his warm and loving wife."

According to Kelly (1992g, A1), this image rehabilitation "required a campaign of behavior modification and media manipulation so elaborate its outline ran to fourteen single-spaced pages." The memo (Goldman et al. 1994, 663; see also Kelly 1992g, A9) lists several recommendations, including "the arranging of an event where 'Bill and Chelsea surprise Hillary on Mother's Day,' " "joint appearances with her friends where Hillary can laugh," and "events where Bill and Hillary can go on dates with the American people."

In the Clintons' view, this was not the construction of a false image but the replacement of a false image with a truer one. A less charitable view is that it was a clear attempt to manipulate voter perceptions in response to information gleaned from focus groups. From our perspective, however, whichever of these views is more accurate, what remains is the question of which, if either, is the "real" picture. Surely there is some irony, if not an oxymoron, in the act of constructing a realistic image.

By tailoring their public performance to emphasize more of what voters appeared to want, the Clintons opened themselves up to questions of their authenticity. In this context, questions concerning their relationship revisited the question of whether what the public saw was fact or a construction. Recall, too, that these questions were raised in the context of other, similar questions concerning the Clinton administration (Was he a new or an old Democrat? Why did he backtrack on some campaign promises, such as the "middle-class tax cut"? and so on).

Any demand for a zone of privacy must be examined in a context that includes whether and what kinds of other questions have been raised about a candidate. It must also take into consideration the nature of the office itself. Candidates who demand a zone of privacy must counter three arguments against that position. First, the presidency is the focal point of the American political system, and a highly public and symbolic office as well. The presidency is an office that sets standards—in policy, in politics, in deportment. Presidents are important public figures in every sense of the word. The increasingly used strategy of "going public" underscores this fact. The president (and his spouse, when she takes a highly public role) cannot expect to have it both ways—to use his high visibility to advance his policy agenda and then complain when the same level of attention is focused on areas he would prefer to keep private. It is unlikely, and perhaps a somewhat disingenuous argument, that one can or should be visible solely on one's own terms.

Second, many candidates (and presidents) meticulously construct their personas for political gain. Advisers carefully give the public (through the media, thus making them complicit) "facts" geared to help it "know" the candidate (or president) in a way he wants to be known. Having done so, candidates and presidents can hardly complain when the public wants to know more than they are willing to tell or searches for evidence of consistency.

Third, the highly symbolic nature of the office and its role in exemplifying the ideals we aspire to result in its occupant being held to a higher standard. Candidates are expected to be consistent and not just to give "lip service" to ideals. Ultimately, issues of consistency are connected to public perceptions of authenticity, integrity, trust, and legitimacy.

A candidate who calls for the public to sacrifice, without giving much evidence of wishing or being able to do so himself, will have difficulty with his presidential leadership, as well as his legitimacy. A president who extols the virtues of public education, does not support the concept of government-supported parental choice between public and private school alternatives, but sends his children to private school raises questions about whether he is governed by a different set of rules from those he would apply to the public. Likewise, a president who presents himself as a family man and isn't raises questions of whether other parts of his self-presentation are authentic.[3]

The Expectation and Monitoring of Virtue

The expectation of virtue works against candidates in another way. While candidates are expected to exemplify our virtues, they are certainly not expected to reflect our vices. Anger, boredom, exhaustion, disgust, impatience, and a host of other human traits must be suppressed, lest the public think badly of a candidate. Candidates rightly fear that an appropriate situational response, such as Ed Muskie's anger at a press attack on his wife (see chapter 6),[4] will be elevated to a trait's status. As a result, not only is the behavior of a candidate self- (and staff-) censored, but the public is deprived of seeing the *range* of the psychology of the person who might be president. The most damaging aspect of this is that the discussion of a candidate's psychology never tries to put together the parts in an overall assessment, which considers not only strengths and weaknesses but when particular traits might be either.

Candidates, presidents, and the American public have also been boxed in by the rise of the *new referendum*. This is the term Brace and Hinkley (1992) give to the constant polling of satisfaction with presidential performance, which allows the public to assess the candidate or president on an event-by-event or almost daily basis. They argue that ongoing instant analysis pushes presidents toward a concentration on short-term rather than long-term goals.

However, the impact of the new referendum is even more pronounced in the area of the relationships between privacy, practice, and performance. The president and his family are constantly monitored by critical observers. Every aspect of presidential behavior is subject to a poll, asking the public what it thinks of it. The degree of privacy afforded by limited-circulation knowledge and the chance to make and recover from missteps are further causalities of the new referendum.

The Changing Role of the Press

The new referendum represents a radical departure from previous practice. The coverage of campaigns and political leaders by the print media developed in the 1920s and 1930s. With this coverage came a series of understandings and "rules" about what was and was not to be reported. Sabato (1991, 25–26) characterizes the period from 1941 to 1965 as one of "lapdog" journalism, in which "mainstream journalists rarely challenged prevailing orthodoxy, accepted at face value much of what those in power told them, and protected politicians by revealing little of their non–official lives, even when private vice affected their public performance."

Reporters operated by a set of well–understood rules that made a candidate's or president's private life off limits. Thus, in 1940, Wendell Willkie could hold a press conference at the apartment of a woman with whom he was engaged in a long–term extramarital relationship, which was widely known by the press.[5] Perhaps one reason this was not raised as an issue by Franklin Roosevelt was that, it is reported, his campaign train made a special stop in Allamuchy, New Jersey, so that he could visit his friend Lucy Mercer, "while reporters . . . looked the other way." [6]

Major breaches in this code of protection began to occur in response to the lies and misinformation surrounding Lyndon Johnson's military buildup and his administration's conduct in the Vietnam War (1964–68), and the code finally broke down in the face of Richard Nixon's illegal activities and his response to public questions during the Watergate (1973–74) period. The press's increasingly aggressive stance toward the Johnson administration over the conduct of the Vietnam War was directly related to the administration's attempt to buttress a failing policy with deception, but it inevitably spilled over to issues of Johnson's own "suitability." The same was true for the Watergate investigation. Inquiries into the criminal misuse of power inevitably reflected on the president's suitability for public office.

What was heretofore "private" behavior began to be considered relevant for making political suitability judgments. In 1974, Wilbur Mills, then an influential member of the Washington legislative establishment, was reported drunk and disorderly at a Washington fountain, frolicking with a burlesque performer. Mills's drinking had long been known by Washington reporters, but it had not been publicly reported. In part, their silence reflected a view that his drinking was a private matter, which gentlemen did not discuss for public comment. It also reflected a view that his drinking habits were not directly relevant to his role as a powerful legislative leader, even though there were occasions when his drinking was evident while he was publicly trying to perform his legislative role.

An important legacy of the 1960s and 1970s was a distrust of two presumptions: first, that leaders could be trusted, and second, that they were necessarily more knowledgeable and policy-competent solely by virtue of their position. As a result, reporters became much more likely, even eager, to stop shielding the private behavior of leaders.

Press-conference confrontations, in which reporters openly challenged the truthfulness of presidents and other administration figures, have left a legacy of skepticism that is still evident in the interviewing styles of several major news reporters. But these developments should not obscure the fact that there is a delicate and ambivalent relationship between the American public and the more aggressive tendencies in political reporting.

The Public's Response to Reporting on Character Issues: Intense Ambivalence

While reporting on the personal lives of leaders has become more wide-spread, it has not been uniformly accepted as a necessary or useful practice among either the public or the press. During the Gary Hart episode, for example, many observers decried questions put to Hart by the press that, in their view, violated not only privacy but decency. Questions about whether Hart had committed adultery, whether he and his wife had an agreement to have a so-called open marriage, and so on were viewed in many quarters as being invasive, inappropriate, and presumptuous. The same feelings were evident when information was brought forward regarding Bill Clinton's relationship with Gennifer Flowers, who said she had an affair with him.

Assessing public reaction to the press's coverage of Clinton's relationship with Gennifer Flowers, the *New York Times* (Tierney 1992, 20) reported that it was mixed. The *Times* reported in the same article that polls showed that "most people considered accusations of marital infidelity an unimportant issue" but also that 45 percent of a nonrandom poll of listeners[7] were "not satisfied with Mr. Clinton's televised confession" on a segment of CBS's *60 Minutes,* during which he and his wife had addressed his relationship with Flowers.

The press has likewise been divided on the reporting of candidates' and presidents' private lives. Anthony Lewis, in an analysis (*New York Times,* 5 May 1987, A31) of the Hart episode, for example, called the question about adultery "the low point" of the campaign.[8] Another columnist, A. M. Rosenthal (*New York Times,* 10 May 1987, A25), wrote that "the *Herald* [which broke the Hart story] damaged journalistic self-respect by skulking around Mr. Hart's house all night, hiding out in bushes." In a letter to the editor (*New York Times,* 22 May 1987, A30), the *Washington Post* reporter who asked Hart the question referred to by Lewis defended his reasons for doing so, in part by noting that the old "gentleman's code" still seemed to be in evidence.

Reporters who pursue these lines of inquiry are not necessarily applauded by the public in whose name these kinds of investigations are conducted. The public appears to believe the charge that the media have been unfair and inappropriate in reporting on the private lives of candidates. In a poll published after Gary Hart withdrew from the presidential campaign, *Time* magazine (May 18, 1987) reported that nearly 50 percent of its representative sample of adults thought that Hart had lied about not having had an affair with Donna Rice. However, 60 percent thought that it had no bearing on his qualifications to be president, and 67 percent thought that it was wrong for the press to write stories about the sex life of a presidential candidate. A poll conducted by the *Miami Herald,* the paper that broke the Hart story, of its own readers reported that 63 percent felt that the press coverage of Hart's personal life had been excessive.[9] In August, three months after Hart had withdrawn his candidacy, he topped a public preference poll with 25 percent, 12 percent more than his nearest rival (*New York Times,* 5 August 1987, A21).

When Hart reentered the campaign in December 1987, he was still the choice of a plurality of Democratic voters, according to a *New York Times/* CBS poll (*New York Times,* 17 December 1987, B16). By January, Hart's name had shown up on a Gallup poll of the ten men most admired by Americans (*New York Times,* 1 January 1988, A17). A further sense of the mixed feelings that the Hart episode engendered among the American public can be found in the following set of public opinion findings: a poll conducted for *Time* magazine found that 59 percent of the respondents felt that Hart was not treated fairly by the press in its investigation into his private life, and in that same poll, 52 percent thought that he should not reenter the campaign (*Time* [December 27, 1987]: 14).

A poll conducted for *Newsweek* magazine ([December 22, 1987]: 14–15) by the Gallup Organization found that Hart was still the most preferred candidate for the Democratic party (31 percent). In this poll, 64 percent rated their opinion of him as "very favorable" or "mostly favorable." At the same time, 40 percent rated their opinion of him as "very unfavorable" or "mostly unfavorable." The respondents were almost evenly split in their opinion of his reentry into the race, with 49 percent finding it "courageous" and 41 percent thinking it "unwise." When asked whether news organizations hold political candidates and public officials to "impossibly high standards," 55 percent thought that they did, while 36 percent felt they were held to a "fair standard." When asked whether news organizations should continue to investigate and report on Hart's private life, 64 percent said no and 28 percent thought they should. Finally, when asked whether the character and judgment Hart showed in his relationship with Donna Rice would be an important factor in the decision to vote for him or not, 70 percent thought it would and only 22 percent thought it would not.

One might conclude from these data, and from the general public reaction to the exploration of Clinton's relationship with Flowers, that the public is, in reality, not very interested in these kinds of issues. But there are comprehensive voting studies that directly contradict this conclusion. Using the University of Michigan's ongoing election-year surveys, a number of studies have shown that presidential candidates are now routinely evaluated by the electorate on personal traits such as honesty, integrity, competence, and leadership. As far back as 1986, in a *New York Times*/CBS poll taken a month before the midterm congressional elections, voters were asked which factor was most important to them in deciding how to cast their votes: "a national issue, a local or state issue, the candidate's political party, or the candidate's character or experience?" Over 40 percent of the sample answered that character and experience would be the most important factor, a response made equally frequently by Democrats and Republicans (*New York Times,* 7 October 1986).

Clearly there is a paradox here—voter interest and acknowledgment of the importance of character issues coupled with a dislike of hearing concrete information about a particular set of character flaws. The paradox is succinctly captured in an interview regarding the media and the Gary Hart story that was aired on the *MacNeil/Lehrer NewsHour* on December 18, 1987 (*MacNeil/Lehrer NewsHour* transcript, 18 December 1987, 8):

Woman: Well, I think his private life is his own business.
Interviewer: It wouldn't affect whether or not you would vote for him?
Woman: Yeah, it makes a big difference to me.
Interviewer: His private life does?
Woman: Yes.
Interviewer: Should the press report on his private life?
Woman: No.
Interviewer: How are you going to know about it?
Woman: I would have felt better if I didn't know about it.
Interviewer: You don't want to know?
Woman: No, I don't.
Interviewer: But it does affect the way you vote, right?
Woman: It certainly does.

Ambivalence is clearly the best characterization of this interview. The woman acknowledges that the information is relevant and important to her evaluation of Hart. At the same time, she criticizes the propriety of this line of press reporting and, in addition, expresses her anger at having been made to consider it because it was published.

The nature of the information being reported, however, is not the only source of ambivalence toward the press. The use of the term *character cops* to describe the press's attention to these issues reflects the presumption of the press's arrogance as well as power. While these concerns do have some basis in fact, the reality of media power is quite different from its appearance. Public skepticism has often been used by candidates and presidents in both parties for their own purposes, with results that suggest the media's vulnerability, not dominance. Gary Hart tried to fuel his reentry into the Democratic Party race by insisting that the press was the issue and not he, and for a time, this line of argument was successful.

The Clinton campaign took the same route as Hart had (*New York Times,* 1992, A1), with his campaign aides frequently referring to "tabloid terrorism." Howell Raines, a reporter covering the Clinton campaign in the aftermath of the Flowers assertions, noted that Clinton, "is reading from the oldest page in the region's populist book. He is running against the newspapers and much of the process is invisible to the public. His Dixie spinners . . . are working the telephones and the campaign plane, exhorting reporters towards self-flagellation and re-education" (1992, sec. 4, E2). Hillary Clinton is reported in the same account to have said that the question of her husband's sex life was the "daughter of Willy Horton" and a diversion that "keeps the real issues out," a response that at once linked the issue of the press coverage of her husband's private life with the Republican's use of television in the 1988 election campaign and tapped into the public's wish to get on with the discussion of "the issues."

Some Dilemmas of Reporting on Character Issues

The question of who's ahead has dominated the media's attention and resources, and as a result, other coverage has suffered. Time and space constraints are another problem. Newspapers have daily deadlines, and broadcast media have limited airtime. Competition also exacerbates the time problems for both broadcast and print media. Sometimes it has the effect of driving stories prematurely into the public arena. The *Miami Herald* reporters who broke the Hart story did so without obtaining incontrovertible evidence that he spent the night with Donna Rice, because of the fear of being scooped.

There is little doubt that these structural pressures have contributed to deficiencies in campaign coverage, but more time or space alone will not necessarily resolve all the difficulties. In the past, a public official literally had to take a drunken midnight swim in a public fountain with a striptease artist before an account was made public. In contrast, during the 1992 campaign some reporters took the position that candidates forfeited any right to privacy once they announced their intention to run for public office. In between these two extremes, rules of appropriateness have yet to be developed.

The motives of journalists who cover character issues are diverse. For some, controversy is enlivening and may serve as a means to make one's professional reputation. Many state that they are simply "doing their job," which they believe is to educate the public about matters of importance relevant to its decisions.

The public sees the media as biased and believes that much of the reporting on character issues reflects such bias. Most journalists reject these charges. In their view, when they report on the private lives of public officials they are, simply, reporting. Which of these views is accurate? Most likely, both views accurately reflect elements of the relationship involved, but there are many complex processes at work, and they need to be more closely examined. Let us start with the nature of the campaign itself.

A presidential election is an important national event, with possibly critical consequences. The person elected will affect millions of lives, for better or worse. Moreover, campaigns are conducted in the context of a zero-sum, winner-take-all context. As a consequence, a premium is placed on candidates putting forward their own best views of what they represent and will try to accomplish. As noted, candidates put themselves forward to be elected, not necessarily to be known.

The reporter's role, of course, differs. Given the market forces that each presidential candidate must contend with, and the fact that only one candidate will become president, reporters are often justified in adopting the view that there is either more or less behind what candidates wish the public to believe. There is, then, an inherent difference of perspective between candidates and reporters. Moreover, it is a difference with psychological implications for both parties. The candidates wish to be seen as the persons they present themselves to be; the media have a responsibility to see if those images accord with who the candidates really are.

This difference in perspective, generated by a winner-take-all market, in the context of an important national event that takes place in a limited time frame, with many, often conflicting stories to be examined and told, gives rise to intense political and psychological pressures. Presidential campaigns are emotional maelstroms for all involved parties. In these circumstances, it is naive to expect that the professional norm of political "neutrality" will be a sufficient buffer.

The difficulties involved in maintaining *neutrality* as a professional stance in complex emotional circumstances can be elucidated by briefly examining its role in the psychoanalytic therapy context. In analytic psychotherapy, the issue of neutrality is connected to the problem of *transference,* that is, the tendency for patients to view their therapists not as they are but in terms of how they appear because of patients' emotionally powerful past experiences. The analyst encourages this transference to some degree, following the "rule of abstinence." That is, the analyst says little about him- or herself (Greenson 1967, 35) as a tactical stance, so that the patient will "fill in" the missing information. This, in turn, provides the analyst with important information about the patient's assumptions, beliefs, and needs and, through them, a greater understanding of the patient's psychological processes and development.

However, the patient's transference onto the analyst has come to be appreciated as only one part of a complex relationship. Analysts, too, have reactions toward their patients and their particular psychologies. This is the important arena of *countertransference.*

Most analysts have some reactions to the patients they see, based on the analyst's own psychology and experiences. A patient who complains that her husband doesn't help enough with the housework may elicit agreement by an analyst because of her own marital or early family circumstances. Ordinarily, these reactions fall into the range of the expectable, and the analyst, being aware of them, is able to make the necessary adjustments so that he or she can maintain the stance of inquiry rather than agreement.

However, in some circumstances patients trigger more intense reactions. An analyst who deals with an angry, demanding patient who rarely accepts responsibility for any of his or her behavior might well feel a range of feelings in response, such as frustration, impatience, or even annoyance. These would be typical feelings. Even understanding that the reasons for such behavior lie deep in the person's emotional history and makeup would not fully negate the ordinary feelings that arise in receiving such treatment. They are, in some respects, *induced* in the analyst by the behavior of the patient, and thus the term *induced countertransference* (Frosh 1990, 70) is often used.

There are important clinical data contained in the analyst's response to these strong currents induced by a patient's psychology. The analyst can gain some appreciation by experiencing through his or her own feelings the responses that the person's behavior gives rise to in others, and this gives important information about that person's interpersonal relations and a clue to how others react to him or her. Still, it is sometimes difficult to manage such feelings, and being aware of them does not always result in the analyst being able to make the necessary adjustments to maintain the stance of inquiry rather than, in this case, response.

In some respects, parallel processes can be observed in the context of presidential elections. In making use of the analytic concepts of neutrality, transference, and countertransference in the context of reporters' observations of presidential character, I am not proposing that reporting is therapy. Rather, I am suggesting that there are parallels in the two processes that may prove helpful in understanding the forces at work during campaigns.

Many discussions of media biases focus on the political attitudes of reporters. Many reporters identify with the Democratic Party. A study conducted by the Freedom Forum, a nonpartisan research group, found that newspaper, radio, and television reporters now identify themselves in larger numbers as Democrats than at any time in the last twenty years. Specifically, in 1971, 35.5 percent of this group identified themselves as Democrats, whereas by 1992 that number had increased to 44.4 percent. This would appear to be a source of possible bias, and that charge has been made.

However, if it were simply a matter of straightforward political views affecting the reporting of news, one would be hard pressed to explain the press's generally gentle treatment of Ronald Reagan or its critical stance toward many aspects of the Clinton administration. These anomalies suggest other factors may be at work.

I suggest that one important factor is the reporter's own psychology as it relates to the characteristics that define presidential performance. In particular, I have in mind a reporter's own responses to presidential character as he or she finds or sees it (the candidate's or president's ambition, honesty, methods, judgment, and general goals). It is at this level of analysis that many distortions can enter into the reporting process.

Journalists who cover political campaigns no doubt have political and policy views, but this does not necessarily mean that specific policy preferences for one candidate over another are the major source of bias. Sabato

(1991, 72–73; see also Elving 1988, 261) has argued that journalistic "feeding frenzies" at the expense of candidates for the presidency have a subtext, the substance of which consists of the journalist's own evaluations of the characters of the candidates. Thus, according to Sabato, the wide negative coverage of George Romney's 1968 campaign remark about having been "brainwashed" reflected in part the press's low regard for this candidate's intelligence. To take another example from Sabato, widespread negative press coverage of Edmund Muskie's 1972 crying episode in the New Hampshire primary had as its subtext journalists' views of Muskie as moody, temperamental, and given to emotional outbursts.

What Sabato is suggesting here (although he does not use this terminology) is that reporters have their own preferences with relation to presidential candidates, but it takes place at the level of character elements rather than political ideology. And where transference occurs, countertransference cannot be far behind.

Many searches into a candidate's life begin with an intent to "unmask" the candidate, a stance that reflects an assumption of some dishonesty. Other reporters go to the opposite extreme and frequently take as given what is told to them. What do these assumptions suggest about journalists' views of candidates or presidents, or powerful and famous figures more generally? What of their views of leadership qualities and judgment? What traits do they value? Do they think intelligence important, a hands-on management style crucial, or a strong sense of authority an advantage?

There has been little professional discussion of these issues, but it is needed. In fairness, however, any discussion of reporters' transference must also acknowledge the role of induced countertransference, the feelings that are stimulated in reporters by the behavior of candidates. To put the matter another way, the stance of professional neutrality may not protect journalists from the ordinary feelings associated with being treated as they often are. When presidents or candidates script even their smallest encounters with the media, when they give incomplete or otherwise misleading information, and when they generally treat reporters with a mixture of fear and contempt, the result is to damage the norm, if not the actuality, of professional neutrality.

Political Psychologists and the Politics of Assessment

I noted in chapter 2 that the construction of psychological explanations of presidential candidates is one area in which extreme caution on the part of analysts is required. Political psychologists are not beyond the concerns noted above with regard to journalists. The combination of powerful psychological theories and academic training in political analysis is a formidable but difficult mix. Suedfeld and Tetlock (1992; see also Tetlock 1992) have already noted the way in which the political preferences of some who conduct research in race relations and international conflict can shape their analyses. The same problem is no less evident in psychological studies of presidential candidates.

Sometimes a particular study reflects a blurring of the line between personal preference and political psychology analysis. Perhaps the best known theory of character and presidential performance is Barber's 1992 theory of presidential character. That theory has been criticized for seeming to equate Democratic candidates with the best person–office fit (the active-positive character type). However, when Barber wrote that George Bush, a Republican, was an active-positive, it seemed to put that concern to rest.

Yet Barber's chapter on George Bush in *Presidential Character* leads to the question of whether the problem of the analyst's own views was not simply transferred from one level of analysis to another, in this case, from character to worldview. In speaking of the connection between President George Bush and son George Bush (his younger self), Barber suggests that in opting for the latter role, Bush "poisoned humanity, here and abroad" (1992a, 458). In another place he talks of Bush "wrapping his arms around those he had just been stabbing in the back." In another spot, it is congressional Democrats who "may well stand tall against this administration's recommendations" (1992a, 460). The symbolism of "standing tall" is positive, especially when it is "against" an alternative and powerful view such as that espoused by "this administration."

In a more recent presentation (1992b), Barber gives further evidence of his disappointment with the worldview and policies of the Bush administration. He faults George Bush for having a managed political persona. However, it is not clear that Bill Clinton's political persona is less consciously developed and constructed, and therefore more authentic, than George Bush's.

Another criticism that Barber makes of George Bush regards Bush's willingness to deal with dictators like President Hafez al-Assad of Syria. However, one wonders what the alternative is, especially if that dealing is in the service of trying to obtain a Middle East peace settlement. Nor is it immediately obvious that a significant part of Bush's response to the invasion of Kuwait can be traced to "Bush the aristocrat . . . obviously supporting the international money-hustlers" (1992a, 477). Ultimately, what is of concern here is not Barber's disappointment per se but the thin and difficult line that separates political psychology analysis from personal political preference.

The difficulties in this kind of analysis don't come from excluding facts. Barber's study of George Bush in *Presidential Character* notes many puzzles and anomalies, evidence of open-minded analysis. Rather, the danger for academics who assess the characters of presidents lies in how the facts are constructed and construed. When Barber notes in a presentation (1992b) that "we are trying to get Clinton to get up on stage at the convention with many Congressman to show the voters what he will accomplish," it raises worries regarding the impact of his political preferences on his analysis. It is a problem that political psychologists, like their counterparts in the media, need to think carefully about.

What Should Be Public? What Should Remain Private?

The attempt to answer the question of which personal characteristics of a candidate are relevant to assessing possible performance as president suffers from an ad hoc and somewhat undiscriminating approach to the problem. Some take the position that everything a candidate does, in both his private and his public life, reflects in some way on his possible enactment of a leadership role. With this perspective, everything is potentially relevant.

There is some plausibility to this position, which borrows its framing assumption from psychoanalytic theory and clinical practice. There, it is accurate (to some degree) that most personal characteristics fit together in a package in some, even if in an indirect, way. In analytic practice, it is often possible to trace some (though not necessarily a causally significant) connection among seemingly disconnected bits of behavior and life history.

However, what is true in psychoanalysis is not necessarily a useful guide for the political arena. The analytic task is both to unravel (where necessary) and to reconstruct (where possible) a life narrative and its attendant psychology. The task of assessing psychological suitability of candidates is much more narrow and focused. In traditional analytic work, time is an ally, provided there is enough of it. In a presidential campaign, given the very heavy press of circumstances, time is always short.

In fact, it is the pressure of time, coupled with the lack of theoretical guidance, that most often leads to the elevation of the tangential to significance. Did Edmund Muskie lose his composure? He's too emotional. Did

Michael Dukakis fail to express his rage when asked a hypothetical question about a hypothetical person who had harmed his wife? He's too controlled.

It's not that these instant assessments are totally wrong in picking up aspects of the candidates. Michael Dukakis is a person who is short on spontaneity when facing policy issues, even hypothetical ones. However, there are many circumstances faced by a president when this would be a virtue, not a fault.

The problem with such quick, one-factor assessments is that they fail to do the hard work of composite and situational analysis. Composite analysis simply means examining some major aspects of the person's psychology and evaluating the package of characteristics of which these aspects are a part. The situational part of the analysis requires the further work of asking how this package, or even individual traits, might work in situations that the president might face. That one characteristic might be connected to presidential performance is an inherently weak argument without a demonstration of real relevance and significance.[10] It is further weakened because it is often used to excuse an arcane search for something, anything, that may become "an issue." Yet among its most damaging effects, in my view, is that it keeps campaign analysts from pursuing the substantive aspects of a candidate's character, tracing its development over time, and seeing the extent to which it has affected the individual's past performance in public roles.

The question is how to distinguish marginal or peripheral connections between character and performance from direct and important ones. The existence of connections per se does not confer behavioral significance. A more stringent requirement is preferable.

One way to approach drawing more specific guidelines is to list areas of a candidate's private behavior that should be open to public scrutiny. Sabato (1991, 218), for example, lists eight such areas of private life. Presumably, these matters relate to candidates' presidential performance. Two of Sabato's areas deal with sexual behavior, two with alcohol or drug use, two with money matters (including anything having to do with public funds), and one each with health and any criminal/civil charges.

Sabato's list is a reasonable attempt to answer the question of what should and should not remain private. However, it is somewhat narrow and not derived from any particular theory of presidential performance. It also has the drawback of not dealing with a whole array of issues that arise out of character but that may not manifest themselves in sex, drugs, or crime.

I have suggested that a candidate's judgment and leadership are the key elements to watch, and that the means of doing so are to be found in a candidate's handling of his ambition, integrity, and relationships. Yet even with this as a guide, it is not enough to say that some behavior is related to leadership, judgment, ambition, or another element. Any analyst who brings forward a piece of behavior as an exemplar has an obligation to specify *how, exactly,* the behavior fits into a pattern that there is some good reason to believe will specifically affect aspects of performance. Will this stop the intrusive and unproductive questions that arise during presidential campaigns? Not entirely. However, it is important to attempt to establish the norm of relevance and provide a theoretical basis for judging it.

Conclusion

Reporters, like the candidates they cover, are judged by many, often conflicting expectations. They are asked to be independent and critical. Yet if they are too critical, they are criticized for fomenting public cynicism. They are criticized for being "too close" to the candidates they cover and, alternatively, for being too hostile. They are distrusted by the candidates they observe and by the public for whom they write. Candidates and presidents complain of their treatment by the press, even as they plan to shape this coverage. In the midst of all these emotional pulls, news reporters must contend with their own professional, political, and psychological values.

Yet for all the difficulties of this role, the press has emerged as a primary source of public understanding of candidates. Reporters often have more direct personal contact with candidates than anyone else, and over a longer period of time. If they are assigned to a particular candidate, they get to see him over time in a variety of different circumstances (see, for example, Goldman, DeFrank, Miller, Murr, and Mathews 1994). Indeed, from the standpoint of the data gathering, reporters are often in a unique position to gather exactly the kind of information that would be enormously helpful in making assessments of the elements that make up psychological suitability. It is a proximity that has, to date, been underutilized.

What is needed to help in defining areas of public and private is a theory that attempts to specify what elements are important to performance and the theoretical basis for putting them forward. Such a framework will not halt inappropriate personal questions. However, one hopes it will force those considering such questions to justify their inquiries not by some broad mandate (e.g., "everything is related" or "the public's right to know") but by the specific relationship of the information sought to job performance.

In the next chapter, I examine why these questions are important and how well they are dealt with during campaigns. I then, in chapter 14, try to provide a series of specific questions to orient those interested in ascertaining psychological suitability. The questions are derived from the theoretical analysis developed in chapters 7 and 8 and are meant to provide a framework for investigation of candidate suitability during presidential campaigns.

THIRTEEN

Election Campaigns as a Tool for Assessing the Psychological Suitability of Presidential Candidates

Professional observers of American politics have become deeply critical of presidential campaigns. They are seen as too long, too expensive, and too shallow. Worse, many believe that the focus of campaigns has little to do with issues of consequence for presidential performance. The primary responsibility for this sorry state of affairs is placed by many on the media, in particular, the press. Driven by pressures to stimulate interest, critics argue, the media focus on sound bites and on controversies that are seen as irrelevant to presidential performance. The focus on presidential character and leadership is a key example, in this view, of the troublesome diversion from substantive discussions of policy choice.

Even scholars who recognize the importance of character and leadership issues are impatient with them. Buchanan (1988, 255) has expressed the wish that character and competence questions could be settled before the nomination, so that the fall campaign could deal with "the issues." Others (Patterson 1993) have suggested, in reaction to what they view as a loss of presidential campaigns' prime function to focus on the issues, a substantial shortening of the campaign cycle. Some are willing to go even farther. One recent proposal (Masters 1992, 5) suggested, "The presidential campaign itself would be limited to three weeks, during which each TV station or cable outlet would be required to devote two hours a night of free time to political candidates."

Far from being too long, I suggest that presidential campaigns are, if anything, barely long enough. While it is probably not feasible to have longer campaigns, I believe it would be a mistake to dramatically shorten them.

However, before we can conclude that presidential campaigns don't serve their purposes, we must first firmly establish what these purposes are. In this chapter I argue that presidential election campaigns serve two basic functions. The first, and traditionally the most focused upon, is public education and discussion of the issues. It is this "textbook" aspect of presidential campaigns that has helped fuel criticisms of the second major function: to select the person best able to lead and govern the country. If the personal qualities, including character, of the person elected to the presidency are important, presidential campaigns are surely the best, if not the only, opportunity the public has to make such judgments.

There is little basis to argue that traditional concerns with candidates' views of the issues are unimportant. The public education function of political campaigns *is* of fundamental importance. However, for many reasons, an exclusive or even primary focus on "the issues" is of limited utility. A focus on the issues, regardless of their importance, is no substitute for learning about the psychology of the person entrusted with the power of the presidency. Similarly, a focus on character and leadership issues is an important supplement to, not a substitute for, debate of policy issues.

The basis for saying this lies in the answer to a key question: What is the relationship, if any, between what citizens learn about candidates during a presidential campaign and what candidates are likely (or may have) to do once elected to office? It seems clear that one major purpose of campaigns is to provide some answer to this question.

In the minds of some, there is too little of a connection between the requirements of campaigning and those of governing. Rose has said:

Campaigning is very different than governing. The effect of forcing ambitious politicians to concentrate upon incessant campaigning is to distract attention away from learning what it really takes to govern. . . . In default of being able to come to grips with government, a President may retreat into campaigning, as Jimmy Carter did during his midterm slump in 1983. But a Rose Garden Strategy that emphasizes looking presidential is no substitute for being presidential. (1987, 54)

I take a somewhat different position. I argue that there are a number of aspects of modern presidential campaigns that throw quite direct light on governance and leadership issues that face any elected president. The problem, in my view, is not so much that what occurs during presidential campaigns is irrelevant to presidential performance but rather that the analyses made and questions asked of candidates do not frame the correspondence with sufficient clarity.

In the sections that follow, I turn first to the question of why concern with the issues is not enough. I then turn to the question of how well presidential campaigns fulfill their second major function, that of facilitating the selection of the "best" from among presidential candidates or, alternatively, at least protecting us from the worse.

Why Isn't a Concern with the Issues Sufficient?

A number of presidential scholars (for example, Cronin 1975; Rose 1988) have pointed to the differences between the textbook presidency and the presidency as it really operates. The same distinction might be made of presidential campaigns. The expectation that substantive issues will (and should) dominate campaigns has traditionally been tied to the role of educating the public on important issues.

The most basic view of the election process is that campaigns represent a time when the country can focus its attention on important public issues and if not resolve them, at least better appreciate them. Few fully accept this view as actuality, but it remains a powerful ideal, and "deviations" from it, such as a concern with character and leadership issues, are criticized.

The public wants to know a candidate's stands on the issues for two related but distinct reasons. First, such information allows citizens to learn more about the problems they face and the implications of alternative policy choices. This is the *educational function*. Second, a candidate's stands on the issues also allow the public to understand what the successful candidate is likely to do once in office. The public can a make a choice related to its collective perception of which policy alternative it favors, which, presumably, the successful candidate will then carry out. This is the *mandate function*.

At the heart of the mandate function is the issue of accountability, which requires some link connecting the expression of alternative candidate views, the evaluation and selection by the public of its choice, and, consequently, the views selected being carried out. There are at least three assumptions embedded in this linkage. One is that candidates do (and should) have well-articulated views on a range of problems facing the country. I term this the *assumption of policy mastery*. A second is that these views provide a reliable guide to actual presidential policies. I term this the *expectation of performance carryover.* A third is that a candidate's views of the issues that he frames during a campaign are fairly representative of the range of problems that he will face and act upon once in office. I term this the *expectation of performance representativeness.* Let us examine these for what they suggest about how realistic it is to have high expectations about the ability of presidential campaigns to carry out their educational and mandate functions.

Some Consequences of the Expectation of Policy Mastery

Since World War II, expectations concerning the presidency have grown enormously. Rose (1988) has argued that one fundamental characteristic of the "postmodern presidency" is that the president must worry about how his policies will play in Peking as well as Peoria. A contemporary president, whether postmodern or not, is expected to be in command of domestic and international economics, geopolitical strategy on an overall and region-by-region basis, details regarding the full array of domestic programs and issues, and the complex interrelationships among all these areas. I refer to this level of comprehensive knowledge as the expectation of policy mastery.

The knowledge required for policy mastery raises the issue of whether public expectations regarding the relationship between knowing where a candidate stands on the issues and the elected candidate's behavior in office are either reasonable or desirable. The *issue of reasonableness* arises because presidents, like citizens, have cognitive limits to their capacity to process information. Experience with some range of issue areas prior to public service is clearly an advantage, but experience may serve to stretch a candidate's limits, not eradicate them.

The *issue of desirability* arises because the expectation of policy mastery in the full range of issues that a candidate might face in office leads to several consequences, not all of which are necessarily beneficial. Expectations of policy mastery lead to a preference that candidates be familiar with a wide range of issues before campaign. This is perhaps a desirable goal, but difficult.

Too many issues and too little time to prepare for them leave candidates relying on advisers and briefing books. The expectation of policy mastery leads to an emphasis on a candidate's appearance of knowledge rather than a deeper understanding. It can also lead to a somewhat misplaced emphasis on knowledge at the expense of learning. It may not be so much what a candidate knows but how well he can learn that is of crucial importance.

And, of course, the focus on learning raises the issue of how well one uses what one knows or learns. As I argued in chapter 8, judgment is the key issue here, not knowledge. Knowledge, while desirable, is not synonymous with good judgment.

The criticism that presidential candidates and the media are increasingly geared to the pithy remark is accurate. But the media's focus on the attention-grabbing quote and candidates' attempts to shape and use this opportunity are not the only problems. Less discussed is the role that expectations of policy mastery play in this tendency. The sound bite can be viewed, after all, as a defense against the expectation of mastery. It conveys the impression of knowledge without necessarily reflecting it.[1]

Few presidential candidates have the capacity to withstand the public's expectation of answers. The more certain a candidate appears, the more he is seen as competent. Ross Perot's terse aphorisms in the 1992 presidential campaign struck a responsive cord in part because they reflected the promise of direct, understandable, and workable answers to public problems. George Stephanopoulos, a close adviser to President Clinton, said of this issue during the campaign that policy specificity was the character issue of the 1992 election. This was a major reason that the Clinton, Perot, and Bush campaigns all published detailed compendiums of their policy positions and plans.

On the face of things, it would appear to be a positive development when candidates deal directly with the issues. However, the expectation of policy mastery can lead to ironic consequences in the educational function of presidential campaigns. The idea that each candidate has policy-dilemma solutions sidesteps the important issue of policy uncertainty and substitutes instead a combination of hope and expectation. When, as often and perhaps inevitably happens, policy does not produce the desired result, the public's disappointment fuels the feeling that it has been misled. Repeating this cycle of hope, expectation, and disappointment is extremely damaging to everyone concerned.

The expectation of policy mastery can lead candidates to hold themselves to a difficult standard. Alternatively, they may come to believe they have achieved mastery when, in fact, they have achieved familiarity. The latter danger might be particularly present in candidates with strong ambition, very high levels of self-esteem, and an idealized view of themselves.

Last, in succumbing to the expectation of policy mastery, candidates often place themselves in a position they later regret. Premature policy closure or the appearance of policy certainty when the circumstances may well change can damage an elected president once in office. Both may fuel increased disappointment or cynicism in citizens who had been led to place their hopes on the candidate's mastery. How and why this can happen is the subject to which I now turn.

From Campaigns to Governing: Why Policies Change

A candidate's policy values and preferences are expected to provide a road map to his behavior as president. The expectation of carryover from campaign to governing applies to both a stronger and a weaker form of policy. A candidate is expected to articulate both general (the weaker form) and specific (the stronger form) approaches to public issues. There are several reasons that candidates' articulations of either are not likely to be quite the road map that textbook views of presidential campaigns appear to expect.[2]

The expression of a candidate's policy values serves two conflicting purposes. One purpose is to unite individuals who might not otherwise agree. The second is to distinguish the candidate from others. These disparate purposes are difficult to satisfy simultaneously at a concrete level of discourse, so candidates understandably opt for two levels of symbolic value discourse. The first and most useful level of symbolic value discourse involves expressions of policy that reflect broad commitments with which many, if not most, can identify. An example would be *constructive engagement* as an overarching principle of U.S. foreign policy. The term implies both involvement and limits, capturing those who subscribe to either; and who, after all, could be against being constructive?

The second level of symbolic value discourse appears more specific but is, in reality, also quite capable of being interpreted in different ways. The policy value of *responsibility* is an illustration. Voiced in a context in which there has been debate regarding the relative weight of citizen and governmental responsibilities, it suggests the candidate understands and supports the concern of those who want to balance the latter with the former. Here, as in the first, more specific articulation, the exact form that responsibility takes in an particular policy, such as welfare reform, can be a matter of fierce debate.

Policy values expressed in terms like *constructive engagement* or in symbolic words like *responsibility* have many meanings in the abstract, but presidents operate in a world that requires concrete manifestations of the values, that is, policies. One difficulty with the textbook view of presidential campaigns is that a candidate's policy values are always easier to express in "equivocal" (symbolic) forms than to implement in the real world of actual choice.

Because presidential candidates are pushed toward symbolic value discourse by the structure of the winner-take-all process, the expectation that the policy values they express will prove a reliable guide to actual policy decisions in an administration is somewhat unrealistic. However, the functions of symbolic value discourse are not the only reason it is difficult to rely on campaign debate as more than a rough guide to actual administration policy. There is an additional set of structural elements, which every president faces, that also helps to make campaigns a questionable guide to administration policy.

We can observe at least five reasons for changes that occur in this area between a campaign and assuming the responsibilities of governing. None of these reasons argues that policy debate is unimportant. Rather, they suggest why a focus on character and leadership issues is needed to fulfill the mandate function of presidential campaigns.

First, in the real world of policy, values compete. A president may prefer "investment," but other compelling values, such as "fiscal responsibility," have their advocates. During the 1992 campaign, candidate Clinton said that if he was elected, he would strongly assert the importance of human rights in American foreign policy. Yet President Clinton, when faced with the option of denying "most favored nation" trading status to China because it had failed to meet minimum human rights standards, chose to reconsider his earlier position and extend that status. That decision was framed by a number of considerations: the need to enlist China as a political ally to pursue helpful policies vis-à-vis North Korea; the need to keep the lines of communication with China open; a concern with losing markets and therefore domestic jobs; the view that more contact rather than less would, in the long run, lead to an improvement of human rights conditions in China; and directly economic matters, including the usefulness to both parties of continued trade relations.

One might argue whether this particular decision represents good judgment or mere expediency. However, that is not my focus here. My point is that judgment is the reflection of choices made in real circumstances, not in the abstract. Knowing where Clinton said he stood regarding human rights and trade was not necessarily the same as knowing the basis for his making a particular judgment on the issue in the context of real and varied presidential responsibilities.

Second, sometimes a president's values can't successfully frame a policy without damaging other important policy values. When this occurs, a president who doesn't want to continue a failing policy (not all presidents are able to pull back in these circumstances) must reconsider whether having his values embedded in this particular policy is worth the price.

Consider in this regard President's Clinton early policy regarding the United Nations. As a candidate, Clinton discussed an increased role for the United Nations in peacekeeping operations and U.S. support for that role. The U.S. contributions he envisioned included more military personnel, logistical support, and financial support. The goal was to maintain the U.S. role in world affairs while increasing the United Nation's capacity for intervention to further humanitarian purposes and international human rights.

In the abstract this seemed a reasonable plan, until it received a test in Somalia. Here President Clinton found that, in committing the United States, he had also signed on to UN goals such as peacekeeping and nation building, which involved the substantial use of American military force to stabilize a long-smoldering military conflict among warring Somalian factions. When this increased level of intervention resulted in the widely publicized death of American soldiers, President Clinton stepped back from his earlier commitments.

Would continued persistence in this policy, in the face of information that it would take more than we were willing to risk, be a sign of good or poor judgment? Candidates campaign as if policy circumstances will remain stable, when in fact, this is simply not a reasonable expectation in many areas. Therefore, while campaigns may elicit a candidate's views on the overall direction or approach he intends to follow, slavish adherence to campaign views when circumstances have substantially shifted would be a sign of rigidity as well as consistency.[3]

Fourth, being president itself may facilitate a more differentiated view of a policy and its implementation. To the candidate, the world is relatively simple, even if his thinking is complex. He will simply do things differently from the other candidates. Once he becomes president, however, he must direct a vast institutional structure, manage demands for his time, and weigh the political and other implications of every action. Weighing alternatives, working through potential benefits and costs related to specific circumstances, and generally trying to appreciate the different interests and values involved in any complex policy dilemma are of a different order of magnitude for presidents and candidates. The role itself may increase demands for cognitive complexity (Tetlock 1984), thus decreasing policy carryover.

Fifth, even if commitment to expressed policy values remains stable from candidacy to presidency, questions of degree and method still have an enormous impact. Consider candidate Clinton's pledge (Clinton and Gore 1992, 164–65) to "end welfare as we know it." This was part of his symbolic value discourse on the issue of responsibility. Central to his view was that individuals on welfare would have to enroll in job training programs and accept available work in either the private or the public sector after two years or risk losing their benefits. However, it wasn't until Clinton became president that he was forced to confront the issue of what would happen if there was no work. His decision that welfare recipients would be given government-financed jobs if they couldn't get employment in the private sector raised strong doubts among some that this was keeping the promise to "end welfare as we know it."[4]

A thorough debate on all the candidates' policy values, their specific programs, *and* specifics of the implementation structure(s) they propose for *each* policy area would be the logical outcome of adherence to the textbook view of campaign functions. It quickly becomes clear that such a requirement would impose vast, probably insurmountable, burdens on the campaign process, the candidates, and the public. In some respects, selecting a candidate on the basis of the public's comfort in his ability to solve problems rather than on the technical aspects of his specific policies makes some sense.

If Not Policy, Why Character and Leadership?

My purpose in laying out the consequences of taking seriously the textbook view of presidential campaign functions is to underscore the many difficulties involved in using that view as a reliable guide to presidential behavior. Discussions of the issues are important but of limited use as a basis for anticipating the concrete world of presidential choice.

Presidents do not merely address old problems. A primary responsibility of presidents is to address new ones. What should a president do if Iraq begins to mass troops on the Kuwait borders? How should the president respond to the seizing of U.S. citizens by a foreign government? The list could be expanded indefinitely, but the point seems obvious: presidents do not only add their views to policy debates that have been incrementally addressed over many years; they must address a host of circumstances on which there has been little debate and for which there may be little time to have one.

This is why addressing the psychology and skills of presidential candidates is such a crucial function of presidential campaigns. Selecting the person best able to handle the responsibilities of the office is not limited to matching the public's policy preferences and the candidates' views. It involves examining presidential responsibilities with an eye toward uncovering the psychology that underlies them.

Lists of presidential responsibilities vary. Cronin (1975, 251) lists, among other items in a job description of the modern presidency, symbolic leadership, priority setting and program design, crisis management, legislative and coalition building, program implementation, and the oversight of government routines. Neustadt (1990, 167–69) has suggested that appraising presidents requires we pay attention to the president's purposes, his "feel" of the nature of power, his stance under pressure, and his legacy. He suggests these criteria for appraising presidents in retrospect, but it is clear that at least the first three can be evaluated prospectively and contemporaneously to some degree.

It would not be difficult to explain the ways in which each of the elements noted by Cronin and Neustadt depends on the psychological characteristics of the person in office. I will, however, note a few for illustrative purposes. Crisis management, a ubiquitous feature in modern presidencies, tests the president's ability to keep calm and to think and act under pressure. This, in turn, requires that the president have the ability to control or modulate his level of anxiety.

To take another illustration, one aspect of legislative and coalition building is the president's ability to mobilize and invest his psychological energies into the pursuit of his goals. This, in turn, requires that he have such energies, that the president's sphere of ambition not be blocked or inhibited by expectations of or anxieties regarding failure. It requires that a president have the ability to persist in his policy quests. Few legislative or political victories are gained without opposition. If the president is deterred from persisting because he cannot tolerate opposition, doubts his abilities (has low self-esteem), would prefer consensus to conflict, or for any number of other psychologically grounded reasons, leadership falters.

The final example is Neustadt's criterion of the president's feel for power. Political power is relational. At its base, the exercise of political power involves choices of how to deal with others to accomplish one's purposes, given the instrumentalities available. A president can reason, demand, threaten, cajole, flatter, reward, or punish in the attempt to accomplish his purposes. Every president has all these methods available to him, yet each president selects his own mix. The methods selected may well be responsive to circumstances. However, not every president is able to correctly match the two. There seem few circumstances where one, and only one, method is demanded. Given that choice is often an option, the particular choice made reflects as much on the president's views of others and what motivates them as it does on "objective circumstances."

My argument is simply that the psychology of the person in the office not only matters but is of basic importance. To the extent that this argument is plausible, the question becomes not whether presidential campaigns should examine such issues but how well they do so. It is to that question that I turn in the following sections.

Presidential Campaigns as a Context to Assess Judgment, Leadership, and Character

In chapter 8, I suggested that there are three fundamental areas of analysis relevant to assessing the psychological suitability of presidential candidates: (1) judgment; (2) political leadership; and (3) the character elements of ambition, integrity, and relatedness. The first, dealing with the candidate's policy understanding and judgment, is the most observable. The second, dealing with presidential leadership and its related components, is the next most publicly observable. How well can, and do, presidential campaigns enlighten the public on all three important matters?

Judgment and Decision Making

Presidential campaigns focus on what, rather than how, candidates think. Campaigns examine candidates' political opinions and worldviews, but while these elements provide the frames for policy and leadership decisions, they reveal little about the actual process of how candidates make decisions. This is unfortunate since, as I noted, the expectation of a strong connection between general worldviews and actual presidential behavior falters on three grounds—the novel event, the shaping power of specific circumstances, and the ways in which decisions ordinarily require the integration of more than one set of considerations.

The dilemma here is that it is precisely the ability to see important factors in a particular context and shape a response accordingly that is one characteristic of good policy and decision judgment. It is judgment that is critical in presidential performance. Yet policy *judgment,* unlike policy *views,* is difficult to assess during a presidential campaign.

If the candidate has been in public life (and sometimes even if he has not), it is possible to examine past policy judgments. This is a different focus from researching his past views on an issue. General policy views are one factor that may inform specific judgments, but assessments of judgment always require a reading of the specific circumstances and how they were handled. The unit of analysis for the assessment of judgment is the decision, not the leader's worldview or political philosophy.

The press has not performed effectively in asking these kinds of questions of some candidates. Although the press has frequently been criticized for being too aggressive in pursuit of character issues, there is reason to suggest the opposite. Coverage of Jesse Jackson in the 1988 presidential campaign, for example, was quite cautious by the standards established for Senators Gary Hart, Joe Biden, and Dan Quayle. Few hard questions were asked about the adequacy of his judgments in connection with his association with the Black Muslims, his running of Operation Push (an antipoverty program), his foreign policy views, or his lack of governing experience.

We cannot really tell in the context of a campaign how a candidate would respond to an armed conflict in South America, a terrorist strike in Europe, or a surge in unemployment or inflation. Candidates don't like to talk about the hypothetical. They often are inhibited from discussing what they would do should an actual domestic and international crisis arise by the fact that they must not appear to be second-guessing a sitting president. So we are left, at best, with indirect indicators of candidates' judgment that must often be sought outside of the traditional policy decision arenas.

Information about candidates' judgment can come to light in at least two ways during a campaign. One way is for the candidate to commit a gross error of judgment, as Gary Hart did in the 1988 primary campaign. Did Gary Hart's judgment in having a relationship with Donna Rice mean that he was unlikely to have good policy judgment about, say, a response to an armed conflict in the Middle East? Not necessarily. But someone who sabotaged his own efforts to obtain a position he ostensibly wanted shows poor judgment and calls into question both his capacity for good judgment and the seriousness of his commitment to his leadership role.

Gross errors of judgment of the kind that Gary Hart made in the middle of his presidential campaign are relatively rare and therefore cannot be depended upon to provide insight into a particular leader. Misstatements and mistakes are much more common but not really revealing of judgment. Gerald Ford's mistaken statement about Soviet domination of Eastern Europe and Jimmy Carter's acknowledgment that he had felt lust in his heart generated commentary and controversy but little information about the important performance attribute of judgment.

There is another way in which issues of judgment get raised in campaigns, and that is by observing candidates' responses to the unexpected. Serious campaigns are carefully planned, but no campaign can anticipate all eventualities. A candidate's response to the unexpected during the "heat of battle" gives some insight into how and how well he may respond in other unforeseen circumstances.

This is one reason that one can readily discern attempts in recent campaigns to reduce the unexpected (as in recent campaign debates, in which format, substance, and style have been meticulously prepared in advance) and, where that is not possible, to blur the line between a candidate's real, spontaneous response and something that looks like it but isn't. When CBS anchorman Dan Rather confronted George Bush on national television about his role in the Iran-Contra affair and Bush asked in return how Rather would feel about having his whole career judged by one incident (referring to Rather's petulant absence from his anchor position one evening because his broadcast had been delayed to allow completion of another program), it had the feel of high drama. Yet a follow-up story in the *New York Times* revealed that both sides had carefully prepared for that brief interview, including role-playing sessions during which Dan Rather was confronted with exactly the same question that George Bush actually asked him on the broadcast.[5]

Questions about judgment must ultimately be tied to the circumstances that confronted a candidate, the way(s) he framed and understood those circumstances, the options that a candidate saw as available, the one(s) he chose and his expectations in doing so, and, finally, the results of his choice.

Political Leadership

In addition to a candidate's judgment, a presidential campaign should seek to clarify a candidate's leadership ability and skills. I have suggested that the process of political leadership can be viewed as including three elements: mobilization, orchestration, and consolidation. The first entails the ability to speak to the issues that concern people in a way that leads them to commit themselves, at least preliminarily. The second focuses on the ways in which the president, as leader, brings people and institutional resources together in an attempt to accomplish his goals. The third refers to the political, policy, and institutional infrastructure and other by-products of this process.

Of the three, presidential campaigns can reasonably be expected to cast direct light only on mobilization and orchestration. Of these two, mobilization is the more accessible. Any candidate demonstrates his ability to mobilize the public in part by doing so. That means activating partisans, volunteers, contributors, and, of course, voters. The candidate does this by projecting a personal and political identity, espousing his view of the nature of the country's political problems and prospects, and conveying the sense to the public that he will be able to accomplish his (and their) purposes.

The ability to do this in the context of a national election has important and direct implications for a president's work and the tools available to him to accomplish it. Presidents must be able to make their case with the public. Strong rhetorical and interpersonal skills are an asset in mobilizing and consolidating public support.

Orchestration, the ability to put together the mobilized elements of one's constituencies while making use of other strategic resources to accomplish leadership purposes, is also on view during campaigns. It takes the form of building, managing, and applying personal and political resources to the goal of winning the nomination and then the election. In this general sense, a candidate's ability to orchestrate a successful campaign will tell us something about his skills in this area of leadership, which should have some applicability should he be elected.

The relationship between the overt level of analysis described above and the "horse-race" aspect of the campaign should not be overlooked. It is tempting and easy to confine the analysis of mobilization skills to the number of received votes or orchestration skills to the number of party constituencies that can be counted as part of one's camp. There is a certain logic to this. Candidates who can't mobilize votes don't gain office.

However, *how* a candidate mobilizes or orchestrates others is at least as important to how he will govern as *whether* he is able to do so. Does the candidate mobilize others by utilizing hope or fear, by being honest about the country's problems and prospects or by choosing optimism over realism? Does he play on people's hopes by making promises that he knows will be difficult (at best) to keep? Does he portray himself as he believes people would like to see him, rather than as he really is?

The pressures of the campaign market create a push to use such methods as making promises that can't be kept or presenting oneself as quite different from how one actually is. Indeed, these pressures may well be another culturally patterned defect (see chapter 3) in our system. However, not all candidates respond to these pressures. Walter Mondale in 1984 said he would have to raise taxes. Paul Tsongas in 1992 talked directly about the problems of large deficits and the need to do something about them. If candidates cannot completely resist these pressures, there is still some analytic mileage in examining the extent to which they are used and to which the candidate is able to avoid succumbing to them. A candidate's ability to do so says something very important about his integrity, ambition, and relatedness.

Candidates who allow themselves to be less than candid about their views, their analysis, and, ultimately, themselves can expect to pay a heavy price should they gain office. Their legitimacy will rest on a false foundation, and they will be hard pressed to explain why they have changed after being elected, further damaging their credibility and legitimacy. Or they may decide to mask the changes they wish to make, in which case they stand the constant danger of being found out for who they really are and what they really think. Maintaining appearances in the presidency then becomes a consuming task, pushing aside the time that would be spent on other, more substantive matters.

Character Elements

Character elements play an important role in presidential performance. The question is whether they are accessible to public observation and analysis. If it is true that intricacies of character can take years to unravel in psychoanalytic work, how, then, can we hope to uncover what we need to know during the relatively brief period of a presidential campaign? In chapters 10 and 11 I tried to demonstrate that it was possible. In this section, I step back and say more clearly why it is possible.

I first emphasize the phrase "what we need to know." Campaigns are not psychoanalytic therapy. Their function is not to reach a deep understanding of a candidate or president. What is needed is enough understanding to make a reasonable judgment regarding the relative strengths and weaknesses of a candidate's psychology and their implications for his performance of presidential responsibilities.

There are at least three reasons to believe that such information is not beyond our reach. First, today there is more coverage of candidates than ever before, across more circumstances and over time. Second, the circumstances of the campaign lend themselves to learning more about these character elements. Third, character elements for most candidates are likely to be more, rather than less, striking than those we see in others in ordinary life.

Coverage refers not only to the enormous range of behavior that is generated by the hourly, daily, weekly, and monthly needs of making a serious bid for a party's nomination and, thereafter, in a presidential campaign. Increasingly, candidates are covered on almost a moment-by-moment basis by C-SPAN, and large numbers of reporters are assigned to the candidates, many of whom travel from morning to night with them and their aides over the many months of a campaign (Goldman et al. 1994). In addition, reporters are dispatched to cover a candidate's present, past, and even distant past.

The nature of campaigns themselves aids the process of revealing character and candidate psychology more generally. A presidential campaign is a high-risk, high-stakes undertaking with no fixed rules, played out in public under the critical eye of observers and opponents for the chance to shape one's country, the world, and perhaps history. As Greenstein (1969, 50, 54, 55, 59) has pointed out:

> The more demanding the political act—the more it is one that calls for an active investment of effort—the greater the likelihood that it will be influenced by the personal characteristics of the actor. . . .
>
> The greater the actor's affective involvement . . . , the greater the likelihood that his psychological characteristics will . . . be exhibited in his behavior. . . .
>
> Ambiguous situations leave room for personal variability to manifest itself. . . .
>
> Certain types of environmental stimuli undoubtedly have a greater "residence" with deeper layers of the personality than do others. . . .
>
> Even when there is little room for personal variability in the instrumental aspects of actions, there is likely to be variation in their expressive aspects.

Certainly, a presidential campaign contains all of these elements that Greenstein lists as stimulating the expression of a leader's inner psychology. To these, however, we can add one more. The psychologies of persons who actively seek the presidency, are likely to be stronger and therefore more observable than that of the ordinary person on the street.[6] Ambition, for example, is likely to be stronger and more manifest among presidential candidates than among average persons, and the self-image of the former is likely to be different from that of the latter. One way in which this can be seen is in the candidate's belief that he is up to the job. The number of people who believe that and are willing to commit themselves, their families, their associates, and their collective histories to intense and not generally friendly scrutiny is rather small, even among professional politicians. In short, as I pointed out in chapter 3, the inner psychologies of those who seek the presidency are not likely to be ordinary, and while inner psychologies may be disguised, they cannot be easily hidden.

Can we see more of the candidate than he may want us to see? In all likelihood, yes. There are limits, especially over time, to the extent that character can be suppressed. As Freud noted:

He that has eyes to see and ears to hear may convince himself that no mortal can keep a secret. If his lips are silent, he chatters with his finger-tips; betrayal oozes out of him at every pore. And thus the task of making conscious the most hidden recesses of the mind is one that is quite possible to accomplish. (1905, 77–78)

In this passage Freud is referring to his methods of gauging the effects of subjects being discussed by his patients. The general methodological point is relevant to presidential campaigns, but I am not suggesting that we watch for candidates tapping their fingers on podiums to denote anxiety.

In presidential campaigns we have to look to more systematic reflections of character and inner psychology. One obvious and easy one is persistent patterns of behavior. In the 1988 presidential campaign, the public learned of Michael Dukakis's steadiness and persistence in a very direct way by observing him over the course of the primary campaign, as he emerged from a crowded primary field, and on through the final election campaign.

In contrast, Senator Robert Dole's explosive temper was well known in Washington circles but was not in public view for the first part of the primary battle as each candidate attempted to appear dignified and therefore more "presidential." However, Dole was not fully able to contain his anger during heated exchanges with George Bush, especially in those that touched on his wife, Elizabeth. The result was a well-publicized evening news bite showing a clearly angry Dole confronting George Bush at an opening session of the Senate. It is hard to remain out of character if the person has a consolidated one.

Somewhat more subtle indicators of character can found in the ways that candidates frame their understandings of what they must do or in the strategies they do (and do not) choose. Other indicators are to be found in how they handle their relationships with others—their advisers, staff, opponents, and colleagues. Yet other indicators are to be found in how they respond to crises.

Consider in this regard concerns about George Bush's "toughness" in the 1988 presidential campaign and his use of negative campaign commercials. We do not know all the details surrounding their use, but the basic public outlines of the decision can be stated. As far back as April 1987 (see *New York Times,* 17 April 1987, A27), Bush aides conceded that their candidate had two major problems, one having to do with his role in the Iran-Contra arms-for-hostages fiasco, the other with the public perception of a certain "weakness of character" (the so-called wimp factor).[7] The questions raised about Bush reflected a concern about his capacity to be strong and effective in a tough, sometimes lethal international environment. Ronald Reagan was said to harbor similar questions and misgivings. It is one thing to call for a kinder, gentler nation, quite another to be inhibited by this wish in a world in which circumstances dictate otherwise.

The campaign commercials that Bush allowed (reluctantly, it was loudly said) resulted in criticism of him for being both negative and inconsistent (he had said we wanted "a kinder, gentler nation"). But ironically enough, the decision to start and continue these ads suggested that Bush as not as indecisive and weak as he had been portrayed. In allowing these commercials to run, Bush demonstrated that he was willing and able to be tough with an opponent.[8] It foreshadowed his capacity for resoluteness and tough-mindedness in responding to the Iraqi invasion of Kuwait.

One can certainly be critical of the tone and substance of Bush's TV spots, but more is involved than issues of fairness and accuracy. We surely expect campaign staffs to put the best possible interpretation on facts surrounding their candidates and not to present their opponents in the best possible light. We also expect that a candidate who commands large resources will respond quickly and pointedly to important inaccuracies or damaging misrepresentations. Dukakis's failure to do so raised questions about his ability to see that there was a problem, his willingness to do something about it, and his ability to mount an effective response.

Did Dukakis's failure to respond adequately suggest that he would also not do so when faced with a major international or domestic crisis? As was the case for Gary Hart, we cannot be certain. It is perhaps an unfairly stringent test, but it does seem that a major fumbling of a challenge results in doubts about capacity that are enough to doom a candidacy. The public seems more concerned about failing to weed out a potentially ineffective or otherwise questionable leader than it is about the possibility of not selecting an adequate or even a good leader because of a mistaken understanding of his capacities.

Consider in this regard Bill Clinton's determined 1992 presidential candidacy, covered in some depth in chapter 10. Shaken by allegations that he had an affair, as well as by questions about his Vietnam draft status, he nonetheless persisted. During the general election campaign, he endured furious assaults on his integrity, judgment, and leadership. At times his negative evaluations in the polls rivaled his level of support among the American public, yet he continued to mount an effective and active counterattack and campaign. It is natural to be disheartened and even thrown off stride by large discouragements, but a strong sense of self and one's ambitions provide a personal reservoir on which to draw in such times.

Presidential campaigns also shed light on important questions of candidates' personal and political identities, their integrity, and their authenticity. Is the candidate really who he says he is? The degree of integration, integrity, and authenticity in a candidate's identity and persona has become a crucial window into psychological suitability. If a candidate cannot be trusted to present himself as he really is, how is it possible to entrust the powers of the presidency to him?

In the last few presidential campaigns, several candidates were undone by inconsistencies that threw their public personas and private behaviors into doubt.[9] Does it matter that Pat Robertson's wife was pregnant before they got married? In general, no. However, the answer changes if the candidate runs on a platform that includes denouncement of premarital sexual activity. In this case, it would matter because it would call into question not only the consistency of his policy views but his authenticity and integrity. Ultimately, it raises questions of character. Does he think he is exempt from the rules that he himself sets up as a guide for others?

Does it matter that candidate Joe Biden freely borrowed from another speech and presented it as his own (*New York Times,* 12 September 1987, A1)? Yes. Does that incident become more significant in the context of an admitted plagiarism in law school (*New York Times,* 18 September 1987, A1)? Of course. Both incidents call into question the candidate's honesty, and the fact that two such incidents are uncovered must lead to questions of what causes this unfortunate pattern. Does it reflect a tendency to bend the rules to get a political advantage? Does it reflect the operation of intense political ambition, which has adversely affected judgment?

Sometimes judgments about authenticity that are finessed by a candidate during the campaign can have damaging consequences when the candidate achieves office. An example of this occurred in connection with candidate Bill Clinton's election to the presidency as a "New Democrat." As noted in chapter 10, this label and Clinton's actions seemed to address the basic public dilemma that he and the other candidates faced: making public policies that were smart, fair, cost-conscious, unbeholden to advocacy-group demands, and effective. After two years with Clinton in office, some of his policies, in particular his economic stimulus package, his policies concerning homosexuals in the military, and his large-scale government health care initiative, led many voters to conclude that he was more like an old Democrat than a new one. It seems reasonable to suggest that one result of this perception, and a corresponding loss of confidence in President Clinton's willingness or ability to resolve the basic public dilemma, was the unprecedented losses he and his party experienced in the 1994 midterm elections.

In contrast, authenticity can be a potent political resource. Ronald Reagan seemed genuinely to be the man he presented himself to be. Recall that when Howard Baker visited Reagan in response to staff concerns that Reagan was seriously out of touch with his responsibilities (see chapter 4), Baker found him "just as he always had been." Whether or not one approved of Reagan's detached management style, the comment does suggest that there was great overlap between the person and the persona. Whether or not one agreed with Reagan's policies, his authenticity counted for something with an electorate tired of pretense and deception.

On occasion, reporters simply don't appreciate that information is readily available to them which could provide crucial insights into the personal characteristics of a candidate. For example, the ability to mobilize and then work with groups and other political leaders who are not necessarily predisposed to the candidate or president (orchestration) is an important aspect of political leadership. However, during campaigns it is primarily mobilization of voter support, not orchestration, that is revealed. Therefore it is critical to look back over a candidate's record. Often this kind of information is available from the candidate's past, especially if he has held elective or appointive office.

One senior news commentator (quoted in Sabato 1991, 221) noted in connection with Gary Hart that the focus on his affair with Donna Rice tended to obscure more important and *obtainable* information:

This is a job where if you are going to be a success at all, you have to be able to build relationships with other political players. This guy had never demonstrated the slightest inclination or capacity to build any kind of relationship with any other politician. Now this is something that we should have been able to write about.

The problem with information regarding character elements, I submit, is not that we are not getting (or cannot get) enough information. It is rather that observers need to have a way of understanding all the information available.

Some Limitations of Assessing Psychological Suitability during Election Campaigns

The assessment of character and leadership during presidential campaigns, even when partially successful, underscores several dilemmas. One arises from ambiguities in the meaning of the behavior that we see. The Biden case provides an illustration. It is clear that Senator Joe Biden borrowed important parts of another leader's speech without attribution and that he also plagiarized a law review article when he was in law school, but what exactly does this say about his character? Does it reflect a strong need to succeed at any cost, a tendency to enter "gray" areas and err in favor of self-interest? Or does it reflect the lack of confidence, skill, or some combination of these factors?

In a world of more information and better theories, the answers to these questions would conceivably have some bearing on a more sophisticated assessment of a candidate's psychological suitability. But the reality is that serious answers to these questions can't be obtained without intimate access to the individual and painstaking research, and neither is likely to be possible during a campaign. There is, therefore, a rough but politically legitimate cutoff point to these questions in a candidacy. *The fact that we cannot fully appreciate or understand in complex detail the personal motivations that underlie questionable behavior does not require citizens to forgo their discomfort and judgments about its existence.*

Another dilemma is found in the fact that character reflects *composite* characteristics. A given character element or derivative may be productive or "successful" in one arena or time but not in others.[10] So, for example, Dukakis's persistent, steady approach to unfolding political events might be helpful for "long-haul" events but less helpful in response to new, dramatic developments. A strong and steady approach is an important dimension of leadership psychology, but so is the capacity for quick, effective response. To take the opposite case, a characteristic that may seem to be a matter of some concern, say, the capacity to be tough, may carry with it more positive implications for some contexts (for example, in standing up to aggressors).

Alternative Venues for Assessing Suitability

During the 1988 presidential campaign, when Gary Hart was forced to withdraw from contention because of allegations of martial infidelity, James Reston of the *New York Times* suggested ignoring the primaries altogether and then went on to note, "Back to the smoke-filled room, you say? Undemocratic? You bet, but not unintelligent or unprecedented. The delegates know more about the records and characters of potential Presidents than all the voters in the primary combined, and would probably come out with candidates that the people could trust and respect" (20 September 1987, E27).

Reston's enthusiasm for the smoke-filled room appears to reflect the assumption that a concern with fielding candidates who can be elected is synonymous with the selection of good candidates. Backstage selections have proved to be no guarantee of effective and psychologically suitable presidential candidates. Even widespread canvassing of professional political opinion is no guarantee that important information regarding psychological suitability will emerge.

Recall the analysis in chapter 6 of the selection of Thomas Eagleton as George McGovern's vice presidential running mate. McGovern says he spent some time checking out his list of candidates, which included Eagleton, "with a broad cross-section of Democratic leaders" and that "many of them gave the highest marks to Mondale, White and Eagleton" (1977, 197). McGovern's old friend Gaylord Nelson also favorably recommended Eagleton. If this is accurate, and there is no indication to the contrary, it means that Eagleton's peers and colleagues were either unaware of his medical history or else unconcerned by it. This is also not a particularly reassuring conclusion for proponents of the structural barriers argument.

To take another example, rumors of Bill Clinton's marital difficulties were more widely known than Eagleton's medical difficulties, as were allegations about Clinton's draft record. In both cases, it is hard to imagine that fellow professionals in the candidate's party would ask tough questions or, more importantly, be able to go beyond the candidate's answers to them. Often the candidate's own staff may not know the truth about an individual's behavior. For example, when answering charges raised against Bill Clinton with regard to his draft status, his closest staff were unaware that he had written a letter to an official at his draft board, thanking him for saving him from the draft (Goldman et al. 1994, 122). Alternatives to public exposure and debate on these issues clearly have their own major problems.

Conclusion

There is no escape from the need to make overall judgments based on mixtures of characteristics that may have different implications under varying circumstances. This would be a difficult and complex undertaking even if there were adequate theories of the relationships of character elements to one another and to political situations. The development of theory can help inform these judgments, but in the end, the judgments cannot be made with certainty.

Character analysis is part of a composite picture that emerges of candidates during a campaign. It is not a substitute for the analysis of candidates' personal and political beliefs. Questions raised about Pat Robertson having fathered a child before marriage were less damaging politically than reports of his apocalyptic views on foreign affairs, his self-stated ability to perform miracles, and his stated belief that he had personal conversations with God and Satan.

The new standards of propriety, as well as the concerns with character, leadership, and judgment, seem, on balance, a necessary and desirable step. They may encourage more prospective care and thought about appropriate behavior by those who would serve in high public office. It does seem likely that major questions of character deficiency can act as a bar to nomination and election, although the lack of such glaring defects does not in itself guarantee success. But if closer scrutiny does keep the virtuous away from politics, it also may help to screen out undesirable candidates.

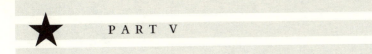

PART V

Assessing Psychological Suitability:
Some Applications

Asking the Right Questions of Presidential Candidates: Some Suggestions and Guidelines

The psychological assessment of presidential candidates is a complex task. It involves developing a set of performance criteria for a role that is embedded in a particular institutional and political setting and specifying the psychological elements that shape the accomplishment of the responsibilities associated with that role. I have, in the preceding chapters, examined in some depth the nature of the issues involved and, where possible, suggested some theoretical approaches of possible usefulness.

Yet it is not to be expected, given the complexity of the issues we have examined, that this work would result in a set of simple decision rules that would allow citizens to survey the factual landscape during a presidential campaign and select those facts with relevance for favoring one candidate over others on the basis of his psychological suitability. Still, if simple decision rules are unlikely to be the result of any analyses in this complicated area, it may still be possible (and useful) to attempt some general guidelines and suggestions.

In this chapter I offer some tentative guidelines and suggestions to frame the analysis of psychological suitability. They are not offered as hard and fast rules. Nor are they meant to be definitive, although taken together they are somewhat comprehensive.[1] If they do prove useful, it will be as a framework that can be modified or supplemented in any particular case.

The guidelines and suggestions are drawn from the preceding chapters. Their primary function is to organize and specify in one place some of the elements we have considered and to suggest some ways by which each area might be elucidated before and during a presidential campaign. Given their purpose, I have framed them in a general rather than a technical way. The areas that are addressed and the questions that are asked do not require in-depth, formal training in the disciplines that gave rise to them. Nonetheless, persons who make use of these guidelines or questions should, at minimum, be familiar with the general theoretical frames of analysis that underlie them.

It is not my intention to suggest that each question be asked of each candidate for every period that I cover. Rather, these are meant to be guiding frameworks that can be modified to fit individual circumstances. The questions are meant to be asked of the candidates themselves and, also important, of others who knew and worked with them in different periods. These multiple strands of data allow analysts not only to build a picture of a candidate's development over time but to compare the candidate's view of himself and his experiences with those of others.

A Note on Anecdotal Evidence

Many of the questions in this section ask the candidate or other interviewee to recall a particular set of circumstances that reflect the material in question. For example, one set of questions reads:

- Did the candidate seem to have strong personal standards of right and wrong, for himself and for others?
- Can a particular set of circumstances that showed these standards in action be recalled?

The purpose of asking for an example or story is that it helps to focus the answer by locating the material in a particular context. This also allows the interviewer to follow up and clarify specific parts of the story or what they reflect. Stories or examples often take the form of anecdotes, so it is important to consider their use as evidence. The analyst of presidential candidates who makes use of anecdotal case material must, like his statistical data–oriented counterparts, address the issue of the quality of the data.[2] There are essentially four areas of concern raised by the use of such material: validity, representativeness, consequence, and meaning.

An anecdote is a story, and anecdotal evidence is a story put forward to support a characterization. The first set of questions that must be addressed concern whether the story is true. Who is telling the story? Was the person there, or is the individual repeating what he or she heard elsewhere? What is the relationship of the person telling the story to the person about whom it is told? What is the individual's motivation in telling the story? What independent evidence is there that the event took place? Does that confirmation differ from the story in any respects? Obviously, independent evidence that any event took place as portrayed buttresses confidence in its utility. But establishing that a particular event did take place is only the first step.

The next question is how representative the incident is. This is a critical but often misunderstood question. In surveys and experiments, the question of representativeness is, in reality, the question of whether this particular result (incident) is representative of a range of classes of behaviors. An experimental effect that showed up only among college sophomores taking psychology courses would raise the question of whether the effect had applicability elsewhere.

This issue also arises with presidents, but in somewhat different ways. The issue is the extent to which the narrative incident is representative of a particular class of this president's behavior. For example, does an anecdote reflecting presidential indecisiveness reflect a more general pattern of indecisiveness, or is it more of a unique event? The density of similar anecdotes adds to the weight of confidence that there is indeed something here that needs to be explained.[3]

The question of the density of examples is related to but does not fully resolve the issue of whether the behavior is consequential. The sampling of behaviors ordinarily taken by presidential scholars is somewhat limited. In the study of individual presidential behaviors, there is little that is comparable to even the ordinary, limited survey. Thus, in studies of presidential behavior, a few behaviors may count for as much as would a much larger set of behaviors (in the average survey sample).

Moreover, even a modest number of instances of a particular presidential behavior (or in some cases, even only one instance of it) may have enormous consequences. George and George (1956) focused on only three instances, across a very long public and political career, in which a full-blown, and perhaps avoidable, crisis was generated by Woodrow Wilson's interior psychology. Yet it would be difficult to argue that in any of these cases the results were inconsequential.

Establishing that an anecdote is accurate and representative of consequential behavior still requires one to document the *meaning* of the element(s) revealed in the anecdote. This is one of the most difficult aspects in making use of the anecdote. Consider, for example, the many anecdotes outlined in chapters 10 and 11 regarding Bill Clinton's anger. Yes, there are enough anecdotes to establish its validity. Yes, it has happened often enough to establish that it is a substantial element in his psychology. Yes, his anger has consequences. Yet it remains to be established just what the function and meaning of Clinton's anger is in his overall psychology. For this we cannot rely on anecdotes, as plentiful, accurate, and consequential as they may be, but must turn to psychological formulations. The researcher who uses any of the following questions must ultimately look to theories to supplement and inform narratives.

Tentative Guidelines for Asking Questions of Presidential Candidates: Five Caveats

Before turning to the guidelines and suggestions offered to assist in the assessment of psychological suitability of presidential candidates, five cautions must be noted. First, the traits I describe should be thought of as being placed on a continuum. However, it is a continuum anchored by general, not specifically calibrated, levels of functioning.

I believe it is possible, for example, to distinguish individuals whose level of ambition is very high, is very low, or falls within the moderate range. It is not always or easily possible to distinguish specific comparative points *within* categories. So while I may be able to tell that candidate X has much higher ambition than candidate Y, it is not so easy to distinguish, relative to each other, two candidates with high (or low) ambition.

Second, and very important, psychological functioning is a *composite* concept. High levels of ambition, for example, do not completely define anyone's character, much less his or her overall psychology. In the sections that follow, each area has its own set of questions, but often questions from one section will have relevance for questions in another. Character elements are interrelated.

For example, there are questions in the section on ambition and others having to do with values in the section on integrity. Yet it is clear from the theory put forward in chapters 7 and 8, as well as from my commentary in this chapter, that ambition must be considered in relation to the framework of a candidate's personal values. In short, relationships among characterological and other psychological traits are important and are, in most cases, the basis on which judgments regarding suitability are ultimately made.

Third, I emphasize the term *good enough* as the basis of psychological suitability. It would be a serious mistake to suppose that any assessment procedure, however sophisticated, can find what doesn't exist, namely, candidates without areas of difficulty or any flaws. Moreover, while it is possible, I believe, to avoid those who are prone to error, it is not likely that we will find candidates (or presidents) who don't make errors. In short, it is important not to confuse an ideal, which may serve as a useful guide (but only that), with what exists in the real world.

Fourth, and related to the third caveat, is the fact that some consequences of character important for presidential performance may not be what are commonly thought of as virtues. They are, nonetheless, necessary. Presidents need to have the capacity to be tough (which is quite different from being ruthless). On occasion, they have to distance themselves from their tendencies toward empathetic attunement with others, if they are not to be paralyzed. In short, too much virtue in candidates, like too little, has its implications for performance, and these need to be thought through. Presidents who worry about being nice or don't think twice about being vicious both show, in their own way, a failing with potentially damaging consequences for performance. Adults are complicated composites. There is no reason to think that presidents, who are adults, will be any different.

Fifth, character and psychological variables are meant to address the issue of psychological suitability. However, psychological suitability is itself one of several suitability issues. A candidate might be perfectly acceptable on psychological grounds but unacceptable on political grounds.

Keeping these concerns in mind, let us now turn to some suggestions and guidelines for assessing psychological suitability. Many of the questions raised below may well be asked of a presidential candidate; however, asking these questions only of the candidate himself would be a serious mistake. Candidates have become adept at answering (even anticipating) tough questions, and the questions offered below are not likely to be an exception. These questions are meant to frame a *broad* inquiry into the candidate's views and record, and that can be accomplished only by also asking them of others in a position to know (because of past or present knowledge). Under no circumstances would it be useful—and it would most likely be counterproductive—to rely solely on the candidate to provide answers.

Suggested Questions for Presidential Candidates: The Candidate's Early Basic Experience

Many candidates have realized that allowing the public to get to know them is an important part of the presidential selection process. This personal information has come to include, in recent years, background stories on the candidate's early years, as well as information on their early political roles (if any). Not surprisingly, candidates have not been content to allow such biographical stories to unfold but have tried to shape them in numerous ways, including putting together their own campaign biographies, whether in books (e.g., Jimmy Carter's *Why Not the Best?* [1975]) or in campaign commercials in the form of autobiographies (e.g., Bill Clinton's story "The Man from Hope," presented at the Democratic national convention).

Analysts should accept such productions for what they are—the candidates' views of themselves as they see themselves and/or would like to be seen. There is nothing necessarily sinister about this wish. Candidates may believe what is written or produced in their name, as well as what they write themselves. But to accept uncritically such biographical materials, produced by candidates with a vested interest in presenting their case, would be analogous to having court proceedings limited to the representations of the plaintiff.

Candidates' constructions of their own biographies are useful and important, as long as it is kept in mind that they represent the candidates' views of their histories. The thoughtful and careful analyst will want to supplement these reflections with those of others in a position to cast some light on a candidate's developmental experiences.

Analysts should exercise the most extreme care in evaluating the relationship between their informants and the subject. Many candidates' parents are unlikely purposely to reveal information that might damage their children's chances. Some have even claimed to have seen distinctly presidential qualities in their children at a very early age.

Analysts should also be careful not to read too much into individual facts in a person's biography. It is the larger patterns that are most useful and accessible. Moreover, developmental analysis is the most difficult of the three levels of analysis and is best done, if at all, by persons with substantial information and the training to make use of it.

One other strategy that would prove helpful in building up understandings of those likely to emerge as candidates is to develop profiles *before* presidential elections. It is usually the case that many potential candidates give indications of their intentions well before (in some cases, years) acting on their presidential ambitions. Candidates who tried and were unsuccessful in the previous election are also good prospects for inclusion in this kind of precampaign data gathering.

The reasons for gathering this kind of detailed background information before the campaign seem fairly clear. First, to attempt to gather such information during a campaign, when there are many candidates and evolving political and policy issues to keep track of, guarantees that detailed examination of a particular candidate's past will not be likely or even necessarily a high priority, given the emphasis in the media on the horse-race aspects of the campaign. This problem emerges even when the selection process has been narrowed to the two (or as was the case in 1992, three) major-party candidates. Second, collecting this kind of data before a campaign makes it more likely that the reflections obtained will be less influenced (for better or worse) by the person's status as a presidential candidate and possible president.

Finally, the questions posed below are meant not only to provide the first, broad steps in framing a more specific picture of the candidate at each of a series of different stages but also to stimulate a series of more specific questions in the minds of any users. Their purpose is to begin to assemble a useful picture of how the candidate developed as a person over time. The life history is the experiential source of the character elements we observe and, as such, can offer important clues to the candidate's ambition, ideals and their consolidation, and relatedness.

With these understandings in mind, let us turn to some broadly framed possible questions:

Early Family Experiences

- What were the candidate's early family circumstances?
- What was/is his mother like?
- What was/is his father like?
- What influences did each parent appear to have on the candidate? How does the candidate see their influence? What particular strengths does he see each as having?
- Were there any unusual separations, deaths, illnesses, or reversals or advances in social and/or economic circumstances during the candidate's childhood?
- What were the candidate's early school experiences like?
- What, if anything, do neighbors or teachers remember about the candidate? What kind of child do they remember him as being? Are there any specific incidents or stories that come to their minds in connection with the candidate?
- Who were the candidate's friends when he was young? How do they recall him? Are there specific incidents or stories that stick in their minds?

High School and Adolescence

- What were the candidate's family circumstances during this period? Had they changed? If so, how?

- Were there any unusual separations, deaths, illnesses, or reversals or advances in social and/or economic circumstances during this period?
- What were the candidate's school experiences like? Did he do well in school? Was he a participant in extracurricular activities?
- What, if anything, do people who came into contact with the candidate (neighbors, teachers, mentors) remember of the candidate during this period? What kind of young person do they remember him as being? Are there any specific incidents or stories that come to mind?
- Who were the candidate's friends during this period? How do they recall him? Are there specific incidents or stories that stick in their minds?
- How did the candidate spend his summers? Did he work? Did he study?

College

- Where did the candidate go to college? What were his intellectual and extracurricular (clubs, athletic teams, fraternities, etc.) experiences there?
- Was he involved in any political clubs or activities? What was his role, if any, in them?
- What, if anything, do people who came into contact with the candidate (neighbors, teachers, students with whom he participated in activities) remember of the candidate during this period? What kind of young man do they remember him as being? Are there any specific incidents or stories that come to mind?
- Who were the candidate's friends during this period? How do they recall him? Are there specific incidents or stories that stick in their minds?

Suggested Questions for Presidential Candidates: The Candidate's Early and Mid-Adulthood Experiences

Immediate Postcollege Years

The young and mid-adulthood years are particularly important for appreciating the ways in which childhood and adolescent character patterns, supplemented (or inhibited) by an individual's skills, are shaped in the context of real, adult world experience into a psychological package that forms the foundation for the candidate's political career. Let us now turn to some possibly useful questions for framing such an inquiry:

- What did the candidate do after college?
- If he attended a graduate program, what kind was it? How did the candidate do?
- Was he involved in any extracurricular activities? If so, what kind, and what was the candidate's role in them?
- If the candidate did not attend a graduate program, what did he do?
- Was the candidate employed? If so, in what capacity?
- What were the candidate's responsibilities? How did he handle them? What talents did he display? What areas, if any, did he have difficulty with?
- How did he respond to setbacks, to successes?
- What were his relationships like with peers, supervisors?
- What, if anything, do people who came into contact with the candidate (coworkers, supervisors) remember of the candidate during this period? What kind of young man do they remember him as being? Are there any specific incidents or stories that come to mind?

Early Political Roles

At some point, by early or middle adulthood, many presidential candidates have had direct political or semipolitical roles.[4] Analysts and others interested in appreciating a candidate's likely approach to presidential responsibilities have largely failed to make sufficient use of the very important information available to them in these areas, especially (but not limited to) circumstances in which a candidate's political experience has included an executive position, for example, that of governor (Carter, Reagan, and Clinton).

There is a wealth of data in these areas that is directly relevant to the candidate's possible performance in the presidential role. It cannot be emphasized too strongly that the failure to make better use of this kind of data, when available, deprives political analysts and the public alike of information that could provide the most useful insights into that person's likely approach to presidential responsibilities.

The Candidate as Person: Early and Mid-Adulthood

- How would one describe the candidate as a person (at any particular stage of his early or mid-adulthood)? Was he flexible, tough, fair, anxious to make his mark, relaxed, solicitous of others (especially those in a position to help him), warm toward others, somewhat reserved, or very goal-oriented?

- How did the candidate feel about his ability to accomplish his goals? Was he generally without doubt? Did he seem periodically to have substantial doubts, or would you describe him as generally confident?
- Would you describe the candidate as somewhat moody, or was he generally a steady, consistent person in temperament and behavior?
- Did the candidate seem to have strong personal standards of right and wrong, for himself and for others? Can a particular set of circumstances that showed these standards in action be recalled?
- Did the candidate appear to have a set of consistent personal and public values that informed his behavior, both privately and in public life? Did you ever know him to deviate from these standards? If so, what were the circumstances?
- Did the candidate invest himself wholeheartedly in his responsibilities?
- What did the candidate do, if anything, to relax? Was he able to enjoy periods away from his responsibilities?

Motivation and Skills

- What political positions or offices did the candidate aspire to or obtain?
- In his attempts to gain a position or office, what methods or strategies stood out?
- What skills, if any, seemed particularly evident or lacking in the candidate at the time?
- What serious questions, if any, were raised about the candidate at the time? How did he respond?
- What responsibilities did the candidate have in each of the offices or positions that he obtained? In retrospect, which were handled well and which were not? Are there any reasons regarding personal or leadership style that help explain why he was more successful in some circumstances than in others?

Every political office or position requires of individuals that they handle conflict, crisis, and more routine operations. For *each* political position or office held, it would be useful (for comparative developmental purposes) to know the following:

Successes and Setbacks

- What were the chief accomplishments of the candidate? How did he accomplish them?
- How did he respond to success? Did he savor it or move quickly on to the next task?
- What skills did he display in achieving his accomplishments?
- Was there a specific instance (or more than one) in which the candidate tried, but failed, to achieve his purposes? How did the candidate account for this at the time? How does he account for it now? How do others familiar with the circumstances account for it? How did the candidate respond to this setback?
- When things did not go well, did the candidate have a tendency, either in public or in private, solely to blame others, or did he fully acknowledge any role he may have had in the circumstances?

Leadership

- Did the candidate seem to have definite points of view? How did he handle disagreement?
- What strategies did the candidate adopt to forward his agenda?
- Was the candidate candid in both his public and private assessment of circumstances, or did he generally avoid mentioning any hard realities?
- When the candidate was in a position of leadership, what was his style? Did the candidate like to be in charge? Did most things revolve around him? What aspects, if any, was the candidate willing to delegate, and to whom? Was the candidate a person who focused on a few big issues, or did he tend to deal with numerous issues? Did the candidate work hard?
- How did the candidate (in each position) handle his relationships with others—with peers, with subordinates, with superiors, with those having independent means of power and influence?
- Was the candidate willing to acknowledge (publicly and privately), in more than a pro forma way, the role that others may have had in achieving his success?
- How did the candidate handle any crisis situations that arose? What was the particular nature of the circumstances? Was the candidate calm, excited, anxious, reassuring to others? How did the crisis turn out?

Decision Making

- Did the candidate generally make decisions by himself, or did he make them after or in conjunction with wide consultation with others?
- How did the candidate function in group decision settings? Did he often take initiative? Did he speak up in support of prevailing views? How did he respond to people who disagreed? Did he ever stand against the views of the group? With what effects? What did others think of the candidate in these settings?
- Was the candidate effective in articulating his views?
- Did the candidate search widely for advice or rely on a few key people? Who were his key advisers? Were they generally like-minded or independent-minded people?
- Did the candidate prefer well-articulated options from which he would choose, or did he prefer to have more free-flowing discussions and then arrive at a conclusion?
- What can be said about the candidate's political and/or policy judgment? Were there occasions when he showed good judgment? What were the issues in that case? Were there any occasions when his judgment seemed somewhat off? What were the issues in that case? How were they resolved?
- In attempting to resolve conflicts arising from different views or interests, what strategies did the candidate employ? Was the candidate able to appreciate the concerns of those who did not share his views? How did he attempt to reconcile, if he tried to, these differences?
- Was the candidate able to make decisions that others might not like, even to the point of being extremely vocal in their opposition, and follow through on those decisions?
- What were the candidate's chief strengths as a decision maker? Did his strength lie in the area of digesting and synthesizing large amounts of information or in creating new approaches to problems? Can any specific circumstances be recalled when these strengths were on display?
- What were candidate's chief areas of difficulty as a decision maker? Can any specific circumstances be recalled when these difficulties manifested themselves?

Suggested Questions for Presidential Candidates: The Candidate as Possible President

In the sections that follow, I stress those aspects of the candidate's personal psychology and approach to leadership and decision making that seem relevant to presidential responsibilities. Many of the questions raised in the preceding sections are relevant to considering the candidate as possible president and will not be repeated here.

The Basic Public Dilemma

Presidential selection and performance take place in a psychological as well as an institutional and political context. Among presidential theorists, Barber has come closest to this idea with his concept of the "climate of expectations" (1992a, 6–7). The climate of expectations has to do with what the public may want from the president, for themselves. They may want, in Barber's view, reassurance (that things will be all right), a sense of progress (that the president will do something), or a sense of legitimacy (that the president is able and justifiably belongs in the role). In reality, it is hard to imagine that the public does not wish all three.

The basic public dilemma concept takes a somewhat different tack. Most presidents, I argue, come to office in a historical context characterized by an unresolved problem involving the relationship between the public and its institutions, political process, or a set of economic, social, or political circumstances. A candidate's responses to particular policy questions are not at issue here. Basic public dilemmas may frame specific policy questions, but the latter are not synonymous with the former.

Looking back to the presidency of Franklin Delano Roosevelt, we can easily see the origins of the basic public dilemma in 1932: a rapid deterioration of the nation's economic and social circumstances, which held damaging consequences for the political order. The dilemma itself, which arose from those circumstances but was not synonymous with them, was how, if at all, the federal government should respond to large-scale private circumstances that would alter the fundamental relationship between government and citizen. So, too, the basic public dilemma of the Reagan presidency is not difficult to frame, coming as that presidency did after the unsuccessful (each in their own ways) ones of Richard Nixon, Gerald Ford, and Jimmy Carter.

The basic public dilemma is, by its nature, likely to change, except in periods of consensus and stable politics. Therefore, the question becomes:

How does one uncover the basic public dilemma? I offer the following questions, in combination with one another, as potentially of some help in this regard:

- Has a really new set of political circumstances arisen in either the domestic or the international arena, in the past five years or so, that requires rethinking of the traditional ways that politics in either (or both) of these areas has been viewed? Does the candidate have any particular experience in either (or both) of these areas?
- Have there been any basic problems evident on the part of the public in relation to its political institutions, and especially the president, in the past six years or so?
- What was the chief failing of the last (two) president(s)? Was there any major problem that was either not addressed or inadequately addressed by the (two) previous administration(s)?
- What major unresolved question(s), which rests on presidential performance, frames American political life?

Character and Presidential Psychology: Temperament

Temperament reflects basic elements of an individual's emotional life. It is strongly rooted in, and related to, both the individual's biology and his or her psychology. We may recall (from chapter 5) that Allport defined temperament in part as equivalent to "an individual's emotional nature, including his susceptibility to emotional stimulation, his customary strength and speed of response, the quality of his prevailing mood" (1937, 54). Let us examine each of these factors briefly.

Susceptibility to emotional stimulation refers to the ability of a candidate to maintain emotional and psychological equilibrium when confronted with situations that trigger arousal. Among the general questions that can be asked here are:

- What evidence emerges from the campaign regarding the candidate's temperament?
- Is the candidate easily excitable?
- Does he have trouble maintaining psychological balance and equilibrium?
- Does it take a lot or a little to throw him off balance?
- Are there specific things that throw the candidate off balance, such as questions regarding his integrity, his competence, his grasp of the issues, his record?

- As far as can be determined, is his behavior in public consonant with his reactions in private? How, if at all, do they differ?

Some presidents have been able to maintain a remarkable sense of inner calm in the face of circumstances that would have caused many others considerable anxiety. Leuchtenburg, in his analysis of Franklin Roosevelt, writes:

F.D.R.'s view of himself and his world freed him from anxieties that other men would have found intolerable. Not even the weightiest responsibilities seemed to disturb his serenity . . . [A reporter noted,] "He seems to have a singularly fortunate faculty for not becoming flustered." Even after two terms in office, *Time* reported that: "He has one priceless attribute: a knack for locking up his and the world's worries in some secret mental compartment and then enjoying himself to the top of his bent." (1988, 14)

Leuchtenburg concludes that "this quality of survival, of physical toughness, of champagne ebullience is one key to the big man."

Perfect calm in the face of situations that would normally make one anxious, angry, or sad is neither the preferred nor the expected response. Many presidents have been known for their periodic outbursts of temper. Dwight Eisenhower's temper was famous (Greenstein 1982, 43–45; 1988, 81). Lyndon Johnson and Richard Nixon were also well known for their tempers, and it appears that William Clinton can be added to that list.

Occasional displays of temper are not, by themselves, psychologically significant. Sometimes presidential anger is constructive and appropriate.[5] However, there are some questions that might be usefully asked regarding candidates' displays of temper:

- Are the candidate's temper outbursts occasional or more regular?
- Are there particular issues that set off the temper displays?
- Does the candidate recover easily, or does he nurse grudges?
- Does he berate or belittle those with little power or likelihood of talking back?
- Is he aware of his temper? Does he try to control it? What methods has he evolved to do so?

Occasional outbursts of temper at the frustrations of office would not be unusual, especially for presidents motivated by the desire for accomplishment. However, an ability to understand and tolerate the frustrations that arise from the nature of the federal system, opposition from those who don't share the president's goals or views, or any number of other possible causes must certainly be considered part of the job.

Chronic anger outbursts reflect chronic internal and easily aroused anger. This, in turn, suggests unresolved psychological issues. These issues can arise from feelings of entitlement (How dare they stand in my way or call what I do into question!), from resentment (Who do they think they are! I won't stand for this!), or from low levels of tolerance for frustration.

Being angry is one thing, but failing to control it is quite another. Failure to control anger can spring from several sources. It can happen because the person lacks the capacity to rein in or modulate feelings, because the person is unable to acknowledge that he gets angry,[6] or because the person feels that he is entitled to his anger and doesn't care about trying to control it.

I now turn to the question of *mood*. Mood refers to a most typical (modal) state of the individual. Ordinarily, it does not reflect some extreme emotional state. People who are perpetually pleased by their lives are not much in touch with life's difficulties and disappointments, including their own. Those who overwhelmingly see their lives as lacking some essential element draw little comfort or pleasure from their efforts. Neither option seems particularly suited for presidential responsibilities. Neither is a modal mood that fluctuates widely, as it did for vice presidential candidate Thomas Eagleton, suitable for the responsibilities of high office, for reasons covered at length in chapter 6.

The kind of mood most useful for presidents is one that could be described as generally positive, in spite of adversity. What does "positive" mean here? It means a general mood tone buoyed by confidence, resilience, and energy. It does not mean that adversity is denied, only that it gets balanced.

Lastly, I consider the variable of *energy levels*. Energy levels are another prime example of a temperament element rooted in biology. Some individuals are able to maintain high levels of energy expenditure over time, without tiring as easily as others who need more sleep.

But energy levels are also shaped by psychology. Ambition increases energy, while depression depletes it. Most modern presidents, including Eisenhower (see Greenstein 1988, 38–42, for an examination of Eisenhower's actual and substantial habits of work), have apparently had substantial levels of energy. Presidents Kennedy, Johnson, Nixon, Bush, and Clinton are all presidents who fit this mold.

Generally speaking, substantial levels and reserves of energy are an important resource for anyone in a top executive position, and the presidency is certainly no exception. Yet like every other trait, excessive patterns of activity raise questions. A president who is always on the go, who finds it impossible to slow down, or who seems starved for stimulation (whether company, information, or activity) raises the question of what function all of this activity plays in his psychic economy. Is it a fear of being alone, the use of activity to define himself (I do, therefore I am), a fear of resting (letting go) because it will be difficult to start up again, or something else?

Character and Presidential Psychology: The Domain of Ambition

Ambition is a major psychological source of achievement. No modern president who sought and won the office—even Ronald Reagan, who is often analyzed in terms of his delegation of responsibilities—was without substantial amounts of it. Political psychologists have tended to view ambition as Lord Acton viewed power: ambition, like power, corrupts, and absolute ambition, like absolute power, corrupts absolutely.

Clinically, as Kohut (1977) has suggested, only the second part of this axiom is accurate. Moderate or even substantial ambition need not corrupt, as long as it is buttressed by a set of skills that enable the person to accomplish his purposes and, most importantly, tempered by realistic and firmly established ideals. So with these things in mind, we can ask the following questions regarding the ambition of presidential candidates:

- Does the candidate have relatively high ambition (keeping in mind the generally high state of ambition for those who seek the presidency)?
- How does the candidate explain his ambition? Does he disown it?
- How does his ambition manifest itself? Does the presidency seem important above all else?
- Are there boundaries the candidate will not cross to be elected? If so, what are they?
- Is there evidence that the candidate is willing to compromise his stated values? How does he explain this?
- Why does the candidate want to be president?
- Is the candidate's ambition linked to any large-scale political, economic, or social design?
- Does the candidate give evidence that he will be satisfied with less than very substantial accomplishment, or must his accomplishments be very large for him to feel satisfaction?
- How does the candidate handle setbacks and disappointments? Does he take them in stride or lash out with blame toward those (other than himself) that he feels are responsible?

Character and Presidential Psychology: Political Skills
(see also previous questions)

Skills are the link between ambition and performance. Some skills relevant to presidential performance are on display to some degree during campaigns, but some are not. Some are particularly useful for the domain of political leadership, others are more relevant to the domain of decision making, and some apply to both.

- What does the candidate view as his major political skills relevant to the presidency? Are they to be found in the areas of public education, public mobilization, bargaining, persuasion, decision making, administration, policy or political orchestration, or policy implementation?
- How will he handle those areas in which he feels he does not have particularly strong skills?

Character and Presidential Psychology: The Domain of Relatedness
(see also previous questions)

- Does the candidate seem to move to accommodate people, stand somewhat apart from them, or not mind conflict with them?
- Does he count many as his friends, or does he tend to be somewhat reserved?
- Does the candidate care a great deal about what people think of him? Does he prefer compromise over conflict?
- Is there a substantial difference between his public and his private behavior? Is he "nice" in public and more hostile in private? Is he more "open" in public and less accessible in private?
- How does the candidate treat those he needs and those he doesn't?

Character and Presidential Psychology: The Domain of
Character Integrity
(see also previous questions)

- How does the candidate view himself, as a person and as a candidate?
- What ideals seem particularly important to the candidate?
- How has the candidate addressed the inevitable conflicts that occur between ambitions and ideals? Is there a particular experience that, in his or others' views, tends to show how he has handled this issue?
- How has the candidate responded when he has been unable to fully realize his ideals? Does he ignore the fact, try to explain it away, feel depressed and depleted, or strive to do better?

- What personal and/or political values seem particularly important to the candidate? How does he address the inevitable conflicts between and among ideals and values in a particular situation posed to him?
- Does he present himself directly and forthrightly?
- Does the candidate seem at ease with himself and the paths and values he has chosen?
- Does he have periods or episodes of self-doubt? Are these exceptions to the general rule or the rule itself?
- How does he handle criticism? Is he very ready to acknowledge it, resistant to hearing it, or will he consider and weigh it?

Character and Presidential Psychology: Decision Making
(see also previous questions)

- What evidence has been or is emerging from the campaign regarding the candidate's judgment?
- Does the candidate give evidence of being able to think well and clearly under pressure?
- Does the candidate rely heavily on his own counsel, or does he tend to place more weight on the views of his advisers?
- Whom does the candidate rely on as advisers? Where are they drawn from? Do any have independent stature, or are their fates linked directly and solely to that of the candidate?
- Does the candidate have particular experience in either domestic or international politics? Who will the candidate draw upon in area(s) where he has less experience?

Character and Presidential Psychology: Political Leadership
(see also previous questions)

- What issues does the candidate see as paramount?
- What are his personal and political goals? What does he want to accomplish? What is his time frame for doing so?
- Which groups does the candidate see as particularly in need of his attention as president?
- What concrete plans, if any, does the candidate have to work with those who now actively oppose him?

Conclusion

Psychological assessment is a complex task, given the nature of campaigns and the fact that behavior can spring from many sources. However, it is made more manageable by six facts. First, there is a great deal of behavior to observe in presidential campaigns. Even more important for psychologically minded observers, the behavior takes place over time and in different circumstances. This important fact carries with it several equally important implications.

It is difficult to be consistently "out of character" for long periods of time. Thus behavior sampled at one point can be checked against behavior at another point (in similar circumstances) for consistency or change. The fact that behavior takes place in different circumstances also allows an examination of the ways in which a candidate's psychology changes (or doesn't) in response to differing conditions.

Second, candidate behavior during a presidential campaign is, by its very nature, relevant (to some degree) to presidential performance. Candidates cannot help but give indications of how they would mobilize the electorate, handle setbacks or successes, or make hard judgments under the difficult circumstances of a campaign environment. Governing is not the same as campaigning (although the differences may become somewhat blurred during certain historical periods), and candidates who become president generally learn more about their new role by being in it and thus may learn new responses or strategies. However, at the basic psychological level of the three character elements we have examined in this study, it would be empirically surprising if a candidate's character changed when he became president.

Third, all the behavior referred to above is much more accessible, given modern technology, than ever before. The problem is not that the public cannot learn enough about the psychology of presidential candidates. It is that it must have a way of appreciating what it is seeing.

Fourth, there is a body of theory on which trained analysts can draw that helps to identify both behaviors and the psychologies they reflect. It is not a cookbook, nor is there a specific formula to be applied, without variation, in all cases. But psychoanalytic theory, broadly defined, supplemented by theories in cognitive, social, and developmental psychology and relevant theory drawn from the field of presidential behavior and political leadership, can provide solid intellectual and empirical grounding for developing psychologically framed and useful profiles of candidates.

Fifth, making psychological assessments of presidential candidates does not require that a full-scale psychologically informed biography be made of each candidate. To be sure, there is not enough time to do so, but that is not the primary reason. A useful psychologically framed profile of a candidate, oriented to the questions that are of direct concern (that is, those related to presidential performance), need not rely on a detailed accounting of the origin and development of the characteristics we might observe. What is needed is a profile that illuminates those aspects of a candidate's psychology that are relevant to the major domains of presidential performance.

Finally, the purpose of psychologically assessing presidential candidates is limited in another important way. We do not have the means, nor is it really necessary for the purposes of assessment, to specifically locate candidates on some measurement scale. For example, it is enough to know that a candidate has a grounded, consolidated sense of self-regard, as opposed to an inflated (or deflated) sense of self. It is enough to know that a candidate falls into an acceptable range; we do not need to calibrate nuances in order to make a useful contribution.

What is important is that profiles, however limited, be composite. This means that individual psychologies come in packages. It is important, in my view, to focus on the three basic character elements and their implications for the candidate's possible performance as president. However, these three elements, and their associated psychological traits, will reflect areas of strength as well as areas in which one would be wise to raise questions.

Most presidential candidates are persons of substantial accomplishment, so in examining them, we are looking at a small and, in some respects, unique sample. High ambition, for example, must be seen to some extent as a given, not a variable. The question then becomes not whether a person has substantial ambition but how he is prepared to satisfy it.

The purpose of psychological assessment is to help select the best from among a generally high-functioning group. This does not mean that any candidate will approach perfection. Every individual history contains disappointment and difficulty as well as satisfaction and success, and every presidential candidate will present a different configuration of strengths and weaknesses. It is important that each be given its due and that we keep in mind that we are seeking good enough individuals with the capacity to become good enough presidents. In the next chapter, I present a psychologically framed portrait of what, exactly, that might entail.

FIFTEEN

Conclusion: The Good Enough President

Every four years, the public selects one person to be president and delegates to him enormous power and equally enormous responsibilities. We expect him to accomplish a great many things. He is held responsible for us in world affairs. He is held responsible for us in his domestic policies. Most of all, he is held responsible for helping us to realize our dreams, satisfy our needs, fulfill our wants, even while allaying our fears.

The president also has other responsibilities. Contemporary American democracy is a discourse of many voices, and we expect him to blend this cacophony into a recognizable, even pleasing, chorus. He must deal both at home and abroad with many who do not share a commitment either to democratic process or, in some cases, to the existence of our government as it is constituted. He must deal with governments abroad who would destroy us—and domestically, with those who would destroy him—in a way that does no violence to the principles he is charged to uphold and the example he is expected to set.

The president is expected to reflect the best in us—what we aspire to but often fail to achieve. We expect him to retain his idealism and compassion even as we expect him to be shrewd and tough. Since we put our trust and faith in him, we expect him to know where he wants to lead and why. We expect him to know what will help us and avoid what will harm us. We want him to be able to place our hopes and fears in a context that will

380

allow us and him to see a solution. In short, we want more than knowledge. We want wisdom.

We have given the president a mixed tool kit to accomplish these purposes. He has enormous power, even command power, but its use must be carefully rationed. In a democracy, command power cannot be substituted for leadership. He must be able to work with others to accomplish his (and our) purposes, even as we ask him to stand on his principles. Ultimately, the issue of psychological suitability boils down to how can we find a person who could possibly accomplish these many, conflicting expectations.

Selecting the Right President: Ideal Type or Good Enough?

In this final chapter of my inquiry into psychological suitability, I draw a portrait and make some concluding remarks. The portrait I have in mind draws on the theory of character put forward in chapter 7, the theory of presidential performance put forward in chapter 8, and the issues of emotional stability discussed in chapters 3 and 4.

I use the term *portrait* for a particular reason. It connotes an image that is, to some degree, representational and to some degree, realistic. The realism in the portrait is a product of the theory. Nonetheless, the theory is, in some respects, provisional. Moreover, like any theory or portrait, some things are emphasized while others remain in the background. Therefore, while it is to be hoped that the portrait does justice to its subject, it cannot be presented as definitive.

I have characterized the portrait that follows as based on theory, and so it is not presented as an *ideal type*. An ideal type can be thought of as a model whose function is to throw into the sharpest possible relief the characteristics of which it is composed. This is done by drawing out and extending each characteristic so that its full conceptual and causal power is highlighted. As Kaplan (1964, 83) notes, "No state in history has been wholly, fully, 'truly' a democracy, just as no male has exhibited all the traits of masculinity in superlative degree—Athens did not extend suffrage to slaves, and even Achilles was given to tears. *But we can conceptualize perfect specimens of any species*" (emphasis added).

Kaplan adds that the fact that "there is nothing in the world corresponding to it does not of itself rob such a concept of scientific usefulness" (1964,

82), which is, generally speaking, to facilitate comparisons and serve as a springboard for hypothesis formulation. Still, he warns against the dangers of confusing ideal types with reality,[1] and those dangers seem particularly important to avoid in the area of psychological suitability. Aside from the particular logic-of-inquiry difficulties that Kaplan points out, the search for more psychologically suitable presidents runs a very strong risk: assessing presidential candidates on how well they measure up to an ideal psychological type risks adding layers of impossible perfection on already extremely high levels of expectation.

In analytic work, the phrase "narcissistic pursuit of perfection" refers to those who can only be satisfied when they feel they have obtained, and others confirm that they have achieved, the pinnacle of what they aspire to accomplish. Their work cannot be merely good, it must be great. The response to it must not only be positive but enthusiastic. Others cannot merely like them, they must admire them.

I use that phrase in this context because public expectations and many theoretical discussions leave the impression that when it comes to presidents, only the ideal will do. Our presidents must have lots of energy, invest it all wisely in the pursuit of their goals, enjoy the exercise of power, gain sustenance from their public roles and responsibilities, and, in general, derive the ultimate meaning of their presidencies from what they do. They are, of course, allowed some minor imperfections. President Franklin Roosevelt's attempt to pack the Supreme Court is seen as a somewhat overreaching but understandable (in view of Roosevelt's feelings that they were stopping his plans for the country) extension of his thrust for results (Barber 1992a, 299). Besides, Barber's argument continues, one has to compare this thrust for results with "the Eisenhowers and Coolidges, guardians of the proper system, [who] may so dignify process that they neglect results."

If a portrait of psychological suitability built on an ideal type simply compounds the problem, what other options are available? I take as my frame Winnicott's (1986, 144) felicitous term *good enough*. The term denotes, above all, sufficiency; that is, one is able enough, smart enough, empathetic enough, and so on. Naturally, the question arises: To what does "enough" refer? The answer is enough, sometimes more than enough, generally to accomplish what needs to be done.

Winnicott developed the term as an adjective preceding "mothering." His point was that mothers (and fathers) did not have to be perfectly attuned to their children, perfectly responsive, perfectly knowledgeable— indeed, perfect in any way. Rather, they had to be good enough. In the context of a child's emotional and physical development, this meant being attentive and attuned to the child's needs, recognizing his or her individuality and acting accordingly, and not allowing the parent's inevitable imperfections—limits of attention, of empathy, of energy—to compromise authentic feelings of love and relatedness.

A Good Enough President: A Portrait

Winnicott's point was that parents need not be perfect, as long as they did adequately enough of the things that needed to be done, enough of the time. What might such a term mean in political life? From the standpoint of a psychoanalytic and psychological framework of analysis, what is a good enough president?

Temperament

Let us start with the most basic building block of presidential performance, temperament. As discussed in chapter 5, temperament is a partially biologically grounded element of individual psychology. It refers, to recall Allport's (1937, 54) definition, to "the characteristic phenomena of an individual's emotional nature, including his susceptibility to emotional stimulation, his customary strength and speed of response, [and] the quality of his prevailing mood, and all peculiarities of fluctuation and intensity in mood." What specifically might this mean for a president?

It must be said again that psychology and experience can and often do modify temperament. Here, too, biology is not destiny. Yet we must be familiar with what may have needed to be modified in the course of development and how this modification was accomplished.

Let us begin with the president's level of physical energy. The presidency is an office of many demands, primarily of time and attention to the myriad problems a president is asked to face and the points of view that surround them. The president needs to have a sufficient store of physical (and emotional) energy to manage these tasks. A president's days are long but need not be grueling. It seems likely that the all-out pace of presidential campaigns is not necessarily a model for conduct within the office. Being at the top is hard, demanding work, but a daily schedule of sixteen-hour days is neither necessary nor desirable.

Energy levels are partially biological. Some individuals simply are able to do more over longer periods of time, without tiring, than others. But physical stamina is also partially psychological. Depression, fear of giving one's all in anxious anticipation of possible failure, the manic pursuit of one's ambitions, and the attempt to substitute action for unwanted feelings are all reasons that an individual's natural levels of activity may be modified. Candidates may invest enormous time and energy primarily because of personal ambition or need. In these cases the psychological formula becomes "I do because I must," "I do, therefore I am good," or "I do so that I don't have time to worry about it." As is the case with every other aspect of the portrait of a good enough president, this one must be analyzed *in relation* to its dynamics and function in the individual's psyche.

An adequate store of physical energy is a necessity, but an abundance is not necessarily a virtue. Lyndon Johnson used to brag that the American people were getting twice their money's worth because he generally put in two eight-hour days in one, punctuated by a mid-afternoon nap. He accomplished a lot, but his presidency floundered. George Bush was an extremely peripatetic president, but that did not save his reelection bid. William Clinton has demonstrated an enormous reserve of energy to invest in his presidency, but at the end of two years, his presidency, too, was floundering. Energy is not a substitute for some of the other, more important characterological elements.

When we see a candidate who is a whirlwind of energy, we need to be less awed by his endurance and more concerned about its psychological meaning. Restless and relentless activity can have many meanings. Sometimes it is associated with a low tolerance for "boredom." In these cases the individual has to be doing something, anything, in order to feel alive. For some, it means taking risks. For some, it requires being with others constantly to avoid being alone. For others, relentless activity and what is done during it are proof of accomplishment, virtue, or both.

Emotional stamina is related to its physical counterpart but refers to a somewhat different class of phenomenon. An individual has a store of physical energy, with a generally consistent level available to him, and the same is true of emotional stamina. The term refers to the capacity of an individual to invest himself in what he needs to do and the psychological capacity to persist in what can sometimes be emotionally draining circumstances. I noted before the many demands on a president for his time and attention. It is absolutely crucial that a president have an abundance of psychological resources to deal with the emotional vicissitudes of the presidency.

What are the emotional vicissitudes of the presidency? At their simplest level, they reflect the fact that every presidential interaction carries with it some emotional analogue. Did the president's approval ratings go up or down? Was the British prime minister difficult to convince of American good intentions in addressing England's dispute in Northern Ireland? Do Iraqi troops massing on the border with Kuwait mean war? These and a thousand other occurrences carry with them a psychological price tag for the president, whether he is fully aware of it or not. Most modern presidents age quickly in their role for just this reason.

Emotional stamina also entails emotional resiliency. It is easier in most cases (but see below) to maintain one's emotional balance when things are going well. Obviously, this experience will be somewhat episodic in the presidency. The president must have the ability to experience but not be paralyzed by the inevitable losses that he will confront. His bills will be stalled in Congress, allies will balk, enemies will try to derail his initiatives, and so on. A president who thrives only on success will be hard pressed to stay the emotional distance.

The president must not only be able to cope with the intense emotional demands for his time, attention, and favorable decisions, he must also be able to handle the *emotional variability* of the demands. He must be able to switch from one emotionally appropriate response to another (given the varied circumstances that he must address in a relatively short period). He must be able to contain his responses without denying them. If he is angry at Senator X for failing to follow through with a commitment, he must be able to be experience (and perhaps express) his anger while not allowing it to contaminate his consideration of, say, a welfare reform bill. He must also be able to experience pleasure and satisfaction at accomplishing one of his purposes without letting that emotional boost color his realistic calculations for getting Congressman Y to change his vote on a forthcoming measure.

The emotional life of the presidency places many responsibilities on the president. He has enormous power to achieve, but also to punish. As noted in chapter 4, the psychology of the White House can exacerbate tendencies toward entitlement, grandiosity, or overall narcissism that a president may have. The presidency requires a person in it who understands his own emotional makeup, its strengths and limitations, and has learned to build on the first and address the second.

The emotional balance and stability of a president are not a matter of temperament alone. Temperament is encased in a character structure, which can either provide the framework for emotional balance and stability or else exacerbate a president's vulnerabilities in this area.

I have suggested that character can be usefully conceptualized as a composite outcome of three basic elements: ambition, character integrity, and relatedness. I emphasize again the importance of the composite nature of character. The character elements are assembled in a package. Examining each alone will give only a limited and perhaps, in some ways, misleading picture.

Ambition

Let me start, however, with ambition. Presidents need ambition. It provides the motivational source of a desire to achieve, and this, in turn, is translated into what they will try to accomplish as president. A president without ambition is like a train without an engine.

Discussions of whether or not a candidate has enough "fire in his belly" confound two different levels of ambition. If a person is not willing to make considerable sacrifices to reach the presidency, he'd best not undertake the effort. However, there is an important difference between those who don't want it enough and those for whom it represents the ultimate personal and professional quest, worth any sacrifice, indignity, or tactic to get.

It is a mistake to think that disorders of ambition are the sole problem for such people. Political psychologists have worried that leaders driven to obtain powerful offices are defined by their need for power, which political psychologists view dynamically as helping to overcome low self-esteem. The psychological equation there is "I have so much power, I must be a good person."

This is, no doubt, a danger. But people are also driven to gain power for other reasons that are likely to be damaging, to them and to us. They may seek power because it is the ultimate validation of their unrealistically *high* self-esteem. Here the psychological equation runs "I have great power and people are deferential, therefore I truly must be the extraordinary person I believe myself to be." Or power can validate a somewhat idealized self-image: "I have been given great power because, knowing my high ideals and wish to help others, I deserve it."

The view that a strong aspiration for power can be used primarily as an *intrapsychic* compensation or mechanism of validation represents a substantial but incomplete understanding of the functions of grandiose ambition. The presidential candidate who aspires to office with grandiose plans for the public is, in many ways, as dangerous as the president who has none. The construction of monumental policy architecture is often meant as a narcissistic tribute to the wisdom, power, compassion, and so forth of the president. Great crises, such as wars or depressions, call for large measures. However, given the history of unintended consequences of even the most idealistically motivated large-scale public programs, one has to ask whether, at this stage of historical development, such sweeping plans, along with the promise that they will work as advertised, without drawbacks, aren't an example of denial in the service of grandiosity.

The psychology of ambition requires us to ask whether there is enough, whether there is too much, and what is its role in the individual's psychic economy. Will the candidate be satisfied with modest accomplishments, does he aspire to more substantial ones, or will only outstanding and monumental ones do?

In good circumstances, children begin life with grandiose ambitions but outgrow them.[2] Gradually, the child modulates his grandiosity in response to suitable, compassionately applied limits—his own, his parents', those imposed by others and by his environment. Some children, however, because of failures to set and maintain strong, appropriate, and principled limits retain their sense that they are different, special, entitled, and ultimately not to be limited by conventional boundaries. These are people whose ambition is still fueled by a fairly primitive sense of their own worth. Their ends therefore justify any means.

Often this leads to tendency to cut corners, to be less than forthcoming, to portray things always in the best possible light (in keeping with their own high views of themselves and their motives), and to be ready to bend the rules when it suits their convenience. Such persons are vulnerable to getting into political (and sometimes legal) trouble. They are so used to skirting and bending the edges of boundaries that it is not surprising when they sometimes cross the line.

The temptations of executive power are not confined to those with too much ambition. Many persons of lesser drive and talents succumb to more blatant forms of abuse. But the talented, highly ambitious candidate represents a particular danger in this regard.

Integrity: Ideals, Identity, and Self-Esteem

What safeguards are there against the dangers of intense ambition? The chief intrapsychic one is the candidate's commitment to a stable and consolidated set of ideals and values. It is for this reason that personal and political identity are so critical to assessment. Except at the extremes, it doesn't really matter psychologically whether a candidate has embraced conservative or liberal ideals and values. What matters, psychologically, is that the person has found some set of ideals, standards that help him to go beyond his own ambitions.

Yet it is not only a matter of expressed ideals. Ideals held only in the abstract are not necessarily a virtue, because their emotional and experiential roots are shallow. To continue to be committed, both publicly and privately, to one's ideals when it is not easy or when one will not be rewarded by others for doing so is among the most significant ethical steps one can take. To have principles is much easier than to stand up for them. Having the courage of one's ideals means that one must be prepared to lose some, or even all, of what one may wish to gain because there are other, more truly important things at stake than the candidate's personal gain. When ambition is tempered by the capacity for commitment to one's ideals under conditions of adversity, ambition is truly in the service of ideals, rather than the other way around.

The tendency of candidates in recent elections to try to increase their chances of being elected by blurring the lines of their political identities has complicated the assessment of their character integrity. It has further been complicated by the work of some academic theorists who believe that identities are transient and disposable, to be tried on and discarded according to convenience. This belief stands the traditional understanding of a rooted and continuing sense of self on its head and confuses persona with identity.

A disposable identity is an oxymoron. It is, psychologically, an empty or shallow shell, available to the individual primarily to be put in the service of his own ambitions. The byword in campaigns is to adapt and wear the persona that works, not the identity that needs to be developed—sometimes under difficult circumstances.

The ability of candidates to take tough, difficult stands is one criterion of a solid sense of ideals and values. The importance of this criterion becomes all the more telling when a candidate is able to resist the impulse to glide over the implications of what he thinks, rather than trying to have it both ways or expressing his ideals and values simply by criticizing opponents. Ultimately, the question of what, at base, a candidate stands for is among the most important that can be asked. It is not a partisan matter of particular policies per se but rather a matter of policies as an expression of what the person really believes, the convictions that he will not compromise, and the methods he will not use. In short, who, really, is he?

The consolidation of identity, built on fidelity to ideals, has another practical implication in connection with issues of boundaries and limits. The person who has reached his sense of identity by standing up for who he is, is also more likely to know who and what he is not. Barber's (1992a, 299) criticism of the "Eisenhowers and Coolidges, guardians of the proper system, [who] may so dignify process that they neglect results" overlooks a very important boundary-setting function of character. It is difficult to imagine Eisenhower (or Coolidge) attempting to pack the Supreme Court as Franklin Roosevelt did. Was Eisenhower devoid of policy ambitions? Clearly not (Greenstein 1982). The point which Roosevelt lost sight of was that the integrity of the chief judicial institution in the country was more important in the long run than whether it did or did not frustrate *his* policies and *his* view of what was best.

The importance of identity in both enabling and setting limits for the individual raises the issue of self-regard or self-esteem. It is a tricky concept. It is clear that too low a level of self-regard is not desirable in presidential candidates. Low self-esteem is too closely associated with fatalistic beliefs, a lack of hope that solutions can be found, and chronic worry that one cannot meet the challenges of the role. However, given the conviction of one's own value now necessary to support a serious candidacy, this does not seem a large concern. (An exception would be the case of a vice presidential candidate chosen more for ticket balance than competence, who succeeds to the office.)

A solidly grounded, continuous sense of oneself as a good enough person is central to character integrity and identity. They are, of course, related. Fidelity to the ideals and values that come to define one's identity helps to develop this sense of self-worth. So does the experience of working toward and accomplishing one's purposes in a direct and ethical way.

Political psychologists have long worried that leaders with low self-esteem would be successful in gaining political power, in part to overcome low estimates of themselves (Lasswell 1948). But Lasswell's case materials were drawn from relatively low-level, local leaders. Presidents were not among them. The issue is important because almost all modern, and many "premodern," presidents have been men of substantial accomplishment. Herbert Hoover, whose presidency is considered by many an abject failure, gained that office in part by his strong and successful world refugee relief work.

Presidents like Hoover had to have a sufficiently strong sense of self to accomplish a great deal in their professional careers. Moreover, success often helps build feelings of self-respect. The question is how to reconcile their accomplishments with the suggestion that they might have suffered from low self-esteem.

One possible answer is to focus on unconsolidated, and therefore labile, self-esteem, not low self-esteem. Such a sense of self-esteem is not incompatible with accomplishment. A person's family experience could have left him with the conviction that he was only as good as his last achievement. Or the individual may never have experienced fighting hard, against odds, and accomplishing a purpose. Or the individual may have never had the consolidating experience of standing up for his ideals under difficult circumstances.

The causes are many, the outcomes similar. The person is susceptible to substantial swings in his view of his own worth, or his worth is closely tied to some external measurement. One clue to this unconsolidated level of self-esteem is the individual's feeling that his accomplishments ultimately don't measure up or somehow fail to satisfy. Such persons often experience periodic doubts about what they are doing or have done.[3] Another clue is the relentless pursuit of validation or achievement.

It seems plausible that candidates who have reached the stage of being able to mount a serious run for the presidency will not ordinarily suffer from substantially low levels of self-worth. They are more likely to be susceptible to either *regular* swings in their self-esteem or an inflated and exaggerated sense of their own self-worth. The latter problem seems a particular danger, since such people often make substantial accomplishments. On the surface, their confidence seems well founded.

There is a question with such people as to whether they really have such highly inflated levels of self-esteem or whether these high levels are compensating for what are, in reality, low levels of self-esteem. This is, admittedly, a difficult clinical question,[4] but as a practical matter in candidate assessment, it makes no real difference. A candidate whose views and behaviors reflect a strength of conviction and a view of his own self-worth that reach the point of being exorbitant is a very risky selection. In contrast to the candidate with too many doubts, this person has too few. Convinced that he knows what's right, what's best for others, he can be unresponsive to others' realistic concerns.

Relatedness

The presidency is a highly personal and personalized institution. A number of observers have noted this "one person at the top" uniqueness, compared to the more numerous and thus diffuse members of other institutions. However, I approach the personal and personalized nature of the presidency from another vantage point. While the president is *the* single person in charge of this singularly critical institution in the American political system, he is never alone. Everywhere the president turns, there are people. There are people whose sole responsibility is to ensure that he is taken care of, protected, informed, appraised, advised, bolstered, kept on track, reminded of deadlines; to speak for him; to find out for him; to do what he can't do and, sometimes, what he shouldn't. The president's world is filled as much with people as it is with policy.

His relationships with Congress, with the press, with the public, with his own party and with the opposition, and with those who support and those who oppose him abroad—these and many more relationships that could be noted—all reflect the profoundly intense relational nature of the presidency. It is not only that this one man is at the center of this Archimedean institution but that his feelings and ways of dealing with all these relationships are also. It is a fact so obvious that its significance has not been fully appreciated.

Political scientists are used to dealing with the president's relationships with others in terms of a series of external concentric circles. At the center is the president, in the first outer ring are his most intimate and trusted advisers, and so on. However, there is another way to approach the relational presidency, and that is to examine the function of others in the president's inner psychology. Here, too, we deal with a series of concentric circles measured by a proximity–distance radius, with the important difference that they are *internal* rather than *external* and organized according to their psychological meaning and significance to the person.

Events, things, and especially people that have special emotional valence for the candidate or president are part of his internal world. In clinical theory, the study of these internal images—how they got there and what they mean—is the study of "object relations."[5] Among the important dimensions of this internal world of objects is whether a particular internal object is "good"—that is, whether it provides available memories and images of warmth, support, firm and loving care, and so forth—or "bad"—providing the opposite. A person can rigidly categorize particular objects on either basis (sometimes this is appropriate) or see the object as having qualities of both.[6]

The individual's internal representational world serves psychological functions.[7] "Bad" objects are constant reminders of what might (or perhaps is likely to) befall the person if he doesn't take appropriate steps. They are associated with difficulty in developing one's ambition; in maintaining fidelity to realistic, satisfying, and self-selected ideals; and in fully trusting others. "Good" objects provide exemplars of worthwhile ambitions and ideals and function to help sustain the individual in developing these.

What has this do with presidential candidates? Simply this: the nature and functions of a candidate's (and president's) internal world of "object relations" shape the external world of the relational presidency. Let me offer some examples.

The adequacy and degree of consolidation of a president's realistic sense of himself as an able, honorable person who stands for who he is make a considerable difference in how he approaches others. A president whose internal world includes important people and experience related to striving toward one's goals and reaching for one's ambitions will be more able to do so himself. A president whose internal object world has not included, for whatever reason, persons or experiences that form the basis of principled adherence to ideals will be much more susceptible to the lure of results, regardless of the process. A president whose internal world is populated by warm, supportive experiential objects (people or experiences) has something to sustain him in tough times, independent of what others on the outside, even his closest advisers, might say.

The president's primary experience with others is critical to how he treats his staff, his advisers, his appointees, and, ultimately, the public. What is the function of these people for the president? Are they *selfobjects,* that is, persons whose primary role is to provide something psychological for the president? Or are they independent persons whom the president feels comfortable asking for their best (views, work, etc.), even if it might not always be fully in accord with his positions or views? When the president's own sense of self is secure and consolidated, he can afford (psychologically) to allow people to be who they are rather than who he emotionally needs them to be.

A skeptic might ask: How would the average person establish a candidate's object relations? The answer does not consist of advice to put the candidate on the couch. Rather, it consists of knowing what to look for and asking the right questions (see, for example, some of the questions in chapter 14, especially those dealing with temperament, relatedness, decision making, and leadership). A candidate's interpersonal relations are fairly visible, consistent, and leave a long and easily remembered trail.

Another clue comes from the candidate's earlier experiences. Ordinarily, a person's early family life is very important in the development of his object relations. But one cannot depend on candidates to provide this information, especially those inclined to present themselves as they would like to be seen. On resigning the presidency, Richard Nixon, in his nationally televised farewell, twice recalled his mother as a "saint." Knowing that his father, Frank, was a stern, argumentative man, one can wonder about the connection between sainthood and martyrdom. But even at a level of analysis closer to the surface, one can wonder what effects being raised by a "saint" may have left. One need not wait for presidential resignations to ask "what might it have been like" questions.

The destination of character analysis for assessing suitability is presidential performance. How will the candidate perform as president? A focus on the candidate's ambition, character integrity, and ways of dealing with others provides strong clues for an answer to this most basic question.

Judgment and Decision Making

At the heart of presidential decision making lies presidential judgment. The president is given the ultimate authority to decide what elements should be given what weight. A president driven by his ambitions, policy or personal, is unlikely to make good judgments; he is too likely to focus on what *he* wants. Similarly, a president with too much confidence in the correctness of his own views is unlikely to take the views of others really seriously.

The president must know when to delay and when to act. Decisions delayed by doubt or lack of resolve become more difficult. Decisions reached too quickly stand the risk of substituting action for thought. Both are normal occupational hazards. In terms of temperament, the president must not be too stimulated or made anxious by the need to decide. A strong, stable, and consolidated sense of self is critical to these tasks. Solid, quiet confidence is to be preferred to the brash assertion that a candidate "can handle it."

Likewise, a stable identity, anchored by a consolidated set of ideals and values, is an absolutely essential partner to the intelligence needed to master information elements that accompany problems. The president's identity, values, ideals, and the experience from which these developed are the ultimate resource for perspective. Intelligence or information mastery alone, without such perspective, is unlikely to result in good judgments.

It is important for the president to be smart. The presidency is no place for shallow thinking. In campaigns, therefore, it is always necessary to try to get underneath or beyond the briefing-book answer, the day's "message." We need to know more about *how* a candidate thinks, as well as *what* he thinks.

But intelligence and judgment do not progress in lockstep. Past a certain, basic level, smarter is not necessarily better. However, there is an important aspect of how a candidate or president thinks that has not received wide attention. Imagine the president as fighter pilot, flying through a long stretch of contested territory. Ahead, below, above, and in back of him are planes from different groups—some friendly, some not; some neutral, some whose motives are unclear. Some are close by and flying parallel, others are following, others trying to overtake. Some are in the far distance, approaching slowly; others are approaching more rapidly. Blips on the horizon could or could not be matters of eventual concern. One cannot be absolutely certain what any of these other planes will do, and of course, the president's plane is also moving.

The metaphor of flying through contested territory may not be perfect, but it does capture a crucial element of political life: the ambiguity of the president's relations with others, even those in his own party. But the most important element of the metaphor involves thinking of each of those other planes—friendly, hostile, neutral, or unknown—as one in a stream of decisions. The president must keep his eye on all, although some require more intense focus than others. Those that are near must be examined differently from those that are far, those that are approaching quickly differently from those one will meet in time. And one must also have one's eye on the horizon, and the overall meaning of it all.

Most discussions of decision making assume a somewhat linear sequence. Yet the reality of presidential decision making would appear to resemble more closely the metaphor above. A president must be able to think well not only sequentially but in multidimensional space.

The talents necessary for this ability have not, as yet, been examined, but we can hazard some suggestions. A certain cognitive and emotional flexibility would seem to be important. A president must be able to switch gears without great stress. He must be able to go from the pleasurable to the difficult and back again, without dwelling on the first and avoiding the second. He must be able to hold things in his mind, focus on them, and work on them. He must be able and willing to see the consequences of his actions (or inaction) across time and circumstance. He must be able to correct his course, not on the basis of political or personal expediency but on the basis of fuller, deeper, richer understanding.

Adherence to any of the above will not result in perfection. Even presidents with solid characterological grounds for making good judgments will err. Judgment by definition involves risk, including the risk of being wrong. Rather than concentrate on whether a candidate or president has made mistakes, one would more usefully inquire carefully into what went wrong.

We don't very often ask presidents to explain their thinking fully. At best, questioners at presidential news conferences get one question and one follow-up. Interviewers suffer from a tendency to cover too much ground too quickly and are inhibited by worries about future access. A good possible venue for asking the kind of detailed reconstruction questions I have in mind here are the televised campaign debates. What went into a candidate's thinking about a particular decision, how he weighed the information, and on what basis he finally came to a decision are important questions, but only if questioners come to the questions with adequate preparation. The point is not to trip up the candidate (although that might happen) but rather to be in an authoritative and independent position to explore his thinking.

Political Leadership

Discussions of political leaders and leadership often stress the fit between what might be politically necessary at a particular historical point and the success and desirability of a particular leader. Carlyle and Erikson are among the best known and most influential proponents of the view that the times make the man. In this section, I do not so much discard their view as seriously modify it. I argue that in institutionally stable and developed democracies such as the United States, it is possible to set out a series of principles governing democratic leadership that apply regardless of historical circumstances, or at least regardless of most circumstances that we have faced to date as a nation.

It is a given that leadership involves a relationship between the leader and public. The public cedes enormous power to its chief executive, who in turn is bound by certain responsibilities and expectations. The public expects the president to know and be able to carry out his responsibilities. This is the expectation of competence, and it is possible to make a useful list of the competencies expected (Buchanan 1987, 101–36). From the perspective of the theory developed in this work, the crucial one is blending ambition and skill.

While competence is no small matter, it is not the only matter. If, at base, leadership is a relationship, then at its heart lie trust and trustworthiness. Trust and trustworthiness are the psychological foundation, the adhesive, of the citizen–leader relationship. In giving their trust, citizens bestow legitimacy. In being trustworthy, leaders earn it.

Why do I place so much emphasis on trust and trustworthiness? Because policy problems are pervasive, and proven answers are in short supply. Realistically, presidents can promise only to address problems, not necessarily to solve them. The expectation that policy can truly solve very difficult, long-standing problems, which may develop in new and complicating ways, has resulted in a large measure of cynicism about government and our presidents. But this is in part because presidents persist in claiming that they will provide what they can't accomplish. Part of the responsibility also lies with the public, who understandably wishes that those claims be true.

But a good deal of the responsibility lies with the candidates themselves. Either because they truly believe in their promises or because they think those promises will further their election chances (or both), they continue to promise rather than educate. Paralleling this trend is the blurring of political identities and the construction of personas for political advantage.

In the end, these trends damage everyone. Candidates gain office but cannot govern. Citizens therefore become less trusting, and as a result, it takes more effort by candidates and presidents to convince citizens that their worst suspicions are untrue. Ultimately, the fabric of democracy is in danger as the psychological adhesive that holds it together loosens.

The good enough president has ambition, even substantial ambition. He believes he can make things better and wants to try. He is not certain that he has all the right answers but believes he has a promising approach. He is willing, indeed, anxious to explain to the public, in an honest, straightforward way, what will be entailed by his plans. He shares with citizens the range of possibilities for success and what it would actually mean in concrete terms. He also candidly explains the risks involved in his efforts and limits of what can be accomplished. He is enough at ease with himself to acknowledge both the contributions that others have made to his views and the real concerns of those who oppose them. He is willing to explain his views without drawing artificial differences between himself and those who share only some of his views. He distinguishes himself from those who oppose his views without demeaning them or their concerns. Most of all, he is willing to stand by what he says, even if it proves unpopular. Ultimately, he subscribes to the belief that gaining public trust by candor is more important than gaining office by deceit.

Sound too good to be true, too perfect to be possible? Not really. I have simply described the consequences of a character development in which the person has found a way to express his aspirations for accomplishment, in a context of well-realized ideals, tempered by a sense of his responsibilities to himself and others. It is perhaps a measure of our current state that this clinically derived characterological outcome, drawn from analytic experience, not from a fantasy of an ideal type, seems so far removed from our realistic expectations.

Character and Performance in Historical Context

I noted above that many leadership theorists support the view that the times make the man. That view has merit, especially when the times are revolutionary and the institutional frameworks of the nations involved are either just developing or reaching the end of their rope. Luther ushered in the Reformation when the old order was failing. Gandhi ushered in a new order when the moral bankruptcy of the colonial system was evident. Lenin in Russia and Mao in China ushered in new political arrangements when the old ones had irretrievably broken down. The breakdown of old orders, whatever their specific arrangements, opens the way for leaders who can aspire to redefine the political culture. There is no doubt in such revolutionary circumstances that the times make the man, just as they allow the man to remake the times.

But how shall we conceptualize our own circumstances here? We have a two-hundred-year-old constitutional, political, social, and economic order that keeps evolving even as it retains essential forms. What can we say of American presidential leadership and context in these circumstances?

I argue that circumstances still matter, but in a less dramatic way than the great man–revolutionary times model would suggest. Given the nature of our system—its institutional strength, its history, and its capacity to evolve—our presidents don't rearrange the political order; they guide it. Occasionally, in special circumstances, they shape it.[8]

One way in which to understand how context matters is in how it shapes the *basic public dilemma*. I conceptualize that dilemma as a fundamental unresolved question concerning public psychology, facing each president on taking office, that has to do with the public's psychological connections to its institutions, leaders, and political process. The nature of the basic public dilemma does not negate the importance of the three character elements analyzed in this volume, but it may point toward relative emphases.

For example, in 1932 the question was whether the government should—and if so, how it could—respond to massive economic and social dislocation. In terms of our characterological model of presidential performance, the emphasis would fall on ambition and the skills associated with innovation and experimentation. On the character integrity level, it would focus on a sense of confidence that one *might* succeed, coupled with a willingness to admit that a particular plan might not. At the relational level, it would entail a capacity to give people hope, to assure them not that everything would be all right but that the president could be trusted to try hard on their behalf.

In the 1992 presidential election, trust and trustworthiness loomed large as the basic public dilemma. In the domain of ambition, this called for someone able and skilled, but not necessarily for a larger-than-life president to draft larger-than-life solutions. Solid competence was good enough. At the relational level, it called for a leader really in touch with the increasing concerns of ordinary citizens and who was not just expressing compassion as a political tool. Finally, in the area of character integrity, it called for a candidate who was honest with himself and others and willing to be seen for what he really was, rather than for what the latest focus group suggested was needed. In short, the particular circumstances of this basic public dilemma emphasized the need for a candidate whose ambitions had been tempered by the hard but honest pursuit of ideals that went beyond self-aggrandizement.

The basic public dilemma represents one way in which context shapes leadership, but there are others. As an illustration, I note two different states of the democratic order, one characterized by consensus and major areas of bipartisan agreement, the other by widespread disagreement and little, if any, consensus.

Obviously, the skills and character elements necessary for effective presidential performance will differ in each of these cases. The president's judgment will still be a crucial element in each case (reinforcing its status as the more crucial of the two performance elements); however, the tasks of leadership and the emphasis on the character elements related to it will differ. In times of consensus, the relational aspects of both character and leadership come to the fore. The ability to orchestrate becomes more central than the ability to mobilize. In times of disagreement, the ability to mobilize becomes paramount, and this entails a leader having a strongly articulated personal and political identity which helps to clarify and present in pure (and perhaps somewhat dramatic) form the core vision that shapes the leader's quest.

In times of consensus, the president's judgment revolves around evaluating the "tried and true" and making adjustments where necessary. Past experience is important because it can and does provide a judgment framework that fits current circumstances. In times of consensual disarray, judgment is, if anything, even more critical. In these circumstances the president is required to extrapolate from a past that, by definition, will not fit the present.

Moreover, it takes more self-confidence to be president in times of disarray than in times of consensus. Yet even in times of disarray, a president's self-confidence is better if it is tempered by a degree of realistic humility than if it is grandiose. The view "I think I can, and I will try" reflects a different characterological calculus than the view "There's no doubt I can, and I will." The latter may accurately reflect the candidate's view of himself but does an injustice to public. The disarray of consensus reflects a view among many that the old ways (whatever they were) are not working, yet what might take their place is unclear. In such circumstances, people seek reassurance, and it is tempting for candidates to inspire faith rather than realistic hope. The former rests on a somewhat unsubstantiated expectation of results, the latter on their possibility rather than their likelihood.

Conclusion

The concern with issues of psychological suitability and presidential character in American politics is likely to remain controversial. It should be kept in mind, however, that public and professional concern with these issues takes place within a context of the democratic selection of political leadership. For most political systems, in most historical periods, information about emotional stability, character, or the leadership ability of persons contending for power, even if available, would be irrelevant. Where political leaders are not freely chosen by citizens, it makes little sense to discuss these issues.

The question of whether this kind of analysis should be attempted seems moot at this point. Analyses of character and its relationship to presidential performance already are an important part of presidential campaigns and seem unlikely to disappear, as long as the discretionary nature of presidential power remains. The question is whether a responsible, useful, and solid theoretical foundation for such analyses can be found. The questions are not trivial, even if the form they have sometimes taken in recent presidential campaigns makes them appear to be so.

What can those of us who observe presidential candidates from the vantage point of individual psychology contribute to the presidential selection process? In my view, our most important contribution lies in asking, and attempting to answer, a set of questions about the behavior of candidates that includes the meaning of that behavior for presidential performance.

Ultimately, however, presidential selection is up to the voters. Character and candidate psychology count. But so do a candidate's political philosophy and specific policy views. It is the voter, not the expert, who assigns these factors specific weight in the constellation of individual and public concerns. This may, on occasion, be a source of frustration to those who weigh these factors by a different calculus. But ultimately, our purposes as psychologically informed analysts can only be to inform, discuss, and, if the circumstances warrant, forewarn.

There are, of course, recommendations contained within these functions, and analysts will reach their own conclusions about which candidate presents the best prospects. Our function, however, is not to substitute our views for the public's but to provide the basis for the public to better consider its own, along with our collective best interests. Any reasonable steps along this important path seem worth the effort and difficulties the journey may entail.

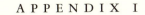

APPENDIX I

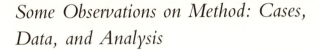

Some Observations on Method: Cases, Data, and Analysis

A Note on the Case Analyses

The core database from which these issues are developed and analyzed is a series of psychologically framed case studies of presidential campaigns in the years 1964, 1972, 1988, and 1992. Given the theoretical concerns of this study, there has been, of necessity, substantial discussion of some psychological characteristics of presidential candidates. However, the objective of these case studies is not primarily to provide detailed, "depth" psychological profiles of particular presidential candidates.

The purpose of these case studies is to illuminate the issues that arise in connection with developing a theory of character and its relationship to presidential performance. The specific psychological configurations of candidates' characters are part, but only a part, of the processes that need to be examined in illuminating such issues. The theoretical analyses put forward in this book are not meant to be judged by how deeply they delve into the psyches of the candidates or presidents involved.

The cases were not selected because issues of psychological suitability necessarily played *the* decisive role in the campaign outcome in each case. In some cases—for example, the impact of George McGovern's choice of Thomas Eagleton as running mate in the 1972 presidential campaign— issues of psychological suitability did not carry the decisive, causal weight of other factors in the outcome of the election. Nor was Gary Hart's aborted presidential bid selected for analysis because it played a decisive role in the final outcome of the 1988 presidential election.

The point here is not to prove that psychological factors always have definitive, causal importance but to begin to examine in detail some specific aspects of assessing the psychological suitability of presidential candidates. Each case was selected, therefore, because it framed, in a direct and accessible way, the conceptual, theoretical, psychological, political, and practical questions arising in the assessment of psychological suitability.[1] A brief explanation of the selection rationale for each case study follows.

There are two case studies each in the parts on assessing "mental health" and on assessing character. Before the presentation of the case studies in each part, there are two theoretical chapters that set the conceptual stage for the case studies which follow. The theoretical chapters that precede the case studies cast a wider conceptual net than the specific circumstances of the case materials. They are meant to provide a framework for analysis, and no attempt is made to reduce the former to the latter or vice versa.

The first two case studies appear in Part 2. They deal with the issue of psychological suitability from the perspective of psychological, or mental, health. The 1964 case study involves a detailed analysis of the attempt to assess the mental health of then–presidential candidate Barry Goldwater. This attempt to assess psychological suitability took the form of a questionnaire that was mailed to all members of the American Psychiatric Association, inviting them to assess the mental health of the Republican candidate. A number of psychiatrists chose to give their observations on this subject, and the results suggest some basic cautionary concerns when assessing psychological suitability.

The second case study in Part 2 deals with the unsuccessful candidacy of Thomas Eagleton in 1972. While Eagleton was a vice presidential, not a presidential, candidate, this case is selected and examined in depth because it is the first time that a candidate for such high public office was revealed to have been hospitalized for psychological problems. The Eagleton case represents an important opportunity to examine several questions of concern to us, especially (1) Is the psychological health of candidates truly something that needs to be worried about? and (2) What does the Eagleton case suggest about the structural barriers argument, which suggests that individuals with substantial problems of psychological functioning are screened out informally during their professional careers?

The second set of case studies appears in Part 3 of the book. These two were selected because they allow us to examine some important aspects of psychological suitability and presidential performance from the standpoint of character and its analysis. The first case study, in chapter 9, deals with the unsuccessful candidacy of Gary Hart in 1988. In that nominating campaign, Hart's candidacy was derailed by revelations that he had spent the weekend with a woman whom he had met at private party while campaigning.

The second case study, in chapters 10 and 11, focuses on the 1992 presidential campaign, and in particular on the candidacy of William J. Clinton who, of course, became president. I examine Clinton as a presidential candidate in chapter 10 and as president in chapter 11. On the surface, this campaign appeared to be one in which the public demanded, and to some extent was responsible for, a lessening of overt appeals to "character issues" (in other words, character attacks). However, a close analysis of the campaign waged by all three candidates suggests that character issues were absolutely central to their election strategies and played a decisive role in the public judgments that were made. Far from signaling the demise of the character issue, I argue that the 1992 election campaign represents a watershed in the relative weight accorded character and policy in the public's electoral judgment, with the outcome not yet decided.

Political psychologists studying leadership and others who study presidents are used to focusing on those who have obtained office. Yet in four detailed case studies (chapters 5, 6, 9, and 10–11), only one candidate whom I analyze, Bill Clinton, actually became president.

Would it not have been better to examine a series of presidential campaigns, select the winner of each campaign, and then proceed to do a detailed comparison of what each election revealed about the winning candidate and how he performed in office? Such an approach would have some advantages but would also suffer from at least three serious drawbacks. First, it would make electoral success, rather than theoretical usefulness, the criterion for case selection. For example, there have been only two modern sitting presidents of whom direct questions of psychological suitability in terms of psychological health were asked. One was Richard Nixon, during the period of the Watergate crisis when his presidency began to unravel. The other was Lyndon Johnson, based on a postpresidency allegation by a former aide that he may have been clinically paranoid.

In neither case was there much case material, beyond the concern (in Nixon's case) or the allegation (in Johnson's case). Concerns or allegations alone do not make theoretically useful and informative case materials. However, in neither case would examination of the campaigns that preceded their respective elections have cast much light on the complex issues surrounding this aspect of psychological suitability. It seemed much more theoretically useful to select the two cases where the issue was raised in a direct and documented way, as a method of exploring the intricacies of the issue.

A similar dynamic is operative in the cases selected regarding the character domain of psychological suitability. Character issues began to receive widespread public attention in the 1984 presidential campaign. To have concentrated only on successful candidates would have meant limiting the analyses to Presidents Reagan, Bush, and Clinton. In many respects, the Hart and Clinton case studies are much more instructive on the issues that surround the assessment of psychological suitability from the perspective of character. Here again, theoretical usefulness rather than electoral success seemed a better criterion. And of course, in focusing on the 1992 election, we have a case in which one of the candidates examined was electorally successful.

Second, adopting a strategy of comparing successful candidates' election campaigns with their presidential performance assumes the existence of a theory that allows such explicit comparisons. However, it is precisely that theory which this analysis is attempting to develop. Therefore, it seemed inadvisable to proceed with such a directly comparative strategy before more fully developing these areas conceptually, theoretically, and empirically.

Third, such a strategy would have made the major focus of this analysis what we learned (or did not learn) about a particular successful presidential candidate during the campaign. That is an important question, but not the only one. By looking at elected candidates, there is little chance to explore the full range of factors relevant to our concerns. Given such a focus, we cannot really explore Type I errors (ruling out on false grounds someone who would have been acceptable). Nor can we explore cases where the screening process apparently worked. Sometimes candidates such as Thomas Eagleton and Gary Hart are unsuccessful for reasons that are very important and instructive for developing a framework for the analysis of psychological suitability. Concentrating only on the electorally successful and ignoring those who tried and failed for reasons relevant to our theoretical concerns is like preparing for war by studying only victories.

A Note on Data and Analysis

The psychological analysis of psychological suitability and presidential performance is a complex undertaking. There are many ways in which it can falter. The psychologically based analysis of leaders has been tarnished by the attempt to explain large ranges of presidential behavior by one or a few "deep" psychological mechanisms,[2] naïveté, and, in some cases, blatant personal bias. How can these difficulties be avoided?

The only basis for making an assessment is to be aware of these dangers and proceed in a straightforward way. This requires that the theoretical basis of one's assessment and the steps through which the analysis proceeds be clearly stated. Such a process does not guarantee the lack of error, but it at least allows theories and analyses to be examined in a systematic way.

A major purpose of this book is to specify behavioral clusters and begin to account for them theoretically, using Greenstein's (1969) phenomenological and dynamic levels of analysis. In this I follow the process described by the Georges (1956, 317–20) as their method of approaching Woodrow Wilson. It consists of an interplay between an immersion in the basic behavioral data, tentative exploration, and use of appropriate psychological theory. First, the analyst becomes thoroughly familiar with the basic behavioral data[3] and the questions that emerge from it. Then he or she examines these data in the context of the psychological theory (or theories) that appears to best explain them. Often in that process the theory must be modified to fit the specific and complex patterns found in an individual life.

The approach employed herein is that of psychologically informed events analysis, guided by theories of presidential leadership in political psychology and comparative psychoanalytic theory. The first step consisted of gathering detailed personal and events data. To do this I depended in part on multiple, cross-checked news accounts of events; multiple, cross-checked biographical accounts; and the words of the candidates themselves.

The use of "public data" deserves some comment here. Each kind of public data is used in a specific way for a limited purpose, with recognition of each method's advantages and limitations. For example, the news and other journalistic accounts are primarily used as documentation of the major facts concerning a particular event: a presidential candidate made a particular pledge, a particular event took place within a certain sequence of events, and so on. The accounts themselves are, for the most part, concerned with describing events and the circumstances surrounding them. This material is an important part of the attempt to use specific "contexts" and "circumstances" in a theoretically useful way. Even so, detailed knowledge of events and the circumstances surrounding them is necessarily limited, so that news accounts can be used only with appreciation and acknowledgment of their limitations.

News accounts provide at least five kinds of important information for the analyst. First, they can be used to establish the basic existence of an event, that it has taken place. Second, the nature of the event and its place in a sequence of events can often provide an analyst with important information from which he or she may begin to construct an understanding of the meaning of the event. Third, news accounts can be used to help establish some of the circumstances surrounding an event. These details, while most likely incomplete, do help to deepen appreciation of the context. Fourth, news accounts may also convey some sense of an actor's understandings of these events, as reflected in his or her public discussions or actions. Fifth, and very important, by following such accounts over time, one can use later accounts and *outcomes* to cross-check the validity of earlier accounts. Differences between earlier and later public portrayals, as well as (often, in light of) the emergence into public discourse of private information relating to the candidate, can be important data for the analyst. They can reveal elements of presidential psychology and style that analysts must take into theoretical account.

Even when cross-checked, news accounts have at least three limitations that must be kept in mind. First, reporters may report events accurately but miss important aspects of an event because those aspects were not evident at the time, or because the reporters did not have access to all that went on, or because they simply didn't appreciate the implications of what they were reporting. Second, a reporter often pieces together his or her understanding of events in the form of a "story," and this subtext can be shaped either by a reporter's attitudes and views or by decisions (strategic or unconscious) on the part of the person(s) on whom the reporter relies. Third, stories can, on occasion, simply be in error. This is a special difficulty for covering presidents, but it also occurs when covering candidates. Both presidents and candidates (and their staffs) try to put the best frame on events. For all these reasons, events data must be *one* of a number of data sources that an analyst uses.

Another important source of data for psychologically informed events and case analysis is the candidate's own stated understanding and experience of the events. Therefore, key sources of supplementary evidence to accounts of events are the transcribed words of the candidates themselves. These include unstructured (but not necessarily unrehearsed) interviews, press conferences, and other spontaneously recorded transactions that are a part of every campaign and presidency.

It is obvious that the presidential candidates involved in the events this book analyzes have private understandings or motivations that they don't reveal (and may not even be aware of). Even so, I believe it would be a mistake to discard totally as unimportant analysis of their publicly stated views and behavior, for several reasons. First, candidates' publicly stated views and behavior may be very useful in revealing, sometimes quite starkly, what they wish to convey about themselves to others. Second, the public statements and overt behavior of candidates may actually reflect what they really think and how they are approaching their attempts to shape or respond to circumstances (a point that is often overlooked in discussions of the methodology surrounding case studies). But both of these reasons bolster the key reason for making use of these data elements, namely, to uncover and assemble a pattern of behaviors with which to construct a theoretically useful framework for explanation and analysis.

Each of these sources of information has its limitations. Formal speeches are good reflections of what candidates or presidents may wish to project or may themselves wish to believe. However, they do not necessarily reflect the conflicting views that may underlie the formal presentation, nor the political or personal calculations that went into it. Similarly, unstructured interviews, while in some ways more revealing of the candidate, are often not completely spontaneous. It is a fact of political life that candidates and presidents spend much time behind the scenes considering how they should approach or respond to public issues or events. Last, the amount of uncalculated information that is reflected in the give-and-take of a question-and-answer format depends in large part on the nature of the format. General questions from supportive or for other reasons uncritical audiences allow a candidate or president more opportunity to respond in preselected ways than in a real debate.

It is likely that more complete knowledge of specific circumstances will emerge in time. Participants may write their memoirs, documentation may emerge from files, and so on. These sources may, in turn, modify an analysis tentatively based on the circumstances, understandings, and motivations involved in the actions and events as described by the original accounts. However, should these additional data sources become available, they must be considered in the light of their own strengths and limitations. Memoirs by or interviews with major actors about past events in which they were involved are shaped by those participants' memories, views, and motives. Memos, reports, and minutes may also be helpful but limited in their usefulness. They may have been made with some particular purpose in mind; and they can be selective and may not cover important aspects of an event, either by omission or by purpose.

No single data source is beyond ambiguity or error. It is for this reason that, in the end, a researcher must rely on a confluence of evidence from several sources. It is the pattern and the density of factual elements which support it that provide the foundation for the theoretical analyses contained herein.

For these same reasons, the case studies presented here must be considered in terms of their purpose. That purpose is not to present a definitive account of the 1964, 1972, 1988, and 1992 presidential campaigns. Rather, it is to isolate and examine those dimensions of each campaign that are relevant to the issues we wish to examine. Specifically, the case studies provide a context in which to examine how issues of psychological suitability are raised and addressed in presidential campaigns, with what results, and with what implications for refining the analysis of character and presidential performance.

A Model of Character: Dynamics, Development, and Implications for Presidential Performance

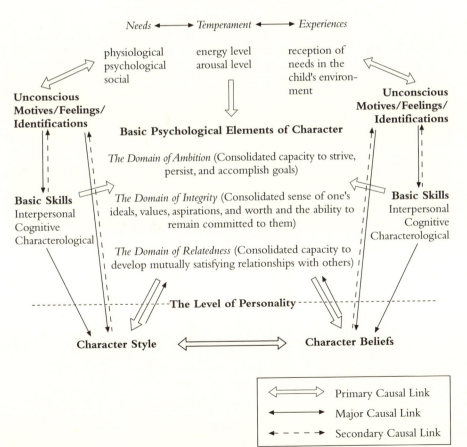

The Basic Foundation of Character

Needs ←——→ *Temperament* ←——→ *Experiences*

physiological   energy level   reception of
psychological   arousal level   needs in the
social   child's environ-
                                             ment

**Unconscious   Unconscious
Motives/Feelings/   Motives/Feelings/
Identifications**   **Identifications**

Basic Psychological Elements of Character

The Domain of Ambition (Consolidated capacity to strive,
persist, and accomplish goals)

Basic Skills   *The Domain of Integrity* (Consolidated sense of one's   **Basic Skills**
Interpersonal   ideals, values, aspirations, and worth and the ability to   Interpersonal
Cognitive   remain committed to them)   Cognitive
Characterological   Characterological

The Domain of Relatedness (Consolidated capacity to
develop mutually satisfying relationships with others)

- - - - - - - - - - - - - - - **The Level of Personality** - - - - - - - - - - - - - -

Character Style ⟸⟹ **Character Beliefs**

⟸⟹ Primary Causal Link
←——→ Major Causal Link
←- - -→ Secondary Causal Link

Character Style ⟵⟹ **Character Beliefs**

Characterological (Autonomous vs. Dependent)   *Mastery Beliefs*

Energy and motivational commitment

Capacity for effectiveness (mastery)—
moves directly toward goals

Secure identity and sense of self—
personal and professional goals shaped
by considered ideals and values

Persistence and resilience—
is able to tolerate setbacks and disagreements

Belief that effort is worthwhile

Belief that setbacks can be overcome

Belief that solutions can be found

Belief that one's skills can be refined and
developed

Cognitive (Analytical vs. Global)   *Identity Beliefs*

Preference for analytical/intuitive

Preference for introspective/reflection

Ability to extrapolate to action

One's values are important guides

One should try to live by one's values

I have been generally successful in living by
my values

I am a good enough person even though I
sometimes fall short as I strive

Interpersonal (Toward vs. Away from People)   *Relationship Beliefs*

Ability to make nonstrategic empathetic
connections with others

Ability to mobilize others, including those
not already disposed toward support

Capacity to work effectively with others,
including those not already disposed toward
support

Real connections with others are possible

People will, on balance, be responsive

People can, in general, be trusted

It is necessary and important to consider
others along with myself

Presidential Performance:
Decision Judgment and Political Leadership

⟵⟹	Primary Causal Link
◄———►	Major Causal Link
◄ – – – ►	Secondary Causal Link

Presidential Performance:
Decision Judgment and Political Leadership

Judgment in Decision Making   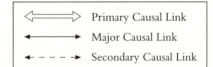   **Political Leadership**

Understanding/diagnosing problems
Ability to place problems in appropriate
judgment frameworks (relies primarily on
cognitive and characterological skills)

Mobilization
Ability to arouse, engage, and direct others
(relies on interpersonal and characterological
skills)

Political and policy judgments
Ability to synthesize, analyze, and draw
appropriate inferences (relies on cognitive,
interpersonal, and characterological skills)

Orchestration
Ability to organize others effectively for
purpose (relies on characterological and
interpersonal skills)

Implementation/Consolidation

Ability to place the results of one's judgments into an appropriate framework for action (relies
primarily on characterological, cognitive, and interpersonal skills)

<table>
<tr><td>⟸⟹</td><td>Primary Causal Link</td></tr>
<tr><td>←——→</td><td>Major Causal Link</td></tr>
<tr><td>←– – –→</td><td>Secondary Causal Link</td></tr>
</table>

APPENDIX 3

Preparing Political Leaders for Power: A Supplement to Assessing Psychological Suitability

I have contended in this book that screening presidential candidates for psychological suitability is an essential undertaking. However, in one important respect that emphasis overlooks another, potentially very important supplemental approach to issues of leadership suitability and performance, namely, *preparing* individuals for leadership roles and the exercise of power in a democracy.[1]

Becoming a presidential candidate is ordinarily the culmination of many years of public service, not its beginning. Consequently, a focus on assessing the psychological suitability of presidential candidates as a means of improving the quality of leadership in that office, though very important, comes rather late in the leadership selection process. Would it not be useful to look seriously at the question of preparing leaders for the exercise of political power, rather than to ask only how we can keep those who are inappropriate from obtaining it?[2]

My point here is not to argue for a special "school for presidents" but rather to examine more broadly the ways in which we might better prepare individuals as they advance through their careers in public service and political life. There are, of course, efforts being made. There are a large number of "schools of public policy" and even more programs in policy analysis, where the tools of decision making and even, on occasion, leadership development are taught. A small number of universities offer courses in professional socialization for specific groups of public officials for limited purposes. Harvard has played host to freshman congressional representatives and new mayors, and the specialized agencies of the government, such as the Pentagon, the Joint Chiefs of Staff, and the federal executive branch, have programs for government officials.

Yet each of these potentially useful vehicles suffers from substantial difficulties as a general model for leadership development as it applies to senior executive positions. Pentagon war games, for example, are designed to give participants experience in dealing with possible real-world problems with lethal consequences that must be solved quickly. These games are played because participants with important real-world responsibilities often do not have time to reflect on the issues that might be involved in such situations. Somewhat ironically, the games simulate reality by running eight hours a day and have many, sometimes conflicting messages coming into the control center and demanding an immediate response. In this case, simulation imitates life, perhaps too well.

Schools of public policy and analysis concentrate on empirical tools to gather data and empirical models by which to make decisions. Wildavsky (1987, xxix–xxx), surveying the curricula of many of them, has noted, "They have similar curricula. They teach microeconomic, quantitative modeling political and organizational studies, and either a practicum on some area of policy or a practicum combined with some effort to teach 'political economy; that is principles for or against government in different contexts.' "

By and large, Wildavsky concludes that the schools have succeeded in creating incrementalists who shy away from the more ambitious plans of those in the political arena. (I am not certain that all similarly trained policy analysts eschew more comprehensive solutions; otherwise how would one explain the quite large and complex Clinton plan for health care reform, presented under the auspices of a large number of government, academic, and foundation policy analysts?) His point is that those who have intelligence (read: the intellectual tools that result in incremental approaches) often lack power, while those who have power often lack intelligence. Only partially tongue in check, Wildavsky notes, "All else failing, the next move may be to train politicians to be analysts" (1987, xxxi). I think he was more correct than he knew.

The tools that Wildavsky cites as the basis for the schools' success, as useful as they can and have been in identifying trends and effects, are not without problems. Perhaps the most important problem is that many deep policy conflicts cannot be adequately addressed by an incrementalism which assumes that general values are shared and therefore that trade-offs will be acceptable to achieve maximum effect. Moreover, the tools of policy analysis tend to downplay the individual's role in *constructing* analysis. This is not an argument against the importance of evidence but a concern that the ways in which evidence is developed, construed, and applied are not a disembodied process.

The willingness to make trade-offs rests on the assumption that people generally agree and will be both willing to accept less of what they want to achieve and satisfied with only some of what they want. Especially in a context where there is fundamental value disagreement in many policy areas and where people feel that a benefit delayed is a benefit denied, the incrementalist approach to policy analysis will be less useful. Such approaches also fail to appreciate the extent to which the ideals, values, beliefs, and personal history of individual decision makers play an important role in the use of data and the construction of their interpretations.

Leadership Education: A Foundation of Ambivalence

Useful preparation for political leadership today consists primarily of on-the-job training. Derek Bok, when he was president of Harvard University, said that in preparation for public service, "politicians and appointed officials seldom receive an in-service education" (1989, 48). He noted that such training as there is "consists of brief orientations programs designed to prepare participants for their next job." He characterized a 1977 initiative by President Jimmy Carter to identify and train a "Senior Executive Service in the federal government" as "generally considered to have been a failure," in part because "little advanced training has occurred."

Bok (1989, 47) attributed the lack of resources devoted to leadership education in part to "longstanding doubts over whether special training is truly necessary for government service." Others are not convinced that it is desirable, even if it proves necessary. There are concerns about the potential "elitism" of leadership development and that specialized preparation may result in an increase in the psychological distance already built into leader–citizen relations.[3]

Even if leadership education and development are desirable, there remain a number of important problems to address. These include theoretical and practical questions regarding the nature, rationale, and (possible) content of such preparation. In this appendix, I begin by asking why demonstrated political success isn't enough. I suggest that the concept of learning enough to gain power is, in some important ways, limited. It may even be counterproductive and instill the wrong "lessons."

Even if there is something that could be learned that would better prepare leaders, a skeptic might ask whether it is possible to educate political leaders. Isn't "leadership education" an oxymoron? These are not cynical questions. Individuals become political leaders well after they reach adulthood, by which time they have developed many deeply rooted ways of doing things. How much change could education, whatever its goals, reasonably be expected to produce? I examine this question from the standpoint of developmental theory and focus on character and the cognitive frames and dynamics that underlie decision making.

Finally, I turn to a discussion of some practical issues concerning leadership education. Specifically, I focus on the goals of such education, the nature of the persons and groups for whom it might be useful, when in their careers it might usefully take place, who might provide it, and what might be the content of such education. I put forward a prototype educational seminar for those in positions of exercising discretionary power.

The Value of Experience: Why Isn't Success Sufficient?

The importance of electoral success in our system leads to some difficult issues in leadership education and development. There is a presumption of competence in success, especially when it is repeated. Therefore, one might ask whether repeated political success doesn't reflect the fact that effective political learning has already taken place. Certainly, it is a fact of political life that leaders who do not master their roles to some degree will not acquire much on-the-job experience. Political leaders are, after all, called upon to perform in ways that can be anticipated only to a limited degree by earlier socialization. Most leadership skills are developed or refined within the context of adulthood, not childhood. Learning by experience is clearly an important method of leadership development.

Experience, however, even that of success, has its limitations. It is more often a variable than a constant. Political leaders differ with regard to how much they can learn, the kind and range of experiences they have, and what they learn from them.[4] Most experience is complex and ambiguous enough to allow individuals with strongly held beliefs (especially those based in character) to presume that their psychological assumptions have been further legitimated.

Time pressures and workloads also tend to undercut the usefulness of experience. Powerful political roles are time- and effort-intensive. Moreover, American leadership culture frequently emphasizes "getting things done," and there is much to do. Allies must be consulted, enemies considered, strategy planned, decisions made, and so on. These pressures provide little time for reflective thinking, even if the leader is so inclined.[5] Thus one study of upper-level political officials in Washington, D.C. (Adams 1978/79), found that one of their chief complaints was that they had very little time to think![6]

It is not to be expected that reflection alone will necessarily result in adequate policies. For some problems there are no "good" solutions (Calabresi and Bobbitt 1979). Even when there are, thorough thinking is an aspect of, but not synonymous with, good policy judgment. The quality of policy thinking must also be considered in the context of leadership skills. As discussed in chapter 8, good policy judgment is one thing, effective leadership another. Still, sustained, thoughtful attention to policy issues would seem to be one ingredient of improving policy judgments, and the lack of time for this element is a cause for concern.

Some Limitations of Political Success as a Learning Experience

Many political successes are the result of narrow but effective forms of political learning, in which the aspiring leader has become adept at "playing the system." This dynamic can be found in the rise of campaign advisers, who set general campaign strategies to target distinct demographic groups with psychological and policy messages. These political advisers micromanage the candidate's presentation of self. In order to win, candidates, in varying degrees, allow it.

Powerful personal and political ambition is another source of narrow political learning that is highly associated with electoral and political success. The paradox here is that strong ambition is related to political learning, but not necessarily the kind preferred by democratic theorists. Lasswell (1948, 54) noted two aspects of those whom he termed *political men*.[7] First, they are strongly oriented toward power at the expense of other concerns and strongly focused on the historic and future possibilities regarding power. In other words, power-oriented leaders will be alert to the nature and operation of power in their environment, a precondition for learning. Second, power-oriented people will be sufficiently capable to "acquire and supply the skills appropriate to the demand," that is, they will develop skills needed to obtain power. In short, the motivated pursuit of power leads to a similarly motivated effort to learn about it.

Development, Consolidation, and Political Careers: Can Leaders Learn?

Any discussion regarding preparing political leaders for their public responsibilities is based on two premises: first, that to do so will be useful, and second, that it is possible. In this section I focus on the latter, emphasizing the two related aspects of leadership functioning that I established in chapter 8 as fundamental to presidential and, more generally, executive performance: (1) character and (2) the cognitive frames and operations that underlie judgment and decision making. The analysis herein focuses on the degree to which persons can develop these more basic levels of psychological functioning.[8]

Development can take the form of either reversal or elaboration. The first can occur when a leader's nonconfirming critical experience leads to a substantial change in the direction of a characteristic—for example, a leader starts out political life as a liberal but, because of a related set of critical experiences, reverses his belief system and becomes a conservative. Elaboration occurs when the leader's understanding of his interpersonal and political world deepens and becomes more highly specified, differentiated, and integrated. It is the second, developmental elaboration that is my chief focus here.

What evidence is there that leaders can and do develop? Is concrete, specific, role-related learning the most that can be expected with regard to preparing persons for higher political roles? It is to these questions that we now turn.

Character

I have analyzed character as the composite organization and functioning of three basic psychological domains: ambition, integrity, and relatedness. A successful outcome of character development would be characterized by ambition and purpose that are tempered by a strong sense of personal ideals and interpersonal values. In most cases, though, individual development is uneven and does not approach the outcome of an "ideal type." This should not be discouraging, unless one hopes to find perfection rather than a preponderance of "virtue" over "vice" in one's political leaders.

The questions before us, then, are how much change is possible or likely in the basic character elements we have examined, and under what circumstances change in character is possible. The clinical literature on personality change that is most relevant to this level of psychological functioning is that of psychoanalytic psychology. It suggests that change is neither quickly nor easily achieved (Strupp 1973). Emotional and behavioral patterns are held in place both by a person's psychological makeup and by the circumstances into which people place or find themselves. Character functioning varies with the individual; hence the range and limits of change and development (Volkan 1987; Chessick 1985). In general, however, adult emotional and behavioral patterns have developed over many years and countless experiences and are maintained by strong internal and external forces.

Yet there is some evidence that leaders can and do become aware over time of their personal patterns and try (not always successfully) to do something about them. For example, in discussing Woodrow Wilson's recurring political difficulties, George and George (1956, 321) note that "Wilson sensed the dangers implicit in his compulsive ambition" and made some "rudimentary effort of finding a means of protecting himself." Unfortunately, Wilson was not able to overcome the damaging political effects of this characterological flaw, and in the culminating effort of his political career (the League of Nations treaty), he went down in defeat.

Mazlish (1972, 125) offers another illustration. Assessing the development of Richard Nixon over the decade spanning 1960 to 1970, he notes some changes: "He has turned his problems and weaknesses into strengths. Racked by indecision, he has learned how to plan and concentrate ahead of time. Faced with the constant need to test himself, he has shown real courage on a number of occasions." One does, however, have to ask whether these changes constituted real development, given the behavior that led to Nixon's impeachment and resignation.

The Nixon and the Wilson examples suggest that leaders can become aware, perhaps with the help of trusted others (Colonel Edward M. House, in Wilson's case), of patterns of personally or politically damaging behavior. However, the examples also suggest how difficult it is for a leader to come to grips with these patterns on his own. This finding is hardly surprising.

Sixty years of clinical work in a wide variety of settings and using varied theoretical techniques have suggested how difficult it is fundamentally to alter basic patterns of behavior in adulthood. However, the clinical picture is by no means bleak. For example, while not everyone can be helped by insight-oriented psychology, the clinical literature over the last sixty years suggests that a substantial number do benefit by becoming more psychologically elaborated, differentiated, and integrated in the course of treatment. If this were not true, psychoanalysis and other forms of psychoanalytic psychotherapy would be unable to justify their clinical existence. One question before us is whether one can harness the techniques of guided insight analysis without necessarily requiring every aspiring political leader to undertake psychoanalysis, as has been suggested by some (Jones 1974).

What does the clinical literature say about how people make basic changes? First, basic change is preceded by some awareness that one's patterns are damaging and need revision. Second, change occurs when people are motivated to attempt it. And third, change occurs when a person gains insight and appreciation of the origins of his or her expectations of the world and others and the ways in which they become self-confirming.

The first two can be considered preliminary to the third. Basically, expectations become modified in the context of experience that does not work out as anticipated. This can be thought of as *corrective disconfirming experience*. The term is derived from Alexander's (1954a; 1954b) work on "corrective emotional experience."[9] Experience that runs counter to assumption can, in the proper context, form the basis of psychological change and development. We can see this principle at work in the second layer of psychological functioning, political beliefs and values, to which we now turn.

Cognitive Frames

One layer of psychological organization and functioning that is central to leadership, and particularly to decision making, consists of a leader's cognitive frames[10] and processes. What a leader believes will influence choices. For the most part, a leader's cognitive frames are accessible to both himself and others. Some beliefs, however, function at a more latent level.

Do the cognitive frames (belief systems) of political leaders develop in either of the two senses we have discussed above? Evidence suggests the answer is yes. Johnson (1977) examined the operational code of former U.S. senator Frank Church at the time of his emergence in politics (1956) and again at mid-career (1972) and found evidence of both continuity and development. The latter was strongly related to changes in the international system, including the Vietnam conflict and a thaw in the cold war that brought about deep changes in his views on Russia and China. In these cases, the beliefs that Senator Church started with were modified in response to external developments in the international system that could not easily have been encompassed within his original cognitive framework.

The importance of disconfirming political experience in the development of belief systems is also illustrated by the case of Richard Nixon. After graduating from law school, Nixon went to Washington and briefly worked for the Office of Price Administration (OPA). Here is how he described the changes in his belief systems over this time:

> I came out of college more liberal than I am today. I became more conservative after my experience at OPA. I also became greatly disillusioned about the bureaucracy and about what the government could do because I saw the terrible paperwork that people had to go through. For the first time when I was in OPA, I saw that there were people in government who were not satisfied with merely interpreting the regulations, enforcing the law that Congress passed, but who actually had a passion to get into business and used their government jobs to that end. That set me to think a lot. (Quoted in Mazlish 1972, 58)

This is Nixon's view of what prompted him to change, but it is instructive because it shows how old lessons and assumptions ran up against disconfirming experience and, as a result, were revised and replaced with new beliefs more consistent with that experience.

A similar reevaluation may be seen in Ronald Reagan's political transformation. He went from being a founding member of Americans for Democratic Action to a conservative anticommunist, at least in part because of his experience while president of the Screen Actors Guild during a time when a supposed attempt to infiltrate the guild was made by communist sympathizers.

Cognitive Dynamics

While cognitive content is clearly important, cognitive frames are not passive filing systems. They are infused with affect and developed over time in response to experience. They are dynamic, motivated psychological constructions.

The relationship of character and cognition to perception and understanding is complicated by perceptual style. Individuals differ, with significant consequences for understanding, in how they view the world. The issue here is not categories that identify content but literally how persons actually see the world. Some persons focus on details, others on whole configurations in viewing the world (Exner 1986). Glad (1983) reviewed Ronald Reagan's style of cognitive operation and suggested the important role that a few basic values, coupled with a tendency to see the world in somewhat global, highly differentiated terms,[11] played in his policy decisions. Finally, some weigh external stimulus properties more heavily, while others give more weight to their own intrapsychic constructions (Witkin, Goodenough, and Karp 1967).

These perceptual styles set the experiential foundation of perception and decision, but it is the logic of *judgment heuristics* that sets the frame of decision calculations. Judgment heuristics refers to the way in which the person actually arrives at an understanding and decision. What information does he or she give importance to, and why? How are these elements considered, integrated, or discarded in arriving at a decision? Tversky and Kahneman (1981) have shown that the way a political problem is presented will lead to a change in a person's calculation and decision, even when the alternatives presented have exact numerical equivalence!

Even if we assume that some form of examination by leaders of the cognitive operations they use in political and policy decision making would, on balance, be beneficial, the question still remains as to how much can be accomplished in this area. Neustadt and May (1986) focused on the appropriateness of the analogies that political decision makers use in their policy thinking and found many instances in which questionable parallels were drawn. They then designed a course at Harvard's Kennedy School of Government for mid- and upper-level government officials that effectively challenged how their students approached decision making, particularly the appropriateness of the historical analogues they used. They thought the course effective. However, some aspects of cognitive routines are firmly anchored in the operation of character elements and not so easily changed (Renshon 1989a). It may prove easier to change *what* leaders think than it is to change *how* they think.

Education for Leadership Development: For Whom, by Whom, and When?

What should the scope of leadership education be, and who should be educated? Who will provide such education, and when should it take place? Finally, there is the most important question of all: What might be the content of leadership education? In the brief sections that follow, I deal with the first three of these issues in turn, and then I move on to the most important question of what should be taught.

For Whom Is Leadership Education Intended?

Is leadership education meant only for the very highest-level policymakers or political leaders? Paige suggests that leadership development training would be particularly appropriate for "all successful candidates for national public office and to other leaders and citizens of national political prominence or promise" (1977, 205). His suggestion raises several questions.

Paige emphasizes the national level. At the time of his discussion, he could not have anticipated the increasing importance of state governments in policymaking (Osborne 1988). Therefore, it would seem prudent to include the state level in any discussion of leadership development, and one might add as a caution that local policymakers and leaders should not be automatically excluded either. In many cases, local decisions can have a large-scale impact.

Paige (1977) focuses on elected leaders; but isn't this too narrow? The only U.S. leaders who are elected at the national level are the president and 535 members of Congress. Is leadership development to be limited primarily to federal legislators?

In my view, this would be a mistake. Leadership development would include those in legislative roles, but there is a substantial degree of discretionary, independent policy and political power in many other roles. Certainly, one would not wish to exclude from consideration other functional policymaking roles in the federal, state, and perhaps local bureaucracies; nor would we wish to exclude, on an a priori basis, judicial roles.

I suggest that we should focus on executive leadership positions and executive dimensions of other political roles.[12] Specifically, I focus on those positions with authority and responsibility to decide and implement policy. My argument is that all positions with discretionary decision-making power involve certain commonalities. These, in turn, allow the possibility of leadership education that transcends specific functional roles.

By Whom Should Leaders Be Educated?

Under whose auspices would such programs be developed? Several possibilities are available. A number of research institutions, such as the Rand Corporation, and universities such as Harvard, the Massachusetts Institute of Technology (MIT), and the University of Chicago have run or are currently operating a variety of in-service or pre-service programs. However, universities are not the only institutions plausibly concerned with and potentially able to provide education for leadership development.

Schmidt (1960) reports the results of a productive collaboration between California's state Democratic and Republican parties and the University of California. Topics included "Leadership and the Discussion Process" and "Parliamentary Procedures and Political Parties," which are somewhat far from the areas developed in this appendix. Nonetheless, the experience left Schmidt with the impression that such an undertaking was both possible and worthwhile. This experiment remains the exception and not the rule.[13]

Another set of institutional prospects for developing programs of leadership education are the various professional associations whose members exercise policymaking or political power. An example is the National Governors Association (NGA), which provides a number of policy and other support services to the nation's governors. A substantial amount of informal and even formal socialization goes on at the various regional and national meetings of the association. The NGA sponsors policy debates and has even published a handbook for new governors (NGA 1978) on governing, as well as a book of reflections by former governors on the same subject (NGA 1981). It is not a large step to move from these initiatives to examining the kinds of leadership development issues we have been discussing.

When Should Leaders Be Educated?

What is the best time to undertake this education? Paige's (1977) discussion leaves the impression that leadership development is best undertaken after the leader has successfully been elected at the national level. I think it should begin earlier in a leader's career and continue throughout it. The ideal view of leadership education is that it is an ongoing learning process. To be sure, we can speak of the general preparation of political leaders as taking place over the entire life cycle, beginning in childhood and progressing through primary, secondary, and college experiences, and so on. This is a broadly accurate reflection of the socialization histories of many (but not all) who rise to positions of policymaking and political importance, but it is questionable whether, beyond the most general educational experiences, there should be comprehensive, special programs for anyone prior to the completion of undergraduate education.

There are several reasons for this view. First, the farther back one begins comprehensive leadership education, however that is defined, the more likely it is that a gap will develop between leaders and citizens. Second, such a policy would have to confront the importance of having a wide-ranging general education as a basis for later, more specialized training. This dilemma can be seen most clearly in medical schools, which to date have required very specialized undergraduate training in the sciences, to the exclusion of other subjects. In order to broaden the basis of a physician's judgment, many premedical curricula are reintroducing nontechnical subjects, and medical school admissions are increasingly allowing less specialized students to enter. Third, while general anticipatory socialization to leadership roles may be valuable, it cannot substitute for attention to leadership development once the person is actually in such a position.

Anticipatory socialization can provide a general approach to the dilemmas of exercising policy or political power, but many of the dilemmas that leaders face arise from the concrete circumstances of making decisions. As noted, it is one thing to favor policy values in the abstract, quite another to have to decide among competing values. Moreover, one can never fully anticipate all the factors that might bear on any decision or the ways in which circumstances may change over time. This is why political gaming, used as a learning exercise for leaders, can have important but only limited impact on how a leader might really decide, given a complex array of real circumstances. For these reasons, anticipatory socialization, however thorough, can never fully address the issues of exercising policymaking or political power.

These observations indicate that education for leadership development, in its specific sense, is the legitimate province of adult, role-related learning. But where in adulthood should such efforts be focused? Should they occur throughout it? If so, how are they to be reconciled with the enormous demands on the leader's time and the equally strong pressures for accomplishment that underlie leadership culture?

One suggestion regarding timing comes from the work of adult development theorists, especially Levinson (1978). Levinson found in his research on adult men that the adult life cycle could be characterized by attempts to build stable life structures, in which the person's aspirations and skills would find a place within the range of possibilities extant in society. Since no single life structure can contain all of these aspirations and skills simultaneously, and since the nature of the elements themselves undergoes change, each stable life structure is the product of changes, in some cases involving the transformation of previous life structures, in some cases simply modifying them. These transitions occurred to some degree in all of Levinson's subjects, in their twenties, thirties, forties, and fifties. The common thread was that the individual, to a greater or lesser degree, began to question aspects of the life structure already established. This suggests that education for leadership development should attempt to take advantage of these apparently natural (within our culture, at least) developmental periods of questioning and consolidation.

The point of focus should obviously be the individual's entry into policymaking or leadership roles. Among the many important questions that could be raised at this stage of development are: What ideals, values, and ambitions does this individual begin with? How do these first experiences in the role affect the individual? As the policymaker moves upward in the organizational hierarchy, the focus would include the consideration of lessons learned and changes in values and beliefs as a result of experience, as well as the dilemmas of practice that arise because of his new responsibilities.

Concepts of Leadership Performance and Preparation

Education implies the existence of specific goals, but in leadership education, the nature of these goals is far from clear. Do we aim for more technical competence, more commitment to democratic values, or better leadership skills? In short, what do we want to prepare leaders in a democracy to do?

The answers to these questions turn on our views of leadership performance. Hermann (1986) has described four views of the political leader: as a "pied piper," a salesperson, a puppet tossed on the winds of fate, and a firefighter. The pied piper recalls the tale of the town tricked out of its children. The leader as salesperson recalls the phrase "caveat emptor." The puppet image is antithetical to our commonsense understanding of the term *leader* and reflects either public anxiety (nothing can be done) or cynical nihilism (our leaders can't do anything anyway). Finally, the firefighter represents an image of some capacity for action (or at least some attempt), but of a reactive kind.

None of these images is particularly positive, and none leads us to a better appreciation of what leadership education might attempt to accomplish. Each presents us with quite a different rationale and direction for leadership preparation. If we assume the first view is the most descriptive of leaders, then our objective may be to desocialize any antidemocratic tendencies on the leader's part. If we assume the second view is more accurate, we may wish to concentrate our energies on educating citizens to be more intelligent "consumers" of leadership. If we assume the third, there will be little point in educating leaders, except perhaps to be more accepting of their fate. If we assume the fourth, we will want to equip our leaders with all the skills necessary to put out the many fires they will have to face.

At some point we need to ask whether the purpose of leadership education is to prepare trained technicians, develop supportive authority figures, train policy experts, or perhaps something else altogether. We have to ask not only what leaders do, if we are to think seriously about preparation, but what special capacities or talents political leadership in a democracy requires, and at present, there is considerable disagreement about this very issue.

I suggested in chapter 8 that decision making and leadership are the two fundamental elements of presidential (executive) performance. In the former arena, I have emphasized a president's judgment. In the latter, I have emphasized a president's ability to mobilize and engage others in the pursuit of policy goals. Both judgment and leadership are essentially built on a set of characterological, interpersonal, and cognitive skills.

Do these essential elements of presidential performance have implications for preparing individuals to exercise political power even if they don't aspire to that office? I believe they do. These are areas that would benefit from consideration throughout the leader's career, in a variety of settings. If decision making, judgment, and leadership are critical to performance, a case can be made for the utility of increasing the leader's knowledge regarding them and his skills at exercising them.

Making Decisions

There is, in the decision-making literature, a gap between the general models we use and the actual processes they are meant to describe. As Allison (1971) has pointed out, there has been some utility over the years in viewing decision makers as "rational actors" who are able to make sophisticated inferences and calculations from complex and ambiguous data. However, in a classic article some years ago, Lindblom (1959) described this model as the perfect description of what no one does.

As they reform the comprehensive rationality model, researchers of political and other forms of decision making have developed more realistic descriptions of the processes involved (George 1980; Janis and Mann 1977). They have also identified some personal, group, and structural factors that either inhibit or facilitate effective decision making. Some decision-making literature concentrates on the steps involved in making high-quality decisions (George 1980; Janis and Mann 1977). Research by cognitive psychologists (Nisbett and Ross 1980; Tversky and Kahneman 1981; Suedfeld 1992) has demonstrated that the way in which a problem is framed and understood has an enormous impact on the decision-making process. Research by social psychologists (Abelson 1959; Janis and Mann 1977) has focused on the complex mix of psychological inducements and inhibitions that affect persons with decision-making responsibility, as well as the unique dynamics that occur when individuals make decisions in groups (Janis 1984; t'Hart 1990), which are a very typical decision-making venue in public policy. Finally, psychoanalytically oriented political psychologists (George 1980) have suggested that an individual's own developmental history and his or her resulting psychological frameworks can have important implications for that person's approach to the decision-making process. Political and other social scientists have explored the ways in which decision makers use (and misuse) historical analogies to provide frameworks for decision analyses (Neustadt and May 1986; Khong 1992).

Familiarizing political leaders with the results of this research would certainly be helpful in preparing them for their work, especially for those in executive positions. Merely acquainting political leaders with these materials, however, is not likely to be enough. Educating leaders to make better decisions by exposing them solely to didactic courses or seminars is like trying to develop good psychoanalysts solely by having them read Freud.

What, then, is needed? Decision makers need periodic in-depth experiences that will allow them not only to confront the dilemmas of their responsibilities but to *reflect* on how they have approached them. This means gaining further appreciation of how they think, how and why they tended to weigh information as they did, and how their own values and motivations have influenced their decision-making processes. The need for this kind of self-knowledge among decision makers is well captured in the following comments of Saul Alinsky, who spent many years organizing radical reform. Here he discusses political activists, but his point is equally applicable to other kinds of leaders:

The one problem that the revolutionary cannot cope with by himself is that he must now and then have the opportunity to reflect and synthesize his thoughts. To gain that privacy in which to figure out what he is doing, why he is doing it, where he is going, what has been wrong with what he has done, and above all to see the relationships of all the episodes and acts as they tie into a general pattern [is extremely difficult]. (Quoted in Paige 1977, 201)

Alinsky suggests that, for most radicals, the most convenient and accessible time to begin this process is while the activist is in jail. One would hope that this undertaking would be accomplished in more congenial surroundings for those who would govern.

I suggest the term *guided self-reflection* for this process, to distinguish it from its psychotherapeutic counterparts on the one hand and from more didactic methods on the other. It would not be a psychotherapeutic process per se, since its direct purpose would not be to alleviate or resolve psychological conflict (although this might be a by-product). Even so, in a modified way it would make use of some analytic techniques that have developed over the past sixty years to encourage the reflective process. It would not be purely didactic, since it would encourage the decision maker to look inward, not only to master a set of strategic skills. The process would aim at developing insight and self-knowledge in connection with making public decisions, as well as increasing leaders' knowledge of the decision process itself.

The purpose of guided self-reflection would not (indeed, could not) be the impossible task of uncovering or eliminating all the many psychological factors that can interfere with good judgment but would rather be that of uncovering and tracing as many connections within the leader's policy thinking as possible, so that he or she will be aware of them.[14] This will require attention to at least two levels. The first would include how leaders gather and organize information relevant to solving particular problems. The second would look more closely at leaders' beliefs, assumptions, and inferences as they proceed through the process of reaching a decision.

Leadership as a Set of Relationships and the Exercise of Power

Exercising political power in a democracy is a matter not only of making the right choices but of implementing policies that effectively carry them out. The basic currency of power is compliance, and its ultimate weapon is force. The basic ingredients of democratic political power are earned legitimacy and authority, which reflect certain kinds of relationships between leaders and citizens.

Psychological processes relevant to leadership (and politics more generally) are interpersonal as well as intrapsychic. The interpersonal world of the leader is complex, for many developmental and institutional reasons. By adulthood, the leader has developed patterns of relating to people. In broad terms, the leader has developed, among other elements, views of whether or not people can be trusted and of whether the world is a hospitable or hostile place. These character beliefs operate at the level of global assumptions, but they alone do not determine the nature of a leader's contemporaneous relationships.

Relationships, like other aspects of individual functioning, generally become more differentiated throughout adulthood. So while relationships reflect a person's basic assumptions, they frequently include a more differentiated set of expectations, as well as relationship-specific behavior. For example, a leader may not trust people in general but may develop an expectation that certain classes of persons or individuals are different.

Trust is only one element of relationships. Whatever the level of basic trust, the leader must still deal with a variety of people important to his or her personal, political, and policy needs. These people, in turn, will have their own personal, political, and policy motives. This increases the complexity of the leader's relationships as he or she gains in stature, visibility, and power. At the same time, the leader's own public and private sets of responsibilities and obligations will also be developing.

Role Conflicts and Ethical Dilemmas

The interpersonal complexities of leadership in a mass society are enormous. Public officials and political leaders must distinguish among their loyalties, obligations, and responsibilities to, among others, themselves, other legitimate centers of political power, their professions (if they come from backgrounds that claim independent professional status and norms), "the public interest," and other relevant elected and appointed leaders. Two results are "role strain" and "role conflict," but at base, these dilemmas raise intense and difficult questions of character, ideals, values, policy goals, and, ultimately, personal and political ethics.

Political leaders are frequently required to make choices that affect themselves and others, often without time to reflect on all the values and considerations that went into them. One result may be that the process by which conflicting values, claims, and preferences have been weighed and decided remains somewhat opaque to a decision maker. The danger is that the full force of the conflictual elements not adequately addressed will spill over inappropriately into other decisions.

Even if the political decision maker recognizes these problems, there may not be an adequate context in which to work them through. In working with groups of high-level city officials in a management development program, I found that many had faced similar dilemmas, but they had no place to discuss and share their experience.[15]

How can leadership education help to address these problems? One obvious way is to provide a forum, away from their ongoing responsibilities, in which leaders can grapple with these and related issues. Many of the dilemmas surrounding the exercise of power, where the leader must balance conflicting motives, values, information, and feelings, are recurring. These issues have a basis not only in the leader's present responsibilities but in his or her developmental history. Both could profitably be explored in a neutral context.

Why would leaders be willing to undertake this somewhat difficult form of personal and political education? One reason is that their roles and work are likely to be key elements in their sense of self. It is the arena in which their ambitions and ideals are engaged. Gaining positions of policy or political leadership is labor-intensive work, to which substantial personal resources are ordinarily committed. Anything that promises to improve their capacity in an area of significant personal investment and importance is likely to gain at least a sympathetic hearing.

It is true that the higher one goes in policy or political hierarchies, the more one is likely to encounter strong ambition. But ambition is rarely the sole motivation of persons in those positions, and even where it dominates, it frequently operates in conjunction with other motivations. Political or policy leadership positions reflect many motivations. One of these is the desire for accomplishment, in the sense not only of having obtained a position but of doing something with it. These motivations are likely to be allies in the process of examining personal, interpersonal, policy, and leadership dilemmas.

A Proposal: The Decision Analysis Seminar— Developing Operational Skills in Policy Leadership and Decision Making

Most public executive development programs concentrate on teaching economic (cost-benefit) tools of analysis as the best method of rationally resolving public policy dilemmas. This approach is helpful but limited. As noted, a major problem with this approach is that many public problems involve dilemmas that are not easily addressed, much less resolved, by the external calculus of costs and benefits. Indeed, it is precisely because individual persons and groups involved in public dilemmas have very different subjective calculations of costs and benefits that a simple utilitarian calculus is unable to resolve many policy dilemmas.

In this section I put forward a suggestion for a prototype educational seminar for persons with discretionary power in formulating and implementing policy. I call it the Decision Analysis Seminar.* The basic idea of the seminar

---

* The Decision Analysis Seminar is copyrighted © 1996 by Stanley A. Renshon, and specific material from it and this appendix may be quoted and copied only with permission.

would be (1) to bring together a diverse group of policymakers to explore problems of substantial importance to them and the wider set of communities in which they operate; (2) to introduce the participants to substantive developments in the fields of political and policy decision making; and (3) to provide an opportunity and a context in which participants can better understand and strengthen their own approaches to making decisions. *This third point is the major purpose of the seminar.* It includes exploring the role that an individual's values and beliefs play in framing the problem, weighing information, and evaluating it, as well as the feelings associated with the exercise of power and the dilemmas that arise in exercising it.

This seminar builds on the decision seminar pioneered by Harold D. Lasswell in 1960. A major purpose of Lasswell's seminar was to bring policymakers in a particular area together to discuss the ways in which larger social and political elements (politics, the economy, the family, and so on) influenced the policy under consideration. In this respect, Lasswell's seminar is entirely opposite to the incremental, parochial curriculum described by Wildavsky, but for Lasswell as for Wildavsky, the focus remains on solving the policy problem *out there.*

The Decision Analysis Seminar takes a somewhat different approach. It would bring together a select group of individuals from a variety of policymaking backgrounds who now have a substantial degree of discretion in policymaking and implementation and can be expected to acquire more in the future. They would work together on an important public policy dilemma, making use of their own experiences.

The specific problem selected for the seminar would concern a major public policy issue in either the domestic or the international arena, depending on the group. One possible topic could be the use of force in post–cold war international relations; another could be reconciling policies that promote diversity with those that promote integration. What is important is that the topics chosen not address issues on which there is already a large consensus. Preexisting consensus on issues is not the best vehicle to explore the ways in which one's own values and experiences shape the construction of understanding.

The Decision Analysis Seminar would proceed along three sequential but overlapping and interrelated tracks:

The Decision Literature Track (First Frame)

As noted, there is now extensive academic literature on the dynamics of policy decision making. Contributions by political scientists, social psychologists, cognitive psychologists, and psychoanalytic psychologists have all provided important information on decision-making processes.[16] While some elements of this vast body of research and findings have filtered into the public domain, most participants will not be conversant with the full range of what each of these perspectives has to offer to assist them as they engage in the business of public policy formulation and decision making over the course of their careers.

One purpose of the Decision Analysis Seminar is to acquaint participants with the many important understandings that each of these psychological frames of decision analysis can bring to their decision-making skills. Another important purpose, however, is to explore the operation of these various dynamics within the context of the ongoing seminar itself. That is, participants not only would become familiar with theories of the ways in which various elements of individual and group psychology affect decision processes but would be given an opportunity in the second part of the seminar to reflect on the operation of these factors, as the group addresses and attempts to resolve the particular policy problem chosen for the seminar's focus.

The Policy Dilemma Track (Second Frame)

Becoming familiar with the theories and tools of high-quality decision making is an important undertaking. However, it is also very important that the appreciation of those tools become more fully integrated into the participant's repertoire of decision-making skills. To accomplish that purpose, the second track of the training seminar focuses on a concrete policy dilemma, specifically chosen for its importance and likelihood of engaging the participants.

The seminar participants will have wide latitude in deciding how best to address the policy issue and in attempting to forge, if possible, a range of understandings of the problem under consideration and its possible solutions. They will have to address and resolve such questions as: How do we frame the problem? What resources and alternatives are available? How do they affect the solutions proposed?

Seminar participants might also be asked to develop policy guidelines and a set of cautions and limiting assumptions for the policy dilemmas under consideration. This should help focus the work of the seminar, as well as providing an analysis, which might be circulated as a working paper, that may help further policy deliberations in this area. In addition, each participant, working on his or her own or as part of a small group, might be asked to undertake a final paper dealing with some aspect of the decision process drawn from the participant's own policy developing/making experiences. These papers might also prove of some value to others, and a mechanism might be found to circulate them more widely.

The information and evaluation search conducted by the seminar to address the problem under consideration will generally follow four separable stages:

1. Problem Framing and Problem Development:
   - What is the problem?
   - What are the various ways in which it can be conceived? What is the appropriate frame of analysis?
   - What factors account for the development of the problem?

2. The Formulation of Policy Alternatives:
   - What are the policy objectives?
   - What is the range of issues and values at stake?
   - How are these issues perceived by the various persons and groups who have an interest in (or will be affected by) this problem?
   - What are the political, social, ethical, and psychological implications of the alternatives suggested?
   - How might these implications be addressed? With what resources?
   - What are the implications of framing the problem in different ways?

3. Policy Implementation:
   - Assuming that a viable policy has been developed, how will it be implemented?
   - What resources will be needed to implement policy?
   - What issues are likely to arise in the implementation process?
   - How will these issues be addressed?

4. Policy Evaluation:
   - How will we know if a policy is accomplishing its purposes?
   - What measures or indicators, both subjective and objective, of failure and success can be developed? What would be the best indicators of success? Of failure?
   - What indicators could be developed to indicate trouble in the implementation process?

- How can information (which develops as the implementation process unfolds) be used to further refine the policy or its implementation?

The Guided Self-Reflection Track (Third Frame)

One of the dominant insights that psychoanalytic psychology provides to those interested in improving the quality of public decision making is that an individual's own experiences, values, assumptions, and emotional needs play an important role in the process. A key question, however, has been how one can translate that insight into a useful, efficient method of analytic insight.

Clearly, most decision makers do not have the time or the interest in being psychoanalyzed. Yet most decision makers would, I think, recognize the importance of becoming more aware of the ways in which their own values, experiences, and psychology play a role in how they approach and engage in the process of making decisions. That understanding is in keeping with some recent work in political decision making (Tetlock 1992; Renshon 1993b) that stresses the importance of an individual's capacity for—and level of—sound judgment in the decision-making process. The emphasis on the individual decision maker's judgment is not a substitute for following effective procedural decision-making routines, but is rather a supplement to those efforts.

The individual participant's subjective approach to the decision-making process will be an important and somewhat unique third track of the Decision Analysis Seminar. The mechanism I have developed is called *guided self-reflection*. Its purpose is to acquaint participants with the specific ways in which they approach the policy formulation and decision-making process.

Guided self-reflection is a technique developed out of an understanding of the psychoanalytic process but is not itself designed to be psychotherapeutic. It does not deal directly with unconscious processes or attempt to delve into the participant's early life or private life. Rather, it is directly related to the immediate and very accessible demands of the individual's public responsibilities.

Several techniques will be used to facilitate this important third level of understanding. These techniques have been developed in the course of my work with New York City's "Top 40" program, an executive training program for high-level New York City public officials. Each participant will be asked to keep a "decision journal" of his or her reactions to the unfolding decision seminar and its processes. The participants will be asked to address specific questions in this journal, designed to tap their own values, beliefs, and assumptions. Of particular interest will be the opportunity for them to reflect on the lessons they have learned about policymaking and leadership and the ways in which these lessons frame their approaches to the decision process.

A central feature of the second part of the seminar would be a series of individual meetings with the instructor to discuss and clarify further the issues that arise from the seminar or the journal in a one-to-one setting. In addition, there will be several sessions of the seminar, strategically placed throughout, devoted to discussing and analyzing the participant's personal reactions to the decision-making process as it unfolds.

The purpose of this third track of the Decision Analysis Seminar would be to sensitize the participants to the ways in which their own developmental experiences and resultant assumptive frames and feelings influence them as they go through the process of making decisions. Among the issues that this track would address are the following (the questions for each issue below are illustrative, not definitive):

1. Individual Responses to Decision-making Responsibilities (Material will be covered primarily in private, individual meetings with participants.):
   - Is making decisions generally easy or difficult for you? What aspects of making decisions come easily to you, and why? Are there any aspects of making decisions that you find somewhat difficult? What makes them difficult?
   - Thinking back on difficult public decisions that you have been involved with, which do you recall as particularly difficult? What made them so? How did you resolve the issues? What did you learn from the experience?

2. Individual Responses to Leadership Roles (Material will be covered both in the general sessions and in private, individual meetings with participants.):
   - How comfortable is the individual with taking the lead in policy matters? What aspects make him/her uncomfortable?
   - Sometimes being in a decision-making position makes one a lightning rod for criticism. Has that happened to participant? How has he/she handled this issue?

- Individuals in leadership roles are often expected to "get something done." Is that a fair expectation? What has been the participant's experience with this issue?
- Another expectation of leaders is that they have solutions, when often they are unsure. Has this ever been the participant's experience? How did he/she handle it?
- Sometimes good policies are not always politically acceptable. How has the participant handled that problem in the past? What lessons has he/she taken from these experiences?

3. Individual Reactions to Problem Formulation:
- How does the participant view the problem? Into what frame is it appropriate to place it?
- On what basis did the participant place the problem into that particular frame? What evidence was used? What weight was assigned to various elements of evidence? On what basis?
- Is this problem similar to others in the participant's experience? How are they alike?
- Is the participant aware of any feelings regarding the problem? Is he/she challenged, put off, indifferent to the problem?

4. Individual Reactions to the Formulation of Policy Alternatives (Participants may wish to share some of this material with others during group sessions devoted to the process. Other material would be covered in individual meetings with the instructor.):
- Do you feel all the relevant policy objectives were fully and fairly dealt with? Which, if any, were not? How do you account for this?
- Do you feel that the range of issues and values at stake in this problem was fully and fairly dealt with? What issues and values would you have given more weight to? On what basis?
- How would you assess the impact of the alternatives suggested on the various persons and groups who have an interest in or will be affected by this problem? On what basis did you reach these understandings?
- Does the participant have a view of the political, social, ethical, or psychological implications of the alternatives suggested that is different from views held by other participants? In what ways does the participant's view differ? What are the bases of these differences?
- How does the participant feel about the decisions being reached by

the group? Does participant feel he/she can support them? Are there any differences that participant feels are worth a fight? What would be the benefits and costs of strongly disagreeing?

5. Individual Responses to Policy Implementation:
   - Is participant comfortable with the implementation strategy being developed? Why or why not?
   - Is participant satisfied that the group has carefully considered all the important issues that are likely to arise in the implementation process? What factors seem particularly important to participant? Why?

6. Individual Responses to Policy Evaluation:
   - How will the participant know if a policy is accomplishing its purposes?
   - What indicators, both subjective and objective, would best measure success or failure?
   - How would the participant know if the policy was running into difficulty?

7. Individual Reactions to the Group's Functioning (Material will be covered primarily in private, individual meetings with participants.):
   - Does the individual generally feel comfortable expressing his/her positions in the group? Are there particular situations where the participant feels less comfortable in doing so? Why does he/she think this is happening?
   - How does the participant feel the group is performing? What does the group seem to be accomplishing? What makes the participant feel that way? Are there any areas of difficulty? If so, what makes the participant think that there are?
   - Does the group seem to have developed a leader? If so, on what basis has this happened? Is this a positive development for the group's purpose?
   - How does the participant feel about his/her own role in the group? Would he/she like it to be different? In what way(s)?
   - How is the participant's experience in this group similar to or different from his/her other experiences in group problem solving?

Conclusion

I asked why leaders should be willing to undertake the kind of professional education we have been discussing. A similar question could be asked of us as citizens: Why should we support programs for developing leadership skills? The answer is that public support for leadership development is a matter of citizen self-interest. In a complex, interdependent world where problems can't always be solved, much less anticipated, we are increasingly dependent on the character, good judgment, and competence of our leaders to solve difficult policy problems. Our current laissez-faire approach to leadership development is consistent with our democratic mythology and its assumption that "every child can become president." As an expression of our idealistic aspirations for equality of leadership opportunity and access, this aphorism has considerable ethical and substantive weight. But as a comment on the universal availability of the complex cognitive, emotional, and character traits essential to effective policymaking and political leadership in a democratic society, it is certainly incorrect.

The fact that political leaders and policymakers require special skills and capacities does not lend itself well to equal opportunity arguments, but this does not necessarily make leadership education an exercise in antidemocratic policy. There is research to suggest that leaders tend to be more supportive of democratic values than are citizens in general (Sniderman 1975), though one could argue that these commitments in principle may not hold in practice. Regardless, those who express concerns about elitism must also address the crucial issues of competence and capacity.

Above all, we need to look at the development of policymakers and political leaders as a policy issue, that is, as an important national problem that requires a comprehensive, integrated approach. We need to think through the problems of leadership development in a way that takes into account the skills and capacities necessary for service in a wide range of important roles in our society, where discretion and judgment are key ingredients. In addition, while applying our efforts to developing policy, we also need to invest resources in developing the people who will be responsible for them. None of this will happen easily or quickly, but the present patchwork of leadership development programs ensures a gap between what is needed and what is done. Democracies not only deserve better, they require it.

★ Notes

Notes to the Prologue

1. Early practitioners (and many later ones) viewed psychoanalysis as a general theory of psychological functioning rather than only a specialized theory of impairment. In commenting on the subtitle of his work with Bullitt on Woodrow Wilson *(A Psychological Study),* Freud wrote that it was justified because it expressed "our conviction that psychoanalysis is nothing but psychology" (1966, xvi). Not surprisingly, given this view of its wider applicability, psychoanalytic theory was, almost from the first, applied outside of the consulting room. Paul Roazen, a historian of the early psychoanalytic movement, reports that the very first psychoanalytic group, consisting of Freud, Alfred Adler, Wilhelm Stekel, Max Kahance, and Rudolph Reitler, began meeting in Freud's waiting room in 1902. According to Roazen (1971, 177; emphasis mine), "the discussions at the meeting were wide-ranging . . . papers by members, reviewed books, *examined historical figures,* presented case materials and raised theoretical subjects." Strachey, for example, in his "Editor's Introduction" to Freud's analysis of Leonardo da Vinci, confirms this and notes, "The minutes of the Vienna Psycho-Analytical Society . . . show that on a meeting of December 11, 1907, Freud made some remarks on psychoanalytic biography" (1910, 60n. 1).

In 1906, a year before his first excursion with his theory into literary analysis, Freud delivered a lecture at a law seminar (Freud 1906) in which he advocated the use of psychoanalysis in legal proceedings to establish the facts and to help determine guilt or innocence by "objective sign." This interest in the social and political contexts of psychoanalytic theory continued, and by 1918, funds had become available to support the publication of several psychoanalytic journals. They were also sufficeint to endow two yearly prizes, one in medicine and the other in *applied psychoanalysis* (Freud 1919a). That same year, Freud indicated his readiness to apply psychoanalytic theory to the problem of war neurosis. The First Psycho-Analytic Conference, held in Budapest in 1918, was, according to Freud, attended by "official representatives of the highest quarters of the European Powers." They were very interested in understanding and curing these war-related disorders, for obvious reasons, and Freud was equally interested in establishing his theory and expanding its domain. The result of these intersecting interests was an agreement to establish psychoanalytic centers to study and treat these disorders. But governement interest in this project waned when the war ended (Freud 1919b), much to Freud's disappointment.

These applications of psychoanalytic theory to social and political settings represent branches and not the major line of development in psychoanalytic theory. However, they do point to the persistent attempts of both Freud and his followers to apply the

439

theory in diverse social settings and not necessarily confine it to the thereapeutic practice. Freud himself encouraged this perspective with his own work in literature, anthropology, and political analysis.

Notes to the Introduction

1. Throughout this book I have adopted the convention of using the masculine pronoun to refer to both individual presidents and the role of president. I do so because, to date, all presidents and major-party presidential candidates have been men, as well as to avoid awkward linguistic conventions.

2. The traditional focus of "informed consent" has been on policy prescriptions or direction. However, this emphasis has tended to obscure another dimension of such consent, that based on the expectation of principled behavior by those chosen to exercise power. Legitimacy in this sense derives not only from the democratic nature of the process itself but from expectations regarding the behavior of the individuals who are temporarily given the power to govern.

3. In the 1990 congressional election Rudy Boschwitz, the incumbent senator from Minnesota, badly blundered by raising this issue. Boschwitz's campaign sent a letter to Jewish groups (with his permission) suggesting that his opponent Paul Wellstone, who is also Jewish but had married a Christian, did not raise his children as Jews. He ended by claiming that Wellstone had "no tie to the [Jewish] community" (*New York Times,* 11 November 1990, A26). Many people were outraged by this attack, and Boschwitz lost the election.

4. Candidates prefer generality to detail, for reasons that are not difficult to discern. General statements give the candidate more flexibility and fewer potential policy adversaries. But there is more than strategic calculation involved. There are an enormous number of potential issues in a presidential race. Most of these issues are complex, have long policy histories, and are not amenable to simple policy solutions. The expectation that a large number of these issues and a set of specific policy approaches to each will be discussed in depth would appear somewhat stringent. We also need to consider the very real possibility that candidates don't discuss a wide range of issues in depth because they may not have immediate or comprehensive solutions to these problems.

5. Among the difficulties that confront efforts to distinguish between character and persona in a campaign context are those that arise from theoretical ambiguities in the concepts themselves and those stemming from candidates' strategically motivated presentations of political self. In 1989, for example, George Bush added to his White House a senior staff member whose sole responsibility was to examine the Bush presidency with a view toward shaping its public messages and image (*New York Times,* 3 October 1989, A18). In the 1992 presidential election, Bill Clinton's chief advisers prepared a detailed memo on the specific "presentation of self" that would be needed to recast his image and a set of specific recommended public behaviors for Clinton and his wife (Kelly 1992g, 1). That document became official campaign strategy for presenting Bill Clinton and his wife to the public during the campaign (Kelly 1992g; *Newsweek* [November/December 1992g]: 4–42, 55–56).

There are several treatments of the rise of image advisers in election campaigns. Sabato (1991) provides an analysis of the rise of these operations in American politics. Two recent books by journalists (Simon 1990; Taylor 1990) provide a close-up examination of these image operations in specific campaigns. The particular implications of these campaigns for what the public needs to know about the candidates and what they get to see has yet to be addressed in any detail.

6. This is a criticism that has been made of Barber's (1972) influential *Presidential Character* (see George 1974a, 276). In the 1987 edition of his book (see Barber 1992a, chap. 13) has sought to anchor more firmly his two character dimensions (active/passive and positive/negative feelings about one's investments) in the psychological literature. However, while he succeeds in showing that a number of psychologists do use one or the other of these dimensions (in some form) in their work, this is not the same as showing that the two dimensions are used together or that they form the basis for a good understanding of character development and functioning. To be fair to Barber, it must be noted that he is a political scientist and has not put himself forward as a clinical psychologist or psychoanalyst. Therefore, he understandably appears to be interested not so much in developing a formal theory of character as in demonstrating the impact of some aspects of character on presidential performance.

7. Paige (1977, 11), for example, noted that of 2,164 articles published in the *American Political Science Review* from 1906 through 1963, the word *leader* or *leadership* appeared in article titles only seventeen times. In the years since Paige noted the relative neglect of political leadership by political scientists, the field of political leadership in political science and especially in political psychology has become more robust. Good examples of this trend are Barber ([1972] 1992a), George (1974a), Burns (1978), Greenstein (1982), Tucker (1981), Kellerman (1984), Hermann (1986), Heifetz (1994), and Skowronek (1993). These scholars differ, of course, in their conceptualizations of leadership, but individually and collectively they have furthered our understanding of leaders and their work.

All psychological studies of political leaders and leadership, including this one, owe a debt to the pioneering work of Lasswell (1930; 1948), Erikson (1958; 1969b), and George and George (1956).

8. I do not take up the important issue of physical health and its impact on psychological suitability in this work. Such an extension of my focus would add a further burden of complexity to the issues we examine. An excellent treatment of the issues involved in assessing and treating the physical health of leaders can be found in Post and Robins (1993).

9. Barber argues that personality shapes performance but then develops his famous fourfold typology of character. This leaves the impression that he views character and personality as somewhat synonymous. I differ somewhat in distinguishing character as the psychological foundation of the larger set of psychological characteristics that I consider personality to encompass.

10. See Greenstein (1969, 42–46) for a list of the circumstances in which leaders, and by analogy, presidential psychology, will have freer reign.

11. A president, of course, is tested upon taking office by many problems for which the public expects at least some partially successful response. In addition, presidents

come to office with their own views of what they wish to do, as well as the public's views of what they were elected to accomplish. The basic public dilemma to which I refer may be, but is not necessarily, related to either of these.

Notes to Chapter One

1. Evidence that public perceptions of a candidate's strengths and weakness in leadership skills and competence weigh heavily are found in numerous studies. For example, Markus (1982) analyzed the 1980 presidential race between incumbent Jimmy Carter and the challenger Ronald Reagan. Using data from the 1980 National Election Study, Markus (1982, 560) found that "the data clearly indicate that Carter's loss can be attributed to pervasive dissatisfaction with his first-term performance and doubt about his personal competence as a political leader."

2. The analysis of psychological suitability owes much to the work of several scholars in political psychology who pioneered in this area. Harold Lasswell's early (1930) discussion of "political man" as one who projected his private motives onto public life and rationalized the result in terms of public interest directly raised the question of leadership motivation. His work drew on early psychoanalytic formulations supplemented by the then-emerging theory of ego psychology. Somewhat later (1948), Lasswell examined the motivation to seek political power. He proposed a class of political men who urgently seek great political power and do so to compensate for low or irregular self-esteem. Lasswell later (1948; 1951) contrasted political man with his concept of the "democratic character." Among political activists, democratic characters sought a number of value outcomes, not just power. Moreover, such character types were willing to share power rather than just accumulate it. Finally, democratic character types among activists were, according to Lasswell, more inclined to be supportive of and practice democratic procedure.

In a somewhat later paper (1959) titled "Political Constitution and Character," Lasswell specifically argued that each system of government presupposed a fit between what its political processes required (psychologically) of people and how well citizens were able to adhere to these requirements, to ensure the ongoing viability of the system. Lasswell was suggesting that there were really two related dimensions involved in the fit between democratic and psychological political processes. One was at the "elite" level and concerned the suitability of those who specialized in political activity (e.g., democratic and political men). This corresponds to the focus of this book, which is presidential leadership. The second, or "mass," level at which a "fit is operative is public's support and tolerance of democratic procedures and their responsibilities and opportunities within that tradition."

George and George (1956), building on Lasswell's insights, asked a crucial question in their seminal study of Woodrow Wilson: How could a man so skilled in obtaining power run into such problems exercising it? Their study represents the first recognition of the rule of composite types, which is to say that presidents, like others, come to office with personality packages, not neat, clinical categories. Their study suggested that Lasswell's concern with low self-esteem was well founded but that the dangers were also tied to specific sets of circumstances.

Greenstein's (1969) careful analysis of the logic of inquiry in the study of personality and politics provided a number of important observations. Following the Georges' inquiry of the circumstances under which certain characterological difficulties might be triggered, Greenstein set out a number of general circumstances in which the personality and character of political leaders might find freer expression. An important insight of his analysis was the need to frame questions of psychological process more closely with context. He argued that the so-called large questions of psychological assessment, such as are reflected in the "great man" theory of political leadership, were ultimately less productive than examining the circumstances of specific linkages.

Barber's influential analysis ([1972] 1992a) of presidential character adopted a modified psychoanalytic framework developed specifically for assessing presidential candidates. His well-known framework views presidential psychology as arising from a president's character, worldview, and political style. Character, in Barber's view, consists of two continua: first, general activity levels, and second, feelings about that activity. He defines "suitability" in terms of the essential fit or lack thereof to be found between a president's character and worldview, on the one hand, and the climate of expectations—what the public needs (a sense of reassurance, progress, or legitimacy)—on the other.

3. The concept of judgment is analyzed at length in chapter 8.

4. An illustration is the problem of dependency and the institutionalization of the poverty cycle that have accompanied income maintenance programs for the poor (Murray 1984). An analysis of New York City's policy of providing housing to all who said they needed it (Dugger 1993) found that the city's initial generous policy had the perverse effect of encouraging many poorer New Yorkers to declare themselves homeless—and that a new system was needed to make sure that only the truly homeless were served.

5. Wattenberg (1991, 108) notes that "welfare spending" has acquired a steadily rising negative connotation and public support for it has dramatically declined. A 1994 *Times-Mirror* poll (Berke 1994) found a "striking decline in public support for social welfare programs," with a 12 percent decline from the previous year in the number of people who thought it the government's business to take care of people who can't take care of themselves. This is one reason why candidate Clinton's promise to "end welfare as we know it" was such a powerful campaign slogan.

6. A related problem here is that many social advocates have inflated and misused data to further their own narrow political agendas. Jenks, in his 1994 study of the homeless, noted that inflated estimates of over three million homeless were repeated as fact when they had no empirical basis. The purpose of these numbers was not to provide a basis for realistic policies but to stimulate a sense of crisis. He quotes (1994, 2) one researcher, Richard White, as calling this "lying for justice," and Jenks notes that "big numbers are politically useful."

7. I use the phrase "broadly conceived" to connote a view of psychoanalytic theory that considers a variety of theoretical perspectives as potentially useful, depending on the problem. The analogy that best seems to fit the circumstances of studies of presidential performance shaped by theories of political psychology is that of theory as a lens. We can liken the use of theory in this context to what occurs during an ophthalmology examination. During the examination, the patient focuses on a particular object while the ophthalmologist slides different lenses into an apparatus, asking the patient whether

each lens helps make objects clearer or not. To carry the analogy one step further, it might be that, through successive refinement, one *composite* formula will best cover both near and far sight. However, it might also prove the case that a different configuration will be needed for each.

Notes to Chapter Two

1. The Group for the Advancement of Psychiatry Task Force Report of the American Psychiatric Association notes that, "given the right circumstances, a psychoanalytically trained psychiatrist (or other professional in human behavior) can come to a rather reliable estimate of the principal motivational forces, the more significant personal conflicts, and the basic psychological adaptive measures of his subject. He may, in fact, be able to do so well in advance of his subject's own knowledge of them" (GAP 1973, 4). What are the right circumstances? According to the report, they consist of "a sustained, confidential professional relationship between the subject (ordinarily a patient) and a participating observer . . . , a relationship in which the subject gradually becomes capable of speaking with extreme candor, of relaxing some of his psychological defenses, and of experiencing, within the framework of the therapeutic sessions, a special kind of regressive relationship called transference." In other words, the right circumstances are found in a therapeutic relationship.

There can be no doubt that in developing an understanding of an individual's psychology, the level and nature of information obtained in analytic circumstances are superior to those obtained outside of it. In such circumstances the analyst gains information from at least five types of data: (1) the spontaneously expressed concerns and understandings of the patient over time; (2) responses to the analyst's framing or clarification of issues or information, as well as any interpretations that might be offered; (3) the nonverbal cues that accompany such information; (4) the patient's behavior with and toward the analyst (including, but not limited to, the transference); and (5) the patient's reaction to the raising of any issues connected to any of the preceding four types. However, the purpose of psychoanalytic treatment and the purpose of assessing psychological suitability are not the same. The purpose of the first is to allow the individual to come to grips with the consequences of his or her experience, while the purpose of the second is to develop a relatively rough understanding of the advantages and limitations of a particular composite of psychological elements. One does not need to obtain the level of information appropriate to the first to accomplish the second.

I have examined the different sources of data available for this undertaking, as well as their advantages and limitations, in appendix 1.

2. Levinson has pointed out that there is no doubt that "public figures, especially candidates for the Presidency, cannot plausibly claim any legal right to be exempt from public knowledge about any aspect of their lives" (1988, 264). To this Elms adds, "The Supreme Court has severely limited a public figure's right to privacy" (1976, 179).

3. This position has both a strong and a weak(er) form. The strongest form of the argument views any private behavior as publicly relevant. For some, every behavior reveals some aspect of the person and is therefore potentially relevant to public performance. For others, a "presumption of privacy" (*New York Times* editorial, 10 September 1988, A20) exists.

4. We can compare this position to that of the mayor of a medium-sized city, who, in comparison, has a much-reduced set of public responsibilities as well as a correspondingly smaller set of organizational and other resources available for power enactment. Under the criteria being proposed, the presumption of privacy would be stronger for mayors than for presidents, stronger for state legislators than for governors, and so on.

5. A U.S. senator, for example, holds a position with more power potential than does a state legislator in terms of the domains of public life each can potentially affect; but a U.S. senator does not have the discretionary power of most governors. The question that arises in considering discretion is how much latitude a leader or official has *on his own* to initiate, carry through, or decide a particular set of issues. A Supreme Court justice has enormous power potential when one considers the range of public life on which he or she may have an effect, but that justice must act in concert with eight others who have equal power potential. So, too, a U.S. senator must share his or her power potential with ninety-nine others. From this perspective, the mayor of a large city may have more discretionary power than a Supreme Court justice, although the latter could reasonably be argued to have a wider scope of power potential. According to the threshold guidelines proposed herein, the greater the discretionary power of the office or position, the weaker the presumption of privacy for that official.

6. The role of local civil judge, for example, has a fairly limited range of power potential and discretion. Local decisions apply only locally, and civil matters are limited in scope. A person in that position does have some discretionary power but is limited by law, precedent, and convention. Consequently, the range of personal characteristics that are typically engaged in enacting that role is limited too. By contrast, the role of a U.S. senator is much more varied, or to put it another way, there are many divergent ways one can choose to enact this particular role. Precedent, law, and convention provide only the broadest outlines for role enactment in this case, thus freeing the person to express a wider range of his own personal characteristics.

7. Fred I. Greenstein has pointed out to me (personal correspondence, 1993) that John Kennedy's well-documented extramarital relationships might well have been related to a machismo element in his character that had implications for his willingness to take risks in other areas, for example, with the Russians over cold war issues. Greenstein suggests, however, that this tendency was tempered to some degree by Kennedy's well-known personal detachment. One might argue, given this combination, that the affairs themselves were an attempt to overcome feelings of emotional detachment.

8. Freud acknowledged that his study of Wilson "did not originate without strong emotions," that he found Wilson "unsympathetic," and that "this aversion increased in the course of years the more I learned about him and the more severely we suffered from the consequences of his intrusion into our destiny" (Freud and Bullitt 1966, xiii, xvi). However, Freud went on to say these feelings "underwent a thorough subjugation" (1966, xvi) to a mixture of "sympathy, but sympathy of a special sort mixed with pity" (xv). This is hardly an auspicious vantage point from which to conduct such an analysis, and it has led some, such as Elms, to make the very sensible suggestion that the analyst "choose a subject towards whom he feels considerable ambivalence rather than harsh antagonism or uncritical adulation" (1976, 179).

9. The following discussion draws on my own psychoanalytic training and practice. I use the word *analyst* in this discussion to denote anyone with advanced psychoanalytic training in psychoanalytic psychotherapy and psychoanalysis. I treat these two areas as forming a continuum characterized by certain commonalities (the use of transference, the attempt to bring to the fore and work through previously unconscious material, and so on) as well as differences (number of weekly sessions, the nature and degree of the analyst's activity, and so on).

10. An exception is Kernberg, Goldstein, Hunt, Bauer, and Blumenthal (1981), whose work with borderline and other highly disturbed patients relies on making their anger manifest through confrontation.

11. There are several technical reasons for this. First, to cast interventions in an authoritative way reflects an assumption of certainty that is usually unwarranted in the complex psychological circumstances of analysis. Second, it may also be difficult for the patient, for many reasons, either to accept or to reject such certainty on the part of the analyst. Third, if the analyst is mistaken, he or she runs the risk of an empathic breach or other psychological harm. Fourth, a directly authoritative intervention tends to require the patient to accept or reject the whole intervention; in such circumstances the patient is not given the option of tentative or partial acceptance.

12. News accounts and reporters have tended to focus on the former, which are of some, but limited, utility. Academic theorists and observers have generally attempted to provide more comprehensive views of candidates' psychological functioning. The latter have had some influence on the former, but the degree to which more comprehensive theoretical views have been used in the public domain remains limited.

13. For these reasons and the practical reasons I outlined in the Introduction, I have relatively little to say in this book about the early developmental origins of the characterological and presidential performance patterns I discuss. Therefore, for example, although I analyze Bill Clinton as a presidential candidate in chapter 10 and as president in chapter 11, I have relatively little to say about Clinton's childhood. I do not analyze in detail the possible meanings of the loss of his biological father, of his relationship to his mother, or of the effects of his mother's absence when he was young or of his stepfather's alcoholism. In wishing to avoid the use of psychoanalytic formulations in this work around the meaning and impact on Bill Clinton (and other presidential candidates I examine herein) of his childhood experiences, I am not denying their importance. On the contrary, I subscribe to the view, based on my own clinical training and experience, that early experiences are, if not determinative, surely very important in shaping adult character and psychology.

Notes to Chapter Three

1. For an earlier formulation of these issues, see Renshon 1983.

2. While a decreased likelihood of nuclear war with the Soviet Union is probably the most important reason for the generally low level of concern about the mental impairment of presidents, it is not the only one. The comparative level of emotional difficulty involved in seriously confronting nuclear war probably contributes to the general public attitude of "it can't happen here" (Rogow 1963, 344), which is a form of denial. Many discussions in this area have been framed by the specter of a presidential

"Dr. Strangelove" following a tortured private vision to nuclear annihilation. Such Hollywood-inspired images give perhaps the most dramatic version of the possibilities involved but, as I argue in the next chapter, not necessarily the most accurate one. Severe impairment comes in many forms, not all of them overly dramatic.

The rise of character issues also has helped focus public attention on the domain of psychological suitability and away from issues of more severe impairment. Not only have character issues been more prevalent in recent presidential campaigns but they are probably, in some respects, easier for the public to confront emotionally than issues of severe impairment. The unfortunate results of presidential "character flaws" may come in the form of unethical or inappropriate exercise of discretionary powers. Often they may be associated with low-quality political and personal judgments. However, ordinarily the impairment of judgment associated with cases of "character flaws" will be less extreme than in cases of severe impairment. This does not make character-based difficulties in judgment desirable, only less likely to be disastrous in a larger public sense (character-based flaws in judgment may, of course, lead to personal or political disasters for a president).

3. The literature on the conceptualization of mental health/illness and the epistemological problems associated with such formulations are immense. Two extremely thoughtful and strong analyses of the difficulties involved may be found in Maklin 1972 and Moore 1975. Some of the discussion that follows draws on their careful analyses.

4. There are actually several different formulations of the medical model, but I will confine my discussion to those aspects relevant to diagnosis and understanding of "disease" entities. For a fuller discussion of the ways in which these models have been employed, see Siegler and Osmond 1974.

5. As Moore (1975, 1489) notes, "Since the concept of mind is intimately connected with our concept of what it is to be a person, predicating mental experiences, actions and intentions to another human being is not only necessary before we say what he has in mind, but also before we think of that being as a person."

6. Moore (1975, 1484) points out, "Although diseases might be *caused* by the presence in the body of some such entity (as a cold may be caused by a virus), and although they might be associated with *symptoms* that are concrete entities (e.g., the fluid present in the sinuses), a physical illness is not identical with its causes or its symptoms." As L. S. King notes (1954, 194), "Diseases are not things in the same sense of rocks or trees, or rivers, diseases . . . are not material." Many concepts in science (forces, electrons, etc.) are given ontological status in spite of the difficulty of specifying their concrete referents; and as Moore (1975, 1484) reminds us, we are not reticent in science or in everyday speech and understanding to confer "thinghood" on abstract qualities such as, "squareness, zoological species, or more to the point perhaps, psychological states."

7. Maklin (1972, 361) argues that the question of whether it is *ever* legitimate to extend or enlarge a concept may be answered without controversy in the affirmative. She then goes on to quote Margolis (1966, 73), who makes the point that "Szasz is absolutely right in holding that Freud reclassified types of suffering. But what he fails to see is that this is a perfectly legitimate (and even necessary) maneuver."

8. Infrequency of occurrence does not imply pathology either. Moore (1975, 1149) asks us to imagine a person with a cubical stomach that, while abnormal in its physical

structure, performs efficiently in digesting food and allows its owner an equally long life as would a "normal" stomach. As these illustrations indicate, normality in the limited sense of frequency may be quite irrelevant to the questions posed by the concepts of health and illness.

9. Lasswell (1930, 27; see also Boorse 1975) noted long ago that the line between health and illness is a gradient, not an abyss. However, clinical work over the last three decades on borderline and other forms of major character disorders have complicated the theoretical gradient considerably.

10. It must be emphasized, however, that these difficulties do not necessarily invalidate the idea of developing a theory of psychological suitability in *one* culture or with regard to one specific political role. It may well be the case that there is no universal way in which specific aspects of psychological well-being manifest themselves in differences across cultures, behavior, or time. However, in raising this point as an argument against any attempt to assess psychological suitability, critics err. Attempting to appraise the concept in one culture and political setting is not dependent on the ability to do so in others. To put it another way, it may well be all right for a Kwakiutl to act as a member of that culture but not a presidential candidate.

11. Szasz's inclusion of legal norms in his list is somewhat puzzling. It is true that forensic psychiatrists and other psychological professionals play a role in the legal system as expert witnesses, but it doesn't follow from this that legal norms underlie their professional assessments. Certainly, clinical theory and training do not rest on legal distinctions regarding capacity; if anything, the relationship is the reverse.

12. The experience of pain poses certain difficulties in attempting to make it a criterion in evaluating suitability. It might be transposed to political contexts via such manifestations as substantial stress, emotional discomfort, or other reflections of intrapsychic, interpersonal, or role conflict. But the capacity to experience these feelings is not necessarily associated with an inability to perform. On the contrary, the failure to experience emotional discomfort may itself result in compromising performance. Nor should it be assumed that psychological pain is equivalent to physical pain. Both are experienced as discomforts and both reflect an injury to or difficulty with some physiological or psychological system, but neither by itself is synonymous with incapacity. Finally, it is still a very open question as to whether emotional discomfort is as "normal" (in both the statistical and functional senses) in the psychological domain as absence of physical pain is for normally functioning persons in the physiological domain.

Similarly, incapacity as a criterion would have to specify a degree of inability. That, in turn, would have to be specifically derived from an understanding of the requirements of particular political roles. The functional requirements for some political roles, such as that of president, include a number of skills and can be conceptualized as involving numerous tasks (see, for example, Cronin 1975, 251, for a representative list of six tasks). Any understanding of psychological suitability would therefore have to distinguish among the range of personal skills as they relate to each proposed task of presidential performance. It would then be possible to begin the process of discerning which skills are really necessary for adequate or better performance as a president from among those that are only useful or that are irrelevant. I take up this task in chapter 8.

13. The third criterion, an increased risk of death, pain, or disability, seems somewhat unsuitable for application in the arena of political leadership. The first might be

useful to the extent that an individual recognizes that the source of his difficulty is himself. However, it is often the case that individuals cannot recognize their own contributions to their difficulties. Moreover, by the time most people reach adulthood, their ways of doing things have become comfortable and seemingly very normal (in more technical terms, *ego syntonic*). As I argue in the next chapter, the White House may be a place that leads its occupants to be particularly unlikely to recognize their own contributions to their personal and political difficulties.

14. It is this phenomenon that lies behind Greenstein's observation (1969, 12) that political scientists look to commonsense explanations for most ordinarily occurring events but look to psychological explanations only when something "out of the ordinary" occurs.

15. In the end, better clues to the relationship of character to power may lie in how the leader approaches power. How, for example, does the leader define "winning"? Is winning everything, the only thing that matters? Can the leader feel comfortable accomplishing some things instead of everything? How does the leader approach and treat those who disagree? Are they viewed as insufferable or misguided fools, or as respectable but wrong?

16. This is a source of paradox in Barber's (1992a) passive-negative presidential type, who does not invest enormous energy in exercising political power. While such a person may not invest a lot of emotional energy in exercising power, the nature of the contemporary American presidency almost guarantees that he must invest heavily to obtain it. Political reality exerts a certain pressure toward at least a moderate investment of time and effort. It is this set of facts that was the basis of Barber's early reformulation of the passive-negative category. A candidate who invests no (or little) personal energy or resources in obtaining the presidency and who has only the sense of duty to sustain him is not likely to spend the time and energy needed to obtain the presidency.

Notes to Chapter Four

1. On the back inside cover of *Mad Majesties,* for example, Rappaport is listed as also the author of *Royal Lovers and Mistresses* and *The Curse of the Romanoffs.*

2. See, for example, Henry 1970 and Macalpine and Hunter 1966. This list is meant to be illustrative, not exhaustive.

3. Mrs. Robert F. Noland generously made available to me a portion of her late husband's notes and data concerning this issue. The points that follow are my interpretations.

4. Some have argued, quite plausibly, that social structure and process and the experiences encountered therein give rise to specific psychological syndromes. It follows therefore that if social structure and process change significantly, so too will the psychological processes they generate. This argument is relevant to narcissistic and borderline character disorders but somewhat less so for other character disorders (e.g., obsessive-compulsive types).

Many of the royal bloodlines that were the basis for political recruitment into major political roles suffered from genetically based impairments as a result of frequent intermarriages. This is clearly not a major cause of psychological disorders in contemporary leadership recruitment patterns. There is some evidence, however, that the borderline and other major character disorders are on the increase and are directly related to aspects of political recruitment. We will take up this point at some length shortly.

5. Beyond the question of how frequently such instances occur lie several other issues of equal importance. Were such leaders impaired before or after assuming office? If they became so or are more likely to become so after obtaining office, then monitoring becomes an important concern. If they were impaired before gaining office, then screening clearly takes on added prominence.

6. I use the term *impairment* here to denote a functional disability of serious proportions. It is possible to be impaired without being substantially disabled. A person who has two drinks may be (slightly) impaired but not totally disabled.

7. A detailed consideration of the amendment and, in particular, Section 4 is beyond the scope of the present study. Background information on the concerns that led to the development of the Twenty-fifth Amendment can be found in the following congressional reports: (1) Senate Committee on the Judiciary, *Presidential Inability and Vacancies in the Office of the Vice President,* S. Rept. 1382, 88th Cong., 2d sess., August 13, 1964; (2) *Presidential Inability and Vacancies in the Office of Vice President,* S. Rept. 66, 89th Cong., 1st sess., February 10, 1965; (3) *Presidential Inability and Vice-Presidential Vacancy,* H. Rept. 203, 89th Cong., 1st sess., March 24, 1965; (4) *Report on Presidential Inability and Vacancies in the Office of the Vice President,* Conference Committee Report 564, 89th Cong., 1st sess., June 30, 1965; and (5) Senate Committee on the Judiciary, *Hearings on Presidential Inability and Vacancies in the Office of the Vice President,* 88th Cong., 2d sess., January 22, 1964. Other useful examinations of the issue are contained in Feerick 1976, Bayh 1968, a book on the issue edited by Thompson (1988), and the discussion in Post and Robins (1993, 171–79).

8. In fairness, however, it should be pointed out that the failure of admitting personnel immediately to distinguish these pseudopatients from their real counterparts is not so surprising. The pseudopatients arrived at the hospital in what appeared to be a state of distress, earnestly claiming to be experiencing psychotic symptoms, such as hearing voices. After they were admitted, the most highly trained staff members in the theory of psychiatry (e.g., psychiatrists) spent the least amount of time with the pseudo patients (or with the other patients). Their failure to make the correct diagnosis may therefore say less about the competence of the theory, as Rosenhan claimed, than about the personnel's commitment and attention to those most in need of help.

There is other evidence available which suggests that even severely regressed (real) patients may have an acute sense of certain vulnerabilities in others, especially in those whose help they may reject, such as therapists. One of the best and most detailed case studies of this problem can be found in Arieti 1974, 551–53. A more literary presentation of these same capacities may be found in Green 1972.

Notes to Chapter Five

1. The survey and its results are questionable on a number of grounds: methodological, clinical, ethical, and political. Therefore, it should be made clear at the outset that our interest in this survey is *not* for what it reveals about Senator Goldwater's mental health.

2. The following points are taken from an unpublished paper by David Ray, written while Ray was a graduate student at Stanford University.

3. This figure is low for a mailed survey; more typical returns, especially with follow-ups, run closer to rates of 50 and 60 percent.

4. My analysis of the questions raised in the cover letter draws on Rogow's (1970) description of it.

5. The study of friendships can give insight into a person's way of organizing interpersonal relationships. Important indicators would include the number, depth, kind, and functions that friendships serve for individuals. An excellent example of the richness of such data for understanding political leaders can be found in Brodie's (1981) analysis of Richard Nixon, especially Nixon's friendship with Bebe Rebozo. Further discussion of the political implications of interpersonal relationships, including patterns of friendships, can be found in Renshon 1989b, 235–38.

6. One additional source of difficulty in diagnostic consensus might be the different clinical views held by those respondents trained in psychoanalytic analysis from those of respondents who are not. In general, psychiatrists have medical training that includes a residency or related experience in psychiatry. Psychoanalysts, in contrast, need not have a medical degree and pursue a postdoctoral training program specifically related to the theory and practice of psychoanalysis. In the *FACT* survey, no distinction is made between those psychiatrists who have also had psychoanalytic training and those who have not. Not all psychiatrists are psychoanalysts, nor must all psychoanalysts be psychiatrists. Even among the psychoanalysts there are differences in theoretical orientation that might well result in different diagnostic sensitivities.

7. This has been a source of disappointment to some psychologically oriented political scientists (Lasswell 1938; Greenstein 1969). Greenson (1967), a well-known psychoanalyst, has noted several reasons for the lack of discussion of political values and issues, most obviously that individual treatment is oriented toward addressing personal and interpersonal, not political, problems. Among the various theories of psychoanalysis and psychiatry, only Sullivan specifically mentions the usefulness of exploring the patient's connections to the external world, including politics (Mullahy 1970, 200). Even here it is in the context of exploring interpersonal connections. Introducing other, nontherapeutic considerations into someone's treatment because of the analyst's own intellectual agenda would raise ethical as well as theoretical questions.

8. One reason for this is the fundamentally different nature of the two domains. Politics is concerned with the "authoritative allocation of values" (Easton 1965, 50), or to put the matter more directly, with "who gets what" (Lasswell 1936). In politics, sharp conflicts are generated by different values, and this is an expected fact of political life even during consensual periods. Political preferences need not rest on objective criteria and frequently do not. In the clinical tradition, theoretical perspectives and the interventions that are derived from them are dependent on systematic evidence and bodies of persuasive findings. One does not settle clinical questions by reference to the legitimacy of personal values, nor can one legitimately move from preference to advocacy on this basis, as one can in politics.

9. No attempt is made here to analyze how representative the points are that I discuss in the sections which follow, since, as noted, the responses do not constitute a

452   *Notes to Chapter Six*

sample. Furthermore, no assumption is made here that the criteria discussed in these sections are the best set of standards by which the psychological suitability of presidential candidates could be assessed.

10. The reasons for this are worth noting. First, the ability to assess the status of a person's (or leader's) intrapsychic and interpersonal functioning is not necessarily limited to psychiatrists. A given psychiatrist, for example, who has completed medical school and specialized in psychiatry, may not necessarily be any more competent to judge these areas by virtue of training or theory than a psychoanalyst who has completed a Ph.D. in clinical psychology and received postdoctoral training in an analytic institute or a political scientist who has had intensive training in relevant psychological theory. Second, while aspects of intrapsychic and interpersonal functioning, which fall within the expertise of psychoanalytic theory and training, are clearly important in assessing psychological suitability, they are not the only aspects of presidential functioning that require analysis. Cognitive characteristics, for example, are clearly important in decision making and judgment, yet while they are related to intrapsychic functioning at the level of character dynamics and interpersonal style, they are not synonymous with either. Clearly, a number of psychological theories will prove relevant for assessing the psychological suitability of leaders, not to mention more traditional concerns with a candidate's ability to handle the political and policy concerns of that office. A number of trained observers other than those with psychiatric training will also be needed.

11. The classic work in this area remains Rokeach 1960.

Notes to Chapter Six

1. These rumors were picked up and reported by the *Washington Times* (2 August 1988) and immediately denied by the Dukakis campaign, which said that Dukakis had never been treated for depression by a physician (*New York Times,* 3 August 1988, 10). The next day, on its front page, the *New York Times* reported a remark made by President Reagan at a news conference in answer to a reporter's question about the rumor: "Look, I'm not going to pick on an invalid" (a remark for which he later apologized). Soon after, Dukakis reversed himself and allowed his personal physician, Gerald R. Plotkin, to hold a press conference and discuss Dukakis's medical history.

2. Both Senator Eagleton and Senator McGovern declined to be interviewed concerning these events. Senator McGovern's description of the events is contained in his autobiography (McGovern 1977, 188–216). Senator Eagleton's view of the events is set forth in several brief interviews with *Time* and *Newsweek,* as well as an appearance on the television news program "Face the Nation." The specific sources for the Eagleton interviews are: "Eagleton's Odyssey," *Time,* 14 August 1972, 14–15; "Self, It Won't Be Easy," *Newsweek,* 7 August 1972, 17–19; and the transcription of Eagleton's appearance on "Face the Nation," 30 July 1972. In addition, case materials for this analysis are drawn from several excellent pieces on the Eagleton affair, among them Loye Miller, Jr., "The Eagleton Affair," *Miami Herald,* 8 December 1972, 30A; Milton Viorst, "Did Eagleton Do Anything Wrong?" *Esquire,* February 1973, 59–63; and the series by Haynes Johnson in the *Washington Post,* December 3–6, 1972. Basic coverage of the unfolding events, which this analysis also draws upon, can be found in the *New York Times,* July 26–27, 1972. Useful supplemental materials can be found in coverage by

major news magazines, for example, "A Crisis Called Eagleton," *Newsweek,* 7 August 1972, 12–16. Another good account within the context of a description of the whole campaign is White 1973, 256–89, which, however, relies on Eagleton's version of certain disputed conversations and events.

3. Mankiewicz's recollection of this important conversation is found in Viorst 1973, 62.

4. The account in the next two paragraphs draws on information contained in Miller 1972, 30A.

5. Miller also reports that Ann Wexler, then chair of the National Democratic Party, had received a call from an acquaintance familiar with St. Louis politics who warned her that Eagleton had been mentally ill and hospitalized because of it several times. Wexler insists she gave this information to Stearns at about 1 p.m. that Thursday afternoon. Stearns is equally insistent that Wexler gave him no such information. It is possible that Stearns, if he did receive the direct warning from Wexler, interpreted that information in light of the information he had received from his sources when he had checked into the rumors.

6. In the same news conference Eagleton reported that "as a younger man, I drove myself too hard" and revealed that when he was running for state attorney general, "I was in many instances my own driver . . . and I pushed myself terribly hard—long hours, day and night."

7. The term *reactive depression* has traditionally referred to a depression brought on by an external event such as some form of loss, while an *endogenous depression* is not directly traceable to some precipitating factor. The third edition of the *Diagnostic and Statistical Manual of Mental Disorders (DSM-III)* does not make this distinction (APA 1980, 205), since many severe depressions are associated with external factors even though not directly attributable to them.

8. The matter of Eagleton's medical records is a small but important tributary of this story. The anonymous informant who alerted the press and the McGovern campaign to Eagleton's difficulties used the phrase "manic-depressive state with suicidal tendencies," apparently reading from some kind of report (Viorst 1973, 142).

Notes to Chapter Seven

1. This formulation differs somewhat from those put forward by other political psychologists. Lasswell's (1930) discussion of "political man," one who projects his private motives onto public life and rationalizes the result in terms of public interest, draws on early psychoanalytic formulations. That model is concerned with showing the operation of unconscious motivation but not with the explication of character functioning itself beyond this single aspect. His later (Lasswell 1948) formulation of political man as one who pursues power as a compensation against low self-esteem delineates one character type found in politics but does not attempt a more general theory of character, political leadership, or their relationship.

Barber's (1992a) well-known typology posits that character consists of an activity continuum and a continuum (positive–negative) that reflects how one feels about what ones undertakes. The problem with the first is that activity levels themselves may reflect other, more basic psychological elements. For example, one may undertake to do more if one has a feeling of effectiveness and capacity. In this case activity level would be a reflection of the character element rather than the basic character element itself. Or it may be the case that activity can have a defensive component. The person who compulsively strives for accomplishment is at once active and driven. There are similar difficulties with Barber's second continuum—how one feels about what one undertakes. This is a derivative of self-esteem, and not necessarily the most reliable one. How well one is actually doing influences how one feels about the effort. By all accounts Richard Nixon, an active-negative in Barber's typology, enjoyed being president, at least until Watergate began to unravel his presidency.

2. Allport's distinction between character and personality reflects some important functional differences between the two. But it also tends to underestimate their connections. Character is the foundation and personality the superstructure, but personality has its roots in character, and the two are not independent entities.

Even at the level of personality, a distinction needs to be drawn between a political persona on the one hand and the political self on the other. The former is a creation, developed and shaped to suit the political currents of the moment. The latter is developed over time in response to the personal need to integrate the private self with public role responsibilities.

3. Freud mentioned character early in his writings (1908) but did not directly take up the subject for eight years (1916a; 1916b; 1916c). In those later papers, character difficulties were considered one aspect of the more general problem of neurosis and were given no special role in Freud's models of psychological functioning. Freud distinguished several "character types," among them those who claimed special privileges in reparation for infantile disadvantages, those "wrecked by success," and those whose Oedipal intentions produced enormous guilt. Somewhat later, Karl Abraham (1927) and Otto Fenichel (1945), Freud's disciples, added the "obsessive-compulsive" character to this list. According to Fenichel, character was "the habitual mode of bringing into harmony the tasks presented by internal demands and by the external world" (1945, 467).

4. This observation does not require each character element to be equally present in all circumstances. Situations may call forth character elements or, alternatively, inhibit them. Some situations might be more highly resonant with a person's history or needs than others and thus more likely to engage character elements. Also, as individuals get older and the circumstances they face change, the ways in which character elements may be expressed can also change. The basic questions regarding character for purposes of assessing psychological suitability—that is, whether, how, and under what circumstances a particular character element will appear—cannot be an a priori matter. They must be settled by reference to observing behavior over time and across circumstances.

5. Some of these (the borderline character disorders) are located toward the psychotic end of the psychological functioning continuum (Giovacchini 1975). Others, such as narcissistic and other self disorders (Kohut 1971; 1977), are more frequently found in the neurotic range of functioning, although they can be associated with areas of substantial psychological difficulty within the personality structure.

6. Early psychoanalytic theory developed a model of character tied to the warding off of unconscious impulses. Even Reich ([1933] 1949), who attempted the most systematic explication of character development, saw it as essentially a defensive psycho-

logical structure (hence his term *character armor*). Indeed, as Gay points out, "In psycho-analytic theory, character is defined as a configuration of stable traits. But this orderly grouping does not necessarily connote a persistent serenity; as a cluster of fixations to which the individual's life history has tethered him, character often stands as organiza-tion of inner conflicts rather than their resolution" (1988, 336).

7. The George and George (1956) study of Woodrow Wilson provides perhaps the classic analysis of this problem in political psychology theory. The Georges' analysis of Wilson started with a puzzle, namely, how a person who was often politically flexible could occasionally become stubborn and self-defeating. It was Wilson's frequent politi-cal successes, therefore, that underscored the need to account for his dramatic policy setbacks. The Georges note that, during his career, Wilson had certain recurring problems, first as president of Princeton, later as governor of New Jersey, and finally as president of the United States. At times, the normally flexible Wilson refused to compromise and, as a result, lost the chance to shape cherished policy goals. George and George trace his rigidity during certain policy conflicts to the inappropriate transfer-ence of early family experience (more specifically, the expectations, beliefs, and styles of relatedness that developed in connection with his father) to adult contexts. But for most of his adult life Wilson functioned at a high level of accomplishment in his work and maintained a number of close personal and professional relationships. These considera-tions are important. They suggest that while Wilson's damaged sense of self-esteem and unresolved conflicts played a role in the three most famous of his policy setbacks, they don't represent a complete portrait of his psychological functioning. Nor, obviously, are they very helpful in explaining his far more numerous political successes and policy accomplishments. Different formulations of the relationship between character and leadership functioning are clearly needed.

8. Wishes and needs can be viewed as basically *intra*personal (within), while their reception by particular others (parents, family, society) is basically *inter*personal (be-tween). I will not review here the enormous and influential psychological literature on needs. Relevant major works are Allport 1937, Maslow 1954, McClelland 1961; see also Hall and Lindzey (1978) for an excellent review of major personality theories and theorists. Freud's theory can be viewed in one respect as resting on a theory of needs. Both the pleasure and reality principles are, in fact, metapsychological statements of basic needs, the former by the id and the latter by the ego.

9. There are two general ways in which solutions developed to deal with this basic developmental dilemma can prove inadequate. First, feelings and wishes that are treated as inappropriate (either developmentally or situationally) may become inhibited. In this situation, the person falters developmentally because anxiety connected to particular wishes limits attempts to master a certain kind or range of experience. Second, a person might apply responses appropriate to one developmental period or circumstance to another circumstance in which those responses are less appropriate.

10. I have reviewed elsewhere (Renshon 1974, 43–58) the relevant theoretical foundations for this assertion as found in the psychoanalytic clinical literature as well as in personality theory and development psychology. Bandura's concept of self-efficacy (1977) develops a behavioral theory of the sense of effectiveness and capacity. His paper reviews the relevant literature from this branch of social-experimental psychology.

11. The concept of consolidation is an important but overlooked aspect of psycho-

logical development and performance. It refers to a level of development that is both *stable* and *resilient*. Lack of consolidation is reflected in wide swings between values, ambivalence between or among values, or a tendency for values to waver in the face of modest setbacks.

12. Ideals represent the more abstract, affect-laden elements of identity, values their more near-experience counterparts. Ideals incorporate identifications and associations that are unlikely to be fully accessible to the individual. They may be made of "part objects," aspects of one or another person or persons whose views were important at the time the ideals were developing. Values represent the more specific, conscious manifestations of ideals. A person's character integrity incorporates both.

13. In addition to character style and character beliefs, consolidated character structures are related to the development of the individual's set of personality traits. Each trait can be seen as a relatively stable pattern of behavior along one of a number of possible trait continua. Every individual can be located among a wide range of personality traits. Some traits, however, will play relatively minor roles in an individual's psychological structure. Others will have much more centrality in his or her overall psychological functioning. The concern of the analyst is to identify those character-based personality traits that are more central and thus potentially more important in understanding the person's approach to experience and behavior. Those personality traits that arise most directly out of the integrated psychological package which reflects the three basic character elements would appear to be a promising area to examine.

This approach differs somewhat from the "big five" approach, which assumes that each of the five traits is an important trait for individuals. I do not employ the "big five" tactic in chapters 11 and 12, which deal with the implications of Bill Clinton's character elements for his performance as a candidate and as president.

14. In putting the words *good* and *bad* in quotes, I do not mean to denigrate their importance in helping to set the child's basic sense of integrity. This basic view of the world as black or white is, in most cases, developmentally supplanted by more complex understandings. My point is not that judgments of good and bad may not ultimately inform both child and adult; they may indeed. Rather, my point speaks to the amount of complex, reflective thinking that may go into process of arriving at such judgments in adulthood.

Notes to Chapter Eight

1. A schematic representation of the overall relationship among the character elements is found in Appendix 2.

2. There are numerous variations in the types of decisions any president faces and in the ways in which presidents organize their information resources. Decisions also vary in their time frames. Some decisions, such as where to place the United States's intercontinental ballistic missiles (ICBMs), are debated for years. Others, such as how to rid Cuba of offensive missiles in 1962, have to be decided in a matter of days. Finally, decisions vary in their location along a public–private continuum. Some presidential decisions are made in the context of public debate; more often, they are the product of small decision groups, and occasionally decisions are made by the president alone.

3. This discussion builds on an earlier analysis of judgment and decision making in the 1991 Persian Gulf War (see Renshon 1993b).

4. All decisions, of course, reflect judgment to some degree. However, minor or routine decisions do not ordinarily raise issues of good or poor judgment. In the case of framing decisions, it is that major judgment and those connected with carrying it out that are the focus of our theoretical attention.

5. An individual might make one or several misjudgments on small matters because the matters did not seem consequential enough to engage concern, or for other reasons. Good judgment does not require perfect judgment. However, numerous instances of misjudgment, especially in connection with the aftereffects of framing decisions, would raise questions about overall judgment.

6. George (1980, 1–3) has discussed the trade-off that often occurs between the quality of a decision and its acceptability. A decision might be sound but not feasible or, alternatively, feasible but not sound. Reconciling these two is a critical task of any president or decision maker. A similar trade-off may be seen to operate between judgment and politics. During the 1992 check-cashing scandal in Congress, some congressmen faulted the House Speaker "for being thoughtful and judicious but not political enough" (Clymer 1992, 1).

7. Decision-making theorists have not looked carefully at the impact of the problem itself. The closest theorists have come is to discuss the leader's definition of the problem (but see Pruitt 1965 for an exception). How the leader defines the problem has implications for both decision-making and political processes. It is also true that perception operates within historical and personal frames that have some factual (real-life) basis.

8. The exact reason that the Russians put missiles into Cuba has been a subject of strong debate (Allison 1971). Khrushchev's son, Sergei, states flatly that "the reason for installing missiles was a single one: the defense of Cuba" (Allyn, Blight, and Welch 1992, 38). My point here is not that the reasons given by the Russians are necessarily the correct ones but rather that the members of the Kennedy decision-making group never seriously considered this possibility, at least in the portions of the meeting for which transcripts are now available.

9. There is an anonymous aphorism that is relevant here: "Good judgment comes from experience. Experience comes from bad judgment." The thrust of this aphorism is that mistaken but corrected judgment is the basis of better judgment. So, too, the concept of skillful judgment suggests that skills in making judgments, like other skills, can be developed and refined.

10. This possibility is raised by Gelb's (1992, A15) analysis of George Bush's mishandling of his January 1992 trip to Japan with executives of the major automobile manufacturers.

11. See Renshon 1993b, 68–71, for an examination of the contributions and limitations of the procedural model of decision making.

12. In a rare exception, Herek, Janis, and Muth (1987; see also Janis 1989, 119–35) studied nineteen major crises since World War II to determine whether good decision procedures resulted in high-quality outcomes. Using content analysis of bibliographic sources, they rated the decision procedures used (1987, 211). Experts then rated the outcomes on two dimensions, increased (or decreased) international tension and favorable

(or unfavorable) outcomes for U.S. interests. They found that "quality of decision-making process is related to the decision's outcome" (Herek, Janis, and Muth 1987, 218).

Two other interesting findings of the Herek et al. study are worth noting. Interestingly, they found that raters of decision outcomes agreed much more about short-term than about long-term effects, which were considered so unreliable that they were omitted from the analysis (1987, 213n. 3). Herek et al. also found that in judging outcomes (e.g., increased world tension, advances for U.S. interests), "the conservative expert was inclined to see more of the outcomes as favorable or neutral, while the liberal saw more of them as negative" (1987, 215). This suggests how political views may frame the evaluation of outcomes, even for scholarly observers.

13. It is a matter of some regret that more attention is not paid to developing specific instances of past policy judgments for candidates who have been in a position to make them. The tendency has been to concentrate on a candidate's policy views, but a more helpful source of information for how a candidate is likely to behave as president would be an in-depth examination of one or a few policy decisions.

14. Describing persons as having some degree of psychological maturity does not mean they are conflict-free. Psychologically developed persons have areas of conflict, emotional and interpersonal difficulties, like everyone else. However, their difficulties take place in the more general context of psychological accomplishment rather than vice versa.

15. The importance of affect in decision making is becoming more widely recognized, but its exact roles are not clear. Some years ago, Abelson (1959) introduced the concept of "hot cognition" to account for the finding that in some areas cognition became suffused with affect and, in doing so, became more salient and powerful in shaping behavior. Janis and Manns' (1977) emphasis on the importance of feelings of hope in reaching optimal political decisions represents a further attempt to integrate the two domains.

Traditional rational-actor theorists of decision making viewed affect as interfering with calculations of "value maximizing," which were, in their view, the essence of rational decision making. In these models, affect can interfere in two ways: first, it can result in people giving inappropriate weight to some consideration, and second, feelings of empathy, for example, would appear to undercut a totally self-interested calculation. As noted in chapter 4, full rational-actor models have given way to "bounded rationality" models (Kinder and Weiss 1978), which place a number of constraints on the assumptions of the "rational actor." Most of these constraints have to do with the cognitive requirements of the full rational-actor model. The role of affect in these modified models is somewhat unclear.

In some models of self-interest, feelings are viewed as simply another datum to be factored into the overall self-interest evaluation. This solves the problem of accounting for affect in some way and perhaps preserves the (self-interest) model, but whether it furthers a theory of the relationship of affect to decision is another issue. Psychoanalytically inclined theorists, by contrast, tend to emphasize affect, especially as it presents itself in the form of impulse. This has the virtue of examining how and why affect influences decisions but appears to limit the role of affect primarily to the expression of unconscious wishes.

16. A president's grandiosity and accompanying sense of invulnerability and entitle-

ment can often reflect an underlying, masked anxiety or an insufficiently consolidated sense of self-esteem. The anxiety may arise from the direct personal and political implications of events themselves or may be related to the steps that may need to be taken if events are viewed clearly and seriously.

17. Support for the view that individuals with a strongly consolidated sense of self-worth tend to be better learners is found in a number of studies. For example, Barber (1992a) argues on the basis of his extensive case studies that active-positive presidents (those characterized by high self-esteem) are better able to learn from experience. This relationship also received strong support in a study by Sniderman of several nationally representative samples of adults, including one of party and political leaders. His intensive study of the impact of self-esteem on political orientations suggested that "low self-esteem clearly inhibits the acquisition of political knowledge" (1975, 161). In both studies, low self-esteem is associated with inhibitions to learning.

18. For an example of strategic empathy in the context of the rational-actor model of international conflict management, see Allison 1971, 256. White (1991) has recently examined the impact of empathetic identifications with Iraq and their implications for American foreign policy.

19. The unshakable belief that one embodies a large collectivity in all of its important respects is, of course, grandiose. It is also difficult to sustain in democracies (with their traditions of opposition and critical dissent). For this reason, this form of strategic empathy is more likely to be found in dictatorships, where there are no institutional or informational alternatives to the leader's beliefs.

20. This is very difficult even when the other shares a similar culture. It is extremely difficult when leaders face each other across cultures, as well as while in conflict over policy interests.

21. This does not mean that immediate feelings are necessarily wrong, only that one needs the capacity to supplement the information they supply.

22. Consistency of character functioning can be as important as its level. A labile sense of self-esteem, for example, can result in episodic performance. Leaders who do well as long as they are amassing power may do less well when they have to share it. Tucker (1977) suggests that Woodrow Wilson's difficulties as president of Princeton University, governor of New Jersey, and president of the United States resulted not from low self-esteem but from swings in his sense of self-esteem (for another view of the origins of Wilson's difficulties, see George and George 1956). Thomas Eagleton's history of clinical depressions, which was revealed during the 1972 presidential campaign, provides another illustration. As I noted in chapter 6, while there was much discussion of Eagleton's depression and its treatment, there was much less discussion of his periods of high activity preceding the depressions. These periods of high tension and great anticipation and activity led to a decline in judgment in at least one documented case—his handling of the questions regarding the existence of any skeletons in his closet posed to him at the time of his selection as a vice presidential candidate.

23. I focus on Neustadt primarily because his classic work is still the best, clearest formulation of these issues.

24. In between are those many policy areas where either political tradition or public necessity requires some pronouncement of policy preference and that may or may not be fully supported by an intense personal investment of time and energy.

25. Kellerman (1983b) adds that Carter was introverted and that this inhibited his capacity to "reach out." Her argument is compatible with the views expressed here.

26. It should be stressed that while the capacity to build and maintain effective relationships is helpful in exercising political power in a democracy, it is no guarantee of success. Good interpersonal relationships cannot overcome strong divergent interests or policy views. So while George Bush was able to maintain a fragile alliance abroad during the Persian Gulf War, he had much less success maintaining a strong governing coalition domestically.

Notes to Chapter Nine

1. The challenge to reporters is contained in a story about Gary Hart that appeared in the Sunday magazine section of the *New York Times* on May 3, 1987, 28–40, 70–71, one day before the story of his relationship with model Donna Rice was reported in the *Miami Herald*. The story, titled, "Gary Hart—The Elusive Front Runner," quotes Hart as saying in response to a question about the rumors of his womanizing, "Follow me around, I don't care . . . I'm serious. If anyone wants to put a tail on me, go ahead. They'd be very bored."

2. The raw data for the chronology of the events and the candidate's reactions to them are taken from both the *New York Times* and the *Miami Herald*. The latter paper first broke the Hart story, and its investigative techniques became an issue. The author wishes to acknowledge the assistance given to him at the Miami Municipal Library by its director and staff.

The candidate's own recorded words are also used as a basis for analysis. This record includes transcripts of news conferences, transcripts of appearances on national news programs, and remarks recorded in the context of news stories that detailed the unfolding events. Hart himself, in a recent autobiography (1993; see also Remnick 1993), has almost nothing to say about this important episode in his public life.

3. This is accurate for differences in functioning not only between borderline and narcissistic character structures but also within each diagnostic category. For example, Meissner (1984, 230–41) notes that reality testing is substantially intact in some of the character types he includes under "borderline characters." He has also noted (1984, 107) that narcissistically vulnerable persons "do not generally show a dramatic regressive crisis, but rather under conditions of severe stress, the regression may be severe and, at times, irreparable." It is this mixed picture that makes differential diagnosis difficult.

4. Cleckley's cases were men and suggest, as does Masterson's use of male pronouns to describe the narcissist in the quote that follows, the tendency to associate narcissism with men. In part this may reflect a social structure in America (and other countries), in which men had a near monopoly on powerful institutional positions. It may also reflect the special patterns of early socialization for men that link ambition, power and success, defined as "getting to the top" without a corresponding emphasis on the means of getting there. Since self-confidence and acceptance, two foundations of narcissism, appear to be an aspect of general psychological development, it seems unlikely that women, as a group, do not have to deal with the developmental issues that accompany them. Rather, in many ways the calculus of ambition and means and their relationship

to power and success has seemed to have, at least in the past, a different configuration for women than for men.

What are the effects on women of more equality of access to traditional institutions associated with power and success? At this point, it is an unanswered question. One possibility is that if the sexes become more equal in their acceptance and pursuit of traditional models of power and success, we will see a convergence between men and women. Or it may be that the ruthlessness associated with gaining and keeping power in this society will be moderated by experience and the new sensibilities that may be brought to the political system.

5. Tartakoff (1966) confirmed these characteristics in a study of individuals who were ambitious, able, and successful in their professional fields. Two dominant leitmotivs of this group were their view of themselves as powerful, even omnipotent, and the sense that they were special and had been or should be singled out for special recognition because of their exceptional talents, abilities, and virtues.

6. Such persons recall Freud's observation in *Group Psychology and the Analysis of the Ego* that the followers will often be more connected to one another and to the leader than he is to them.

7. Walter Mondale had started building his campaign two years earlier, around the same time that Senator Edward Kennedy announced he would not run for the Democratic Party's 1984 nomination. Kennedy did so citing his duty to his children and his recently completed separation from his wife Joan and denying that his decision had anything to do with lingering questions about his behavior at Chappaquiddick (*New York Times,* 2 December 1982, A1). A news report the previous day, however, had noted that Kennedy and his poll taker had conducted surveys gauging the effects of a campaign commercial that depicted Senator Kennedy's character in a positive light, the results of which neither the candidate or his poll taker would discuss (*New York Times,* 1 December 1982, A1).

8. Walter Mondale's campaign ran two commercial spots during this period that questioned Hart's experience and substance. The first spot pictured the highly symbolic but nonexistent White House "red phone" (a symbolic stand-in for the actual hot-line apparatus) and asked whether voters wouldn't prefer to have an experienced former vice president at the helm. The second spot attacked Hart's "new ideas" by borrowing the slogan of a fast-food commercial and asking of Hart, "Where's the beef?" This attack directly implied that Hart's ideas, when examined, were insubstantial. An essentially parallel argument was evolving at that time about the authenticity of his personal and political identity.

9. In addition, questions were raised about the circumstances surrounding Hart's naval reserve commission, the actual nature of his work in a position that he listed, and the fact that he appears to have changed the way he signed his name. A complete account of the discrepancies and the varying explanations put forward by Senator Hart are contained in a story titled, "Persistent Questions about Discrepancies on Hart Background." The article notes, "No one has proved that Mr. Hart is not telling the truth. But the questions persist because some of the answers given by Mr. Hart contain discrepancies" *(New York Times,* 24 March 1984, A28).

10. Exactly what might be concealed in one form of writing versus another is not made clear.

11. One major TV network news commentator, when interviewing Hart about his name change and Kennedy-like mannerisms, thought it appropriate to ask him, "Will you do your Ted Kennedy imitation for us now?" (*New York Times*, 16 March 1984, A24).

12. One thinks here of the early adolescent pastime of writing one's name in many different ways, seeing which "looks" more like the self one aspires to become. A similar change took place with Woodrow Wilson, whose first name (Thomas) was dropped by the president. George and George (1956, 19) note that after college, "a casualty of this period was his first name, Thomas. After experimenting with various ways to sign his name, he decided that 'Woodrow Wilson' was the most euphonious possibility."

13. It is also the case that public acknowledgment itself has developed as one strategy for escaping more serious political consequences.

14. One is also left to wonder whether, when Hart refers to the separations from his wife, he means separation as a state of mind, a legal status, or a private, mutual agreement.

15. A detailed account of the process that led the *Miami Herald* reporters to follow Hart's friend Donna Rice from Miami to Washington, D.C., where she met and spent the night with him, is found in that paper's 10 May 1987 edition on page 1A. A detailed account of the confrontation between Hart and the *Miami Herald* reporters in Washington and the subsequent unfolding of events are also to be found in news stories in the *New York Times*, the *Washington Post*, and the *Miami Herald* for the period from May 3, 1987, to Hart's withdrawal from the campaign on May 8, 1987.

16. The interview with Donna Rice took on place May 4, 1987, in Miami. The interview is reported in the Tuesday, 5 May 1987, edition of the *Miami Herald* on page 1A.

17. Ironically, one of the pictures that accompanies the Hart story in the May 3 *New York Times* shows Hart making a call from a pay phone at the airport in Des Moines, Iowa.

18. An exposition of the various accounts given by the persons involved, with accompanying maps and diagrams, is in the *Miami Herald*, 5 May 1987, 19A.

19. A more detailed explication of the evidence of Hart's relationship with another Washington woman is contained in a front-page story in the *Washington Post*, 16 December 1987. The analysis of the evidence appears on page 31 of the *Post*.

20. The partial acknowledgment came in the context of an interview on ABC's *Nightline* program on September 8, 1987, after Hart had reentered the Democratic Party primary race. The exchange regarding the reasons for Hart's earlier withdrawal from the presidential race is as follows (Hart 1987c, 8):

> *Koppel:* Is it not true, . . . what has . . . come to be kind of the accepted history of this relatively recent story . . . that Gary Hart finally decided to pull out when someone from the *Washington Post* called your press secretary, Kevin Sweeney, and said, "Look, we're about to go with another story relating to another woman with whom Senator Hart is alleged to have had a long-standing affair?
> *Senator Hart:* That's only partially the case.

21. Hart's admission that he had talked with Donna Rice about coming to Washington on the weekend in question is contained in his press conference, as reported by

the *Miami Herald* in a story titled, "The Points at Issue" (7 May 1991, 30A). Hart's friend William Broadhurst had previously said that it was he who arranged for Rice to come to Washington and that Hart wasn't even aware that she would be there.

22. The issue, while legitimate, did serve a purpose for Hart. In his September 8, 1987, *Nightline* interview (ABC transcript, 9) Hart says of his wish to continue to be part of the campaign, "I hope by getting what I think are irrelevant issues behind us, and certainly privacy issues behind us, and focusing frankly on what I think is a new issue, and that is the privacy of political figures . . . I can make that contribution."

23. Not all sins are equal, nor do sins a candidate commits in the course of a campaign have the same meaning as those, say, committed as a child, a young adult, or, under certain circumstances, even early in a political career. The exact importance of "past transgressions" is a complex matter, as is the public's attitude toward them. One presidential contender in 1988, Albert Gore, who became vice president in 1992, admitted that he had tried marijuana as a young adult, which appeared to do his candidacy no immediate harm; nor did Kitty Dukakis's admission that she was addicted to diet pills (among other things) harm her husband's campaign. In contrast, a Reagan nominee for the Supreme Court, Douglas Ginsberg, had to be withdrawn when it was discovered that he had tried marijuana somewhat later in his career. And suspicions of cover-ups (such as those perceived to have been applied to Ted Kennedy's behavior at Chappaquiddick) or other forms of dishonesty, unethical behavior on the margins of legality (as, for example, in the business dealings of vice presidential candidate Geraldine Ferraro's husband), or questions of character involving authenticity (Gary Hart's adoption of Kennedy-like mannerisms) have proved politically damaging.

24. The relationship between Franklin Delano Roosevelt and Lucy Mercer Rutherford contrasts in this regard with the many brief relationships of John F. Kennedy.

Notes to Chapter Ten

1. In this chapter I distinguish between information that was generally available during the campaign and that which became evident only after Clinton was in office. I do not analyze Clinton's campaign-related behavior retrospectively from the vantage point of his presidency, nor have I brought forward the evidence regarding the developmental origins of the characteristics I discuss. This is in keeping with the focus of this chapter, which is to examine the extent to which the presidential campaign allowed us to make assessments of the "presenting characteristics" (phenomonology) and psychological relationships underlying those characteristics (the dynamic level of analysis). In examining evidence of the three character elements, I rely on information that was widely publicized at the time or easily available to those interested in appraising Clinton. Because of space limitations and the limited purposes of this chapter, I report *representative* illustrations of the key character elements rather than a comprehensive detailing of all the data available to support the observations. This chapter builds on my previous work (Renshon 1993c; 1995), and readers interested in a more comprehensive, developmentally framed analysis of President Clinton's character and presidential performance are referred elsewhere (Renshon 1995; 1996).

2. Indeed, Levin reports that Clinton was president of so many of his high school activity clubs that the principal of Hot Springs High School, Johnnie Mae Mackey,

limited the number of organizations that a student could join, "or Bill would have been president of them all" (1992, 30). Clinton was also involved in a large number of community organizations and was called on by them frequently. Levin (1992, 32) reports the recollection of Edith Irons, a teacher who had a substantial impact on Bill Clinton, that at one point the principal was also forced to limit Bill's community service activities because she feared they were distracting him from his schoolwork.

3. I leave aside here the question of whether or not this information was organized in categories that reflected deep or creative integration pointing toward the successful resolution of policy dilemmas. On this issue, see Suedfeld and Wallace 1995.

4. An important question is how much of Clinton's response was a part of his strategy and how much reflected his real conviction that he was not really the person depicted by press stories. There seems little doubt that Clinton's portrayal of himself as a victim was one of a number of tactics used by his campaign to manage a substantial credibility problem. In this strategy, he clearly recalls Gary Hart's efforts along the same lines.

5. Some attribute Clinton's movement toward others as an expected outcome of having grown up as the child of an alcoholic father, but there is evidence that it may have preceded that experience. George Wright, Jr., a childhood friend of Clinton, recalls that at age six, "he [Clinton] . . . wanted to be everybody's friend." Wright goes on to recall, "It seemed to upset him if someone in the group he went into didn't seem to like him. It would trouble him so much that he seemed to be asking himself, 'What do I have to do to make this person like me?' I can remember that from when I was six years old" (1993, 28). Clinton's mother did not marry her second husband, Roger (who had problems with alcohol), until 1950, when Bill Clinton was four years old. It is possible that Roger's difficulties with alcohol had substantially manifested themselves that early in the marriage. It is also the case that Clinton's mother, Virginia Kelley, had, by her own admission (Kelley 1994), a tendency to drink and gamble somewhat to excess. However, to the extent that these factors played a role, they followed another most important developmental experience, the fact that Clinton's mother left him in Hope with his grandparents while she pursued her studies in nursing outside the state during a critical developmental period for him (ages two to four). This loss, coupled with the realization, which would not have been difficult for a child that age to come to, that he had no father (as other children had), seems to me a more adequate explanation of Clinton's turn toward others.

6. It is possible that Clinton's high level of confidence masks a deeper sense of insecurity. One line of argument for this view is that high levels of self-confidence are by themselves suspect. The drawback of such a line of reasoning is that it relies on an assumption (too much of something indicates its opposite) and provides no data to support the proposition. Another line of argument points to Clinton's difficulty in making decisions, which I discuss at length in the next chapter. Ordinarily, people with high self-confidence do not have great difficulty reaching decisions. However, as I argue when I take up this question, I believe Clinton's reluctance to make decisions has more to do with his dislike of limits than a real lack of self-confidence. Moreover, any argument about Clinton's lack of self-confidence must explain the many strands of evidence (such as his reaction to the teleprompter incident, described on p. 283 above) which support the view that overall he does have high self-confidence.

7. The draft deferment controversy is an instructive small case study that raises a number of interesting and important issues regarding Clinton's psychology. It is not the only such controversy that could have been chosen. I have specifically chosen not to analyze the allegations made regarding Gennifer Flowers and Clinton's relationship with her, for three main reasons. First, the draft issue is more comprehensive and publicly documented. Second, there is not much to be learned about Clinton by examining the Gennifer Flowers controversy that could not be learned by looking at the draft issue or other issues. Last, an emphasis on sex-related scandals might well leave the erroneous impression that only these kinds of controversies and issues are revealing of candidates' psychology, or that they are always important.

Limitations on space in this chapter and its more general purposes preclude a full chronology and analysis of the draft issue, which, however, is undertaken elsewhere (Renshon 1996). Kelly (1992a–d) contains of good overview of the draft story up to December 15, 1992. Goldman et al. (1994, 39, 112–25) present a view of the controversy from the standpoint of an inside observer of the Clinton campaign, which, however, appears to accept at face value Clinton's explanation of it.

8. For example, a chronology of Clinton's draft status from March 20, 1968, when he graduated from Georgetown, until he received a high number in the draft lottery on December 1, 1969, which appeared as part of a story in the *New York Times* in February 1992 (Rosenbaum 1992b), did not contain the important fact (see below) that Clinton actually did receive an induction notice in April 1969. That fact only emerged in April 1992 and was not widely reported. Another example is the news story that broke in the *New York Times* on September 19, 1992, reporting that Clinton asked for and received help (contrary to his earlier assertions) in securing an ROTC slot from the office of Senator J. William Fulbright (Suro 1992). The story first appeared in March 1992 in the *Arkansas Democrat* and was followed the same month by the *New York Post*. However, the significance of the story was not appreciated when it first came to the public's attention.

9. Brown's book is polemically anti-Clinton, but it contains some limited material that is useful, such as the Holmes affidavit, which is not easily obtained elsewhere (but see Oakley 1994, 535–36).

10. One possible source of guilt is Clinton's two-year battle to escape the draft by means that in some cases included misleading others as to his views and intentions. The fact that several of his friends died in Vietnam while he had avoided serving through such methods may also have been an important factor.

11. One other possibility is that Clinton actually did not begin to appreciate how his views would have been seen by the colonel until after he had successfully obtained his deferment. The failure to see this obvious point, given the strong feelings in the military about war objectors and draft resisters, is striking. If accurate, it means that Clinton most likely had to work very hard psychologically to keep himself from recognizing the obvious.

12. The variable that comes closest to validation is respect. However, the two are not synonymous. Respect reflects an acknowledgment and appreciation from others of accomplishment (including how it was done) but makes no necessary connection between this acknowledgment and what is central to the person's self-definition. It is that connection which is central to the concept of validation.

Validation is a more comprehensive concept than respect, affection, or, more generally, a need for external assurances or reassurances of one's positive self-image. It is an acknowledgment by others of those things that the person views as most important about himself. It differs from affection in that one need not be liked to be validated, although for some people, being liked is an important source of validation. When the need to be liked develops as a primary source of personal validation, it leaves the person dependent on doing what will bring others good feelings toward him, rather than their respectful acknowledgment of what he feels is central to his own view of himself. It is also important to distinguish validation that becomes connected to the acquisition and imposition of power. There the psychological equation is "I'm acknowledged because I am powerful." This leaves open the question of whether one could be so acknowledged for accomplishment other than power (beauty, wealth, etc.).

Notes to Chapter Eleven

1. This chapter, like chapter 10, relies substantially on publicly available data such as multiple and cross-checked news accounts to establish that a particular event did or did not happen. It also relies on President Clinton's own words, whether from his press conferences or other interviews or as they are quoted in other reliable sources. In addition, this chapter makes use of two behind-the-scenes accounts that have recently become available, one by Woodward (1994), the other by Drew (1994). Both books are based on extensive interviews with high- (and more modest-) ranking members of the White House staff, including those with daily and direct access to the president.

Both books have been characterized in a number of reviews as descriptive; that is, they have no theoretical framework anchoring their work. Nor, in the interest of being fair and objective about a controversial president, do they argue a point of view. Drew, in characterizing her book, says, "This is a genre of middle-distance journalism, intended to catch events and people's involvement in them or reactions to them while they are still fresh and before they have been fuzzed over, and retouched, in recollection. *It is intended to offer the analysis and perspective of someone close to the events, seeing them unfiltered*" (Drew 1994, 438; emphasis mine). Both books have been characterized as very useful source material for those with a scholarly or other interest in writing about Clinton. I have used them exactly in that way, as *one* more evidentiary strand.

This chapter lays no claim to being a definitive account of Clinton's presidency. Rather, it makes use of public data to suggest some preliminary and provisional aspects of Clinton's approach to his presidency. It is likely that the theoretical formulations and analyses in this chapter will be modified by further information. To what extent must await further data. For a more detailed analysis of the methodological and data issues that face a psychologically or psychoanalytically framed study of the presidency, see the Appendix 1 herein and also "Bill Clinton's Character and Presidency: A Note on Method" in Renshon 1996.

2. Drew (1994, 343) argues that when President Clinton referred to the labor unions that opposed NAFTA (not all did) as "muscle-bound," he did so in a calculated manner, not spontaneously. She compares the incident to the one during the campaign when Clinton took on the black rap singer Sister Souljah, who had, in her song lyrics, suggested killing whites. My argument is that the highly publicized and, when a more

substantial portion of the public record of Clinton's relationships with these groups is examined, unrepresentative nature of these events makes them more symbolic than representative.

3. The "Friends of Bill" (FOB) are a network that Clinton began developing early. It has reached proportions that are almost without precedent in the modern presidency. For the most part, these friends are extremely supportive of the man and his accomplishments, and in a number of cases, one can discern among them strong tendencies toward uncritical idealization (see Levin 1992 and a number of the recollections in Dumas 1993).

4. The word *grandiose* carries with it implications that require further explanation. In clinical usage, the word refers to behavior or expectations that far outstrip the person's ability to accomplish them. The reasons for this may lie in the capacities of the person, the nature of the circumstances, or some combination of the two. An analysis of grandiose elements in a president's behavior must address two additional factors. First, the ambition to achieve large ends, coupled with a determination to see that ambition through to its conclusion, can sometimes result in the achievement of those ends that may have seemed grandiose at inception. Second, grandiose ambitions may be a consciously used political tool. A president who wishes to promote large-scale social or policy change may reason that any change, even moderate change, is difficult to accomplish. Given this, one strategy is to attempt large change with the expectation of getting at least some change.

One problem with the latter formulation is that it argues that Clinton's policy aspirations are merely a strategic artifact. If there is a character, as opposed to a politically based grandiose, element in Clinton's approach to presidential leadership or policy making, it should make itself manifest in a number of circumstances. The careful documentation of these occasions, should they be present, would constitute important pieces of evidence. Resolving this issue requires the analyst to examine to what extent either (or both) hypothesis about grandiose elements is *consistent* with both relevant theory and other behavioral data.

5. A person who lacked any capacity for empathetic attunement would have difficulty making any strategic calculations in this area. Similarly, a president who is too empathetically attuned to others might have difficulties connected to the inhibition of action. Acts of leadership may require the temporary suppression of empathetic attunement. Effective presidents must have some capacities of empathetic attunement but also find ways to make use of these insights in pursuit of their personal or political goals. This is not by itself suspect.

6. One anonymous reviewer of this manuscript suggested that it might well turn out, given more data and further analysis, that Clinton is a "skillful Machiavellian." This possibility cannot be dismissed out of hand. Still, it is important to distinguish how Clinton may appear to the outside observer from how he views himself and operates internally. It may well be that the *effects* of Clinton's psychology, viewed from the outside, seem (or actually are) somewhat Machiavellian, but it is still important to understanding Clinton's psychology that nothing may be further from his mind. The true Machiavellian ruler covers his manipulations under the guise of benevolence. One cannot rule out the plausible possibility that Clinton's Machiavellianism, if it exists, is masked primarily from himself.

7. See Renshon 1996 for a fuller analysis of President Clinton's anger and its role in his overall psychology. Generally, my argument is that President Clinton's anger has a number of dynamic and developmental sources. One is the need to keep himself under control so he can be validated for being the person he sees himself as being. A person gets validated for being friendly, open, sincere, and so on. Anger runs counter to this presentation of self. The irony is that by trying to suppress this aspect of himself, he creates more of what he seeks to avoid. The public outbursts and the frequent private tantrums reflect both the amount of anger in Clinton and his difficulty in always keeping it under control. The second origin, in my view, lies in the experiences of Clinton's childhood. These factors are developed in Renshon 1996.

8. The failure to achieve fully all that he sets out to do has many causes. Political resistance must certainly be counted among the very important factors here, but it is not the whole story. The resistance is a function of several other factors, including the scale, direction, and financial and political basis of Clinton's policy ambitions.

9. It is not enough to note that a president has a high or moderate (or low) level of achievement orientation, although that is a beginning. It is also important to specify more clearly the nature and components of this achievement. For example, what specifically is the role of initiative in the overall "achievement package"? Is the number of initiatives important, or their content? How does the president actually define accomplishment, and why? By anchoring major character-based traits in the president's actual character configurations, answers to such questions may emerge with greater clarity.

10. There are also risks in using a "satisficing" strategy for ameliorating social problems, the chief being that modest policy architecture may prove insufficient. However, in some respects the "maximizing" and "satisficing" alternatives do not address the most important issue, which is to create policies that address important problems in a fair and cost-efficient way and that really make headway in resolving the difficulties without creating a host of new ones in their place.

11. Blumenthal comments that Clinton's "imperiousness can be seen in the design of a White House that would not challenge him when he chooses indecision." Of Mack McLarty, Clinton's childhood friend and former chief of staff, Blumenthal notes, "He is not . . . a peer as other Presidents have had peers; he would be the old (self-protective) friend as manager." Blumenthal suggests that "Clinton is acting as his own chief of staff" and that a number of Clinton's friends have speculated that "he put McLarty in the slot in order to retain control" (1993b, 37).

12. Hillary Clinton's role in the White House and especially the nature of her relationship with the president as adviser are important but complicated matters that cannot be adequately addressed here. These matters are taken up in Renshon 1996.

13. While Clinton is definitely not averse to risks, he clearly makes what are in his mind calculated, not reckless, risks. For example, Clinton had enough self-confidence to risk public defeat by running for the presidency against a then-popular president. However, this risk was not reckless. We do not yet know the basis of Clinton's personal and political calculations in this matter. It is possible that his polling information suggested Bush's vulnerability and he decided on this basis to run. In doing so, though, he was hedging his political bets; he was, after all, still a sitting governor. And his

calculations might well have included the belief that a strong run against Bush, even if unsuccessful, would have made him a front-runner in 1996. Bush, of course, could not succeed himself in 1996, and no strong Republican contender (such as a widely respected vice president) was immediately obvious.

14. The sense of being above or perhaps beyond limits has implications for the person's relationship to many issues of boundaries and boundary setting that arise in powerful executive positions like the presidency. Difficulties in setting and maintaining boundaries have a great deal to do with such issues as honesty and integrity. These have been particularly difficult issues for Clinton and his administration. Clinton is himself under investigation for the series of public and private transactions that have been lumped together under the name Whitewater. Hillary Clinton has had to respond to allegations that the boundaries of propriety between her public and private roles were breached by allowing a well-connected friend to help her make one hundred thousand dollars in the commodities market, under circumstances that are still not fully resolved. Two years into President Clinton's administration, his secretary of transportation, secretary of commerce, former secretary of agriculture, and secretary of Housing and Urban Development are all being investigated, by either the Justice Department or by special, independent counsels, for improper or illegal behavior. For a more focused analysis of these issues, see Renshon 1996.

Notes to Chapter Twelve

1. I mean this phrase in both an empirical and a normative way. Part of the problem is that presidents, candidates, and reporters have different interests and responsibilities (Kumar 1995). Presidents and candidates are interested in putting the best face on themselves and their efforts, while the press's responsibility is to examine these claims fairly but critically.

2. Consider the area of a president's judgment about a complex and controversial issue. Such issues raise complicated problems of "value trade-offs," including (but not limited to) the preferable versus the possible. Is it appropriate for the president to share with the public his precise thinking as he addresses the various complexities of a specific problem? Should he share his frustrations, disappointments, or fears as they arise and before they are resolved? Or should he share with the public his own personal process, as it is in process? One could answer no on the strategic grounds that doing so would damage public confidence in him. Alternatively, one could answer yes by stretching the "public's right to know" argument to include this pre-decision process. However, from the perspective of the psychological functions of privacy and of decision-making theory, one could more easily suggest that time is and should be "private," except for those whom the president invites to share his deliberation.

While presidents certainly have the right to counsel of their choice and time to work through their own understandings, feelings, and calculations regarding an issue, it is also true that presidential judgments and decisions are, in a democracy, ultimately subject to review and evaluation. Included in the process is the right to ask, "Did you consider *x?*" or "Why didn't you do *y?*" Such questions raise the issue of what elements went into a presidential decision and by what calculus it was reached.

3. This is not an argument for a robotic president who must act uniformly, regard-

less of the circumstances (such rigidity itself would be cause for concern). Rather, the point is that a president is elected in part on the assumption that the person he presents himself to the public as being is not a political construction. When the Watergate tapes were released, many were taken aback by the level of the discourse on them. Expecting high-level discussion of important issues, they instead heard a level of talk one would expect to find in a corner tavern and certainly not in the White House. Similarly, when a president portrays himself as a caring, empathetic person but then is revealed to be abrasive and even, on occasion, abusive to his staff, questions are raised about who exactly the president is.

4. Lest the point be misinterpreted, I want to make clear distinctions between anger and rage and between reactive (circumstantial) and chronic anger. Rage and chronic anger have very different implications for behavior, especially presidential performance. Neither would appear to be particularly productive for either the president's judgment or his political leadership.

5. The story is contained in an article that appeared in the *New York Times,* titled, "In Praise of Wendell Willkie, a 'Womanizer' " (*New York Times,* 12 September 1987, 27).

6. This quote, along with a poll of readers' responses to questions regarding the private morality of political leaders, is contained in a *Life* magazine report titled, "Sex and the Presidency" (August 1987): 70–75.

7. These were TV viewers who responded to an invitation by CBS to call a toll-free number to register their opinions after President Bush's State of the Union address.

8. A response to this view by the reporter who asked Hart the question about adultery is contained in a letter to the editor (*New York Times,* 22 May 1987, A30). The reporter pointed out that it was Hart's behavior that had prompted the question.

9. The poll is described in the *Miami Herald,* 5 May 1987, B1. The results of the poll, along with a sampling of readers' comments, are to be found in the *Miami Herald,* 7 May 1987, B1.

10. If a matter is both private and irrelevant to presidential performance (for example, whether a candidate sleeps in the nude or, as President Clinton was asked [and answered], whether he wears jockey or boxer shorts), there is no legitimate basis for inquiry or discussion.

Notes to Chapter Thirteen

1. The sound bite has been repeatedly criticized for not presenting enough information, but sometimes this criticism is misplaced. The essence of an informative news bite is the ability to convey a complex fusion of facts and concerns that accurately frame and underscore a set of "truths" in condensed form. The Quayle–Bentsen vice presidential debate in the 1988 election, which aroused so much commentary, is a case in point. In that debate, Dan Quayle sought to compare himself to John F. Kennedy and was rebuffed by his opponent ("Senator, you're no John Kennedy"). In this brief exchange we saw a candidate, overeager to add stature to a career whose depth and accomplishments had been publicly questioned, reach for a questionable comparison and be told of its inappropriateness in a way that raised the same doubts anew. The exchange succinctly and accurately captured a set of concerns about then Senator Quayle's

qualifications to be vice president, at the same time containing illustrations of their basis.

2. I exempt from this discussion cases where a candidate takes a position that he knows he will not or cannot follow through on. That circumstance goes directly to the candidate's sense of ideals and values as they help to define his character integrity and shape his ambition.

3. Consider also candidate Clinton's criticism of President George Bush for being too soft on dictators. Clinton wrote (with Al Gore, 1992, 138) that Bush "casts a blind eye on Syria's human rights abuses and its support for terrorism." Clinton pledged that, as president, he would neither coddle nor cozy up to dictators such as Hafez al-Assad; yet in October 1994, President Clinton visited Syria, which is on the list of states that knowingly support terrorist organizations. Had the president gone back on his campaign pledge? Yes. Were there substantial reasons for doing so? Perhaps; Israel and the Palestine Liberation Organization (PLO) had reached a historic accord, and Jordan and Israel had signed a second historic accord soon thereafter, while Syria had begun to talk with Israel about its views on reaching an accord. Clinton says he went to Syria to help move along the negotiations between Israel and Syria, to broaden the Middle East peace process.

Was it worth modifying a campaign pledge under those circumstances? Perhaps, since there was the possibility of gaining important movement toward a wider Middle East peace. Would adherence to the campaign pledge in this particular case be a sign of consistency or shortsightedness? Was the possibility of broadening the Middle East peace process worth some risk? Individuals will differ on the answers to these questions, but they make the point that it cannot be reasonably expected that campaign positions will never be open to change in response to circumstances.

4. A similar circumstance occurred when candidate Clinton called for a comprehensive, universal health care plan (Clinton and Gore 1992, 108–11). The four-page outline contained in the Clinton campaign book did not bear a close resemblance to the complex, thirteen-hundred-page health care program the administration put before Congress in October 1993. That proposal went down to defeat in large part because the scope and complexity of the plan raised many questions that there was not adequate time to understand, debate, and resolve. The Clinton health care plan was certainly *related* to the values and positions expressed by the candidate during the campaign, and even to the more specific points he made about what he thought such a plan should cover. However, there were many alternative mechanisms available to realize these goals, and each of them had a set of cost and benefits associated with it.

Candidate Clinton had never outlined these options. It is possible that he wanted to keep details vague until after his election. It is also quite likely that he didn't know which of these options he would choose and had no time or saw no reason to immerse himself in the details necessary to make such choices. Moreover, the presidential campaign was about not just health care reform but a range of other issues. The same points about the lack of detailed prescriptions for implementing candidates' policy values in the form of specific programs could be made for many, if not most, policy areas. Even if candidates do express specific policy values, and even if they further specify policy aims (as Clinton did with health care), there remains the very large area of the means by which these programs will be put into effect (implementation).

5. The point here is not that candidates shouldn't prepare for public events but that spontaneous and prepared behaviors have different meanings and significance. There are good reasons for wanting to know how a candidate responds to the unexpected, since political events cannot always be anticipated, yet the development of debates for the past few election campaigns and incidents like the furiously rehearsed "spontaneous" interview between Dan Rather and George Bush suggest that citizens are getting fewer opportunities to make these assessments.

6. In discussing the possibility of assessing national leaders at a distance, Wedge, who performed such analyses for the Central Intelligence Agency, notes, "In my experience, almost all leaders of major nations are men of strong character—hence, the personality assessment of them is less problematical than for the common run of man" (1968, 25).

7. It is possible that the latter questions arose in part because of Bush's long history in positions that required him to avoid public exposure and controversy (e.g., director of the CIA, ambassador to China). It may also have developed from Bush's leadership style of working intensively, but privately, to mobilize and build agreement. Whatever its origins, the public's view of Bush was that of a slightly effete "preppy" with a quiet, noncharismatic leadership style.

8. The question here, it is important to note, was not whether Bush was a "tough character" but whether he was a character who could be tough.

9. A political campaign requires citizens to evaluate and respond to the political persona as well as to the leader as a person. Part of the task of a presidential candidate is publicly to give voice to a political self, that part of a candidate's personal and political identity which expresses (among other things) a vision of the future as well as plans for the present. There is nothing inherently sinister in this. The candidate's political self has its own developmental line as well as its own personal and political functions. The elaboration of a professional identity and style is a normal part of adult development, and the presentation of a political persona is a legitimate part of the leadership selection process. It therefore deserves consideration on its own grounds.

But assessment problems arise here because although character will always find expression in a candidate's political style and identity, the two are not synonymous. Like character, the leader's political self can find expression in a variety of ways. Some presidential candidates stress their activism (J. F. Kennedy), others their seriousness (Dukakis), and others make use of their geniality (Reagan). The political self can be viewed, therefore, as the way in which skills and character have been integrated into an approach to the task of political leadership.

10. As Hargrove (1974, 76) notes, excellent political skills can be used for destructive purposes.

Notes to Chapter Fourteen

1. The questions put forward in this chapter are meant to supplement, not replace, other forms of information gathering, such as a candidate's written record (speeches, writings, etc.).

2. For the statistically minded, the issues concern the validity and reliability of data, which are affected by such things as sampling, indicator construction, using statistical

tests appropriate to the data, and so on. By now, the difficulties that attend these and other elements of validity and reliability are well known. That is why researchers familiar with the comparative utility of the alternative methods available do not make absolute judgments but rather informed choices.

3. A related but somewhat different question is whether this incident reflects something about this president or about presidents more generally. To answer this question, the researcher must locate and examine instances of this behavior across presidencies, being careful to ensure that the behaviors presented as belonging to a particular category do in fact belong, even though they might differ in some surface respects.

4. I am thinking here of Dwight D. Eisenhower's role in the military and, later, as university president. Also illustrative would be Ross Perot's role in attempting to reform the Texas school system.

5. Appropriateness is an important consideration in the analysis of anger. This is one reason that Michael Dukakis faltered in the eyes of the public, when he gave a very unemotional and measured response to a reporter's question about how he would feel toward a criminal who had harmed his wife. It is also why Senator Ed Muskie's loss of emotional control (crying) when defending his wife raised the question of whether anger, rather than tears, would have been a more appropriate response.

6. Greenstein notes (1984, 43), for example, that "Eisenhower's awareness and attempts to control his temper distinguished him from Richard Nixon. For Eisenhower, there was no denial of angry impulses. Nixon appears sometimes to have repressed anger, driving it from consciousness, only to have it surface in outbursts that conveyed the impression of meanness of spirit."

Notes to Chapter Fifteen

1. There are many reasons for being careful in presenting and using portraits or any other kind of model. The reader is referred to Kaplan 1964, 273–88, for a very useful discussion of models and their limitations in social science.

2. The child raised in favorable circumstances begins life with the unconscious view that all is his or hers and everything is possible. This is Freud's stage of "infantile narcissism" and what Kohut viewed as "untamed grandiosity."

3. Unconsolidated, labile self-esteem is most likely to be expressed privately, not publicly, which requires the researcher to gather or make use of data from those who know or have worked with the candidate.

4. In the treatment of such grandiose character structures, often over many years, these elevated claims to special importance can be somewhat modified. This suggests that the grandiose-self structure is a construction, meant to cover a primary deficit. However, it is also true that psychological structures, once developed, begin to function and further develop autonomously. A grandiose-self structure, fed over time by repeated successes, will have a very potent psychological and behavioral reality.

5. *Object* is the technical term for representations of the external world, including events, things, and persons, that find a place in an individual's intrapsychic life. The term denotes that the object begins as an external, separate entity. However, there are a number of more technical arguments about the development of the capacity to experience and internalize objects and about their various functions once they have been

internalized that will not concern us here. The interested reader is referred to Goldberg 1988 and Mahler 1968 for two representative but very distinctive views.

6. The rough preponderance of each object type in the individual's internal representational life is significant, but so are the primary objects, those that had a disproportionate impact because of their role in the individual's development.

7. To use Kohut's (1977) term, they are *selfobjects,* objects in which the self and the former external object have been fused. This type of object relationship can be distinguished from *true objects,* which remain separate and identifiable as such to the person. For a discussion of the distinction, see Goldberg 1988, 206.

8. Guiding and shaping are still processes that produce important and powerful effects. As I suggested in chapter 1, presidents are still important even though not every president is a "great man," nor every circumstance redefining.

Notes to Appendix 1

1. One problem with the case-study method is that of cumulative results. Different individuals employing different criteria and focusing on different theoretical problems may arrive at substantively worthwhile understandings that cannot easily be integrated into a larger theoretical framework. This is a justified concern, especially in the context of validating theories. However, it may be less justified in the "context of discovery," the purpose of which is not to validate theories but to uncover the factors that might lead to their development. On the distinction between the context of discovery and validation, see Kaplan 1964, 12–18.

2. An extreme example of this is deMause's (1977, 28) assertion that then-president Jimmy Carter would lead the United States into a war because of a "distancing mother" and an unresolved birth trauma.

3. The Georges were aided in their search by the existence of, and their access to, a great deal of published and unpublished data about their subject. Much of this kind of data—personal letters, diaries, etc.—is not available to researchers at this point, so a first step must be the gathering and analysis of publicly available materials.

Notes to Appendix 3

1. Certain observations on decision-making training are drawn from my role as long-term consultant to the New York City Department of Personnel's Top 40 program, a two-year training program for top-level public officials. That agency bears no responsibility for the views expressed in this appendix.

2. Some time ago, in a chapter titled, "The Politics of Prevention," Harold Lasswell pointed out that "the problem of politics is less to solve conflicts than to prevent them" (1930, 197).

3. I have examined the currents in American political culture that help to account for the general ambivalence regarding leadership training and development and refer the interested reader to Renshon 1990.

4. It is not only that decision environments and most major political problems are complex and frequently ambiguous (Dror 1986; George 1980) but that political leaders may draw inappropriate present–past parallels (Neustadt and May 1986; Khong 1992).

5. The problem of busy lives raises a practical issue for leadership development, namely, when there will be time for it. The higher in office decision makers go, the more demands there are on their time. Many efforts to provide systematic, developmental experience therefore must contend with continuing operational responsibilities. For this and other reasons, mid-career developmental efforts are likely to have some advantages. Having said this, it is important to keep in mind that treating the issue of leadership development seriously will require more attention to very senior decision makers too.

6. The "culture of leadership action" sometimes puts presidents and other policymakers and leaders in a position where understandable public sentiment to "do something" is at variance with productive policy. A good example appears to be the 1992 recession, which economists agree was the result of long-term trends and causes that could not be resolved by a short-term fix (which, if attempted, might even have resulted in a worsening of the situation). Yet powerful demands for results, or the promise of them, were generated because it was an election year. A policymaker may be put in the position of doing things immediately that may help, at least marginally, but that sacrifice longer-term solutions.

The public's preference for seeing the leader "in action" has spawned a corresponding public relations emphasis in presidential campaigns. It is a rare political commercial that shows a candidate thinking rather than doing. Action is frequently associated in the public mind with being "on top of things." Furthermore, activity is equated with the leader having a direction and being willing to take it. In a society where there is no consensus regarding direction and where there are pervasive public fears about the loss of its ability to influence events, the perception of leadership activity is a powerful psychological and political force.

7. In his early work (1930; 1948; 1951), Lasswell distinguished between two broad political types, "political man" and "democratic character." The first were oriented toward the pursuit of a single value—power—and might be seen in a variety of political roles: "agitator," "theorist," "administrator," and so on. The second character type was oriented toward the pursuit of multiple values, power being one among many. Lasswell's work is often misread and misunderstood as saying that persons in politics are oriented toward power and are thus "political men." This is true, however, only for those who pursue power single-mindedly.

8. The term *learning* is reserved for relatively context-specific acquisition of information and approaches to political action (for example, the appropriate time for a junior U.S. senator to make a maiden speech). *Development,* by contrast, refers to the integration of understandings that significantly alter the leader's ways of thinking and acting.

9. Alexander's (1954a; 1954b) controversial experiments in providing such corrective experiences have tended to obscure his basic insight. The analyst, by not necessarily responding as the patient expects (technically, the transference), helps bring the patient's assumptions (and his or her corresponding feelings) to the fore for discussion and understanding. It is this process that underlies basic psychoanalytically oriented psychotherapeutic work.

10. There are several ways to analyze cognitive frames, which include beliefs, values, schemas, and attitudes. A number of frameworks for analyzing political belief systems are available (see, e.g., Inglehart 1988; Lane 1969; Putnam 1973). Among the

most useful is the "operational code" framework, first developed by Leites (1951), revised and systematized by George (1969), and further developed by Holsti (1982).

11. The concept of black-and-white thinking raises some issues from the standpoint of the meaning of differentiation. One could argue that the use of two large categories (black or white) shows relatively high differentiation between the categories. Things are put into one or the other category, but the more complex relationships that might exist between the categories are downplayed, if seen at all. The two categories are clearly (in the mind) differentiated, and one would never mistake something that is black for something that is white and vice versa. From the standpoint of cognitive complexity theory, however (Suedfeld 1992), the existence of two rather global categories reflects a lack of differentiation. In the latter understanding, differentiation reflects seeing various elements of a situation (complexity) and fitting them together in appropriate ways (integration).

12. Do we prepare persons only for formal roles, and if so, how do we encourage preparation for a variety of within-role possibilities? Or should we try to isolate the key elements of leadership performance and focus our attention on these? In fact, both approaches are needed. It makes no sense to educate judges to act as governors.

13. Political parties provide programs of campaign and issue development for candidates, as well as orientation sessions for newly elected officials. In general, though, the contributions of the political parties to education for leadership development are short term and strategic. Political parties could undertake more effective, professional (rather than partisan) socialization of their leadership. To do so, they would have to look beyond winning the next election and move instead toward a comprehensive, long-term approach. The public's concern with issues of competence and character might provide one inducment, but in our highly partisan, contested, and dissentious period, such an initiative seems unlikely.

14. Decision making can never be a totally transparent activity. Allison began his classic book on the Cuban missile crisis by quoting John F. Kennedy's observation that "the essence of ultimate decision remains impenetrable to the observer—often, indeed, to the decider himself. . . . There will always be the dark and tangled stretches in the decision-making process—mysterious even to those who may be most intimately involved" (1971, i).

15. For example, one participant relayed a story of being asked by his superior to represent his agency's position at a public hearing for a policy to which he was intensely opposed and that he felt, on both policy and personal grounds, was detrimental to the community involved. That community was made up largely of Americans of African descent and was also this official's community of origin. Furthermore, the official felt that he was being asked to perform this role in part because of his race and his policy credentials. This conflict raised intense dilemmas for him, and he was at a loss as to where to turn for help. As he soon discovered, his predicament was not unusual, and once his story was on the table, many others in the class were able to discuss similar experiences. What had heretofore been private was transformed into a shared experience, with corresponding increases in consideration of the complex issues involved.

This story is meant to be both representative of a class of problems and illustrative of the benefits of having contexts where these issues can be raised and considered. Early socialization is not of much help here. Political life is not easily lived by the Golden

Rule, nor is any list of moral virtues likely to be helpful to leaders facing complex and frequently agonizing value trade-offs.

16. Standard works on the decision-making process include Abelson 1959; Allison 1971; Burke and Greenstein 1989; George 1969; 1974b; 1975; 1980; Herek, Janis, and Muth 1987; Janis 1984; 1989; Janis and Mann 1977; Kinder and Weiss 1978; Lindblom 1959; and Paige 1968. This list is meant to be representative, not exhaustive.

Bibliography

Abelson, Robert P. 1959. "Models of Resolutions of Belief Dilemmas." *Journal of Conflict Resolution* 3:342–52.

Abraham, Karl. 1927. "Character Formation on the Genital Level of Libido Development." Chap. 20 in *Karl Abraham: Selected Papers on Psycho-Analysis*. London: Hogarth.

Adams, B. 1978/79. "The Limits of Muddling Through: Does Anyone in Washington Really Think Anymore?" *Public Administration Review* 22:35–43.

Alexander, Franz. 1954a. "Some Quantitative Aspects of Psychoanalytic Technique." *Journal of the American Psychoanalytic Association* 2:685–701.

————. 1954b. "Psychoanalysis and Psychotherapy." *Journal of the American Psychoanalytic Association* 2:722–33.

Allison, G. T. 1971. *Essence of Decision: Explaining the Cuban Missile Crisis*. Boston: Little, Brown.

Allport, G. 1937. *Patterns and Growth in Personality*. New York: Holt, Rinehart & Winston.

Allyn, Bruce J., James G. Blight, and David A. Welch. 1992. *Back to the Brink: Proceedings of the Moscow Conference on the Cuban Missile Crisis*. 27–28 January 1989. Cambridge, Mass.: Harvard University Center for Science and International Affairs.

Altman, L. 1991. "President's Condition Was Worse than Revealed." *New York Times*, 23 May, B12.

American Psychiatric Association (APA). 1980. *Diagnostic and Statistical Manual of Mental Disorders (DSM-III)*. 3d ed. Washington, D.C.: American Psychiatric Association.

————. 1994. *Diagnostic and Statistical Manual of Mental Disorders (DSM-IV)*. Fourth Edition. Washington, D.C.: American Psychiatric Association.

Apple, R. W., Jr. 1993. "7 Nations' Leaders Open Tokyo Talks; Expectations Low." *New York Times*, 8 July, A1.

Arieti, Silvano. 1974. *Interpretation of Schizophrenia*. New York: Basic Books.

Balint, Michael. 1968. *The Basic Fault*. New York: Brunner/Mazel.

Bandura, Albert. 1977. "Self-Efficacy: Towards a Unifying Theory of Behavioral Change." *Psychological Review* 84: 191–215.

Barber, James D. 1965. *The Lawmakers*. New Haven: Yale University Press.

————. [1972] 1992a. *Presidential Character: Predicting Performance in the White House*. 4th ed. Englewood Cliffs, N.J.: Prentice Hall.

————. 1992b. "Today's Relevance of Psychological Politics." Paper presented to the Annual Meeting of the International Society of Political Psychology, San Francisco, July 3–7.

Barton, W. E. 1968. "Diagnosis by Mail." *American Journal of Psychiatry* 124:140–42.

Baudry, Francis. 1984. "Character: A Concept in Search of an Identity." *Journal of the American Psychoanalytic Association* 32:455–77.

———. 1989. "Character, Character Type, and Character Organization." *Journal of the American Psychoanalytic Association* 37:655–85.

Bayh, Birch. 1968. *One Heartbeat Away: Presidential Disability and Succession.* Indianapolis: Bobbs-Merrill.

Benedict, R. 1934. *Patterns of Culture.* Boston: Houghton Mifflin.

Bennett, Lance W. 1995. "The Cueless Public: Bill Clinton Meets the New American Voter." Pp. 91–112 in *The Clinton Presidency: Campaigning, Governing and the Psychology of Leadership,* edited by Stanley A. Renshon. Boulder, Colo.: Westview.

Berke, Richard L. 1992a. "Easing Friction, Clinton Meets with Jackson." *New York Times,* 23 November, A14.

———. 1992b. "Many Will Escape Ethics Restriction." *New York Times,* 9 December, A1.

———. 1993a. "Advisors Looking Askance at Pledge for 25% Staff Cut." *New York Times,* 7 January, A18.

———. 1993b. "An Inauguration Designed to Play to the Cameras." *New York Times,* 18 January, A11.

———. 1994. "Survey Finds Voters in U.S. Rootless and Self-Absorbed." *New York Times,* 21 September, A21.

Blalock, H. M. 1960. *Social Statistics.* New York: McGraw-Hill.

Blight, James G., David Lewis, and David A. Welch. 1991. *Cuba between the Superpowers.* Providence, R.I.: Center for Foreign Policy Development, Brown University.

Blumenthal, Sidney. 1993a. "Letter from Washington: Rendezvousing with Destiny." *New Yorker* (March 8): 38–44.

———. 1993b. "Letter from Washington: Dave." *New Yorker* (June 28): 31–43.

———. 1994. "Letter from Washington: The Education of a President." *New Yorker* (January 24): 31–43.

Bok, Derek. 1989. "A Daring and Complicated Strategy." *Harvard Magazine,* May–June, 47–58.

Boorse, C. 1975. "On the Distinction between Health and Illness." Philosophy and Public Affairs 5:54–62.

Boroson, W. 1964. "What Psychiatrists Say about Goldwater." *FACT* 4:24–64.

Bowlby, J. 1969. *Attachment and Loss.* Vol. 1, *Attachment.* New York: Basic Books.

Brace, Paul, and Barbara Hinckley. 1992. *Follow the Leader: Opinion Polls and the Modern President.* New York: Basic Books.

Bradsher, Keith. 1993. "Controllers Ban Lifted by Clinton." *New York Times,* 13 August, A17.

Brodie, F. 1981. *Richard Nixon: The Shaping of His Character.* New York: Norton.

Brown, Floyd G. 1992. *"Slick Willy": Why America Cannot Trust Bill Clinton.* Annapolis, Md.: Annapolis Publishing.

Browning, R. P., and H. E. Jacob. 1964. "Power Motivation and the Political Personality." *Public Opinion Quarterly* 28:75–90.

Brummett, John. 1994. *High Wire: The Education of Bill Clinton.* New York: Hyperion.

Buchanan, B. 1987. *The Citizen's Presidency.* Washington, D.C.: Congressional Quarterly Press.

———. 1988. "Sizing Up the Candidates." *PS: Political Science and Politics* (spring):250–55.

Burke, J., and F. Greenstein. 1989. *How Presidents Test Reality: Decisions on Vietnam, 1954 and 1965.* New York: Russell Sage.

Burns, J. 1978. *Leadership.* New York. Harper & Row.

Calabresi, G., and P. Bobbitt. 1979. *Tragic Choices.* New York: Norton.

Campbell, Angus, Phillip E. Converse, Warren Miller, and Donald E. Stokes. 1960. *The American Voter.* New York: Wiley.

Campbell, Angus, Gerald Gurrin, and Warren E. Miller. 1954. *The Voter Decides.* Evanston, Ill.: Row, Peterson & Co.

Carlyle, Thomas. 1907. *On Heroes, Hero-Worship, and the Heroic in History.* Boston: Houghton Mifflin.

Carter, Jimmy. 1975. *Why Not the Best?* New York: Bantam Books.

Chessick, R. D. 1985. *Psychology of the Self and the Treatment of Narcissism.* New York: Jason Aronson.

Citrin, Jack. 1974. "Comment: The Political Relevance of Trust in Government." *American Political Science Review* 68:973–1001.

Cleckley, H. M. [1941] 1976. *The Mask of Sanity.* 5th ed. St. Louis: C. V. Mosby.

Clift, Eleanor. 1993. "Playing Hardball." *Newsweek,* 19 April, 24.

Clinton, Bill. 1992. "A Letter by Clinton on His Draft Deferment: 'A War I Opposed and Despised.' " *New York Times,* 13 February, A25.

———. 1993a. "Excerpts from an Interview with Clinton after the Air Strikes." *New York Times,* 14 January, A10.

———. 1993b. "Excerpts from Clinton's News Conference in the Rose Garden." *New York Times,* 15 May, A8.

———. 1993c. "Excerpts from Clinton's Question and Answer Session in the Rose Garden." *New York Times,* 28 May, A14.

———. 1993d. "Excerpts from Clinton News Conference: 'The U.S. Should Lead' on Bosnia." *New York Times,* 24 April, A7.

Clinton, Bill, and Al Gore. 1992. *Putting People First: How We All Change America.* New York: Times Books.

Clymer, Adam. 1987. "The Momentous Decision Not to Run for President." *New York Times,* 22 February, C2.

———. 1992. "Leadership and Its Limits." *New York Times,* 1 May, A1.

Costa, Paul T., and Thomas A. Widiger, eds. 1995. *Personality Disorders and the Five Factor Model of Personality.* Washington, D.C.: APA Press.

Cronin, Thomas. 1975. *The State of the Presidency.* 2d ed. Boston: Little, Brown.

Curran, W. 1969. "Public Psychiatry and Political Libel." *American Journal of Political Health* 59:2260–72.

Davies, J. C. 1963. *Human Nature and Politics.* New York: Wiley.

deMause, Lloyd. 1977. "Jimmy Carter and the American Fantasy." Pp. 9–31 in *Jimmy Carter and the American Fantasy,* edited by L. deMause and Henry Edel. New York: Two Continents/Psychohistory Press.

Destler, I. M. 1988. "Reagan and the World: An 'Awesome Stubbornness.' " Pp. 241–61 in *The Reagan Legacy: Promise and Performance,* edited by Charles O. Jones. Chatham, N.J.: Chatham House.

Deutsch, H. 1942. "Some Forms of Emotional Disturbance and Their Relationship to Schizophrenia." *Psychoanalytic Quarterly* 2:301–21.

Dionne, E. J., Jr. 1987. "Gary Hart: The Elusive Front Runner." *New York Times Magazine,* 3 May, 28–40, 70–71.

Dowd, Maureen. 1992. "How a Battered Clinton Has Stayed Alive." *New York Times,* 16 March, A1.

———. 1993. "Washington Is Star-Struck as Hollywood Gets Serious." *New York Times,* 9 May, A1.

Drew, Elizabeth. 1994. *On the Edge: The Clinton Presidency.* New York: Simon & Schuster.

Dror, Y. 1967. "The Improvement of Leadership in Developing Countries." *Civilizations* 112:72–79.

———. 1986. *Policymaking under Adversity.* New Brunswick, N.J.: Transaction Books.

Dugger, Celia W. 1993. "New Rules Tighten Access to Shelter in New York City." *New York Times,* 11 August, A1.

Dumas, Ernest. 1993. Introduction to *The Clintons of Arkansas: An Introduction by Those Who Know Them Best,* compiled and edited by Ernest Dumas. Fayetteville, Ark.: University of Arkansas Press.

Eagleton, Barbara, with Winzola McLendon. 1992. "Mrs. Eagleton's Own Story: A Wife's View of the Most Dramatic Personal Crisis." *Ladies Home Journal,* 11 October, 153–57.

Eagleton, Thomas. 1972a. Transcript of Eagleton's appearance on CBS's *Face the Nation,* 30 July, 239–46.

———. 1972b. Transcript of Eagleton interview: "Self, It Won't Be Easy." *Newsweek* (August 7):17–19.

Easton, D. 1965. *A Framework for Political Analysis.* Englewood Cliffs, N.J.: Prentice-Hall.

Elms, Alan C. 1976. *Personality in Politics.* New York: Harcourt Brace Jovanovich.

Elving, D. 1988. "Candidates, the Need to Know, and the Press." *PS: Political Science and Politics* (spring):257–62.

Erikson, E. H. 1956. "The Problem of Ego Identity." *Journal of the American Psychoanalytic Association* 4:56–121.

———. 1958. *Young Man Luther: A Study of Psychoanalysis and History.* New York: Norton.

———. 1969a. "Review of Thomas Woodrow Wilson: Twenty-Eighth President of the United States: A Psychological Study, by Sigmund Freud and William C. Bullitt." *International Journal of Psycho-Analysis* 68:462–68.

———. 1969b. *Gandhi's Truth: On the Origins of Militant Nonviolence.* New York: Norton.

———. 1980. *Identity and the Life Cycle.* New York: Norton.

Evans, Rowland, and Robert Novak. 1966. *Lyndon B. Johnson: The Exercise of Power.* New York: New American Library.

Exner, J. E. 1986. *The Rorschach: A Comprehensive System.* Vol. 1, *Basic Foundations.* 2d ed. New York: Wiley.

Feerick, John D. 1976. *The Twenty-fifth Amendment: Its Complete History and Earliest Applications.* New York: Fordham University Press.

Fenichel, O. 1945. *The Psychoanalytic Theory of Neurosis.* New York: Norton.

Fenno, Richard. 1959. *The President's Cabinet.* Cambridge, Mass.: Harvard University Press.

Fieve, Ronald. 1975. *Moodswing.* New York: Bantam Books.

Fiske, S. T., and P. W. Linville. 1980. "What Does the Schema Concept Buy Us?" *Personality and Social Psychology Bulletin* 6:543–47.

Fitzgerald, R., ed. 1977. *Human Needs and Politics.* Elmsford, N.Y.: Pergamon.

Freud, S. 1905. "Fragment of an Analysis of a Case of Hysteria." *Standard Edition* 7:7–122.

———. 1906. "Psycho-Analysis and the Establishment of the Facts in Legal Proceedings." *Standard Edition* 9:99–114.

———. 1908. "Character and Anal Eroticism." *Standard Edition* 9:167–76.

———. 1911. "Psychoanalytic Notes upon an Autobiographical Account of a Case of Paranoia (Dementia Paranoides)." *Standard Edition* 12:35–84.

———. 1916a. "Some Character Types Met in Psycho-Analytic Work: The 'Exceptions.'" *Standard Edition* 14:311–15.

———. 1916b. "Some Character Types Met in Psycho-Analytic Work: Those Wrecked by Success." *Standard Edition* 14:316–31.

———. 1916c. "Some Character Types Met in Psycho-Analytic Work: Criminals from the Sense of Guilt." *Standard Edition* 14:332–36.

———. 1916d. "Some Character Types Met in Psycho-Analytic Work." *Standard Edition* 14:309–36.

———. 1919a. "A Note on Psycho-Analytic Publications and Prizes." *Standard Edition* 17:267–70.

———. 1919b. "Four Prefaces: (A) Psycho-Analysis and the War Neuroses." *Standard Edition* 17:205–10.

———. 1921. "Group Psychology and the Analysis of the Ego." *Standard Edition* 18:69–143.

Freud, S., and W. Bullitt. 1966. *Thomas Woodrow Wilson: A Psychological Study.* New York: Avon Books.

Friedman, Thomas L. 1992. "Professor Elect on T.V.: More Than Just a Talk Show." *New York Times,* 18 December, B12.

———. 1993a. "Clinton Aide Demurs on White House Staff Cuts and Recovery Plans." *New York Times,* 13 January, A17.

———. 1993b. "Clinton Trimming Lower-Level Aides." *New York Times,* 10 February, A1.

Frosh, John. 1990. *Psychodynamic Psychiatry.* Vol. 1. Madison, Conn.: International Universities Press.

Gay, Peter 1988. *Freud: A Life for Our Time.* New York: Norton.

Gaylin, W. 1973. "What's Normal?" *New York Times Magazine,* 1 April, 14, 54–57.

Gelb, Lawrence. 1992. "Three Wine Mice." *New York Times,* 12 January, A15.

George, Alexander L. 1969. "The 'Operational Code': A Neglected Approach to the Study of Political Leadership and Decision Making." *International Studies Quarterly* 13:190–222.

———. 1974a. "Assessing Presidential Character." *World Politics* 26:234–82.

———. 1974b. "Adaptation to Stress in Political Decision Making: The Individual,

Small Group, and Organizational Context." Pp. 176–245 in *Coping and Adaptation,* edited by George V. Coelho, David A. Hamberg, and John E. Adams. New York: Basic Books.

———. 1975. *Towards a More Soundly Based Foreign Policy: Making Better Use of Information.* Report to the Commission on the Organization of Government for the Conduct of Foreign Policy. Washington, D.C.: U.S. Government Printing Office.

———. 1980. *Presidential Decision Making in Foreign Policy: The Effective Use of Information and Advice.* Boulder, Colo.: Westview.

George, Alexander L., and Juliette George. 1956. *Woodrow Wilson and Colonel House: A Personality Study.* New York: John Day.

Gergen, Kenneth. 1991. *The Saturated Self.* New York: Basic Books.

Gerzon, M. 1992. "He's No Gary Hart." *New York Times,* 23 January, A23.

Gilbert, G. M. 1950. *Psychology of Dictatorship: Based on an Examination of the Leaders of Nazi Germany.* New York: Ronald Press.

Ginzburg, R. 1964. "Goldwater: The Man and the Menace." *Fact* 4:2–4.

Giovacchini, Peter. 1975. *Psychoanalysis of Character Disorders.* New York: Jason Aronson.

Glad, B. 1983. "Black-and-White Thinking: Ronald Reagan's Approach to Foreign Policy." *Political Psychology* 4:33–76.

Goffman, E. 1959. *The Presentation of Self in Everyday Life.* Garden City, N.Y.: Doubleday.

Goldberg, Arnold. 1988. *A Fresh Look at Psychoanalysis: The View from Self Psychology.* Hillsdale, N.J.: Analytic Press.

Goldman, Peter, Thomas M. DeFrank, Mark Miller, Andrew Murr, and Tom Mathews. 1994. *Quest for the Presidency 1992.* College Station: Texas A & M University Press.

Goodwin, Richard N. 1988a. *Remembering America: A Voice from the Sixties.* Boston: Little, Brown.

———. 1988b. "President Lyndon Johnson: The War Within." *New York Times Magazine,* 21 August, 35–38, 42, 48.

Green, H. 1972. *I Never Promised You a Rose Garden.* New York: Signet.

Greenberg, Jay R., and Stephen A. Mitchell. 1983. *Object Relations in Psychoanalytic Theory.* Cambridge, Mass.: Harvard University Press.

Greenson, R. 1967. *The Technique and Practice of Psychoanalysis.* Vol. 1. New York: International Universities Press.

Greenstein, Fred I. 1968. "Private Disorder and Public Order: A Proposal for the Collaboration between Psychoanalysts and Political Scientists." *Psychoanalytic Quarterly* 37:261–81.

———. 1969. *Personality and Politics.* Chicago: Markham.

———. 1982. *The Hidden Hand Presidency.* New York: Basic Books.

———. 1988. "Dwight D. Eisenhower: Leadership Theorist in the White House." Pp. 76–107 in *Leadership in the Modern Presidency,* edited by Fred I. Greenstein. Cambridge, Mass.: Harvard University Press.

Grey, J., and J. Fiscalini. 1987. "Parallel Process as Transference-Countertransference." *Psychoanalytic Psychology* 4:131–44.

Group for the Advancement of Psychiatry: Committee on Governmental Agencies (GAP: CGA). 1973. *The VIP with Psychiatric Impairment*. New York: Scribner's.

Halberstam, Michael J. 1972. "Who's Medically Fit for the White House?" *New York Times* Magazine, 22 October, 39–40, 100–107.

Hall, Calvin S., and Gardner Lindzey. 1978. *Theories of Personality*. 3d ed. New York: Wiley.

Hargrove, Erwin C. 1974. *The Power of the Modern Presidency*. Philadelphia: Temple University Press.

Harlow, H. F., and M. K. Harlow. 1962. "Social Deprivation in Monkeys." *Scientific American* 207:136–46.

Hart, Gary. 1987a. Transcript of remarks to Newspaper Publishers Association. *New York Times*, 6 May, B8.

———. 1987b. Transcript of statement withdrawing candidacy. *New York Times*, 9 May, A9.

———. 1987c. Transcript of interview on ABC's *Nightline*, 8 September, 2–13.

———. 1987d. Transcript of interview on ABC's *Nightline*, 15 December, 2–15.

———. 1987e. Transcript of statement on reentering the primary race. *New York Times*, 16 December, B7.

———. 1987f. Transcript of interview on CBS's *60 Minutes*, 20 December, 1–6.

———. 1993. *The Good Fight*. New York: Random House.

Heifetz, Ronald. 1994. *Leadership without Easy Answers*. Cambridge, Mass.: Harvard University Press.

Henry, William D. 1970. "The Psychiatrric Illness of Lord Casterleagh." *Practioner* 204:318–23.

Herbers, John. 1973. "State of Nixon's Health Is a Dimension of Watergate Affair Constantly Being Gauged." *New York Times*, 4 December, A36.

———. 1980. "Panel Blames Lawmakers for Aid Crisis," *New York Times*, 25 August, A24.

Herek, Greg, Irving Janis, and Paul Muth. 1987. "Decision Making during International Crises: Is the Quality of Process Related to Outcome?" *Journal of Conflict Resolution* 31:203–26.

Hermann, Margaret G. 1979. "Indicators of Stress in Policymakers during Foreign Policy Crises." *Political Psychology* 1:27–46.

———. 1986. "Ingredients of Leadership." Pp. 167–92 in *Political Psychology*, edited by M. G. Hermann. San Francisco: Jossey-Bass.

Holsti, O. R. 1982. "The Operational Code Approach: Problems and Some Solutions." Pp. 75–90 in *Cognitive Dynamics and International Politics*, edited by C. Jonsson. New York: St. Martin's.

Hook, S. 1955. *The Hero in History*. Boston: Beacon.

Horney, K. 1937. *The Neurotic Personality of Our Times*. New York: Norton.

Hutschnecker, A. A. 1973. "A Suggestion: Psychiatry at High Levels of Government." *New York Times*, 4 July, A22.

———. 1974. *The Drive for Power*. New York: Evans.

Ifill, G. 1992a. "Vietnam War Draft Status Becomes Issue for Clinton." *New York Times*, 17 February, A1.

Ifill, G. 1992b. "A Front Runner in Trouble, Clinton Portrays Himself as a Victim of Attacks." *New York Times,* 10 February, A14.

———. 1992c. "Clinton Thanked Colonel in '69 For 'Saving Me from the Draft.' " *New York Times,* 13 February, A1.

———. 1992d. "Questioned about Trust, Clinton Turns Angry." *New York Times,* 24 March, A21.

———. 1992e. "Clinton Resists Being Labeled a Liberal." *New York Times,* 28 July, A11.

———. 1992f. "Clinton Expands Position on the Draft." *New York Times,* 20 September, A26.

———. 1993a. "Globe-Trotting Clinton Faces Trip's Side Effects." *New York Times,* 9 July, A8.

———. 1996. "Democrats Drop Donor's Session with President." *New York Times,* 2 May, A1.

———. 1994. "Clinton and Japan Chief Say Trade Talks Fail; U.S. Threatens Action." *New York Times,* 12 February, A1.

Inglehart, R. 1988. "The Renaissance of Political Culture." *American Political Science Review* 82:1203–30.

Jahoda, M. 1958. *Current Concepts of Positive Mental Health.* New York: Basic Books.

Janis, I. 1984. *Victims of Groupthink.* 2d ed. Boston: Houghton Mifflin.

———. 1989. *Crucial Decisions: Leadership in Policy Making and Crisis Management.* New York: Free Press.

Janis, I., and L. Mann. 1977. *Decision Making: A Psychological Analysis of Conflict, Choice and Commitment.* New York: Free Press.

Jenks, Christopher. 1994. *The Homeless.* New York: Basic Books.

Johnson, Haynes. 1972. Series on Thomas Eagleton. *Washington Post,* 3–6 December.

Johnson, L. 1977. "Operational Codes and the Prediction of Leadership Behavior: Frank Church at Mid-Career." Pp. 80–119 in *A Psychological Examination of Political Leaders,* edited by M. G. Hermann. New York: Free Press.

Jones, Charles O., ed. 1988. *The Reagan Legacy: Promise and Performance.* Chatham, N.J.: Chatham House.

Jones, Ernst. 1974. "Can Civilization Be Saved?" Pp. 234–53. In Ernst Jones, *Psycho-Myth, Psycho-History,* vol. 1. New York: Hillstone.

Kantor, Robert E., and William G. Herron. 1968. "Paranoia and High Office." *Mental Hygiene* 52:507–11.

Kaplan, Abraham. 1964. *The Conduct of Inquiry: Methodology for Behavioral Science.* San Francisco: Chandler.

Kearns, Doris. 1976. *Lyndon Johnson and the American Dream.* New York: Harper & Row.

Kellerman, B. 1983a. "Leadership as a Political Act." Pp. 63–89 in *Political Leadership: Multidisciplinary Perspectives,* edited by B. Kellerman. Englewood Cliffs, N.J.: Prentice-Hall.

———. 1983b. "Introversion in the Oval Office." *Presidential Studies Quarterly* (spring): 383–99.

Kelley, Virginia, with James Morgan. 1994. *Leading with My Heart.* New York: Simon & Schuster.

———. 1984. *The Political Presidency*. New York: Oxford University Press.

Kelley, Michael. 1992a. "Day After 'Final Word on Draft,' Clinton Faces Renewed Questions." *New York Times,* 3 September, A20.

———. 1992b. "Clinton Says He Was Told of Draft Aid." *New York Times,* 5 September, A7.

———. 1992c. "Clinton Readies Answer to Bush on Draft Issue." *New York Times,* 15 September, A1.

———. 1992d. "Clinton Again Faces Draft Issues as He Returns to New Hampshire." *New York Times,* 27 September, A20.

———. 1992e. "William Jefferson Clinton: A Man Who Wants to Be Liked, and Is." *New York Times,* 7 November, A1.

———. 1992f. "After 13 Months, Clinton Relaxes." *New York Times,* 8 November, A28.

———. 1992g. "The Making of a First Family: A Blueprint." *New York Times,* 14 November, A1.

———. 1993a. "President Moves in Favor of Labor." *New York Times,* 3 February, A17.

———. 1993b. "Hillary Clinton's Health Panel Invites Ideas from the Invited." *New York Times,* 13 March, A7.

Kenney, P. J., and T. W. Rice. 1988. "Presidential Prenomination Preferences and Candidate Evaluations." *American Political Science Review* 82:1309–19.

Kernberg, O. 1975. *Borderline Conditions and Pathological Narcissism*. New York: Jason Aronson.

———. 1976. *Object Relations and Clinical Psychoanalysis*. New York: Jason Aronson.

———. 1984. *Severe Personality Disorders*. New Haven: Yale University Press.

Kernberg, O., E. Goldstein, A. Hunt, S. Bauer, and R. Blumenthal. 1981. "Diagnosing Borderline Personality Disorder." *Journal of Nervous and Mental Disease* 169:225–31.

Kernell, Samuel. 1986. *Going Public: New Strategies of Presidential Leadership*. Washington, D.C.: Congressional Quarterly Press.

Khong, Yuen Foong. 1992. *Analogies at War*. Princeton, N.J.: Princeton University Press.

Kilborn, Peter T. 1993. "Buoyed but Wary, Union Chiefs Gather." *New York Times,* 15 February, C4.

Kinder, Donald R., and J. A. Weiss. 1978. "In Lieu of Rationality: Psychological Perspectives on Foreign Policy Decision Making." *Journal of Conflict Resolution* 22:707–35.

King, C. D. 1945. "The Meaning of Normal." *Yale Journal of Biology and Medicine* 17:493–94.

King, L. S. 1954. "What Is Disease?" *Philosophy of Science* 21:193–203.

Klein, Joe. 1993. "Slow Motion." *Newsweek* 24 May, 16.

Knutson, J. N. 1972. *The Human Basis of the Polity*. Chicago: Aldine.

Kohut, H. 1965. "A Statement on the Use of Psychiatric Opinions in the Political Realm." *Journal of the American Psychoanalytic Association* 13:450.

———. 1971. *The Analysis of the Self*. New York: International Universities Press.

———. 1977. *The Restoration of the Self*. New York: International Universities Press.

Krosnick, Jon, and Margaret G. Hermann. 1993. "Report on the 1991 Ohio State Summer Institute in Political Psychology." *Political Psychology* 13:363–73.

Krosnick, Jon A., and Donald Kinder. 1990. "Altering the Foundations of Support for the President through Priming." *American Political Science Review* 84:497–512.

Kucharski, A. 1984. "On Being Sick and Famous." *Political Psychology* 5:69–82.

Kumar, Martha Joynt. 1995. "President Clinton Meets the Media: Communications Shaped by Predictable Patterns." Pp. 167–94 in *The Clinton Presidency: Campaigning, Governing, and the Psychology of Leadership,* edited by Stanley A. Renshon. Boulder, Colo.: Westview.

Labaton, Stephen. 1993a. "Ron Brown Gala Raises Questions." *New York Times,* 13 January, A1.

———. 1993b. "Commerce Nominee Cancels Party Planned by Companies." *New York Times,* 14 January, A1.

Ladd, E. C. 1993. "The 1992 Vote for President Clinton: Another Brittle Mandate?" *Political Science Quarterly* 108:1–28.

Lane, R. E. 1969. *Political Thinking and Consciousness.* New York: Markham.

Lasswell, H. D. 1930. *Psychopathology and Politics.* Chicago: University of Chicago Press.

———. 1936. *Politics: Who Gets What, When, How.* New York: McGraw-Hill.

———. 1938. "What Psychiatrists and Political Scientists Can Learn from Each Other." *Psychiatry* 1:33–39.

———. 1948. *Power and Personality.* New York: Norton.

———. 1951. *The Political Writings of Harold D. Lasswell.* Chicago: Free Press.

———. 1959. "Political Constitution and Character." *Psychoanalysis and the Psychoanalytic Review* 46:3–18.

———. 1960. "Techniques of Decision Seminars." *Midwest Journal of Political Science* 4:213–36.

———. 1964. "The Selective Effects of Personality on Political Participation." Pp. 197–225 in *Studies in the Scope and Method of "the Authoritarian Personality,"* edited by D. Christie and M. Jahoda. New York: Free Press of Glencoe.

———. 1968. "A Note on 'Types' of Political Personality: Nuclear, Co-Relational, Developmental." *Journal of Social Issues* 24:81–91.

Lee, R. V. 1974. "When Insanity Holds the Scepter." *New York Times,* 24 April, A22.

Leites, N. 1951. *The Operational Code of the Politburo.* New York: McGraw-Hill.

Leuchtenburg, William E. 1988. "Franklin D. Roosevelt: The First Modern President." Pp. 7–40 in *Leadership in the Modern Presidency,* edited by Fred I. Greenstein. Cambridge, Mass.: Harvard University Press.

Levin, Robert E. 1992. *Bill Clinton: The Inside Story.* New York: SPI Books.

Levinson, Daniel. 1978. *The Seasons of a Man's Life.* New York: Knopf.

Levinson, S. 1988. "Public Lives and the Limits of Privacy." *PS: Political Science and Politics* (spring): 263–68.

Levitt, Morton, and Ben Rubenstein. 1970. "Normality as a Factor in Contemporary Political Life." *Political Science Quarterly* 2:171–84.

Lindblom, C. 1959. "The Science of Muddling Through." *Public Administration Review* 9:79–99.

Lodge, Milton, and Kathleen McGraw, eds. 1994. *Political Judgment.* Ann Arbor: University of Michigan Press.

Lowi, Theodore. 1984. *The Personal Presidency: Power Invested, Promise Unfulfilled.* Ithaca, N.Y.: Cornell University Press.

Macalpine, Ida, and Richard Hunter. 1966. "The 'Insanity' of King George III: A Classic Case of Porphyria." *British Medical Journal,* January, 65–71.

MacNeil/Lehrer NewsHour. 1987. Transcript of program, 18 December.

Mahler, Margaret. 1968. *On Human Symbiosis and the Vicissitudes of Individuation.* New York: International Universities Press.

Maklin, R. 1972. "Mental Health and Mental Illness: Some Problems of Definition and Concept Formulation." *Philosophy of Science* 39:341–65.

Mansfield, Harvey C., Jr. 1989. *Taming the Prince: The Ambivalence of Modern Executive Power.* New York: Free Press.

Maraniss, David. 1995. *First in His Class: A Biography of Bill Clinton.* New York: Random House.

March, James G. 1966. "The Power of Power." Pp. 39–70 in *Varieties of Political Theory,* edited by David Easton. Englewood Cliffs, N.J.: Prentice-Hall.

———. 1978. "Bounded Rationality, Ambiguity, and the Engineering of Choice." *Bell Journal of Economics* 9:587–608.

Margolis, J. 1966. *Psychoanalysis and Morality.* New York: Random House.

Markus, Gregory. 1982. "Political Attitudes during an Election Year: A Report on the 1980 NES Panel Study." *American Political Science Review* 76:538–60.

Maslow, A. 1954. *Motivation and Personality.* New York: Harper & Brothers.

Masters, Roger D. 1992. "Let's Elect the President in Three Weeks." University of Calfornia-Berkeley *Public Affairs Report,* 5 January.

Masterson, J. F. 1988. *The Search for the Real Self.* New York: Free Press.

Mayer, Jane, and Doyle McManus. 1988. *Landslide: The Unmaking of the President, 1984–1988.* Boston: Houghton Mifflin.

Mazlish, B. 1972. *In Search of Nixon.* New York: Basic Books.

McClelland, D. C. 1961. *The Achieving Society.* Princeton, N.J.: Van Nostrand.

McGovern, G. 1977. *Grassroots: The Autobiography of George McGovern.* New York: Random House.

McGuire, W., ed. 1978. *The Freud–Jung Letters.* Translated by Ralph Manheim and R.F.C. Hull. Princeton, N.J.: Princeton University Press.

Meissner, W. W. 1984. *The Borderline Spectrum: Differential Diagnosis and Development Issues.* New York: Jason Aronson.

Merelman, R. M. 1971. "The Development of Policy Thinking in Adolescence." *American Political Science Review* 65:1033–47.

Milbrath, Lester, and M. L. Goel. 1977. *Political Participation.* 2d ed. Chicago: Rand McNally.

Miller, A. H. 1974. "Trust in Government 1964–70." *American Political Science Review* 68:951–72.

Miller, A. H., and M. P. Wattenberg. 1985. "Throwing the Rascals Out: Policy and Performance Evaluations of Presidential Candidates 1952–1980." *American Political Science Review* 79:359–72.

Miller, A. H., M. P. Wattenberg, and O. Malanchuk. 1986. "Schematic Assessment of Presidential Candidates." *American Political Science Review* 80:521–40.

Miller, Loye, Jr. 1972. "The Eagleton Affair." *Miami Herald,* 8 December, 30A.

Moore, M. S. 1975. "Some Myths about 'Mental Illness.' " *Archives of General Psychiatry* 32:1483–97.

Moore, Rudi, Jr. 1993. "They're Killing Me Out Here." Pp. 85–94 in *The Clintons of Arkansas: An Introduction by Those Who Know Them Best,* compiled and edited by Ernest Dumas. Fayetteville, Ark.: University of Arkansas Press.

Moynihan, Daniel P. 1969. *Maximum Feasible Misunderstanding.* New York: Macmillan.

Mullahy, P. 1970. *Psychoanalysis and Interpersonal Psychiatry: The Contributions of Harry Stack Sullivan.* New York: Science House.

Murray, Charles. 1984. *Losing Ground.* New York: Basic Books.

National Governors Association. 1978. *Governing the American States: A Handbook for New Governors.* Washington, D.C.: Center for Policy Research, National Governors Association.

———. 1981. *Reflections on Being Governor.* Washington, D.C.: Center for Policy Research, National Governors Association.

Nelson, Bryce. 1988. "The Political Kiss of Death." *New York Times,* 7 August, A23.

Neustadt, R. [1960] 1990. *Presidential Power and the Modern Presidents: The Politics of Leadership from Roosevelt to Reagan.* New York: Free Press.

Neustadt, R., and E. R. May. 1986. *Thinking in Time: The Uses of History for Decision Makers.* New York: Free Press.

Nie, N., S. Verba, and R. Petrocik. 1976. *The Changing American Voter.* Cambridge, Mass.: Harvard University Press.

Nisbett, R. E., and L. Ross. 1980. *Human Inference: Strategies and Shortcomings in Social Judgment.* Englewood Cliffs, N.J.: Prentice-Hall.

Noland, R. L. 1966. "Presidential Disability and the Proposed Constitutional Amendment." *American Psychologist* 21:232–33.

Oakley, Meredith L. 1994. *On the Make: The Rise of Bill Clinton.* Washington, D.C.: Regnery.

Osborne, David, and Ted Gaebler. 1992. *Reinventing Government: How the Entrepreneurial Spirit Is Transforming the Public Sector.* Reading, Mass.: Addison-Wesley.

Osborne, T. 1988. *Laboratories of Democracy.* Cambridge, Mass.: MIT Press.

Paige, G. D. 1968. *The Korean Decision.* New York: Free Press.

———. 1977. *The Scientific Study of Political Leadership.* New York: Free Press.

Patrick, J. J. 1977. "Political Socialization and Political Education in Schools." Pp. 190–222 in *Handbook of Political Socialization: Theory and Research,* edited by S. A. Renshon. New York: Free Press.

Patterson, Thomas E. 1987. "Television and Presidential Politics: A Proposal to Restructure Television Communication in Election Campaigns." Pp. 302–29 in *Presidential Selection,* edited by Alexander Heard and Michael Nelson. Durham, N. C:. Duke University Press.

———. 1993. *Out of Order.* New York: Knopf.

Pious, Richard M. 1979. *The American Presidency.* New York: Basic Books.

Pollack, Andrew. 1993. "U.S. Appears to Retreat from Setting Targets to Increase Japan's Imports." *New York Times,* 10 July, A4.

Pomper, Gerald. 1993. "The Presidential Election." Pp. 132–56 in *The Election of 1992,* edited by Gerald M. Pomper, F. Chris Atterton, Ross. K. Baker, Walter Dean Burnham, Kathleen A. Frankovic, Marjorie R. Hershey, and Wilson Carey McWilliams. Chatham, N.J.; Chatham House.

Post, J. M. 1991. "Saddam Hussein of Iraq: A Political Psychology Profile." *Political Psychology* 12:279–90.

———. 1993. "Current Concepts of the Narcissistic Personality: Implications for Political Psychology. *Political Psychology* 14:99–121.

Post, Jerrold M., and Robert S. Robins. 1993. *When Illness Strikes the Leader: The Dilemma of the Captive King*. New Haven: Yale University Press.

Prince, M. 1912. "Roosevelt as Analyzed by the New Psychology." New York Times Sunday Magazine, May, part 4, 1.

Pruitt, Dean G. 1965. "Definition of the Situation as Determinant of International Action." In *International Behavior: A Social Psychological Perspective,* edited by Herbert C. Kelman. New York: Holt, Rinehart and Winston.

Pryor, Senator David. 1992. *Introduction to Bill Clinton: The Inside Story* by Robert E. Levin. New York: SPI Books.

Putnam, R. 1973. *The Beliefs of Politicians*. New Haven: Yale University Press.

Raines, Howell. 1992. "In Re: Clinton, Battle Report from the Ramparts of the Privacy Zone." *New York Times,* 2 February, sec. 4, E1.

Rappoport, A. S. 1910. *Mad Majesties: Or Raving Rulers and Submissive Subjects*. New York: Brentano.

Ray, D. 1976. "The Psychiatric Assessment of Political Leaders: The Goldwater Case and Beyond." Unpublished seminar paper, Stanford University.

Redlich, F. C., and D. X. Freedman. 1966. *The Theory and Practice of Psychiatry*. New York: Basic Books.

Reedy, George E. 1970. *The Twilight of the Presidency*. Cleveland and New York: World.

Reich, W. [1933] 1949. *Character Analysis*. New York: Farrar, Straus & Young.

Reischauer, Richard D. 1993. Letter from the Director of the Congressional Budget Office to House Majority Leader Richard Gephart (with eleven-page analysis of CBO estimates of H.R. 3400, *The Government Reform and Savings Act of 1993*). November 15. Available from the Congressional Budget Office.

Remnick, David. 1993. "Gary Hart in Exile." *New Yorker* (April 19): 41–49.

Renshon, Stanley A. 1974. *Psychological Needs and Political Behavior: A Theory of Personality and Political Efficacy*. New York: Free Press.

———. 1983. "Assessing Political Leaders: The Criterion of Mental Health." Pp. 229–59 in *Leadership: Multidisciplinary Perspectives,* edited by B. Kellerman. Englewood Cliffs, N.J.: Prentice-Hall.

———. 1989a. "Beneath the Mask: The Character Issue in Presidential Campaigns." *Thesis* 1:22–35.

———. 1989b. "Psychological Perspectives on Theories of Adult Development and the Political Socialization of Leaders." Pp. 203–64 in *Adult Political Socialization: A Sourcebook,* edited by Roberta I. Sigel. Chicago: University of Chicago Press.

———. 1990. "Educating Political Leaders in a Democracy." Pp. 313–45 in *Political Socialization, Citizenship Education and Democracy,* edited by Orit Ichilov. New York: Teachers College Press.

———. 1993a. "How to Select a Good President: Some Observations." *Political Psychology* 3:549–54.

Renshon, Stanley A. 1993b. "Good Judgment and the Lack Thereof in the Gulf War: A Preliminary Psychological Model with Some Applications." Pp. 67–105 in *The Political Psychology of the Gulf War: Leaders, Publics, and the Process of Conflict*, edited by Stanley A. Renshon. Pittsburgh: University of Pittsburgh Press.

———. 1993c. "A Preliminary Assessment of the Clinton Presidency: Character, Leadership and Performance." Paper presented to the Annual Meeting of the American Political Science Association, Washington, D.C., 2–5 September.

———. 1995. "Character, Judgment, and Political Leadership: Promise, Prospects, and Problems of the Clinton Presidency." Pp. 57–87 in *The Clinton Presidency: Campaigning, Governing and the Psychology of Leadership*, edited by Stanley A. Renshon. Boulder, Colo.: Westview.

———. 1996. *High Hopes: The Clinton Presidency and the Politics of Ambition*. New York: New York University Press.

Roazen, P. 1971. *Freud and His Followers*. New York: Meridian Books.

Roberts, Steven V. 1988a. "Book Gives Aides' Conflicting Views of President." *New York Times*, 15 September, A29.

———. 1988b. "Former Aide Questions Signing of Reagan's Initials." *New York Times*, 16 September, 1988, A16.

Robins, R. S. 1977a. "Introduction to the Topic of Psychopathology and Political Leadership." Pp. 1–34 in *Psychopathology and Political Leadership*, edited by R. S. Robins. New Orleans: Tulane University Press.

———. 1977b. "Recruitment of Pathological Deviants into Political Leadership." Pp. 53–78 in *Psychopathology and Political Leadership*, edited by R. S. Robins. New Orleans: Tulane University Press.

Rogow, A. 1963. *James Forrestal: A Study of Personality, Politics, and Policy*. New York: Macmillan.

———. 1970. *The Psychiatrists*. New York: Putnam.

Rokeach, M. 1960. *The Open and Closed Mind*. New York: Basic Books.

Rose, Richard. 1987. "Learning to Govern or Learning to Campaign?" Pp. 43–73 in *Presidential Selection*, edited by Alexander Heard and Michael Nelson. Durham, N.C.: Duke University Press.

———. 1988. *The Postmodern Presidency*. Chatham, N.J.: Chatham House.

Rosenbaum, David E. 1992a. "Clinton Leads Experts in Discussion of Economy." *New York Times*, 15 December, A1.

———. 1992b. "Clinton Could Have Known Draft Was Unlikely for Him." *New York Times*, 14 February, A1.

Rosenhan, D. H. 1973. "On Being Sane in Insane Places." *Science* 179:250–58.

Rosenthal, Andrew. 1988. "Dukakis Releases Medical Details to Stop Rumors on Mental Health." *New York Times*, 8 August, A1.

Sabato, L. 1991. *Feeding Frenzy: How Attack Journalism Has Transformed American Politics*. New York: Free Press.

Safire, William. 1975. *Before the Fall: An Inside View of the Pre-Watergate White House*. New York: Doubleday.

Sanger, David E. 1993. "Clinton Achieves Trade Framework in Japanese Pact." *New York Times*, 10 July, A1.

Schlesinger, Arthur M., Jr. 1973. *The Imperial Presidency*. Boston: Houghton Mifflin.

————. 1974. "Can Psychiatry Save the Republic?" *Saturday Review* (September 7): 10–16.

Schmidt, W. H. 1960. "Developing a University Bi-Partisan Political Program." *Journal of Social Issues* 16:48–52.

Sears, David O., and Carolyn L. Funk. 1991. "Graduate Education in Political Psychology." *Political Psychology* 12:345–62.

Seifman, David. 1979. "Her Message: Prez Is Happy . . . & Healthy." *New York Post,* 23 July, 1.

Shapiro, D. 1965. *Neurotic Styles.* New York: Basic Books.

Sheehy, Gail. 1984. "The Hidden Hart." *Vanity Fair* (July): 80–101.

————. 1987. "The Road to Bimini." *Vanity Fair* (September): 132–39, 188–94.

Sidney, Hugh. 1987. "The Presidency: Upstairs at the White House." *Time* (May 18): 20.

Siegler, M., and H. Osmond. 1974. *Models of Madness, Models of Medicine.* New York: Macmillan.

Simon, H. A. 1957. *Models of Man.* New York: Wiley.

Simon, Robert. 1990. *Road Show.* New York: Farrar, Straus & Giroux.

Simpson, E. 1971. *Democracy's Stepchildren.* San Francisco: Jossey-Bass.

Singer, J. David. 1968. "Man and World Politics: The Psycho-Culture Interface." *Journal of Social Issues* 24:127–56.

Skowronek, Stephen. 1993. *The Politics That Presidents Make.* Cambridge, Mass.: Harvard University Press.

Smelser, Neil J. 1968. "Personality and the Explanation of Political Phenomena at the Social-System Level: A Methodological Statement." *Journal of Social Issues* 24:111–25.

Smith, M. B. 1977. "Metapsychology, Politics, and Human Needs." Pp. 124–41 in *Human Needs and Politics,* edited by R. Fitzgerald. Elmsford, N.Y.: Pergamon.

Smith, Stephen A. 1993. "Compromise, Consensus, and Consistency." Pp. 1–16 in *The Clintons of Arkansas: An Introduction by Those Who Know Them Best,* compiled and edited by Ernest Dumas. Fayetteville, Ark.: University of Arkansas Press.

Smith, Terence. 1979. "Schlesinger and Adams Last Cabinet Aides to Go; Changes 'Please' Carter." *New York Times,* 21 July, A1.

Sniderman, P. 1975. *Personality and Democratic Politics.* Berkeley: University of California Press.

Sperlich, Peter W. 1975. "Bargaining and Overload: An Essay on Presidential Power." Pp. 406–30 in *Perspectives on the Presidency,* edited by Aaron Wildavsky. Boston: Little Brown.

Spitz, R. 1945. "Hospitalism." *Psychoanalytic Study of the Child* 1:53–74.

Stainbrook, E. 1976. "White House Needs a Psychiatrist in Residence." *Los Angeles Times,* 1 October, 33A.

Staley, Carolyn. 1993. "The Music of Friendship." Pp. 34–41 in *The Clintons of Arkansas: An Introduction by Those Who Know Them Best,* compiled and edited by Ernest Dumas. Fayetteville, Ark.: University of Arkansas Press.

Sternberg, Robert J. 1979. "The Nature of Mental Abilities." *American Psychologist* 34, 214–30.

Stone, Michael H., ed. 1986. *Essential Papers on Borderline Disorders: One Hundred Years at the Border.* New York: New York University Press.

Storr, A. 1969. *Churchill: Four Faces of the Man.* London: Allen Lane.

————. 1990. *Solitude.* New York: Free Press.

Strachey, James. 1910. "Editor's Introduction." *Standard Edition* 11:59–62.

Strupp, Hans H. 1973. *Psychotherapy: Clinical, Research, and Theoretical Issues.* New York: Jason Aronson.

Suedfeld, Peter. 1992. "Cognitive Managers and Their Critics." *Political Psychology* 13:435–53.

Suedfeld, Peter, and Philip E. Tetlock. 1992. "Psychologists as Policy Advocates: The Roots of Controversy." Pp. 1–30 in *Psychology and Social Policy,* edited by Peter Suedfeld and Philip E. Tetlock. New York: Hemisphere.

Suedfeld, Peter, and Michael D. Wallace. 1995. "President Clinton as a Cognitive Manager." Pp. 215–34 in *The Clinton Presidency: Campaigning, Governing, and the Psychology of Leadership,* edited by Stanley A. Renshon. Boulder, Colo.: Westview.

Sullivan, Harry S. 1953. *The Interpersonal Theory of Psychiatry.* New York: Norton.

Suro, Robert. 1992. "Senate Office Helped Clinton on Draft, Aides Acknowledge." *New York Times,* 19 September, A1.

Swift, E. K., and K. Finegold. 1992. "Has Clinton Said Enough?" *New York Times,* 23 January, A23.

Szasz, T. 1960. "The Myth of Mental Illness." *American Psychologist* 15:113–18.

Tartakoff, H. H. 1966. "The Normal Personality in Our Culture and the Nobel Prize Complex." Pp. 222–52 in *Psychoanalysis: A General Psychology,* edited by R. M. Lowenstein, L. Newman, M. Schur, and A. Solnit. New York: International Universities Press.

Taylor, Paul. 1990. *See How They Run: Electing the President in an Age of Mediaocracy.* New York: Knopf.

Tetlock, Philip. 1984. "Cognitive Style and Political Belief Systems in the British House of Commons." *Journal of Personality and Social Psychology* 45:118–26.

————. 1992. "Good Judgment in International Politics: Three Psychological Perspectives." *Political Psychology* 13:517–40.

————. 1994. "Political Psychology or Politicized Psychology: Is the Scientific Road to Hell Paved with Good Moral Intentions?" *Political Psychology* 3:509–29.

Thach, Charles C., Jr. [1923] 1969. *The Creation of the Presidency, 1775–1889.* New York: De Capo Press.

't Hart, Paul. 1990. *Groupthink in Government: A Study of Small Groups and Policy Failure.* Rockland, Mass.: Swets and Zeitlinger.

Thiselton, T. F. 1903. *Royalty in All Ages: The Amusements, Eccentricities, Accomplishments, Superstitions, and Frolics of Kings and Queens of Europe.* London: John C. Nimmo.

Thompson, Kenneth W., ed. 1988. *Papers on Presidential Disability and the Twenty-fifth Amendment.* Lanham, Md.: University Press of America.

Tierney, John. 1991. "Now, Journalists Renege on Election Promises." *New York Times,* 31 January, A12.

————. 1992. "Grace under Pressure? It's Working for Clinton." *New York Times,* 2 March, A20.

Toner, Robin. 1988. "Candidates' Health Discussed." *New York Times,* 3 August, A10.

————. 1992a. "Clinton Candidacy Is Shaken by War He Disdained." *New York Times,* 13 February, A25.

————— 1992b. "AIDS Protester Provokes Clinton's Anger." *New York Times,* 27 March, A21.

Torre, Mottram. 1968. "Psychiatric Disability in High Office." *American Journal of Psychotherapy* 3:626–35.

Tractenberg, Mark. 1985. "White House Tapes and the Cuban Missile Crisis." *International Security* 10:164–203.

Tucker, Robert C. 1965. "The Dictator and Totalitarianism." *World Politics* 17:555–83.

—————. 1981. *Politics as Leadership.* Columbia: University of Missouri Press.

—————. 1977. "The Georges' Wilson Reexamined: An Essay on Psychobiography." *American Political Science Review* 71:606–18.

Tulis, Jeffrey. 1987. *The Rhetorical Presidency.* Princeton, N.J.: Princeton University Press.

Tversky, A., and D. Kahneman. 1981. "The Framing of Decisions and the Psychology of Choice." *Science* 211:453–58.

Valenti, Jack. 1988. "Letter to the Editor: The War Within." *New York Times Magazine,* 11 September, 8.

Viorst, M. 1973. "Did Eagleton Do Anything Wrong?" *Esquire* (February): 59–63.

Volkan, Vamik D. 1987. *Six Steps in the Treatment of Borderline Personality Organization.* Northvale, N.J.: Jason Aronson.

Waite, R. 1977. *The Psychopathic God: Adolf Hitler.* New York: Basic Books.

Wattenberg, Martin P. 1990. *The Decline of American Political Parties: 1952–1988.* Cambridge, Mass.: Harvard University Press.

—————. 1991. *The Rise of Candidate Centered Politics: Presidential Elections of the 1980s.* Cambridge, Mass.: Harvard University Press.

Wayne, Stephen. 1977. "Working in the White House: Psychological Dimensions of the Job." Paper presented to the Annual Meeting of the Southern Political Science Association, New Orleans, November 3–5.

—————. 1993. "President Bush Goes to War: A Psychological Assessment at a Distance." Pp. 29–48 in *The Political Psychology of the Gulf War: Leaders, Publics, and the Process of Conflict,* edited by Stanley A. Renshon. Pittsburgh: University of Pittsburgh Press.

Weaver, Warren, Jr. 1988. "Ex-Aides Assail Depiction of Johnson as Paranoic." *New York Times,* 24 August, A19.

Wedge, Bryant. 1968. "Khrushchev at a Distance: A Study of Public Personality." *Trans-Action* (October): 24–28.

Weinraub, Bernard. 1987. "Walter Mondale on Not Saying, 'I Told You So.' " *New York Times,* 4 March, B5.

Welch, David A., and James G. Blight. 1987/88. "The Eleventh Hour of the Cuban Missile Crisis: An Introduction to the ExComm Transcripts." *International Security,* Winter, 5–92.

Wenner, Jann S., and William Greider. 1993. "President Clinton: The Rolling Stone Interview." *Rolling Stone* (December 9): 40–45, 80–81.

White, Ralph K. 1983. "Empathizing with the U.S.S.R." *Political Psychology* 4:121–37.

—————. 1991. "Empathizing with Saddam Hussein." *Political Psychology* 12:291–308.

White, Theodore H. 1973. *The Making of the President: 1972.* New York: Bantam Books.

White, Theodore H. 1975. *Breach of Faith: The Fall of Richard Nixon.* New York: Atheneum.

Wildavsky, Aaron. 1987. *Speaking Truth to Power: The Art and Craft of Policy Analysis.* New Brunswick, N.J.: Transaction Books.

Wilson, William J. 1987. *The Truly Disadvantaged: The Inner City, the Underclass, and Public Policy.* Chicago: University of Chicago Press.

Wines, Michael. 1993. "Clinton, Who Opposed 'Soft Money,' Got Plenty." *New York Times,* 19 March, A19.

Winnicott, D. W. 1958. "The Capacity to Be Alone." *International Journal of Psycho-Analysis* 39:416–20.

———. 1965. *The Maturational Process and the Facilitating Environment.* New York: International Universities Press.

———. 1986. *Home Is Where We Start From: Essays by a Psychoanalyst.* New York: Norton.

Witkin, H., D. R. Goodenough, and S. A. Karp. 1967. "Stability of Cognitive Style from Childhood to Young Adulthood." *Journal of Personality and Social Psychology* 7, 291–300.

Witkin, R. 1940. *Psychological Differentiation.* New York: Wiley.

Wolf, Ernest S. 1988. *Treating the Self: Elements of Clinical Self Psychology.* New York: Guilford.

Woodward, Bob. 1994. *The Agenda.* New York: Random House.

Wright, George, Jr. 1993. "Everyone's Friend." Pp. 28–29 in *The Clintons of Arkansas: An Introduction by Those Who Know Them Best,* compiled and edited by Ernest Dumas. Fayetteville, Ark.: University of Arkansas Press.

General (Unattributed) Newspaper Articles and News Magazine Stories

"The Bill Clinton Nobody Knows." 1992. *The Economist* (November 7): 38.

"Clinton Denounces New Report of Affair." 1992. *New York Times,* 24 January, A14.

"A Crisis Called Eagleton." 1972. *Newsweek* (August 7): 12–16.

"Eagleton's Odyssey." 1972. *Time* (August): 14–15.

"Heckler Stirs Clinton Anger: Excerpts from the Exchange." 1992. *New York Times,* 28 March, D9.

"Manhattan Project, 1992." 1992. *Newsweek* (November/December): 40–42, 55–56.

Miami Herald. 1987–88. May 4, 1987–January 12, 1988.

New York Times. 1987–88. May 4, 1987–January 12, 1988.

New York Times. 1972. July 26–27.

Subject Index

Subject Index 501

★ Name Index

Elving, D., 327–28
Erikson, E. H., 45, 57, 84, 92, 189, 202, 395
Evans, R., 199
Exner, J. E., 476

Feerick, J. D., 450
Fenichel, O., 110, 182, 454
Fenno, R., 223
Fieve, R., 91, 97, 173–74
Fiscalini, J., 135
Fiske, S. T., 141
Freud, S., 44–45, 50–53, 57–59, 84, 108, 110, 182, 193, 350, 454–55, 461, 473
Friedman, T. L., 283, 295
Frosh, J., 327
Funk, C., 57–58

Gaebler, T., 256
Gay, P., 454–55
Gaylin, W., 76, 91, 95, 97, 149, 168–69
Gelb, L., 457
George, A., 51, 57, 63, 86, 113, 142, 145, 156, 164, 190, 197, 253, 361, 442, 455, 457, 462
George, J., 63, 164, 190, 361, 442, 455, 462
Gergen, D., 192
Gerzon, M., 313
Gilbert, G. M., 91
Ginzburg, R., 124–25, 127
Giovacchini, P., 455
Glad, B., 476
Goel, M., 149
Goffman, E., 315
Goldberg, A., 193, 474
Goldman, P., 265–66, 317, 332, 349, 355, 465
Goodenough, D. R., 476
Goodwin, R. N., 102, 106, 109
Gore, A., 261, 342
Green, H., 450
Greenberg, J. R., 193
Greenson, R., 326, 451
Greenstein, F. I., 41–42, 63, 130, 191, 294, 349, 373–74, 389, 442, 449, 451, 473, 476–77
Greider, W., 66, 284–86
Grey, J., 135
Group for the Advancement of Psychiatry:

Committee on Governmental Agencies, 91, 96
Gurrin, G., 38

Hall, C. S., 455
Hargrove, E., 472
Hart, G., 242–45, 252, 460
Heifetz, R., 441
Henry, W. D., 97, 449
Herbers, J., 36, 101, 106–7
Herek, G., 457–58
Hermann, M. G., 58, 138–39, 156
Herron, W. G., 90
Hinckley, B., 319
Holsti, O. R., 475
Hook, S., 41
Horney, K., 45, 81, 193, 262
Hunt, A., 446
Huth, P., 457–58
Hutschnecker, A. A., 90

Ifill, G., 260–61, 264–66, 269, 281–82, 294, 301, 313
Inglehart, R., 475

Jackson, C., 269–70
Jacob, H. E., 117
Jahoda, M., 81, 88
Janis, I., 86, 115, 145, 172, 457–58
Jenks, C., 443
Johnson, H., 452–53
Johnson, L., 475–76
Jones, E., 198

Kahneman, D., 141
Kantor, R. E., 90
Kaplan, A., 381–82, 473
Kearns, D., 96, 102, 106, 199–200
Kellerman, B., 198, 205, 460
Kelley, V., 465
Kelly, M., 66, 262, 268, 270, 287, 295, 301, 317
Kenney, P. J., 179
Kernberg, O., 135, 446
Kernell, S., 86
Kilborn, P. T., 287
Kindner, D. R., 458
King, C. D., 83
King, L. S., 83, 447
Klein, J., 262

Knutson, J. N., 200
Kohut, H., 45, 127, 129, 186–87, 190, 193, 258, 454, 473–74
Krosnick, J. A., 58, 179
Kumar, M., 469

Labaton, S., 294
Ladd, E. C., 37
Larson, J., 159–60
Lasswell, H. D., 57, 91, 93, 130, 140, 148–49, 164, 190, 206, 236, 389, 442, 446, 450, 453–54
Lebow, N., 457
Leites, N., 475
Leuchtenburg, W., 373
Levin, R. E., 258–59, 464, 466–67
Levinson, S., 164
Levitt, M., 94
Lewin, K., 91
Lewis, A., 321
Lewis, D., 209
Lindblom, C., 476–77
Lindsey, B., 302
Lindzey, G., 455
Linville, P. W., 141
Loab, W., 151
Lodge, M., 440
Lowi, T., 440

Macalpine, I., 449
Mahler, M., 473–74
Maklin, R., 445, 447
Malanchuk, O., 179
Mankiewicz, F., 157, 175
Mann, I., 86, 115, 145, 172, 457–58
Mansfield, H. C., Jr., 440
Maraniss, D., 257, 266, 268
March, J. G., 114
Margolis, J., 79, 447
Markus, G., 179, 442
Maslow, A., 455
Masters, R. D., 334
Masterson, J. F., 235, 460
Mathews, T., 265, 317, 332, 349, 355, 465
May, E. R., 474
Mayer, J., 101
Mazlish, B., 475
McClelland, D. C., 455
McGovern, G., 150–53, 158–59, 169–70, 452

McGraw, K., 440
McGuire, W., 440
McManus, D., 101
Meissner, W. W., 111, 235, 460
Menninger, K., 169
Milbrath, L., 149
Miller, A. H., 179
Miller, L., Jr., 452–53
Miller, M., 66, 159, 160, 265, 317, 332, 349, 355, 465
Miller, W., 33, 38
Mitchell, S. A., 193
Moore, M. S., 84–85, 447
Moore, R., Jr., 259
Moynihan, D. P., 36
Mullahy, P., 451
Murr, A., 265, 317, 332, 349, 355, 465
Murray, C., 443
Muth, R., 457–58

Naughton, J. M., 158–59
Nelson, B., 32
Neustadt, R., 116–17, 197, 343, 474
Nisbett, R. E., 477
Noland, R. L., 98–99, 148, 449
Novak, R., 199

Oakley, M. L., 257, 465
Osborne, T., 256

Paige, G. D., 113
Parker, M., 270
Patterson, T. E., 314, 334
Pious, R. M., 225
Pollack, A., 301
Post, J., 92, 112, 450
Prince, M., 439–40
Pryor, D., 258
Putnam, R., 475

Raines, H., 324
Rappoport, A. S., 98
Ray, D., 451
Reedy, G., 100, 118–19
Reich, W., 454–55
Reischauer, R. D., 300
Remnick, D., 460
Renshon, S., 92, 195, 198, 200, 294, 446, 451, 455, 457, 463, 465, 468–69
Reston, J., 354–55